Sunda and Sahul

Sunda and Sahul

Sunda and Sahul

Prehistoric Studies in Southeast Asia, Melanesia and Australia

edited by

J. ALLEN
J. GOLSON
R. JONES

*Department of Prehistory, Australian National University,
Canberra, Australia*

1977

ACADEMIC PRESS
London · New York · San Francisco
A Subsidiary of Harcourt Brace Jovanovich, Publishers

ACADEMIC PRESS INC. (LONDON) LTD.
24/28 Oval Road,
London NW1

United States Edition published by
ACADEMIC PRESS INC.
111 Fifth Avenue
New York, New York 10003

Library of Congress Catalog Card Number: 77–74808
ISBN 0–12–051250–5

Printed in Great Britain by Galliard (Printers) Ltd, Great Yarmouth, Norfolk

This Book is Dedicated to the

Memory of

Carl O. Sauer

and

Ole A. Christensen

PREFACE

Late in 1974 we were invited by Professor Cyril Belshaw of the University of British Columbia to organise a symposium in the Social Sciences section of the 13th Pacific Science Congress to be held in Vancouver, Canada in August 1975. Based at an Australian University and with our research programme centred on an Australian-Melanesian axis, we accepted the invitation as an opportunity to explore some of the general themes which we felt linked the prehistory of our own area with that of Southeast Asia on the northern side of the Wallace Line.

In organising the symposium, we consciously sought a limited number of scholars currently working on the sorts of questions outlined in the introduction to this book. Although the bulk of such people would label themselves archaeologists, we have come to recognise in this part of the world, with its own particular problems, the need to co-operate with ecologists, geographers, anthropologists, geologists and zoologists, just to mention a few of the related sciences. Some of the contributors were previously known to us only through their writings. The symposium which resulted was one of those rare occasions where the stimulus of new data and new ideas proved thoroughly infectious. The publication of these papers and others invited later is the result of the meeting, and we trust that this book will play its part in contributing to the growing interest in the prehistory of Sunda and Sahul, a region in which the data now begin to challenge conventional views of world prehistory.

There was however a shadow cast by the news of the death of Carl Sauer, news which for some of us revived our memory of the death of a colleague,

Ole Christensen, only eight months previously. In a conference gathering where dialogue, debate and friendship so conspicuously transcended the generations, it was unanimously agreed to dedicate this book to the memory of these two fellow scholars, the first long an authority in his field, the second on the threshold of his career.

Carl Sauer was a major figure in American geography for over half a century, whose interests brought him into close and fruitful association with ethnographers and historians of human societies. The environmental insights he provided for the students of man have had a substantial impact on the historical and social sciences, while his concern with man as a central figure on the natural stage has in its turn influenced the biological sciences. Among his many contributions to the study of the interaction between man and his environment, those on the role of fire, the seashore as an optimum habitat and the tropical origins of agriculture relate in particular to central issues identified and discussed at the Vancouver symposium, many of whose members acknowledged Sauer's personal or intellectual influence on their work and writing.

Ole Christensen, a Canadian citizen of Danish birth whose parents settled in rural Alberta, shared, like Sauer, in the North American frontier tradition. As an archaeological student at Calgary, he was attracted by economically and ecologically oriented aspects of his discipline and developed an interest in pursuing research of this character in tropical agricultural systems. At the time of his tragic death in a car accident, he was a doctoral student of the Department of Prehistory at the Australian National University. He had just completed major fieldwork into the settlement and economy of a New Guinea Highlands valley over a period of 10,000 years and was focusing on the preserved plant remains to document the development of horticulture in the region and its environmental impact.

Acknowledgements

Concerning the Congress itself, we editors would like to thank Stevie Stephens and her husband Peter Rayher for offering us the hospitality of their house, and for giving us the facilities of office and work base. In her professional capacity in the Anthropology Museum, Simon Fraser University, we thank Dr Stephens for introducing us to archaeological colleagues at both universities in the city. Fares of most participants were met by their own institutions or privately, but some funds from the Australian Academy of Science were crucial additions which allowed several people to attend, who otherwise would not have been able to. We personally would like to thank our own Research School of Pacific Studies and the 13th Pacific Science Congress organising committee for our fares. Cyril Belshaw and the staff at the Congress provided constant support behind the scenes.

Concerning this book Maureen Johnson worked for long hours to type the text, maintaining her enthusiasm despite the pressures of inconsistent editors and short deadlines. She was assisted by Lois White, who typed the bibliographies and captions, and by Carol Joyce. Winifred Mumford supervised the layout as well as drawing the illustrations. Dragi Markovic prepared the photographs, and Eleanor Crosby the index. Peter Brown assisted with the setting-up of the final text.

David Harris established initial contact with Academic Press. Finally we thank Anthony Watkinson for his encouragement and above all his patience.

J.A.

J.G.

R.J.

Department of Prehistory
Research School of Pacific Studies
Australian National University
Canberra
February, 1977

CONTENTS

SUNDA AND SAHUL: AN INTRODUCTION

RHYS JONES

Department of Prehistory
Australian National University

> Who knows the early history of our Globe?
> and how many spaces of land now isolated
> were formerly continents? .... Some day
> we will amuse ourselves in this research
> if that suits us (Diderot, *Supplément au*
> *voyage de Bougainville* 1796).

To a world where there are no lands left to
discover, biogeographers have done us a favour.
Where once there was a Prester John, presiding over
a country beset by infidels and winged dragons; or
a Commodore Anson conversing with giants on the
Patagonian pampas; or even a thick skinned matelot
from Le Havre, Nicholas Baudin, cursing his ship-
mate citizen savants, as he gingerly rounded the
southeastern bastion of a half unknown Terra
Australis; we now have coloured photographs of the
Earth from the Moon, tourist charter flights to
Antarctica or wild wallabies in Wales - George
Borrow where are you now? Even Karta, that island
of the dead (Lat. 36°S.; Long. 138°E.), where
Ngurunderi once walked in the Dreamtime, is reduced
to a few municipalities of soldier settler townships,
the dense bush which so intrigued Flinders having
been bulldozed away to provide cheese for nearby
Adelaide. Yet in this unromantic age, new landscapes
appear - Gondwanaland, Behringia, the Littorina Sea,
Old Melanesia, some floating across the globe like
one of Gulliver's islands, others rising or falling
beneath the waves like Atlantis, each populated by
strange animals and plants, acting out their lives
in stone.

The most famous of these lands, and perhaps the first named is Wallacea, that group of islands lying between the continental shelves of Asia and Australia, the geographical distribution of whose biota enabled Alfred Russel Wallace (1869) and others, to elucidate so much about their history. 'Sunda' and 'Sahul', the names now given to the two shelves flanking this dividing zone, has been chosen for this book as an expression of intellectual debt to the great biogeographers and biohistorians of the past, as a device to stimulate minds to fantasy, and as a symbol of a focus - the Australianists to look to the tropical north of their continent and beyond, and those working in Southeast Asia to consider the relevance to their own problems of new prehistoric data emerging from the southern continent and its daughter islands.

The region had an auspicious start in the annals of world prehistory with the discovery by Dubois in 1891 of the human fossil now assigned to *Homo erectus* in mid-Pleistocene deposits on the banks of the Solo River in Java. Legend has it that Dubois had considered that the most likely place for the origins of man was within the tropical forested zone of the world; and that the Dutch East Indies was the only substantial area of this type access- ible to him as a civil servant. Colonial history has in fact played a considerable role in the development of prehistoric studies in the region - Colani and other French workers carrying out their pioneering work in the limestone caves of the then Indo-China; van Stein Callenfels and van Heekeren in Dutch Indonesia; the British Tweedie and Harrison in Malaya and Sarawak; Beyer and later Fox in the Philippines. Perhaps we should also include Golson, White and Allen in the last days of Australian New Guinea, Boriskovskii in North Vietnam and products of the Cambridge school in Australia and New Zealand. This tended to produce fragmented prehistories which looked towards their various metropolitan intellectual centres rather than across political boundaries

where often similar archaeological manifestations
had been analysed according to different traditions.
It is within such a context, that previous Pacific
Science Congresses have played an important role,
providing a forum of mutual discussion and the
possibilities for regional synthesis. McCarthy's
paper at the 1938 Singapore Congress of Far Eastern
Prehistorians, called 'A comparison of the prehistory
of Australia with that of Indo-China, the Malay
Peninsula and Archipelago' (1940), shows that
extending hands across the Wallace Line is not a
new phenomenon. Despite the establishment of
basic sequences and the definition of some of the
fundamental problems that all this work produced,
there developed a curious pessimism about the
status of Southeast Asia and Australia in world
prehistory, the reasons for which being discussed
in the first section of this book.

Research during the past 20 years has
revolutionised the picture. A new generation of
field workers entering the fray armed with
techniques such as radiocarbon dating are freed
from having to look over their shoulders at
comparative sequences established elsewhere, in
order to give a chronological base to their work.
The pressure of new discoveries, and the problems
that they expose have been well expressed in
W.W. Howells' splendid new book *The Pacific
Islanders* (1973). It is to him and his fellow
protagonists in the second section of this book,
that we look for an understanding of the
implications of such finds as the possible
40,000 year old Niah skull, the Tabon skull and
the 26,000 year old Lake Mungo I skeleton, for
the evolution of modern man - and what echo within
the genetic cauldron of Southeast Asia do the
skulls of Kow Swamp reflect? In Australia, we are
now facing a prehistory which extends back to the
limits of the radiocarbon dating method. Evidence
of meals of fish and shellfish back to 35,000 years
ago, of the manufacture of bone tools at 20,000, of

edge ground axes at 24,000, of boomerangs and
barbed wooden spears at 10,000, of rock art older
than 13,000, of burial with ochre and grave goods
back to 25,000 - 30,000 (cf. Mulvaney 1975; Jones
in press); all stress the fact that many of the
key criteria by which we judge the emergence of
modern human cultures - complex technology, art,
religion and vanity are now as old in Australia
as they have previously been shown to be in Western
Europe. This is not to assert any kind of
regional chauvinism, but rather to remind ourselves
that both the peninsulas, on opposite edges of the
vast Asiatic continent, were reverberating to the
same fundamental cultural advances being made in
the time period 50,000 to 30,000 years ago.

Carl Sauer (1952), predicted that the tropics
of Southeast Asia and the Malay Peninsula would
eventually prove to be an independent and perhaps
even the oldest centre of plant domestication. Now
at last on several fronts, from the 12,000 year old
edible seeds of north Thailand to the 12,000 year
old pottery of Japan, important discoveries are
being made, indicating the majestic antiquity of
such systems within the region, and outlining the
causes for their development. From all these
indications it seems as if the Southeast Asian-
Australian region was indeed a major innovative
centre of the late Pleistocene world, an
investigation of whose prehistory is essential
to an understanding of the physical and cultural
evolution of modern man (Golson 1972). It is time
to look at the geographical background to these
developments and see how it may have influenced
them. Such an interplay of geography and history
forms the main theme of this volume.

Firstly, there is the tropical Indo-Malayan
rainforest - the world's richest reservoir of
edible plants, large pristine remnants of which
can still be studied in New Guinea and in the
highlands of Southeast Asia. This forest, its

floristic and geographical diversity, its resources
edible and useful to man, its transformation and
simplification by fire, axe and other artifice,
its present role as a refuge for its specialist
exploiters, and its past one as a nursery for
horticulture - is the theme of several papers from
Yen in Thailand and Hutterer and the Petersons in
the Philippines, to Golson, Ohtsuka and Harris in
New Guinea and Australia. In 1971, Golson pointed
out how similar were many of the plants used by
hunters of tropical Australia to those also
important economically in Southeast Asia - the
various forms of *Dioscorea* yams; the tubers of
Colocasia taro and *Tacca* arrowroot; the starchy
pith of the palms; the poisonous, cancer forming,
but leachable nuts of the Cycads; the fruits of
Terminalia, Eugenia and *Pandanus*. If one fact
has emerged clearly during the past decade's
research, it is that the traditional division into
exclusive economic categories of hunters or of
farmers does not make much sense in our region
(Jones 1975; Allen in press). Here, we seem to
be faced with a series of clines from food
gathering through to full horticulture.
Ethnographically, we can investigate them in the
face to face economic exchanges between forest and
open land dwellers in the Philippines, or along
the more gradual cline on the peninsula, islands
and plateau linking Australia and New Guinea. In
the prehistoric record, we see such transitions
operating diachronically, sites such as those in
northwest Thailand and the Wahgi swamp perhaps
being destined to give us a profound understanding
of some of the decisive pathways towards
horticulture.

The second main factor to consider is the
pattern of land and water, the region constituting
the world's largest archipelago stretching more
than 8000 km southeast of the Asian mainland, with
islands ranging in size from mere dots on the map
to the 7,500,000 km^2 of Australia. Yet this

pattern which we now see on the map is but a single
state in a dynamic process controlled largely by
the glacio-eustatic budget of the world's water.
Periodically, over the past few million years, the
continental shelves were exposed and drowned,
alternatively allowing new opportunities for
colonisation by the fauna of the enlarging islands
or adjacent continents, and conversely squeezing
them during a rise in sea level. Or could it be
for hunters and gatherers that the reverse was true -
that the archipelagic state had a higher exploitable
productivity than the continental one? An 'ice
age', measured in terms of temperature has little
meaning in our region, except on the tops of the
highest New Guinea mountains (Hope *et al*. 1976),
but the converse aspect in the formation of the
great polar ice sheets - not the freezing of the
water itself, but rather its removal from the cycle
of atmospheric circulation and ultimately from the
sea - had an immense effect. It is strange to
think that the same process, which in driving
Irish ice across the mouth of Paviland Cave in
Wales caused its abandonment some 20,000 years ago,
gave other men on the obverse side of the globe,
the opportunity to cross the salty marshes to Cave
Bay Cave, Tasmania; or that when Palaeo-Indians
were moving north on the fresh gravel sheets of
Michigan, contemporary Hoabinhian forest
dwellers were seeing their great valleys being
steadily drowned by the rising sea, Kangaroo
Island was being forsaken, and the Tasmanians and
the Kaiadilt isolated to pursue their lonely
histories until met by their George Augustus
Robinsons or their Norman Tindales.

    The tropical sea shore is a rich resource
zone, and in our region we perhaps have a unique
opportunity for observing the operation of hunting
and gathering societies able to use both this
shoreline and the products of the forest behind.
Meehan's paper on the Gidjingali of Arnhem Land,
Tindale's on the Kaiadilt, the Petersons' on the

Agta of the Philippines and Bowdler on coastal
Australians in general, will discuss aspects of
such economies capable of supporting what Tindale
once called 'the metropolitan centres of population'
of the hunting and gathering world.

Some water straits were never closed during
the period under review and to get to these
islands, men had to cross various distances of
sea. These acts of colonisation are of intense
interest and we have to consider such variables
as the rate of successful crossings; the probabilities
against the survival of individuals in new ecological
conditions; and more fundamentally the probabilities
against the survival of viable populations when the
number of colonists at any one time is extremely
low, down indeed to the limiting case, as John
Calaby (pers. comm.) once put it, of the single
pregnant girl clinging to a mangrove raft swept
across the last water gap to Australia! But once
established as a viable human bridgehead, we then
have to consider the speed within which man
occupied the new ecological vacuum, the effects
of the founder principle on the genetic make-up
of the new population, and the impact that this
human predation and new fire regime had on the
recipient biota. These issues are discussed by
Birdsell, whose previous classic paper on the
topic in 1957 is still the touchstone for those
of us who have tried to document them in the field
record.

Watercraft transform man from being an element
in a continental fauna to, borrowing Diamond's
phrase, a mammalian supertramp. Indeed on the
eastern flank of the region lying on the boundary
of the world's greatest archipelago and its
greatest ocean, we have cultures whose powers
of cross-water dispersal rivalled even those of
the wandering Albatross or the famous Mutton Bird.
A trend of improving watercraft, slowly changes
the sea from being a barrier into a highway,

resulting in fundamentally different rhythms of the histories of the men using them. This dynamic linkage of men and of materials by trade and movement, sets up its own cultural momentum leading to new levels of social integration.

The interplay of tropical forest and of shoreline, of land and of sea, of hunters and horticulturalists, of diversity genetically, culturally and historically - these are the themes of Sunda and Sahul.

REFERENCES

Allen, J. in press (1977) The hunting neolithic: adaptations to the food quest in prehistoric Papua New Guinea. In J.V.S. Megaw (ed.) *Hunters, gatherers and first farmers beyond Europe.* Leicester: Leicester University Press

Birdsell, J. 1957 Some population problems involving Pleistocene man. *Cold Spring Harbor Symposia in Quantitative Biology* 22:47-70

Diderot, D. 1796 [1935] *Supplément au voyage de Bougainville.* Paris: Librairie E. Droz, Baltimore: The John Hopkins Press, Oxford: University Press and London: Humphrey Milford

Golson, J. 1971 Australian Aboriginal food plants: some ecological and culture-historical implications. In D.J. Mulvaney and J. Golson (eds) *Aboriginal man and environment in Australia*:196-238. Canberra: Australian National University Press

        1972 *The remarkable history of Indo-Pacific man: missing chapters from every world prehistory,* (Fifth David Rivett Memorial Lecture). *Search* 3:13-21; *Journal of Pacific History* 7:5-25

Hope, G.S., J.A. Peterson, I. Allison and U. Radok (eds) 1976 *The equatorial glaciers of New Guinea*. Rotterdam: Balkema

Howells, W.W. 1973 *The Pacific Islanders*. London: Weidenfeld and Nicolson and New York: Scribner

Jones, R. 1975 The neolithic palaeolithic and the hunting gardeners: man and land in the Antipodes. In R.P. Suggate and M.M. Cresswell (eds) *Quaternary studies: selected papers from IX INQUA Congress, Christchurch, New Zealand, 2-10 December 1973*:21-34. Wellington: Royal Society of New Zealand, Bulletin 13

      in press (1977) *Australia felix*: the discovery of a Pleistocene prehistory. *Journal of Human Evolution* 6

McCarthy, F.D. 1940 Comparison of the prehistory of Australia with that of Indo-China, the Malay Peninsula, and Archipelago. In F.N. Chasen and M.W.F. Tweedie (eds) *Proceedings of the Third Congress of Prehistorians of the Far East*:30-50. Singapore: Government Printer

Mulvaney, D.J. 1975 *The prehistory of Australia*, (rev.ed.) Ringwood (Victoria): Penguin Books

Sauer, C.O. 1952 *Agricultural origins and dispersals*. New York: American Geographical Society, Bowman Memorial Lectures

Wallace, A.R. 1869 *The Malay Archipelago*. London: Macmillan

CRUDE, COLOURLESS AND UNENTERPRISING?
PREHISTORIANS AND THEIR VIEWS ON THE
STONE AGE OF SUNDA AND SAHUL

J. PETER WHITE

Department of Anthropology
University of Sydney

Writing of the earlier Australian industries
one of the world's eminent prehistorians said in
1968:

> The crude and rather colourless nature of this
> industry may serve to remind us that the original
> Australian aborigines issued from one of the most
> unenterprising parts of the late Pleistocene
> world (Clark 1968:21-2).

Now there are clearly two sets of somewhat
emotive adjectives in this statement - 'crude and
rather colourless' and 'most unenterprising', and it
is the consideration of these and their implications
that I wish to undertake here.

Let me stress two things however. Firstly,
this is a paper about the history of ideas; to use
some trendy jargon, it will explore the parameters
of a paradigm, with a view to understanding where we
are and possibly suggesting one or two ideas about
where we might go. Secondly, this paper is about
stone tools. As Sir Mortimer Wheeler once said of
early man in India 'his solitary memorial is an
infinitude of stones' (1959:34), and his comments
indeed apply generally to the Sunda-Sahul area. If
we cannot usefully employ the stone tools, we cut
out a very large part of our direct data from the
past, data which provide many of the foundations of
our more theoretically oriented upper stories.

Well, what of these crude, colourless and
unenterprising lumps of rock?

Let me point out that Grahame Clark is not
alone in his views, especially of Sundaland stone
industries. Chard talks of 'the underdeveloped
status of technology' in Eastern Asia, with its
'rather crude local industries' (1969:103, 109),
statements which are repeated in the more recent
edition of the same book, in which he talks also of
the 'very monotonous archaeological remains' of
Australia (1975:161). Others who make similar
statements include Gifford and Shutler (1956:66-7),
van Heekeren (1972), L.S.B. Leakey (1934:72-3)
although most of these statements were removed from
later editions of his book, and Movius (1948:411),
while other books less directly concerned with
prehistory, or whose authors have less direct
knowledge of the material simply take their cue
from the experts. In this latter category I would
include, for example, Pfeiffer (1969:132), the
eminent historian G. Coèdes (1966:13), Vayson de
Pradenne (1941) and de Sonneville-Bordes (1967). In
short, stone tools in this part of the world have
had a pretty bad press.

Were the statements simply restricted to stone
tools, with the aim of making comparisons between
those from this part of the world and elsewhere, it
might be easy to overlook them, but such is not the
case. Poor stone tools, it seems, are merely
indicators of the wider cultural situation. To
quote the American prehistorian who has been longest
concerned with the earlier stone materials of
Southeast Asia:

Perhaps the most important single conclusion to
be drawn from the implications of the new
archaeological material brought to light during
the last fifteen years in southern and eastern
Asia is that this area cannot be considered in
any sense 'progressive' from a cultural point of

view (Movius 1948:411).

It is the same stone tools which cause Clark
and Piggott to talk of the area's 'cultural
development' as being 'somewhat retarded' (1965:49),
and similar implications litter the literature.

On what basis are such statements made?
Initially, of course, we may be reminded of Wheeler's
'infinitude of stones' and the fact that since they
are such a large part of our record, people have
assumed they must convey cultural information. This
attitude tends to be codified, perhaps often almost
subconsciously, into belief that changes in the form
and patterning of stone tools *do* mark stages in
human cultural evolution and illustrate the
increasing complexity of man's technology and his
increasing control over the environment. Marvin
Harris puts this very nicely when he says 'Our
interest...is not primarily in the stone tools
themselves, but rather in what these tools and their
evolutionary modifications can tell us about the
general and specific evolution of sociocultural
systems' (1971:156). Grahame Clark's logic is even
clearer. Archaeologists concentrate on stone tools,
as he says, not only 'for lack of evidence bearing
more directly on habits and mode of life' but also
because they are 'eloquent memorials of human
achievement reflecting in their evolution that
progress in discrimination and dexterity which...
played so important a part in "the development of
mind"' (1946:31). A similar attitude may be seen in
Clark's later definition and use of technological
modes (1970:68; 1969:29) and in his statement that:

> it would be surprising if no broad degree of
> correlation existed between the appearance of
> successive advances in the manufacture of flint
> and stone tools and the emergence of progressively
> more advanced types of men (1969:31).

This is to say that stone tools can be used in some
ways fairly directly as markers of not only cultural

but even biological advance. I would certainly suggest that Clark speaks here for a great many prehistorians.

It is therefore now in order to raise the question of how prehistorians measure changes in stone tools. What criteria are being used to demonstrate that change, evolution and progress have occurred? Harris (1971:170) following Bordaz (1970) suggests four:
1. Higher standards of workmanship - i.e. finer detail, greater symmetry, smoother finish.
2. An increase in the number of items in the tool kit.
3. Tools are increasingly specialised.
4. More tools are made from the same quantity of raw material.

These may be conflated into two general criteria: an increase in the number of formally identifiable 'types' (2 and 3) and an increase in the technological competence involved in making the tools (1 and 4). It is the second of these which Clark primarily uses to distinguish his various modes (1970:68-79), although he notes that new forms also occur in association with these modes. Carleton Coon, on the other hand, is inclined to stress the increasing number of types (e.g. 1967:81, 96-104) as also are van Heekeren (1972:47) and Isaac (1972:176, 186). But it is these two criteria that are used by almost all students of the Palaeolithic. Man's progress through the first 2.5 million years of his existence can be characterised by the exhibition of his increasing technological control over material, its more economic use and increasingly elaborated formal patterning. Initially, indeed, our very recognition of stones as tools depends precisely on the recognition of formal patterning: stones are tools if they are altered and shaped to a set and regular pattern. 'Pattern' here is unquestionably macroscopic morphological pattern. As Bordaz,

writing specifically on tools of the stone age, says,
'archaeological typology...essentially uses the
formal attributes of the artefacts' (1970:41) and
the basic classifications for example, of Breuil,
Bordes, Bohmers, de Sonneville-Bordes, McBurney and
Coles and Higgs for the Old World, of McCarthy for
Australia and of Duff for New Zealand and the
Pacific will of course at once spring to mind.

The increasing number of formal types is well
documented for the Palaeolithic as a whole, although
within short sequences the pattern is now less
clearly established than used to be claimed (compare,
for example, M. Leakey 1971, with L. Leakey 1951).
What does this increase in formal types mean? Here,
prehistorians are somewhat at a loss for an answer.
Clark casts the whole into an evolutionary mould.
'Man and his way of life are both ultimately the
product of natural selection' (1970:61), and he has
no doubt that both the adoption of new modes of
stone working and the new types that occur allow
man both to expand the range of his settlements
(1970:82-3), to exploit a wider range of
environments (1970:84-5) and to do so more
efficiently - that is (if I understand him
correctly) to produce the same return with less
effort. Clark's formulation is the most explicit I
have found:

> The fact that the production of artifacts was
> subject to the evolutionary process has obvious
> implications for the methodology of archaeology.
> In particular, it high-lights the need to focus
> attention on progressive changes in basic
> processes such as working flint, potting, or
> metallurgy... Imperfect though competition
> between communities may have been, it seems
> evident *that those people flourished most, and*
> *therefore left the main impression on the*
> *archaeological record, that were most efficient*
> *not merely at a technical level but in terms of*
> *social achievement.* Natural selection must

always and necessarily have favoured those who
showed themselves most adaptable to circumstances
as these arose and most capable of exerting
themselves effectively (Clark 1970:97 [my
italics]).

In the same vein, Coon points out that, over
time, men 'invented more and more efficient
implements, some purely utilitarian and others of
a partly aesthetic character' (1967:81). Kottak's
wide-ranging text summarises the general trends in
stone tool making throughout the Palaeolithic as
demonstrating '*Homo*'s ever-increasing reliance on
technological means of adaptation' (1974:129).
Other trends are 'the production of more tools per
capita and the functional differentiation of tools.
With functional specialization usually comes greater
efficiency in doing necessary jobs'. Finally, 'one
can sum up trends in the evolution of technology by
saying that with increasing tool manufacture,
functional differentiation and specialization, and
efficiency, *Homo* has been able to increase the range
of environments he can cope with, and...has
undergone a population explosion which makes him
the most successful primate' (1974:129, 131).

The correlation between number of tool types,
efficiency and increasing population is also
supported, in a more sophisticated fashion, by
Isaac:

Now the Lower Palaeolithic might legitimately be
characterized as a situation involving a low
density network of population (bands) with
considerable variability in the permutations of
a very restricted number of artefact traits,
while the Late Pleistocene and Holocene are
perhaps characterized by higher population
densities, greatly increased numbers of traits
and increasingly diverse regional combinations
of these traits (Isaac 1972:186).

The implications of such statements seem to me
to be clearly that progress is measured by
increasing complexity. Conversely then, if such
complexity - formal and technological - is *not*
observed in the record, then that area or period
will have a lower population density and must be
un-progressive, retarded or backward.

Also explicit in prehistorians' discussions is
the notion that increased complexity is the mark of
increased efficiency, and I think it is now
important to raise the question of just what is
meant by the use of the term 'efficiency'. Although
the prehistorians who use the term have neither
defined it nor demonstrated directly how it applies
to the data, I believe that by it they embody two
concepts which Leslie White has termed *efficiency*
and *economy*. *Efficiency* is determined by the rate
of appropriation of plant and animal energies;
economy is measured in units of energy required for
the production of the tool (L. White 1959:53-4).
It is, of course, obvious that operationally these
are intimately related: a tool which is somewhat
more efficient in operation but much less economical
to produce is, overall, less *effective*, to use one
term to summarise the product of both concepts.
Effectiveness, according to Leslie White (1959:49),
can be measured by observing the amount of energy
harnessed i.e. the amount of human need-serving
goods and services produced per unit of human
labour, and he goes on to point out that:

> the tool or instrument that makes possible the
> greater product per unit of energy expended will
> tend to replace one yielding the lesser product
> in processes where the efficient and economical
> production of goods is the primary consideration
> (1959:55).

If we see this principle of White's occurring
through the operation of natural selection within
the technological world, as Grahame Clark would

have us believe, and which would certainly remove
any teleological implications from White's
statement, then I think we have found the basis for
all claims for the increasing effectiveness of
human control of energy throughout the Palaeolithic.
This greater effectiveness as White himself says
'consisted of adding new tools to the cultural
tradition and in the improvement of ones in use'
(1959:55).

We might ask, however, what measures we can
use to investigate the effectiveness of 'new' and/or
'improved' tool types. The mere existence of
different forms will hardly do since this assumes
what we are trying to test. The simple fact of
adoption of a new manufacturing technique will not
do either since we need other data - experimental
reproduction, investigation of the energy
requirements for assembling the technology of the
new technique, knowledge of the *social* energy
involved - before we can evaluate it. While some
measure of the *economy* of a new situation may not be
too difficult to gain, I suggest that measures of
stone tool *efficiency* are in fact very difficult.

The obvious measures seem to me to be i) an
increase in population, and/or ii) a decrease in
the amount of time spent on subsistence activities.

Both these are, as we know, not at all easy to
measure accurately from archaeological data
especially within the relatively small spatio-
temporal framework within which this problem must
be studied. It is all very well to show that the
world human population has increased during the
Pleistocene and that this has gone along with a
total increase in technological complexity
(measured in some as yet unspecified way by summing
all the material from a given time) but this
demonstrates only that there is a temporal
correlation between the two, and not that there is a
cause and effect relationship. We need, in fact, to

look at some specific, small-scale situations.

Now, on the basis of what I have said so far, if we have two populations occupying similar environments at similar energy-harnessing levels (i.e. both hunting fishing and gathering, or both agricultural), then if the tools of one group are more effective, we would expect it to have either greater population density *or* more leisure time. I will now examine two situations from Sunda and Sahul which might assist us.

The first case, which has been explored in detail by Rhys Jones (in press), contrasts the Tasmanian and southern Australian Aboriginal lifeways at the time of European contact. His elaborate analysis demonstrates that although Tasmanian material culture - including the stone tools - was vastly simpler than its Australian counterpart, in terms of both the number of classes of objects and their technological complexity, the population densities of ecologically equivalent areas were almost precisely the same. Population levels, as he says, were proportional to resources and not to technology. Jones does, however, believe that the more elaborate mainland technology resulted in an increase in leisure time.

He contrasts in particular the large-scale and lengthy religious ceremonies observed throughout the mainland with their complete absence in Tasmania and suggests that 'the siphoning off of the manhours gained by the deployment of a new technology into non-productive activities' was a powerful homeostatic mechanism for maintaining population at environmentally safe levels. Jones is referring here directly to the formal groups of stone tools which were added to the basic Australian tool-kit around 4-6000 years ago and which are categorised as the 'Australian small-tool tradition'. How did this new technology increase leisure time? Jones is unable to demonstrate this effect directly, but

refers to other cases. Of the two examples which
he cites, namely the introduction of steel axes to
the Yir Yoront and the invention (or introduction)
of shell fishhooks in coastal New South Wales about
2000 years ago, the first demonstrates that new
tools allowed certain tasks to be completed quicker,
while we may *infer* from the second that the change
allowed (or caused) a shift in sex-roles in relation
to fishing. Both increased male 'leisure' time, at
least on a day-to-day basis. It is much less clear,
however, in what ways these or other technological
changes, especially in stone tools, created the
situation whereby scores of men could suspend food-
getting activities *for several weeks* in order to
carry out ceremonies, which they presumably had not
been able to do before they acquired the new stone
tools.

In a situation where stone tools seem to be
used primarily for maintenance activities, it is
difficult to determine their effect on food
procurement, and even more on food transport and
storage, especially since it is clear that we are
dealing *not* with day-to-day increments in leisure
time (the Tasmanians had plenty of that), but with
longer term ones. This is not to deny the contrast
in religious elaboration, only its technological
underpinnings. Perhaps we should question the
correctness of the basic propositions which Jones
espouses, that a technology which has more elements,
which is morphologically complex and contains an
apparently greater range of task specific tools is
more effective in extracting energy. What if, in
Leslie White's terms, the tools were similarly, or
even more, *efficient*, but less *economical*? Can we
conceive of the production of the majority of the
material aspects of a culture as forming part of
the 'non-productive' or 'leisure' activities which
kept Australians from too great an emphasis on
extractive tasks and from over-exploiting their
environment? Certainly, to restrict my comments to
stone tools, it remains to be shown that a Bondi

point is a more efficient *and* economical knife or
barb than a simple flake, or that a hafted and
ground stone axe blade is more efficient *and* economical
than a hand-held chopper, at least within hunter-
gatherer economies. There is, of course, the classic
case of Kimberley points being adopted by the
Wardaman (Davidson 1935): the points were both less
efficient in use and less economical in terms of
energy expended in their production or acquisition
than those which they replaced. Are *they*, rather
than steel axes, a better example of stone age
practices, not only in the Antipodes but even in
more 'normal' parts of the world?

   The second case I want to look at is not as
precise in its contrasts as the Australian one but
it does exemplify the lack of necessary correlation
between stone tool morphology and efficiency in
harnessing energy. This is the situation in the
New Guinea Highlands, about which I have written
elsewhere (J.P. White 1971, 1972). The aspect I
wish to stress concerns the continuity of the stone
technology and the discontinuity in energy
harnessing. From several sites in the Highlands we
now have a technological tradition reaching back to
the Pleistocene. Within this time span we find a
stone technology which, if anything, becomes *less*
complex over time. Around 10,000 years ago, we find
ground stone axe-adzes, waisted blades and flaked
tools retouched in a variety of ways; by 1000 years
ago, waisted blades are not being made and the use
of simple unretouched flakes has become a great deal
more common; within recorded history, all flake tools
were unretouched (White and Thomas 1972). Over the
same period, there has been a marked economic shift
from a largely gathering and cultivating economy to
one involving complex forms of agriculture which
support much higher population densities. On our
current data, this change is largely unreflected in
the wooden tools and negatively reflected (if I may
use such a term) in the stone tools (cf Golson, in
press). The New Guinea case is not a unique one,

as Hayden (this volume) has pointed out. I suspect,
with him, that in this part of the world at least,
and probably more widely, it may belong with the
majority rather than being an exception when we
consider changes in energy harnessing and their
reflection in the technological record.

In this context, let me also draw attention to
one other interesting fact. Let us contrast the
history of Southeast Asia, that technologically
backward, culturally retarded and isolated corner of
the world over the last 50,000 years, with the
'northern parts of the Lower Palaeolithic world
(which witnessed) the genesis and rise of the
Advanced Palaeolithic cultures on which the future
development of mankind was largely to depend'
(Clark 1961:41). For the earlier part of the period,
say 50,000-15,000 BP, we can certainly find more
stone tools, more types of stone tools and more
complex ways of making stone tools, around and
especially north and east of the Mediterranean than
we can in Southeast Asia. We are unable to say from
this, however, that greater energy per capita is
being harnessed or that this area is more advanced,
since we find that the exploitation of new,
biological sources of energy occurs synchronously
in both areas (Fagan 1974:202-46). This in turn
implies, I think, that population densities in the
two areas must have reached a similar order of
magnitude, despite quite marked differences in the
morphological complexity of the stone tool remains.
As Sahlins says:

> For the greater part of human history labour has
> been more significant than tools, the intelligent
> efforts of the producer more decisive than his
> simple equipment (1972:81).

I have now, I trust, supported to some extent
the proposition that there is no necessary
relationship between stone tool morphology and
efficiency of energy harnessing. If so, we may then

ask why has this correlation been made by
prehistorians, and in the areas where it does
exist, what does increasing complexity of tool
morphology mean?

The first question is explicable in terms of
history and geography. Most early work on stone
tools was carried out in Europe by natural
scientists, whose approach to the classification
of specimens was through the study of their form.
Right from the early nineteenth century, when the
Three Age System was first systematised, the
concept of increasing technology and formal
complexity formed the cornerstone of archaeological
classification. This concept was, as Daniel (1943)
has shown, not only useful for ordering material
but also a reasonable account of the real history
of technology in the area. If, overall, history
was the history of technological progress (*pace*
Childe) then each stage must be a part of it and
more elaborate tools, whether in stone, bronze or
iron, must naturally be progressive.

The application of these views on a world-wide
basis is less surprising. Scientists work within
the paradigms they are used to, until 'surprises'
cause them to think afresh. Remember simply the
'surprise' caused by the discovery of 20,000 year
old ground axes in Arnhem Land and the time it is
taking for the implications of them to alter our
thinking; remember also the strenuous efforts made
to classify both Sunda and Sahul industries into
classic European taxons so that, for example, even
in 1969 Australian stone industries could be
classified by an Australian worker as 'Mesolithic,
verging on Neolithic' (Abbie 1969:105). As has
been said many times in Australia over the last
few years, Eurocentric models are clearly inadequate
for this part of the world.

The second question that I raised is much more
difficult to answer. If we cannot believe that

increasing complexity of tool form equals increasing
extractive efficiency what can we believe about it?
Let me quote again from Grahame Clark:

> In the elaboration and refinement of these tools
> on which he depended so largely for his place in
> the world, early man displayed the capacity to
> progress, to accumulate improvements, that
> distinguished him from the non-human primates.
> It may be asked how far the improvement of the
> hand-axe was dictated by purely functional
> considerations, and how far an aesthetic element
> had entered in. Certainly there was functional
> advance; more effective tools were made from
> smaller quantities of raw material. Equally,
> surely the tools became more graceful, smoother
> and pleasanter to handle. One may feel sure that
> whatever the economic gain from technical
> improvement, pride of craftsmanship in the mere
> process of production was a major factor. It
> would be perverse to account for the finest
> hand-axes in terms of their function alone, since
> they were better made than large numbers which
> must presumably have been adequate. The cult of
> excellence, the determination to make things as
> perfect as they could be made, even if at a
> purely utilitarian level perfection might seem
> excessive, is something which began thus early
> in the history of man (Clark & Piggott 1965:51).

I would in fact carry this statement a good
deal further and suggest that the majority of stone
tool forms were not necessary, in a utilitarian
sense, at all. If wooden spears and fire could kill
off Australia's Pleistocene megafauna, what is the
conceivable necessity for stone spear points?
(Peterson 1971:244).

In relation to other aspects of man's material
culture we do not regard increasing complexity as a
necessary sign of modernity or progress. In
discussing art, or burial or clothing, we do not

demand 'efficiency': we accept elaboration at some times, simplicity at others. Why not with stone tools?

ACKNOWLEDGEMENTS

This paper has benefited from discussion at seminars at the Universities of Sydney and New England. I am especially grateful to Iain Davidson, Brian Hayden, Jack Golson and Rhys Jones, without wishing to implicate them or anyone else.

Attendance at the Congress was made possible by grants from the University of Sydney and the Australian Academy of Science, both of which bodies I thank.

REFERENCES

Abbie, A.A. 1969 *The original Australians.* Wellington: Reed

Bordaz, J. 1970 *Tools of the Old and New Stone Age.* Garden City (N.Y.): Natural History Press

Chard, C. 1969 *Man in prehistory.* New York: McGraw-Hill

            1975 *Man in prehistory,* (2nd ed.) New York: McGraw-Hill

Clark, J.G.D. 1946 *From Savagery to Civilization.* London: Cobbett Press

            1961 *World prehistory: an outline.* Cambridge: Cambridge University Press

            1968 Australian Stone Age. In K. Jazdzewski (ed.) *Liber Iosepho Kostrzewski*

octogenario a veneratoribus dicatus:17-28.
Warsaw: Ossolineum, Polish Academy of Sciences

1969 *World prehistory: a new outline*. Cambridge: Cambridge University Press

1970 *Aspects of prehistory*. Berkeley: University of California Press

and S. Piggott 1965 *Prehistoric societies*. London: Hutchinson

Clarke, D.L. (ed.) 1972 *Models in archaeology*. London: Methuen

Coèdes, G. 1966 *The making of South East Asia*. London: Routledge and Kegan Paul

Coon, C.S. 1967 *The history of man*. Harmondsworth (Middlesex): Penguin Books

Daniel, G. 1943 *The Three Ages*. Cambridge: Cambridge University Press

Davidson, D.S. 1935 Archaeological problems of northern Australia. *Journal of the Royal Anthropological Institute* 65:145-84

Fagan, B. 1974 *Men of the earth*. Boston: Little Brown

Gifford, E.W. and Dick Shutler Jr. 1956 *Archaeological excavations in New Caledonia*. Berkeley and Los Angeles: University of California Press, Anthropological Records 18(1)

Golson, J. in press Simple tools and complex technology: agriculture and agricultural implements in the New Guinea highlands. In Wright in press

Heekeren, H.R. van 1972 *The Stone Age of Indonesia*, (2nd ed.) The Hague: Nijhoff

Harris, M. 1971 *Culture, man and nature*. New York: Crowell

Isaac, G.L. 1972   Early phases of human behaviour:
     models in Lower Palaeolithic archaeology.   In
     Clarke 1972:167-99

Jones, R. in press   The Tasmanian paradox.   In
     Wright in press

Kottak, C.P. 1974   *Anthropology*.   New York:
     Random House

Leakey, L.S.B. 1934   *Adam's ancestors*.   London:
     Methuen

               1951   *Olduvai Gorge*.   Cambridge:
     Cambridge University Press

Leakey, M.D. 1971   *Olduvai Gorge*,(vol.3).   Cambridge:
     Cambridge University Press

Movius, H.L. Jr. 1948   The Lower Palaeolithic
     cultures of southern and eastern Asia.
     *Transactions of the American Philosophical
     Society* n.s.38:329-420

Peterson, N. 1971   Open sites and the ethnographic
     approach to the archaeology of hunter-gatherers.
     In D.J. Mulvaney and J. Golson (eds) *Aboriginal
     man and environment in Australia*:239-48.
     Canberra: Australian National University Press

Pfeiffer, J. 1969   *The emergence of man*.   New York:
     Harper and Row

Pradenne, A. Vayson de 1941   *Prehistory*.   London:
     Scientific Book Club

Sahlins, M. 1972   *Stone Age economics*.   Chicago and
     New York: Aldine-Atherton

Sonneville-Bordes, D. de 1967   *La préhistoire moderne*.
     Périgeux: Fanlac

Wheeler, Sir Mortimer 1959   *Early India and Pakistan*.
     London: Thames and Hudson

White, J.P. 1971   New Guinea: the first phase in
     Oceanic settlement.   In R.C. Green and M. Kelly
     (eds) *Studies in Oceanic culture history*,

(vol.2):45-52. Honolulu: Bernice P. Bishop
Museum, Department of Anthropology, Pacific
Anthropological Records No.12

            1972 *Ol tumbuna*. Canberra: Australian
National University, Research School of Pacific
Studies, Department of Prehistory, *Terra
Australis* 2

            and D.H. Thomas 1972 What mean these
stones? In Clarke 1972:275-308

White, L.A. 1959 *The evolution of culture*. New
      York: McGraw-Hill

Wright, R.V.S. (ed.) in press *Stone tools as
      cultural markers: change, evolution and
      complexity*. Canberra: Australian Institute
      of Aboriginal Studies

REINTERPRETING THE SOUTHEAST ASIAN PALAEOLITHIC[1]

KARL L. HUTTERER

*Museum of Anthropology
The University of Michigan*

INTRODUCTION

Although the history of palaeolithic research in Southeast Asia goes back to the end of the 19th century, during the past two decades the number of researchers interested in Pleistocene cultures and peoples of Southeast Asia and, consequently, the number of field investigations conducted in various countries of the region has increased markedly. Nevertheless, our information about the Southeast Asian palaeolithic is still remarkably poor and our understanding of this period is very inadequate. This is unfortunate because hominid settlement in this part of the world is of great antiquity and palaeolithic research could, therefore, not only enlighten us about the culture-history of that area but also contribute greatly to our general understanding of man and his bio-social evolution.

This paper attempts a critical examination of the information on hand and the current interpretations of it. After surveying current syntheses and their supporting evidence, I conclude that the study of the palaeolithic of Southeast Asia is still largely Euro-centric in bias. This not only gives a very peculiar twist to our view of cultural developments in the area, but it also has been misdirecting our research. On the basis of ecological as well as cultural-processual considerations, I consider Southeast Asia as an important focal area of human biological and cultural evolution. Concomitantly, I suggest that further research turn away from the traditional

typological approach and concentrate rather on a
combination of stratigraphic, ecological, and
processual variables.

THE TRADITIONAL VIEW

Two countries of Southeast Asia have been
credited with long palaeolithic sequences:
Indonesia and Burma. Research on Early Man in
Indonesia started about half a century earlier than
in Burma and has produced both hominid fossils and
artifact assemblages, while no fossils have yet been
reported from the mainland. The evidence from
Indonesia has recently been summarised by the late
van Heekeren (1972, 1975). A simplified synopsis
of his geological, palaeontological and archaeological
sequences is given in Fig.1.

		Geol. Deposits	Fossil Fauna	Fossil Man	Archaeology
PLEISTOCENE	Late Upper	Cave deposits	sub—Recent	Niah, Wadjak Homo sapiens	Pebble—and—flake industries
		Solo terraces	Ngandong	Homo erectus soloensis	Ngandong Bone Industry
	Early Upper	Notopuro beds Baksoka terraces	Trinil ?	Homo erectus erectus ?	Sangiran Flake Ind. Patijitanian
	Late Middle	Kabuh beds	Trinil	Homo erectus erectus Meganthropus palaejavanicus	?
	Early Middle	Putjangan beds	Djetis	Homo erectus robustus Meganthropus palaejavanicus	?

Fig.1. Indonesian geological, palaeontological and archaeological
sequences (after van Heekeren 1972, 1975).

Van Heekeren recognises a sequence of at least
five distinct grades of Pleistocene hominids. He
associates a sequence of distinct and different
lithic tool industries with the later three types
of hominids (*Homo erectus erectus*, *Homo erectus
soloensis*, *Homo sapiens*). Since none of these
industries has been found actually associated with
human fossils, their respective chronological
positions have always been open to question and van
Heekeren has repeatedly modified his views.
Basically, however, his sequence starts with the
Patjitanian, a pebble-and-flake tool industry
which he positions in the late Middle or early
Upper Pleistocene and associates with *Homo erectus*.
This is followed by a flake industry horizon - the
Sangiran in Java and the Tjabengè in Sulawesi -
which is also associated with *Homo erectus*. The
next youngest horizon is represented, at least in
Java, by a flake-and-bone tool industry, named the
Ngandong Industry, which he sees associated with
Solo Man, an advanced *Homo erectus* or a primitive
neanderthaloid type. Finally, early *Homo sapiens*,
represented by Wadjak Man and the skull from Niah,
is related to a pebble-and-flake tool industry
found in the lower layers of Niah Cave in North
Borneo.

Van Heekeren largely skirts the issue of
Pleistocene environments and how they may have
affected Early Man and his culture. He assumes
that '*Homo erectus* was a roving collector of food,
plant and animal, over a wide area. He probably
lived in small self-contained groups, widely
dispersed and highly mobile. Isolation in
tropical forests and lack of contact with the
outside world give little chance for the adoption
of the achievements of others' (van Heekeren 1972:
75). He quotes at length from Movius (1955:539) to
the effect that since 'the region seems to have been
a marginal area of cultural retardation, it is
unlikely that it played a vital and dynamic role in
Early Man evolution'.

Burma is the other country of Southeast Asia
with a long palaeolithic sequence. Based on his
fieldwork carried out in 1937-38 and on geological
and palaeontological evidence supplied by H. de Terra
and Teilhard de Chardin, Hallam L. Movius produced
his classical statement on the Stone Age of Burma
in 1943. He distinguished two major palaeolithic
periods: The Early Anyathian, which he subdivided
into three phases, and the Late Anyathian, which he
subdivided into two phases. He correlated those
phases with terraces of the Irrawaddy River and
putative pluvial and dry periods of the Burmese
Pleistocene (see Fig.2).

			Geol. Deposits	Climate	Archaeology
POST PLEIS-TOCENE			Terrace 5 deposition	interpluvial	Neolithic
PLEISTOCENE	Upper		Terrace 4 deposition	pluvial	Late Anyathian 2
			Terrace 3 erosion	interpluvial	Late Anyathian 1
			Terrace 2 deposition	pluvial	Early Anyathian 3
	Middle		Terrace 1 erosion	interpluvial	Early Anyathian 2
			Lateritic gravel deposition	pluvial	Early Anyathian 1

Fig.2. The palaeolithic sequence in Burma correlated with·
climatic changes and geological deposits along the Irrawaddy
River (after Movius 1943).

Movius based his archaeological divisions both
on correlations with the geological age of the river
terraces and on typological differences between tool
assemblages of different phases. He admitted,

however, that the typological differences are very
slight indeed. Lithic artifacts of the Early
Anyathian, made of silicified tuff, fossil wood
and occasional quartz and quartzite, consist
primarily of rather large choppers and chopping
tools and a few flakes and cores. Artifacts of the
Late Anyathian consist of the same range of forms,
with an apparent tendency toward smaller tools and
some edge retouch. Since all assemblages were
recovered from secondary deposits, there is no
cultural information apart from aspects of lithic
technology. For geological reasons, the Anyathian
sequence is believed to start sometime in the
Middle Pleistocene, somewhat earlier than the
oldest cultural remains from Java.

The early work in Java and Burma as well as
contemporaneous research in China stimulated a
search for palaeolithic artifacts and human remains
in many parts of Southeast Asia. Putatively
palaeolithic stone tools have been found at Kota
Tampan in Malaya in a gravel terrace of the Perak
River (Collings 1938; Sieveking 1958, 1962). A
similar lithic complex has been reported from the
Meklong River in Thailand (van Heekeren 1948;
Heider 1958; Sørensen 1962). There are also reports
of palaeolithic finds from the islands of Flores
and Timor (Maringer and Verhoeven 1970a, 1970b,
1972, 1975; Glover and Glover 1970; Almeida and
Zbyszewski 1967) and from other parts of Indonesia
(Soejono 1961). There have also been claims of
palaeolithic finds from Laos (Fromaget 1937, 1940a;
Fromaget and Saurin 1936; Saurin 1968) and from
Cambodia (Saurin 1966). Boriskovskii (1966b, 1967)
has attributed a Lower Palaeolithic age to stone
tools found at Mt Do near Thanh-hoa in the
Democratic Republic of Vietnam, and similar claims
have been made for sites in northern Luzon,
Philippines (von Koenigswald 1958; Fox 1973; Fox
and Peralta 1974). Finally, important excavations
of late Upper Pleistocene deposits have been carried
out in Niah Cave, Sarawak, N. Borneo (Harrisson

1957, 1959) and Tabon Cave on Palawan, Philippines
(Fox 1967, 1970).

In his 'Early Man and Pleistocene Stratigraphy
in Southern and Eastern Asia', published in 1944,
Movius made systematic comparisons and suggested
correlations between the geological and
palaeontological sequences and archaeological
assemblages from four areas: the N. Punjab region
in northwest India, the middle Irrawaddy River in
Burma, the island of Java, and northern China.
This first systematisation of palaeolithic data from
the area (see Fig.3) was to have enormous impact on
subsequent research. Of equal importance was the
fact that Movius made a superficial comparison
with the Lower Palaeolithic of Europe and Africa
and saw pronounced differences in technological
traditions. India south of the Punjab, Asia to the
west of India, Europe and Africa were characterised
by the presence of hand-axes, while the area from
the Punjab eastward through China was characterised
by the absence of true hand-axes and the use of
pebble-tools. Movius also felt that the rate of
technological progress was infinitely slower in the
east than the west. Although Movius remained
relatively cautious in his judgements, the
secondary literature elevated his assessments to the
level of categorical statements and distinguished
between a 'hand-axe tradition' in the west and a
'chopper-chopping tool tradition' in the east,
separated by 'Movius' Line' (Coon 1965:48).

Movius' interpretation and integration of
palaeolithic materials of the Far East became an
important guide for archaeologists in Southeast
Asia. The author himself only slightly amplified
and modified his views in subsequent statements
(Movius 1949, 1955). By and large, his ideas can be
summarised as follows:

   1. There are two major cultural complexes during
      the Lower Palaeolithic: the Chellean-Acheulean

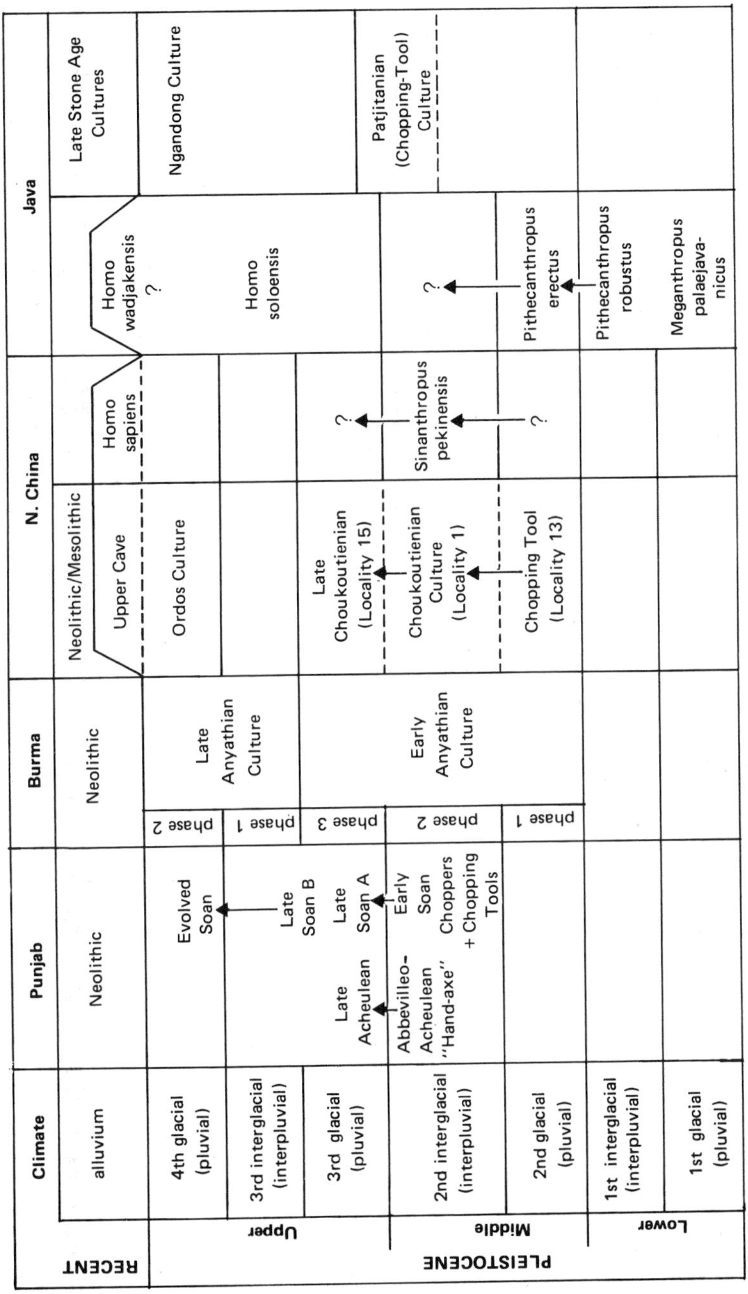

	Climate	Punjab	Burma	N. China	Java
RECENT	alluvium	Neolithic	Neolithic	Neolithic/Mesolithic	Late Stone Age Cultures
Upper (PLEISTOCENE)	4th glacial (pluvial)	Evolved Soan	Late Anyathian Culture (phase 2)	Upper Cave — Homo sapiens	Homo wadjakensis ?
	3rd interglacial (interpluvial)	Late Soan B (phase 1)	Late Anyathian Culture (phase 1)	Ordos Culture	Ngandong Culture — Homo soloensis
	3rd glacial (pluvial)	Late Soan A (phase 3)	Early Anyathian Culture (phase 3)	Late Choukoutienian (Locality 15)	
Middle	2nd interglacial (interpluvial)	Early Soan / Choppers + Chopping Tools (phase 2)	Early Anyathian Culture (phase 2)	Choukoutienian Culture (Locality 1) — Sinanthropus pekinensis	Patjitanian (Chopping-Tool) Culture — Pithecanthropus erectus
		Late Acheulean / Abbevilleo–Acheulean "Hand-axe" (phase 1)	Early Anyathian Culture (phase 1)	Chopping Tool (Locality 13)	Pithecanthropus robustus
	2nd glacial (pluvial)				Meganthropus palaejavanicus
Lower	1st interglacial (interpluvial)				
	1st glacial (pluvial)				

Fig.3. Southern and Eastern Asian sequences according to Movius (1944).

hand-axe complex in Europe, Africa and Western Asia;
and the chopper-chopping tool complex in Southeastern
and Eastern Asia.

2. The tool inventory of the chopper-chopping
tool complex is remarkably similar throughout
the area of its occurrence and consists of a very
high proportion of core tools made on pebbles
(choppers, chopping tools, hand-adzes) as well as
plain, unmodified flakes and unprepared cores.

3. In spite of over-all similarities, there are
at least four distinct culture provinces
within the chopper-chopping tool area: a Western
Area - represented by the Soan Culture of northwest
India; a Northern Area - represented by the
Choukoutienian Culture of north China; a Central
Area - represented by the Anyathian Culture of Burma;
and a Southern Area - represented by the Patjitanian
Culture of Java and possibly the Tampanian of Malaya.

4. The earliest cultural manifestations in
Southeast Asia are found in phase 1 of the
Early Anyathian which is correlated with the second
pluvial period, or the early Middle Pleistocene.

5. Both on geological and typological grounds,
the Patjitanian culture of Java is considered
to be more recent, dating from the second
interpluvial period, that is the late Middle or
possibly early Upper Pleistocene.

6. The chopper-chopping tool industry shows
similarities with a pre-hand-axe horizon in
Africa. However, while the developments in Europe
and Africa goes on to hand-axe and flake and blade
tool technologies, the chopper-chopping tool
complex in the Far East persists throughout the
whole Pleistocene with almost no change. This is an
indication of stagnation.

7. The Patjitanian of Java was probably the
culture of *Pithecanthropus erectus* or his
descendants as the related Choukoutienian was the
culture of *Pithecanthropus pekinensis*. In this
context Movius (1949:408) thinks that:

it may well be that one of the most vital reasons

why the cultures considered here are different
from classical developments found elsewhere
possibly lies in the fact that we are also dealing
with men belonging to a different branch of the
human stock from that found outside the Far East.

Understandably, many Asians have heard racist over-
tones in this statement.

CRITIQUE

As influential as Movius' synthesis of the Far
Eastern Palaeolithic has been, increasing criticism
of the far-flung scheme has arisen during the last
decade (Boriskovskii 1973; Fox 1973; Fox and
Peralta 1974; Ghosh 1971, 1973; Harrisson 1973, 1975;
Mulvaney 1970). Most of the criticisms are related
to problems of lithic typology, the distribution of
specific tool types, and questions of Pleistocene
stratigraphy and chronology. While there is some
agreement about the general topics that need
rethinking and renewed research, little useful
direction has been offered for new investigations.
The various statements primarily reflect a growing
awareness that Movius' admirable synthesis has often
been used uncritically as a crutch to overcome some
fundamental inadequacies of the palaeolithic data
from this region of the world. Closer inspection
reveals that the evidence for palaeolithic cultures
in Southeast Asia is very meagre, often highly
ambiguous, and in many cases quite useless. It is,
therefore, worthwhile to devote some time to a
brief critical overview of the field evidence as it
has become available up to 1975 in order to judge
its soundness and bearing.

Indonesia and Sarawak

All the reputedly 'Patjitanian' tools reported
from Indonesia before 1970 were either collected

from the gravel beds of rivers and streams or were
picked from eroding faces of river terraces. None
of the tools was associated with human fossils,
none was found in a securely datable position, and
probably none was found within the context of a
primary archaeological deposit. In spite of the
large number of artifacts collected - von Koenigswald
and Tweedie in 1938 gathered some 3000 at the type
locality along the Baksoka River in Java (van
Heekeren 1972:35) - the sample of lithic artifacts
is extremely poor. Being derived from secondary
fluviatile deposits, the assemblages must have been
subject to more or less severe sorting through
water action and other geological processes. In
addition, picked up from the surface without the
benefit of the strict controls usually applied in
excavations, the artifact collections were probably
subject to further selection by the collectors
(local inhabitants, often children) who were likely
to favour the larger specimens. Thus, the various
collections labelled 'Patjitanian' are not only not
securely located in space and time, they do not
even provide a sound basis for a purely technological
assessment of the industry, if indeed they all
relate to a single industry or lithic tradition.

The situation has improved somewhat recently
because of excavations in 1965 in Flores by
Maringer and Verhoeven (1970b) and re-examination
of, and excavations at the Patjitanian type locality
in Java in 1972-73 by Bartstra (1973a, 1973b).
Unfortunately, neither of the projects has been
reported on fully so far, and the preliminary
reports give no information as to the archaeological
nature of the deposits. Maringer and Verhoeven
report fossil bone of *Stegodon trigonocephalus*
stratigraphically associated with pebble tools
(choppers, a hand-axe, a hammer stone), flake tools,
blade tools, cores and what they consider to be
debitage. On the basis of geological and
Palaeontological evidence, the age of the deposits
is assumed to be late Middle or early Upper

Pleistocene. However, no radiometric dates have
been announced so far. The excavators see
similarities between the industry from Flores and
both the Sangiran and Patjitanian industries from
Java. The preliminary report does not say how large
the excavation was, but it may be significant that
only 74 artifacts were recovered.

Bartstra's preliminary announcements (1973a,
1973b) of his excavations in the Baksoka Valley in
Java indicate that, as suggested by earlier
investigators, the valley does have a system of
three terraces. However, the origin of the terraces
may not be related to erosional processes in
connection with Pleistocene pluvial and interpluvial
periods but rather to local uplifting which took
place no earlier than the Upper Pleistocene. Stone
tools occurring on all three terraces show a large
variety of forms throughout, ranging from large
unifacial pebble tools to true bifaces and a large
number of rather sophisticated tools made on small
flakes such as scrapers, gravers, and borers. The
precise dating of the terraces is still open, but
an Upper Pleistocene date for the high terrace and
a post-Pleistocene date for the low terrace is
probable.

The quality of the evidence for other purported
palaeolithic industries from Indonesia is hardly
better than for the Patjitanian. The so-called
Sangiran Flake Industry (van Heekeren 1972:48-51)
is known primarily from surface collections of
eroding gravel beds of presumed Upper Pleistocene
age. Von Koenigswald reports (von Koenigswald and
Ghosh 1973) that he conducted limited excavations
at Sangiran in 1935 in which he recovered 123 stone
tools, but important technical information about
the excavation which would make it possible to
evaluate the results is not available. There is,
again, no direct association with human fossils,
and control of the archaeological context is
highly questionable. It must be mentioned here

however, that von Koenigswald claims that in his
Sangiran excavation the artifacts were stratigraphically
associated with elements of the Trinil fauna,
specifically *Axis lydekkeri* (von Koenigswald and
Ghosh 1973:1).

The Ngandong Industry is the only palaeolithic
assemblage ostensibly associated with human fossils
(van Heekeren 1972:58-9). However, the crucial
evidence in this case is also derived from surface
collections, and specific questions of association,
composition of the assemblage, and dating remain.
Similarly the Tjabengè Industry (van Heekeren 1958,
1972:69-72), a flake tool industry from Sulawesi,
has been collected only from the surface and even
its geological correlation with the strata on top of
which it has been found is uncertain, as is the
association with mammalian fossils found on the same
surface.

Since the material evidence is so dismally weak,
it is not surprising that the excavations at Niah
Cave in northwest Borneo[2] created much excitement
and raised great expectations. At the so-called
'Great Cave of Niah', a cavern with some 26 acres
(10.5 ha) of floor space, Tom Harrisson excavated
stratified archaeological deposits of some four
metres depth. The nature of the deposits ranges
from burial assemblages of the early second
millennium AD through 'neolithic' burial assemblages
to 'palaeolithic' habitation remains. The potential
importance of Niah Cave lies in its deep
stratigraphic sequence containing radiometrically
datable materials, and the association of both human
bones and a wide range of food remains with the
artifacts. Much of the excavation programme was
carried out before 1960, but to date only the food
remains and the 'neolithic' burials have been
reported on in detail. For the rest, only very
sketchy preliminary reports are available (Harrisson
1957, 1958, 1959, 1967, 1973; Solheim 1958) which
give tantalising bits of information without

providing the necessary background evidence to substantiate the extraordinary claims and implications raised. There is some suggestion in the publications that the cave was excavated in arbitrary levels with an apparent disregard for natural stratigraphy. This may explain why not a single drawing or photograph of a stratigraphic profile has been published to date. If this suspicion is true, then the published sequence of tool assemblages as well as the 39,600 BC date for the *Homo sapiens sapiens* skull are suspect. This date would make the Niah skull the earliest true *H. sapiens* find in the world. This does not agree well with the advanced modern morphology of the specimen, especially its facial gracility (Brothwell 1960).[3]

Although no published figure is available it appears that the actual number of stone tools excavated at Niah is extremely small. Indeed, for some years, the chief excavator of the site used a single flake to define a whole archaeological horizon below the 40,000 BC date. Typology and cultural relationships of this flake were determined as follows (Harrisson 1959:3):

> I showed this with other Niah tools at the Glasgow Meeting of the British Association for the Advancement of Science, 1958. Dr. T.T. Paterson, who pioneered research on the Sohan palaeolithic culture of northwest India, examined the tools with Dr. Kenneth Oakley and gave as his considered opinion that it appeared equivalent to the 'Mid-Sohan' - that is 'middle palaeolithic' - of his Indian experience.

In more recent publications Harrisson (1972, 1973) dissociated himself from the Soan identifications as well as from most other typological affiliations of the lithic artifacts from Niah. In any case, we are forced at present to disregard the material from Niah Cave until further information becomes available.

Burma

Similar critical remarks hold true for the 'palaeolithic' finds from Burma as for the Patjitanian. The Anyathian implements were all collected from the surface, and their geological association with the Pleistocene river terraces appears anything but certain. Again, the artifacts were not found in the context of primary archaeological deposits, and whatever ended up in the collecting bags of the archaeologists was probably subject to both natural and human sorting. In addition, the total number of artifacts available for the definition of some of the stages of the Anyathian is less than satisfactory (Table 1).

Arch. stage	Number of artifacts found	Number of localities
Early Anyathian 1	23	3
Early Anyathian 2	ca. 100	1
Early Anyathian 3	ca. 400	6
Late Anyathian 1	16	3
Late Anyathian 2	73	3

Table 1.

Sixteen or 23 stone tools provide an insufficient basis for the definition of an archaeological period under any circumstances, but especially when the stratigraphic situation is insecure and when basically similar forms of implements may occur all the way from a postulated mid-Pleistocene to a mid-Recent date.

Malaya

An extensive critique of Ann de G. Sieveking's excavation at Kota Tampan on the Perak River (Sieveking 1958, 1962) has recently been published

by Harrisson (1975). Harrisson disputes the early
Middle Pleistocene date of the parental gravel bed
and argues for a late Upper Pleistocene age. He
feels that the excavator was overly generous in
attributing artifactual character to many of the
254 collected specimens, and he is of the opinion
that, whatever indisputable tools there are from
this site, they show a Hoabinhian technology,
although some Patjitanian similarities are possible.

Cambodia, Vietnam, Thailand

Saurin (1966) claims a long palaeolithic
sequence in eastern Cambodia going back to the
second glacial period and associated with a system
of four terraces along the Mekong River. The same
caveats have to be applied to his claims as to
Movius' interpretations of the Burmese materials.
In fact, Saurin interprets both his geological and
archaeological evidence in a way closely related to
the Anyathian research, and he sees close
similarities between the development of the
Palaeolithic in Burma and in Cambodia.

Turning to Vietnam, the supposedly palaeolithic
assemblage from Mt Do (Boriskovskii 1966a, 1966b,
1967) was collected from the surface of a fairly
large area of basalt outcrops. There is not even
any claim of a geological association with Pleistocene
geological deposits. Rather, the collection is
evaluated and dated purely on typological grounds.
Boriskovskii points to the absence of certain
typical Hoabinhian forms and makes some improbable
comparisons with Lower Palaeolithic industries from
Europe. On this basis he claims an Abbevillian-
early Acheulean affinity and postulates a Lower
Palaeolithic date. In spite of Boriskovskii's
disclaimers it seems possible that lithic properties
of basalt, the predominant raw material employed at
Mt Do, account for some salient peculiarities of the
assemblage. Generally, the 'Clactonian'
characteristics which Boriskovskii detects in the

Mt Do assemblage indicate probably no more than the
rather amorphous character of the industry, an
element which it shares with innumerable other stone
industries from Southeast Asia.

In Thailand, van Heekeren (1948) found six
pebble tools *in situ* in fluviatile gravels of a
terrace of the Meklong River. He assumed the terrace
to be of Middle Pleistocene age and evaluated the
stone tools as belonging to a Lower Palaeolithic
industry. In evaluating van Heekeren's assessment
it must be kept in mind that the finds were made
under the difficult circumstances of a wartime
prison labour camp, and three of the six specimens
were subsequently lost. When Heider (1958)
reinvestigated the area he was able to collect
artifacts only from surface exposures of the terrace
gravels. He gathered 104 pebble tools and four
flakes but says that 'a small number of the specimens
collected along the Kwae Noi should not be considered
artifacts' (Heider 1958:65) and admits (1958:66)
that the artifacts 'were found neither in reliable
geological nor cultural context'. Von Koenigswald
(von Koenigswald and Ghosh 1973:30) suspects that
these finds belong to the Hoabinhian complex.

Philippines

Beyer (1947, 1948) was the first to claim
palaeolithic stone tools from several places in the
Philippines, but the evidence he presented was
extremely meagre. Von Koenigswald's two trips to
Northern Luzon in 1957 and 1958 yielded only about
a dozen pebble tools, all collected from the surface.
On the basis of his collection, he proposed a
'Cabalwanian Culture' (von Koenigswald 1958). Von
Koenigswald himself felt unsure about the dating
saying only that 'the geological evidence is such
that one might conclude that it is of Pleistocene
antiquity' (1958:70). Nevertheless, there has
always been a strong feeling among Philippine
prehistorians that these implements are of mid-

Pleistocene date. This belief eventually stimulated
more extensive field investigations beginning in
1971 (Fox 1973; Fox and Peralta 1974).

Surveys have so far yielded a profusion of
extinct vertebrate fauna in the same general area
where the stone tools·are being found, and at least
68 localities have been located where stone tools
have eroded out of the ground. However, excavations
to date have not contributed much information that
would help to interpret the surface finds. Not a
single indisputable *in situ* association between
artifacts and fossil fauna has been reported. The
excavators themselves admit that they are having
great difficulty interpreting the archaeological as
well as the geological stratigraphy. Although Fox
claims that the archaeological localities represent
kill sites, no evidence has yet been presented which
would unequivocally support such an interpretation.
For the time being, the chronological position as
well as the wider archaeological context of the
Cagayan stone tools has to remain open.

The situation is much better for Tabon Cave
on the island of Palawan with an archaeological
sequence extending from about 40,000 to 9000 BP
(Fox 1967, 1970, 1973). Although detailed reports
of the extensive excavations are still eagerly
awaited, there appears to be no real reason to
doubt Fox's general description of the sequence as
a relatively unchanging industry of undifferentiated
flakes with little retouch, some utilised cores,
and very few pebble tools.[4] It should also be
mentioned here, however, that the dating of the
Tabon skull has always been considered highly
uncertain.

Résumé

It is necessary now to summarise this critical
survey and to amplify it with other related
archaeological information.

1. On the basis of fossil evidence there is no doubt that hominids in Southeast Asia were present at a very early date, possibly as early as two million years ago if the recent radiometric dates for Java can be substantiated (Jacob 1972; Jacob and Curtis 1971).

2. Unless *Homo erectus* in Southeast Asia was markedly different in his cultural capacity from his cousin in Africa, we must expect to find archaeological deposits with a chronological range similar to that indicated for the human fossils.

3. Regardless of the status of Niah skull, *Homo sapiens sapiens* must also have made a relatively early appearance in Southeast Asia, because he is present in Australia by at least 30,000 years ago (Jones 1973; Thorne this volume).

4. It is quite possible that some of the archaeological finds discussed in this paper are indeed of at least early Middle Pleistocene age. However, we do not have any sound evidence as to which ones might qualify; and even if we did know, the nature of the archaeological material collected would provide little or no cultural or social information.

5. Nevertheless, because of the great repetitiveness in basic patterns of the finds, Movius' claim for a lack of substantial change in lithic technology throughout the Pleistocene may well prove correct.

6. There are some reasonably well dated assemblages, excavated under varying conditions of archaeological control and often insufficiently documented, of Upper and terminal Pleistocene age. The primary component of the lithic industries of these assemblages invariably seems to be a large number of morphologically undifferentiated and rarely modified flakes with a small percentage of core and/or pebble tools.

7. A similar technological substrate has been shown to be present during the late Pleistocene in New Guinea and Australia, although specific tool forms such as 'waisted blades' and 'ground axes'

seem to be added in some areas (Jones 1973; Lampert 1975; Mulvaney 1969).

8. The highly generalised tool technology of the Upper Pleistocene shows great geographical and chronological persistence lasting well into Recent, and in some cases even historic times (Dunn 1964; Fox 1970; Glover 1971; van Heekeren and Knuth 1967; Hutterer 1974; Peterson 1974).

DISCUSSION

Typology as a problem

A reconsideration of the Palaeolithic of Southeast Asia should appropriately start with a critical rethinking of the problem of typology, since most previous studies have used typological comparison of lithic assemblages as one of their principal analytical tools. The various typologies previously used had generally two things in common: they were arrived at on the basis of intuitive sorting and they were more or less closely patterned after European models. The latter is especially significant since the theoretical framework employed in most traditional studies of Southeast Asian prehistory was almost universally diffusionistic, and, until recently, it was generally taken for granted that palaeolithic developments in the Far East would follow those in Europe. Even after it became clear that many specific tool types which were considered important 'type fossils' in Europe did not occur in the Far East at all, it was still generally held that at least the overall trend of technological development would have to follow that of Europe, namely a development from core tool industries to flake tool industries, to blade tool industries, and eventually to microlithic industries. While these gross patterns were held to be indicative of the general stage and period of cultural development,

specific typological differences among individual
assemblages of the same technological stage were
taken to reflect different archaeological cultures
and traditions.

The accumulation of new field data has not done
much to clarify the question of cultural traditions
and relationships, nor has it helped to establish
orderly typological sequences within the region.   It
is necessary, therefore, to return to a very basic
question. What variables influence the form and
composition of lithic assemblages and the
distribution of particular assemblages over time
and space? The explicit investigation of this
problem as a general theoretical issue in
archaeology is still in its infancy, but it is
already clear that numerous and highly complex
interrelations and interactions of cultural and
environmental variables are involved (Binford and
Binford 1966; Bordes 1961; Hayden this volume; White
this volume; White and Thomas 1972).

When working with archaeological artifacts, we
are constantly reminded that we are dealing with
human behaviour only in a very roundabout way. The
artifacts themselves are, of course, not behaviour
but only the material debitage of it. Nevertheless,
they do reflect, more or less well, human behaviour
as it is related to and conditioned by the
environment on the one hand and the cultural-
cognitive system on the other. Not all classes of
artifacts are equally good indicators of all areas
of human organisation. By their very nature, those
groups of artifacts which Binford (1962) labels
'technomic' are less sensitive to the ideological
and strictly social aspects of human existence than
to the aspects of technology, subsistence, and
physical survival within a given environment.
Palaeolithic stone tools belong to this category,
and they are probably even less satisfactory
indicators of the ideological life and social
organisation of prehistoric groups than, say,

artifacts of wood or clay, since the physical
properties of the raw material set rather narrow
limits for non-functional expression. It is,
therefore, often quite useless to speculate about
formal typological similarities and differences
among lithic assemblages as indications of cultural
relationships or the lack of a relationship between
the human populations who produce the artifacts.
The primary areas of information stone tools are
able to convey are: i) the technology by which they
were produced; ii) functions they were employed
for; and iii) the contexts in which they were
discarded.

Thus, one of the most crucial pieces of
evidence to be established in the analysis of lithic
artifacts is their function. In Southeast Asia, a
number of investigators have taken note of the
apparently generalised nature of most of the late
Pleistocene and post-Pleistocene lithic assemblages
and have postulated that the stone tools must have
been complemented by an array of tools made of
organic raw materials, principally wood and bamboo
(Gorman 1970; van Heekeren 1972; Solheim 1970).
Slowly, some evidence for this hypothesis is being
accumulated. Only very limited investigations of
edge damage have been undertaken so far suggesting
that woodworking is a prevalent functional role for
flakes studied (Gorman 1970; Hutterer 1974; Peterson
1974). It is quite difficult to relate either flake
tools or pebble tools directly to primary subsistence
activities. With very few exceptions, there is
nothing that could qualify as projectile points,[5]
hardly anything that would make an efficient digging
tool, and certainly nothing that might serve as a
container. By way of elimination then, if the
tools were not used for extractive (subsistence)
purposes, they must have been used for maintenance
(manufacturing) purposes. (I am disregarding the
possibility of symbolic or ritual function.)

I have suggested elsewhere (Hutterer 1976) that

the predominance of generalised lithic technologies
in Southeast Asia is related to the rain forest
environment, the primary habitat of ethnographic
hunters-and-gatherers in the region. Humid tropical
environments are characterised by extremely high
biological diversity and a very dispersed distribution
of individual species. Consequently, hunters and
collectors in the humid tropics must utilise a wide
variety of plant and animal resources to meet their
nutritional needs. Since many of the plant and
animal species utilised are not only widely spaced
but are also very specialised in habitat and
behaviour, societies of hunters and collectors are
forced to employ a wide array of specialised gear,
which must be either carried from place to place or
manufactured when needed. This situation makes it
unlikely that stone could be employed as a universal
raw material. The energy outlay involved in the
procurement of the raw material and the manufacture
and curation (repair, transport, etc.) of stone
tools would in many cases make it highly
uneconomical to employ them extensively as extractive
implements. However, most tropical areas provide a
variety of vines, hardwoods, and especially the
highly versatile bamboos as raw materials for making
tools. These materials are ubiquitous, thus
lessening the problem of procurement, and since they
are light-weight, they can easily be transported.
They are also easily worked with stone tools that
fulfill only a minimum of formal requirements (shape
and angle of edge, perhaps overall size) and which
can thus usually be produced quickly and nearly
anywhere from various kinds of stone.

To date, only a handful of detailed studies of
lithic industries from the area of Southeast Asia
and New Guinea is available and these concern
flake tools. White (1967, 1969, 1972; White and
Thomas 1972) specifically investigated problems of
formal typology of both ethnographic and
archaeological flake assemblages from New Guinea.
Gorman (1971b) limited his investigation to

functional aspects of the flake component of the
lithic assemblage from Spirit Cave in northwestern
Thailand. The results of both studies may be used
in support of the foregoing discussion, however.
Woodworking was indicated as a primary role of flake
tools in both instances. The ethnographic research
in New Guinea indicated that flakes would meet all
the requirements for functional tools if they
fulfilled a very limited number of conditions
primarily concerning the shape of a potential
working edge. No further modification of the flake
to conform to standardised overall forms was
necessary. The only major formal distinction made
by ethnographic informants concerned the relative
size of the flakes.

To the best of my knowledge no similar studies
have yet been made or published with regard to
pebble tools (but see Hayden this volume). However,
it stands to reason that pebble tools also were used
primarily for woodworking. In most cases, where
detailed descriptions and illustrations are
available, it is evident that the tools are very
steeply flaked. Thus they would not make good
cutting implements and would not be efficient for
the killing and butchering of meat (unless one wants
to make mince meat or to crush bones). On the other
hand, a steep edge angle is essential for woodworking
tools as it reduces wear and cuts down on the need
for resharpening and tool replacement. However, it
is quite possible that because of the size of pebble
tools and the mechanics involved in handling them,
edge angle is much less important in determining
function than it is for flake tools. Like Western
hand-axes, pebble tools may represent a very
generalised class of implement. The dichotomy
between lithic tools for woodworking and non-lithic
tools for other purposes need not be expressed
equally strongly in all industries of Southeast
Asia, not even in lithic assemblages of the same
period or the same region. Much may depend on
such variables as general availability of suitable

lithic raw materials within an area, closeness of a
site to a source of raw material, and type of site
(e.g. base camp, hunting/collecting camp). It is
known however, that large areas of Southeast Asia
are not blessed with good cryptocrystalline
minerals. It is in those areas that one would
expect the dichotomy to be strongest. In any
event, it would not be reasonable to claim that *all*
flake and pebble tools in Southeast Asia were used
exclusively for woodworking.[6]

In general, it is probable that pebble tools
match the functional range of flake tools fairly
closely, being designed primarily for heavy-duty
work. If this reasoning is correct it would make
little sense to expect individual lithic traditions
to consist primarily either of pebble tools or
flake tools. On the other hand, it would not be
surprising if there were considerable differences
in the relative proportions of flakes and pebble
tools among assemblages even of the same tradition.
The differences between assemblages would reflect
differences in site-specific activities. Thus the
composition of specific lithic assemblages should
correlate with other aspects of the sites with which
they are associated: location of the site with
regard to certain resources, amount and nature of
food remains, size of site, density of archaeological
material relative to length of occupational period,
and so forth. For example one would expect, if a
site was visited primarily in connection with heavy-
duty woodwork, to find a relatively small number of
stone tools generally but a relatively high
proportion of pebble tools among them. The amount
of food remains would also be relatively limited
and the number and variety of plant and animal
species present would probably be considerably less
than in a site regularly used for habitation. In a
habitation site of the same group, on the other hand,
pebble tools might be totally absent while flake
tools abounded, and food remains would be
concentrated with the number of species represented

being relatively large. Similarly the composition
of lithic assemblages of the same social group
could vary considerably between coastal and interior
sites.

According to this view the form of most stone
tools in Southeast Asia, or more precisely the
relative lack of recurrent forms, is related
primarily to environmental and functional variables.
This means that similarities as well as differences
between lithic assemblages may have little to do
with cultural-cognitive similarities or differences
between the groups that produced the stone tools.
In other words morphological characteristics and
composition of lithic assemblages by themselves
should not be used to make inferences about
cultural relationships, socio-cultural development,
or chronology.

It is worthwhile to leave the time boundaries
of the Pleistocene for a moment and ask what the
Hoabinhian phenomenon may mean in this context.
The Hoabinhian has variously been defined as a
'culture' (Matthews 1966), a 'tradition' (Dunn 1970),
and a 'techno-complex' (Gorman 1970). Gorman chooses
the concept of 'techno-complex' because he doubts
'whether the sites are the remains of any single
cultural group' (1970:81) and he feels that 'the
wide distribution of Hoabinhian traits reflects an
early Southeast Asian techno-complex, widely
diffused and reflecting common ecological
adaptations to the Southeast Asian humid tropics'
(1970:82). Primarily due to historical accident in
the pursuit of archaeological research, the
designation 'Hoabinhian' has essentially been
restricted to post-Pleistocene sites on the mainland
of Southeast Asia and on the island of Sumatra
(Solheim 1974). At this time there is little
indication that either the temporal or geographical
restrictions are justified. It is not demonstrable
that the lithic technology of 'Hoabinhian' sites is
qualitatively different from technologies found

throughout Pleistocene Southeast Asia, nor can it
be shown that the relative scarcity of certain types
of 'Hoabinhian' pebble tools in many of the islands
is indicative of a lack of cultural relationships
with mainland populations.[7]   Some have claimed that
'Hoabinhian' sites evidence a major ecological
reorientation compared to palaeolithic sites
(Gorman 1971a).   While the ecological orientation
of early 'Hoabinhian' populations (that is, early
Holocene populations) may be correctly perceived,
it is not possible to establish a contrast with
earlier Pleistocene populations until we have more
and better archaeological data from that period.
However, owing to the nature of the environment in
much of Southeast Asia, it is entirely probable
that both a 'broad spectrum' exploitative pattern
and a certain amount of plant manipulation are of
Pleistocene antiquity in this region (Hutterer 1976).
All in all, it is questionable whether the term
'Hoabinhian' reflects a meaningful archaeological
category.

It was asked earlier whether a lack of change
in lithic technology reflects general cultural
stagnation.   On the basis of the argument presented
in this paper, the answer has to be 'no'.   Since
stone tools in the Southeast Asian tropics are seen
as primarily related to maintenance, it is
conceivable that the subsistence economy, and with
it the extractive technology, could undergo radical
changes without visibly affecting the basic
typological patterns of the stone tools.   What might
well reflect such changes however, are such things
as relative proportions of flake and pebble tools
in the assemblages, patterns of site utilisation,
spatial distribution patterns of stone tools,
overall settlement patterns, etc.   There is now
some archaeological field evidence to suggest that
the typology of stone tools is a misleading
indicator even for such fundamental cultural
developments as major changes in the subsistence
economy.   Glover (1971) reports from Timor the

persistence of an essentially undifferentiated
flake assemblage for several thousand years beyond
the date for which there is indication of the
introduction of agriculture. And White reports
from New Guinea (1972:148) that, over a period of
approximately 10,000 years, the stone tool technology
remained essentially the same while the subsistence
economy was becoming more complex and intensified
from gathering and horticulture to agriculture.

The 'Palaeolithic' sequence

The foregoing discussion has been concerned
primarily with hunting-and-gathering cultures in a
humid tropical environment, regardless of
chronological considerations. The wide distribution
of implied climatological and phytogeographical
conditions through much of Southeast Asia can,
however, be assumed only for terminal Pleistocene
and post-Pleistocene times. World-wide Quaternary
research is presently very much in flux. It is
clear that many of the older assumptions concerning
the sequence of major climatic cycles as well as
world-wide correlations of regional climatic
sequences are inadequate (Flint 1971). The
interpretation of the Pleistocene in Southeast Asia
itself seems to have undergone some cyclical
changes. Researchers of the 1930s and 1940s saw
evidence for major climatic fluctuations within a
framework of pluvial and interpluvial stages closely
correlated with the classical four stages of the
central European alpine Pleistocene sequence (e.g.
de Terra 1943a, 1943b). More recently, the
tendency was to see Southeast Asia only slightly
affected by world-wide Pleistocene climatic
fluctuations and to infer only minor environmental
change (e.g. Gorman 1970). This trend may now be
reversing itself again, for some evidence seems to
be accumulating from a variety of sources to indicate
that climatic conditions in the region during the
Pleistocene fluctuated more widely than has
previously been assumed (Verstappen 1975).

Particularly, it seems that 'drier conditions with
lower precipitation values and a longer dry season,
have occurred in Malesia during the Pleistocene
glacials' (1975:28). While many details are still
unclear, it must be assumed that such conditions
would have had incisive effects on landforms and on
the distribution of fauna and flora. There is
evidence however, for the uninterrupted existence
of two large cores of rain forest since Miocene
times, one on the Sunda Shelf covering the present
areas of Malaya, Sumatra, Borneo and the westernmost tip of Java, and the other on the northernmost
portion of the Sahul Shelf, covering much of what is
now New Guinea. For these areas it may well be
possible to extend the considerations presented here
about tropical forest hunters some way back into the
Pleistocene.

The situation is somewhat more difficult for
those areas which apparently did undergo several
episodes of relative aridity, such as most of
mainland Southeast Asia, the Philippines, Sulawesi,
most of Java, the Moluccas and the Lesser Sundas.
Phytological conditions during the drier interludes
may have varied from monsoon forest to savannah,
with the attendant faunal complexes of browsers and
grazers. It must also be remembered however, that
the situation fluctuated between drier episodes
during glacial periods and wet rain forest
conditions during interglacial periods. It is not
possible at present to speculate how such changes
might have affected various cultural and social
patterns of hunting-and-gathering populations in
the area. As long as the palaeoclimatological and
palaeontological evidence is so vague and reliable
archaeological information essentially non-existent,
it may be best to hold the problem in abeyance.
Nevertheless one point must be made: even radically
different ecological conditions need not necessarily
call for a radically different lithic technology.
Even under extremely arid conditions such as
prevail in the interior of Australia, lithic

technologies may be extremely simple, essentially maintenance related, and highly conservative (Gould 1973, 1974; Gould *et al.* 1971), although the ecological and cultural-processual reasons there may be quite different.

While our present data are insufficient to reconstruct in detail a sequence of Pleistocene environments for any area of Southeast Asia or to correlate securely geological strata and archaeological assemblages, there are some vague archaeological hints to indicate that Pleistocene lithic technologies may actually have undergone more change than is commonly acknowledged. The first collectors of 'Patjitanian' tools in Java already were aware of the fact that the archaeological deposits along the Baksoka River contained not only pebble tools but also '"complete Chellean" hand-axes, flake tools and a few crude blades' (van Heekeren 1972:35). Bartstra (1973a) recently pointed to the fact that his excavation yielded, in addition to pebble and undifferentiated flake tools, some hand-axes as well as some specialised smaller flake implements. The same claims are made by Maringer and Verhoeven (1970b) for their material from Flores. This would imply a change from more complex industries in Middle or Upper Pleistocene times to less complex industries during the late Upper Pleistocene and early Holocene. More information is needed to demonstrate whether such changes did in fact occur and whether they may be related to changing environments during the earlier periods of the Pleistocene.

Finally, a word should be said about what might be expected of the very oldest archaeological material to be found in Southeast Asia. A consensus seems to be emerging which places the lower Sangiran hominid as a transitional form between australopithecines and *Homo erectus* (Pilbeam 1972).[8] This agrees well with the redating of the Djetis beds to nearly two million

years ago. Since we are dealing with a relatively
early stage in the evolution of cognitive and
manipulative abilities, it would not be unreasonable
to expect that the material culture of this hominid
would be quite simple and his stone tools relatively
crude. However, such a prediction might easily
prove wrong. In any case it should be fruitful to
study the rapidly accumulating artifactual material
of early hominids in Africa, not so much for the
purpose of simplistic typological comparison, but
rather to gain an understanding of the cultural
capabilities and adaptive flexibility of hominids
of that stage of development.

SUMMARY

The somewhat diverse considerations and
speculations of this paper may now be summarised.
It is abundantly clear that our evidence of
Pleistocene cultures from Southeast Asia is exceedingly weak. Much of the material on hand was
collected without even the most fundamental
archaeological controls, and traditional reconstructions of the Southeast Asian Palaeolithic
were based largely on unfounded typological
comparison. The apparent homogeneity, simplicity,
and conservatism of lithic industries documented at
least for parts of the Upper Pleistocene and the
Recent periods, has nothing to do with cultural
homogeneity and cultural retardation. Rather, it
has to be explained on ecological and cultural-
processual grounds. For earlier periods of the
Pleistocene, the palaeoenvironmental and
archaeological information is so meagre that it is
difficult at present to make predictions. It seems
quite likely, however, that cultural traditions
through the greater part of the Pleistocene were
more varied than has been assumed in the literature.

FOOTNOTES

[1] An earlier version of this paper was read at the
   Midwest Conference on Asian Affairs, Athens, Ohio,
23-25 October 1975. I thank Henry T. Wright and
William K. Macdonald for the critical reading of the
earlier draft. The present version has also
profited from discussions at the conference.

[2] Although North Borneo (Sabah), Brunei and Sarawak
   are politically not part of Indonesia they are
included here for obvious geographical reasons.

[3] This is not to dispute that modern *Homo sapiens*
   may have been present in Southeast Asia at a very
early date. In fact, this may have to be postulated
because of his presence in Australia at least 30,000
years ago (Jones 1973; Thorne this volume). It must
also be mentioned here that the oldest known population
of Australia does have a very modern morphology of
the skull (Thorne 1971), but this does not, by
itself, demonstrate the antiquity of the Niah skull.

[4] However, J. Kress (pers comm), who has excavated
   at Tabon, disputes Fox's description of the
technological sequence. The awaited publication
of a report by Kress may change the assessment of
the Palawan finds.

[5] Among the post-Pleistocene lithic assemblages are
   a few that contain either flaked or ground
projectile points (e.g. Beyer 1948; van Heekeren
1972; Levy 1943; Mulvaney and Soejono 1970). Also
the claim of morphological indistinctness does not
apply to all assemblages. Some lithic industries
with a relatively strong blade component have been
reported (e.g. van Heekeren 1972; van Heekeren and
Knuth 1967; Scheans *et al.* 1970). However, it is
possible that these latter assemblages were produced
by agriculturists.

[6] Semenov (1971) thinks that the unifacially flaked

'sumatraliths', commonly found in the large coastal
middens of Sumatra, were used as wedges and hand-axes
to pry open shells and extract the molluscs.
W. Peterson (pers comm) has informed me that, in his
experience, pebble tools show a wide range of edge
angles, with unifacially flaked choppers generally
having edges around 30°-40°, bifacial chopping tools
having edges around 60°, and the so-called 'flat-
iron choppers' and 'horse-hoof cores' having edges
of 90° and more.

[7] The essential technological similarity between
   palaeolithic (Pleistocene) and 'Hoabinhian' stone
tools is well illustrated by recurring confusion
and disputes over whether some surface finds should
be assigned to one or the other chronological and
cultural complex (see, for instance, van Heekeren
1972:44-7; van Heekeren and Knuth 1967:197;
von Koenigswald and Ghosh 1973).

[8] The classification of this hominid has presented
   some problems, and it has variously been
identified as '*Meganthropus palaeojavanicus*',
'*Paranthropus palaeojavanicus*', and '*Pithecanthropus
palaeojavanicus*' (Day 1965). Whatever one's
position may be about the developmental significance
of this hominid, the rules of zoological systematics
hardly permit to give it the status of a separate
generic form.

REFERENCES

Almeida, A. de and G. Zbyszewski 1967 A
     contribution to the study of the prehistory
     of Portuguese Timor - lithic industries.
     In Solheim 1967:55-67

Bartstra, G-J. 1973a *The Patjitanian culture:
     preliminary report of a new research.* In
     Chicago 1973

1973b Short account of the 1973 investigations on the palaeolithic Patjitanian culture, Java, Indonesia. *Newsletter of the Committee on Palaeolithic Research in Southern and Eastern Asia* 1

and W.A. Casparie (eds) 1975 *Modern Quaternary research in Southeast Asia.* Rotterdam: Balkema

Beyer, H.O. 1947 Outline review of Philippine archaeology by islands and provinces. *Philippine Journal of Science* 77:205-374

1948 *Philippine and East Asian archaeology and its relation to the origin of the Pacific Islands population.* Quezon City: National Research Council of the Philippines, Bulletin 29

Binford, L.R. 1962 Archaeology as anthropology. *American Antiquity* 28:217-25

and S.R. Binford 1966 A preliminary analysis of functional variability in the Mousterian of Levallois facies. *American Anthropologist* 68(2:2)(special publication): 238-95

Bordes, F.H. 1961 Mousterian cultures in France. *Science* 134:803-10

Boriskovskii, P.I. 1966a Basic problems of the prehistoric archaeology of Vietnam. *Asian Perspectives* 9:83-5

1966b *Vietnam in primeval times,* (in Russian). Moscow-Leningrad: Nauka. (Translated in *Soviet Anthropology and Archaeology* 7(2):14-32; 7(3):3-19; 8(3):214-57; 8(4):355-66; 9(2):154-72; 9(3):226-64, over the years 1968-71)

1967 Problems of the palaeolithic and of the mesolithic of Southeast Asia. In Solheim 1967:41-6

1973 *Some problems of paleolithic of southern and south-east Asia.* In Chicago 1973

Brothwell, D.R. 1960 Upper Pleistocene human skull from Niah caves. *Sarawak Museum Journal* 9:323-49

Chicago 1973 Papers read at 9th International Congress of Anthropological and Ethnological Sciences

Collings, H.D. 1938 A Pleistocene site in the Malay Peninsula. *Nature* 143:575

Coon, C.S. 1965 *The living races of man.* New York: Knopf

Day, M.H. 1965 *Guide to fossil man.* Cleveland and New York: The World Publishing Co.

Dunn, F.L. 1964 Excavations at Gua Kechil, Pahang. *Journal of the Malaysian Branch, Royal Asiatic Society* 37(2):87-124

1970 Cultural evolution in the late Pleistocene and Holocene of Southeast Asia. *American Anthropologist* 72:1041-54

Flint, R.F. 1971 *Glacial and Quaternary geology.* New York: Wiley

Fox, R.B. 1967 Excavation in the Tabon Caves and some problems in Philippine chronology. In M.D. Zamora (ed.) *Studies in Philippine Anthropology*:88-116. Quezon City: Alemar-Phoenix

1970 *The Tabon Caves: archaeological explorations and excavations on Palawan Island, Philippines.* Manila: National Museum

1973 *The Philippine paleolithic.* Paper read at Conference on the Early Paleolithic of East Asia, McGill University, Montreal

and J.T. Peralta 1974 Preliminary report on the palaeolithic archaeology of Cagayan

Valley, Philippines, and the Cabalwanian
Industry. In Seminar 1974:100-47

Fromaget, J. 1937 Aperçu sur la stratigraphie
et l'anthropologie préhistorique des
formations récentes dans la chaîne annamitique
et le Haut Laos. In *Congrès préhistorique de
France: compte rendu de la douzième session,
Toulouse-Foix, 1936*. Paris: Société
préhistorique française

          1940a Les récentes découvertes
anthropologiques dans les formations préhistoriques
de la chaîne annamitique. In F.N. Chasen and
M.W.F. Tweedie (eds) *Proceedings of the Third
Congress of Prehistorians of the Far East*:51-9.
Singapore: Government Printer

          1940b La stratigraphie des dépôts
préhistoriques de Tam Hang (chaîne annamitique
septentrionale) et ses difficultés. As above:
60-70

          and E. Saurin 1936 Note préliminaire
sur les formations cénozoïques et les plus
récentes de la chaîne annamitique septentrionale
et du Haut Laos: stratigraphie, préhistoire,
anthropologie. *Bulletin du Service Géologique
de l'Indochine* 22(3)

Ghosh, A.K. 1971 Ordering of lower palaeolithic
traditions in South and South-East Asia.
*Archaeology and Physical Anthropology in
Oceania* 6:87-101

          1973 *Chopper/chopping and bifacial
traditions in South and Southeast Asia - a
reappraisal*. In Chicago 1973

Glover, I.C. 1971 Prehistoric research in Timor.
In D.J. Mulvaney and J. Golson (eds)
Aboriginal man and environment in Australia:
158-81. Canberra: Australian National
University Press

          and E.A. Glover 1970 Pleistocene

flaked stone tools from Timor and Flores. *Mankind* 7(3):188-90

Gorman, C.F. 1970   Excavations at Spirit Cave, north Thailand: some interim interpretations. *Asian Perspectives* 13:80-107

1971a   The Hoabinhian and after: subsistence patterns in Southeast Asia during the late Pleistocene and early Recent periods. *World Archaeology* 2:300-20

1971b   Prehistoric research in northern Thailand: a cultural-chronographic sequence from the late Pleistocene to the early Recent period.   PhD dissertation, University of Hawaii, Honolulu

Gould, R.A. 1973   *Australian archaeology in ecological and ethnographic perspective.* Andover (Mass.): Warner Modular Publications No.7

1974   *The Australian Desert Culture.* Paper read at the 73rd Annual Meeting of the American Anthropological Association, Mexico City

, D.A. Koster and A.H.L. Sontz 1971 The lithic assemblage of the Western Desert Aborigines of Australia.   *American Antiquity* 36:149-69

Harrisson, T. 1957   The Great Cave of Niah: a preliminary report on Bornean prehistory. *Man* 58:161-2

1958   Carbon-14 dated palaeoliths from Borneo.   *Nature* 181:792

1959   New archaeological and ethnological results from Niah caves, Sarawak.   *Man* 59:1-8

1965   50,000 years of stone age culture in Borneo.   In *Smithsonian Report for 1964:*521-30.   Washington: Smithsonian

Institution

  1967 Niah caves, Sarawak. In
Solheim 1967:77-8

  1972 The Borneo Stone Age - in
the light of recent research. *Sarawak
Museum Journal* 20:385-412

  1973 *Present status and problems
for paleolithic studies in Borneo and
adjacent islands.* In Chicago 1973

  1975 Discovery and excavations at
Kota Tampan, Perak (1936-54). In Bartstra
and Casparie 1975:53-70

Heekeren, H.R. van 1948 Prehistoric discoveries
 in Siam, 1943-44. *Proceedings of the
 Prehistoric Society* 14:24-32

  1958 The Tjabengè flake
industry from south Celebes. *Asian
Perspectives* 2:77-81

  1972 *The Stone Age of
Indonesia,* (2nd ed.). The Hague: Nijhoff

  1975 Chronology of the
Indonesian prehistory. In Bartstra and
Casparie 1975:47-51

  and Count Eigil Knuth 1967
*Archaeological excavations in Thailand, I:
Sai-Yok.* Copenhagen: Munksgaard

Heider, K.G. 1958 A pebble-tool complex in
 Thailand. *Asian Perspectives* 2:63-7

Hutterer, K.L. 1974 The evolution of Philippine
 lowland societies. *Mankind* 9(4):287-99

  1976 An evolutionary approach to
the Southeast Asian cultural sequence.
Current Anthropology 17:221-42

Jacob, T. 1972 The absolute date of the Djetis
 beds at Modjokerto. *Antiquity* 44:148

and G.H. Curtis 1971 Preliminary
potassium-argon dating of early man in Java.
*Contributions of the University of
California Archaeological Research Facility
(Berkeley)* 12:50

Jones, R. 1973 Emerging picture of Pleistocene
Australians. *Nature* 246:278-81

Koenigswald, G.H.R. von 1958 Preliminary report
on a newly-discovered stone age culture from
northern Luzon, Philippine Islands. *Asian
Perspectives* 2:69-70

and A.K. Ghosh 1973 Stone
implements from the Trinil beds of Sangiran,
central Java. *Proceedings of the Koninklijke
Nederlandsche Akademie van Wettenschappen*
(series B)76(1):1-34

Lampert, R.J. 1975 Trends in Australian prehistoric
research. *Antiquity* 49:197-206

Levy, P. 1943 *Recherches préhistoriques dans la
région de Mlu Prei.* Hanoi: École Française
d'Extrême-Orient, Publications Vol.30

Maringer, J. and Th. Verhoeven 1970a Die
Oberflächenfunde aus dem Fossilgebiet von
Mengeruda und Olabula auf Flores, Indonesien.
Anthropos 65:530-46

1970b Die
Steinartefakte aus der Stegodon-Fossilschicht
von Mengeruda auf Flores, Indonesien.
Anthropos 65:229-47

1972 Steingeräte
aus dem Waiklau-Trockenbett bei Maumere auf
Flores, Indonesien: eine Patjitanian-artige
Industrie auf der Insel Flores. *Anthropos*
67:129-37

1975 Die
Oberflächenfunde von Marokoak auf Flores,
Indonesien. *Anthropos* 70:97-104

Matthews, J.M. 1966   A review of the 'Hoabinhian'
    in Indo-China. *Asian Perspectives* 9:86-95

Movius, H.L., Jr. 1943   The Stone Age of Burma.
    *Transactions of the American Philosophical
    Society* 32:341-93

            1944 *Early man and Pleistocene
    stratigraphy in southern and eastern Asia.*
    Cambridge (Mass.): Harvard University, Papers
    of the Peabody Museum of American Archaeology
    and Ethnology 19(3)

            1949   The lower palaeolithic
    cultures of southern and eastern Asia.
    *Transactions of the American Philosophical
    Society* 38:329-420

            1955   Paleolithic archaeology of
    southern and eastern Asia, exclusive of India.
    Journal of World History 2:257-82, 520-53

Mulvaney, D.J. 1969 *The prehistory of Australia.*
    London: Thames and Hudson

            1970   The Patjitanian Industry:
    some observations. *Mankind* 7(3):184-7

            and R.P. Soejono 1970   The
    Australian-Indonesian archaeological
    expedition to Sulawesi. *Asian Perspectives*
    13:163-77

Peterson, W.E. 1974 Summary report of two
    archaeological sites from north-eastern Luzon.
    *Archaeology and Physical Anthropology in
    Oceania* 9:26-35

Pilbeam, D. 1972 *The ascent of man.* New York:
    Macmillan

Saurin, E. 1966 Le paléolithique de Cambodge
    oriental. *Asian Perspectives* 9:96-110

            1968   La géologie du Quaternaire et
    les industries préhistoriques en Indochine.
    In Solheim 1968:63-84

Scheans, D.J., K.L. Hutterer and R.L. Cherry 1970
A newly discovered blade industry from the
central Philippines. *Asian Perspectives* 13:
179-81

Semenov, S.A. 1971 A contribution to the question
of certain stone age implements of Southeast
Asia. *Soviet Anthropology and Archaeology* 10
(1):82-8

Seminar 1974 *Proceedings of the First Regional
Seminar on Southeast Asian Prehistory and
Archaeology*. Manila: National Museum of the
Philippines

Sieveking, A. 1958 The palaeolithic industry of
Kota Tampan, Perak, northwestern Malaya.
Asian Perspectives 2:91-102

                1962 The palaeolithic industry of
Kota Tampan, Perak, Malaya. *Proceedings of
the Prehistoric Society* 28:103-39

Soejono, R.P. 1961 Preliminary notes on new finds
of lower palaeolithic implements from
Indonesia. *Asian Perspectives* 5:217-32

Solheim, W.G., II 1958 The present state of the
'Palaeolithic' in Borneo. *Asian Perspectives*
2:83-90

                (ed.) 1967 *Archaeology at the
Eleventh Pacific Science Congress*. Honolulu:
University of Hawaii, Social Science Research
Institute, Asian and Pacific Archaeology
Series No.1

                1970 Northern Thailand,
Southeast Asia, and world prehistory.
Asian Perpsectives 13:145-62

                1974 The Hoabinhian and
Island Southeast Asia. In Seminar 1974:19-26

Sørensen, P. 1962 The Thai-Danish prehistoric
expedition, 1960-1962, II: a preliminary
report of the expedition 1960-1961 to the

Kanchanaburi Province, western Thailand.
Folk 4:28-45

Terra, H. de 1943a Pleistocene geology and early
man in Java. *Transactions of the American
Philosophical Society* 32:437-64

          1943b The Pleistocene of Burma.
*Transactions of the American Philosophical
Society* 32:271-339

Thorne, A.G. 1971 Mungo and Kow Swamp: morphological
variation in Pleistocene Australians. *Mankind*
8(2):85-9

Verstappen, H. Th. 1975 On palaeo climates and
landform development in Malesia. In Bartstra
and Casparie 1975:3-35

White, J.P. 1967 Ethno-archaeology in New Guinea:
two examples. *Mankind* 6(9):409-14

          1969 Typologies for some prehistoric
flaked stone artefacts of the Australian New
Guinea highlands. *Archaeology and Physical
Anthropology in Oceania* 4:18-46

          1972 *Ol tumbuna: archaeological
excavations in the eastern central highlands,
Papua New Guinea.* Canberra: Australian
National University, Research School of
Pacific Studies, Department of Prehistory,
Terra Australis 2

          and D.H. Thomas 1972 What mean these
stones? In D.L. Clarke (ed.) *Models in
archaeology*:275-308. London: Methuen

STICKS AND STONES AND GROUND EDGE AXES:
THE UPPER PALAEOLITHIC IN SOUTHEAST ASIA?

BRIAN HAYDEN

Department of Archaeology
Simon Fraser University

Europeans have long had some difficulty in fitting the inscrutable orient - or at least the Southeast Asia portion of it, as well as Australia into their world concepts, and in this prehistory has not been spared. Palaeolithic, Mesolithic or Neolithic do not fit particularly well. This has been due in part to poor formulation of the terms in the first place, and in part due to some rather disturbing differences.

However, before we dismiss European evolutionary concepts as ethnocentric and revert to a kind of Boasian particularism, where everything is different and no generalisations can be proffered, a closer examination of Southeast Asian prehistory can be made to see if some general evolutionary tendencies might not be observable, and to see what these tendencies have in common with prehistory further west. We have some basis for suspecting that parallel developments were taking place, since both hemispheres started out with an essentially identical tool kit nearly a million years ago (Saurin 1966:108), and both appear to have domesticated plants synchronously, about 9000 years ago. Also both areas developed bronze metallurgy about 5000 years ago. What I try to establish is that these synchronous events were largely the result of more detailed parallel evolutionary trends in the two hemispheres (as opposed to periodic massive diffusion events), and I attempt to flesh out the basic similarities in evolutionary trends in prehistoric technology, and to propose an explanation for such trends.

BACKGROUND

The history of trying to fit terms of
European origin to the situation in Southeast Asia
and Australia is long and abundant. I will only
sketch some of the highlights here. The Dutch and
the French took the initiative, after attention was
directed to the area in 1891 when Eugene Dubois
unearthed the world's first real proof of an ape-
man from the Trinil beds in Java. At the end of
the decade, the École Française d'Extrême-Orient
and the Service Géologique de l'Indochine were
established - the leading agencies in prehistoric
research during the first half of the coming century.
In 1902 Mansuy identified the Somrong Sen 'neolithic'
culture; and in 1906 the Bacsonian culture with
parallel grooved pebbles and edge ground axes and
pottery appearing in upper levels was defined.

The 1920s and 1930s however, proved to be the
Golden Age of prehistory in Southeast Asia. In
Indonesia Tweedie discovered the first Lower
Palaeolithic tools in the region on Java, and
attracted such luminaries as von Koenigswald,
Movius, and Teilhard de Chardin into more detailed
research on what later became known as the
Patjitanian. Another industry, the Sangiran,
considered to be Upper Pleistocene in age and
consisting of small flake tools alone, was found on
Java, Sulawesi and the Philippines. In 1924 van
Stein Callenfels in a bout of evolutionary paranoia
attempted to demonstrate that the Palaeolithic,
Mesolithic and Neolithic were all represented in
Indonesia, and by 1925 Mansuy (1925:36-7) could
confidently write about Magdalenian Cro-Magnon
populations migrating across Eurasia to the caves of
Vietnam, carrying with them a new technology.

The Palaeolithic was thought to be absent on
the mainland until the 1920s. Then Frommaget found
a massive Lower Palaeolithic-like industry associated
with probable pithecanthropine bone fragments.

From 1926-1931, Colani and Mansuy founded and pursued the Hoabinhian, through numerous poorly excavated and published sites. This industry was considered 'Mesolithic' on the basis of its associated fauna. It could be identified by the dominance of unifacial tools made on pebbles and large flakes, by the presence of sumatraliths (a particular unifacial pebble type), grinding stones, short axes, abundant use of red ochre, and generally crude workmanship of flaked stone tools (Matthews 1966a:86; Gorman 1970:82). Gorman has recently added subsistence and other criteria to this list, but these are too situationally specific and would exclude many traditional Hoabinhian industries from being considered as such.[1]

It is now evident that aside from the alpha and omega (the early pebble tool cultures and the full Neolithic) no matter how most of the intervening terms for evolutionary stages were *traditionally* defined, they did not fit the Southeast Asian situation, and the immediate reaction of ethnocentric Europeans was to view events in the region as slow or even backward (J.G.D. Clark 1968:21-2; Movius 1948:411). In reality what this difference reflects is perhaps simply more a tendency to use unmodified flakes with requisite tool features for work at hand (J.P. White 1967:409; Strathern 1969; Hayden in press; Patte 1936:293) rather than the systematic modification of flakes for specific tasks. The lack of extremely cold weather in the Southeast Asia/Australia region may have also reduced the need for as great a variety of specialised stone tools (e.g. hide scrapers) at comparable technological levels; and I will argue that alternate solutions to common problems also played a role.

In Australia, the quandry over whether to assign groups to the Palaeolithic or Mesolithic, or even Neolithic, has long persisted (Ascher 1961:

317-8). The chipped stone vs. ground stone
distinction is clearly inadequate as a criterion
for assigning cultures to these evolutionary
stages, as are most other traditional criteria
which have been applied to the region. Again,
using European criteria, Colani and most of her
contemporaries concluded that the Hoabinhian was
'Mesolithic' because all fauna associated with the
industry was recent, which indicated to them a
post-glacial age. Van Heekeren (1957:67), Saurin
(1969:29), Boriskovskii (in Solheim 1962) and
others maintained this position up through the
1960s. However recent research has shown that the
regional fauna has not changed significantly in the
past 40,000 years (Solheim 1969:129; Gorman 1970:
88; Harrisson 1970:32-3) and very little in the
preceding Pleistocene.

Discrete technological changes used in Eurasia/
Africa to mark the Lower, Middle and Upper
Palaeolithic, such as the disappearance of hand-
axes and the production of blades cannot properly
be applied to Southeast Asia or Australia because
these occidental 'marker' traits never developed
extensively in the latter areas. Nor can lithic
morphological criteria, such as ground axes -
traditionally associated with domestication - be
used. In the first place, we do not know in any
certain fashion when domestication began in the
region, nor which groups adopted it and which
abstained - and it is important to remember that
many autochthonous groups never adopted it. In the
second place ground stone materials which used to
be, and often still are, equated with the Neolithic
and Neolithic economies (Tweedie 1953:61), go back
to at least 23,000 years ago and these occurrences
are surprisingly, in Australia (C. White 1971).

Thus we find ourselves in the midst of seeming
chaos in attempting to apply traditional European
definitions of prehistoric evolutionary stages to
the Southeast Asia/Australia region. In view of

this it is not surprising that a separate
evolutionary terminology has been proposed for the
region (Solheim 1970:153-4, 1972:39). However I
would suggest that despite the technological and
environmental differences, very similar types of
phenomena were occurring in Eurasia and Southeast
Asia from about 1,000,000 to about 10,000 years BP,
and probably later.

Aside from changes in specific forms of tools
(core tools to flakes to blades), I see three
broad trends in the general evolution of Eurasian
technology as possibly applicable to Southeast
Asia/Australia and as potentially important for our
understanding of cultural evolution. In the West
these are overall, uni-directional trends which are
well documented or readily inferred:

1. Increasing variety or 'specialisation' of
        tools (probably loosely related to
increasingly varied functional roles of tools)
(Leroi-Gourhan 1964:196-200). Although this trend
now appears more attenuated due to recent research
at Olduvai, it still appears valid in overall form,
particularly if regularity of occurrence of
specialised tool types is taken into consideration
(see Bordes *et al.* 1972:21).
2. Increasingly economical use of raw material
        material (as measured in amount of cutting
edge per pound of raw material) (Leroi-Gourhan
1964:190-6).
3. A *generally* increasing complexity of overall
        subsistence technology, which in absolute
terms *must* progress from the level of the
termiting stick and unmodified throwing stone to
the intricate and complex gadget technologies of
the Mesolithic. As an aside - both as a logically
prior stage, and from archaeological evidence - the
European Upper Palaeolithic was quite complex
technologically. With its blade stone technology
it also ranked high in terms of cutting edge per
pound of raw material; and was obviously

specialised.

The above trends are fairly clear in terms of
general evolution in Eurasian prehistory. I do not
wish to maintain that situational changes or other
influences might not have created temporary
reversals among specific groups.

SOUTHEAST ASIA/AUSTRALIA

If the three evolutionary trends documented
for Eurasian prehistory are expressions of a more
fundamental aspect of human behaviour, we can
expect to find similar long term trends in all
major areas of the world with sufficient time depth
for human occupation. If substantiated, it might
even be possible to advance suggestions as to the
specific aspects of human nature which are
responsible for those trends. I suggest that no
better test case can be found than the Southeast
Asia/Australia region, an area long heralded as a
cultural backwater of the world, where very little
changed throughout the Middle and Upper Pleistocene,
and Holocene (Movius 1948:411; J.G.D. Clark 1968:
21-2; Clark and Piggott 1965:49). Or did it?

There are several aspects of the regional
prehistory that I would like to examine. In
particular, I would like to focus on the Hoabinhian,
which apparently evolves insensibly from earlier
forms of chopper/chopping tool industries (Solheim
1970:150). There are no recently excavated
stratified deposits of the early or middle Hoabinhian.
The only data available consists of Colani's original
excavations in the 1930s, which were crude by
contemporary standards, but adequate for examining
the broad issues of change being discussed here.

Increasing functional variety and specialisation of lithic tools

This is a particularly important topic, since this seems to be what various authors have in mind when they refer to the 'uninventiveness' of Southeast Asia and Australia, and particularly mainland Southeast Asia.

Colani (1927:47-59, 70; Saurin 1969:29) divided the Hoabinhian into three phases based on her excavation of dozens of caves. Her techniques may have been crude, but there is little doubt, especially from her description of the deep deposits at Sao Dong and Trieng Xen that the technological trends which she observed in the successive deposits correspond to meaningful changes. The earliest form of Hoabinhian that she recognised was called the 'archaic' and was characterised by massive pebble tools which were always unifacial. The second Hoabinhian phase was termed the 'intermediate' and was characterised by a reduction in the size of pebble tools and the appearance of bifacial working, and occasional edge ground tools. The third, or 'late' stage was characterised by smaller scrapers, grattoirs, knives, piercers, rare sawn and *polished* pieces, frequent shell artifacts, and towards the end, very probably pottery. The heavier pieces of the intermediate period also continue. Of particular interest is the addition to the more recent Hoabinhian assemblages of a rare, but potentially important tool: the bifacially edge ground slate knife, the importance of which is explained later. Gorman claimed to have discovered 'archaeologically unique' examples of this tool in his Spirit Cave Hoabinhian (1971:314), but a close examination of the literature shows that there are other edge ground knives found at Trieng-Xen (Intermediate Hoabinhian level, Colani 1927:29), Lang-Neo (Most Recent Hoabinhian, Colani 1927:42), Som-Jo (Most Recent Hoabinhian, Colani 1927:47), and Phuc-Luong

(Colani 1930a:268).

Solheim (1970:150, 1972:39) followed Colani
when he proposed his early, middle and late stages
for the Hoabinhian and her division into earlier
and later assemblages has been generally accepted
(Saurin 1969:29).

Temporally, what kind of time span are we
looking at? Originally, it was thought that the
Hoabinhian was a brief, relatively recent
'mesolithic' cultural tradition. Some thought that
it only dated back to 2000 BC. This view changed
radically with two events: Gorman's excavations of
Spirit Cave which dated the more recent forms back
to the 12th millennium BP, and the dating of ground
stone axes in northern Australia to 19-23,000 BP.
In using the Australian data, I am assuming for a
number of reasons that Australia formed part of the
Hoabinhian province during at least part of the
Pleistocene.[2] Early dates for ground stone
implements also occur in New Guinea and Borneo
(White, Crook and Ruxton 1970:168; Harrisson 1970:
40; Mulvaney 1975:193; Golson 1971:126-31). These
facts together with data from Colani's excavations
indicating an indigenous evolution of edge grinding
and polishing, as well as the development and
manufacture of quadrilateral adzes in North Vietnam,[3]
all point to the occurrence of the Intermediate
Hoabinhian sometime before 20,000 BP (see also
Golson 1971:130). On this basis, Solheim's
suggested initial date for the earliest Hoabinhian
of about 40,000 or 50,000 BP (1970:150, 1972:39)
does not seem unreasonable.

What we have then, from about 40 or 50,000 to
10,000 years ago or so, is a definite, overall
increase in lithic technological diversity, in a
culture which has rather mistakenly been referred
to in ultra-conservative terms. Other industries
in island Southeast Asia, as well as Australia,
exhibit this same tendency (Mulvaney 1975:172-80),

210; van Heekeren 1957). Thus the first
evolutionary trend - that of increasing tool
specialisation - is confirmed, even if its lithic
expression is not as extreme as that of glacial
Western Europe.

Increasingly economical use of raw material over time

Here again, the traditional European world view
sees Southeast Asia as backward since the Hoabinhian
only gets to the flake tool stage and never develops
blades or further refinements. Australia fares a
little better than continental Southeast Asia since
microliths become popular at one point (apparently
independently [Pearce 1974]), and blades make a
limited appearance. But the popular European view
of backwardness is sorely mistaken, and the genius
of the Far East is manifest. Pressures - for
whatever reasons - to conserve raw material can be
resolved in several ways. One is to break up the
material more finely or more regularly, thereby
yielding more cutting edge per pound. Another
solution is to obtain tools which can be
sharpened and resharpened more frequently without
loss in working effectiveness. The ultimate
expression of this last solution is edge ground
tools, which compared to chipped stone analogues,
last indefinitely. This is a much more effective
economy of raw material than blade technology, and
interestingly it probably dates back to the same
general time period when blade technology became so
widespread. Given the early Australian dates, and
the *in situ* development sequence in North Vietnam,[3]
and perhaps throughout the region, dates for the
initial development of edge grinding around 30,000
years ago do not seem at all out of place. Thus,
the second evolutionary trend, that of increasing
economy of raw material over time, is even more
pronounced in Southeast Asia/Australia than in
Eurasia, and apparently begins to become
significant at about the same time, about 30,000
years ago.

Increasing complexity of overall subsistence technology

This may seem like a motherhood issue,[4] but as noted previously many have been reluctant to accord it much status in Southeast Asia or Australia. I will here elaborate some of my views on the regional subsistence behaviour and technology over time. Specifically, I will treat the beginnings of technology, inferences about the functions of stone tools which my own ethnographic work in Australia has produced, and finally inferences others have made regarding 'incipient domestication'.

Firstly, one must assume that at some point in prehistory there simply was no material technology. Given this fact, it seems reasonable to assume that additions to the stone tool inventory, in a *very general* way at least, are related to increments in some other aspects of technology. This would be especially true if stone tools were needed in the manufacture of the wooden, bone, and basket components of technology - which I wish to maintain - and if all other conditions were equal. Given the increase in stone tool complexity from the earliest to the latest Hoabinhian, I feel rather confident in assuming an increase in the overall technological inventory. What was the nature of this increase in complexity? A rather lengthy digression is needed here to deal with the question.

My ethnographic work in Australia and a review of the world literature on the use of stone tools among hunter/gatherers enables a good guess to part of the answer. The earlier stages of the Hoabinhian and Australian technologies have core tools. Among the Western Desert groups with whom I worked, core tools are always used for woodworking. It is very significant that the rest of the Australian ethnography supports this conclusion as well (for a résumé, see Hayden in press). Furthermore, the gradual replacement of these large chipped tools in

the Hoabinhian, and their gradual evolution into
ground edge axe forms makes this same woodworking
functional attribution for early Hoabinhian core
tools seem very probable. Assuming that Hoabinhian
core tools were used for woodworking, what kinds of
woodworking were engaged in? In Australia chopping
implements were principally used for procuring wood
and for shaping such tools as spears, digging sticks,
throwing sticks, fighting sticks and bowls. Branches
were also cut with these tools when shelter was
needed. A brief recourse to hunter/gatherer
ethnographies of the world indicates the near
universality of many of these implements, and they
can be viewed as the rudimentary exploitative tool
kit of all generalised hunter/gatherers. These
tools are also known to extend relatively far back
into the Palaeolithic (J.D. Clark 1970:142-3; Fagan
1972:203; Movius 1950). On this basis, I think we
can minimally infer that early Hoabinhian core tools
were being used to produce spears, throwing sticks
and digging sticks and perhaps bowls or other items
as well. In effect, little more than core tools
and perhaps an occasional primary flake are needed
to produce any of these items. In the warm
tropical climates this basic technology must have
been largely adequate for a very extended time
period. Viewed from this perspective, Solheim's
division of the Southeast Asian (and Hoabinhian)
sequence into lithic and lignic stages is very
misleading, since it seems dubious that stone tools
were significantly dissociated from woodworking
activities during these periods. Given this as an
initial point of departure, I tend to view the
addition of various kinds of flake tools to later
assemblages as the result of either the addition of
more varied and more intricate wooden items to the
technological inventory (such as basketry, snares,
traps, barbed spears, ritual paraphernalia), or
the refinement of workmanship on already existing
wooden implement types, or both.

Ethnography continues to support such

inferences, since flake tools are also used almost
entirely for woodworking in the region, and the use
of chipped stone tools for skin working in the past
seems improbable (Hayden in press). An increased
consumption of wood can also be logically linked to
the developing Hoabinhian ground stone technology,
as will be explained in the next section.

    There is further evidence of increasing
complexity in overall subsistence technology in the
Intermediate and Late Hoabinhian. Ground stone
mortars, pestles, and grinders become established
during these periods. As Peterson (1968:567) has
noted, these have many functions but they generally
serve to process types of food which are often
otherwise inedible, or at least unpalatable, such
as cartilage, seeds with tough glumes, fibrous
roots and vegetables. Tindale and Maegraith (1931:
286) also observed that the Ramona natives at
Encounter Bay used pitted hand pounding stones,
similar to the Hoabinhian types, for pounding rush
fibre for string. If the manufacture of string or
cordage on a relatively large scale can be inferred
from these implements, it seems that some kind of
netting such as used by some Australian Aboriginal
groups for fishing or snaring could be further
inferred for the Hoabinhian. Use of all these
types of ground stone processing equipment would
therefore expand the subsistence base. Moreover
there are a number of indications that seeds may
have begun to be utilised during this time period.
In addition to the grinders and mortars, we can
note that cereals were widely used in Australia and
that the grinding technology dates back to about
18,000 BP (Kamminga and Allen 1973:48; Allen 1974:
315; Mulvaney 1975:133, 152; Tindale in press). As
noted previously, Australia appears to be in the
Hoabinhian province in the late Pleistocene. Meat
protein seems to have been scarce in the Hoabinhian
diet according to Colani and others (Colani 1927:7,
19, 38, 31; Matthews 1961:18; Mansuy 1909:543; van
Heekeren and Knuth 1967:106; Boriskovskii 1969-1970:

239) and the use of cereal seeds would have been
nutritionally advantageous as well as increasing
the reliability of the food supply; Colani
graphically describes the rich grasslands around
some of the Hoabinhian sites (1931:302, 325).
Furthermore, there are a number of engravings on
stone and bone from Hoabinhian deposits, of which
Colani suggests that five depict grasses with
leaves, while five others seem to represent
different plants (Colani 1931:406). One additional
finely polished leg bone from Lam-gan cave in Hoa
Binh depicts an engraved stalk and leaves which
Colani suggests portrays a cereal plant (1930b).
Finally, as mentioned earlier, Gorman excavated
three ground slate knife fragments at Spirit Cave
(1971:314). Comparing his specimen to a ground
stone Javanese rice harvesting knife, Gorman
implied that the archaeological specimens may have
been used to harvest rice, although there was no
evidence of rice at the site. If this and similar
knives from other Hoabinhian deposits (some of which
are crescentic in shape and even more like the
Javanese knife that Gorman illustrates) were grain
harvesting knives - which does not seem improbable
- they may have been used for reaping wild or
domestic rice as well as other cereals, wild or
domestic.

   I emphasise the use of cereal grains because
their use as a staple is not at all obvious,
requires special technological items for processing,
and was probably developed relatively recently as
far as the Pleistocene goes. As such, it nicely
supports the contention that subsistence technology
became increasingly more complex over time, and has
many more important ramifications for further
evolutionary developments. To recapitulate, the
other indicators supporting the trend of increasing
complexity of subsistence technology are: the
increase in frequency and complexity of flake stone
tools, and the introduction of ground stone knives,
mortars, pestles and grinders. Worked bone objects

also increase in variety and frequency in the
Hoabinhian; however they cannot be tied as firmly
to subsistence activities, nor can we be certain
that their absence is due to cultural rather than
preservational factors.

Because Tasmania was cut off from the rest of
the Australian and Southeast Asia region about
10,000 years ago, comparison of its subsistence
technology with that of the rest of Australia may
provide us with a *general* indication of the kinds
of technological changes that occurred over time in
the region. For instance, some of the items
Tasmanians lacked in the 19th century and which I
see as probably lacking 10,000 years ago were: the
spear-thrower; hafted adzes, axes and knives - in
fact hafting in general; stone tipped spears; net
bags and net snares; ground edge tools; boomerangs;
shields; the dingo and possibly the ability to make
fire. Jones (in press) has recently emphasised
these differences and some of their evolutionary
implications for culture.

Obviously, with intensive subsistence
strategies, previously exploited resources would
continue to be exploited, and it is unrealistic to
see the use of plants such as nuts, beans, peppers,
cucumbers and water chestnuts as evidence of
'incipient domestication', or to claim that these
plants were only used at very late stages of
cultural evolution, when man 'discovered' their
usefulness (as per Solheim 1970:150, 1972:37).
Given the high reliance of hunter/gatherers on
plant food, and the scarcity of animal protein on
the mainland, it seems most unlikely that hunter/
gatherers at *any* period would have been unaware of
such readily obvious resources, or not made
immediate use of them.

To summarise up to this point, I have
hopefully demonstrated similar evolutionary trends
in Eurasia and Southeast Asia/Australia in terms of

increasing lithic diversity or 'specialisation',
economy of lithic raw material, and complexity of
overall subsistence technology.

ZIPF'S PRINCIPLE AND SOURCES OF CHANGE

I would like to present my views on why I
think these overall, uni-directional tendencies
exist in the human record (at the risk of being
given the epithet of a palaeopsychologist!). To do
this it is necessary to deal with assumptions
regarding principles around which man's behaviour
is and has been structured. The two questions we
must pose are:

1. Why would people increasingly economise lithic
   material over a period of 2 million years or
more?
2. Why would people develop a more and more
   complex technology over that same period?

The answer to the first question is relatively
simple. Given a nomadic existence and restricted
availability of stone types suitable for tools,
there is a rather limited amount of lithic raw
material that can be carried comfortably about in
order to effect repairs in one's technological
repertory or to replace broken items in the
repertory such as spears and digging sticks, which
are vital to subsistence procurement. When the
wooden technological repertory is simple and consists,
for example, only of spears, throwing sticks and
digging sticks - the hunter/gatherer basics - the
rate of wood consumption is low. Some wooden
implements may have to be replaced every three
weeks or so per adult, and use of stone is
correspondingly sporadic. Lithic consumption is
thus also low. Under these circumstances carrying
around a single core tool per person (or family),
and perhaps a few primary flakes, may totally

satisfy woodworking needs of the group until it can
return to a quarry site.

However, when the wooden (and/or bone)
component of the technology expands, consumption
and replacement of wood goes up, and in general
this means that for a given resharpening mode,
the consumption of lithic material goes up. If
this trend continues, one must reach a point at
which no more lithic material can be comfortably
carried around. Increases in wood consumption
beyond such a point would necessitate more
economical use of the stone being carried about,
which means stretching the cutting edges per pound.
The more gadget oriented and wood consuming one's
technology, the more one needs to stretch lithic
resources.[5] And this, I maintain, eventually leads
to increased emphasis on flakes and then blades in
the West, and to grinding techniques of sharpening
stone in the East. Perhaps it is possible to
establish a rough threshold at which it becomes
useful to adopt ground stone tools - which have
laborious maintenance drawbacks, and which
according to my observations in Australia do not
seem to provide any significant increase in working
efficiency (in terms of time or energy) over chipped
stone analogues.

In the Western Desert of Australia, I found
that people used chipped stone chopping implements
for procuring wood and roughing out tools. In
terms of the above proposal, this made sense
because the wooden inventory was simple and the
replacement of items which consumed very large
amounts of lithic material (such as spearthrowers
and hard wood bowls) occurred very infrequently
(less than once a year), in addition to which
replacement of such items could probably be fore-
seen relatively far in advance and planned for.
Clearly, for such infrequent occasions it made little
sense to laboriously maintain a ground stone axe.
That the maintenance of ground edge axes was

laborious and tedious was indicated by several
Walbiri old men who described their fathers as
constantly sitting around campsites grinding and
grinding away, sharpening their axes. Chipped
stone chopping tools are much more readily
resharpened, and if not needed in the immediate
future, can be discarded without much loss of
effort investment. Interestingly, the Walbiri,
immediately to the north of the Western Desert
Pintubi, generally used ground edge axes. It was
attempting to explain this disparity which
eventually led me to the explanation proffered
above. The Walbiri, in effect had a number of
supplementary wooden implements in their material
inventory which the Western Desert people did not.
Perhaps most important among these was the non-
returning boomerang. Unlike simple throwing
sticks, these boomerangs usually require
considerable thinning of thick pieces of mulga, an
extremely hard wood. They therefore consume large
quantities of stone material. They also
undoubtedly had a relatively high replacement rate
due to breakage and loss, being thrown at game or
into flocks of birds. This rate of wood and lithic
consumption was without doubt higher than that of
Western Desert groups, and was apparently
sufficiently higher to make long lasting types of
lithic tools worth the effort required to maintain
them. Like boomerangs, throwing clubs with bulbous
ends (waddies) also require an excessive amount of
woodworking in manufacture, and probably had
similarly high replacement rates. If this general
'threshold' of lithic economy in any way
approximates the point at which it becomes worthwhile to shift to ground edge tools, we should find
a good positive correlation between the absence of
edge ground axes and the lack of such lithic
consuming items as boomerangs and throwing clubs.
Although Davidson and McCarthy's data is dated and
somewhat inaccurate for the Western Desert region
around the Pintubi, it is the best synthesis
available, and will serve as a very crude test of

the proposition. Obviously the boomerang and
throwing club are not the only possible high
consumers of lithic materials - and depending on
manufacturing frequencies, they need not
necessarily be high consumers - but they are the
most apparent high lithic consumers in Australia.
Using Davidson and McCarthy's (1957) distribution
figures to compare the occurrence of ground edge
axes versus boomerangs and throwing clubs
demonstrates a surprisingly good correlation between
the relevant categories (Fig.1). Where boomerangs

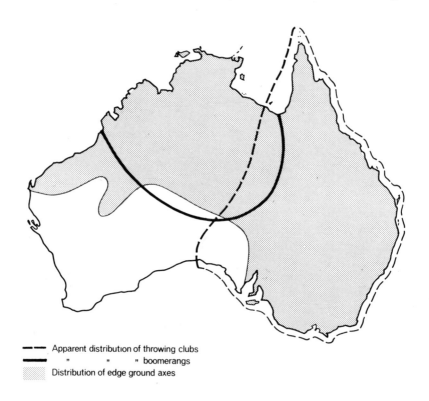

--- Apparent distribution of throwing clubs
━━ "   "   " boomerangs
▨▨ Distribution of edge ground axes

Fig.1. Comparative distributions of edge ground axes and items
requiring large amounts of stone for manufacture (from Davidson
1957:396,426).

or throwing clubs occur, so do ground edge axes;
where they are absent, so are ground edge axes.
This limited test, which does not even take into
account frequency of manufacture, but only
presence/absence data, provides important support
for the proposed interpretation, and gives us a
more tangible idea of what was going on in the
Hoabinhian when ground edge tools appeared: I am
not saying that Hoabinhians had boomerangs; only
that they were engaging in woodworking activity
above a certain threshold point. For Australia,
the above interpretation is much more tenable, I
think, than other attempts to explain the lack of
edge ground axes in given locations. These
alternate explanations include the lack of suitable
stone (consider the extensive trade routes!); the
lack of watercraft or large trees to climb (Helms
1890:274; Tindale 1950:270); and historical
diffusion models which totally ignore the role of
differential adaptiveness (Davidson and McCarthy
1957:427).

Thus, economy of lithic raw material can be
generally viewed as principally a function of the
rate of use of stone materials, which in Southeast
Asia/Australia is a function principally of wood
and bone technological inventories and their rates
of replacement.

The second question - why human cultures
slowly but steadily increased their material
inventories, especially in subsistence technology
- is not so easily answered. However, I have two
suggestions which probably reflect the situation
rather accurately.

At the outset, it should be realised that we
are dealing with a delicate balance; change was so
slow for the first million or more years that the
systems must have been relatively stable. However,
there can be little doubt that periodic resource
shortages, while probably infrequent, did occur

(Hayden 1975). Times of resource shortage can
reasonably be viewed as sufficient motivation for
persons to cast around for new food resources and
new ways of obtaining food. Exploration of new
resource alternatives during most of the Pleistocene
was probably confined to the investigation of *minor*
variations of already known resources and/or
processing techniques. In most cases these
'emergency' ration resources were probably the
already known, less palatable foods, or foods that
required otherwise excessive effort to procure or
process. Given such undesirable qualities,
innovative strategies making use of these resources
might be remembered but unused, or else entirely
forgotten due to infrequent use (e.g. every 10-20-
50 years), probably only to be rediscovered again.

Maximum retention of resource innovation makes
adaptive sense for *all* periods in the past *to the
extent practicable and feasible*, because broader
resource potential leads to an increase in the
reliability of the resource base. However, during
the Pleistocene, rates of innovation would have been
low due to a number of factors such as low overall
population, small group sizes, low cranial and
mental capacities, and the infrequent and short
term nature of periods of stress. Retention rates
were probably also low due to these same factors.
It seems reasonable to assume finite limits on the
amount of information a family or small band could
maintain regarding the general techniques of
exploitation, and more importantly, the specifics
of their environment and possible exploitative
technology.

I would suggest that at the earliest end of
this technological spectrum (close to the termiting
stick extreme), the balance between retained and
non-retained strategies was limited to only the
most regularly used, generalised subsistence
strategies, as well perhaps as strategies for
obtaining the most desired foods, and that this

balance point was advanced to include more and more
complex strategies only as cranial and mental
capacities increased. There were also drawbacks to
the new techniques which will be discussed below.

Thus we can expect a slowly expanding repertory
of subsistence strategies over time, even though
subsistence options which required inordinate work
according to prevailing standards might only be
used in times of resource crisis, and might be
used so infrequently that they were repeatedly
dropped from the subsistence repertory and
rediscovered. Thus, attempts to increase resource
reliability can be seen to result in increase in
technological complexity over time.[6]

The other suggestion which I have complements
the first. This proposition concerns sedentism and
may be introduced with an interrogation. Given
enough quantity and variety of resources at a
particular location, why would anyone be nomadic?
Intuitively the normal response is that they would
not, because being constantly nomadic requires a
considerable outlay in effort and energy which
sedentism does not, and must eventually become
burdensome even to the point where the arthritic,
sick, and aged must be left behind and given up.
Nomadic foraging is basically a pain in the ass
once the novelty wears off - or more correctly, a
pain in the foot. Ethnographic observations also
support this notion. Lee (1969:60) observed that
one of the basic strategies of Bushman groups is to
reduce work in the form of travel as much as
possible. We know that conditions approximating
full sedentism, or extreme semi-sedentism, could be
attained at the hunter-gatherer level in some
relatively rich areas, for we have archaeological
evidence of this among some North American Archaic
and Eurasian Mesolithic groups, as well as some
ethnographic occurrences such as the Northwest
Coast Indians and some coastal Australians.
However, it also seems relatively clear that

possibly with very rare exceptions, the *extensive*
procurement of the most easily obtainable resources
at the hunter/gatherer level was incapable of
supporting sedentary groups. What sedentism
generally demands at the hunter/gatherer level is a
very *intensive* exploitation of the environment.
This means not only securing all the easily
obtained and obvious resources, but also culling
the unobvious, the latent, the minute, and often
the incredibly abundant resources - resources which
without a sophisticated technology and special
apparatuses are painstaking to collect or unpalatable
in an unprocessed form. Without a sophisticated
technology which could efficiently harvest or
process these unobvious resources, it was far
easier to pluck and prey upon those obtained with
little effort, even though it was necessary to
move frequently in order to forage with facility.
Unobvious resources were left for emergency fares,
if used at all. They were therefore useless as
staples until sophisticated technological advances
occurred. Resources which fall under this
unobvious category probably included cereal grains,
vegetables containing semi-toxic substances
removable by parboiling, fish, rodents, many birds,
and other dimunuitive land and aquatic animals. As
an example of the impact of intensive exploitation,
the use of wild cereals alone could provide enough
potential food in some areas to permit full
sedentism (see Harlan 1967). But superficially,
the potential was far from obvious: the resource
consisted of tiny grains which it was difficult to
collect or even obtain a mouthful of, and at that
it would have been a dry, hard mouthful full of
sharp glumes and husks. Moreover, boiling was
entirely lacking in Aboriginal Australia as well as
hunter/gatherer groups in the Philippines (Fernandez
and Lynch 1972:298) and the Andaman Islands.
Boiling is a simple technological step, but a very
unobvious one and one that was probably not used
until very late in the Pleistocene. The intensive
exploitation of other unobvious resources as

staples requires considerable sophistication in wood
and bone technology and considerable investment in
effort, such as in the construction and maintenance
of nets, fishing gear, weirs, baskets, traps, snares,
boomerangs and other gadgets which are known to
occur in the Mesolithic and other late Palaeolithic
manifestations. To further complicate matters, many
of these technology laden subsistence strategies
required considerable sedentism before they could
be adopted. One could not simply transport all
one's nets, traps, weirs, grinding slabs and other
paraphernalia wherever one went. It was at least
necessary to leave material at a given site and
return often enough to make fabrication of the
gadgets worthwhile.

These were the drawbacks to intensive
subsistence exploitation: it demanded additional
investment of labour in new technology; it was
untried; it was not obvious; it often constituted
hard work (as in seed grinding); and it sometimes
demanded semi-sedentary conditions which did not
necessarily exist. These factors were a successful
immediate deterrent to increasing the intensity of
exploitation and technology, and therefore were a
deterrent to sedentism in many areas. Once
temporary shortages were past, even if some groups
had relied on some intensive subsistence techniques
to cull what sparse food they could in times of
stress, they reverted to the easier extensive
foraging techniques and technology.

I have argued that the effort saved by not
having to move constantly generally requires
intensive means of subsistence procurement. It is
reasonable to assume that in areas where the
frequency of nomadic moves could be reduced
appreciably by the deployment of one or more
intensive techniques, that the constant, although
perhaps slight, pressure to reduce effort by
reducing the frequency of moving would eventually
militate in favour of adopting more intensive and

broader spectrum (more reliable) forms of
exploitation. Obviously, emic perceptions of the
full range of options involved may have been an
important factor as well. But when recognised, by
culling a little more out of the local environment,
groups could postpone the next move making it
easier on everyone, particularly the aged, and the
women who carried infants and most of the material
items of the family. Once such subsistence
techniques were developed to relatively efficient
degrees, other groups might also find them
advantageous and adopt them under the same
motivation: witness the rapid spread of the bow and
arrow. What is this behavioural principle? I
suggest that it is simply Zipf's principle (1949)
as applied to sedentism. This states that all other
things being equal, given two ways of arriving at
the same goal, man more often than not chooses the
way involving the least effort.

Given either this proposition or the
motivation to increase resource reliability as
discussed previously, the long term developments
which I have been discussing inevitably followed
once man became a technologically flexible animal.
This does not mean that all hunter/gatherers were
capable of attaining near sedentary conditions even
with extremely intensive exploitation strategies;
for even with these strategies some areas of the
world were only barely habitable. It does mean
that where the potential was present for greater
sedentism, man eventually tended to evolve
culturally in that direction.

In conclusion I would like to suggest that
what the Europeans have termed Lower, Middle and
Upper Palaeolithic and Mesolithic are in reality
stages in the development of the trends we have
been talking about, and that Southeast Asia and
Australia passed through the same stages more or
less contemporaneously, although solving common
problems in different ways. Finally, I would

suggest that planting behaviour in relation to
food staples does not make much sense given
extensive nomadic foraging and that it only makes
sense under conditions of intensive foraging and
near sedentism. Interestingly, the Petersons'
study of near sedentary Philippine hunter/gatherers
(see this volume) indicates that at first it may
have been the old and otherwise economically
unproductive members of the bands who engaged in
planting and horticultural activities under
sedentary conditions. I would not argue that
intensive exploitation and sedentism are sufficient
conditions for the development of planting
behaviour and domestication, but I certainly feel
that they are necessary, together with some other
situational factors. It seems to me that this is
why domestication did not take place during the
Palaeolithic, and why the stochastic development of
technology along the trends I have outlined led
inexorably to the development of domesticated
plants and animals in a number of areas of the
world synchronously. Terminal Pleistocene hunter/
gatherers in many parts of the world had simply
crossed a critical threshold of technological
complexity and sedentism and established new
relationships with other factors which made planting
and domestication profitable.[7] Again I emphasise
that this is definitely not all of the puzzle. It
takes us to the brink of explanation only. It
explains why domestication did not occur prior to
this time, but does not explain why domestication
occurred afterward. There are definitely other
factors involved, since some intensive hunter/
gatherer systems appear to have stabilised, as
along the North American West Coast - this might be
referred to as the West Coast model - whereas other
intensive hunter/gatherer systems went on to
develop planting and domestication as in the case of
some Mesolithic groups in the Near East. Filling
in this last part of the puzzle may be somewhat
easier given the data base presented here, but it
is still far from being resolved as an evolutionary
problem.

FOOTNOTES

[1] In accord with Gorman (1971) and Solheim (1970,
   1972), I will consider the Bacsonian a local
Hoabinhian manifestation for the purposes of this
paper.

[2] McCarthy (1940, 1944:263) argued that early
   Australian lithic industries were derived from
the Hoabinhian on a typological basis. Tindale
(1957) concurred, and even named some of the tool
types in his early Kartan industry after Hoabinhian
types (e.g. sumatraliths). Subsequent syntheses
have tended to reinforce these similarities
(Mulvaney 1975:174). In fact, there are numerous
typological affinities between early Australian
industries and the Hoabinhian tradition, including
the presence of pebble tools (sumatraliths and
others), pitted hand pounding stones, edge ground
axes, grinding stones, small round mortars (Colani
1927; Kamminga and Allen 1973), and an overall
orientation of both lithic traditions toward using
naturally occurring features of chipped or broken
stone for working purposes, as opposed to
modification of the stone (Patte 1936:293; Hayden
in press). Regarding this last point, J.P. White
(1967:409) and Strathern (1969) have made similar
observations about New Guinea assemblages. Matthews
(1966b) has pointed out metrical differences between
Australian and Hoabinhian tool types, but the
overall resemblances of the industries cannot be
denied. There are other material traits as well
which serve to reinforce the relationship between
the Hoabinhian and early Australian manifestations.
These include: the abundant use of red ochre, the
intensive reliance on shellfish and deposition of
middens, and perhaps most strikingly of all the
occurrence in some Hoabinhian sites of carved flat
slabs of stone which bear remarkable resemblances
to some stone Australian churingas, even to the
point of similar motifs (Colani 1927:plate 12).
Colani has interpreted these as unspecified cult
objects.

Extending the geographical scope also tends to reinforce the impression that the Hoabinhian had a wide sphere of influence. For instance, there are definite chipped stone shouldered axes from Hoabinhian contexts. This type is unusual and should have good style diagnostic properties. At Sao Dong (Colani 1927:plate 3, No.8), one of the classic Hoabinhian sites, there is at least one example; at Da-phuc there are notched-shouldered axes with ground edges, and the same obtains at Lang-Vanh (Colani 1930a:268, 269); they are also found at Gua Debu (Cheng 1957:60). Waisted axes are recorded in chipped stone form from the opposite ends of the Hoabinhian sphere: Szechwan (Cheng 1957:60), and New Guinea, where they date back to 26,000 BP (White, Crook and Ruxton 1970). Morphologically similar specimens have also been identified in the Kartan assemblages of Kangaroo Island, South Australia (Lampert 1975). Some of these waisted types are remarkably similar to shouldered adzes, particularly White's figure 3b of the New Guinea artifacts, and the series makes it easy to envisage the development of shouldered axes from waisted axes. The early occurrence of edge ground tools in Borneo and New Guinea also adds to the impression of homogeneity in the region. When one adds to these factors the proximity of Southeast Asia to Australia and the prevalence of the Hoabinhian in Southeast Asia, one has a relatively tight case for viewing Australia as a southern Hoabinhian province during at least some part of the Late Pleistocene.

[3] Early authors, especially Mansuy (1925:28, 30) saw in the advent of edge ground tools a new technology introduced by invaders from the north. However, as with similar contemporaneous interpretations of the European Upper Palaeolithic (due to invasions), there is data in the excavation reports, which indicate indigenous evolution. In fact, if one were to attempt to discover a developmental sequence for the invention and

development of edge-grinding and more advanced
forms, what one would look for in the archaeological
record is exactly what has been found in the
Vietnamese Hoabinhian caves. Mansuy's ideas were
followed by other researchers (Colani 1931; Chang
1959), however, as the Hoabinhian sequence
suggests, and as the Australian dates allow,
edge grinding was almost certainly an *in situ*
regional development, owing nothing to northern
influences. The grinding process first appears in
the Intermediate Hoabinhian at such sites as Sao
Dong and Trieng Xen, occurring generally only along
the very edges of the tools. Grinding area appears
to be gradually extended in later assemblages,
especially in the Late Hoabinhian, until it covers
nearly the complete surface of some edge ground
tools. Moreover, there are a number of indications
that this grinding process was successively refined
within the Hoabinhian zone of North Vietnam,
culminating in the classical 'Upper Neolithic'
polished quadrangular stone tools. Mansuy
originally postulated a continuous development from
the Bacsonian to the Neolithic, although the
interpretation was questioned by Patte due to
uncontrolled mixing of deposits at some sites
(Patte 1936:291). Nevertheless, at Duong Thuoc,
one of the major Bacsonian sites, and San-Xa,
neither of which have evidence of mixing, a range
of ground types occur, with grinding extending
over more surface on some specimens and nearly
covering entire specimens in a few extreme cases
(Mansuy 1924, 1925:26-32). The same is true at
Lang-Vanh (Colani 1927).

The problem of where the quadrangular adzes
came from has been the point of departure for more
than one historical reconstruction depicting
migrations into Southeast Asia. In the Thai
Hoabinhian at Spirit Cave, they are patently
intrusive or diffused elements. This would seem to
support migration theories such as Heine-Geldern,
van Heekeren, Stein-Callenfels, van der Hoop and

Chang propose. However the Hoabinhian sphere was very large, and the quadrangular adze may well have developed in a restricted local area. I would again argue that if one set out to locate archaeological evidence for the in place development of the quadrangular adze from the edge ground adze, one would look for exactly what was found by Colani in a number of caves in Hoa Binh.

As Colani herself notes (1927:61) the method for making adzes with straight sides, ethnographically observed in Manchuria, is to saw along the line where one wishes to create the edge of the tool, and then simply break off the unwanted portion, much as in glass cutting. Now such saw marks begin to appear sporadically in the latest deposits in the Hoa Binh caves (which are south of the Bac Son region). Saw marks on stone appear at X-Kham, Sao Dong (both very important sites), Lang Neo and Lang Vo (Colani 1927:17, 22, 38, 43, 50), while being generally absent from the Bac Son sites - there is only one saw mark from Bac Son (although this is on an edge ground axe!), and Colani often refers to the presence and absence of saw marks in contrasting the Hoabinhian and Bacsonian (1927:61). Moreover, at Sao Dong, one of the cut pieces has been ground ('polished'), and at Lang Vo there is a bifacially chipped adze, unground, with both of its lateral sides bearing cut marks along the straight edges. The cross-section appears rectangular. Most recently, Solheim (1972:39) strongly implied that quadrangular adzes most likely developed in Formosa. If this assessment is warranted, it would appear that Formosa was not unique. Taken with other evidence of the *in situ* development of Neolithic adze forms in the Hoabinhian, I think that the above data is about what one would expect an indigenous development to look like in the archaeological record. The fact that transition forms are not abundant is to be expected from the general spurt-like nature of cultural evolution.

[4] This apparently means 'something no one would really argue against' (eds).

[5] In climates where the use of hides became intensive the lithic requirements of skin preparation might also be a significant factor in increasing stone consumption. Groups which reap large amounts of cereals might have similarly high stone requirements for reaping knives. As per the following argument, I might add that it seems plausible that the greater suitability of knapped cryptocrystalline edges for meat and hide processing may have rendered the development of blade technology (versus ground edge technology) more suitable for high lithic consuming groups in glacial, Eurasian environments; whereas groups consuming primarily large quantities of wood, as in Southeast Asia, would have been better served by ground stone options. The raw material on which stone is being used is undoubtedly very important as a factor affecting lithic transformations, but the issue is too complex to deal with in detail in this exploratory paper. Briefly, however (and perhaps minimally), the three variables which I see dominating changes in technological modes are: frequency of manufacture (consumption requirements); raw materials being worked; and availability of various lithic raw materials. These should be interpreted broadly, and may combine differentially for different tool types within assemblages.

[6] This does not necessarily mean that overall resource reliability did increase significantly during the Pleistocene, for it may well be the case that resource advantages accrued from technological innovation were sooner or later compensated for by increases in population density. Such increases could certainly be expected during periods of minimal stress, which were probably frequent and of long duration. Thus a moving equilibrium between population and resources may have characterised palaeolithic populations, even though short term

improvements were sought and attained in many cases.

[7] In this respect, Braidwood's (Braidwood and Willey 1962:342) rather simplistic statement that domestication occurred when culture was ready for it, is probably partly correct, and Binford's (1968: 322) critique of Braidwood's stand is probably too extreme.

REFERENCES

Allen, H. 1974 The Bagundji of the Darling Basin: cereal gatherers in an uncertain environment. *World Archaeology* 5:309-22

Ascher, R. 1961 Analogy in archaeological interpretation. *Southwestern Journal of Anthropology* 17:317-25

Binford, L.R. 1968 Post-Pleistocene adaptations. In S.R. and L.R. Binford (eds) *New perspectives in archaeology*:313-41. Chicago: Aldine

Bordes, F., J. Rigaud and D. de Sonneville-Bordes 1972 Des buts, problèmes et limites de l'archéologie paléolithique. *Quaternaria* 16:15-34

Boriskovskii, P.I. 1969-70 Vietnam in primeval times, (part IV). *Soviet Anthropology and Archaeology* 8(3):214-57

Braidwood, R.J. and G. Willey 1962 Conclusions and afterthoughts. In R.J. Braidwood and G. Willey (eds) *Courses toward urban life*: 330-59. Chicago: Aldine

Chang, Kwang-chih 1959 A working hypothesis for the early cultural history of China. *Bulletin of the Institute of Ethnology, Academica Sinica* 7:75-103

Cheng, Te-kun 1957 *Archaeological studies in Szechwan*. Cambridge: Cambridge University Press

Clark, J.D. 1970 *The prehistory of Africa*. London: Thames and Hudson

Clark, J.G.D. 1968 Australian Stone Age. In K. Jazdzewski (ed.) *Liber Iosepho Kostrzewski octogenario a veneratoribus dicatus*:17-28. Warsaw: Ossolineum, Polish Academy of Sciences

            and S. Piggott 1965 *Prehistoric societies*. London: Hutchinson

Colani, M. 1927 *L'âge de la pierre dans la province de Hoa-Binh (Tonkin)*. Hanoi: Mémoires du Service Géologique de l'Indochine 14(1)

            1930a Quelques stations hoabinhiennes. *Bulletin de l'Ecole Francaise d'Extrême-Orient* 29:261-72

            1930b Gravures primitives sur pierre et sur os. *Bulletin de l'Ecole Francaise d'Extrême-Orient* 29:273-87

            1931 Recherches sur le préhistorique indochinois. *Bulletin de l'Ecole Francaise d'Extrême-Orient* 30:299-422

Davidson, D.S. and F.D. McCarthy 1957 The distribution and chronology of some important types of stone implements in Western Australia. *Anthropos* 52:390-458

Fagan, B. 1972 *In the beginning*. Boston: Little, Brown

Fernandez, C. and F. Lynch 1972 Tasaday. *Philippine Sociological Review* 20:275-330

Golson, J. 1971 Both sides of the Wallace Line: Australia, New Guinea, and Asian prehistory. *Archaeology and Physical Anthropology in Oceania* 6:124-44

Gorman, C. 1970 Excavations at Spirit Cave,
     north Thailand: some interim interpretations.
     Asian Perspectives 13:79-107

          1971 The Hoabinhian and after:
     subsistence patterns in Southeast Asia
     during the late Pleistocene and early
     Recent periods. *World Archaeology* 2:300-20

Harlan, J. 1967 A wild wheat harvest in Turkey.
     Archaeology 20:197-201

Harrisson, T. 1970 The prehistory of Borneo.
     Asian Perspectives 13:17-45

Hayden, B. 1975 The carrying capacity dilemma.
     In A.C. Swedlund (ed.) *Population studies
     in archaeology and biological anthropology:
     a symposium*:11-21. *American Antiquity* 40
     (2:2), *Memoirs of the Society for American
     Archaeology* 30

          in press Stone tool functions in the
     Western Desert. In Wright in press

Heekeren, H.R. van 1957 *The Stone Age of
     Indonesia*. The Hague: Nijhoff

               and Count Eigil Knuth 1967
     *Archaeological excavations in Thailand, I:
     Sai Yok*. Copenhagen: Munksgaard

Helms, R. 1890 Anthropology. *Transactions of
     the Royal Society of South Australia* 14:237-
     332

Jones, R. in press The Tasmanian paradox. In
     Wright in press

Kamminga, J. and H. Allen 1973 *Alligator Rivers
     environmental fact-finding study: report of
     the archaeological survey*. [Darwin:
     Department of the Northern Territory]
     (limited distribution)

Lampert, R.J. 1975 A preliminary report on some waisted blades found on Kangaroo Island, South Australia. *Australian Archaeology* 2: 45-8

Lee, R.B. 1969 !Kung Bushman subsistence: an input-output analysis. In A.P. Vayda (ed.) *Environment and cultural behavior*:47-79. Garden City (N.Y.): Natural History Press

Leroi-Gourhan, A. 1964 *Le geste et la parole: technique et langage.* Paris: Editions Albin Michel

McCarthy, F.D. 1940 Comparison of the prehistory of Australia with that of Indo-China, the Malay Peninsula, and the Netherlands East Indies. In F.N. Chasen and M.W.F. Tweedie (eds) *Proceedings of the Third Congress of Prehistorians of the Far East*:30-50. Singapore: Government Printer

    1944 The *windang*, or edge-ground uniface pebble axe, in eastern Australia. *Records of the Australian Museum, Sydney* 21:261-3

Mansuy, H. 1909 Gisement préhistorique de la caverne de Pho-Binh-Gia (Tonkin). *L'Anthropologie* 20:532-43

    1924 *Contribution à l'étude de la préhistoire de l'Indochine, IV: stations préhistoriques dans les cavernes du massif calcaire de Bac-Son (Tonkin).* Hanoi: Mémoires du Service Géologique de l'Indochine 11(2)

    1925 *Contribution à l'étude de la préhistoire de l'Indochine, V: nouvelles découvertes dans les cavernes du massif calcaire de Bac-Son (Tonkin).* Hanoi: Mémoires du Service Géologique de l'Indochine 12(1)

Matthews, J.M. 1961 *A check-list of Hoabinhian sites excavated in Malaya 1860-1939.* Kuala Lumpur: University of Malaya, Department of History, Papers on Southeast Asian Subjects 3

1966a A review of the 'Hoabinhian' in Indochina. *Asian Perspectives* 9:86-95

1966b The Hoabinhian affinities of some Australian assemblages. *Archaeology and Physical Anthropology in Oceania* 1:5-22

Movius, H.L. Jr. 1948 The lower palaeolithic cultures of southern and eastern Asia. *Transactions of the American Philosophical Society* 38:329-420

1950 A wooden spear of Third Interglacial age from Lower Saxony. *Southwestern Journal of Anthropology* 6: 139-42

Mulvaney, D.J. 1975 *The prehistory of Australia,* (rev.ed.) Ringwood (Victoria): Penguin Books

and J. Golson (eds) 1971 *Aboriginal man and environment in Australia.* Canberra: Australian National University Press

Patte, E. 1936 L'Indochine préhistorique. *Revue Anthropologique* 48:277-93

Pearce, R.H. 1974 Spatial and temporal distribution of Australian backed blades. *Mankind* 9(4):300-9

Peterson, N. 1968 The pestle and mortar: an ethnographic analogy for archaeology in Arnhem Land. *Mankind* 6(11):567-70

Saurin, E. 1966 Le paléolithique du Cambodge oriental. *Asian Perspectives* 9:96-100

1969 Les recherches préhistoriques au Cambodge, Laos, et Viet Nam (1877-1966). *Asian Perspectives* 12:27-41

Solheim, W.G., II 1962   Southeast Asia (including
P.I. Boriskovsky's report). *Asian
Perspectives* 6:21-33

            1969   Reworking Southeast Asian
prehistory. *Paideuma* 15:125-39

            1970   Northern Thailand, South-
east Asia, and world prehistory. *Asian
Perspectives* 13:145-62

            1972   An earlier agricultural
revolution. *Scientific American* 226:34-41

Stein Callenfels, P.V. van 1924   Het eerste
palaeolithische werktuig in den Archipel.
Oudheidkundig Verslag 1924:127-33.   Bandung:
Oudheidkundige Dienst in Indonesie

Strathern, M. 1969   Stone axes and flake tools:
evaluations from two New Guinea highlands
societies. *Proceedings of the Prehistoric
Society* 35:311-29

Tindale, N.B. 1950   Palaeolithic *kodj* axe of the
Aborigines and its distribution in
Australia. *Records of the South Australian
Museum* 9:257-74

            1957   Culture succession in south-
eastern Australia from late Pleistocene to
the present. *Records of the South
Australian Museum* 13:1-50

            in press   Adaptive significance of
the Panara or grass seed culture of
Australia. In Wright in press

            and B. Maegraith 1931   Traces of an
extinct aboriginal population on Kangaroo
Island. *Records of the South Australian
Museum* 4:275-91

Tweedie, W.M.F. 1953   The stone age in Malaya.
*Journal of the Malayan Branch, Royal Asiatic
Society* 26:3-90

White, C. 1971 Man and environment in northwest Arnhem Land. In Mulvaney and Golson 1971: 141-57

White, J.P. 1967 Ethno-archaeology in New Guinea: two examples. *Mankind* 6(9):409-14

                    K.A.W. Crook and B.P. Ruxton 1970 Kosipe: a late Pleistocene site in the Papuan highlands. *Proceedings of the Prehistoric Society* 36:152-70

Wright, R.V.S. (ed.) in press *Stone tools as cultural markers: change, evolution and complexity*. Canberra: Australian Institute of Aboriginal Studies

Zipf, G.K. 1949 *Human behavior and the principle of least effort*. Reading (Mass.): Addison-Wesley

PART 2

PEOPLING THE NEW LANDS

The movement of men from Sundaland into the
small islands of eastern Indonesia and eventually to
the island continent of Greater Australia - Australia
with New Guinea and Tasmania joined at times of low
sea level - is one of the dramatic episodes of world
Pleistocene history. To comprehend it requires
attention to more than the narrowly archaeological
evidence. The group of papers that follow deal with
relevant questions of Pleistocene sea levels and
shorelines, primitive watercraft, ecological
adaptation and the nature of hunter-gatherer
colonisation of new territories.

Birdsell's contribution raises these issues in
the context of exploring why this settlement of
Greater Australia should have led to the complex
situation presented by the physical anthropology of
its contemporary inhabitants. In doing so he brings
together in a single statement the major formulations
he has made in a lifetime's work on Australia and its
settlement. Like Birdsell, two of the other
contributors write from the same position of long
experience: Howells on the physical anthropological
dilemma, seen in a wider geographical frame, Tindale
on the historical implications of the culture of an
isolated island community.

Three other papers are by newer scholars in this
field. They provide an injection of new evidence
from the points of view of human palaeontology,
archaeology and coastal geomorphology in terms of
which the major issues raised by Birdsell must be
discussed. Although we are left with no concensus

of opinion as to the manner and means of the initial colonisation of Sahul, this truly reflects the open nature of the debate in this area of research and the intense commitment of the debaters themselves.

THE RECALIBRATION OF A PARADIGM FOR THE FIRST PEOPLING OF GREATER AUSTRALIA

JOSEPH B. BIRDSELL

Department of Anthropology
University of California
Los Angeles

The initial peopling of an empty continental landmass is a dynamic microevolutionary event. The date of arrival is important. The means of transport is significant in terms of the development of technology in prehistory. The manner in which the new lands were settled and the kinds of cultural, and possibly physical, adaptations required for successful occupancy are worthy of speculation if direct investigation proves too difficult. Finally the identity of the first peoples is of considerable interest in the reconstruction, both in subsequent evolution in the initially saturated continent and in looking backward to throw some light on the longer phases of evolution of mainland populations from which the immigrants are derived. The first peopling of Greater Australia involves these major issues, and others at a finer scale.

As the result of extended fieldwork with living Aborigines in 1938 and 1939 I proposed a model for the populating of Australia involving three waves of differing kinds of populations and extending over the whole of the last glaciation. Its details were published (Birdsell 1949) at a time when prehistory was little known in Greater Australia and before radiometric techniques of dating had been established. Therefore this early paradigm was in a sense structured primarily around the biological evidence of differences between the regional populations within Australia.

The three types of populations visualised as

contributing to the modern populations of Australia,
Tasmania and New Guinea commenced with an initial
wave of Oceanic Negritos who saturated the regions
to carrying capacity as determined by their
technological adaptation.   Their arrival was
estimated to have been in the early part of the
last glaciation, when the eustatic lowering of sea
level made movements from the Sunda Shelf to the
emergent Sahul Shelf less hazardous than periods of
high, or normal, sea level. This is the interval
and these are the people with whom this paper is
primarily concerned.

Subsequently in the model a second kind of
population, called the Murrayian, reached Greater
Australia and in the areas most favourable for
their penetration, such as Australia proper, rolled
back the original inhabitants, whose traces today
survive only in a few marginal areas.   The
Murrayians themselves are best represented by the
historic Aborigines of the Murray drainage system
and the adjacent coastal regions.

A third wave of peoples, called the
Carpentarians from their preponderant position
around the Gulf of that name in north Australia,
arrived in the terminal portion of the last
glaciation, and so were the last of the Pleistocene
migrants to reach Greater Australia. The impact of
seafaring peoples in the Recent Period, such as
Malays, Micronesians, or Polynesians, is of no
concern here.

THE DISCOVERY OF GREATER AUSTRALIA

Variation in Pleistocene sea levels in the region

It has long been known that worldwide sea
levels fluctuated with the withdrawal of water to
form the great glacial ice masses during each ice

advance in the Pleistocene. That much was evident
when the original paradigm was constructed. But it
might be noted that at that time palaeoanthropologists
were not concerned much with matters so far removed
from anatomy. Many workers still believed that the
Tasmanians reached their island homeland by voyages
from unspecified points of origin in the Melanesian
chain of islands. The types of watercraft used
were not considered and the time of arrival left
unspecified. Today prehistorians (e.g. Bowdler
this volume; Jones this volume) have provided ample
evidence that the Tasmanians' ancestors populated
mainland Australia, and that the Tasmanians
themselves walked overland on the Bassian Shelf to
reach the terminal southern peninsula which
subsequently, with rising sea level, became isolated
as the island of Tasmania.

Current estimates of the oscillations of
eustatic sea level for the last 120,000 years have
recently been provided by J. Chappell (1976). He
includes estimates of the withdrawal of water from
the ocean and reconstructs palaeoshorelines as
modified by the water-load effects on continental
shelves and ocean basins. From 120,000 years ago
until the beginning of the Recent, some 10,000 years
ago, the surface of the sea always lay below present
levels. But during this extended interval there
were six oscillations in which the level was
considerably lower than at other times. Perhaps
for the entirety of the last glaciation the
generalised average shoreline lay about 50 m below
present levels. But at two intervals, one centring
on the time span about 53,000 years ago and the
other about 20,000 years ago, water levels dropped
considerably below the average, possibly reaching
depths 120-150 m below the present surface. The
import of Chappell's findings for the recalibration
of the original model are evident. The whole of
the last glaciation would have been generally
favourable for primitive watercraft to island-hop
from the western shelf to the eastern one.

Admittedly there were likely intervals of time
between each step of the overall voyaging, and hence
possibly many generations of human time were involved
in the total trip. Nevertheless two more than
ordinarily favourable intervals arose when sea level
dropped well below the average levels. As will be
seen in the next section on prehistory, the last
interval centring about 20,000 years ago is too
late to have affected the initial peopling of
Greater Australia, although it may have facilitated
movements of the last peoples, the Carpentarians.
Whether the first arrival in the new lands began
about 53,000 years ago will of course depend upon
subsequent findings by prehistorians. The present
data do not conflict with such a suggestion, but
the earlier time spans have not yet been thoroughly
investigated, so that only tentative approval can
be extended in this direction. It may even prove
in the long run that the general lowering of sea
level with the emergence of the shelves is the most
important factor, and that further drops in sea
level little affected the distance of water gaps
between the islands which extended between them.

Current data from prehistory in Greater Australia

In 1929 Hale and Tindale (1929) conducted the
first scientific archaeological excavation in
Australia. At Devon Downs, on the lower Murray
River, they found superimposed cultural layers in
an archaeological context for the first time on the
continent. No dating was available then, but
subsequent radiocarbon dating established that the
earliest occupation was beyond 5000 BP (Mulvaney
1975:118). Their work was a scientific landmark
and stood alone until the late 1950s when a flood
of stratified sites began to be excavated and
published, giving the first perspectives of
Australian prehistory and reaching back to the
terminal Pleistocene. The original model had been
constructed without the benefit of this knowledge.

Today a very respectable time depth has been shown for both continental Australia and New Guinea. Very recently the same has been found true in Tasmania. In all three segments of Greater Australia, man's occupancy has been found to extend well back into the Upper Pleistocene. Beginning with the northern segment, the oldest site presently known in what is now Papua New Guinea is in the eastern mountains at Kosipe. The dating for this deposit of charcoal and artifacts is c. 26,000 BP. The elevation of the site is around 2000 m so it is quite clear that the mountainous interior was occupied this early, implying that the occupancy of the New Guinea lowlands was some millennia prior to this time.

The present continent of Australia has numerous sites of human occupancy dating to 20,000 BP or earlier. They are found in the central north, the southeast, southern coastal and extreme southwest regions. Obviously the continent carried a saturation population well before such times. One of the most important of the sites occurred at Lake Mungo, in western New South Wales. Lake Mungo is but one of five closely associated, now extinct, lakes lying in a chain and known together as the Willandra Lakes system. The stratigraphic relationships and palaeoclimatology of the Willandra Lakes were under study by J.M. Bowler before the important skeletal finds made there could warp any judgement on chronology (Bowler *et al*. 1970; Bowler 1971, 1976). The chain of lakes was filled by overflow waters of the Lachlan River flooding out through an anabranch during periods climatically more favourable than the present. This series of freshwater bodies contained a fauna of both fish and shellfish upon which the local inhabitants lived. Aboriginal occupancy of this region was possible roughly between 40,000 and 20,000 years BP. The maximum stand of the lakes was reached by 32,000 years BP. Cultural remains from these lakeshore sites are extensive and include a variety of simple

percussion types of artifacts reminiscent of other
early sites on the continent and those on the
island of Tasmania. It is not going too far to
call the artifacts Tasmanian-like.

To date, Lake Mungo has yielded the fossilised
remains of three human individuals. Of these only
the first has been described in print. Mungo I
according to Thorne (1976, this volume) is a young
adult female, modern in type and fitting into the
extreme gracile end of the modern Aboriginal
distribution. Dated at about 25,000 years BP, it
might be questioned whether this cremated specimen
shows any affinities with the historical Tasmanians,
whose ancestors must have been present and perhaps
even preponderant, on that portion of the mainland
during that period of time. While Thorne does not
examine this problem, the meagre remains of Mungo I
do show one character pointing in the direction of
the Tasmanian Aborigines. The left orbit has the
very low height of 27 mm (Thorne 1971, 1976), which
excludes it from the mainland range of Aboriginal
females and barely includes it in the lowest portion
of the Tasmanian females. On the other hand, the
vault is more like that of Victorian Aborigines in
historic times than it is that of the Tasmanians.
The other two individuals found at Mungo have not
yet been described, although they are all said to
be 'modern' in type. This term primarily
distinguishes them from the archaic Kow Swamp
population, which, dated from about 10,000 years
BP, is rather extreme in form for an Australian
Aboriginal population. The paradox that the later
Kow Swamp archaic population succeeded the very
modern type of population sampled at Mungo at much
earlier times has not been solved. (On this
question see Thorne this volume.)

Cultural remains suggest that a date of 40,000
years BP is to be expected in several areas of
Australia. Dates approximating this occur at Outer
Arumpo, the most southerly lake in the Willandra

chain. There charcoal has been dated at 36,000
years BP. At Keilor in southern Victoria the
picture has not yet clarified, but there are
indications that cultural remains have been found
in situ in alluvium for which 40,000 years BP is a
probable date (Bowler 1976). Thus at these sites,
and elsewhere in Australia, there is ample evidence
that the last great drop in sea level of about
20,000 years ago was not responsible for the initial
populating of Greater Australia.

It is more difficult to make sensible
projections about the earliest occupancy of this
region. Bowler again (1976) leads the way with
some tentative conclusions. The deposits of the
Golgol lunette at Lake Mungo are estimated to have
an age of from 100,000 to 120,000 years ago and
although carefully examined for evidence, there is
no indication of the presence of man on the lake
shores of that time. On the east coast of Australia
there are two systems of coastal barriers or dune
ridges. An inner and earlier one, which again may
have been constructed about 120,000 years ago, has
yielded no evidence of human occupancy. This type
of negative evidence is not yet compelling however,
so that it would be premature to claim too much for
it. Nevertheless by Chappell's reckonings the
initial eustatic lowering of sea level began 120,000
years ago, so that at any time thereafter there is
a possibility that men reached Greater Australia.
The answer must result from the future activity of
the diligent prehistorians of this area.

One of the most exciting discoveries in the
prehistory of the Pleistocene continent has
recently been discovered in its Tasmanian segment.
There Bowdler (1974), excavating in a cave site on
Hunter Island a short distance off the coast of
northwestern Tasmania, found ancient cultural
deposits. In strata 80 to 100 cm below the surface
she found two pieces of flaked quartz and, more
impressively, a bone point, ground and polished

into usable form. The date of 18,500 years BP for
these finds is now to be supplemented by one of
c. 23,000 for lower deposits (Bowdler this volume).
Thus the occupancy of Tasmania not only begins to
show very respectable antiquity, but since this is
many millennia before the Bassian shelf was flooded
by rising waters, it proves beyond any possible
doubt that Tasmanian Aborigines were 'overlanders',
that they were a normal part of a continental
population of Australia of their times and that
their ancestors held sway there. It is now up to
those anthropologists who believe otherwise to
demonstrate that their beliefs are viable.

*A major problem in the present-day distributions of
peoples in the remnants of Greater Australia*

One of the major problems of the peopling of
Greater Australia involves an adequate explanation
for the great unevenness in the distribution of
different types of populations in the present day
remnants of the former great continent, New Guinea,
Australia and Tasmania. The whole of New Guinea,
and for that matter outer Melanesia, is peopled by
diverse types of essentially Negritoid populations.
It matters little what terms are used to label
them, for in essence they are derived from a basic
population of Oceanic Negritos, variously admixed
with other later waves of migrants.

In very sharp contrast to the peoples of
Melanesia are the continental Australians. For the
moment lumping them together as 'Australomorphs'
and ignoring the regional differences evident on
the continent, it is sufficient to say that they
stand in marked contrast to the shorter, frizzly-
haired Negritoid peoples to their north. Since
both New Guinea and Australia were once broadly
joined by the now submerged Sahul Shelf, the very
evident question is can these great population
differences be accounted for in any reasonable terms
of a) the sequencing of peoples, b) the

differential survival of different types of
populations in very different environments, c) even
the possibility that men preferentially chose one
ecological scene over another. It is possible that
a study of the routes and waterways through which
these people must have come will in a small way
reflect upon this problem.

Aside from this major problem, there remains
the origin of the Aborigines of Tasmania, who stand
apart from Victorian Aborigines in a number of minor
but nonetheless taxonomically relevant ways. Having
reached Tasmania overland, they once more represent
a populational difference that must be fitted into
the sequencing of peoples into Greater Australia.
Those current investigators who still think that
the Tasmanians can be explained away as a
consequence of millennia of isolation and some
mutational changes would do well to re-examine the
probable consequences of mutational pressure on
short-term evolution.

*The probable routes for Pleistocene watercraft
between the Sunda Shelf and the Sahul Shelf*

The seas between these two emergent landmasses
were island-studded. The majority of the large
islands are high and mountainous, but a few chains
of low islands also exist. The patterning of these
landmasses is not random. Two sizable chains of
large islands extend between the two emergent shelves
(Fig.1). In the north, the route leaving the Sunda
Shelf for Sulawesi (R-1) with its various terminal
options, passes through a series of islands to
reach New Guinea either at the region of the present
Bird's Head or the Sahul Shelf near the Aru Islands.
R-1, with its three major options, in all cases
involves water crossings of 65 km and more. A more
southerly passage (R-2) with two major options, is
in some ways more attractive, because the initial
water gaps are considerably smaller. But again its
terminal stages involve stretches of more than 65 km

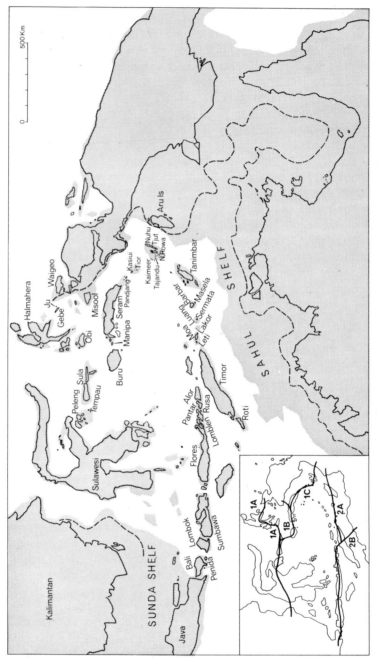

Fig.1. Routes from Sunda to Sahul. This map locates the major islands mentioned in the text.

of water to be crossed, even with a maximum eustatic
sea level lowering of 150 m.

All five optional routes were hazardous, and
since it is evident that they were traversed
successfully from time to time, it seems probable
that the watercraft used in the late Pleistocene
were superior to those found in recent times in
Australia and Tasmania. It is highly probable that
there was a constant if somewhat straggling trickle
of small groups of human beings over all or most of
the routes. The size of the watercraft likely to
have been used suggests that the groups consisted
of small biological families.

In Fig.1 the small and non-essential islands
have been omitted and the two main routes, R-1
and R-2, have been shown with their terminal
options. The expanse of the emergent landmasses
with a drop of 80 fathoms or around 150 m in sea
level is shown by the lightly stippled area in the
figure. The 25 fathom line, close to 50 m, is
shown dotted for the two shelves where distances of
water gaps are affected.

Table 1 gives relevant information about the
stages on the two routes, and their variants, at
times of maximum sea level, under the following
heads:

    1. *Target distance*: an estimate of the shortest
       distance between stages along the routes.
    2. *Target height*: visibility of target islands
       in terms of their elevation plus 150 m for
lowered sea level. This is expressed as 1500 + m
for any land above that height and to the nearest
25 m for land below. Note in this connection for
example, that Meati Miarang (R-2A), though a low
island, is visible at 22.5 km according to
mariners' charts.
    3. *Target width*: extent of the barrier interposed
       by the target island, which is relevant to the

Stages	Target Distance (in km)	Target Height (in m)	Target Width (in degrees)
Route 1: from Sunda Shelf at Kalimantan			
Sulawesi	42	1500+	135
Peleng	10	1125	125
Tempau	4	300	135
Sula	1	1500+	140
Variant A: from Sula			
Obi	93	1500+	30
Halmahera	35	1500+	120
Gebe	30	550	20
Ju	7	250	45
Uta	1	175	95
Sahul Shelf at Waigeo	18	1075	100+
Variant B: from Sula			
Buru	69	1500+	65
Manipa	26	650	30
Seram	5	1500+	95
Sahul Shelf at Misool	68	650	140
Variant C: from Seram			
Pandjang/Manawoka	8	500	65
Kasiui	19	500	20
Baam	5	225	45
Tioor	6	525	80
Uran	13	150	50
Kaimeer	45	300	5
Kur	11	575	30
Tajandu	29	275	40
Nuhu Rowa	14	250	125
Nuhu Tjut	3	950	165
Sahul Shelf at Aru Is	103	375	190+

Stages	Target Distance (in km)	Target Height (in m)	Target Width (in degrees)
Route 2: from Sunda Shelf at Bali			
Penida	6	450	120
Lombok/Sumbawa	19	1500+	75
Flores/Lomblen	3	1500+	115
Rusa	8	475	60
Pantar	2	1250	115
Alor	0.2	1500+	200
Timor/Roti	29	1500+	140
Variant A: from Timor/Roti			
Leti	35	550	15
Moa	2	525	110
Lakor	1	150	125
Meati Miarang	16	150	50
Luang	11	400	35
Sermata	2	550	45
Babar	63	975	25
Masela	8	350	80
Tanimbar	74	375	60
Sahul Shelf near Aru Is	98	375	120+
Variant B: from Timor/Roti			
Sahul Shelf at Fantome Bank	87	150	180

Table 1. Routes from Sunda to Sahul. Target islands, distances, heights and widths.

question of the precision of navigation and amount of control over the process of watercraft required along different stretches of the routes. It is expressed as the angle (to the nearest 5°) subtended by the target island at the point on the home island from which the measurement of shortest distance was made. When the target island offers a larger target from another point on the home island than this, it is indicated by a + sign behind the angle.

All three factors must be taken into account
together when assessing any one value in the table.
Thus low elevation and small target width become
less important the shorter the target distance.

Fig.2 graphs the number and extent of water
gaps to be crossed along the two routes, with
hachuring of those in excess of 30 km.   The
following comments can be made:

   1. *Route 1A*: of the ten water gaps to be
      traversed, four exceed 30 km, one barely. Of
these far and away the most difficult passage would
be from Sula to Obi, a distance of nearly 95 km.
   2. *Route 1B*: this requires fewer stages, eight
      in all, and while it has three water gaps in
excess of 30 km, two of these are shorter than the
maximum crossings on any of the alternative routes
between the two shelves. This makes it highly
probable that R-1B was relatively heavily used by
Pleistocene migrants to Sahul.
   3. *Route 1C*: this requires no less than 18 stages,
      imposes two major water gaps and involves a
number of crossings to low islands in its terminal
stages. All in all, it seems considerably less
attractive than the optional R-1B.
   4. *Route 2*: the passage from the Sunda to the
      Sahul Shelf by this route has a different
character from Route 1 and its options. From the
Sunda Shelf at its southern part, all the water gaps
are small and as a result, the landing fronts broad,
until the island of Timor is reached. In all cases
progress is from one large high island to another.
   5. *Route 2A*: requiring 17 stages overall, this
      route contains no less than four steps in
excess of 30 km and three of these occur in the
last four steps necessary for arrival on the Sahul
Shelf. In a general way this route seems less
attractive than the three options presented for
Route 1.
   6. *Route 2B*: although the Timor Sea contains a
      channel more than 1.5 km in depth running

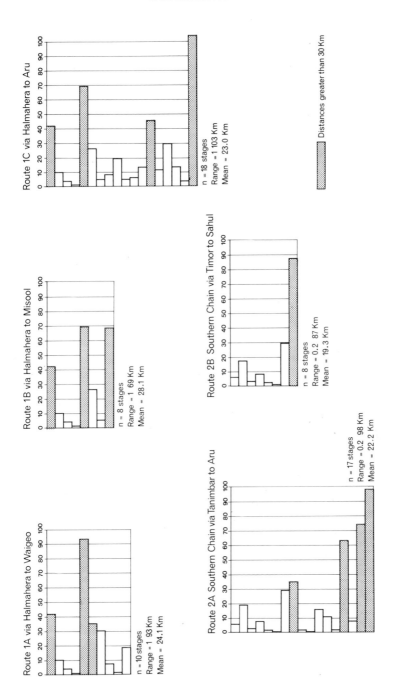

Fig.2. Routes from Sunda to Sahul. Graphs of stages and distances.

next to the island, this route seems to have much
to recommend it both in terms of the number of
water crossings required and the extent of the
biggest of these. It would seem probable that with
the maximum eustatic drops approximating 150 m, both
around 53,000 years ago and again around 20,000 years
ago, some of the earliest migrants from the Sunda
Shelf should have reached the Sahul Shelf in the
general region of the present-day Kimberleys of
northwest Australia.

*Changes in the water gaps with the eustatic sea level
25 fathoms (nearly 50 m) below the present surface*

Chappell (1976) indicates that for the last
120,000 years eustatic sea level has oscillated
around a generalised level of about 25 fathoms or
nearly 50 m below the present-day surface. This
depression of water level is very much less than
the maximum drop postulated during the preceding
discussion of the problem. The difference in the
two levels did not appreciably affect the water gaps
between high islands, which in general plunge
steeply into the sea to great depths. Much more
important differences are to be found on the
emergent shelves and perhaps some of the banks
submerged at present levels.

All three variants of Route 1 show an increased
water gap between Kalimantan and Sulawesi of from
42 to 87 km. This doubles the magnitude of the gap
at the very first stage of Route 1. The gaps to be
crossed between the intervening high islands along
R-1A show little increase, and it is not until the
terminal portions of the route that much further
difference is to be noted. With a maximum lowering
of sea level the distance between Uta and Waigeo
was a modest 18 km; under the more average conditions
the distance rises to 39 km. Under these
circumstances landfall must then be made at Balabalaba,
a small island of some elevation. There remains a
very short water gap across present-day Bougainville

Pass, before landfall is finally made on the island
of Waigeo. The gap in the central portion of the
route between Obi and Halmahera remains as
formidable as it was at the lowest sea level. The
changes in this route are thus not severe except
at the very first water gap between Kalimantan and
Sulawesi.

The 25 fathom sea level does not seriously
affect R-1B in its terminal stages from Seram to
Misool. As before, the water gap between Kalimantan
and Sulawesi is more than doubled, but the water to
be spanned between the high islands remains
virtually constant. The gap between Sula and Buru
is a very difficult one with a maximum drop of sea
level and remains so under these new conditions.
The final gap from Seram to Misool, which stood at
68 km under the previous conditions, now only
increases to 84 km. While this pathway now has
three stages well in excess of 65 km to be covered
by primitive watercraft, it still has but eight
crossings and hence remains a likely route for
Pleistocene migrants.

In summary a sea level standing 25 fathoms
below the present level increases the difficulties
of all three variants of R-1, but primarily in the
initial step proceeding from Kalimantan to Sulawesi.
What appear to be the great stumbling blocks in the
middle of the routes, that is making landfall on
Obi on R-1A and reaching Buru on R-1B and R-1C,
remain the most precarious parts. These would be
dangerous crossings at best and the losses among
early voyagers must have been considerable.

As already noted, the more southerly island
route R-2 is more attractive than the northern
route as far as the island of Timor. A sea level
dropping to only 25 fathoms below the present level
would have no effect on this portion of the route.

However in continuing on R-2A via Tanimbar to

the Sahul Shelf, there are ten further crossings
of which three of the last four are formidable at
maximum sea level drop. With the higher sea level
the gap from Sermata to Babar remains little
changed at 63 km. The next to last crossing from
Masela to Tanimbar remains close to its earlier
value of 74 km. The configuration of the Sahul
Shelf just to the west of the present Aru Islands
is such that there is little difference between the
distances to be traversed at the two levels of
eustatic drop. With the smaller drop the distance
increases to but 103 km. This is of course a very
considerable gap to be traversed, but its risks
have not been changed greatly with the more modest
drop in eustatic sea level. Presumably Pleistocene
voyagers successfully used this route.

R-2B, terminating in a final crossing from
Timor to the adjacent Sahul Shelf, was the most
attractive of all the feasible routes at the
minimum sea level. But with water standing higher
this terminal crossing, which formerly amounted to
87 km, now becomes greatly broadened. A successful
arrival on the low-lying Sahul Shelf now involves
an initial crossing from Timor to the Troubadour
Reefs, a distance of 193 km. From this stopping
point it remains another 69 km to the Sahul Shelf
proper. These are great distances, and it is
unlikely that the Sahul Shelf could be seen from
Roti Island at a distance of nearly 260 km. There
are other routes between Timor and the Sahul Shelf
when the sea stood at the 25 fathom level, but they
involve even greater distances. Thus R-2B, which
seemed so favourable for Pleistocene migrants when
sea level stood at its lowest below the present
level, now becomes excessively formidable. These
considerations suggest that it could only have
been used systematically during the periods of
minimum sea level, for a few millennia about 53,000
years ago and a further few about 20,000 years ago.
This route may be discounted as being of no great
importance after the initial peopling of Greater

Australia.

Problems on landing on the Sahul Shelf

Quite aside from the difficulties involved in the various routes themselves, the actual scene of landing on the Sahul Shelf imposes some problematical hardships. With sea level oscillating over some scores of metres in depth, even through millennia, the nature of the emergent shelf comes into some question (Chappell and Thom this volume). Presumably the tidal reaches of the shelf, even those involving coral-building organisms, could and did react to changes of sea level at this rate. Nonetheless the country behind the strand must have approximated the tidal mud banks which characterise the low-lying country on the southern shores of the Gulf of Carpentaria in present-day north Australia. Except for that portion of the Sahul Shelf lying in the vicinity of the present-day Aru Islands, relatively few rivers would have flowed across its emergent surface to reach the sea. Therefore the adaptive transition of the island-hoppers to the realities of the shelf may have been a difficult one. This would be particularly true of those voyagers who might have crossed from Timor directly to the Sahul Shelf.

One further point deserves consideration, and that is the availability of stores of fresh water. Potable water is not always present in low-lying mud banks in the present-day scene, and there is a very real question as to how the voyagers reaching the Sahul Shelf via R-2B would have fared in this respect. Presumably the other four optimal routes would have yielded freshwater resources upon the landing of the travellers in suitable places.

Routes to the Philippines

Feasible routes to the Philippine archipelago at low sea level are not a major concern here. For

once those islands were reached, migrants would
have to turn southward and traverse a long chain of
small islands to reach the north end of Sulawesi.
Thereafter they would be on the main Route 1 and no
further along than if they had passed directly over
from Kalimantan to Sulawesi.

On the other hand, the early peopling of the
Philippines may give some evidence as to what kinds
of people first moved out from the Sunda Shelf
toward the Sahul. With sea level lowered to 80
fathoms (150 m) the present island of Palawan would
have been firmly attached to the northern end of
Kalimantan. Migrants on that route would still have
the crossing of Mindoro Strait before reaching the
island of Mindoro proper. But the distance is only
18 km and could even have been shortened by island
hopping *en route*. A southern gateway to the
Philippines leads to the island of Mindanao and
involves an additional water jump at Sibutu Pass.
Lying between the present-day islands of Sobiti and
Tawitawi, this water gap would have been but 18 km
at lowest sea level and so no serious obstacle.
Thus the Philippine archipelago would have been far
more accessible to Pleistocene immigrants than was
Greater Australia.

If the more generalised shoreline of a depth
of 25 fathoms is considered, the route to Palawan
would only have required a little island hopping
over short stretches of water. Much the same can
be said for access to Mindanao, for while
considerable numbers of water gaps were involved,
they were short in distance and would hardly impede
the movements of Pleistocene travellers.

*Is route choice to Greater Australia a matter for
computer simulation?*

A seeming wealth of data is available for input
in such a computer analysis, including the number of
water gaps at given levels of sea, the distances

involved, the visibility of land ahead, and angular measures of accuracy needed to make landfall. These factors suggest that a computer simulation involving a minimum-risk solution might be attractive.

The data that are lacking at the present time are of major magnitude. The factors described above are static, the missing ones dynamic. Required for even a reasonable simulation is detailed knowledge of surface wind upon primitive watercraft. It can be assumed that travelling would have been done on the northwest monsoonal winds, in short during the favourable season to move from west to east. But at this time the picture remains complicated by a paucity of local current data, large gaps in the knowledge of local tidal effects, and the compounding of monsoonal winds upon both of these factors of major magnitude. It should be pointed out that the emergence of the two shelves, the Sahul to the east and the Sunda to the west, may very well have changed magnitudes and possibly even directions of each or all of the three missing components to the problem. For the present it seems that elegant solutions to the question are out of reach and consolation can be taken only in the fact that many small groups of people succeeded in moving from west to east to reach Greater Australia during the last glaciation of the Pleistocene.

One further source of present-day indeterminancy in the whole problem lies in the fact that the waters between the Sunda and Sahul Shelves occur in a region of great tectonic activity, both past and present. There are some suggestions that water gaps may have been smaller in the past, for it is otherwise difficult to explain the presence of a Middle Pleistocene stegodon as far south as Timor. Such animals either swam across Wallace's Line, or were assisted in their passage by a great number of stepping-stone islands and land bridges which are no longer evident in the region. Thus there is a very distinct possibility that the late Pleistocene

topography of this region was different from today
and possibly served to shorten some of the long
water gaps noted earlier.

One other source of error in the data upon
which these analyses are dependent involves the
very low density of soundings throughout most of
the region. While in some regions the inshore
waters are heavily sounded, most of the main water
gaps show a great paucity of data. Therefore it is
perfectly possible, indeed quite probable, that
some of the water gaps which appear with present-day
sea levels may have been broken in late Pleistocene
times by a series of emergent banks and shoals which
served to give some relief to travellers over the
longer water gaps. Indeed, active tectonic shifts
may have quite altered the picture, but these can
hardly be reconstructed today. These kinds of
missing data produce one type of systematic error.
Their effects would be to shorten the water gaps as
they have been plotted from today's maps. But even
with favourable bias in this direction, great
hazards faced the primitive voyagers.

MODELS FOR PLEISTOCENE WATERCRAFT

At this time archaeology provides no information
as to the types of watercraft which might have been
used in the crossings from the Sunda to the Sahul
Shelf, so it is appropriate to seek watercraft among
the hunters and gatherers of the region which might
have served for models in earlier time. All were
constructed with simple percussion stone tools and
none of the advanced forms, such as the dugouts
introduced in recent millennia, which required
polished stone tools, have been included in this
survey.

The Tasmanian Aborigines were technologically
the simplest people in the region and used at least

two types of watercraft. At a level of sheer
expediency, they used driftwood logs for simple
water crossings. More elaborate craft were
fabricated either from bark or bundles of reeds.
According to Robinson (in Plomley 1966:119):

> These catamarans are ingeniously constructed of
> the bark of the tea-tree shrub and when properly
> made are perfectly safe and are able to brave a
> rough sea. They cannot sink from the buoyancy
> of the material and the way in which they are
> constructed prevents them from upsetting. The
> catamaran is made of short pieces of bark, some
> not above a foot in length, which when collected
> in a mass are tied together with long grass...

In Robinson's travels the Aborigines constantly and
quickly constructed them for the crossing of rivers.
They were also made with stringy bark (*Eucalyptus
obliqua*, *E. regnans*). The bark catamarans were made
of three bundles tapering toward each extremity, so
that when lashed together both the bow and stern
were somewhat upturned. At times they were made
entirely of rushes, when five bundles were lashed
together. The Tasmanian catamarans were not only
used upon island rivers but extensively brought
into service along the coasts and used to reach
offshore but nearby islands. In the southern
coastal regions these catamarans were about the
size of a whale boat and carried as many as seven
or eight people, with their dogs and spears
(Robinson in Plomley 1966:379). Data indicate that
the best of them, those of tea-tree paper bark,
could not venture much more than 8-16 km off the
coast (Jones 1976:246-8) and that these trips were
very dangerous ventures. Robinson's informants
told him that many hundreds of Aborigines had been
lost on such island excursions. The catamaran was
given some headway by the use of spears as pole
paddles. These simple but effective craft had a
very great disadvantage, in that the bark became
saturated and lost its buoyancy in under six hours
(Jones 1976:246).

Technically, the construction of a catamaran was rather simple, since all that was involved in the stripping of bark from the tree was at most some form of stone chopper. The bundles were fastened together with some type of cordage, itself a very ancient invention. Hence this type of watercraft may go far back into the Pleistocene, but for evident reasons it does not seem suitable to carry migrants from the Sunda to the Sahul Shelf, where many water gaps exceed the maximum range of 16 km. While logs might show greater periods of buoyancy, very little controlled headway could be made with them, aside from pure current riding.

The Aborigines of continental Australia possessed a number of kinds of watercraft that deserve examination. One of these made from a large sheet of thick bark stripped from a river red gum, *Eucalyptus camaldulensis*, can be quickly dismissed since it was adapted only for use in still waters and was limited virtually to the Murray and Darling River drainages. Its manufacture and use are described by Edwards (1972:7).

Another type of bark canoe was used in the coastal waters from Victoria in the south, up the east coast and around the north coastal districts. This is the tied bark canoe, made of thinner bark. To quote the process of manufacture from Edwards (1972:7, 9):

> To make these canoes, the Aborigines moved a cylinder of bark three metres to five metres long from a tall straight eucalypt, usually a stringybark, *Eucalyptus obliqua*. After the heavy sheet had been prised off, it was laid on logs. The rough outer surface was stripped and the ends thinned in preparation for tying. A small fire lit under the sheet rendered the sappy bark pliable, and at the appropriate moment it was turned inside out and the ends bunched and securely tied with bark cord.

Thin saplings inserted at regular intervals
across the canoe maintained the shape of the
bark to the desired width. Cord ties held the
spreaders in place. Further strengthening was
achieved by forcing pliant branches into the
body of the craft to act as ribs. The tied bark
canoe, although an unsophisticated type, was a
decided improvement on the simple Murray Valley
form because its greater depth and rigidity
increased seaworthiness although it too became
waterlogged after prolonged use.

This craft again involved only simple technology but
its relatively low freeboard limited its use to
sheltered waters and it cannot be considered a
likely candidate for Pleistocene water crossings of
any extent.

The northern coast of Australia and the tropics
of the Queensland coast contained a superior
watercraft, the sewn bark canoe. As described in
Edwards (1972:9-10):

The sewn canoe was constructed from broad
strips of bark obtained from one or two species
of eucalypt from whose trunks they were easily
peeled in the wet season. In some instances
only a single sheet of bark was used, but this
was unusual. Most canoes were built by
extending one piece of bark length-wise from
bow to stern along one side, and sewing two
sheets together to form the other side. The
two sides of the canoe thus formed were joined
along the bow, stern and keel and then caulked
with gum. To give additional freeboard, the
bow and stern were raised by sewing more strips
of bark onto the sides. A network of ties,
stretchers, braces and ribs was employed to
maintain the shape of the boat. Small poles of
mangrove wood were lashed along the gunwales
to prevent the sides from collapsing. When
completed, pieces of bark were laid along the
bottom of the canoe to give added strength and

to afford a dry protected floor.

This type of watercraft contains many obvious advances over the others previously described and it is clearly more seaworthy. One voyage is recorded from the Pellew Islands to landfall at the Macarthur River over 32 km of open water. Presumably the crossing was during a favourable time. Craft such as these might well have the potential, aided by currents, winds and tides, to make the crossings necessary to travel from the Sunda to the Sahul Shelf.

There is one note of caution to be sounded. On a distributional basis the sewn canoe is found along the Australian coasts in the north and tropical east in such a way as to suggest, according to the age-area theory, that it may be relatively late introduction into Australian waters. There is no assurance that this type of watercraft was available to Pleistocene voyagers, although it is the only one found in Australia or Tasmania which has sufficient potential to make it speculatively attractive. Such craft can have clean lines and be paddled with sufficient headway to give considerable control to its users. It is not just a tide-rider but allows for some maritime determinism in the hands of its operators. Unfortunately such craft as these are apt to leave little archaeological evidence of either their presence or their passage. The heavy choppers likely to have been used to cut out the outline of the bark sides served so many other functions as to be a nonspecific indicator of this particular role. The wedges used to prise the bark off the bole are not apt to be preserved under most circumstances. So if an early marine-oriented Pleistocene people had utilised such efficient watercraft, direct evidence is not likely to be recorded. It is conceivable that upon arrival at the Sahul Shelf, and during subsequent adaptation to a life of a land hunter and forager, this type of craft might have become forgotten. It

is possible, then, but certainly difficult to prove,
that all of the craft described before the sewn
bark canoe have been reinvented in Australia and
Tasmania in later times and are not directly
related to those of the original immigrants.

Rafts are unsuitable for the purposes of
crossing extensive water gaps, but in their modern
usage Australian Aborigines found them adequate for
a complex type of marine adaptation. On the northwest coast of Australia at King Sound and Collier
Bay, at least four tribal groups lived almost
exclusively on marine products afforded through
skilful raft exploitation. The Djaui tribe lived
only on Sunday Island and the other adjacent smaller
islands in Sunday Strait. The Ongkarango likewise
exploited a series of islands to the east of the
Djaui and lying just off the mainland. They also
extended inward on the mainland some 16 km to the
Kimbolton Range. To the north lay a third tribe,
the Emede, who were also primarily an island-
exploiting people. Further to the north and living
almost entirely on a group of islands well offshore
were the so-called Montgomery Islanders, the
Jaudjibaia tribesmen. In all four tribes the
adaptation was almost entirely marine and so they
may provide the best models for the kinds of
peoples involved in moving from the Sunda to the
Sahul Shelf in the Pleistocene.

The construction of the light mangrove double
raft is described by Love (1936:7):

The *kalum* is made with the help of a stone axe,
and a handy-sized piece of stone as a hammer.
Light poles of soft mangrove wood, about ten
feet in length, are cut down and tapered at the
two extremities with the stone axe. Usually
about nine poles are used for the lower raft
and about seven for the upper raft. These poles
are nailed together with hardwood pegs, of about
a foot long. The pegs are chopped from a hard-

wood tree with the stone axe, split longitudinally
to make them the easier to drive, and hammered,
with a stone, through one pole into the next.
Each successive pole is just hammered into the
last with three or four pegs. When the two
sections of the double raft are completed, they
are placed, one lapping over the other, small
ends to the centre. They are not fastened
together, the navigator relying on his weight
to hold the two sections together in the sea.
The paddle is a piece of red mangrove, cut so
that the spreading root makes a blade, a very
poor and rough paddle; but the Worora man is
skilful and graceful in his use of it, dipping
for a few strokes on one side, then changing
over to the other side.

While the Worora are primarily a land-oriented
tribe, the *kalum* is used on the inlets and still
waters of estuaries.

Unfortunately very little is known about these
rafting peoples. Even so it is clear that they
became highly adept at moving from island to island.
They are quite literally tide-riders, for this is a
region where some of the world's highest tides, from
9-12 m between changes, occur and the currents
generated are rapid: 8-10 knots are certainly
achieved in some constricted passages. Quite
obviously the *kalum* cannot progress against such
currents and must ride with them.

Essentially the Aboriginal procedure seems to
have involved pushing offshore into a current,
riding with it to a desired destination and then
making feeble headway to move out of the current
into still shore water. The implications of this
kind of tide-riding are profound. Without clocks
or chronometers, these coastal Aborigines learned
the full timing of tidal variation. Beyond that
they knew the direction and velocity of the currents
they rode, for otherwise they could not control

their destination. For a people with no written
records and no instruments other than their primary
senses, this is an extraordinary achievement. Even
though the *kalum* may not have been the watercraft
by which men moved outward from the Sunda Shelf to
finally reach Sahul, nevertheless this degree of
marine adaptation must have been maintained by all
the peoples involved in this venture, and at all
times, until disembarking upon the Sahul Shelf.

   In general most of the travel by such rafts
was of a magnitude of 8-16 km but there is some
evidence that the Montgomery Islanders successfully
voyaged for greater distances in working their
seasonal round in their outer islands. How
unfortunate it is for present purposes that no
careful observer documented in detail the skills of
these raft-using peoples.

   The Kaiadilt of Bentinck Island, in the southern
portion of the Gulf of Carpentaria, were also
rafters, using a single triangular raft made of
light mangrove wood. Tindale (1962) returned with
parties of Kaiadilt to the island from which they
were taken in 1949 and saw the rafts in their
proper use. They again are subject to waterlogging
and so are hauled out of the water after each short
period of use and dried out on a northern, steeply
sloping beach where they will receive a maximum of
solar radiation (see Tindale this volume). The
single triangular raft is presumably a precursor of
the more specialised *kalum* found in the northwest
coastal districts. It suffices for fishing and
foraging in the tidal zone around low Bentinck
Island, but it really would not fit the role of a
watercraft capable of making major water crossings.

   Tindale (1962) obtained a recounting of one
incident in which the head of the *dolnoro* fleeing
the main island with his women and children for a
small adjacent island, Allen Island, foundered and
14 of the 19 individuals drowned. Presumably he

could not pick a safe time for the trip and was
overtaken by a storm. This and one other such
episode allowed Tindale to calculate that inter-
island travel in his admittedly small series of
events showed a mortality rate of 50% among the
voyagers. The double raft of the west coast seems
to provide a much greater margin of safety than
these figures indicate.

Alternative kinds of watercraft

There are two requirements for primitive watercraft to cross extended gaps of water up to 100 km
successfully. First, the buoyancy must be sufficient
to allow the craft not to founder through becoming
waterlogged. Second, the craft must be capable of
sufficient headway at the operator's option to
position itself successfully in tide-riding, so as
to make landfall, even on a small goal, a fairly
secure proposition. Since Malay praus, fairly
sophisticated hulled watercraft with sails, only
average four to five knots on the northwest monsoonal
winds, it is unlikely that Pleistocene watercraft
did half as well. If a Pleistocene voyager averaged
two knots, a crossing of 100 km should require
approximately 30 hours. Therefore extended crossings
would likely need some sort of receptacle for the
storage of water. Food would not be necessary, but
some water would seem a requirement.

The limitation of materials found in Australia
and Tasmania need not have affected migrants setting
out on the long, many-staged trip from the Sunda
Shelf. What materials may have been used in
Pleistocene watercraft of course remain totally
speculative. Nonetheless it is perhaps worth
noting the distribution of two eucalypts outside of
Australia (Penfold and Willis 1961). *Eucalyptus
deglupta* Blume extends from New Britain in the east,
through New Guinea and the Moluccas, into Mindanao
in the Philippines. It is a large tree, growing up
to 58 m in height and 1.5 m in diameter. It has a

smooth deciduous reddish bark, but nothing is known
of its adaptability for canoe making. It is perhaps
most noteworthy in having crossed Wallace's Line,
from east to west.

A second extra-Australian tree, *Eucalyptus alba*
Reinw. ex Blume, extends from southern New Guinea
westwards through Timor and Flores to Solor. It
thus occurs along the easterly portion of Route 2.
The tree is smallish, growing to only 18 m with a
smooth white decorticating bark. This is one of the
few deciduous species of eucalypt and so accords in
this habit with most of the forest trees of the area.
Again nothing is known of its suitability for canoe
making, but its size seems too small to yield
suitable materials for such projects.

A type of material not found in Australia
consists of the tropical bamboos. From the point of
view of a Pleistocene boat builder, bamboos have
certain important properties. The shafts of these
grasses are coated in silica and so are essentially
impervious to water. Craft made from them would
not be subject to waterlogging. The shaft contains
internal nodes which seal off sections into air-
filled compartments. If bamboo were to be
substituted for light mangrove, the resulting raft
would have no problems as a result of loss of
buoyancy, would float higher and presumably handle
at least as well. Instead of pegging, lashing the
shafts together with cordage would seem required.
Cordage was however certainly technologically
feasible and present by late Pleistocene times.

The definitive monograph on the bamboos by Munro
(1868) provides a wealth of material about these
useful grasses, whose distribution is suggestive with
regard to the early peopling of Greater Australia.
Remembering that Munro is primarily concerned with
the taxonomy of these plants and that collectors
seldom give complete distributions, it is nonetheless
significant that they seem to pattern in our area in

a clear-cut fashion. No fewer than seven genera,
comprising 35 species, may have some relevance to
the problem at hand. Representing the former Sunda
Shelf, the present island of Java has no fewer than
four genera of bamboo, consisting of 13 species.
Presumably the ancient Sunda Shelf in the late
Pleistocene would have been similarly endowed with
these plants. Route 1, especially at its eastern
end in such islands as Seram, Amboina and Manipa,
today has three genera of bamboos, comprising 12
species in all. Since some of these same species
also occur in Java, it is tempting to conclude that
most of the high islands along Route 1 grow bamboos
of one kind or another and that the distribution is
nearly continuous. This conclusion is strengthened
by the presence of three genera, consisting of 11
species, in the Philippines. The plants seem to have
distributions concordant with high rainfall regimes.

Munro gives no records of any bamboo species in
any of the islands along Route 2, once Java has been
left, but this must be viewed as negative evidence.
It need not be surprising however, when it is
recalled that many of these islands have a
deciduous forest fauna and so presumably
insufficient rainfall for bamboos to prosper.

If the ancient immigrants to Greater Australia
used bamboo as a material for rafts and
'catamarans', then it seems clear that they could
have traversed Route 1 and its various options.
This of course assumes that climatic conditions
have not changed greatly since the late Pleistocene.
At the same time it gives the interesting counter
suggestion that some other materials may have been
utilised by the travellers along Route 2, but it is
not evident what these may have been. There could
be a useful role for experimental archaeology here.

THE SETTLEMENT OF GREATER AUSTRALIA

*The palaeogeography of the island chains and the
Sahul Shelf*

The reconstruction of palaeoclimates is a
complex task and at best provides speculative models.
Empirical data for the late Pleistocene climate of
the Sahul Shelf are largely lacking at this time.
It is fortunate that Nix and Kalma (1972) have
developed a complex model involving light, thermal
and moisture regimes for the Sahul area and have
interpreted it in terms of dominant flora. At the
time of maximum exposure of the Sahul Shelf's
surface they predict that it would have been covered
with the following sequence of flora in a transect
from south to north. The shelf in the area of the
present Gulf of Carpentaria would have been
essentially scrubland. Then to the north would lie
a moderately wide belt of low open woodland.
Further north this would be succeeded by woodland
proper, while the shelf adjacent to New Guinea would
consist of broadleaf open forest. This floral
pattern would have occurred at the maximum drops of
sea level of Chappell (1976) of around 53,000 and
20,000 years ago. In essence the shelf would have
been covered with vegetation very like that in the
northern third of continental Australia today.

A further development of the model of Nix and
Kalma closely corresponds to the generalised sea
level of 25 fathoms below present. The shelf is
considerably reduced in size and in its interior
is a sizable body of water, certainly brackish and
perhaps, with high evaporation and a reduced flow
of rivers from northern Australia, even saline.
The sequence of floras in these conditions shows that
most of the present Gulf of Carpentaria would be
covered by low open woodland and the remaining
portion of the shelf largely by woodland proper. In
both of these conditions closed forest, or
tropical rain forest, would be extensive and

continuous from one end of New Guinea to the
other. But whereas at the maximum extension of the
Sahul Shelf most of the Bird's Head was open
broadleaf forest, and so provided a broad continuum
with the major portion of the Shelf, during the
more generalised condition with sea level standing
25 fathoms below the present, the Bird's Head is
totally covered with rainforest, as is most of the
rest of New Guinea. Insofar as various populations
of migrants may have had ecological adaptations, or
cultural preferences, for a given kind of environment,
these changes of course have potential importance for
the unravelling of their movements.

Returning to the two arcs of islands that
connect the Sunda Shelf to the Sahul Shelf, today
the northern chain, comprising Route 1 for the
immigrants, is largely covered with broadleaf evergreen forests, that is, rainforests. It has been
relatively little altered by the inroads of modern
agriculturalists. But the southern chain, consisting
of Route 2 through Timor, falls into a regime of
lower rainfall and its original cover was broadleaf
deciduous forest. The latter islands, then, are
much more like the environment found in north
Australia, while those falling along Route 1
approximate the conditions now prevailing in New
Guinea. These points will be referred to again in
discussing the first peoples to reach the Sahul
Shelf.

*On the rate of expansion of a new people in an
empty continent*

Even in the face of a total lack of data
bearing on the point, it must be assumed that the
migrants to the Sahul Shelf came highly adapted to
a maritime life along the fringing tidal stretches
of the islands, both high and low, which they
traversed to reach their landfall in Greater
Australia. They would have earned their livelihood
primarily from the sea and their maritime knowledge

must even have exceeded that of the tide-riding
rafters of northwest Australia, since the water gaps
they traversed were very much wider. They must have
been a highly specialised Pleistocene people for
whom few models remain today, and those largely
unstudied.

Most stages of both Routes 1 and 2 would
probably have involved uni-directional movements,
always toward the east on the northwest monsoon,
and few returns save where the water gaps are very
short. It seems probable too that with each new
group arriving at a further island, a long period
of local adaptation to wind, water and tides must
have been required. In learning such intricacies
by which relatively safe crossings might be made
yet further ahead, it does seem reasonable to
consider that perhaps a generation of time may have
been involved. Thus depending on the routes chosen,
a minimum of eight generations to a maximum of 18
would be involved. But great time depth is
available, and even if as few as four or as many as
nine centuries were involved in the crossing of the
intervening waters between the shelves, the time
would have been well spent in terms of increasing
security through refining local knowledge
adaptively.

Once arriving on the Sahul shores, two
ecological options lay before the immigrants. They
could continue in their own marine oriented life or
gradually adapt to a more terrestrial economy in an
environment very like that of the northern portion
of the present continent of Australia. It is clear
from Tindale's (1962, this volume) work that the
Kaiadilt of Bentinck Island, who might well serve
as models for ancient migrants, found a very
successful life-style in low islands. With
virtually no resources provided by the barren island
on which their residence was based, they collected
richly from the tidal zone and the seas on all
sides. Their way of life was such that this small

population was well scattered, with each *dolnoro*
or local group small in numbers. Yet the overall
density supported by this small island was the
highest yet recorded for Australia. So the
resources of the tidal zone can support large
numbers of people on a high protein diet, presumably
without the great fluctuation in food availability
that may occur with a terrestial life-style. It
seems clear, then, that the coast of the Sahul
Shelf must have been heavily populated by people
retaining that kind of way of earning their economic
livelihood.

But population pressures would build as both
Routes 1 and 2 fed continuing family groups in to
the Bird's Head of New Guinea and especially the
Sahul Shelf. Somewhere in the process there would
have been pressure to exploit terrestrial resources,
and so a different kind of ecological adjustment
would have been explored and found attractive.
Certainly the initially empty spaces and the
unexploited plant and animal life would have had
attractions to even a committed coastal people.

Given a sufficiency of time, terrestrial
adaptations would have brought larger and larger
groups of people inland to live in a way reminiscent
of modern Australian Aborigines, although presumably
with a less sophisticated technology initially.
Once this stage was attained, there arises the
interesting question as to how long it would take a
land-oriented population to fill the interior of
Greater Australia to carrying capacity. Fortunately
this has been in a general way worked out (Birdsell
1957). Without reviewing the methodology involved
in the model, it is sufficient here to point out
that the time is surprisingly small and would vary,
according to the variables in the model, from less
than 1000 years to a little over four millennia.
The land surface considered in this model was
limited to present-day Australia and Tasmania. It
did not include New Guinea. Adding the emergent

shelves and New Guinea and recognising that an abrupt ecological shift would have been required to penetrate the New Guinea rainforests, it is still possible to conjecture that five millennia after the first landing on the Sahul Shelf, the whole of the landmass of Greater Australia would have been populated at carrying capacity by a population of hunters and gatherers.

Evidence that the populations of hunters are maintained at carrying capacity

Early European contacts with the hunting and gathering peoples of all continents were so biassed that the early observers' literature treats them as really little better than animals. Anthropology has long passed through any such views, and it is now realised that these economically simple peoples, and all of the Pleistocene occupants of Greater Australia, lived in fact in a skilfully regulated state of homeostasis. Such peoples were in equilibrium with their environment and this balanced condition was maintained, despite some fluctuations, by a rather complex series of actions, beliefs and traditions. There is evidence that this type of population control was self-consciously practised and involved, among other things, preferential female infanticide where that was deemed appropriate to the end.

In Aboriginal Australia the nature of these man-land equilibria has been evident for some time (Birdsell 1953). Population densities varied with the support base provided by the local scene, but everywhere social units tended toward a kind of constancy, save in the richest environments. Thus the so-called 'magical numbers' include an average family size of about five, a band size of 25 in the less rich environments, and a dialectal tribal size approaching the generalised figure of 500 persons. New research now in process by the writer utilises a greater wealth of data than the original study,

and so the results are more compelling. Preliminary
figures indicate a coefficient of correlation of
0.96 between the area occupied by each dialectal
tribe and some 65 of the environmental variables
affecting their land. In the final stages of
analysis an input of yet further data gives every
reason to hope that this coefficient of correlation
will rise to 0.98. This very satisfactory value
indicates that only 4% of the total variance in the
system is unexplained. It is evidence for the
highly structured nature of Aboriginal occupancy of
Australia, that an appropriate homeostasis of
population numbers in a given landscape was
rigorously realised and that these results were
obtained through the working of a complex system of
behaviour within a simple economy.

WHO WERE THE FIRST MIGRANTS TO REACH
GREATER AUSTRALIA?

The importance of the rapid saturation of
empty space by an incoming people lies primarily in
the fact that all of Greater Australia would have
been fully populated by whatever kind of people
came across in the first few millennia. How then
did the very different populations of New Guinea
become differentiated from those of Australia? The
easy explanation that these very diverse peoples
arose out of local evolution and differentiation
simply will not do. Evolution is not so easy. So
the problem is to determine what kinds of peoples
did migrate from the Sunda to the Sahul Shelf during
the 60, 80, or perhaps 100 millennia in which such
movements could and probably did occur.

This is a question of considerable difficulty,
for there is no very exact way of determining how
much the first migrants to Greater Australia have
contributed to its present inhabitants. The issue
is further complicated by the fact that traits

which are very clear-cut among living people, such
as spirally curled hair, are absent among the relics
of prehistory, and judgements on fossil crania must
be based upon other criteria. In the long run, and
in a perfect world, the evidence from living peoples
in Greater Australia, and the prehistoric crania
ultimately to be discovered there, should tell a
single story. As yet, the two kinds of data have
not been shown to be concordant, for they yield
different types of information.

The situation is confounded by the vast variety
of terms used to describe one and the same people
in the area of consideration. It would be futile
to review these terms in their variety, but
certainly some new common language of communication
is desirable. As a starting point, perhaps a series
of residential terms should be used in the broadest
sense. Thus the Aboriginal inhabitants of Australia
can be called 'Australians'. Likewise the residents
of Papua New Guinea and the eastward chain of
islands can be called 'Melanesians'. Such terms
are both bland and, in their limited sense, specific.
They do not imply that either the 'Australians' or
the 'Melanesians' are homogeneous in their origins,
but they do allow reference to specific populations
as they were at the time of contact.

In trying to unravel past contributions to
living populations, it is wise to proceed by referring
to populations that lived as entities either in times
past or in different places. Certainly the peopling
of Greater Australia must take into account *Homo
soloensis*, who inhabited Java as the last of the
pithecanthropine populations. The dating of this
species has varied over time. Originally described
as Upper Pleistocene in date, largely because of the
fauna associated with it, it was logically considered
to have perhaps direct connection with the later
peoples who moved into Greater Australia to become
both 'Australians' and 'Melanesians'. But recently,
though not yet in published form, Curtis working at

the Radiometric Laboratory in Berkeley, California,
has orally provided audiences with a date of
300,000 ± 300,000 years as appropriate for Solo man.
He has emphasised that the error in the date is
very great, but that it perhaps represents a
correct figure of magnitude for these hominids. He
had promised (pers. comm.) to proceed with better
samples and attempt a further dating for these
important finds.

As it now stands, Solo man seems to represent a
population of the late Middle Pleistocene, possibly
contemporary with the Chinese pithecanthropines from
Choukoutien. They are thus placed very much earlier
in time than previously estimated, and there is now
no evidence that they have directly contributed
through migration to the populations of Greater
Australia. This does not preclude the possibility
that pithecanthropine genes flowed into some of the
subsequent populations in Sundaland and so hitched
a ride to the Sahul Shelf in later migrant
populations.

The evidence which precludes Solo man from
migrating to Greater Australia is all negative in
character. Time depth as it is now known is not
sufficient to allow for Middle Pleistocene
migrants. Bowler's (1976) indications that two
likely types of sites dated to about 100,000 years
ago show no human occupancy in Australia are to the
point. Nor have any artifacts of the type which
seem to characterise the pithecanthropine time
horizons of Java yet been discovered in Greater
Australia. There remain the further suspicions
that pithecanthropines simply had not yet evolved
sufficiently technologically to construct watercraft
adequate for the crossings involved between the two
shelves, to achieve the type of marine adaptation
necessary, or to develop the insights as to time,
tides, and currents to make the venture feasible.
All in all, it seems reasonable to exclude Solo man
from having reached Greater Australia and hence

having been its first inhabitant.

On the probabilities that the Oceanic Negritos
reached Greater Australia as the first immigrants

It may seem curious that a people who today are
to be numbered in very few thousands may have
contributed their genes to literally millions of
later decendants. The Oceanic Negritos, as they
have generally been called, are a diminutive people,
with men frequently 150 cm or even less in stature.
They have a tightly, spirally curled hair form which
sometimes even takes the extreme variant form of
'peppercorn', as commonly seen among the Bushmen of
South Africa. Their skin is dark in colour. Their
features, both cranial and facial, are infantile in
character. At least one group, those on the
Andaman Islands, are characterised by a very rare
morphological condition known as steatopygia. The
condition represents an abnormal accumulation of
fat on the buttocks and upper thighs, particularly in
women. It is not simply a condition of corpulency.
It is only found in certain Negroid populations
among the peoples of the world. It again occurs as
a kind of racial marker among the Bushmen of South
Africa and their pastoral relatives, the Hottentots.
Traces of it are found in the diminutive Negroids
of the Congo rainforests. It seems to serve as a
genetic marker linking the Oceanic Negritos with the
far distant African peoples.

There are but three living groups of Oceanic
Negritos. The Andaman Islanders have gone virtually
to extinction but represent the type population in
its least modified form. True, such neolithic
elements as dugout canoes, bows and pottery reached
them, but their physical type was very little
modified by neolithic tropical Mongoloids. On the
mainland of Southeast Asia, in the mountainous area
of Perak in the centre of the Malay Peninsula, live
the remaining Semang. They are surrounded by
tropical Mongoloids; some gene flow has modified

their type, but there can be little doubt that
originally they were much like the Andamanese.
Finally on a number of the islands of the Philippine
archipelago live a group of Negritos called Aeta
(Ag:ta) who like the Semang have been genetically
influenced by their agricultural Mongoloid neighbours.
Still, in reconstructing earlier populations in any
area, it is necessary to discount the results of
modern gene flow between differing populations and,
at least in one's mind, to reconstitute the original
types.   In terms of such an exercise, there can be
little doubt that the Andamanese, the Semang and the
Aeta formed a single group quite properly known as
the Oceanic Negritos.

It is unfortunate that thus far prehistory has
little to say about the time of first appearance of
the Oceanic Negritos in tropical Southeast Asia.
It is presumed from their cultural adaptations that
the rainforests, that is evergreen broadleaf forests,
were a preferred environment, although there is no
reason to believe that they could not have existed
well outside this particular scene.   The fact that
all three existing groups today inhabit rainforests
is more a function of pressures from other peoples,
particularly agriculturalists, who have left them
undisturbed only in this environment.   This is not
the place to explore the ambiguities introduced by
W.W. Howells (1973) who, on the dubious basis of
measures of generalised distance, separated the
Andamanese, indicated in his exercise to be true
Africans and, paradoxically, closest to Middle
Dynastic Egyptians, from the other two groups, the
Semang and the Aeta.   By claiming no relationship
between the Andamanese and these two groups of
Negritos, he has departed from Occam's precept, for
his scheme requires the independent evolution two
times of the most extreme form of hair known among
men.   That this should occur twice is genetically
doubtful, that it should occur among neighbouring
peoples in Southeast Asia goes beyond good judgement.

Since evidence from prehistory remains inconclusive, it is best to turn to the patterning of Negritoid traits visible among the living peoples of Greater Australia. They are not evenly distributed. To the south, the now extinct Tasmanians showed a derived form of Negritoid hair with rather open spiral curls, growing to at least shoulder length. But this hair form was uniform among them and there is little reason to doubt that it was derived from some Oceanic Negritoid source, for the plea of independent mutation is thin and genetically untenable. It has been used by some with little knowledge of population genetics.

On the mainland of Australia the Aborigines by and large can be classed as 'Australians', barring a few special areas. On the rainforest plateaus behind Cairns in northeast Queensland 12 tribes of diminutive Aborigines showed a quite high frequency of derived Negritoid hair forms, although in more attenuated form than in the Tasmanians (Birdsell 1967). Their stature was reduced compared to other 'Australians' and an infantile cast of features was common among them. The evidence on the living, shown in many metrical and morphological characters, supports the belief that this rainforest area sheltered a relict group of original migrants, now much modified by millennia of gene flow. The inhabitants of Melville and Bathurst Islands, a short distance off the coast of Arnhem Land in northern Australia, might also be considered to show very residual signs of a Negritic component. Their stature is somewhat reduced, their hair form somewhat curlier than in adjacent mainland tribes. For Australia itself, then, it would appear that whatever vestiges of an original Oceanic Negritic component may have survived, it is visible only in marginal areas, whether this be in terms of geographical distance, separation by water or isolation through abrupt changes in ecological factors such as vegetation.

Turning to New Guinea and outer Melanesia, the
contrast is enormous. Everywhere hair form is of a
strongly derived Negritoid form, becoming
attenuated only in those coastal populations where
visible Micronesian or Polynesian genetic influence
has been strong. Thus the peoples of this
portion of Greater Australia show a very different
set of components of origin to those in Australia
and Tasmania. Throughout Melanesia population
stature is short to moderately short. While
children and women frequently have a kind of
Negritoid cast to their facial features, most men
show Australomorphic visages. The mystery is then,
how Melanesia could have retained so much of an
original Negritoid component, which survived only
marginally in Australia.

The reality of Greater Australia precludes any
idea that present-day Melanesia and Australia were
settled separately by different peoples. Two of
the options of northerly Route 1 fed into the Bird's
Head of New Guinea, while the third option reached the
Sahul Shelf at about the site of the present Aru
Islands. The only practical option of Route 2
carried migrants to near the latter point. Further,
during the prevailing sea level of 25 fathoms below
present surface, all four of these optional routes
reached the open forested north flank of the Sahul
Shelf. To have entered Australia during the bulk of
the time available during the last glaciation,
migrants would need to have skirted that portion of
the Sahul Shelf lying south of New Guinea and finally
would have reached Australia only in the general
region of the tip of present day Cape York
Peninsula. Thus the topography of the Sahul Shelf
would have tended to thrust migrants into the New
Guinea portion of the conjoined landmasses.

But given time, the original migrants would have
reached all portions of Greater Australia, and as
indicated earlier, rapidly filled it to carrying
capacity. The present indications are that these first

arrivals were Oceanic Negritos, or possibly Oceanic
Negritoids. This last matter must be resolved through
the findings of prehistorians and the very delicate
interpretation as to whether gracile skulls belong to
unmixed Oceanic Negritos, slightly mixed ones, or so
visibly mixed populations that they must be called
Negritoid. The criteria by which these separate
judgements must be made have not yet been developed,
since the problem has not been of general interest
among biological anthropologists.

There are several factors in favour of the
proposition that the first migrants to Greater
Australia were unmixed Oceanic Negritos. First, the
Andaman Islanders have remained virtually unaltered
by population admixture, although receiving some
aspects of neolithic technology, presumably carried
by Mongoloids. This would put that interface of
contact rather late in time. .Second, both the
Semang and the Aeta retain a surprisingly high
proportion of Negritic characters considering they
have been inundated by Mongoloid agriculturalists
for some millennia. As reconstituted, they must have
been good Oceanic Negritos when arriving at their
present domains. Third, it follows as a corollary
from the last proposition, that if the Aeta of the
Philippines were unmixed, or relatively little
mixed, when they left Kalimantan to reach the
Philippine archipelago, then some and perhaps most
of the populations on the Sunda Shelf at that time
would also have been Oceanic Negritos, unmixed or
very little mixed in character. These were the
considerations which led to the presumption in the
writer's original model (Birdsell 1949) that the
first immigrants were Oceanic Negritos, rather than
a mixed Negritoid set of populations.

Evidence from the fossil crania of Southeast Asia

There are no Pleistocene finds which can be
considered Oceanic Negritos of unmixed form. The
skull from the cave of Niah in north Borneo has

been well reported by Brothwell (1960) and is of
interest here, not only because of its early dating,
40,000 years BP, but because of its undoubted
gracility. Enough of the vault and a portion of
the face of this individual is preserved to tell
something about its population affiliations:
Brothwell concludes that it most resembles the
Tasmanians. Certainly the likenesses are suggestive.
But one may differ with Brothwell on his ageing of
the specimen. Two traits are involved in this
question. First, the basioccipital suture is
fully lapsed, indicating adulthood for the
specimen. Second, the maxillary third molars are
unerupted. Brothwell gives greater weight to the
second trait, and so calls the skull immature.
Perhaps influenced by a rate in excess of 16% of
unerupted third molars among the Negritoid tribes of
the Cairns area, I incline to the view that in
populations of this kind where infantilism is a
component, more weight should be given to the
closure of the basioccipital suture. I conclude
therefore, that the skull of Niah is a young adult,
and a remarkably gracile one. This would suggest
that it has a higher Negritoid component than does
the average Tasmanian. Crania many millennia
earlier than this are needed from the Sunda Shelf
to determine the population characteristics of
the earliest migrants to Greater Australia.

The skulls from Wadjak in Java are undated but
generally regarded as late Upper Pleistocene or
early Recent Period. Current attempts at amino-acid
dating may give a better fix in time for these
important finds. Wadjak I, a nearly complete skull,
has been regarded by Weidenreich (1945), among
others, as being virtually identical with the Keilor
skull from southern Victoria, for which a radiocarbon
age of around 13,000 BP has recently been reported
(e.g. Mulvaney 1975:201). I have gone on record
(1967:148) as indicating that both could be
considered good examples, if outsized, for the type
of Aborigines of southern Australia, the Murrayians.

Howells (1973) following the printout of his
computer programs, classes Keilor as Tasmanian, and
both as Melanesians. Thus in his confusing
terminology Wadjak also would be a Melanesian. This
is not the place to review this controversy in
detail, but it suffices here to note that Wadjak
presumably is later in time than Niah, and so the
evidence from the Sunda Shelf is that a Negritoid
kind of individual appears here in the record of
prehistory earlier than a Murrayian. Obviously a
great deal more material is needed from the Sunda
region, extending back further in time, before any
firm statements can be made on this general issue.
Nevertheless present evidence is concordant with
the idea that the Oceanic Negritos, or possibly
Negritoids, were the first immigrants to Greater
Australia.

The Tabon frontal bone from Palawan is of
uncertain date. It is not Negritoid, but rather,
Australomorphic in a general way, and marks the
passage of a pre-Mongoloid population from Borneo
to the Philippines. Dated and replicated similar
finds could be of considerable interpretive value
for the peopling of the whole region.

A major unsolved problem

Since there can be no doubt that the whole of
Greater Australia was overrun and populated to
saturation by the first immigrants to the empty
landmass, it still remains to explain how through
the passage of many millennia Melanesia is so
predominantly populated by Negritoid peoples of
one kind or another, while Australia and Tasmania
show but marginal traces of this kind of humanity
and were populated instead by full-sized
'Australians'. With the hypothesis that the
Negritos were the earliest, it follows that in
Australia they must have been driven to the verge
of extinction, for the traces remaining are both
residual and marginal. There is nothing in the

array of microevolutionary forces other than
migration to explain this great level of difference
between the two populations. Other factors must
be invoked.

The island of New Guinea has always maintained
a core of rainforest rising from low altitudes
toward the alpine region. This was true even
during the great eustatic drop in sea level, but
with the amelioration of climate, rainforests
descended further toward normal sea level, as in
the Recent Period. It is attractive to speculate
that Oceanic Negritos could adapt better to rainforest than other, full-sized peoples and
consequently maintained themselves there less
influenced by later gene flow from subsequent
comers. In effect this would result in the original
population in Melanesia being protected from
inundation by later waves of 'Australian' types of
peoples.

On the other hand, the idea carries the
corollary that in Australia proper the Murrayians,
who are postulated (Birdsell 1949) as the second
wave of populations to reach Greater Australia,
overrode the earlier Negritos, swamped them out and
essentially extirpated them, save in the few
marginal areas mentioned earlier. It is difficult
to conceive what kinds of superiorities would allow
this process to proceed to conclusion. True, the
Murrayians were a much heavier and stronger people
than the Negritos, but as modern types of men, both
must have been skilled in flexibly adaptive
behaviour. There remains the possibility that
differences in technology allowed for different
densities to develop in similar environments. But
the gap in technology between the first and second
immigrants to Australia must have been considerable
to have given this result. Unfortunately
prehistorians have not yet pushed archaeological
discoveries in Australia sufficiently beyond the
25 millennia period really to indicate the lithic

competence of the first inhabitants there. It is
not really to be expected that the primary tools of
the first people would differ too much from those
used around Lake Mungo 25 millennia ago. More
likely there would have been a difference in the
wooden implements constructed with the stone tools.
The problem is of a major magnitude and at present
no solutions are at hand.

*The evidence for Negritoids on Routes 1 and 2 from
the Sunda Shelf to the Sahul Shelf*

The great disparity between the populations of
present-day New Guinea and those of Australia to
the south confound simple explanations for the
origin of the differences. If it could be
demonstrated that the original Negrito population
only moved over Route 1 to reach New Guinea and
did not progress via Route 2 to reach the Sahul
entry to lands to the south, some sort of explanatory
hypothesis might be structured. It would involve
differential movements of contrasting populations
across the two routes to Greater Australia.

Therefore even at this late date, when all the
islands intervening between the shelves have been
swamped by tropical agricultural Mongoloids, it
seems worthwhile to look for residual evidence of
earlier waves of people. The character of the
island populations along Route 1 is so consistently
tropical Mongoloid that no convincing claims have
been made for the passage of earlier peoples through
this region. This is somewhat surprising, since
the northern chain of islands is essentially
covered with evergreen broadleaf forests and a
relatively small proportion of the rainforest has
been cleared for agriculture. No evidence for
residues of a Negritoid population have been brought
forward and all traces of pre-agricultural peoples
on this northern arc of islands seem to have been
swamped out by later incoming Indonesian farmers.

Route 2, beginning at Bali and leading through
the Timor archipelago to the Sahul Shelf near the
present Aru Islands, is today densely populated by
agricultural peoples of primarily tropical
Mongoloid origin. Its original plant cover was in
the main deciduous broadleaf forest, but much of
this has of course been cut down. Under these
circumstances one would hardly expect to find
survivals of the passage of earlier peoples. Yet
in Sumba, Flores, Alor and Timor there remain today
undoubted traces of a Negritoid people who must
remain as markers for the earlier passage of less
mixed Negritos. Keers (1948) in an extensive
anthropometric survey of thousands of males in this
region provides ample evidence in terms of the high
frequency of derived Negritoid hair forms, and to
some degree in Negritoid facial morphology, that
these islands were once populated in pre-Mongoloid
times by the first immigrants to the Sahul Shelf to
the east. His metrical data are not particularly
convincing, for all the peoples of the region are
short. But the hair form alone, as a marker trait,
provides an ample demonstration of the fact.

These data do not demonstrate that the original
Negritic immigrants to Greater Australia only used
Route 2, but they do indicate that these earliest
peoples reached the Sahul Shelf south of present-
day New Guinea and so had equal access both to the
high forested landmasses to the north and to the
drier, more lightly wooded portions of the Shelf
leading directly into present-day continental
Australia. Therefore these data do not help
explain the extreme differences between the
populations of modern New Guinea and Australia, but
they do indicate that both areas were open to these
earliest of migrants.

The problem of population replacement

Derived from the preceding problem is a major
one concerning the dynamics between an established

continental population intermittently assailed by
raft loads of incoming peoples of different
populational character. It is easy to suppose that
a second wave of immigrants across the islands to
the Sahul Shelf would have been quickly and simple
absorbed by those already in possession of Greater
Australia. But the present distribution of peoples
in New Guinea, as contrasted to Australia, indicates
that it could not have happened this way. Limiting
the problem to Australia for the moment and assuming
that the original inhabitants numbered something
over 200,000 persons at carrying capacity, the
question involved is how to replace them with
perhaps 250,000 individuals of very different
biological makeup. The real problem is how to get
the second wave of people ashore on the Sahul Shelf
without losing their populational characteristics.

One unlikely solution, which is not pressed in
this place, would be to refer the change in
population types back to the Sunda Shelf. There,
slow but massive gene flow into a basic population
of Oceanic Negritos could in time change them into
Tasmanian-like Negritoids, who then, with the
passage of further millennia accompanied by massive
gene flow, moved further in the direction of the
present-day Murrayians, among whom a low
frequency of individuals showed derived forms of
Negritoid hair. This solution saves the
embarrassment of storming the beaches on the Sahul
Shelf and so perhaps is to be preferred. Very
clearly the problem will not be solved until
large collections of cranial materials are
obtainable from the Sunda Shelf and stretching
far back into time. This proposal has its own
difficulties, for if one visualises a continuum of
change on the mainland of Southeast Asia, it
becomes curious that the populations crystallise
out so clearly in Greater Australia. Of course a
modified version might be invoked, in which the
biological change in time was not on a gradual
continuum but contained large nodes of genetic

change accomplished in rather few millennia. This
model would give the appearance of three separate
types of populations straggling across the islands
to the Sahul Shelf, but it still involves the
problem of getting them ashore in sufficient numbers
to replace earlier populations. At this point it
seems wise to await the recovery of further
materials by prehistorians, and it is hoped that
they will work the Sunda Shelf area intensively.

REFERENCES

Birdsell, J.B. 1949 The racial origin of the
    extinct Tasmanians. *Records of the Queen
    Victoria Museum, Launceston* 2(3):105-22

            1953 Some environmental and cultural
    factors influencing the structuring of
    Australian Aboriginal populations. *The American
    Naturalist* 87:171-207

            1957 Some population problems
    involving Pleistocene man. *Cold Spring Harbor
    Symposia on Quantitative Biology* 22:47-69

            1967 Preliminary data on the
    trihybrid origin of the Australian Aborigines.
    *Archaeology and Physical Anthropology in
    Oceania* 2:100-55

Bowdler, S. 1974 Pleistocene date for man in
    Tasmania. *Nature* 252:697-8

Bowler, J.M. 1971 Pleistocene salinities and
    climatic change: evidence from lakes and
    lunettes in southeastern Australia. In
    D.J. Mulvaney and J. Golson (eds) *Aboriginal
    man and environment in Australia*:47-75.
    Canberra: Australian National University
    Press

            1976 Recent developments in
    reconstructing late Quaternary environments

in Australia. In Kirk and Thorne 1976:55-77

    R. Jones, H. Allen and A.G. Thorne
1970 Pleistocene human remains from Australia:
a living site and human cremation from Lake
Mungo, western New South Wales. *World
Archaeology* 2:39-60

Brothwell, D.R. 1960 Upper Pleistocene human
skull from Niah Caves, Sarawak. *Sarawak
Museum Journal* 9:323-49

Chappell, J.M.A. 1976 Aspects of late Quaternary
palaeogeography of the Australian-east
Indonesian region. In Kirk and Thorne 1976:
11-22

Edwards, R. 1972 *Aboriginal bark canoes of the
Murray Valley*. Adelaide: Rigby

Hale, H.M. and N.B. Tindale 1930 Notes on some
human remains in the lower Murray Valley,
S.A. *Records of the South Australian Museum*
4:145-218

Howells, W.W. 1973 *Cranial variation in man: a
study by multivariate analysis of patterns
of differences among recent human populations.*
Cambridge (Mass.): Harvard University, Peabody
Museum of American Archaeology and Ethnology,
Papers vol.67

    1976 Multivariate analysis in the
problem of Australian origins. In Kirk and
Thorne 1976:141-60

Jones, R. 1976 Tasmania: aquatic machines and offshore islands. In G. de G. Sieveking,
I.H. Longworth and K.E. Wilson (eds) *Problems
in economic and social archaeology*:235-63.
London: Duckworth

Keers, W. 1948 *An anthropological survey of the
eastern Little Sunda Islands; the Negritos
of the eastern Little Sunda Islands; the
Proto-Malay of the Netherlands East Indies.*

Amsterdam: Koninklijke Vereeniging Indisch
Instituut, Mededeling no.74, Afd. Volkenkunde
no.26

Kirk, R.L. and A.G. Thorne (eds) 1976 *The origin
of the Australians*. Canberra: Australian
Institute of Aboriginal Studies

Love, J.R.B. 1936 *Stone age bushmen of today*.
London: Blackie

Mulvaney, D.J. 1975 *The prehistory of Australia*,
(rev.ed.). Ringwood (Vic.): Penguin Books

Munro, W. 1868 *A monograph of the Bambusaceae
including description of all the species*.
London: Linnaean Society (New York: Johnson
Reprint Corporation, 1966)

Nix, H.A. and J.D. Kalma 1972 Climate as a
dominant control in the biogeography of
northern Australia and New Guinea. In
D. Walker (ed.) *Bridge and barrier: the
natural and cultural history of Torres Strait*:
61-91. Canberra: Australian National
University, Research School of Pacific Studies,
Department of Biogeography and Geomorphology,
Publication BG/3

Penfold, A.R. and J.W. Willis 1961 *The eucalypts:
botany, cultivation, chemistry and utilization*.
London: Leonard Hill

Plomley, N.J.B. 1966 *Friendly mission: the
Tasmanian journals and papers of George Augustus
Robinson, 1829-1834*. Hobart: Tasmanian
Historical Research Association

Svendrup, H.S., M.W. Johnson and R.H. Fleming 1961
*The oceans: their physics, chemistry, and
general biology*, (10th printing). Englewood
Cliffs (N.J.): Prentice-Hall

Thorne, A.G. 1971 Mungo and Kow Swamp: morphological
variation in Pleistocene Australians. *Mankind*
8(2):85-9

1976 Morphological contrasts in Pleistocene Australians. In Kirk and Thorne 1976:95-112

Tindale, N.B. 1962 Some population changes among the Kaiadilt of Bentinck Island, Queensland. *Records of the South Australian Museum* 14(2): 297-336

1974 *Aboriginal tribes of Australia.* Berkeley: University of California Press and Canberra: Australian National University Press

Weidenreich, F. 1945 The Keilor skull: a Wadjak type from southeast Australia. *American Journal of Physical Anthropology* 3:21-32

THE SOURCES OF HUMAN VARIATION
IN MELANESIA AND AUSTRALIA

W.W. HOWELLS

Department of Anthropology
Peabody Museum
Harvard University

The biological origins of the Australo-
Melanesians involve their crossing of the Sunda-
Sahul gap, and events before and after. Hard fact
and demonstrable interpretation are still in short
supply; however, what has been learned in the last
quarter century has begun to set limits on possible
reconstructions of the story. I want here
primarily to consider the meaning of biological
variation as we know it in the living Australian
and Melanesian Aborigines.

Before 1950 dates were unknown in the region,
and anthropologists (myself among them) tended to
approach racial history and development by trying
to discern a workable scheme of separate races or
types, to represent ancestral strains in a
population. Events were seen as the hybridising of
such strains, once 'purer', following their
migration from different original homes. 'Racial'
formation almost seemed to have its own processes:
mutation and selection were mentioned, but their
specific operation was little considered; genetic
drift was hardly recognised, and hybridising, or
gene flow on a massive scale, was king.[1]

After 1950 more attention was given to the
possible effects of adaptation and selection (e.g.
Coon *et al.* 1950) and to the implications of human
genetics (e.g. Boyd 1950), as well as to
evolutionary biology and population genetics in
general. Blood genetic traits came in for greatly
expanded investigation, notably by Australian

workers. They have served increasingly as a
vehicle for studies in microevolution, such as
patterns of differentiation and genetic drift,
though unfortunately they have shed no light on
selective processes. They have also emphasised
the genetic variation existing within local
populations, as well as, especially in the Pacific,
between such local populations, something
incompatible with earlier 'pure race' ideas. Today
such internally varying groupings as 'Mongoloids',
American Indians or 'Australoids' would be viewed,
I think, not as adulterated versions of once purer
races but as large aggregates of related small
populations mutually differentiated by still badly
measured effects of selection, drift and gene flow.
Of course some of the subgroups may have been
subjected to more recent gene flow from foreign
population complexes ('mixture'); and of course
the distinctions among major population complexes
(like Mongoloid or Australoid) had to arise
originally in geographically distant areas. But it
is hard to see the latter as at any time purer; and
in general the process of differentiation would
always have been local and continuous, and no local
population would, earlier or now, represent
anything 'purer' than any other.[2]

Taking into account all of this together with
what we now know about the past - the existence of
a population more than 30,000 years ago (Thorne
this volume) already differentiated into the
morphology of the present day in the Australasian
region - it seems timely to cast afresh some of the
questions about biological variation in Australo-
Melanesian populations. Such questions are:

1. What are the degrees of within-group and
   between-group variation?
2. What are the causes of these?
3. Does the variation suggest the presence of
   more than one distinct parent population or
not?

4. What are the origins of the existing
   differentiation?
5. Does our knowledge of variation in the many
   traits studied suggest a taxonomy for Southwest Pacific populations, or is the information too
uneven?
6. What have been the most useful traits or
   kinds of variation for the study of either
population structure or history?
7. Can we infer anything from present physical
   or genetic traits and their variation as to
variation or differentiation in the past?

Answers to such questions are spotty at best,
but these and others should be reflected in work
and analysis in the future.

VARIATION IN METRIC TRAITS

Traditionally, that is by subjective
impression, Australians and Melanesians are
separable in morphological appearance. There are,
as we shall see, serological differences as well;
in these there is something of a border area across
northern Australia, and perhaps in morphology as
well. Cranially however, it can be shown by
intensive multivariate analysis (of South Australians,
Tasmanians and Tolais (Howells 1973b)) that there is
a close community of skull form, to which other
Melanesian populations adhere (Howells 1976a).
This form is quite distinct from that of
Polynesians, pre-contact Guamanians, Formosan
Aborigines and various East Asiatics, being less
distant from, though not really close to, European
(Norwegian) and Ainu crania. There is nothing
subjective about this assessment, which sets off an
Australo-Melanesian population complex from anything
to the immediate east, north or west, all of which
seems to belong to a broad and varied Mongoloid
population complex, as traditional views would

indicate.

A simpler but wider multivariate analysis on the living (Howells 1970), using few measurements but many Pacific samples, gives a result somewhat different but not basically so, the information being slighter by far than with the crania. Melanesians and Australians are differentiated: all the Australian samples group together but are joined by certain samples from western (New Britain) and southern (northern New Caledonia, Loyalties) Melanesia. Otherwise, Melanesians tend to overlap with Micronesians, with the focus of overlap being in the central Solomons but also the north coast of New Guinea. Polynesia, with Fiji, forms a separate group.

Grossly, this reworking of simple anthropometry gives results which gather Australian populations together (with no particular pattern) and indicate that the most Australian-like Melanesians are in New Britain and New Caledonia, opposite ends of Island Melanesia. The intergrading, such as it is, of central Melanesia and Micronesia would conform to an explanation of gene flow from Micronesia (or Polynesia) at any past time. This would be the essential direction of flow. It is my subjective judgment that central Solomons populations are indeed somewhat less 'Melanesian' in appearance, while the Micronesians suggest a reciprocal Melanesian contribution only in spots. At present I feel (from observation) that the Micronesians (at least in Palau, Truk, Ponape, Nauru, Gilberts and Marshalls) are not very diverse in outward appearance and, while not closely similar to Polynesians (Marshallese and Gilbertese perhaps most so) would fall in the same way into a diffuse set of populations perhaps best denoted as Proto-Mongoloid.

Local diversity in outward appearance, especially in New Guinea, is a commonplace, seeming

to exceed what anthropometry suggests. However in
a few areas village-by-village studies, notably
Friedlaender's (1975) in Bougainville, have
demonstrated the reality of high local diversity in
physique, as in genetic traits.

VARIATION IN BLOOD GENETIC TRAITS

Blood genetic information can be used in ways
that measured variates cannot, or are less suitable
for (as vice versa). Such ways are the study of
drift and of possible mutation or selection, but
above all that of genetic variation itself and its
patterns of differentiation. From the better
mapped red cell antigens, it has long been obvious
that diversity in Melanesia is high, which is
evident especially in systematic work in a limited
area, by one man or team. In Bougainville
Friedlaender (1975) sampled villages of three
language stocks (one Austronesian, two Papuan),
finding both local diversity and general
heterozygosity to be high. He saw no grounds in
environmental or other differences to suggest
selective forces causing differentiation, but did
find that generalised genetic distances corresponded
moderately well to linguistic distances though not
as well as the anthropometric distances. He
concluded therefore that the diversity reflected
genetic drift, patterned by the actual genealogical
relations among communities within this area,
fostered by a high degree of social isolation which
is the norm among these self-sufficient farming
villages. The antiquity of occupation of the area
by the original (language?) groups, which were
doubtless far from genetically uniform to begin,
seems considerable.

For New Guinea Booth and Taylor (1976) did
cluster analyses of a somewhat looser set of samples,
also getting good correspondences between different

genetic networks and language relationships. For
Australia little has been done of this kind. From
general knowledge however, it seems evident that
Australia, especially when the northern rim is
excluded, has distinctly less genetic diversity
than Melanesia, with less heterozygosity. This is
partly because of various alleles present elsewhere
but missing here (e.g. B of the ABO system)
apparently through loss and partly because of less
social isolation: compare Tindale's (1953) general
figure of about 15% of intertribal marriages with
Friedlaender's approximate average of 5% inter-
language marriages in Bougainville. Thus if the
local diversity within Australia is less than in
Melanesia there are good reasons for it, and the
interest lies more in the diversity between
Australia and Melanesia.

There have been some attempts to organise the
genetic diversity into genealogy at higher than
regional levels, and thus into history, with no
results as promising as that attending anthropometric
data. Robert Feldman (1974) who has kindly allowed
reference to his unpublished results, has made a
valiant effort to form distance trees from the
tabulations compiled in mimeographed form for
Melanesia, without getting an informative pattern.
Cavalli-Sforza and Edwards, in various publications
(e.g. 1965, 1967) have made world-wide trees on the
assumption of constant gene substitution over time.
While results have emerged, various difficulties
such as the meaning of local diversity within the
major groups (read 'Australians' etc) themselves,
geographic differences in heterozygosity at a
given locus, and the likelihood that drift is
neither steady nor without interference by
selection, make such trees a dubious proposition
(Harpending 1974; Harpending and Chasko in press;
Howells 1976b).

But we might throw the baby out with the
bathwater. The above observations and reservations

apply to gene frequencies, and also to attempts to
base generalised figures on them, for the long-known
polymorphisms, mostly red cell antigens, in which
most or all alleles are universal. It remains
possible (though this may be hope springing eternal)
that certain newly found polymorphisms, mainly in
serum proteins and enzymes and read by electro-
phoresis, may be more informative for population
history (Kirk 1975, 1976; Blake and Omoto 1975).
In these, some alleles or variants have restricted
distributions.[3] In the Gm system of the
immunoglobulins, haplotypes have been detected which
may be unique to a population (e.g. Gm^{xg} of the
Ainu); while Gm^{zab}, with high frequencies in New
Guinea and present in other parts of Melanesia, is
absent in (much of ?) Bougainville, and in Australia
excepting the north. In the enzyme phosphoglucomutase loci (Blake and Omoto 1975) variants 3
and 7 at the PGM_1 locus occur in Southeast Asia;
variant 3 has been found in New Guinea, Fiji and
Micronesia while variant 7 is known for the western
but not the eastern Carolines; both are missing from
Australia excepting the north. At the PGM_2 locus,
variants 9 and 10 have been found as rarities widely
in New Guinea but are missing from Australia, while
variant 3 is so far unique to Australia, again
excepting the north. More general mapping will be
needed before considering whether such variants
represent mutations of limited spread in Oceania or
earlier mutations brought by separate migrating
communities. The evidence points to a very long
separation between New Guinea and sub-Carpentarian
Australia. In any case, examinations of these data
(Kirk 1976) and of the more familiar antigenic
systems (Simmons 1976 and references there quoted)
has given no evidence of ancestral connections for
Australians (Ainu, Negrito, Veddoid, etc).

There are a few other traits, genetically
unanalysed, which would appear to antedate any
Australian-Melanesian separation, pointing to an
ultimate common origin. In physiology, Macfarlane

(1976) has pointed to the high rate of water
turnover characteristic of central Australian
Aborigines, and also the ability of rapid suppression
of sweating in a moisture-saturated environment (in
his tests, an arm bag). Melanesians are intermediate
to Australians and Europeans in both. He suggests
that these are genetic adaptations retained from an
original moist wooded homeland (i.e. Indonesia) and
not lost in the drier Australian environment.
Another trait is juvenile blond hair. This 'tawny'
hair has long been remarked on as though it were an
Australian specialty. But it occurs in New Guinea
over an unknown extent, and it is common from one
end of Island Melanesia to the other (and a few
other places where Melanesian admixture may be
suspected, e.g. Yap and Ontong Java). Finally
there is the basic likeness in cranial morphology.
This of course has local variation although the
degree cannot be measured well for lack of skeletal
material. Giles (1976) finds regional variation in
Australia, with some tendency for northern samples
to form a distinct group, as others (e.g. Fenner
1939) also reported; however Larnach and Macintosh
(1970) found Queensland crania to be indistinguishable
from those further south, and specifically to show
nothing of a 'Negrito' character.

ORIGINS OF DIFFERENTIATION

In what has surely been a complicated history
of Australo-Melanesian populations we can say very
little about causes of variety. Genetic drift gives
every sign of having been influential in producing a
real intergroup diversity, but we do not know if we
might consider it responsible for all the variety in
the Southwest Pacific. Selection here is virtually
undemonstrated: short stature in New Guinea 'pygmies'
might be partly a genetic modification. Gajdusek
(1970) believes it is adaptive for work and for
protein conservation in high altitudes and difficult

terrain and reports that the shortness is at least
partly reversible in individuals brought to the
coast and given diets fuller in protein. Mutation
might account for the local origin and spread of
some rare genes described above but can hardly be
seen as an important agent of differentiation.
Should we then turn to migration, in both its senses:
movement of distinct peoples into the area on one
hand and mixture, or gene flow, on the other? This
brings us back to some traditional hypotheses.

Does the variety among the existing Australo-
Melanesians warrant the suggestion of more than one
ultimate parental population, i.e. two or more
'races', migrating from different homes (e.g.
Birdsell 1967), as against a nexus of populations
having the normal variation of such sub-populations
within the area of the whole?[4]

Coon (1962) recognised an Australoid subspecies
for the peoples concerned (within a general hypothesis
of parallel hominid evolution in separate major
geographic zones), comprising three races: Australoid,
Melanesian-Tasmania, Negrito. These three however,
specifically had a single common origin,
differentiating from unclear causes to produce such
distinctions as Australian straight hair. Birdsell
(1967) has denounced this as 'easy evolution' and
presents an unexceptionable statement of the nature
of race and of population differences in the Pacific,
together with the complexities of local evolution.
He believes that Australian regional differences
must be viewed as a product of selection but
primarily of hybridisation among his three
hypothetical immigrant elements: Negrito, Ainu-like
Murrayians, and dark linear Carpentarians (from
India?). While I am doubtful of all this, it must
be said that no one has had so wide an experience
of the physical characters of the Aborigines.

I was also not persuaded by Coon's idea of a
common origin for Australians, Melanesians and

'Negritos' before analysis convinced me of the
essential cranial uniformity of all these populations
(including Philippine Negritos on the evidence) but
clearly and unexpectedly excluding the Andamanese.
This is the hardest evidence I know of as to basic
unity of this whole population complex. Evolutionary
factors of local differentiation, other than
hybridising, deserve consideration in view of the
now known period of some 30,000 years of occupation
of the area. There are, of course, some difficulties
to the notion of a simple, uniform local drifting
away from a single parental form. One is the
apparent greater resemblance of Tasmanians to
Melanesians than to mainland Australians; another
is the particular resemblance, in crania and in the
living, of some New Caledonians, at the far end of
Melanesia, to Australians.

The main question remains whether all
populations in the area fall into one range of
variation, with no real hiatus. There is nothing
that absolutely denies it. Unlike cranial form,
stature or body size appears to have been labile
enough to allow pygmies. Gene frequency differences
are unreliable: small and isolated populations are
subject to marked drift effects, possibly resulting
in outright gene loss.[5] Settler groups on larger
islands like New Guinea and Bougainville obviously
have maintained internal genetic variation and
heterozygosity, making it available for variation
between groups later segregating themselves within
the main population. So in Melanesia the high
local diversity appears to be a product of time and
of social factors of group isolation; these may be
exceptional in Melanesia, just as the diversity of
Papuan languages is exceptional. In this picture
however, Australia differs: there has been gene loss
(out of a general Australo-Melanesian matrix?), and
local variation seems to be less. One or two
alleles may be Australian mutants. It is hardly
possible to demonstrate all this scientifically,
real understanding of genetic processes in man being

almost non-existent. But the body of information
seems to point to such interpretations.

One final observation is important: Australo-
Melanesian variation did not arise entirely within
30,000 years from a single parent or set of gene
frequencies. Local populations of the homeland
were surely genetically and morphologically varied
to begin with. We should not imagine within-group
or between-group variation diminishing steadily as
we go back in time, any more than we should imagine
'pure' parental races.

VARIATION IN PREHISTORY

On the one hand we have a persistence of
cranial form over 25,000 years demonstrated at Lake
Mungo in western New South Wales; nothing is known
for Melanesia. On the other hand we must assume
genetic variation among immigrant bands themselves.
Even if we imagined a single early parental band
for the whole region, which we hardly can, time
would have varied and distorted the genetic traits
of its progeny, so that we could not restore its
gene frequencies, as we apparently can its cranial
form. Linguists may safely reconstruct a Proto-
Austronesian for example, but nobody, fortunately,
has tried to reconstruct a Proto-ABO system, in
spite of genetic trees attempted.

All this implies a parent population complex,
perhaps not as varied as the whole present Australo-
Melanesian gamut, but with the potential to produce
it, existing in Old Melanesia (Howells 1973a)
before (and after) early groups crossed Wallacea;
that is, in Indonesia before this was invaded by
the now predominant Mongoloids, and extending from
the time of this invasion back to some period
earlier than 40,000 BP. Evidence of the Old
Melanesians consists of Australian and Melanesian-

like populations (and Papuan languages) in eastern
Indonesia, and of Philippine Negritos, who are not
everywhere of pygmy size, especially in northern
Luzon where they are more nearly 'Melanesian' in
stature (information from R.B. Fox, J. Treloggen
Peterson and W. Peterson).

For the past, Old Melanesia has the undated
Wadjak crania, the 40,000 year old Niah Cave skull,
and the Tabon Cave frontal and mandible.[6] This is
not enough to suggest the variety that may have
existed among local populations, but is enough to
suggest that they belonged to one general group of
Australo-Melanesian morphology. It is not likely
that during the whole period such populations were
more varied than the recent populations of Australia
and Melanesia, nor is it likely there was any other
source for the latter than Old Melanesia - the land
mass of Sunda, the Philippines, Sulawesi, the
Moluccas and the Lesser Sundas. Just as the last
named smaller land masses were occupied by migrant
groups, so some groups - samples of the whole
complex - reached Sahul, probably at different
points. Doubtless some nearer parts of Island
Melanesia (the Bismarcks and probably Bougainville)
were reached in the same early period as New Guinea
and Australia, but the full occupation of Melanesia
is another, later story, for linguists and
archaeologists to help with (e.g. Shutler and Marck
1975). But the time scale is evidently enough
(from data like Friedlaender's) to allow for
biological differentiation, mostly by drift, to have
been added to imported variation in such places as
New Guinea and Bougainville.

As to central and southern Australia, where
variation seems less and where there are some
differences in outer morphology and blood, there is
the special factor of movement out of the generally
wet tropics of Old Melanesia into a new biogeographic
zone (Golson and others, in Mulvaney and Golson
1971). Still, Australians exhibit what Macfarlane,

as discussed above, considers to be physiological
adaptations to damp tropics and share with
Melanesians a basic cranial pattern and juvenile
blondness.

Other such indicators of likeness or difference,
like those in serum proteins, are sure to emerge.
But we have got away from the simple use of 'types'
or 'races' only to find that there is no end to the
data needed. The straightforward taxonomic tools
for the systematics of other animals - let us say
birds - do not serve for man, certainly in a region
like this. Surveys of human variation - detailed
anthropometry, dermatoglyphics and so on - take too
much effort to have covered more than patches. And
in blood genetic traits the possibilities have
expanded so that the blood taking will have to be
repeated over much of the territory already covered,
let alone in populations never tested, before there
is wide comparability of areas and before various
important distributions can be seen with any
confidence. But only this work will plot the
variation in a way to make the past more
intelligible.

FOOTNOTES

[1] I do not deny that this is a simplification; and
in fact various German, Austrian and Swiss
anthropologists stressed isolation, inbreeding and
selection as important in Melanesian diversity (see
Swindler 1962). However, my statement would
represent the views of so thoughtful and experienced
a scholar as Hooton (1946). He believed that
primary races of modern man first differentiated and
dispersed between 15,000 and 20,000 years ago, with
subraces continuing to develop by the same processes:
isolation and inbreeding. The Whites were probably
the first form of modern man; Australians were a
composite race, mainly archaic White plus Tasmanoid

Negrito and some Melanesian. Melanesians were
essentially Oceanic Negroids, representatives of
the major Negroid race with some admixtures.

[2] This should not be taken to mean that differences
    as abrupt as those between eastern Melanesians,
Fijians, Micronesians and Polynesians could arise
by extreme sampling error (the founder principle)
from a parent Melanesian population, as has been
suggested. If an untutored observer of the United
States population suggested such a process for
Blacks and Whites and their intermediates he would
surely be thought quaint.

[3] In the red cells, the Diego factor has long had
    status as a Mongoloid marker.

[4] Birdsell, in arguing against the hypothesis of
    homogeneity or a single origin for the Australians,
suggests that this would demand that no local
population deviate from the population taken as a
whole to a statistically significant degree. This
is a misconception of the nature of local populations,
which throughout nature accumulate genetic differences,
let alone environmentally caused phenotypic
differences. They are not to be looked on as random
samples from a statistical universe, to be tested in
the above fashion.

[5] Founder groups in other organisms, e.g. *Drosophila*,
    may undergo drastic loss of genetic variation and
subsequently regenerate it, but apparently by
processes involving interaction and balance in the
whole genotype (Mayr 1963), not generally operating
on single systems like blood group loci - at any
rate, processes unstudied in man.

[6] Macintosh (1972) has diagnosed the mandible as
    'Australian' and of large size; I (Howells 1976a)
have found the frontal, by multivariate analysis
using 13 measurements, to be closest to Ainus or
Tasmanians, and exclude Andamanese as a possible

population for it.

REFERENCES

Birdsell, J.B. 1967 Preliminary data on the trihybrid origin of the Australian Aborigines. *Archaeology and Physical Anthropology in Oceania* 2:100-55

Blake, N.M. and K. Omoto 1975 Phosphoglucomutase types in the Asian-Pacific area: a critical review including new phenotypes. *Annals of Human Genetics* 38:251-73

Booth, P.B. and H.W. Taylor 1976 Genetic distance analysis of some New Guinea populations: an evaluation. In Kirk and Thorne 1976:415-30

Boyd, W.C. 1950 *Genetics and the races of man.* Boston: Little, Brown

Cavalli-Sforza, L.L. and A.W.F. Edwards 1965 Analysis of human evolution. In S.J. Geerts (ed.) *Genetics today*, vol.3:923-33. London: Pergamon

                                    1967
Phylogenetic analysis: models and estimation procedures. *Evolution* 21:550-70

Coon, C.S. 1962 *The origin of races.* New York: Knopf

          , S.M. Garn and J.B. Birdsell 1950 *Races: a study of the problems of race formation in man.* Springfield (Ill.): C.C. Thomas

Feldman, R. 1974 *A statistical analysis of blood group genetic data from 49 Melanesian populations.* Unpublished study in graduate work, Harvard University

Fenner, F.J. 1939 The Australian Aboriginal skull:

its non-metrical morphological characters.
*Transactions of the Royal Society of South
Australia* 63:248-306

Friedlaender, J.S. 1975 *Patterns of human
variation: the demography, genetics and
phenetics of Bougainville Islanders.* Cambridge
(Mass.): Harvard University Press

Gajdusek, D.C. 1970 Psychological and physiological
characteristics of stone age man. *Engineering
and Science* 33:26-52

Giles, E. 1976 Cranial variation in Australia and
neighbouring areas. In Kirk and Thorne 1976:
161-72

Harpending, H. 1974 Genetic structure of small
populations. *Annual Review of Anthropology*
3:229-43

           and W. Chasko, Jr. in press
Heterozygosity and population structure in
southern Africa. In E. Giles and
J.S. Friedlaender (eds) *The measures of man:
methodologies in biological anthropology:*
chapter 9. Cambridge (Mass.): Schenkman

Hooton, E.A. 1946 *Up from the ape,* (rev.ed.)
New York: Macmillan

Howells, W.W. 1970 Anthropometric grouping
analysis of Pacific peoples. *Archaeology and
Physical Anthropology in Oceania* 5:192-217

           1973a *The Pacific Islanders.*
London: Weidenfeld and Nicolson and New York:
Scribner

           1973b *Cranial variation in man: a
study by multivariate analysis of patterns of
differences among recent human populations.*
Cambridge (Mass.): Harvard University, Peabody
Museum of American Archaeology and Ethnology,
Papers vol.67

           1976a Multivariate analysis in the

problem of Australian origins.   In Kirk and
Thorne 1976:141-60

   1976b   Explaining modern man:
evolutionists versus migrationists.   *Journal
of Human Evolution* 5:477-96

Kirk, R.L. 1975   Isozyme variants as markers of
   population movement in man.   In C.L. Markert
   (ed.) *Isozymes, IV: Genetics and evolution*:
   169-80.   New York: Academic Press

   1976   Serum protein and enzyme markers
as indicators of population affinities in
Australia and the western Pacific.   In Kirk
and Thorne 1976:329-46

   and A.G. Thorne (eds) 1976   *The origin
of the Australians*.   Canberra: Australian
Institute of Aboriginal Studies

Larnach, S.L. and N.W.G. Macintosh 1970   *The
   craniology of the Aborigines of Queensland*.
   Sydney: University of Sydney, Oceania
   Monographs No.15

Macfarlane, W.V. 1976   Aboriginal palaeophysiology.
   In Kirk and Thorne 1976:183-94

Macintosh, N.W.G. 1972   Radiocarbon dating as a
   pointer in time to the arrival and history of
   man in Australia and islands to the north west.
   In *Proceedings of the 8th International
   Conference on Radiocarbon Dating, Wellington,
   New Zealand, October 1972*, (vol.1):XLIV-LVI.
   Wellington: Royal Society of New Zealand

Mayr, E. 1963   *Animal species and evolution*.
   Cambridge (Mass.): Belknap Press of
   Harvard University Press

Mulvaney, D.J. and J. Golson (eds) 1971
   *Aboriginal man and environment in
   Australia*.   Canberra: Australian National
   University Press

Shutler, R., Jr. and J.C. Marck 1975 On the
    dispersal of the Austronesian horticulturalists.
    Archaeology and Physical Anthropology in Oceania
    10:81-112

Simmons, R.T. 1976 The biological origin of
    Australian Aboriginals: an examination of blood
    group genes and gene frequencies for possible
    evidence in populations from Australia to
    Eurasia.   In Kirk and Thorne 1976:307-28

Swindler, D.R. 1962 A racial study of west
    Nakanai.   In W. Goodenough (ed.) *New Britain
    studies*.   Philadelphia: University of
    Pennsylvania Museum, Museum Monographs

Tindale, N.B. 1953 Tribal and intertribal marriage
    among Australian Aboriginals. *Human Biology*
    25:169-90

SEPARATION OR RECONCILIATION? BIOLOGICAL CLUES TO THE DEVELOPMENT OF AUSTRALIAN SOCIETY

A.G. THORNE

Department of Prehistory
Australian National University

INTRODUCTION

While sufficient human biological remains have
been recovered and dated to establish that populations
of *Homo* have inhabited Asia and Southeast Asia for
most if not all of the Pleistocene period, we are
by no means able to define the details of morphological variation across the area for any of that
period or indeed beyond the limits of the excavations
or collecting sites that produced the fossils. These
difficulties are most acute for the later parts of
the Pleistocene, centring perhaps about 100,000 to
150,000 years ago, when it would seem that either
the process of morphological change accelerated or
that the physical forms in the area underwent major
alteration.

It is not surprising then that despite numerous
efforts, both theoretical and experimental, to
reconstruct the earliest movements of man into
Sahul, the landmass embracing Australia and New
Guinea, our understanding of the biological aspects
of prehistoric events is still largely guesswork.
While the earliest cultural and physical data that
we have at present are suggestive, they are often
more confusing than illuminating. The biological
evidence suffers badly in this respect, in terms of
the geographic areas whence it has been derived and
because of its limited chronological span.

Much of the available biological information
has recently been brought together (Kirk and Thorne
1976). Detailed statements can now be made about
the late Holocene human biological histories of

Australia, New Guinea, parts of Melanesia and
Southeast Asia, particularly from blood genetic
studies. However very little information is
available, from skeletal sources, pointing to the
physical status and variation of the people who
first stepped off the eastern shores of Sundaland
and established new societies in the Pacific. For
that part of the Pleistocene covering the period
of the Sunda-to-Sahul movement there is a little
evidence from various parts of Sundaland -
Indonesia, Malaysia and the Philippines - but for
the whole of the Sahul area and its inhabitable
resultant landmasses there is skeletal evidence
from Australia only.

I want first to look at these southerly Sahul
remains and then indicate how we might put them
into some Sundaland context.

THE SAHUL EVIDENCE

The last decade has seen rapid expansion in
the human fossil record in Australia and most of
the new material is Pleistocene in age. Apart from
the Talgai cranium from Queensland, the first
significant example of an early Australian, and the
recent skeletal and dental remains excavated in
Devils Lair in Western Australia (Davies 1968, 1973;
Freedman 1976; Allbrook 1976) the fossil evidence
has come from a relatively small area of the southeastern corner of the continent. Given the great
range of skeletal, superficial and whole body
characteristics in contemporary Aboriginal
Australians, whether these result from adaptive,
nutritional, random genetic or founding
characteristics, this geographic concentration is
important in making an assessment of the variation
of the remains from this area, which is a narrow
zone approximately 500 km long, bounded by Lake
Nitchie in the northwest and Keilor in the southeast.

The collection consists of the Cohuna and Keilor
crania, the isolated Mossgiel and Lake Nitchie
skeletons, the three Lake Mungo individuals and the
Kow Swamp skeletal series.

The metrical features of the majority of the
Australian prehistoric crania have been recorded
(Macintosh 1971; Thorne 1975, 1976). These data
have recently been compared via a multivariate
study (Thorne and Wilson in press) with each other
and with a series of near-contemporary Aboriginal
remains from southeastern Australia. The results
of the analysis are shown diagrammatically in Fig.1.
A major conclusion from the analysis is that two
groups of fossil crania can be distinguished.

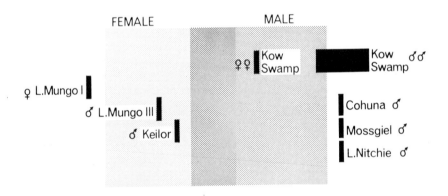

Fig.1. Comparison of southeastern Australian fossil crania
with near-contemporary Aboriginal populations of both sexes
from the same region (stippled areas). The manner in which
the fossil crania lie outside both extremes of the near-
contemporary ranges distinguishes two groups of fossil crania.

Lake Mungo I and Keilor constitute one group,
deviating from the near-contemporary series in terms
of size and, in the case of Lake Mungo I, a complex

of dimensions in the posterior and basal parts of
the cranium. The skull of the male Lake Mungo III
skeleton (Bowler and Thorne 1976) was not available
for the analysis but has been included in Fig.1 to
indicate its probable position in relation to near-
contemporary crania and other fossil individuals.
Sufficient of those metrical characteristics which
lead to a statistical exclusion of Lake Mungo I
from the (female) comparative crania are preserved
in Lake Mungo III for us to be confident that it too
can be excluded from the (male) comparative series.

The second group to be distinguished includes
the population from Kow Swamp (including the Cohuna
cranium) and the Mossgiel and Lake Nitchie
individuals. Apart from a strong trend for
increased size in these fossils, the diagnostic
criteria for this group centre on fronto-facial
dimensions. They demonstrate that 'major morphological changes have occurred in the facial and
frontal regions of Aboriginal crania from northern
Victoria in the last 9-10,000 years' (Thorne and
Wilson in press).

The demonstration of two morphometric extremes
in Australian fossil crania is paralleled to some
extent by non-metrical evidence, although as yet no
statistical assessment based on these characters
has been completed. The non-metrical features of
the Keilor cranium appear to be consistent with
near-contemporary forms of southeastern Australia.
The same features in Lake Mungo I and III are
unusual, when taken together, in that while no
single character lies outside the range observed in
more recent samples the combined incidence of non-
metrical features in these two individuals creates
a picture of extreme gracility or modernity. In
terms of Fig.1 the female Lake Mungo I is ultra-
feminine and, were it not for femoral and pelvic
evidence, one could be tempted to diagnose Lake
Mungo III as female. What is so striking about the
Lake Mungo population in the period 25-30,000 years

ago, assuming that present evidence is confirmed by
new finds, is its morphological delicacy, compared
to late Holocene morphologies from the same general
area and more particularly to the late Pleistocene
and early Holocene populations resident nearby -
Cohuna, Kow Swamp, Lake Nitchie and Mossgiel. I
have described elsewhere (Thorne 1976) those non-
metrical features of the Kow Swamp crania that
indicate divergence from near-contemporary series
from eastern and southern Australia. The bulk of
these relate to characteristics that are to be
interpreted as functions of robusticity and/or an
osteological primitivity.

A parallel and probably related feature is
vault bone thickness. All the Lake Mungo
individuals, including the fragmentary Lake Mungo II
(Bowler *et al.* 1970), possess very thin cranial
vault bones, compared to late Holocene series. By
contrast, all the other early skeletal individuals
demonstrate thickened vaults and mandibles, and in
the case of the infants, juveniles and adults from
Kow Swamp, the thickening is pronounced in the facial
and frontal regions.

Theories of origin

Whether the two Pleistocene cranial groups are
to be interpreted in terms of gracility-robusticity
or modernity-primitivity, or some combination of
these, the choice that can be made at present is
finally one of taste (or bias) and I do not wish to
debate this issue in detail here. What is important
is that the metrical and non-metrical contrasts
relate to general theories put forward to explain
Australian origins and also to the morphological
contrasts that I believe are visible in the skeletal
evidence from Sundaland, whence it may be assumed
the earliest migrants came. The available skeletal
evidence can be forced into several of the
theoretical moulds that are currently used to
explain Australian origins. Put simply, the

existing fossils support a variety of hybrid and
homogenetic concepts. There is one exception, the
trihybrid theory proposed by Birdsell (1949, 1967,
this volume). This is perhaps due to the fact that
it is the most explicit and detailed construct and
is therefore more readily open to criticism.

The data adduced in support of Birdsell's
threefold migration sequence are not convincing.
Analysis of recent skeletal material from northeast
Queensland fails to separate Birdsell's 'Barrineans'
from the surrounding Australoid population
(Macintosh and Larnach 1973, 1976). Similarly the
prehistoric evidence from Tasmania, at West Point
(Thorne 1967, 1971a:318) and Mount Cameron West
(Wallace and Doran 1976), falls within a generalised
southeast Australian range. The mainland Australian
fossil evidence is similarly lacking in metrical or
non-metrical features that demonstrate a specifically
Negritic as opposed to a general Aboriginal clinical
or regional component in the Australian physical
background. It should be remembered that outside
Australia the 'group called Negrito are polyphyletic,
and their gene pools are no more similar than two
random populations of the western Pacific' (Kirk and
Thorne 1976:5). The difficulty of assigning a
'Carpentarian' element to northern Australian
physical diversity lies in the absence of fossil
evidence for this group in Sundaland and the need
to define the contributions that Indonesia
(including Macassar) and southern New Guinea have
made to the Australian gene pool in recent times,
even during the historic period. Removing the first
and final components of Birdsell's tripartite scheme
leaves the 'Murrayian' element as the sole
contributor to the Australian gene pool (Thorne
1971a, 1971b).

Fig.2 illustrates three basic migrational
models through which the Australian fossil evidence
might be viewed, in terms of the ranges of
osteological characteristics seen in Pleistocene

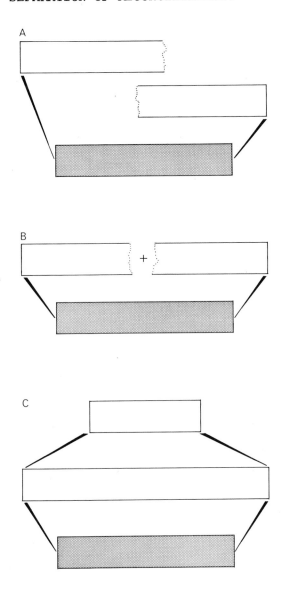

Fig.2. Three basic models for populating Pleistocene Australia.
Figs 2a and 2b represent models of hybridising populations based
on temporally and spatially separated groups who merged to form
the modern population. Fig.2c represents a single migrant stock
which underwent substantial phases of change in the past, within
Australia. Prehistoric populations are represented by open bars
and the modern population by stippled bars.

and late Holocene Australians. The diagram is a
simplified version of a wide range of explanations
that could be proposed. Figs 2a and 2b postulate
hybrid models, based on time and space respectively,
while Fig.2c envisages a single migrant stock that
underwent substantial phases of change after its
arrival in Australia. In each case the basal bar
represents the morphological range exhibited in
ethnographic times, a range narrower than during
the late Pleistocene.

   The case of Fig.2a illustrates one of the
traditional explanations of physical diversity, the
sequential movement of two distinct groups, in terms
of their cranial morphologies, into Australia. If
these movements to Sahul stemmed from populations
occupying approximately the same area of Sundaland,
the migrations are likely to be separated by a
considerable time period. As noted above the
differences between Keilor-Lake Mungo and Mossgiel-
Lake Nitchie-Kow Swamp are extreme, insofar as they
lie outside the extensive range of form demonstrated
by near-contemporary crania. The known
representatives of one of these extremes - Keilor
and Lake Mungo - surround the representatives of
the other spatially and chronologically, so it is
possible, even probable, that the fossils presently
available represent some mixing or fusion in Sahul
of the two original migrant streams. If this
proved to be the case one would envisage the original
stocks as even more distinct, particularly in
Sundaland. The degree of morphological change
involved is unlikely to have occurred overnight.
It should also be pointed out that, morphologically,
it is impossible to suggest which migrant stock
arrived first.

   The second possibility (Fig.2b) represents a
situation whereby the major components of Australian
morphology entered the continent and/or New Guinea
at approximately the same period, but from
different source areas. Birdsell (this volume)

describes a series of alternative paths to Greater
Australia that would allow the two groups to enter
the Sahul region at different points, subsequently
fusing, at least geographically, in the southeast
of Australia proper by late Pleistocene times.
Identification of these points of entry could be
difficult to establish, certainly in the detail
involved in Birdsell's routes to Australia and New
Guinea. Not only would the submergence of large
areas of the Sahul Shelf destroy the earliest
skeletal evidence of the landings but possibilities
such as fusion or selection resulting from sea
level rise might reduce our capacity to distinguish
founding populations osteologically.

The third possibility suggested here (Fig.2c)
envisages a single founding population. Unlike the
models in Figs 2a and 2b, where reduction in
morphological variation is explicable through the
selective extinction or phenotypic suppression of
the Pleistocene extremes as a function of the fusion
of two groups, the model in Fig.2c requires an
adaptive and/or random genetic explanation for the
constricted variation of post-Pleistocene times.
The skeletal variation of the founding population
cannot be known but given the relatively restricted
range of tropical environments from which the
crossing was made it might be expected to have been
narrow, compared to contemporary Australian
continental variation. The late Pleistocene fossil
evidence, indicating greater variability than in
Holocene times, would imply that the spread of
populations around and across the continent involved
a series of physical adaptations, in addition to a
complex of genetic effects.

At the end of the Pleistocene, or soon after,
there was a reduction in skeletal, certainly cranial,
variability. Factors in this process would relate
to effects on the population produced by the rise
and stabilisation of sea levels - the extinction or
constriction of certain environments and reduction

of gene flow from the Sahul Shelf, New Guinea and
the Bassian plain. In addition, the relatively
rapid environmental changes in some inland areas of
the southeastern parts of the continent in late
Pleistocene times (Bowler 1976) can be expected to
have been reflected morphologically, probably
somewhat later.

It should be pointed out that in terms of
Fig.2c it is most unlikely that the Lake Mungo
population could be closely related chronologically
to the initial migrant stock. It would be difficult
to conceive of morphological trends, random or
adaptive, that could lead in less than 10,000 years
to morphologies such as that at Kow Swamp. A much
greater period would be required for the development
of Kow Swamp-like characteristics from a Lake Mungo-
like base. For this reason the Lake Mungo form
represents either a departure from some morphological
norm that was more like Kow Swamp or the Lake Mungo
evidence indicates the maintenance of a morphology
that earlier had led to Kow Swamp-like forms in
other areas. It would thus be unreasonable to
suggest that the Lake Mungo people that we know of
had only recently arrived in that area, fresh from
the Sahul shores, well on their way to populating
the continent as fast as humanly (or statistically)
possible.

In my view it is not possible at present, on
the limited data available, to make any choice from
among the theoretical possibilities outlined above.
Without knowing when the earliest occupation of the
continent occurred we remain ignorant of the period.
in which morphological change could have taken place
before the populations represented by the known
fossils inhabited what is now southern New South
Wales and northern Victoria. But given the present
data and the substantial variation they represent,
I suspect that the period of change was lengthy,
whatever its cause. The existing skeletal evidence
is quite consistent with occupation of the continent

60,000, 80,000 or even 120,000 years ago.

The suggestion by Bowdler (this volume) that occupation of the continent developed from a prolonged coastal adaptation might provide some of the time and/or geographical isolation necessary for the development of substantial variation, based either on sequential migration and fusion or internal fission by a single founding population. Repeated movement around the coast and then inland via the major river systems might also explain why such extreme variation occurs in similar and contiguous environments.

THE SUNDA EVIDENCE

For the general period in Sundaland in which it is likely that migration to the east began there is no known fossil evidence. A few fossils have been recovered that are likely to postdate that event and that do not conform to the contemporary forms from the area. These are the Niah, Wajak and Tabon remains. The Niah cranium, dated around 40,000 years, exhibits a number of Australoid features (Brothwell 1960) and in terms of its general structure would appear to fit within the morphological type represented by the Lake Mungo skeletons. The Australian appearance of the Wajak remains, particularly the similarity of Wajak I to the Keilor cranium, has been noted by several authors (Weidenreich 1945; Coon 1963:405-6). Of the Tabon fossils (Fox 1970) it has been suggested that both the frontal and mandibular fragments are Australoid (Howells 1973:179; Jelinek 1976) and although the specific features have not been detailed, it is clear that whatever the Australoid features of Tabon are, they are not characteristics of heaviness. Thus all these fossils are likely to point in the direction of the Lake Mungo-Keilor end of the Australian fossil morphological range.

Nothing in late Pleistocene Sundaland, such as there is, suggests the more robust forms from Pleistocene Australia. Either the robust element, Pleistocene and ethnographic, developed in Australia or we have not yet found the robust ancestral form in late Pleistocene Sundaland. I believe the second possibility to be the case.

Further evidence of populations contributing to what was to become the Australian genetic makeup, directly and indirectly, is to be found further back in time in Sundaland and in mainland Asia. However, because the crossing by man of the Sunda-Sahul water barrier comes very late in the period of human occupancy of the Southeast Asian region it is common for the earliest inhabitants of that area to be set aside as somehow lying outside the equation. This attitude stems largely from the forumulations of conventional taxonomy - an early and relatively well-known *Homo erectus* population from central and eastern Java that disappears, to be replaced much later by an ill-understood *H. sapiens* population that gives rise, in part, to the Sahul colonists.

Fig.3 summarises the majority of the fossils contributing to the two major sequences that can be recognised in east Asia and Southeast Asia. The sequences have a simple geographical distribution, one purely Chinese and the other Indonesian-Australian. The bulk of these hominids have been known for some time, but the major barriers to definitive discussion of the material remain, not only in the need to obtain expanded samples but also in the need to date precisely those fossils that are available. The chronological problem is most acute for the east Asian evidence.

Apart from purely geographic considerations, Fig.3 summarises the evidence for the simple scheme proposed by Coon (1963:Chapters 9-10) to explain the derivation of recent populations of the area.

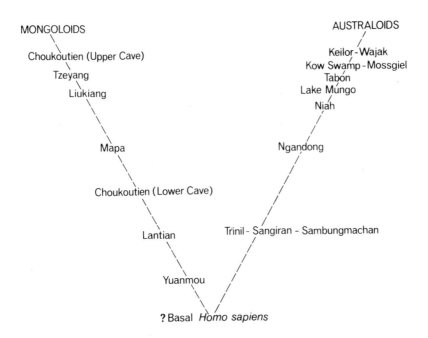

Fig.3. Hominid sequences in Asia and Australasia. For explanation see text.

He has suggested two lineages – *Sinanthropus* and the Mongoloids and *Pithecanthropus* and the Australoids. The scheme does not appear to have won acceptance, largely because it creates two important taxonomic difficulties. These are closely related and concern taxonomy at the specific level on the one hand and the subspecific (or racial) level on the other.

To take the species issue first, there is now general agreement that *Homo erectus* is a chronospecies, giving rise to *H. sapiens* directly. The great majority of the fossil data on which *H. erectus* is based stem from Asia, essentially north China and Java, and there are at present no serious candidates for pre-*Homo* or non *erectus/sapiens* hominids in the fossil record from that area. There

is some agreement on where the species boundary
lies - in terms of Fig.3 somewhere between the Lower
Cave material from Choukoutien and Mapa in the
Chinese sequence and between Ngandong and all later
material from Indonesia-Australia. In terms of
this Pleistocene evidence, then, why do we persist
with two species, other than for reasons of
anatomical shorthand or chronological convenience?
Indeed, referring some or all of the Asian erectines
to *sapiens* has been proposed (Bilsborough 1976;
Buettner-Janusch 1973). If the total fossil
population known from the area were to be regarded
as *H. sapiens* it would clear the way to some
solution of subspecific problems.

To turn to the subspecific argument, a
reluctance to accept a racial classification,
whereby Middle Pleistocene hominids from China and
Java are regarded as Mongoloids and Australoids
respectively, lies to a large extent in the
problems this creates for non-Asian fossils. These
fossils include the Neanderthaloids and, in the
absence of clear evidence for the long-term
physical histories of at least two of the other
major contemporary divisions of mankind, the early
Caucasians and Negroids. Part of this reluctance
also relates to notions that modern racial groups
are of relatively recent development and that they
arose at about the same time. However at the risk
of suggesting that, taxonomically, the tail has
been wagging the dog, the east Asian and Indonesian-
Australian data appear to support the existence of
basic, stable and distinguishable features in the
two areas over long periods.

Two populations, represented by the fossils
from Mapa and Kow Swamp, demonstrate the persistence
of these regional characteristics. The Mapa
specimen, admittedly of uncertain age, preserves
morphological characteristics typical of its region
at a much earlier time. The Kow Swamp population,
and material from nearby sites, exhibits a similar

persistence of regional (Javan) characteristics.
In both cases these features are frontofacial, the
posterior areas of the crania reflecting substantial
modification (or modernisation).

The development of the modern morphological
features of mainland Asia are likely to have
occurred gradually, in an area of relative
geographic stability, large uninterrupted land
areas and relatively high population densities. It
is likely also that substantial samples will be
required to define the course of those changes
leading to the modern Mongoloids. By contrast a
clear view of the changes that took place in island
Southeast Asia should require a smaller sample, if
the modification of long-standing populations in
that area is a function of a rapid influx of new
genes from mainland Asia. The variation in the
hominid remains from Australia points to a
relatively sudden influx of new morphologies into
Sundaland in the late Pleistocene but the parent
stocks of the Australian fossils are not yet visible.

REFERENCES

Allbrook, D. 1976 A human hip bone from Devil's
    Lair, Western Australia. *Archaeology and
    Physical Anthropology in Oceania* 11:48-50

Bilsborough, A. 1976 Patterns of evolution in
    Middle Pleistocene hominids. *Journal of Human
    Evolution* 5:423-39

Birdsell, J.B. 1949 The racial origin of the
    extinct Tasmanians. *Records of the Queen
    Victoria Museum, Launceston* 2:105-22

        1967 Preliminary data on the
    trihybrid origin of the Australian Aborigines.
    *Archaeology and Physical Anthropology in
    Oceania* 2:100-55

Bowler, J.M. 1976 Recent developments in reconstructing late Quaternary environments in Australia. In Kirk and Thorne 1976:55-77

R. Jones, H. Allen and A.G. Thorne 1970 Pleistocene human remains from Australia: a living site and human cremation from Lake Mungo, western New South Wales. *World Archaeology* 2:39-60

and A.G. Thorne 1976 Human remains from Lake Mungo: discovery and excavation of Lake Mungo III. In Kirk and Thorne 1976: 127-38

Brothwell, D.R. 1960 Upper Pleistocene human skull from Niah Caves, Sarawak. *Sarawak Museum Journal* 9:323-49

Buettner-Janusch, J. 1973 *Physical anthropology: a perspective.* New York: Wiley

Coon, C.S. 1963 *The origin of races.* London: Cape

Davies, P.L. 1968 An 8,000 to 12,000 years old human tooth from Western Australia. *Archaeology and Physical Anthropology in Oceania* 3:33-40

1973 A human tooth from Devil's Lair. In C.E. Dortch and D. Merrilees Human occupation of Devil's Lair, Western Australia, during the Pleistocene:115. *Archaeology and Physical Anthropology in Oceania* 8:89-115

Fox, R.B. 1970 *The Tabon Caves.* Manila: National Museum, Monograph No.1

Freedman, L. 1976 A deciduous human incisor tooth from Devil's Lair, Western Australia. *Archaeology and Physical Anthropology in Oceania* 11:45-7

Howells, W.W. 1973 *The Pacific Islanders.* London: Weidenfeld and Nicolson

Jelinek, J. 1976 A contribution to the origin of *Homo sapiens sapiens.* *Journal of Human Evolution* 5:497-500

Kirk, R.L. and A.G. Thorne (eds) 1976 *The origin of the Australians*. Canberra: Australian Institute of Aboriginal Studies

Macintosh, N.W.G. 1971 Analysis of an Aboriginal skeleton and pierced tooth necklace from Lake Nitchie, Australia. *Anthropologie* 9:49-52

     and S.L. Larnach 1973 A cranial study of the Aborigines of Queensland with a contrast between Australian and New Guinea crania. In R.L. Kirk (ed.) *The human biology of Aborigines in Cape York*:1-12. Canberra: Australian Institute of Aboriginal Studies

     1976 Aboriginal affinities looked at in world context. In Kirk and Thorne 1976:113-26

Thorne, A.G. 1967 *The racial affinities of the Tasmanian Aborigines: some new skeletal evidence*. Unpublished MA thesis, University of Sydney

     1971a The racial affinities and origins of the Australian Aborigines. In D.J. Mulvaney and J. Golson (eds) *Aboriginal man and environment in Australia*:316-25. Canberra: Australian National University Press

     1971b Mungo and Kow Swamp: morphological variation in Pleistocene Australians. *Mankind* 8(2):85-9

     1975 *Kow Swamp and Lake Mungo: towards an osteology of early man in Australia*. Unpublished PhD thesis, University of Sydney

     1976 Morphological contrasts in Pleistocene Australians. In Kirk and Thorne 1976:95-112

     and S.R. Wilson in press Pleistocene and Recent Australians: a multivariate comparison. *Journal of Human Evolution*

Wallace, A.G. and G.A. Doran 1976 Early man in

Tasmania: new skeletal evidence. In Kirk
and Thorne 1976:173-82

Weidenreich, F. 1945 The Keilor skull: a Wadjak
skull from southeast Australia. *American
Journal of Physical Anthropology* 3:21-32

THE COASTAL COLONISATION OF AUSTRALIA

SANDRA BOWDLER

Department of Prehistory
Australian National University

It is over a decade since the Pleistocene occupation of Australia by man was conclusively demonstrated, and many archaeological sites of late Pleistocene age have been discovered since then. It is now possible to attempt some sort of synthesis of this data, to examine early Australian man-land relationships and to test some of the assertions that have been made about the initial occupation of the southern continent.

The basic hypothesis of this paper is that Australia was colonised by people adapted to a coastal way of life; that initial colonising routes were around the coasts and thence up the major river systems; and that non-aquatic adaptations, such as desert and montane economies, came relatively late in the sequence. It is further argued that the early Australian colonists were not big game hunters, and that analogies drawn with the peopling of the New World are misleading.

As early as 1957 Birdsell (1957:47) set himself the problem of estimating 'the time required for a population to expand across a former barrier into an unoccupied area and to saturate it to carrying capacity'. He set forward two models of penetration of Australia, one incorporating advancing waves of migration from the north across the continent (1957: 56, Fig.2), the other based on two lines of entry from the north, converging somewhere near Mount Isa, and pressing on in a more or less straight line to Tasmania (1957:58, Fig.3). He concluded that 'the most likely estimate, based upon the assumption that a horde of 25 persons represented the normal

colonising unit and that the budding off occurred
when a population reached 60% of its carrying
capacity, gives the surprisingly short period of
2204 years of total elapsed time'. I do not wish
here to dissect Birdsell's methodology, but two
points may be noted. Firstly, his argument is
based on the two related and dubious assumptions
that the Aboriginal population in the ethnographic
present reflected maximum saturation of Australia
relative to its carrying capacity; and that this
stood at 300,000 persons (1957:67). Secondly, more
recent demographic work suggests that Birdsell was
overly sanguine in his expectations of survival
potentials of small colonising groups (McArthur
1976). In general however, he has reiterated his
view that 'since the intrinsic rate of increase in
man allows it, human populations should be
considered to reach the culturally effective
carrying capacity of a given environment within
very short time periods' (1968, and this volume).

A quick glance through some recent syntheses
would suggest that Birdsell's predictions of rapid
adaptation and saturation of Pleistocene Australia
have been sustained by recent archaeological
findings. Jones for instance asserts that 'by at
least 20,000 BP man was occupying almost all of the
principal ecological zones of Greater Australia
(1973:281). This view is echoed by Mulvaney:
'during the Pleistocene, therefore, man penetrated
to the extremities of Greater Australia and
exploited various ecological niches, including
rugged mountain terrain' (1975:161, also 147); and
Shawcross: 'the adaptation and diversification of
the early Australians must have been extremely
rapid' (1975:31). Jones also suggests that 'by at
least 25,000 BP the distinctive Australian economic
system was already in train in some places' (1973:
281). One might well ask, what is the 'distinctive
Australian economic system' in a country so
ecologically diverse? It would appear however, that
there is a consensus in support of Birdsell's

predictions of rapid adaptation and saturation; but a rigorous scrutiny of the evidence does not in fact support these generalisations.

The notion of early saturation is also pivotal to arguments of stress effects due to post-glacial sea level rise:

One outstanding environmental feature of Australia between about 19,000 and 5,000 years ago is the shrinking of the continent due to eustatic rises in sea level. Consequences for human migration and land settlement were far-reaching. ...regions larger than modern tribal territories disappeared, and even within some human generations, losses would have been evident. It must be conjectured that this required adaptive efforts and a consolatory philosophy... (Mulvaney 1975:136).

Blainey conjectures an even more dramatic, more traumatic picture:

In one way or another the rising seas disturbed the life of every Australian for thousands of years. Salt water drowned perhaps one-seventh of the land. ...A tribe living so far from the coast that it had never heard of the sea could not escape these events. ...Languages, marriage patterns, genetics, religion, mythology, and warfare - all must have been affected by the rising of the seas around Australia. ...Every tribal group on the coast 15,000 years ago must have slowly lost its entire territory. Compelled to move inland, in order to survive, a tribe entered territory to which few or none of its members normally had right of access. ...The slow exodus of refugees, the sorting out of peoples and the struggle for territories probably led to many wounds and deaths as well as new alliances. The violent deaths - if widespread - must have cushioned the pressure on foodstuffs in some of the places of retreat (1975:89-91).

I would argue that not only is this doomsday
libretto based on the mistaken concept of continental
saturation, but also a misconceived demographic
model of Aboriginal Australia in the ethnographic
present. In some parts of Australia indeed the
rising of the seas may have had a beneficial issue:
an extension of coastline, and hence of protein-rich
coastal resources. This is particularly true when
we are dealing with coastally-oriented economies.

In what follows I first present a model of
coastal demography and land-use in the ethnographic
present. I then present a rigorous examination of
the available archaeological data, using as a
springboard my own work in the western Bass Strait
area.

ETHNOGRAPHIC AUSTRALIANS ON THE GROUND

It is easily demonstrated that 'in general the
coastal tribes were more sedentary than most and
their population densities were high by Australian
standards' (Meggitt 1966:60). This may be extended
to the riverine dwellers of the Darling-Murray
basins. Maddock (1974:22-3) gives the following
estimates:

Gidgingali (Arnhem Land):	2 persons to 2.5 sq km
Wanindiljaugwa (Arnhem Land):	1 person to 8 sq km
Walbiri (Central Australia):	1 person to 90 sq km
Aranda (Central Australia):	1 person to 32 sq km
Sydney Aborigines:	5-10 persons to 2.5 sq km
Murray River Aborigines:	3-4 persons to 1.5 km of river

Allen (1974:313, 318) gives a slightly higher figure
for the Murray basin (3 persons per kilometre of
river frontage) and suggests a less dense population
for the Darling basin of one person per 1 to 3

kilometres of river. He further comments that 'the
western slopes of the eastern highlands of New South
Wales seem to have been a less productive environment
for Aborigines than the Darling basin and the
population was less dense and more mobile'. For
the other side of these highlands, Flood (1973:41)
states that 'there is considerable evidence for a
denser population along the coastal strip than in
the immediate hinterland', the former being
expressed by the figure for the Sydney Aborigines
above, also computed at 4 persons per mile of coast
(Lawrence 1968:187).

     Tasmania must be regarded as Australia's
ultimate maritime province. Jones' exhaustive
review of the Tasmanian ethnographic literature
prompted his conclusions that 'there was no tribe
nor group of bands that lived totally inland and did
not at some time of the year forage on the seashore'.
He continues:

   I estimate that one third of Tasmania's land area
   was not used or even occupied by the Aborigines.
   To calculate population densities we can either
   take the whole island or consider the inhabited
   regions only. For the inhabited region, the
   population density was 4-5 to 6 square miles
   (10-15 sq.km) per person, and for the whole of
   the island, 5 to 8.5 square miles (12-20 sq.km
   per person) (Jones 1974:329).

     It is almost superfluous to explain high coastal
population densities; the productive capacity of a
usually well-watered strip of land allied with the
protein-rich produce of the littoral is self-evident.
Tindale (1974:111) has commented on the 'continuing
renewal by the sea of its supplies' and argues that
the dense populations of the Murray are attributable
to its fish and shellfish resources.

     Coastal and riverine populations are generally

described as not only denser on the ground than
others but also as more sedentary, less mobile.
This does not mean however that they were immobile;
Stanner says that in general, 'the members of a
local group clustered in good times and dispersed in
bad' (1965:5), and the most fertile environments
had their leaner seasons. Stanner (1965:2) also
makes the distinction between 'estate' and 'range':

> The estate was the traditionally recognised locus
> ('country', 'home', 'ground', 'dreaming place')
> of some kind of patrilineal descent group forming
> the core or nucleus of the territorial group. ...
> The range was the tract or orbit over which the
> group, including its nucleus and adherents,
> ordinarily hunted and foraged to maintain life.

Clearly, if we are dealing with areas where
traditional society has disintegrated, the
archaeologist or ethnographer will have difficulties
identifying loci of 'some kind(s) of patrilineal
descent group'. Furthermore, Hiatt emphasises the
economic unimportance of the estate, and reports
that amongst the Anbara, 'at any given camp the
majority of members were living *outside* their
estate' (1968:101, his emphasis). I do want to make
the distinction however, between the territory over
which day to day foraging might take place,
especially in the more productive periods, and the
potential area over which dispersal might occur in
leaner months, or over which more long-term hunting
parties might venture. I will therefore use the
terms 'core territory' for the former and 'range'
for the latter.

As an example, let us take the south coast of
New South Wales, including the Sydney region. As
we have seen, the latter carried one of the densest
Australian populations, which is usually held to
have been one of the most sedentary: 'people who
exploited a shoreline whose bounty offered little
seasonal inducement to move' (Lampert 1975:203).
Some movement there was however. Poiner (1976:201)

has carried out a thorough survey of the ethnographic literature and says:

> ...the population appeared to decrease along familiar shores during winter but opinion was divided whether there was a move inland or to other coastal situations. A conclusion that the move was in both directions seemed appropriate. Movement inland was not confined to winter months but it was during this time that it was most strongly expressed.

(See also her diagram (Poiner 1976:Fig.5)).

Let us say then that the *core territories* of the local groups were located right on the coast, and represent focal points for clustering in good times; and the *range* of the groups extended to the hills, and represented potential dispersal areas in the leaner months. The Darling basin is one of the few places for which estimates of seasonally differing population densities are available. Allen (1974:313) has calculated that during the summer there was an average density of one person per kilometre of river frontage, but one person per 3 kilometres during the winter. The average range then must have been 3 times the average core territory.

Extrapolating from these well-documented areas to the continent generally we may set up a demographic and territorial model which postulates dense populations with core territories clustered on the coast, and less dense populations with core territories further inland. The ranges of the respective populations form a kind of buffering zone between the two sets of core territories. Mulvaney's and Blainey's conjectures however demand an evenly distributed population, with a sort of domino effect whereby the rising seas push back peoples into equally densely inhabited areas. Both Blainey and Mulvaney talk about losses of territory, and Blainey mentions tribal groups 'compelled to move inland'.

For the coastal groups, there is no loss of effective
resource zones because they simply follow the
retreating coastline. Only in areas such as the
Gulf of Carpentaria with a wide shallow offshore
profile need the retreating hunter-fishers make
noticeable inroads into the territories of others.
Stanner (1965:2) is quite explicit that a range
'might extend by common understanding into the
territories of neighbours prepared to share food and
water with the distressed'.

   If it be accepted that coasts are capable of
supporting much denser populations than other areas,
then some groups will have benefited by the post-
glacially rising seas. This can be demonstrated for
the Bass Strait region, as depicted in Fig.1. Here

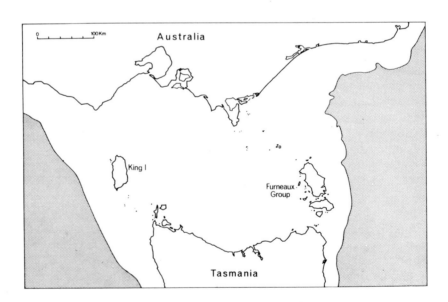

Fig.1. Hypothetical Bassian Plain at the 100 metre submarine
contour, giving 750 km of coast at that time compared with the
present-day coastlines of 450 km for southern Victoria and 550 km
for north Tasmania.

the modern shoreline is contrasted with where the
coast would have been at the height of the last
glaciation about 18-20,000 years ago, assuming a
lowering of sea level of at least 100 m (Jennings
1971:4). It will be immediately seen that there is
a large loss of land involved with the sea reaching
its present level. During the time of lowered sea
level, the land bridge would have incorporated some
15,000,000 hectares. After Tasmania was severed,
within the same region we have only c. 1,250,000
hectares on the Victorian side and c. 3,000,000
hectares on the Tasmanian side: a loss of some 70%.
If we look at the actual coastlines however, there
is a gain of some 30%: from c. 750 km to 450 km on
the Victorian side and 550 km on the Tasmanian side.
Which was more significant - the loss of land or
gain of coastline?

I have so far eschewed examining the
archaeological evidence. A demographic model based
on data from the ethnographic present, no matter how
detailed, needs to be tested against data from the
period under discussion: the late Pleistocene and
early Holocene. Otherwise we shall be assuming that
the inhabitants of Australia were indeed an unchanging
people in an unchanging land.

ARCHAEOLOGICAL EVIDENCE IN THE GROUND

Some twenty sites on the mainland of Tasmania
have been radiocarbon dated, and until recently,
the oldest was 8700±200 BP (Reber 1965:266; see also
Reber 1967; Jones 1968; Lourandos 1970; Gill 1968;
Sigleo and Colhoun 1975; Tasmanian Museum and Art
Gallery 1975:20; Wallace and Doran 1976). All these
sites except two are coastal or estuarine shell
middens, either open sites or shelters. About half
were first occupied between about 8-6000 years ago:
a good fit for estimates of the sea reaching its
present level (Thom and Chappell 1975). The two

non-coastal sites are Flowery Gully and Crown
Lagoon. The former was destroyed by quarrying
operations before any proper investigation could be
carried out, so little can be said about it. It was
a cave site with rich faunal remains, but its
identification as an archaeological site rests on a
single bone artifact. It was situated near
Beaconsfield on the Tamar estuary about 20 km from
the present coast, and contained a faunal assemblage
composed of terrestrial species. A radiocarbon date
of 7080±420 BP was obtained (Gill 1968). Crown
Lagoon is a clearly archaeological site stratified
in a lunette about 30 km inland from the present-
day east coast of Tasmania. Intensive use of this
site began about 5000 years ago (4860±95 BP:
Lourandos 1970:62). A claim has been put forward
for the Pleistocene occupation of the Old Beach
site on the Derwent estuary. All that can be
confidently said here is that a half-dozen stone
artifacts were found in a wind-deposited sand
horizon in excess of 6000 years old; certainly there
are none of the well-defined hearths and activity
areas described by Lourandos for Crown Lagoon, and
the dating of the relevant stratigraphic unit at Old
Beach remains to my mind problematical (Sigleo and
Colhoun 1975; cf. Lourandos 1970:64-6).

Jones (1966:8, 1968:200, 1971:593) has long
put forward the view that during the late Pleistocene
much of Tasmania was inhospitable, that man was
restricted to a narrow coastal fringe by dense
rainforest, practising a well-developed littoral
economy as shown in the earliest levels of Rocky
Cape, and that most Tasmanian glacial sites are now
under the sea. Certainly all the available evidence
agrees with the notion of man arriving at the present
coast at its approximate time of formation, but new
climatic and archaeological data suggest a revision
of the notion that man was thus *restricted* to the
Pleistocene coastline.

A recently discovered site is the Beginners

Luck Cave in the Florentine Valley in the interior southwest, uninhabited in the ethnographic present. The archaeological component appears to represent sporadic occupation associated with a modern fauna, the largest animal represented being the brush wallaby (*Macropus rufogriseus*). Associated charcoal has been dated to 12,600±200 BP (Goede and Murray 1976).

Cave Bay Cave on Hunter Island, just off the northwest tip of Tasmania, which is producing an archaeological and climatic sequence embracing the last 23,000 years (Bowdler 1974a, 1974b, 1975b), has provided significant data for ancient Tasmanian settlement. The archaeological evidence here is not continuous, but bone is preserved throughout, as is pollen. The latter is being investigated by Dr Geoffrey Hope and some preliminary results will be mentioned here. The basic sequence is diagrammatically represented in Fig.2. Bedrock of the site was not reached and it is conceivable that there is evidence of human occupation below the level reached by my excavations. The lowest evidence found however, consists of at least three hearthy layers dated between 22,750±420 BP (ANU-1498) and 20,850± 290 BP (ANU-1612). There is some sporadic evidence for human occupation just above these layers associated with what seems to have been a period of heavy roof-fall. This may represent the height of the last glaciation, and could correlate with the date of 18,550±600 BP (ANU-1361) obtained from a trial trench in the very back of the cave.

Between this period and c. 7000 BP there is only one clear manifestation of man: a small isolated hearth dated to 15,400±330 BP (ANU-1613). No artifacts were associated with it; and the bulk of the bone in the layers dated between c. 18,000 and 7000 BP can be attributed to the work of the Tasmanian devil and Tasmanian wolf or Thylacine. There is also a mass of rodent material best interpreted as the remnants of regurgitated owl pellets.

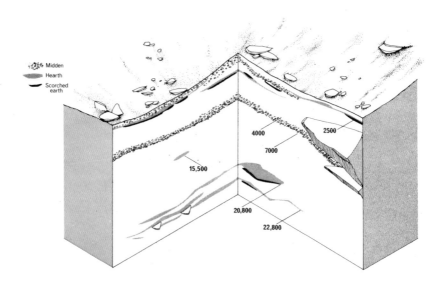

Midden
Hearth
Scorched earth

4000
2500
7000
15,500
20,800
22,800

Fig.2. Cave Bay Cave stratigraphic section showing dated features.

The top layers of the deposit comprise two shell middens sandwiching another archaeologically sterile layer. The bottom of the lower midden has been dated to 7180±90 BP (ANU-1552).   It is similar in content to the lower levels of Rocky Cape South and represents a well-developed littoral economy. I have argued elsewhere (1974a:8, 1975b) that the subsequent culturally sterile layer represents the abandonment of the island when it became an island proper, and that the uppermost midden layer represents the maritime discovery of Hunter Island; I will not pursue these arguments further here.

The archaeological record from Cave Bay Cave serves to clarify one point: with the rise in sea level at the end of the Pleistocene, the gain in coastline in the Bass Strait region was more

important to man than the loss of land. Little or
no use was made of the latter. Cave Bay Cave was
effectively unoccupied from c. 18,000 BP until the
sea reached its present level c. 7000 years ago.
There is no basis for Lourandos' (1970:121) statement that 'at that time, [during the last
glaciation] the area of greatest terrestrial
occupation appears to have been in Bass Strait
across the now drowned land bridge with its
extension to King Island'. Little archaeological
evidence has been found on King Island or the
islands of the Furneaux group, unoccupied and
unvisited in the ethnographic present. The
palaeontological site Ranga Cave on Flinders Island
contained no evidence of man's presence; the top
part of the deposits there are dated to c. 8000 BP
(Hope 1973:167-70). Jones (1976:256) suggests that
'the abundant charcoal in the top layers may
indicate the occasional presence of man and his
firesticks somewhere in the neighbourhood at that
time'. Apart from this somewhat flimsy negative
evidence, only a 'handful of stone tools' (Jones
1976:257) from Flinders and Cape Barren Islands
evince man's presence. By contrast, we have not
only a shell midden appearing in Cave Bay Cave
7000 years ago, but all the other dates mentioned
above for sites such as Rocky Cape, where man
appears on the modern Tasmanian coastline with a
well-developed coastal economy just as the sea
reached its present level. Clearly late Pleistocene
man was living on the coast; but why did he make so
little use of the terrestrial resources of the
exposed Bassian plain?

The pollen evidence from Cave Bay Cave does not
support Jones' contention that 'the narrow forested
fringe along the wet and cold west coast would
probably have consisted of rain forest, and any
human occupation would have been tightly coastal'
(1968:200). If the prevailing winds were westerly
at the time, as they are now, rain forest pollen
would register in the Cave Bay deposits; but they

do not, until c. 10,000 BP in a minor way, and at
c. 7000 BP in full strength (Bowdler and Hope 1976).
The archaeological evidence from Cave Bay dated to
between c. 22,800 and c. 21,000 BP suggests
fleeting transitory visits, and we might envisage
the site as a temporary hunting bivouac rather than
a home base camp: an outlier site within the range
of the local group but well away from its core
territory. But why is even this use of the site
restricted to this relatively short period of time?

Two further hypotheses present themselves:
firstly, the period subsequent to c. 21,000 BP
represents full glacial conditions. Would the
Bassian plain have been too uncomfortable for man?
The pollen evidence suggests a cold but dry
environment; how much colder is difficult to say,
as it is to know the tolerance of the people
concerned. We may look to the ethnographic
Tasmanians and in particular the Big River tribe,
who foraged over the largely subalpine regions of
central Tasmania, sometimes throughout the year,
where mean winter temperatures are not much above
7°C (Jones 1974:342-3; Langford 1965:9, and Map 3).
And perhaps more to the point, why was Cave Bay not
reoccupied during the period of climatic
amelioration after 11,500 BP? (Macphail and
Peterson 1975). There is more evidence, slight
though it is, for man's presence between c. 21,000
and c. 18,000 BP.

A second line of thought might suggest that the
Bassian plain was unproductive of resources during
the pleniglacial period, but the Cave Bay faunal
sequence shows that game was at least as abundant
after c. 18,000 BP as before. Table 1 gives
preliminary minimum numbers for potential game
mammals determined from one of the excavated
trenches (Trench V).

My own interpretation is that Pleistocene man
in Tasmania was marine-oriented, one might say by

	c. 7,000–18,000 BP	c. 18,000–23,000 BP
Macropus cf. *rufogriseus* brush wallaby	32	11
Thylogale billardierii Tasmanian pademelon	3	2
Bettongia gaimardi eastern bettong	2	0
Trichosurus vulpecula brush-tailed possum	1	0
Pseudocheirus peregrinus ring-tailed possum	4	0
Vombatus ursinus common wombat	2	1
Perameles gunnii barred bandicoot	13	7
Dasyurus maculatus tiger cat	3	5
D. viverrinus native cat (quoll)	6	2
	66	28

Table 1. Minimum numbers of some marsupials represented in the lower levels of Cave Bay Cave, Trench V.

choice, rather than by environmental imposition. Not only did he follow the rising seas inward, he also followed the retreating seas outward. If we accept an interstadial sea level higher at c. 25,000 BP than subsequently, then at 23,000 BP the coast may not have been all that far from Hunter Hill (Thom 1972:220; Colhoun 1975:13, 22, 29 and Fig.2). We could then interpret the early occupation levels at Cave Bay Cave as representing rare hunting forays by a basically coastal people into the hinterland; or alternatively, the results of a kind of lag effect of people following the receding shoreline.

Certain it is that no environmental barrier was keeping people away from Hunter Hill, yet it was effectively abandoned for at least 10,000 years.

This gives rise to further speculation about the Pleistocene economy of the inhabitants of Australia generally. Is the Bass Strait region peculiar, or can we demonstrate a more general phenomenon?

Archaeological evidence for eastern New South Wales presents an identical situation, and is furthermore one of the archaeologically best sampled areas of Australia. Nearly fifty sites have been excavated on the coastal strip and the eastern slopes of the Great Dividing Range: in the New England area (McBryde 1974; Campbell 1972; Connah 1975), the Hunter River valley (Moore 1970), the Sydney-Royal National Park region (Megaw 1965, 1974; Megaw and Wright 1966; Megaw and Roberts 1974; Nippard and Megaw 1966; Wade 1967; Bowdler 1971; Glover 1974; Poiner 1974; Tracey 1974) and the South Coast (Lampert 1966, 1971a, 1971b; Bowdler 1970, 1976; Emerson 1973; Flood 1973). More than two-thirds of these sites have been radiocarbon dated.

Only two sites can confidently be said to have been occupied before the period when the sea began to approximate its present level: Burrill Lake and Bass Point (Lampert 1971a; Bowdler 1970, 1976). Furthermore, Lampert and Hughes (1974:232-3, Fig.2) have shown that at these two sites there was considerable intensification of occupation in the period c. 6000-4000 BP. Many other sites were occupied for the first time at this period, such as Curracurang (main shelter, Megaw 1965:203), Currarong shelters 1 and 2 (Lampert 1971a:34; Philip Hughes pers. comm.), Bobadeen (Moore 1970:48), Seelands (McBryde 1974:373), Clybucca 3 (Connah 1975:29).

With such a large number of sites sampled and

dated, the conclusion is warranted that the area constituting the modern coastal strip of New South Wales was unexploited during the Pleistocene, the only evidence being for sporadic visits to the sites of Burrill Lake and Bass Point. The offshore profile here is particularly steep, and the coast-line during the period 18,000-20,000 BP would have been only 24 to 32 km away (Lampert and Hughes 1974:Fig.1). The large number of sites on the modern coastline dating to within the period when the sea reached its present level strongly supports an hypothesis of coastal dwellers pushed back by the rising sea. And it may be noted that there is no evidence that there was anyone already there for them to impinge on.

PLEISTOCENE ADAPTATIONS...?
(Fig.3)

It is generally accepted that the original Australian colonists came from Southeast Asia, and that the route must have at all times involved the crossing of a water barrier at least 50 to 100 km wide (Jennings 1971:6). It follows from this that, whether the journey was made accidentally or by design, these early colonists must have possessed watercraft of some sort and have been coastal dwellers practising a coastal economy.

If Australia was settled by people already adapted to coastal conditions, it seems most likely that their routes of diffusion would have been along the Pleistocene coastlines. Their previous mode of subsistence and technology would need little modification to exploit the marine resources abounding on the new country's extensive littorals. The unique Australian fauna on the other hand must have taken some getting used to; and Golson (1971, esp. Table 15:15) has pointed out that while they would have found many familiar edible plants in the tropical

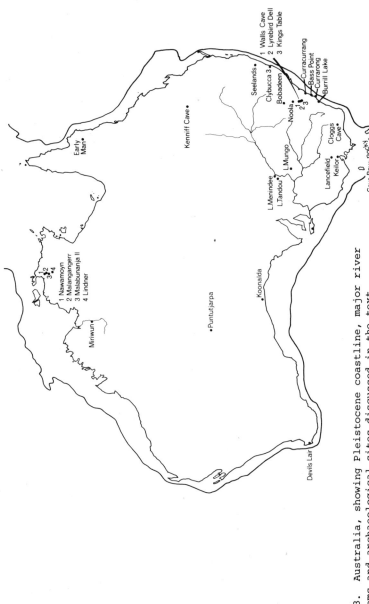

Fig.3. Australia, showing Pleistocene coastline, major river
systems and archaeological sites discussed in the text.

regions, these decrease enormously to the south.
This hypothesis of coastal migration reinforces
suggestions that the truly oldest Australian sites
are now under the sea, but can be tested against the
evidence from the oldest sites which we do have.

The oldest sites so far dated in Australia are
a series of sites in the Willandra Lakes region,
including Lake Mungo, in western New South Wales,
and the somewhat enigmatic river terraces at Keilor
near modern Melbourne. Given coastal migration
routes, the best access to these areas would have
been up the major river systems from the south.
This may also have required little modification of
economic strategy or technology, since if we look
closely at the economic evidence from the older
dated Willandra sites, it can be interpreted as
representing a coastal economy 'transliterated' to
a freshwater situation. There is of course some
difficulty in defining exactly just what a 'coastal
economy' consists of; I have in mind here a
generalised model drawn from diverse sources. There
is Jones' summary of the diet of modern coastal
Arnhem Landers (1975); ethnographic descriptions of
coastal Cape Yorkers (e.g. Lawrence 1968:155, 175,
223); and evidence from relatively recent coastal
midden sites (e.g. Lampert 1971a; Bowdler 1970,
1976). The general picture is one of heavy
dependence on marine resources especially scale fish
and shellfish, and little systematic hunting of
terrestrial mammals with smaller ones being of
greater importance than larger ones. Some foraging
away from the coast, perhaps seasonally determined,
might be expected, with consequent greater reliance
on land fauna on such forays (cf. Poiner 1976).

The oldest firmly dated Willandra sites with
clearly associated economic remains are Mungo 1,
Mungo 2 and Leaghur 1. All date from a time when
these now dried-up lakes were full of water and
supported scale fish and shellfish populations; and
when they would have been connected with the larger

riverine systems of the Darling-Murray basins.
Mungo 1 is dated to 26,250±1120 BP and produced
freshwater mussel shells (*Velesunio ambiguus*)
together with the remains of 130 fish (*Plectroplites
ambiguus* [?], golden perch) and 18 small mammals,
the largest being the hare wallaby (*Lagorchestes* sp.).
Also present were 2 lizards, 3 unidentified birds
and 29 fragments of emu eggshell (Allen 1972:266-7,
267a). Table 2 makes a comparison between the
structure of the vertebrate suite excavated from the
Bass Point shell midden on the New South Wales coast
and that of Mungo 1. This ignores meat poundage
contribution and the like; and of course it is
clearly ridiculous to compare two sites so widely
separated in time, space and environment. What it
does suggest however, is that similar energy
expenditures were being put into capturing aquatic
vertebrates. Mungo 2 is the oldest of the group
(32,750±1250 BP) and contained only freshwater
mussels and stone artifacts (Barbetti and Allen
1972). Leaghur 1 is a fairly substantial midden of
freshwater mussel shells dated by two samples to
c. 25,000 (27,160±900 BP; 24,020±$^{1480}_{1250}$ BP) and
containing only a few bones including the mandible
of a rat-kangaroo or small wallaby and the bone of a
small bird (Allen 1972:283-4).

	Mungo 1		Bass Point	
	Minimum numbers	As %	Minimum numbers	As %
Fish	130	85	252	78
Seal	—	—	11	3
Land Mammal	18	12	33[1]	10
Lizard	2	1	7	2
Bird	3	2	20[2]	6

[1] Largest: swamp wallaby *(Macropus bicolor)*

[2] Muttonbird 15, penguin 1, unidentified 4.

Table 2. Comparison of vertebrate faunal suites from Mungo I
(Allen 1972:167a) and Bass Point (Bowdler 1970:93-4, Tables 4,6).

A further group of Willandra sites cluster around a date of c. 15,000 BP and present a similar economic picture, with one significant addition. This is the period when the lake systems had begun to dry up, and grindstones appear in the artifact assemblages for the first time, implying the collection of cereals (Allen 1972:351). Otherwise, the impression of a transliterated coastal economy is reinforced and the appearance of grindstones is the only evidence of modification of that economy.

Allen (1972:348-9) concludes that giant marsupials in the Darling basin had become extinct by 30,000 BP and appears to base his claim on the absence of their remains from the above sites. By implication then he is attributing their demise to over-predation by human hunters. It seems to me unlikely that people who relied on big game to the extent that they wiped out entire populations would then turn their attention to shellfish, fish and the smaller mammals, and ignore the intermediate sizes of animals available. Only at Mulurulu IIIA dated to 15,120±235 BP are there any numbers at all of the larger available game: one each of three different sorts of kangaroo and one wallaby out of 72 mammals (Allen 1972:305-9).

Some other dated sites in the Murray-Darling basin may be briefly mentioned. Tandou Creek I is a midden composed of freshwater mussels dated to 12,350±170 BP; grindstones and a crayfish gastrolith were associated (Allen 1972:235-9). A similar midden on the banks of the Murray River near Redcliffs, Victoria is dated to 11,250±240 BP. Five middens on the west side of Lake Victoria span the period c. 12,000 to 18,200±800 BP, but only one of these yielded faunal remains other than freshwater mussel shell. Two dentary fragments of the nail-tailed wallaby (*Onychogalea fraenata*) and a crayfish gastrolith were found in the midden dated 15,300± 500 BP (Gill 1973:58; Marshall 1973:162).

Mention must also be made of those persistent
bêtes noires of Australian prehistory, Keilor and
Lake Menindee. Extinct giant marsupial remains
occur at both sites, but in both cases convincing
evidence of their association with man remains to
be produced. There are 'humanly-struck flakes'
from Keilor in a horizon 30,000-40,000 years old
(Mulvaney 1975:146), but no associated dietary
remains. At Lake Menindee, some artifacts were
found in a horizon dated to 26,300±1500 BP and
18,800±800 BP; associated fauna includes freshwater
mussel shells, and *probably* the extinct macropod
Macropus ferragus (Jones 1968:187, 203; Allen 1972:
220-8; see also Marshall 1973:169).

Most other dated Australian Pleistocene sites
are either caves or shelters. I have drawn attention
elsewhere (Bowdler 1975a) to the fact that not only
are the numbers of such sites occupied during the
Pleistocene far fewer than those occupied in recent
times, but the nature of the evidence in the case of
the former is in most cases exceedingly sparse.

A number of sites have been dated to between
c. 25,000 and c. 15,000 BP. Some may, by their
geographical location, be interpreted as riverine
sites to which the coastal economy of the early
colonists was easily adapted. Sites excavated in
Arnhem Land have all been sandstone rockshelters, so
unfortunately faunal remains have only been preserved
from recent levels. The oldest dated sites are
Nawamoyn and Malangangerr on the estuarine plain
near the modern East Alligator River. There are
two basal dates from Malangangerr: 24,800±1600 BP
and 22,900±1000 BP. The top of this early layer
was dated to 18,000±400 BP, but only 10 cms above
this, the bottom of the upper midden layer was
dated to 5980±140 BP (White 1967:131, 136). White
suggests there was a similar stratigraphic break at
Nawamoyn, though only two dates were obtained there,
the lowest basal date being 21,450±380 BP, the other
dating the lowest part of the upper midden layer to

7110±130 BP (White 1967:196, 201).

Climatic evidence has now accumulated to
suggest a period of considerable aridity in this
region beginning c. 18,000 BP (Bowler *et al.* 1976).
It is possible that the early inhabitants of the
plains sites were exploiting a river system which
then dried up considerably, and they retreated to
the coast.[1]

Miriwun rockshelter in the Ord Valley, northwest Australia, has more direct evidence for
aquatic resource exploitation. Faunal remains were
preserved here from an occupation sequence spanning
nearly 18,000 years and include the remains of fish
and freshwater mussels (Dortch 1972, in press).

Kenniff Cave was the first firmly dated
Pleistocene site reported for Australia, and was
probably first occupied somewhat before 19,000
years ago (Mulvaney and Joyce 1965; Mulvaney 1975:
288). Its geographical location is suggestive, as
it is situated near the headwaters of the Darling
River system (Mulvaney and Joyce 1965:Map 1). No
other site in the region has anything like the
same antiquity (Mulvaney and Joyce 1965; John
Beaton pers. comm.). The lower levels of Kenniff
are perhaps representative of an early, tentative
attempt at non-riverine/coastal exploitation by
people based on the upper reaches of the Darling
system.

A number of sites around the southern fringes
of the continent have evidence of extremely low
intensity occupation, and perhaps tentative
exploration of differing resource zones especially
in the period 25,000 to 15,000 BP. Three sites
bear marked similarities to Cave Bay Cave and the
later Florentine Valley site in having sparse
direct evidence of man's presence, and faunal
remains preserved which may be interpreted as the
work of non-human predators. They are Devil's Lair

in the southwest tip of Western Australia, the
Seton site on Kangaroo Island, South Australia, and
Cloggs Cave near Buchan in Victoria. Devil's Lair
has evidence of man's presence dated to 24,600±800
BP and earlier (Dortch and Merrilees 1973:97, and
Charles Dortch pers. comm.). The site is now 5 km
from the present coast and during the height of the
last glaciation would never have been further than
25 km from the sea. Human occupation seems to have
been sparse at all times, even if all the faunal
remains are interpreted as being humanly deposited,
which is open to argument (Baynes *et al*. 1975:114).
The site could well represent extremely sporadic
foraging back into the hinterland by people based
on the Pleistocene coastline.

There are two clear phases of occupation in
the Seton site. The earlier is an extremely thin
band of charcoal containing six stone artifacts and
dated to 16,100±100 BP. This is separated by about
80 cms of culturally sterile deposit from the
uppermost and considerably richer human occupation
horizon dated to 10,940±160 BP (Lampert 1972, in
press and pers. comm.). Humanly deposited faunal
remains in the upper levels include predominantly
grey kangaroo (*Macropus fuliginosus*), together with
marine shell and emu eggshell fragments. There is
some clustering of *Macropus* cf. *fuliginosus* or *rufus*
and the extinct macropodid *Sthenurus* sp. around the
lower cultural horizon, but a confident ascription
of these to a human agency may not be made (Hope
et al. forthcoming).

Evidence for human occupation is sparsest of
all in the Cloggs Cave site. Between levels dated
to 17,720±840 BP and 8720±230 BP only 70 artifacts
or manuports were recovered (Flood 1974:177, 181,
Figs 2, 3) and none of the faunal remains are
attributable to man (Hope in Flood 1973:XIV, 5-7;
Flood 1973:287). Sediment analysis also showed very
little organic carbon content in the lower levels
(Flood 1973:XV, 14, Table XV:1).

Awaiting publication is the 'Early Man' site
near Laura on the Cape York Peninsula. It appears
to be of similar antiquity to Seton and Cloggs Cave,
with occupational evidence beginning after c. 17,000
and before c. 13,000 BP. Faunal remains are preserved
here and consist mainly of small mammals (Rosenfeld
1975 and pers. comm.).

Some other early sites with no faunal remains
may be mentioned. Bass Point and Burrill Lake were
described above; on the western slopes of the Blue
Mountains is Kings Table. This site has been dated
to 22,240±1000 BP: the horizon dated contained one
flake. Above this a date of 14,534±300 BP was
obtained, and the deposits sandwiched between the
two dates contained a grand total of 11 primary
flakes. This works out at one flake per 700 years
for the volume of deposit excavated; sufficient
detail is not provided to ascertain what percentage
of the total deposit this represents (Stockton and
Holland 1974:42, Table 3; Stockton 1973:3).

Roughly mid-way between Kangaroo Island and
the southwest tip of the continent is Koonalda Cave
on the Nullarbor Plain. This extraordinary site was
visited by man probably between 22,000 and 15,000
years ago (there are some dating problems: Wright
1971:28). The sole apparent economic use of the
cave was to extract flint from deep under the earth
to manufacture into stone tools (Wright 1971:28 and
passim); the only evidence of any other activity
carried out here is wall markings. During the
period under discussion, the cave was some 180 km
from the coast. Wright (1971:15) comments:

If the pattern of ethnographic times prevailed
we should assume that in the late Pleistocene
the cave lay on the northern fringes of a human
territory which was then extended to include the
now submerged coastal plain.

About 15,000 years ago the Willandra lakes

began to dry out, and we might look to this period
for the emergence of what Gould (1971:174)
characterises as 'the Australian Desert culture'.
It is about this time that grindstones first appear
in the Darling basin sites, suggesting the
beginnings of grass-seed exploitation. The oldest
site from central Australia so far reported is the
Puntutjarpa rockshelter in the western desert. A
basal date of 10,170±230 BP was obtained and
faunal remains were present throughout. The most
common bones were those of 'medium-sized kangaroos'
(Gould 1971:162; Tedford in Gould 1968:185). This
date may well be not far off the *terminus post quem*
for true desert adaptation.

At about this period, 12-10,000 BP, other
environments begin to be more efficiently exploited.
A number of sites in the Blue Mountains are occupied
for the first time: Noola (Tindale 1961; Bermingham
1966), Walls Cave and Lyrebird Dell (Stockton and
Holland 1974:40). This may well represent
penetration from the west, given the lack of evidence
for occupation to the east at this time. The Seton
site shows intensive exploitation of large land
fauna for the first time about 10,000 years ago,
and the Tombs (near Kenniff Cave) is first occupied
about 9000 years ago (Mulvaney and Joyce 1965). It
is when the sea approximates its present level
however, say between 8000 and 6000 years ago, that
we are confronted with a plethora of sites on the
present day coastlines.

Although some non-coastal/riverine adaptations
were made in the last stages of the Pleistocene, it
is apparent that away from the coast and the main
river systems man was very thin on the ground before
the sea reached its present level. Clearly, the
post-glacial rising of the seas cannot have had
anything like the drastic demographic effects
envisaged by Mulvaney and Blainey, and in some areas
at least, would have had a beneficial effect in
extending coastal resources.

MAN, MEGAFAUNA AND THE MISLEADING AMERICAN ANALOGY

The hunting of big game seems to be a relatively recent adaptation if we restrict our- selves to consideration of the evidence available. Indeed, Allen (1972:213) discussing the recent site, Burke's Cave, evinces surprise at the rarity of such specialised kangaroo hunting sites, and finds only Crown Lagoon and Puntutjarpa to be comparable. Puntutjarpa is the oldest of the three; the only site of similar age with any numbers of kangaroos representing economic data is the upper cultural horizon of the Seton site. Older sites with convincing associations of man and fauna demonstrate the systematic hunting of nothing larger than wallabies. It seems therefore unlikely that man had a direct role in the extinction of the larger marsupials, which is not to discount an indirect role by the use of fire (e.g. Jones 1968:205-11; Merrilees 1968).

One of the main stimuli to the hypothesis of man's role by hunting pressure in the extinction of some marsupial species has come from work done in America, especially that of Martin (Jones 1968:204). In terms of the model presented here, the American analogy is untenable; but let us first quickly review the current situation in the New World.

Man's association with, and predation of, large extinct mammal species in the Americas was dramatically demonstrated as long ago as 1927 (Hester 1967:170). Martin (1966, 1967a, 1967b, 1973) has since sought to demonstrate that man was *the* decisive factor in the demise of the American megafauna, by showing that this demise coincided with the advent of man about 12,000 years ago, and that no convincing climatic change could be brought forward to account for such a demise at that time.

Arguments have of course been brought to bear against Martin's thesis. One is that although

there is no doubt that some at least of the extinct
species were hunted, they formed but a portion of
the total diet, and the dramatic kill sites
represent but a segment of an overall economic
round (Guilday 1967:137; Bryan 1975:156). This
argument would suggest that to invoke overkill, one
must demonstrate specialisation. A further
difficulty, raised by Howells (1973:141 fn) is the
report of dates of the order of 20,000 BP for man
in South America (MacNeish 1971). Recent reviews
of the evidence however, suggest it is inconclusive,
and that man's penetration of the New World south
from Alaska is unlikely to have occurred much before
14,000 to 12,000 years ago (Haynes 1974; Lynch 1974;
Klein 1975).

What does seem clear however, is that America
was peopled from the northwest, that the colonists
entered the new territory by land across Bering
Strait, and they probably derived from north Asian
cultures adapted to big game hunting. Martin's
(1973) model of the colonisation of the New World
by a series of 'bow waves' radiating down from the
north may well be valid for a continent colonised
by land, by people with a land-based economy.
Australia on the other hand was colonised by sea
from an island world by people who probably derived
from cultures adapted to fishing and shellfish
gathering. In America, the kill site came first
and the overkill hypothesis was generated
subsequently; in Australia, we have an overkill
hypothesis, but are still waiting for the kill site.[2]
Indeed, it is ironic that assertions about man's
role in the extinction of Australian Pleistocene
fauna are now being used to bolster the American
argument! (Lynch 1974:371, quoting Gould 1973:5).

CONCLUSIONS

The synthesis presented here may be thought to

be premature, the evidence is fragmentary and vast areas of Australia remain unexplored. I have also chosen to sidestep discussion of New Guinea, which was after all part of Greater Australia during the Pleistocene.[3] One reason is that much interesting data is still to be published; another is its environmental distinctiveness from most of modern Australia.

For Australia, I have presented a model which most economically explains the data available: that the continent was colonised by sea, by people with a coastal economy which underwent little modification for many millennia. Such modification in the initial stages merely involved a shift from marine to freshwater aquatic resource exploitation, and areas away from the coasts and major river/ lacustrine environments were unpopulated till rather late in the day. This model argues against an early population saturation of the continent, and suggests a peripheral rather than a radiational or 'bow wave' penetration by the early colonists.

I have said little about technology.[4] It is becoming a truism that early Australian stone industries show 'an immense conservatism and a surprising uniformity' (Howells 1973:127), yet it has been suggested that early economic adaptations were extremely rapid. As archaeologists, we like to think that technology has something to do with economy; a conservative technology therefore makes more sense if associated with a slow-adapting, conservative economy. Indeed, I have suggested that we might look to the group of Willandra lakes sites dated to c. 15,000 BP for the beginnings of the Australian desert culture: the period when the lakes began to dry up in earnest, and grindstones make their first appearance in the region.[5]

This also brings us to the question of environmental pressure. The period 20,000 to 15,000 BP was a time of major climatic change, and the

Australian colonists would have been faced with an
environment certainly different, and possibly
harsher, than that initially encountered. At c.
18,000 BP, the height of the last glaciation, sea
levels were at their lowest, the temperature at its
coldest, and a period of considerable aridity got
under way. Man's reactions seem to have varied.
Some sites were abandoned at c. 18,000 BP (Cave Bay
Cave, Malangangerr, Nawamoyn); others were first
occupied not long after this time, but very sparsely
(Cloggs Cave, the Seton site), suggesting not very
successful attempts to cope with new environments.
More successful exploitation of different
environments seems to have come with climatic
amelioration (the Blue Mountains, the upper levels
of the Seton site).

The model presented here generates predictions
which may be tested in various field situations.
We would expect to find sites older than say 12,000
BP only near Pleistocene coastlines, on major river
systems or lakes connected to the latter. Sites
showing successful desert or montane adaptations
will only be of the order of 12,000 years old.
Ultimately, we may be able to carry out the
definitive test: archaeological exploration of the
submarine continental shelf.

ACKNOWLEDGEMENTS

The ideas presented here benefited greatly
from discussions I had with Jeannette Hope,
Geoffrey Hope, Philip Hughes and Marjorie Sullivan.
The original stimulus arose from discussions with
Rhys Jones. For permission to use unpublished data
and/or correcting me on certain points I wish to
thank John Beaton, John Clegg, Charles Dortch,
Albert Goede, Ronald Lampert, Peter Murray, Andrée
Rosenfeld and Eugene Stockton. I am particularly
grateful to Jack Golson for reading earlier drafts

and for his very constructive criticisms.

FOOTNOTES

[1] I have not discussed two other old sites from the
   Alligator River region. These are Malakunanja
II, with stone tools the only evidence of man,
dated to 18,040±320 BP, and the Lindner site, also
without faunal remains, dated to 19,900±280 BP.
Whether there is an occupational hiatus in these
sites as in White's is hard to say; no artifact
densities or distributions through time are
included in the report, so no assessment of
occupational intensity can be made (Kamminga and
Allen 1973:48-9, 95-6).

[2] Lancefield in Victoria was initially hailed as
   such a site, but it now appears that there is no
evidence of association between man and the
megafauna there. I have not discussed it in the
text as it is still being analysed (Richard Wright
pers. comm.).

[3] Mention should perhaps be made however of the
   important site of Kosipe. Here evidence for
man's presence has been found in the Papuan highlands, some 2000 m above sea level and dated to
c. 26,000 years ago. Perhaps non-coastal adaptations
were more rapid in this region, no doubt more
ecologically familiar to the colonists. The
excavators however interpret the site as one visited
occasionally for the seasonal exploitation of
pandanus by hunter-gatherers based on the Papuan
lowlands: 'Kosipe...documents one type of short-
term exploitation of an area' (White *et al.* 1970:
159-60, 167-9).

[4] Lampert (1976) has independently reviewed the
   Pleistocene stone industries of Australia, and
his conclusions in some ways parallel those arrived

at here.

[5] Grindstones dated to 18,040 BP were recovered
   from Malakunanja II in the Alligator River area
of Arnhem Land (footnote 1, above). This coincides
with the onset of aridity in the region, and the
abandonment of Malangangerr and Nawamoyn, and may
be an earlier example of reaction to environmental
stress.

REFERENCES

Allen, H. 1972 *Where the crow flies backwards:
man and land in the Darling basin.* Unpublished
PhD thesis, Australian National University,
Canberra

           1974 The Bagundji of the Darling basin:
cereal gatherers in an uncertain environment.
World Archaeology 5:309-22

Barbetti, M. and H. Allen 1972 Prehistoric man at
Lake Mungo, Australia, by 32,000 BP. *Nature*
240:46-8

Baynes, A., D. Merrilees and J.K. Porter 1975
Mammal remains from the upper levels of a late
Pleistocene deposit in Devil's Lair, Western
Australia. *Journal of the Royal Society of
Western Australia* 58:97-126

Bermingham, A. 1966 Victoria natural radiocarbon
measurements I. *Radiocarbon* 8:507-21

Birdsell, J.B. 1957 Some population problems
involving Pleistocene man. *Cold Spring Harbor
Symposia on Quantitative Biology* 22:47-69

           1968 Some predictions for the
Pleistocene based on equilibrium systems among
recent hunter-gatherers. In Lee and DeVore
1968:229-40

Blainey, G. 1975 *Triumph of the nomads*. Melbourne: Macmillan

Bowdler, S. 1970 *Bass Point: the excavation of a southeast Australian shell midden showing cultural and economic change*. Unpublished BA (Hons.) thesis, University of Sydney

1971 Balls Head: the excavation of a Port Jackson rockshelter. *Records of the Australian Museum, Sydney* 28(7):117-28

1974a An account of an archaeological reconnaissance of Hunter's Isles, northwest Tasmania, 1973/4. *Records of the Queen Victoria Museum, Launceston* 54:1-22

1974b Pleistocene date for man in Tasmania. *Nature* 252:697-8

1975a Caves and Aboriginal man. *Australian Natural History* 18:216-9

1975b Further radiocarbon dates from Cave Bay Cave, Hunter Island, northwest Tasmania. *Australian Archaeology* 3:24-6

1976 Hook, line and dillybag: an interpretation of an Australian coastal shell midden. *Mankind* 10(4):248-58

and G.S. Hope 1976 *New evidence for Pleistocene environments in northwest Tasmania*. Paper delivered at 47th Congress of the Australian and New Zealand Association for the Advancement of Science, Hobart, May 1976 (*Abstracts* vol.2:391. Hobart: University of Tasmania)

Bowler, J.M., G.S. Hope, J.N. Jennings, G. Singh and D. Walker 1976 Late Quaternary climates of Australia and New Guinea. *Quaternary Research* 6:359-94

Bryan, A.C. 1975 Paleoenvironments and cultural diversity in late Pleistocene South America: a rejoinder to Vance Haynes and a reply to

Thomas Lynch. *Quaternary Research* 5:151-9

Campbell, V. 1972 Some radiocarbon dates for
    Aboriginal shell middens in the lower Macleay
    valley, New South Wales. *Mankind* 8(4):283-6

Colhoun, E.A. 1975 *A Quaternary climatic curve
    for Tasmania.* Paper delivered at the
    Australasian Conference on Climate and Climatic
    Change (Royal Meteorological Society), Monash
    University, Melbourne, December 1975

Connah, G. 1975 Current research at the Department
    of Prehistory and Archaeology, University of
    New England. *Australian Archaeology* 3:28-31

Dortch, C.E. 1972 Archaeological work in the Ord
    Reservoir area, east Kimberley. *Australian
    Institute of Aboriginal Studies Newsletter*
    3(4):13-8

        in press Early and late stone
    industrial phases in Western Australian. In
    Wright in press

        and D. Merrilees 1973 Human
    occupation of Devil's Lair, Western Australia,
    during the Pleistocene. *Archaeology and
    Physical Anthropology in Oceania* 8:89-115

Emerson, P.L. 1973 *Hooka Point: a disturbed site.*
    Unpublished BA (Hons.) thesis, University of
    Sydney

Flood J.M. 1973 *The moth hunters: investigations
    towards a prehistory of the southeastern
    highlands of Australia.* Unpublished PhD
    thesis, Australian National University, Canberra

        1974 Pleistocene man at Cloggs Cave: his
    tool kit and environment. *Mankind* 9(3):175-88

Gill, E.D. 1968 Aboriginal bone implement from
    fossil bone bed, Tasmania. *Records of the
    Queen Victoria Museum, Launceston* 31:1-4

        1973 Geology and geomorphology of the

Murray River region between Mildura and Renmark, Australia. *Memoirs of the National Museum of Victoria* 34:1-97

Glover, E. 1974 Report on the excavation of a second rockshelter at Curracurang Cove, New South Wales. In Megaw (ed.) 1974:13-18

Goede, A. and P. Murray 1976 *Pleistocene man in south-central Tasmania: evidence from a Florentine Valley site*. Paper presented at 47th Congress of the Australian and New Zealand Association for the Advancement of Science, Hobart, May 1976 (*Abstracts* vol.2: 396. Hobart: University of Tasmania)

Golson, J. 1971 Australian Aboriginal food plants: some ecological and culture-historical implications. In Mulvaney and Golson 1971:196-238

Gould, R.A. 1968 Preliminary report on excavations at Puntutjarpa rockshelter near the Warburton Range, Western Australia. *Archaeology and Physical Anthropology in Oceania* 3:161-85

            1971 The archaeologist as ethnographer: a case from the Western Desert of Australia. *World Archaeology* 3:143-77

            1973 *Australian archaeology in ecological and ethnographic perspective*. Andover (Mass.): Warner Modular Publications No.7

Guilday, J.E. 1967 Differential extinction during late Pleistocene and Recent times. In Martin and Wright 1967:121-40

Haynes, C.V. 1974 Paleoenvironments and cultural diversity in late Pleistocene South America: a reply to A.L. Bryan. *Quaternary Research* 4: 378-82

Hester, J.J. 1967 The agency of man in animal extinctions. In Martin and Wright 1967: 169-92

Hiatt, L.R. 1968   Ownership of land among the
    Australian Aborigines.   In Lee and DeVore
    1968:99-102

Hope, J.H. 1973   Mammals of the Bass Strait Islands.
    Proceedings of the Royal Society of Victoria
    85:163-95

              , R.J. Lampert, L. Edmondson, M.J. Smith
    and G. van Tets forthcoming   *The late
    Pleistocene fauna of Seton rockshelter, Kangaroo
    Island, South Australia*

Howells, W.W. 1973   *The Pacific Islanders.*
    Wellington: Reed

Jennings, J.N. 1971   Sea level changes and land
    links.   In Mulvaney and Golson 1971:1-13

Jones, R. 1966   A speculative archaeological
    sequence for northwest Tasmania.   *Records of
    the Queen Victoria Museum, Launceston* 25:1-12

         1968   The geographical background to the
    arrival of man in Australia and Tasmania.
    *Archaeology and Physical Anthropology in
    Oceania* 3:186-215

         1971   *Rocky Cape and the problem of
    the Tasmanians.*   Unpublished PhD thesis,
    University of Sydney

         1973   Emerging picture of Pleistocene
    Australians.   *Nature* 246:278-81

         1974   Tasmanian tribes.   In Tindale
    1974:319-54

         1975   *Why did the Tasmanians stop eating
    fish?*   Paper delivered at Seminar on Ethno-
    archaeology, School of American Research,
    Santa Fe, November 1975

         1976   Tasmania: aquatic machines and off-
    shore islands.   In G. de G. Sieveking,
    I.H. Longworth and K.E. Wilson (eds) *Problems
    in economic and social archaeology*:235-63.

London: Duckworth

Kamminga, J. and H. Allen 1973 *Alligator Rivers environmental fact-finding study: report of the archaeological survey.* [Darwin: Department of the Northern Territory] (limited distribution)

Klein, R.G. 1975 The relevance of Old World archaeology to the first entry of man into the New World. *Quaternary Research* 5:391-4

Lampert, R.J. 1966 An excavation at Durras North, New South Wales. *Archaeology and Physical Anthropology in Oceania* 1:83-118

1971a *Burrill Lake and Currarong.* Canberra: Australian National University, Research School of Pacific Studies, Department of Prehistory, *Terra Australis* 1

1971b Coastal Aborigines of south-eastern Australia. In Mulvaney and Golson 1971:114-32

1972 A carbon date for the Aboriginal occupation of Kangaroo Island, South Australia. *Mankind* 8(3):223-4

1975 Trends in Australian prehistoric research. *Antiquity* 49:197-206

1976 *Variation in Australia's Pleistocene stone industries.* Paper delivered at 9th Congress of the International Union of Pre- and Protohistoric Sciences, Nice, September 1976 (*Abstracts symposium XVIII*:44. Nice: Université de Nice)

in press Kangaroo Island and the antiquity of Australians. In Wright in press

and P.J. Hughes 1974 Sea level change and Aboriginal coastal adaptations in southern New South Wales. *Archaeology and Physical Anthropology in Oceania* 9:226-35

Langford, J. 1965 Weather and climate. In J.L. Davies (ed.) *Atlas of Tasmania*:2-11.

Hobart: Lands and Survey Department

Lawrence, R. 1968 *Aboriginal habitat and economy.*
Canberra: Australian National University, School
of General Studies, Department of Geography,
Occasional Paper No.6

Lee, R.B. and I. DeVore (eds) 1968 *Man the hunter.*
Chicago: Aldine

Lourandos, H. 1970 *Coast and hinterland: the
archaeological sites of eastern Tasmania.*
Unpublished MA thesis, Australian National
University, Canberra

Lynch, T.F. 1974 The antiquity of man in South
America. *Quaternary Research* 4:356-77

McArthur, N. 1976 Computer simulations of small
populations. *Australian Archaeology* 4:53-7

McBryde, I. 1974 *Aboriginal prehistory in New
England.* Sydney: Sydney University Press

MacNeish, R.S. 1971 Early man in the Andes.
Scientific American 224:36-46

Macphail, M.K. and J.A. Peterson 1975 New
deglaciation dates from Tasmania. *Search* 6:
127-9

Maddock, K. 1974 *The Australian Aborigines: a
portrait of their society.* London: Penguin
Press

Marshall, L.G. 1973 Fossil vertebrate faunas from
the Lake Victoria region, southwest New South
Wales, Australia. *Memoirs of the National
Museum of Victoria* 34:151-73

Martin, P.S. 1966 Africa and Pleistocene overkill.
Nature 212:339-42

        1967a Pleistocene overkill. *Natural
History* 76(10):32-8

        1967b Prehistoric overkill. In Martin
and Wright 1967:75-120

1973   The discovery of America.   *Science*
179:969-74

and H.E. Wright Jr. (eds) 1967
Pleistocene extinctions: the search for a cause.
New Haven and London: Yale University Press

Megaw, J.V.S. 1965   Excavations in the Royal
National Park, New South Wales.   *Oceania*
35(3):202-7

1974   The recent archaeology of
the south Sydney district: a summary.   In
Megaw (ed.) 1974:35-8

(ed.) 1974   *The recent archaeology
of the Sydney district: excavations 1964-1967.*
Canberra: Australian Institute of Aboriginal
Studies

and A. Roberts 1974   The 1967
excavations at Wattamolla Cove, Royal National
Park, New South Wales.   In Megaw (ed.) 1974:
1-12

and R.V.S. Wright 1966   The
excavation of an Aboriginal rockshelter on
Gymea Bay, Port Hacking, New South Wales.
Archaeology and Physical Anthropology in Oceania
1:23-50

Meggitt, M.J. 1966   Indigenous forms of government
among the Australian Aborigines.   In I. Hogbin
and L.R. Hiatt (eds) *Readings in Australian
and Pacific anthropology*:57-74.   Melbourne:
Melbourne University Press

Merrilees, D. 1968 · Man the destroyer: late
Quaternary changes in the Australian marsupial
fauna.   *Journal of the Royal Society of Western
Australia* 51:1-24

Moore, D.R. 1970   Results of an archaeological
survey of the Hunter River valley, New South
Wales, Australia.   *Records of the Australian
Museum, Sydney* 28(2):25-64

Mulvaney, D.J. 1975 *The prehistory of Australia*, (rev.ed.) Ringwood (Vic.): Penguin Books

              and J. Golson (eds) 1971 *Aboriginal man and environment in Australia*. Canberra: Australian National University Press

              and E.B. Joyce 1965 Archaeological and geomorphological investigations on Mt Moffatt station, Queensland, Australia. *Proceedings of the Prehistoric Society* 31:147-212

Nippard, A.P. and J.V.S. Megaw 1966 Note on the discovery of a core of 'horsehoof' type at Wattamolla, New South Wales. *Mankind* 6(8):359-62

Poiner, G. 1974 The trial excavation of an estuarine rockshelter at Yowie Bay. In Megaw (ed.) 1974:28-34

              1976 The process of the year among Aborigines of the central and south coast of New South Wales. *Archaeology and Physical Anthropology in Oceania* 11:186-206

Reber, G. 1965 Aboriginal carbon dates from Tasmania. *Mankind* 6(6):264-8

              1967 New Aboriginal carbon dates from Tasmania. *Mankind* 6(9):435-7

Rosenfeld, A. 1975 The Early Man sites: Laura, 1974. *Australian Institute of Aboriginal Studies Newsletter* n.s. 3:37-40

Shawcross, W. 1975 Thirty thousand years and more. *Hemisphere* 19:26-31

Sigleo, W.R. and E.A. Colhoun 1975 Glacial age man in southeastern Tasmania: evidence from the Old Beach site. *Search* 6:300-2

Stanner, W.E.H. 1965 Aboriginal territorial organisation: estate, range, domain and regime. *Oceania* 36(1):1-26

Stockton, E.D. 1973 *King's Table Shelter*. Report to New South Wales Department of National

Parks and Wildlife, Sydney, March 1973

        and W. Holland 1974   Cultural sites
and their environments in the Blue Mountains.
*Archaeology and Physical Anthropology in
Oceania* 9:36-65

Tasmanian Museum and Art Gallery 1975   *Annual
report 1974-75.* Hobart

Thom, B.G. 1972   The dilemma of high interstadial
sea levels during the last glaciation.
Progress in Geography 5:170-246

        and J. Chappell 1975   Holocene sea
levels relative to Australia. *Search* 6:90-3

Tindale, N.B. 1961   Archaeological excavations of
Noola rockshelter. *Records of the South
Australian Museum* 14(1):193-6

        1974   *Aboriginal tribes of Australia.*
Berkeley: University of California Press and
Canberra: Australian National University Press

Tracey, R. 1974   Three minor sites near Curracurang
Cove, with a preliminary note on a rockshelter
at Newport, New South Wales. In Megaw (ed.)
1974:19-27

Wade, J.P. 1967   The excavation of a rockshelter
at Connel's Point, New South Wales. *Archaeology
and Physical Anthropology in Oceania* 2:35-40

Wallace, A.G. and G.A. Doran 1976   Early man in
Tasmania: new skeletal evidence. In R.L. Kirk
and A.G. Thorne (eds) *The origin of the
Australians*:173-82. Canberra: Australian
Institute of Aboriginal Studies

White, C. 1967   *Plateau and plain: prehistoric
investigations in Arnhem Land, Northern
Territory.* Unpublished PhD thesis,
Australian National University, Canberra

White, J.P., K.A.W. Crook and B.P. Ruxton 1970
Kosipe: a late Pleistocene site in the

Papuan highlands. *Proceedings of the Prehistoric Society* 36:152-70

Wright, R.V.S. 1971 *Archaeology of the Gallus Site, Koonalda Cave.* Canberra: Australian Institute of Aboriginal Studies

       (ed.) in press *Stone tools as cultural markers: change, evolution and complexity.* Canberra: Australian Institute of Aboriginal Studies

FURTHER REPORT ON THE KAIADILT PEOPLE
OF BENTINCK ISLAND, GULF OF CARPENTARIA
QUEENSLAND

NORMAN B. TINDALE

South Australian Museum
Adelaide

The Kaiadilt people are grouped as a small
isolated tribe of eight ['dolnoro']¹ or hordes,
with a population of no more than 123 at its
latest peak in the year 1942 (Tindale 1962a,
1962b), who lived for a long time on Bentinck
Island off the southern shore of the Gulf of
Carpentaria (139° 29'E. 17°3'S.). Their lowly
island was formed when cut off from the mainland
by the rise of sea level during the Flandrian
Transgression of post-glacial times, perhaps some
8000 years ago, and the seas around it are still
shallow. In 1802 the explorer Matthew Flinders
made contact with the islanders, but subsequently
these shy and retiring people successfully hid
away while there were several temporary occupations
of adjoining Sweers Island by Europeans and by
mainland Aborigines. In 1949 the Kaiadilt were
induced to move to the Mornington Island mission
settlement.

Bentinck Island has an estimated area of
140 km², or with lesser used outlying islets
and sandbanks, no more than 180 km². The Kaiadilt
exploited the littoral, finding the bulk of their
sustenance within the actic zone of the shore,
spending moonlight nights of low tide in the
gathering of marine products. In the periods of
half tide in daylight they speared fish by
walking about within stone-walled fish traps
and by searching in mangrove-covered muddy bays
and the small estuaries of tidal creeks, often
using rolls of beach vines and grass as crude

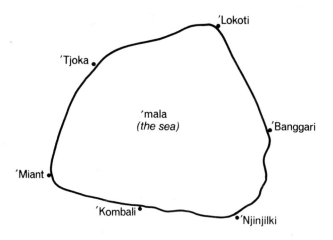

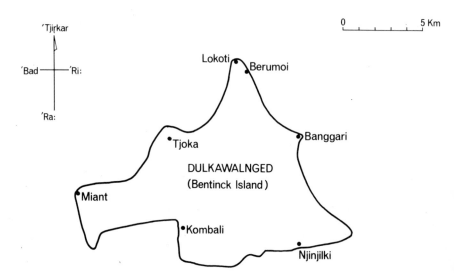

Fig.1. Drawing by Djorangarangati burantant, a 21 year old
Kaiadilt man, showing his concept of his country. Below is
a comparative sketch map of Bentinck Island.

barriers and net substitutes to trap fish. There
is an old stone trap at Njinjilki (Fig.1) near
the small fresh water lake of that name which
Flinders saw in 1802. Men with spears in simple
spearthrowers stood on reefs overlooking deeper
channels hoping to spear a marine turtle or even
a dugong. For the latter, heavy spears of
Tilia wood [ómboroŋk] were used. Their womenfolk
gathered the smaller fish which were left in the
traps as the water drained away, and dug for
cockles which formed an appreciable part of their
diet. *Melo* shell containers were filled from the
meagre supplies of fresh water that seeped from
the sand dune domes at the low-tide margin in
favourable places. Each place was known and
treasured as a prime resource of the horde
claiming the territory in which it lay.

Fig.1 shows a Kaiadilt man's concept of his
country, together with a sketch map illustrating
a few of the place names which he gave when he
drew his map. The population density of this
tribe was high for a food-gathering community.
In 1940, the last year when all the people were
present, and when there were manifest signs of
overpopulation, the density was 0.66 per km^2 of
land and reef surface. Considering that their
food came to a very great degree from the sea
margins alone, the density in practice was of the
order of 2.7 per km^2. This is one of the highest
known for a living stone tool using people
entirely dependent on foraging for their
sustenance.

Their camps were placed usually just above
the next prospective high tide mark, on sandy
beaches; and their day shelters were under the
half shade of the *Casuarina* trees which define
the inner margin of the beach. Only during the
chill southerly storms of the southeast trade
winds in July and August and the tropical cyclones
which occasionally blow with violence over the

area did they retreat to the higher lands, as
much as 10-15 m above sea level, and to the
somewhat higher stabilised, vegetation-covered
sandhills, there to take refuge in leaf- and
twig-lined pits, covered with whatever branches of
timber and bark or grass they could find around
them. On normal cool nights when they felt the
chill of heavy dews, and on occasions when
mosquitoes were about, they tended to sleep
sitting up, with legs folded, under a personal
tall grass tuft (Fig.2) tied at the top to form
a cone. They used a small smoky fire at the
entrance for mosquito deterrence, or a somewhat
warmer fire against the chill. In temperate
weather, with a steady trade wind blowing, a
roll of beach vines placed to windward was all
that was necessary for sheltering their small
night fires and themselves. On such occasions
they lay usually on their sides, with their
bellies absorbing sufficient warmth for bodily
comfort. A piece of driftwood, the blade of a
raft paddle, or even a small pole, was their
pillow.

GEOLOGICAL CONSIDERATIONS

Evidence gathered during my 1963 expedition
to the island, after publication of earlier papers,
showed former camps, comprising banks of food
shells, in many places at the ancient Three-Metre
shoreline. These could be distinguished from more
recent inland sites, where people had lived within
the memories of my informants and which were still
known to them by name as ones to be used during
times of high seas. At such times the northwest
monsoon winds tend to bank up the sea so that the
general level may rise as much as two metres,
flooding wide areas of claypan and the vegetation-
free lowlands on laterite gravel which cover large
areas of the interior of Bentinck Island.

Best evidence for the presence of the people

Fig.2. A personal sleeping shelter at Njinjilki, May 1960;
scene at dawn.

at an early date was the finding of a crude
bifacial stone tool of *mariwa* type (Tindale 1949,
1962a:286) known to the islanders as ['tjilaŋand],
which was *in situ* in deposits which had been
planed during the mid-Recent high sea levels
between about 6000 and 3800 BP and subsequently
exposed by lateral gully erosion. There is a
distinct probability that the sea, since
Three-Metre times, has reduced some areas by
lateral erosion and undermining of older soft
sediments. While laterite plateau lands are
present, there is also in some places a core of
older Pleistocene or earlier marine sediments. On
Sweers Island to the southeast, the highest point,
with an elevation of 31 m, is an old coral reef
in situ with a superficial covering of more recent

terrestrial sediments at the summit. It was from
this locally considerable elevation that Flinders
surveyed the, to him, bleak prospect of the land
he was exploring. Whether this coral reef is to
be ascribed to a recent elevation, through faulting,
or is the protected result of earlier eustatic sea
levels, or both, must await further research.

Fig.3 is intended to illustrate the hypothetical
former shore of the Sahul Shelf at a time prior to
the Flandrian Transgression. It suggests a reduced
area of mangrove-margined shallow sea or large
lake into which must have fed much of the river
drainage of the southern New Guinea highlands west
of Torres Strait and the many rivers of inland
Queensland, some of these latter with less water
than today. Even so, together with those from
the eastern Northern Territory, they make an
impressive list of over thirty major river systems.

If theories are valid, that during colder
times there was a shift of latitudinal belts of
greater aridity towards the tropics, then the
southern areas of the Sahul Shelf must have been
much drier than at present (cf. Nix and Kalma
1972:84-86) except along the littoral. Such
aridity probably was ameliorated always on the
eastern margin of the shelf because of a relatively
narrow corridor of wetter lands and even patches
of rainforest, such as are today kept alive by
the onshore winds from the Coral Sea impinging on
the eastern coast of the Australian continent.
This would provide a restricted corridor of more
attractive country for penetration, one along
which major invasions of the Australian continent
may have been made by successive waves of people,
such as are suggested both by the distribution
of cultural elements and by Birdsell's (1949)
classification of its inhabitants into Barrineans,
Murrayians and Carpentarians. I recently reviewed
some of this evidence, pointing to a riverine
corridor extending southward along the western

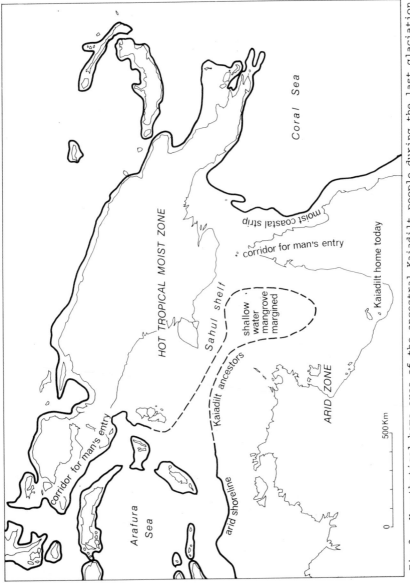

Fig. 3. Hypothetical home area of the ancestral Kaiadilt people during the last glaciation.

side of the Great Dividing Range (Tindale 1974:75
and Fig.24).

SOME EVIDENCE FOR THE ANTIQUITY OF
THE KAIADILT TYPE OF PEOPLE

A possibility exists that the Kaiadilt are
descendants of a very old people who occupied a
niche along the unattractive shores of the Sahul
Shelf as far back as the later stages of the last
glaciation and found refuge on their island by
retreating south as the gradual filling of the
Gulf of Carpentaria proceeded during the Flandrian
events between 10,000 and 6000 years ago. Evidence
for this that can be marshalled is rather
fragmentary at present but when the items are
linked together they seem to point in this
direction.

Physical characteristics

The physical form of the Kaiadilt is
different from that of the people of the adjoining
island, Mornington, situated at the northern end
of the Wellesley group. The Lardiil of the latter
island find them so different that they see little
physical affinity with them, unlike their feelings
for the peoples of the mainland.

The Kaiadilt people differ from all other
Australians, except the folk of two small separate
and isolated tribal enclaves within a range of
about 200 and 400 km, namely the Karawa and the
Tagalag, in the possession of a very high ratio
of type B blood (40%), a type totally absent in
over 98% of the Australian people (Simmons *et al.*
1964). The two exceptional groups may be
considered relict, once sharing fully in the
special characteristics of the Bentinck Island
people but now partly absorbed into the commonality

of the Carpentarian Australians of the mainland
north. The Karawa, who have about 10% of type B
blood, live in a relatively rugged, perhaps
refuge area, north of the Barkly Tableland.

The Kaiadilt also differ serologically from
all Australians in the total absence of type A
blood, which is present throughout the rest of
Australia as well as among the adjoining Lardiil
people of Mornington Island. Serologists who
have analysed the data collected by Peter Aitken
and myself on the islands (Curtain *et al.* 1966,
1972; Simmons *et al.* 1962, 1964) all emphasise
the distinctiveness of the Kaiadilt but differ
in the interpretations of the significance of the
serum and blood findings. A personal analysis in
terms of the possible antiquity of the Bentinck
Island stock is given in some of the following
paragraphs.

Blond hair is a physical trait occurring in
many Kaiadilt boys and most girls. It persists
into late puberty in the case of youths and often
to beyond first pregnancy in the case of women.
In this respect the Kaiadilt resemble the
innermost Western Desert people, whose possession
of a similar blond hair trait has been described
by Birdsell (1950:297-308); Abbie (1969) describes
the same trait among generally displaced Aborigines.
In adults of more mature years the hair is dark,
often almost black, and this colour persists
without greyness well into late middle age and
even later. One woman, Windjarukuarungati
burantan (Sf 13 of my 1960 population list,
Tindale 1962b:322) showed no signs of grey even
at the estimated age of between 60 and 62 years.
Unlike the Murrayian Aborigines, men do not
develop frontal baldness and even in old age
there is no development of the excessive body
hair so characteristic of southern Australians of
Murrayian type. In this character they resemble
rather the Carpentarians and the Western Desert

peoples.

The language of the Kaiadilt seems to be of a type found chiefly in the southern parts of the continent, possibly indicating relative antiquity in a separation between people who drifted to the south and the ancestors of the Kaiadilt who remained in the area near the Sahul Shelf. Some clues appear in the vocabulary, although the study of such is sometimes considered unfashionable.

Take as an example the Kaiadilt word for water. Fresh water, a precious substance, is ['ŋoko], spring water is ['matjiri 'ŋoko]. The base appears elsewhere on the adjoining coast of the Gulf of Carpentaria as ['ŋogo] among the Mara people and as ['koko] among the Nungubuju.

In a southerly direction the root of this word seems to be absent in a wide belt along the eastern coast and west of the Great Dividing Range for 1100 km, being replaced, in the intervening area west of the Divide, by words like ['kamu] to the east and ['kwadja] to the southwest.

Then in the south ['ŋoko] reappears, as among the Punthamara of the Grey Range in southwestern Queensland, as ['ŋoka] and thereafter extends southwesterly among a whole series of tribes for another 1000 km and more, as far as the Tanganekald on the Coorong coast of South Australia, thus spanning the continent with a wide gap in the middle. Some collected versions from the south are:

'noka	PUNTHAMARA	'noko	BARKINDJI	'peroŋuko	NGARKAT
'noko	KULA	'nuko,'nako *also* 'ŋuku	MARAURA	'ŋuke	JARILDEKALD
'nok:o	NAUALKO	'ŋuk:o *and* 'ŋok:o	NGAIAWANG	'peraŋoke *and* 'peramu'kui	TANGANEKALD
				'ŋu'ke	RAMINDJERI

The words in the above table are from a list of about 500 which have been gathered from all parts of Australia and from the literature. South of the Tanganekald the term for water, as foreshadowed in the southern tribes, is ['pare] or ['pari]. For the present study the seeming significance is that the Kaiadilt word may be a very old relict one in the north.

In some of the Kaiadilt vocabulary there is obvious resemblance to Janggal of the small Forsyth Island to the west, although the latter speakers, like the Lardiil of Mornington Island, seem in the main, to possess the more rugged and different physical form approximating that of the Murrayian of the south. Perhaps this implies that an earlier adoption of the Junggal language by Murrayians preceded the present dominance of the Carpentarian physical type in areas extending widely along the coastal areas of Arnhem Land and to some adjoining inland areas of the Northern Territory.

Division of territory

The territorial subdivision of the Kaiadilt tribe is into eight *dolnoro* or clan-like groups, with rather strict territorial limits to each. The senior man in each *dolnoro* was recognised as the ['dolnorodaŋka] or leading man. This man claimed the right to a share of all major food items, especially dugong and turtle, taken within the recognised area of his *dolnoro*, the limits of which extended out to sea as far as it was possible to gather food at lowest tides. He also claimed rights to all the mineral deposits of implement stone, pipeclay and red ochre. Fig.4 shows the younger brother of the *dolnorodangka* of the northernmost *dolnoro* on the island standing on the outcrop of jasperoid rocks which are his to exploit. It is at Bandaro, near the spring on the beach at Berumoi (Fig.1). Inland, beyond the

Fig.4. Outcrop of jasperoid rock at Bandaro, 1.6 km south of
the northern tip of Bentinck Island;   source of *tjilangand* fist
axes and stone hammers, and held by the local *dolnorodangka*.

fixed sand dunes, there is a deposit of the best
red ochre available on the island.

    The *dolnorodangka* seems to have more authority
than is generally the case in other Australian
tribes, wherein it is difficult to define any
regular form of chieftainship.

Social organisation and customs

    The social organisation of the Kaiadilt
differs very markedly from any on the adjoining
islands and the nearby parts of the mainland,
within a radius of more than 1000 km. There are
no signs of a class (section) system. Instead
their marriage arrangements are governed by
kinship terms, much like the southern inhabitants

of the Western Desert, for example the Pitjandjara
(Tindale 1972). However unlike them, there seems
to be no formal distinction between generations.
Instead there are names for the various types of
marriage, with close ones considered undesirable,
and more distant ones considered good. Limitations
in the supply of women at any given time seem to
have led to expedient marriages of several types,
in addition to the 'best'. The cited ideal
marriage was one where a girl infant, who stood
in the classificatory position of mother's
mother's brother's daughter's daughter to the
adult prospective bridegroom, was placed on his
lap in a ritual gesture of coitus. Henceforth
he would nurse her from time to time, until she
was beyond puberty. During this period he would
provide her parents with food and other gifts,
ostensibly for the growing child.

Since the removal of the Kaiadilt to
Mornington Island they have been attempting,
rather unsuccessfully, to relate their system to
that of the Lardiil, who do use class (section)
terms.

Although the Kaiadilt practise a form of
circumcision and subincision on their young males,
like many Australians to the south and west, these
are not secret rites associated with exclusively
male ceremonial activities, as is universal on
the mainland. Instead they are open surgical
procedures, in which women take an active part
along with the men.

The Kaiadilt recognise the primary dominance
of the moon on their lives, linking it with the
tides, whose ebbs at neap and king times govern
most of their activities as food gatherers. At
first sight of ['Balundein] or ['Baludein], the
new moon each month, they address it, enumerating
their needs for lower than ever tides to expose
outer reefs where special shellfish and other

foods may be obtained. They demand the absence
of night fogs, which frequently make night
excursions, far from the shore, more than
hazardous. They also appeal for bright moonlight
to help them on their way. The greatest neap
tides occur during the hours of darkness in the
Gulf, emphasising their dependence on the favours
of the moon.

It may be significant that on neighbouring
Mornington Island it is highly improper for anyone
to notice the new moon, or even to look in its
direction.

Technology

The Kaiadilt still retain knowledge of the
making and use of a crude form of one of man's
most ancient stone tools, the *tjilangand* bifacial
fist-axe (Figs 5 and 6). These, together with
simple stone flakes and fist-axe-profiled shell
knives, known to them as ['nara], and stout half
cockle shells, comprise their cutting tool kit.
As shown in Figs 5 and 6, another piece of
jasperoid rock forms a hammer with which the
tjilangand is made, and the sole of the foot may
constitute a convenient support for the implement
during manufacture. Principal uses of the
tjilangand include the trimming of the driftwood
poles used for their rafts, the cutting of shorter
lengths of hardwood in the making of weapons such
as throwing clubs, and old ones may serve for
hammering oysters off rocks. In the latter use,
a short sharp-pointed stick is held in the same
hand as the stone so that after the oyster is
opened a flick of the stick shoots the oyster
flesh into the *Melo* shell dish supported in the
other hand, along with the burning bark torch
which helps to light the way of the woman as
she gathers her food in the soft light of the
moon.

Figs 5,6. Tadulkingati matali, the oldest living Kaiadilt man,
aged 60 years, making a *tjilangand* fist axe, June 1963.

Nara knives are made from stout pieces of *Melo diadema*, the baler shell. Such shells are shaped with the teeth to produce the proper edge for cutting and scraping (Fig.7). In practice a pad of paperbark or hammered *Eucalyptus* bark is folded over the edge to be trimmed. This seems to prevent injury to the teeth by jarring. Fig.8 shows a *nara* and the method of using it to trim the surface of a mangrove stem in the making of a paddle for a raft. For clarity, the bark wrappings around the handle end, sometimes dispensed with, are omitted from the drawing.

Fig.7. Cutting edge of a prospective *nara*, of *Melo diadema* shell, being nibbled. A strip of bark is used to avoid jarring of the teeth. Minakuri, Bentinck Island, Kaiadilt tribe, May 1960.

Women use massive Crassatellid cockle shells, which are commonly found in mangrove swamps, as domestic knives and as scrapers for fish. The distal edge of the cockle shell serves as knife

'Nara knife

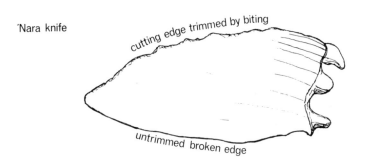

cutting edge trimmed by biting

untrimmed broken edge

Melo diadema shell knife as used in trimming a paddle

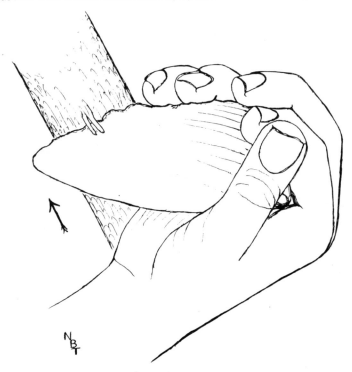

Fig.8. *Nara*, and mode of use by thrusting away and to the left when trimming the shaft of a paddle, *bilir*, of mangrove wood. Bentinck Island, Kaiadilt tribe.

and the hinge and end may be wrapped in bark as
handle or cushion for the hand, if much work is
to be done. The shells and the knives, both known
as ['tubalt], were seldom trimmed in any fashion.
Archaeological ones are often characterised by
signs of wear or injury on the cutting edge.

Archaeologically, a single *karta*-like
implement (Tindale 1937:48, 1968:635-6; Mulvaney
1961:67-9) of local jasperoid rock (Fig.9), well

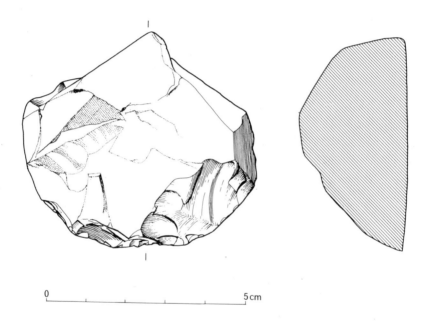

0   5cm

Fig.9. *Karta* or *kodja* axe-like jasperoid implement from Berumoi
Spring, north end of Bentinck Island. Archaeological specimen
A.55483 in South Australian Museum.

trimmed on the part which would have not been
concealed under the hafting, was found beside
Berumoi Spring. In many ways the specimen reminds
one of the *kodja* axe heads found on the south
coast of Australia, as archaeological examples,
and still in use in parts of Australia west of

the Great Australian Bight with blackboy resin joining them to sharpened stick handles (Tindale 1950; Mulvaney 1969:92-3). Sticks of hardwood used as the handles there would match exactly with the ones used in gathering oysters at the other end of the continent. In Western Australia their purpose was however, different, since they helped a man in gaining a purchase by being driven into the bark of trees when the user of the *kodja* was climbing.

In their technology the Kaiadilt differ in one important aspect from the Aborigines of the more southern parts of Australia. When working with their simple tools, *tjilangand* fist-axes and *nara* knives, they tend to push their implements away from them, sometimes with a tendency to move from right to left as they work (Fig.8). In this regard they differ from the main body of Australians, who tend always to pull their stone tools towards them, whether it be a resin-hafted chisel of *tula* or of *kandi* type, a horsehoof-like core implement held in the hand as an adze, maul or chopping tool, as in the Western Desert, a *tjimbila* bifacial knife, or even the round-pointed woman's knife, used as a scraper and, turned over, often employed as a form of spatula or flat spoon (cf. O'Connell 1974).

The difference between 'pullers' and 'pushers' has not been appreciated in Australian anthropology, but is quite as fundamental as the difference between the Japanese pull saw and pull plane and the European pushing tools of similar breed. My attention was first drawn to this difference when observing the method used by the Ingura of Groote Eylandt of pushing a stone *leilira* knife which they called ['uladjaria] (Tindale 1925:95, 124 and Fig. 41a), for they also are pushers, but the significance of their actions was not then fully appreciated.

Absent from the Kaiadilt kit are all the more specialised stone tools so characteristic of

mainland Australia; the hafted *juan* knives
(Tindale 1957:17-22; Mulvaney 1961:75-9), as well
as the bifacial projectile points, known widely
in northwestern Australia as *tjimbila* but traded
widely across the Western Desert to serve as
knives for circumcision rites, as among the Nakako
and the Pitjandjara, Ngadadjara and Jangkundjara
(Tindale 1974:82-3). Absent also are the resin-
hafted chisels, whether the simpler flaked
discoidal *kandi* type, common in the Western Desert
(Tindale 1965:133-9, 152-4), or the more
sophisticated *tula* (Mulvaney 1969:72-4, 113-6,
plates 21-2). None of the microlithic crescents
and triangular implements, one form of which
survived into the present day in the Birdsville
area of western Queensland as an engraving tool
(Tindale 1945), are known.

At first I was puzzled by the seeming
absence of the large discoidal flake implements
which are so characteristic of the Tartangan
culture phase (Tindale 1957:9-16) wherever it
occurs in Australia, from perhaps 20,000 years ago
down to about 5500 BP in the lower Murray Valley
and up to modern times in Tasmania. They also
remain an element in the cultures of the Western
Desert, being still a working tool among the Nakako,
but relegated to a ritual function linked with
circumcision among the Mangala, Njamal and
Indjibandi of Western Australia, where survival
of the resin-hafted tool has probably depended on
the highly secret role it has in the initiation of
young men. They are known among the Mangala as
jimari (Tindale 1957:13) whereas in the eastern
parts of the desert they are *tjimari*, a term
which in places further north sometimes appears
as a general term for other kinds of cutting tools,
presumably the term having survived the transformation
in the styles of cutting tool. On further study it
seemed likely that the Kaiadilt, having never left
the shorelines of the Sahul Shelf, have always had
at their command the large swamp and mangrove

shells which are of the same general shape as the
jimari and provide the same range of services.
They had no need to make a substitute in stone.

Summary

It appears that the Kaiadilt have long been
removed from the main currents of culture change
in the rest of Australia. There were traces of
foreign visitors, as recorded by Flinders, and
Flinders' own visit is remembered in mythic form,
along with stories of a being called *Katjuruku*
who came up an estuary north of Tjoka (Fig.1) and
swallowed an unwary member of the tribe, took
him by way of the south coast to an anchorage on
the northern tip of Sweers Island and there, after
some time, released him unharmed. While we were
on Sweers Island with our Kaiadilt companions,
they took us to the remembered camp of the mainland
Aborigines who had accompanied white men on a
temporary visit or period of occupation there. One
of them picked up the wooden remains of a
boomerang, a weapon which they knew, and also a
single unifacial *leilira* knife blade made from
quartzite found near Redbanks. To the Karawa,
in whose territory the mines are situated and
who have used them up to the present day, they
are ['kulunja] (Tindale 1974:122) and ['babakana]
when traded to Mornington Island. McCourt (1975:
112) figures two very representative specimens
in colour. His name *kulunga* for them should be
interpreted as *kalundja* or, as told to me by a
Karawa man, *kulunja*. The Bentinck Island men
denied that they had ever used such a knife.

THE PREHISTORY OF THE ANCESTORS
OF THE KAIADILT

The Kaiadilt people of today possess only a
minimal aid to navigation, namely a raft of

driftwood poles lashed together to form an
elongated triangular craft, with the small ends of
the poles pointed in the one direction. A bed of
dried grass called a ['walpu] may be placed over
the poles and provide a relatively dry ride when
the sea is calm. The craft can be propelled
laboriously with a paddle ['walpu bilir] (Fig.10).

Fig.10. *Walpu* or raft, of lashed-together poles, overlaid with
grass, being paddled at Njinjilki, Bentinck Island, Kaiadilt
tribe, June 1963.

This implement serves chiefly to propel the craft
out to where a tidal current can be found to
assist in riding from one island to the next.
Such rafts become waterlogged after a few hours
of immersion and have to be hauled up and dried
out. The two-strand ropes which hold the poles
together tend to chafe rather readily and break in
choppy seas. Hence every raftsman wears a belt
formed of coils of the rope, wound around his

middle, against time of need.

Navigation over distances of even a few kilometres was hazardous and mortality could be high when sudden emergencies arose, as on two well recorded occasions of hastily planned flight after combat on the island, involving voyages to Allen Island, a distance of 13 km (Tindale 1962b:310). On both occasions there were drownings, at casualty rates of 20% and 74%, among the 15 and 19 persons, respectively, who commenced the voyages.

Unless the equipment such as the Kaiadilt use is an impoverished one, due to the lack of suitable floatable timbers in their relatively sterile and arid environment, their ancestors may have been able to make the passage from the Sunda to the Sahul Shelf lands only during some cold phase of the last glaciation when sea levels were low enough to reduce to a minimum the water gaps between the islands bridging the space between the Asiatic and Australian continents, and even then such barriers would have been formidable (Birdsell this volume). Assuming that the greater part of the northwestern coast of Australia was drier and more inhospitable than it is now around 18° S.Lat. it may have been even less able to provide floatable timbers for rafts than today, where none occurs along 1000 km of west Australian coastline south of King Sound, western Kimberley. Along the presumably shallow mangrove-lined shores of the then minimal forerunner of the Gulf of Carpentaria, there would have been small chance of sea-borne coastal movements towards the southwest. Remaining in their littoral environment, even as it extended further eastward and south, they might have kept apart from other migrants, who, passing along the northern side of the Gulf area, took more favourable routes near to the eastern margin of their new home, and thus found their way down the aforementioned riverine corridor leading south into the eastern heart of Australia.

To sum up, it is not possible at this time to
do more than point to some of the many interesting
problems facing the anthropologist, ethnographer
and archaeologist in Australia. Whereas a
generation ago it was difficult to convince anyone
that man had a past in Australia, we now know he
has been on the Australian continent since well
back in the last glaciation, and that there is
still much to be learned about him and about his
forebears on the Sunda side of the region. We
are faced with a dilemma that there is no positive
evidence to identify the Kaiadilt with any
particular people in Sundaland, and it seems
likely that none live there today. Is there a
possibility that the Kaiadilt may be the
relatively unmixed and unaltered descendants of a
Wadjak-like people who once foraged widely along
the shores and reefs of Southeast Asia and
Sundaland?

It is suggested that the ancestors of the
Kaiadilt represent a type that has stood apart
from the general flow of people who, over 50,000
years and more, have entered into Australia and
today are represented as admixtures of the three
basic types, Barrinean, Murrayian and Carpentarian,
and perhaps even a fourth, the Western Desert
type. Even over the past thousands of years since
the coldest days of the Ice Age they have not
mixed enough either to learn other ways of tool
making or to have lost their special physical
characteristics. I believe that their earlier
home, after they first landed on the Australian
continent, was along the southern littoral of the
ever-expanding Gulf of Carpentaria, as indicated
in Fig.3. In the immediate past of this century
the Kaiadilt were making their last stand on
Bentinck Island, a sterile remnant of their former
domain.

FOOTNOTE

1 When placed in square brackets Kaiadilt and
   other Aboriginal words are indicated to be
specific tribal terms, spelled out in the
International Phonetic Alphabet. Terms which have
been adopted (or should be) as general descriptive
terms by anthropologists are shown in italics.

REFERENCES

Abbie, A.A. 1969 *The original Australians.*
     London: Muller

Birdsell, J.B. 1949 Racial origins of the extinct
     Tasmanians. *Records of the Queen Victoria
     Museum, Launceston* 2(3):105-22

                    1950 Some implications of the
     genetical concept of race in terms of spatial
     analysis. *Cold Spring Harbor Symposia on
     Quantitative Biology* 15:259-314

Curtain, C.C., N.B. Tindale and R.T. Simmons 1966
     Genetically determined blood protein factors
     in Australian Aborigines of Bentinck,
     Mornington and Forsyth Islands and the mainland,
     Gulf of Carpentaria. *Archaeology and Physical
     Anthropology in Oceania* 1:74-80

                    , E. van Loghem, H.H. Fudenberg,
     N.B. Tindale, R.T. Simmons, R.L. Doherty and
     G. Vos 1972 Distribution of the immunoglobulin
     markers at the IgG1, IgG2, IgG3, IgA2, and
     κ-chain loci in Australian Aborigines:
     comparison with New Guinea populations.
     American Journal of Human Genetics 24:145-55

McCourt, T. 1975 *Aboriginal artefacts.* Adelaide:
     Rigby

Mulvaney, D.J. 1961 The Stone Age of Australia.
     Proceedings of the Prehistoric Society 27:56-107

1969 *The prehistory of Australia.*
London: Thames and Hudson

Nix, H.A. and J.D. Kalma 1972 Climate as a dominant
control in the biogeography of northern
Australia and New Guinea. In D. Walker (ed.)
*Bridge and barrier: the natural and cultural
history of Torres Strait*:61-91. Canberra:
Australian National University, Research School
of Pacific Studies, Department of Biogeography
and Geomorphology, Publication BG/3

O'Connell, J.F. 1974 Spoons, knives and scrapers:
the function of *yilugwa* in central Australia.
Mankind 9(3):189-94

Simmons, R.T., N.B. Tindale and J.B. Birdsell 1962
A blood group genetical survey in Australian
Aborigines of Bentinck, Mornington and Forsyth
Islands, Gulf of Carpentaria. *American Journal
of Physical Anthropology* 20:303-20

, J.J. Graydon and N.B. Tindale 1964
Further blood group genetical studies on
Australian Aborigines of Bentinck, Mornington
and Forsyth Islands and the mainland, Gulf of
Carpentaria, together with frequencies for
natives of the Western Desert, Western
Australia. *Oceania* 35(1):66-80

Tindale, N.B. 1925 Natives of Groote Eylandt and
of the west coast of the Gulf of Carpentaria.
Records of the South Australian Museum 3:61-134

1937 Relationship of the extinct
Kangaroo Island culture with cultures of
Australia, Tasmania and Malaya. *Records of
the South Australian Museum* 6(1):39-60

1945 Microlithic mounted stone
engraver from western Queensland. *Queensland
Naturalist* 12(5):83-4

1949 Large biface implements from
Mornington Island, Queensland, and from south
western Australia. *Records of the South
Australian Museum* 9(2):157-66

1950   Palaeolithic *kodj* axe of the
Aborigines and its distribution in Australia.
Records of the South Australian Museum 9(3):
257-74

1957   Culture succession in southeastern Australia from late Pleistocene to the
present. *Records of the South Australian
Museum* 13(1):1-49

1962a   Geographical knowledge of the
Kaiadilt people of Bentinck Island, Queensland.
Records of the South Australian Museum 14(2):
259-96

1962b   Some population changes among
the Kaiadilt people of Bentinck Island,
Queensland. *Records of the South Australian
Museum* 14(2):297-336

1965   Stone implement making among
the Nakako, Ngadadjara and Pitjandjara of the
Great Western Desert. *Records of the South
Australian Museum* 15(1):131-64

1968   Nomenclature of archaeological
cultures and associated implements in Australia.
Records of the South Australian Museum 15(4):
615-40

1972   Pitjandjara.   In M.G. Bicchieri
(ed.) *Hunters and gatherers today*:217-68.   New
York: Holt, Rinehart and Winston

1974   *Aboriginal tribes of Australia.*
Berkeley: University of California Press and
Canberra: Australian National University Press

SEA LEVELS AND COASTS

J. CHAPPELL
Department of Geography
Australian National University

and

B.G. THOM
Department of Geography
Faculty of Military Studies
RMC Duntroon
Royal Military College Duntroon

INTRODUCTION

Quaternary sea level changes are important in the ecologic history of the Sahul-Sunda region, and are especially significant for human prehistory. Consequences of glacio-eustatism can be gauged, in a static sense, from the fact that many sea passages in the region were substantially narrowed during glacial low sea levels, and, in a dynamic sense, by the high rates of shoreline migration across broad shelves of the region during transgressions and regressions. Thus, not only did the distances across which men must have voyaged change considerably, but also the ecology of coastal lands must have varied between times of eustatic rise and eustatic fall. Shoreline migration rates ranged up to several hundred metres laterally per 10 years, which must place significant stress on littoral and near-shore biota.

Glacio-eustatic changes over the last 130,000 years are now sufficiently known for mean coastal position to be estimated for any 5000 year epoch. For the period 130,000 to 240,000 the same is becoming possible for any 10,000 year epoch. This level of precision seems adequate for most palaeogeographic questions currently being asked, for times beyond about 20,000 years BP. However

questions entailing a finer level of detail arise
when we approach the Holocene Period, where the
archaeology of prehistoric man is more detailed
and where pace of identified cultural change is
accelerating. In the sea level context, such finer
scale questions are to do with changing dimensions
of islands, detailed variations of coasts, and
changes of near-coastal waterways. It becomes
necessary to analyse cases individually, as there is
no reason to believe that different regions have
experienced identical changes of Holocene sea level.

BROAD SCALE EUSTATISM OVER LAST 250,000 YEARS

Discounting vertical crustal movements in
tectonically active zones and glacio-isostically
rebounding areas, the globe as a whole has
experienced similar glacio-eustatic changes. The
amplitude of these changes varies globally, due to
hydro-isostatic effects (Walcott 1972; Chappell
1974a) and near the glaciated regions themselves is
further influenced by gravitational potential of the
icecaps (Farrell and Clark in press). Evidence for
the eustatic patterns come from two principal
sources, being flights of raised coral reefs and
δo^{18} changes in deep sea cores. Flights of coral
reef terraces in New Guinea, Barbados, the Ryukyu
Islands, and Timor record successive marine
transgressions and regressions. Radiometric dating
by Th^{230}/U^{234} shows that these fluctuations
occurred synchronously in all four places. The
islands are tectonically rising and uplift rate in
each case is estimated from the elevation of the
120,000 year old reef. This is an internationally
accepted datum for the last interglacial climax,
when sea level is estimated to have stood between
5 and 8 metres above the present (see reviews by
Bloom *et al.* 1974; Chappell and Veeh in press).
The glacio-eustatic changes are estimated by sub-
tracting tectonic uplift from the coral terrace

records of transgressions and regressions. Results
compare closely between the four cases. The New
Guinea record is the most complete, and is the
basis of Fig.1, which is the curve published
earlier (Chappell 1976) slightly modified by more
recent data of Chappell and Veeh (in press).
Reinforcing data with less resolution come from
δO^{18} analysis of deep sea cores, performed
principally by Shackleton and Opdyke (1973) and
Emiliani (1966). Relationships between these and
the coral reef records are explained by Chappell
(1974b).

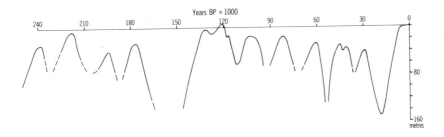

Fig.1. Sea level changes for the last 250,000 years (from
Chappell 1976; see also Chappell and Veeh in press).

As indicated above, the magnitude of these
glacio-eustatic fluctuations varied globally, due
to isostatic adjustments to the changing oceanic
load. However the Sunda-Sahul region is reasonably
homogeneous in this respect and Fig.1 is broadly
applicable throughout. Differences will arise
between the broad shelves and the islands without
shelves, due to variations of isostatic effects at
ocean margins. These differences must be reckoned
with when examining finer scale sea level changes
during Holocene times, as will be explained shortly.

HOLOCENE SEA LEVEL VARIATIONS

Before the advent of Th^{230}/U^{234} dating, applied
to ancient coral reefs, it appeared that Holocene
sea levels were more easily determined than Upper
Pleistocene ones. Now that the chronology of the
last 250,000 years is accessible, Holocene changes
have become more debated than earlier variations
because limits of resolution sought are much finer.
When shoreline movements of only a few metres
vertically are being considered, the effects of small
earth movements and of wave climate variations are
substantial. In analysis of Holocene coastal
stratigraphies the likely influences of storms are
usually considered, as are tectonic effects in
seismic areas. However, a persistent belief in
global eustatism has often suppressed acceptance of
non-tectonic differential movements. Such factors
include isostatic movements and variations of tidal
range arising from changing coastline geometries
during Holocene times. The belief that coasts
remote from tectonic zones are equal, *vis à vis* sea
level, has led to Holocene eustatic curves being
compiled from data from many different places. Such
curves show oscillations or 'wriggles' about their
main trend with amplitudes of several metres (e.g.
Fairbridge 1961). In contrast other curves have
been produced from dated progradational stratigraphy
in a single area. In many of these cases wriggles
around the main trend have not been detected (e.g.
Scholl *et al.* 1969; Bloom 1970). In other such
cases Holocene oscillations have been claimed (e.g.
Mörner 1971; Tooley 1974; Schofield 1960) although
interpretation sometimes is based on supra-tidal
deposits which do not have a proven invariate
relationship with a tidal datum.

The possible existence of these sea level
wriggles confuses identification of the hydrosphere
surface for any given moment because if rapid
oscillations had occurred then all sources of dating
uncertainty would have to be eliminated for global

analysis to be possible. At present many C^{14} dates
from shorelines in different regions cannot be
compared directly, when resolution within a few
hundred years is being sought, because of natural
variations of C^{14} in ocean waters and use of
different bases for the age calculation, as well as
sample contamination problems (see review by
Mangerud 1972; Gillespie and Polach in press). It
is therefore suggested that the questions about
Holocene sea levels be settled in two stages:
firstly, compile smoothed (moving average) curves
for different areas and explain their differences,
and secondly, examine details of the best documented
records to discover, by correlation, whether any
Holocene oscillations occurred globally.
Illustrative data are shown in Figs 2a and b,
respectively.

    The smoothed curves in Fig.2a are from
continental coasts of Australia, England, Sweden and
oceanic islands of Micronesia and Bermuda. Marked
divergence between these illustrates the point that
Holocene eustatic changes cannot be identified by
compiling shoreline heights and ages from many
different places, even if they are tectonically
inactive. Differences in Fig.2a are mostly
explainable in isostatic terms. The Australian and
Micronesian curves differ by the amount predicted
by isostatic theory, which also predicts the
steeper descent of the Australian curve relative to
those from the north Atlantic region, prior to
8000 BP (Chappell 1974a). The difference between
Bermuda and west England may similarly represent
isostatic differential between oceanic and
continental coasts. The reasons for differences
between the west England and south Sweden curves
are more obscure and may indicate either that
isostatic corrections should be applied to the
English data, or that such corrections to the
Swedish data applied by Mörner (1969) are incorrect,
or both.

These last two curves differ substantially in their unsmoothed original forms (Fig.2b) and illustrate the second problem, of identifying eustatic wriggles about the main trends. The detailed curves show very poor correspondence in both timing and amplitude of minor oscillations. The differences are disturbing because these are two of the most closely documented sequences of Holocene shoreline changes. Such oscillations seem unexplainable in isostatic terms which can account only for divergences of smoothed trends. Whether any of these minor transgression-regression wriggles in Fig.2b are real can be tested only by global correlations. It is noteworthy that no well-correlating sequences in widely separated regions are yet reported, although similarities between their respective curves and sequences elsewhere are claimed by Mörner (1971) and by Tooley (1974). Cook and Polach (1973) amplify this·lack of correlation by drawing attention to non-correspondence between areas of Holocene chenier ridges in different parts of the world and similar ridges in Broad Sound, Queensland.

To conclude this section, it is clear that simple global statements about Holocene sea levels are not possible. Ideally, a history must be established for each region of interest. Failing this, smoothed curves may be estimated after taking hydro-isostatic factors into account, following the principles in Chappell (1974a). Minor wriggles about the smoothed trend cannot be suggested. If these occurred however, it is unlikely that their amplitude much exceeded one metre.

Thus, for the Sunda-Sahul region the basic course of Holocene eustatic change lies between the southeast Australia and Micronesia curves of Fig.2a. The actual course of change relative to any coast will vary with local isostatic and tectonic movements. These can be generalised as follows. For northern Australia with its broad shelves, sea level change

A: Smoothed sea level curves (1000-yr moving average)

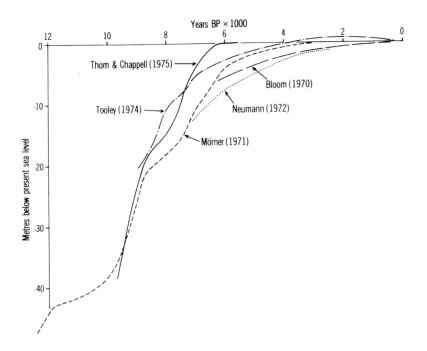

B: Selected detailed sea level curves

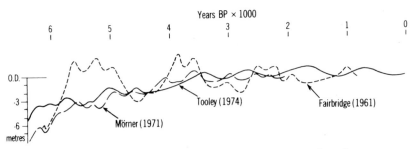

Fig.2.   Holocene sea levels.   Fig.2a compares sea level curves
from southeast Australia (Thom and Chappell 1975), Micronesia
(Bloom 1970), Bermuda (Neumann 1972), Sweden (Mörner 1971), and
western England (Tooley 1974).   The primary curves for Sweden
and western England have been smoothed by taking 1000 year moving
averages.   Fig.2b shows detailed curves of relative sea level
changes for these two countries, again from Mörner (1971) and
Tooley (1974).   The synthetic 'global' curve of Fairbridge (1961),
shown for comparison, must now be discounted.   The problem of
identifying true eustatic changes of small amplitude is apparent.

should resemble the southeast Australian curve, although the highest point achieved by the transgression and the timing of this will vary with regional isostatic movements. A maximum of about one to two metres above present between 4000 and 6000 BP is likely. Islands towards the margins of the shelves may show no Holocene strandline above present due to continuing isostatic depression.

It must be noted that the tectonic islands of the Sunda and Banda arcs are generally rising, as indicated by the existence of raised Pleistocene reef terraces. The distribution of these is reviewed by Katili (1973). Uplift rates have not been determined outside of northeast New Guinea however, except for the north coast of Timor and adjacent Atauro Island, where the rate is 0.5 m per 1000 years (Chappell and Veeh in press). The Holocene transgression will have terminated about 6000 years ago relative to these rising islands, which have been emerging since then.

BIOGEOGRAPHIC CONSEQUENCES OF LATE QUATERNARY SEA LEVEL CHANGES

Sea level changes can be readily translated into shoreline variations. A good approximation to the shoreline at any moment can be reckoned as the bathymetric contour corresponding to sea level for a given moment, as given in Fig.1. This curve is tied at 17,000 BP to a sea level of -150 m; this value for the northern Australian region differs from other parts of the globe for isostatic reasons (Chappell 1974a). In principle, ancient shorelines on broad shelves estimated in this way should be corrected for isostatic flexure of the shelf itself: however the magnitude of the correction in general is no greater than the uncertainty associated with the sea level curve at the present time.

The consequences of changing shoreline geography in late Pleistocene times for prehistoric migrations in Sunda and Sahul have often been discussed (see Birdsell this volume). Possible ecologic consequences in coastlands of very low declivity, which here are the very broad Sunda and Sahul Shelves, have not received corresponding attention. Yet the rapid rates of lateral migration of shorelines - rates around several hundred metres per decade - must have stressed the coastal biota. Whether this imposed significantly different limitations on late Pleistocene human communities on the coastal fringe, as compared with Holocene human activities, is a matter for a kind of speculation for which we are not well qualified. However we shall conclude by sketching possible differences between present coasts and those which may have occurred when transgression and regression rates were maximal.

Given the high mean rates of shoreline migration, the general question arises of the character of the coastal biota and of continuance of various of its compounds. Bearing on the issue are questions of coastal geometry and of the process of migration of different geomorphic zones of the coastal fringe. Specifically these questions are:

1. Were intertidal and high tidal zones so broad that habitats were sufficiently long-standing for elements of the biota to reproduce at their site of growth, or even to reproduce at all?
2. Did shorelines move continuously or in episodes tens of years or more apart?
3. Were there habitats different from those of today and did these affect the sorts of site location for prehistoric human encampments?

A clue to these unknown late Pleistocene environments is furnished by tropical coastal low-lands which have prograded rapidly in Holocene times, such as those described from Broad Sound, Queensland, by Cook and Polach (1973) and from the Cambridge

Gulf-Ord River estuary by Thom *et al.* (1975). In
both areas depositional processes have formed broad
progradational plains in mid to late Holocene times.
Progradation is dominated by deposition of silts
and clays in front of and behind sand and shelly
beach ridges. Episodic development indicated by
the beach ridges may be due to variations in
sediment supply (as demonstrated for similar ridges
in the Mississippi delta by Todd (1968)) or by
minor sea level changes (as claimed by Schofield
(1960) for beach ridges in New Zealand) or by
temporal clustering of storms, perhaps at random.
However sea level has been virtually constant during
deposition (within ± one metre). Thus progradation
is the product of excessive sediment supply.
Stratigraphically the sequence is composed of
intertidal muds and sands, overlain by dark grey
muds rich in mangrove fragments and capped by grey-
brown mottled muds (Fig.3a). The upper mud is
vegetated only adjacent to tidal creeks, estuarine
shores and below high water spring tide level,
seaward of the outmost beach ridge (Cook and Polach
1973:Fig 3). Vast bare high-tidal flats with
hypersaline interstitial waters and localised
evaporite deposits lie landward of the outer
vegetated fringe. These flats stand at about high
water spring tide level. Thom *et al.* (1975) argue
that this elevation and the absence of vegetation
are a function of both sediment supply and duration
of sea level still-stand. Thus in areas of
relatively slow input of fine grained sediment, the
transition from sub-tidal, to vegetated intertidal,
to bare high-tidal requires a still-stand of up to
several thousand years.

During Pleistocene sea level regressions on the
broad shelves of Sunda and Sahul, the sediment
inputs from the land to the shoreface are likely to
be lower than present, because continual regression
of river mouths results in proportionally more
sediment being stored in the alluvial valley and
upper delta. Thus the coastal geomorphology during

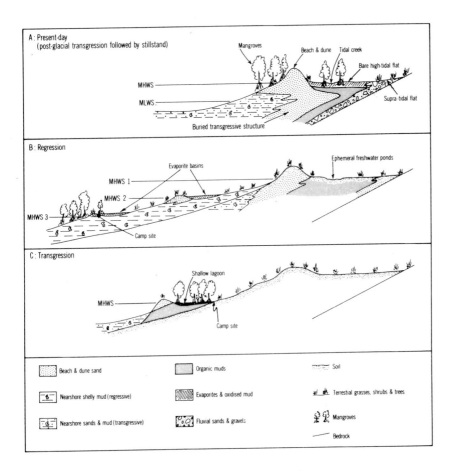

Fig.3. Mangrove coasts of low relief. Fig.3a is a present example of prograding coast in the Joseph Bonaparte Gulf, Western Australia (from Thom *et al*. 1975). Fig.3b is a hypothetical regression case with the horizontal scale several km. Fig.3c is a hypothetical rapid transgression case with the scale comparable with Fig.3a. Vertical scale is approximated by a 6-8 m tidal range, thus all diagrams have a gross vertical exaggeration.

rapid regression will differ from the Holocene case (Fig.3a) because of this factor alone. On the biologic side however, it must be noted that the maximum vertical rate of sea level change of 1.0 to 1.5 m per 100 years is insufficient to prevent

establishment, growth and reproduction of the
coastal organisms, including mangroves. The more
dominant mangroves, especially *Avicennia* and
Rhizophora, are capable of growing in the upper 3 m
of the 8 m spring tidal range in the Cambridge Gulf
(Thom *et al.* 1975). These grow as dense thickets or
forests on newly accreted mud surfaces close to mean
high water level.

Fig.3 compares the present coastal pattern
typical of the Joseph Bonaparte Gulf (Fig.3a from
Thom *et al.* 1975) with the likely case during a
major regression (Fig.3b) and a major transgression
(Fig.3c). In the regressional case, three
sedimentary facies would dominate the shore zone:
nearshore muds, beach shelly sands, and tidal flat
sands and muds. The beachface and nearshore zone
of mud accumulation would have a very low gradient
and between mean sea level and high neap tide level
would be densely covered by mangrove scrub.
Progradation would be periodically interrupted by
storm erosion, which would rework coarser sediment
into beach ridges or cheniers. With falling sea
level there would be no tendency for these ridges to
be rolled back over the tidal flats; instead, mud
flat accretion seawards would promote formation of
new ridges. These would have low relief, with a
broad overwash apron extending onto the muddy tidal
flats to landward. Under rapid regression these
flats would be intertidal and vegetated by
halophytes rather than high-tidal, bare and
hypersaline as the Holocene flats are. Shallow
lagoons are likely within the tidal flats. As these
were left stranded by sea level fall, they would
become hypersaline, and during regression across
the broadest shelves, there may have been broad
expanses of abandoned hypersaline flats. Maximum
biotic production (crustacean, molluscan and fish)
is envisaged seawards of the active beach, and human
encampments, although periodically threatened by
cyclone inundation, would possibly have been best
situated along the beach ridge, as long as it was

sufficiently large to store fresh water.

In the case of a transgression, geomorphic and
ecologic conditions may be considerably different.
Three facies are suggested: nearshore sands grading
into muds well below low spring tide level, beach
washover and tidal delta sands and shelly sands, and
lagoonal muds and tidal flats organic muds. With
sea level rapidly rising (1.3 - 1.5 m per 100 years)
wave action will consistently rework the nearshore
zone, producing a steeper slope. Little or no
mangrove is envisaged on the seaward beach face.
The model of Bruun (1962) relating shoreline position
to sea level rise involves constant beachface retreat
and deposition offshore. We suggest that significant
retrogradation occurs only with a cluster of storms
after a period of vertical accretion of beach and
dune sediment. Lacking protection of seaward
mangroves, sand is swept landwards by storms across
lagoon and tidal flat muds, and a new low-relief
ridge forms with the stump of the old ridge now
being quickly reworked into the new beach face.
Landwards of the re-positioned ridge, muds will
accumulate and mangroves will grow densely where
sediment supply is adequate, and lagoons will occur
elsewhere, which should be well flushed through
active tidal inlets. During transgression a richer
estuarine biota can be expected compared with a
regression, on a seasonally dry tropical coast, as
hypersaline conditions should be absent. Encampments
now are more likely to be on the landward side of
the lagoons and not on the beach ridges, which in
the wet season in particular would suffer frequent
wave overwash. Freshwater stress should be less
acute also, as beach ridges remaining from the
previous regression should lie landwards of the
lagoon and should be shallow reservoirs of rainwater.

To summarise, we have dwelled a little on low
coastlands, because these formed the major fraction
of shorelines in Sahul-Arafura during prehistoric
migration and settlement. The central regions of

the broad shelves are generally of low relief and were occupied by rapidly migrating shores from 120,000 to 6000 years ago. A major fraction of this shore must have been of the periodically shifting beach ridge and mangrove types summarised in Fig.3. Although such coastal fringes have adjacent food resources, freshwater stress must have been high and the environment would have offered little permanence of tenure to early human settlements.

REFERENCES

Bloom, A.L. 1970 Paludal stratigraphy of Truk, Ponape and Kusaie, eastern Caroline islands. *Bulletin of the Geological Society of America* 81:1895-1904

        , W.S. Broecker, J. Chappell, R.K. Matthews and K.J. Mesolella 1974 Quaternary sea level fluctuations on a tectonic coast: new $^{230}Th/^{234}U$ dates from the Huon Peninsula, New Guinea. *Quaternary Research* 4:185-205

Bruun, P. 1962 Sea level rise as a cause of shore erosion. *Proceedings of the American Society of Civil Engineers* 88:117-30

Chappell, J. 1974a Late Quaternary glacio- and hydro-isostasy, on a layered earth. *Quaternary Research* 4:429-40

        1974b Geology of coral terraces on Huon Peninsula, New Guinea: a study of Quaternary tectonic movements and sea level changes. *Bulletin of the Geological Society of America* 85:553-70

        1976 Aspects of late Quaternary palaeogeography of the Australian-east Indonesian region. In R.L. Kirk and A.G. Thorne

(eds) *The origin of the Australians*:11-22.
Canberra: Australian Institute of Aboriginal
Studies

——— and H.H. Veeh in press   Upper
Quaternary tectonic movements and sea level
changes at Timor and Atauro Island. *Bulletin
of the Geological Society of America*

Cook, P.J. and H. Polach 1973   A chenier sequence
at Broad Sound, Queensland and evidence against
Holocene high sea level. *Marine Geology* 14:
253-68

Emiliani, C. 1966   Paleotemperature analysis of
Caribbean cores P 6304-8 and P 6304-9 and a
generalized temperature curve for the last
425,000 years. *Journal of Geology* 74:109-26

Fairbridge, R.W. 1961   Eustatic changes in sea level.
Physics and Chemistry of the Earth 14:99-185

Farrell, W.E. and J.A. Clark in press   On postglacial
sea level. *Geophysical Journal*

Gillespie, R. and H. Polach in press   Suitability
of marine shells for radiocarbon dating of
Australian prehistory.   In *Proceedings of the
9th International Conference on Radiocarbon
Dating, University of California, Los Angeles
and San Diego, June 1976*.   Berkeley and Los
Angeles: University of California Press

Katili, J.A. 1973   On fitting certain geological
and geophysical features of the Indonesian
island arc to the new global tectonics.   In
P.J. Coleman (ed.) *The western Pacific: island
arcs, marginal seas, geochemistry*:287-305.
Nedlands: University of Western Australia Press

Mangerud, J. 1972   Radiocarbon dating of marine
shells, including a discussion of apparent age
of recent shells from Norway. *Boreas* 1:143-72

Mörner, N.A. 1969 *The late Quaternary history of
the Kattegat sea and the Swedish west coast.*

Stockholm: Sveriges Geologiska Undersökning, Årsbok 63(3) (Publication Series C No.640)

　　　　1971　Late Quaternary isostatic, eustatic and climatic changes. *Quaternaria* 14:65-83

Neumann, A.C. 1972　Quaternary sea level history of Bermuda and the Bahamas. *Abstracts of the Second National Conference of the American Quaternary Association, Miami, Florida*:41-4

Schofield, J. 1960　Sea-level fluctuations during the last 4000 years as recorded by a chenier plain, Firth of Thames, New Zealand. *New Zealand Journal of Geology and Geophysics* 3:467-85

Scholl, D.W., F.C. Craighead and M. Stuiver 1969 Florida submergence curve revised: its relation to coastal sedimentation rates. *Science* 163:562-4

Shackleton, N.J. and N.D. Opdyke 1973　Oxygen isotope and paleomagnetic stratigraphy of equatorial Pacific core V28-238; oxygen isotope temperature and ice volume over a 10^5 year and 10^6 year scale. *Quaternary Research* 3:39-55

Thom, B.G. and J. Chappell 1975　Holocene sea levels relative to Australia. *Search* 6:90-3

　　　　, L.O. Wright and J.M. Coleman 1975 Mangrove ecology and deltaic-estuarine geomorphology: Cambridge Gulf-Ord River, Western Australia. *Journal of Ecology* 63: 203-32

Todd, T.W. 1968　Dynamic diversions: influence of longshore current-tidal flow interaction on chenier and barrier island plains. *Journal of Sedimentary Petrology* 38:734-46

Tooley, M.J. 1974　Sea-level changes during the last 9000 years in north-west England. *Geographical Journal* 140:18-42

Walcott, R.I. 1972 Past sea levels, eustasy and
    deformation of the earth. *Quaternary Research*
    2:1-14

PART 3

BIRDS AND BOATS

Denis Diderot put into the mind of one of his dialoguists the thought that has struck everyone contemplating the tiny islands of the Pacific Ocean:

Who put these men there? What communication formerly linked them with the rest of their species? What becomes of them multiplying in a space of no more than a league in diameter? (*Supplément au voyage de Bougainville* 1796:108).

Matthew Flinders posed another question, when on leaving the coast of southeastern Australia which had on it an Aboriginal population, he reached Tasmania also populated, yet between the two in the stormy seas of Bass Strait, were large islands, totally uninhabited:

it was difficult to suppose, that men should have reached the more distant land, and not have attained the islands intermediately situated; nor was it admissable that, having reached them, they perished for want of food (*A Voyage to Terra Australis* 1814, London, cxxxvi-cxxxvii).

Ancient mariners have always held migratory birds in awe. The papers in this section begin with Diamond's development of a biogeographical model, based on the cross-water dispersal powers of birds to colonise islands. The implications of the model for examining human prehistory, touched upon by Diamond, are explored further by Jones, dealing with an isolated population having a very limited maritime technology.

The crucial difference between birds and men which emerges here can be summed up in the word culture. Cultural preference and cultural inheritance of technology and ideas eventually enabled man to loosen the bonds of biological constraint. The third contribution demonstrates how the sea, once mastered, may become an aid to man's evolution rather than a controlling factor. Nevertheless this, as Diamond shows, can be also true of birds.

DISTRIBUTIONAL STRATEGIES

JARED M. DIAMOND

Physiology Department
University of California
Los Angeles

INTRODUCTION

Study of distributions of plant and animal species may be relevant to understanding distributions of human populations for two reasons. At a general level many of the types of questions, methods, models, and concepts characteristic of plant and animal studies recur in anthropology. In some specific situations similar selective forces may have operated on plant or animal and human populations, with similar consequences.

In this article I discuss what is meant by a distributional strategy, what selective forces ultimately determine it, and what properties of a species subject to these forces are the proximate causes of the species distribution. These general considerations will then be illustrated by several types of distributional patterns of Melanesian bird species. Finally I shall mention some human distributional patterns that may be understood in similar terms.

STRATEGIES

When we talk of 'distributional strategy', the root 'distribution' has a familiar meaning: the distribution of a species is simply its pattern of abundance in space and time. The use of the word 'strategy' however, needs some justification in this context. Normally, i.e. in human contexts, a

strategy connotes three elements: the operation of
thought processes, a preconceived goal, and a
weighing of alternative means of achieving this goal
in order to assess which means is most suitable.
Recently ecologists and biogeographers have found it
profitable to discuss plant and animal species as if
they too adopted strategies. For instance a modern
ecologist unashamedly reasons, 'A bird species of
unstable habitats must adopt a strategy of rapid
reproduction'. Or: 'A high ratio of search time to
pursuit time is an optimal foraging strategy for a
predator on large, hard-to-capture prey'.

Until recently, such anthropomorphic reasoning
about plants and animals was considered dangerous
and naive. It is now clear that the language of
strategy is a profitable shorthand for describing
both evolutionary phenomena and behavioural phenomena.
At the evolutionary level species and individuals
vary in their adaptations; the adaptations of some
species (or individuals) permit them to leave more
offspring than other species in a particular
situation; the former species therefore come to
outnumber the latter in that situation. Thus one
can describe evolution as having goals, such as
long survival or large number of surviving offspring.
The probability of achieving these goals is a
function of biological adaptations, which are
analogous to the alternative means of achieving
goals. The weighing of alternative strategies is
made by natural selection rather than by thought
processes. When we say that 'a bird species of
unstable habitats must adopt a strategy of rapid
reproduction', this is shorthand for something like
the following: 'Species and individuals vary in
their reproductive rates. The more unstable the
habitat, the higher is the probability of local
extinction or death due to random factors. Also,
the smaller the population, the higher is the
probability of local extinction due to random factors.
The higher the reproductive rate, the briefer is the
period between arrival of a few colonists at a vacant

piece of habitat and the achievement of a large population size saturating this habitat. Extinction probabilities are higher during this interval than when a large population is achieved. The longer this interval and the fewer the pieces of suitable habitat at any moment, the higher is the likelihood that a species may happen to disappear from all habitat pieces simultaneously. Therefore in unstable habitats natural selection leads to preferential survival of species with high reproductive rates.'

Once one understands that the one sentence about strategy stands for these seven sentences of lengthy prose the language of strategy greatly facilitates discussion. Similar reasoning applies to behavioural strategies of single individuals. When we say that a clam whose shell is tapped closes its shell in order to protect itself from predators, we do not imply that the clam consciously envisions a scenario involving starfish and decides accordingly on a course of action more likely to result in its survival than alternative courses. Instead we imply that the clam's nervous system is programmed genetically (or sometimes in higher species, programmed through learning experiences in early life) and that such programs are closely related to survival probability (Mayr 1974).

The widespread acceptance of the meaning and potential value of strategic thinking in ecology is due largely to the work of the late Robert MacArthur (e.g. 1958, 1972), and has proved a liberating force.

DISTRIBUTIONAL STRATEGIES OF SOME BIRD POPULATIONS

What selective forces ultimately determine the relative values of different strategies, and what types of choices do strategies entail? In general

terms the ultimate determinants of a species'
strategy are the physical parameters of its
environment, such as temperature, light, water, and
minerals; the resource production spectrum, such as
(for a frugivorous bird) the relative production
rates of fruits of different sizes and hardness;
the biological matrix of other species which prey
on, compete with, and feed the given species; and
the fluctuations of all these parameters in space
and time. These selective forces shape the species'
properties which are the proximate causes of its
distributional pattern. Among these properties are:
the foraging technique (e.g. for an insectivorous
bird, whether it catches insects by sallying, .
hovering, plucking, or gleening); the resource
utilisation function (e.g. for a frugivorous bird,
what proportions of fruits of different sizes and
hardness it selects in its diet); the life table,
i.e. the birth and death probabilities as a function
of age; the abundance in the steady-state; the
'fundamental niche', i.e. the values of the above
parameters in the absence of competing species that
utilise some of the same resources or that behave
aggressively towards the given species; and the
'actual niche', i.e. the values of the above
parameters as a function of the competing species
pool.

     To illustrate the meaning of these general
considerations, let us consider some types of
distributional strategies among Melanesian bird
species.

Supertramps

     In the Bismarck Archipelago just east of New
Guinea live two very similar species of flycatchers:
the Golden Whistler (*Pachycephala pectoralis*) and
the Black-tailed Whistler (*Pachycephala melanura*).
Both are of similar size and appearance, catch
insects by similar plucking movements, and occupy
a fairly similar range of habitats. Of several

hundred Melanesian islands that have been well
explored ornithologically, none supports both
species of whistler. Instead, their distributions
form a complicated checkerboard (Fig.1). The two
species often occur to the mutual exclusion of each
other on islands only a few miles apart. In general
the Golden Whistler is found on the larger islands,
while the Black-tailed Whistler is found on small
islands or on islands recently defaunated by the
volcanic explosions and tidal waves that occur
frequently in this part of the world.

The Black-tailed Whistler is typical of a group
of a dozen species called supertramps (Diamond 1974,
1975). Taxonomically these are varied (pigeons,
honeyeaters, flycatchers, a white-eye, a thrush,
and a starling), but all appear to share essentially
the same distributional strategy. They reproduce
rapidly: one pair has been observed to raise six
broods in six months! They do not limit their
reproduction but continue to breed rapidly even
after their populations have saturated an island.
The excess juveniles fly away, often over the ocean,
in search of unoccupied habitats. The supertramps
are not especially well adapted to any one
particular habitat, but instead are moderately
adapted to a wide range of conditions: from sea
level to the summits of mountains, from coral atolls
without fresh water to the perpetually dripping moss
forest, from savannah to rainforest, from open sun
to the deep shade of the forest interior, from near
the ground to the forest canopy. Although supertramps multiply rapidly and become abundant when
resources are abundant, they may be more prone than
other bird species to starve when resource levels
are low.

The supertramp strategy is appropriate to
existence on small islands. Since any plant or
animal faces a finite risk of extinction due to
population fluctuations, and this risk increases
with decreasing population size (MacArthur and

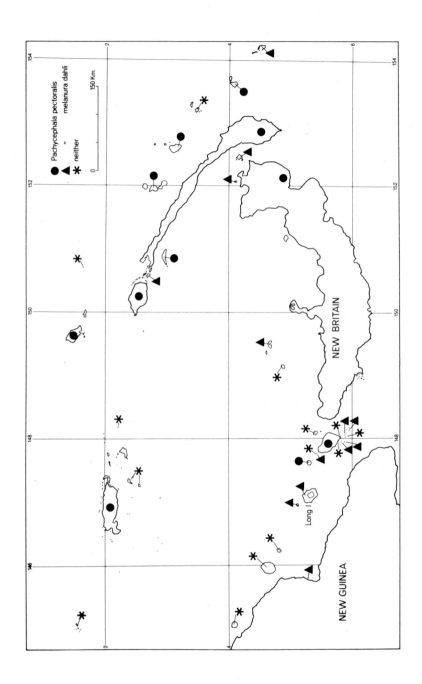

Wilson 1967), populations on small islands go
extinct frequently (Mayr 1965; Diamond 1969). A
strategy for existence on small islands must therefore include three ingredients: sending out many
colonists, so as rapidly to recolonise islands on
which there have been recent extinctions;
reproducing rapidly, so that a recently arrived
colonist pair can quickly fill an island with offspring and reduce the initially very high risk of
population extinction; and maintaining an abundant
population. Supertramps do generate many colonists
because of the rapid breeding of adults and
instinctively programmed dispersal of juveniles,
most of whom are doomed to failure but a few of
whom strike it rich by finding an empty island.
Their rapid breeding also minimises the period
during which a growing colonist population is
smallest and exposed to highest risk of extinction.
The supertramps' abundant populations and ability
to occupy any habitat help reduce risk of extinction
in the steady-state. For the same reasons supertramps are among the first birds to colonise and
fill islands that have been defaunated by volcanic
explosions or tidal waves (Diamond 1974). The
supertramps keep one step ahead of extinction: by
the time another tidal wave or explosion strikes or
another small-island population fluctuates out of
existence, the dispersing juveniles have already
assured the survival of the species by finding
other recently emptied islands. However the supertramps are excluded from larger, older, or more

Fig.1. Checkerboard distributions of *Pachycephala* flycatcher
species on islands of the Bismarck archipelago. Islands whose
flycatcher faunas are known are designated by ● (the overexploiter *Pachycephala pectoralis* resident), ▲ (the supertramp
Pachycephala melanura dahli resident), or ✱ (neither of these
two species resident). Note that no island supports both
species, and that almost all islands with ● are larger than
almost any island with ▲ , except for the medium-large Long
Island, devastated by a volcanic explosion two centuries ago
and recolonised by *Pachycephala melanura* (from Diamond 1975,
with permission of Harvard University Press).

stable islands by superior competitors, as will now
be discussed.

Overexploiters

The Golden Whistler is typical of a group of
species whose strategy is in many respects opposite
to the supertramp strategy. Birds such as the Golden
Whistler raise few broods and regulate their breeding
closely. They are usually habitat specialists, very
well adapted to some narrow range of habitats and
absent from others. They cannot increase their
numbers very rapidly when resources are abundant,
but they manage to survive better than supertramps
when resources are scarce. They are suspected of
overexploiting their resources to gain a competitive
advantage over species like supertramps (Diamond
1974, 1975). That is, birds like the Golden
Whistler may catch insects so efficiently as to
depress sustainable yields of insects, thereby
starving out the Black-tailed Whistler. They may
also devote much energy to aggressive behaviour.
The price however, is that Golden Whistlers cannot
maintain as high population densities as can Black-
tailed Whistlers. In other cases, the dispersing
juvenile supertramps that bombard the shores of all
islands of the New Guinea region are excluded from
the larger islands because of low resource levels
caused not just by one competitor but by a
constellation of competitors, each a habitat
specialist. For instance, the supertramp fruit
dove *Ptilinopus solomonensis*, which occupies all
habitats of recently exploded volcanoes, is replaced
on older islands by the combination of *Ptilinopus
rivoli* in the mountains, *Ptilinopus superbus* in
lowland forest, and *Ptilinopus insolitus* in lowland
second-growth.

I have described the supertramp strategy and
the overexploiter strategy in qualitative terms.
The reader who wishes to see how these anecdotal
interpretations actually emerge from mathematical

models and detailed analyses of community structure
will find such models and analyses in the following
papers: MacArthur and Wilson (1967:Chapter 4) for
analysis of extinction probabilities as a function
of population size and of life-table parameters;
Levins and Culver (1971) and Horn and MacArthur
(1972) for analysis of frequency of occurrence in
checkerboard distributions as a function of
competitive ability and dispersal rates;   and
Diamond (1975) for analysis of the overexploiter
strategy in terms of population growth rate,
resource harvesting rate, susceptibility to
starvation, and capacity for self-regulation of
abundance.

Land-bridge relict populations

An intriguing distributional pattern in many
animal species, and one that was duplicated by the
Aboriginal population of Tasmania (below; see also
Jones this volume), is encountered on so-called
land-bridge islands. During the Pleistocene, when
much water was locked up in glaciers, sea level was
at least 100 m lower than at present. Consequently,
islands that now are separated from a continent by
shallow water less than 100 m deep formed part of
the adjacent continent during the Pleistocene.
Examples of such 'land-bridge islands' are Britain
off Europe, Trinidad off South America, Fernando Po
off Africa, Borneo, Formosa, and Ceylon off Asia,
and Aru off New Guinea.

Ever since the science of zoogeography was
founded by Alfred Russell Wallace (1876),
codiscoverer of evolution with Darwin, it has been
realised that the distinction between land-bridge
islands and oceanic islands (islands that never had
land-bridges to continents) is important in understanding distributions of species that have
difficulty dispersing over the ocean (see
Darlington 1957:Chapter 8, for details). For
example flightless mammals like the rhinoceros,

tiger, elephant and gibbon occur on the large
Indonesian islands that had Pleistocene land-bridges
to Asia, but are absent from islands beyond the
100 m ocean contour. The obvious interpretation is
that these mammals walked to Borneo, Java, or
Sumatra over dry land more than 10,000 years ago
and have persisted since.

Fig.2 exhibits a similar distributional
pattern for a New Guinea bird species, the Frilled
Monarch (*Monarcha telescophthalmus*). This flycatcher
occurs today on all seven of the large islands

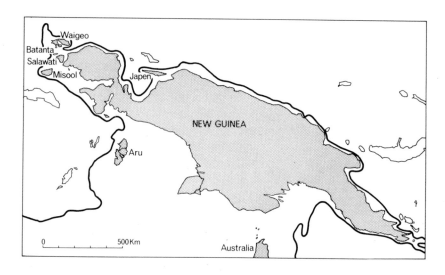

Fig.2. Distribution of the flycatcher *Monarcha telescophthalmus*
(shaded islands). The heavy line is the contour of 200 m ocean
depth, which is very close to the 100 m contour. The whole area
within the heavy line formed a single landmass at times of lower
sea level during the Pleistocene. Thus, present-day islands
within this line are 'land-bridge islands'. Note that this
flycatcher now occurs on every large (>450 sq km) land-bridge
island named on the map, but on no oceanic island nor on any
small land-bridge island, not even ones within a few hundred
yards of New Guinea. The cockatoo *Probosciger aterrimus* has the
same distribution. Both species are capable of normal flight,
and the cockatoo is a strong flier (from Diamond 1975, with
permission of Harvard University Press).

(> 450 sq km in area) that had Pleistocene land-
bridges to New Guinea, but is on no smaller land-
bridge island nor on any oceanic island regardless
of size. Dozens of other New Guinea bird species
are similarly absent from all oceanic islands, and
are present on varying numbers of large land-bridge
islands (Diamond 1972, 1973). For example the
Beautiful Fruit-Dove (*Ptilinopus pulchellus*) is on
four of the seven large land-bridge islands. The
New Guinea Harpy Eagle (*Harpyopsis novaeguineae*) is
on not a single land-bridge or oceanic island and
is confined to New Guinea itself. Virtually all of
these bird species are physically easily capable of
flying to dozens of islands from which they are
absent. The Harpy Eagle for instance, may soar
160 km overland each day in the course of its normal
foraging, yet is absent from large islands a few
kilometres from New Guinea. Most of these species
must have been present on most land-bridge islands
when they formed part of New Guinea. Why are they
now absent from varying numbers of large land-bridge
islands and all small ones? And why don't they now
simply fly to these islands and to the oceanic
islands?

If one accepts for the moment as an unexplained
but given fact that these bird species refuse to fly
across water gaps, then their differing distributions
can be understood in terms of differing extinction
probabilities. A species isolated on an island for
10,000 years runs a finite risk of extinction due to
population fluctuations and environmental catastrophes.
Simple mathematical models (MacArthur and Wilson
1967; Leigh 1975) lead to the prediction that
extinction probability increases with decreasing
population size and with increasing temporal
coefficient of variation of population size.
Extinction probability also increases with decreasing
reproductive potential, since a slowly reproducing
species whose population was reduced by one disaster
may be finished off by a second disaster happening
before its population has recovered. In agreement

with these predictions, most of the bird species
that survived on few or none of the large New Guinea
land-bridge islands fall into one or more of four
categories: species with low population densities
because of large territory requirements (e.g. the
Harpy Eagle); species with low population densities
because of specialised habitat requirements; species
with high coefficients of variation of abundance
because of dependence on spatially and temporally
patchy food supplies; and species of low reproductive
potential (possibly true of most of the species).
On New Guinea land-bridge islands smaller than about
130 sq km practically no bird population survives
10,000 years in isolation, and all species on small
land-bridge islands are derived from recent overwater colonists.

   Similar considerations underlie the differential
survival of mammal species stranded on land-bridge
islands. The best analysed case (Brown 1971) is
provided not by islands in the ocean but by virtual
islands of habitat. Out of the Great Basin Desert
of Nevada and Utah rise 17 mountain ranges whose
upper slopes support pinyon-juniper woodlands now
isolated from each other by the 'sea' of desert
surrounding the base of each mountain. At times of
cooler Pleistocene climates, when the woodland
descended to lower elevations and was continuous
over the Great Basin, small woodland mammals must
have had a continuous distribution. When rising
temperatures drove the woodland up the mountains,
the woodland mammals became stranded on their
mountain tops as on land-bridge islands, and numerous
populations have gone extinct in the last 10,000
years. As with birds of New Guinea land-bridge
islands, the smallest mountain tops have lost the
most mammal species, and the species that naturally
live at low population densities (carnivores, large
species, species of specialised habitats) have
survived on the fewest mountain tops.

   For these small mammals of woodland, dispersal

across desert is virtually a physical impossibility.
In contrast dispersal across a few kilometres of
water would be a trivial effort for most New Guinea
bird species. The failure of so many species to
colonise oceanic islands or to recolonise land-bridge
islands on which populations disappeared must be
due to a behavioural program, about whose underlying
selective forces we can only speculate. Colonising
success depends on many attributes, of which ability
or willingness to fly across water is only one. For
instance colonists must also have high reproductive
potential, or they will be unlikely to survive the
initial colonising phase of low abundance or to
recover from occasional population crashes. If
dispersing juveniles of a species initially varied
with respect to genes that programmed them for or
against crossing water, the relative frequencies of
these genes would come to depend on the subsequent
colonising success of the juveniles. If most
juveniles that flew across water failed to found
successful populations, the water-crossing gene
would be selected out of existence, and the surviving
population would consist of individuals programmed
not to cross water. This may be what has happened
among the land-bridge relict bird species, most of
which are doomed by low reproductive potential to
be poor colonists. In short, behavioural
characteristics, such as the tendency to disperse,
are subject to natural selection, just as are
morphological characteristics (cf. Wilson 1975).

DISTRIBUTIONAL STRATEGIES OF SOME HUMAN POPULATIONS

In this final section we consider three problems
of human distributional strategies analogous to the
cases discussed for Melanesian birds.

Human supertramps

In archipelagoes where many competing species

are present, Melanesian bird supertramps are confined
to small or remote islands and excluded from large
islands. As one proceeds successively eastwards
into the Pacific from New Guinea to the Bismarcks,
then the Solomons, then the New Hebrides, then Fiji,
bird species become fewer. Supertramps then begin
to occupy large islands, because there are now fewer
competitors. For instance the pigeons *Macropygia
mackinlayi* and *Ptilinopus solomonensis* are confined
to small islands of the New Guinea region and the
Bismarcks but are on large and small islands of the
Solomons. The pigeon *Ducula pacifica* is on small
outlying islets of the Bismarcks and Solomons but
is on large and small islands of the New Hebrides.

Among human groups, the Polynesians exhibit a
similar distribution. As far east as the Fiji
archipelago, the people of the large islands are
mainly Melanesians, but Polynesians occur on small
or outlying islands (e.g. Rennell and Nukumanu in
the Solomons and Tikopia in the Santa Cruz group).
At the time of European discovery Melanesians had
not yet reached the more remote archipelagoes of
the Pacific (Samoa, Tahiti, Hawaii, New Zealand)
and here Polynesians settled large islands as well
as small islands. Polynesians resemble supertramp
bird species and differ from Melanesians in at least
one attribute, superior overwater dispersal ability.
It would be interesting to examine just how
Melanesians excluded Polynesians from large islands
wherever the distributions of the two groups over-
lapped. One also wonders whether Polynesians and
Melanesians contrast in other traits distinguishing
supertramps from overexploiters, such as population
growth rate and self-regulation of population. The
analogy may be weakened by the fact that Polynesians
had passed their peak colonising or 'supertramp'
phase before European discovery.

A somewhat similar situation arises in the
straits between New Guinea and New Britain (Fig.3).
Long Island in these straits underwent a cataclysmic

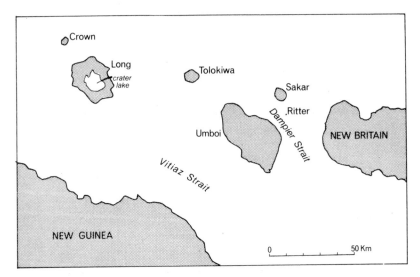

Fig.3. Map of Long Island and vicinity, near New Guinea. The
human population and fauna of Long Island were destroyed in a
volcanic explosion two centuries ago. Birds and man have
recolonised Long mainly from Tolokiwa, Umboi, Sakar, and New
Britain, not from New Guinea, despite New Guinea's proximity
and much greater area. This differential colonisation is not
due to prevailing winds and currents, which reverse direction
twice a year.

volcanic explosion about two centuries ago. The
bird fauna that has re-established itself on Long
Island consists of supertramps plus species from
the Bismarck islands of Tolokiwa, Umboi, Sakar and
New Britain, to the east. The paucity of colonists
derived from New Guinea is striking, since New
Guinea is 20 times larger and several times closer
to Long Island than is New Britain. The explanation
for this pattern seems to be that many New Guinea
species rarely cross water gaps, but that all New
Britain species were initially derived by overwater
colonisation from New Guinea and were thus pre-
selected from New Guinea's pool of superior
colonists. Since the explosion man has also
recolonised Long Island, beginning about a century
ago. As true of Long Island's birds, the human

colonists have mainly come from Tolokiwa, Umboi,
Sakar, and New Britain. Few people have arrived
from the much larger populations on the New Guinea
mainland, clearly visible only 50 km from Long
Island. The people of the small Bismarck islands
are much better seafarers than those of the New
Guinea coast, so much so that Bismarck people were
still acting as the sea-going traders for the
adjacent part of the New Guinea coast until a few
decades ago. It may be that something similar to
the so-called taxon cycle that Wilson (1961)
described for colonising Melanesian ants also
operates for peoples of the Pacific. According to
this formulation, colonists are preferentially drawn
from populations of high growth rate but low
competitive ability, such as populations of coasts
and of 'stepping-stone' islands. After colonists
establish themselves on a large island, they
gradually withdraw into the island's interior and
lose their dispersal ability and high growth rate.
In genetic terms this cycle involves a switch from
so-called r selection to so-called K selection
(MacArthur and Wilson 1967).

Adaptive significance of population self-regulation

Species differ in the extent to which they
self-regulate their population density. We have
noted that overexploiters are thought to self-
regulate much more than do supertramps, and that
the adaptive value of self-regulation is higher in
stable habitats than in unstable habitats.

Humans practise a wide range of customs that
have the effect of limiting population growth, such
as infanticide, sexual taboos during lactation,
restrictions on who can marry whom or on who can
marry at all, etc. In some situations intertribal
differences in self-regulatory practices have been
suggested as being of adaptive significance. For
example Wagley (1969) compared social structure and
resilience in two Tupí speaking Amerindian tribes

of Brazil, the Tapirapé and the Tenetehara. The
latter have survived the shock of European contact
and disease well and are now nearly as numerous as
when discovered three centuries ago. Within 40
years of contact, the former people declined in
numbers by 90%, their social structure disintegrated,
and extinction seemed likely soon to follow. The
technologies of these tribes are similar, but their
social practices related to population regulation
and population density are quite different. The
Tapirapé restrict family size to three children
(not more than two of the same sex), practise
infanticide, observe a complex set of food taboos,
and have a complex ceremonial life that cannot
function in a village of less than 200 people and
that impedes formation of new villages. In contrast
the Tenetehara do not limit family size. Their
social structure makes it easy for groups to split
off and found new villages, and they were even
initially more numerous than the Tapirapé. In
biological language one can describe the Tapirapé
as having low reproductive potential, low resilience
(i.e. ability to recover only slowly from a population
decline), high ability to self-regulate, and
adaptations suitable to a very stable environment
and low maintained population density, while the
Tenetehara tend towards the opposite qualities.
These differing strategies may help explain why the
Tenetehara recovered from the mortality due to
European-introduced diseases, while the Tapirapé
population crashed and did not rebound.

The Tasmanians: a human land-bridge relict population

A human distributional pattern similar to Fig.2
has been discussed by Jones (this volume; also in
Golson 1972:381-2). Off the southeast corner of
Australia is a series of islands that lie in the
shallow waters of Bass Strait and that formed part
of the Australian mainland during the Pleistocene
(Fig.4). At the time of European discovery the only
inhabited islands were the largest one, Tasmania,

plus some smaller islands very close to Tasmania.

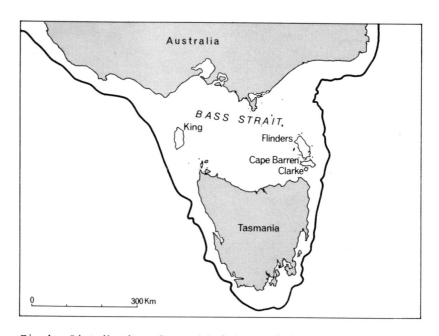

Fig.4. Distribution of man (shaded areas) in the vicinity of Bass
Strait (separating southeastern Australia from Tasmania), at the
time of European discovery. The heavy line is the contour of 100 m
ocean depth. All the area within the heavy line formed a single
landmass during Pleistocene times when sea level was lower. In
modern times native Australians occurred only on the two largest
fragments of this former landmass, Australia and Tasmania, although
there is archaeological evidence of man on the smaller islands in
the Pleistocene. Men spread over the Bassian Shelf when it was
above water, but the populations that post-Pleistocene flooding
left stranded on the smaller islands (e.g. Flinders, King, Cape
Barren, Clarke) fluctuated out of existence or abandoned the
islands, and recolonisation over all but the narrowest water gaps
was impossible. Many animal and plant species (e.g. the Spotted
Quail-Thrush *Cinclosoma punctatum*) have the same distribution, and
presumably for the same reason.

The paperbark canoe-rafts of the Aborigines were
inadequate for reaching more distant, medium-sized
islands, such as Flinders and King. These two
islands have yielded archaeological remains of man
probably dating from Pleistocene land-bridge times,

but not from more recently. The population of
Tasmania itself was at least several thousand, but
the largest of the recently uninhabited islands
could not have supported more than 500 people, given
its area and assuming population densities as on
Tasmania. The obvious interpretation is that when
rising sea levels inundated most of Bass Strait, the
only island on which the stranded human population
was large enough to maintain itself indefinitely was
Tasmania. The populations on the smaller islands
fluctuated out of existence, or else consciously
abandoned the islands at time of land-bridge
severance, and the limited water-crossing abilities
of the Tasmanians prevented recolonisation.

This situation may have been almost unique in
the modern world (but see discussion of Bentinck
islanders by Tindale this volume), since the recent
peoples of other land-bridge archipelagoes had
boats sufficient to permit recolonisation of islands
of which populations transiently disappeared.
However the archaeological record from areas like
the Greater Sunda Islands and the Japanese
archipelago may yield evidence of similar patterns,
existing at times when man's water-crossing
technology was less well developed than it was among
primitive peoples recently extant.

ACKNOWLEDGEMENTS

I thank Drs Sharon Kaufman-Diamond, John
Terrell and Rhys Jones for suggestions.

REFERENCES

Brown, J. 1971 Mammals on mountaintops:
    nonequilibrium insular biogeography. *American
    Naturalist* 105:467-78

Cody, M.L. and J.M. Diamond (eds) 1975 *Ecology and evolution of communities.* Cambridge (Mass.): Belknap Press of Harvard University Press

Darlington, P.J. 1957 *Zoogeography: the geographical distribution of animals.* New York: Wiley

Diamond, J.M. 1969 Avifaunal equilibria and species turnover rates on the Channel Islands of California. *Proceedings of the National Academy of Sciences, U.S.A.* 64:57-63

————— 1972 Biogeographic kinetics: estimation of relaxation times for avifaunas of southwest Pacific islands. *Proceedings of the National Academy of Sciences, U.S.A.* 69:3199-3203

————— 1973 Distributional ecology of New Guinea birds. *Science* 179:759-69

————— 1974 Colonization of exploded volcanic islands by birds: the supertramp strategy. *Science* 184:803-6

————— 1975 Assembly of species communities. In Cody and Diamond 1975:342-444

Golson, J. 1972 Land connections, sea barriers and the relationship of Australian and New Guinea prehistory. In D. Walker (ed.) *Bridge and barrier: the natural and cultural history of Torres Strait*:375-97. Canberra: Australian National University, Research School of Pacific Studies, Department of Biogeography and Geomorphology, Publication BG/3

Horn, H.S. and R.H. MacArthur 1972 Competition among fugitive species in a Harlequin environment. *Ecology* 53:749-52

Leigh, E.G., Jr. 1975 Population fluctuations, community stability, and environmental variability. In Cody and Diamond 1975:51-73

Levins, R. and D. Culver 1971 Regional coexistence

of species, and competition between rare species. *Proceedings of the National Academy of Sciences, U.S.A.* 68:1246-8

MacArthur, R.H. 1958 Population ecology of some warblers of northeastern coniferous forests. *Ecology* 39:599-619

1972 *Geographical ecology.* New York: Harper and Row

and E.O. Wilson 1967 *The theory of island biogeography.* Princeton: Princeton University Press

Mayr, E. 1965 Avifauna: turnover on islands. *Science* 150:1587-8

1974 Teleological and teleonomic: a new analysis. *Boston Studies in the Philosophy of Science* 14:91-117

Wagley, C. 1969 Cultural influences on population: a comparison of two Tupí tribes. In A.P. Vayda (ed.) *Environment and cultural behavior.* Garden City (N.Y.): Natural History Press

Wallace, A.R. 1876 *The geographical distribution of animals.* London: Macmillan

Wilson, E.O. 1961 The nature of the taxon cycle in the Melanesian ant fauna. *American Naturalist* 95:169-93

1975 *Sociobiology: the new synthesis.* Cambridge (Mass.): Belknap Press of Harvard University Press

MAN AS AN ELEMENT OF A CONTINENTAL FAUNA:
THE CASE OF THE SUNDERING OF THE BASSIAN BRIDGE

RHYS JONES

Department of Prehistory
Australian National University

'Life is an offensive against the repetitious
mechanism of the universe' (Alfred North
Whitehead).[1]

Biogeographers have shown that the number of
species on an island tends to approach an equilibrium
position when the rates of immigration and of
extinction equal one another (MacArthur and Wilson
1967). Since the immigration rate to any particular
island decreases the further away it is from the
source of its colonists, and the extinction rate
increases inversely to an island's area, it follows
that small isolated islands have the least number
of species on them, whereas large ones close to a
source of potential immigrants have the largest
(e.g. MacArthur and Wilson 1967; Diamond 1972, 1973
and this volume). Displacement from equilibrium by
some natural event, such as a volcanic eruption
wiping out part of an island's fauna giving an
opportunity for recolonisation, or conversely a sea
level rise 'squeezing' the existing fauna by
reducing the island's area, results in a corrective
trend or 'relaxation' back to the predicted
equilibrium through the differential operation of
the two rates. Such relaxations proceed
exponentially, the highest rates occurring on the
smallest islands (Diamond 1972, this volume).

Continental islands (Darlington 1957) are those
that have been periodically joined to and separated
from their parent continents by glacio-eustatic sea
level changes. The fauna of such islands will

appear depauperate compared to those of their
continents; but unless enough time has elapsed for
relaxation to have been virtually completed, they
will appear species rich, compared to similarly
situated and sized oceanic islands, whose species
recruitment has been effected entirely across water
gaps (Darlington 1957; Diamond 1972, this volume).
This relative richness is however only a temporary
thing, for in the fullness of time, the number of
species will inexorably approach equilibrium which
is a function of the geography of an island and not
its history.

Different species have differential rates of
immigration and of extinction, some having high
powers of dispersal across water, others being
virtually landlocked. The risk of a particular
species becoming extinct on a given island will
depend on aspects of its biology such as its habitat
requirements and patterns of reproduction.
Nevertheless, in the limiting case, for every
species, there is a minimum size of island below
which, given a reasonable length of time, the
probabilities of its survival are negligible.

Taking the philosophical view that man,
behaviourally as well as physically, is an animal,
these biological forces must be operating on him
too, but to demonstrate the fact and to calibrate
the parameters of area, distance and 'relaxation
time' in his case, several historical conditions
have to be met. The men concerned must have watercraft of such limited performance that their
colonising ability across water, is negligible;
they must be participants in the drowning of a
continental shelf where the patterns of final island
sizes and inter-island distances are sufficiently
diverse for the formulation of general statements;
and there must be enough time in the new state, for
consummation of the effects of biological forces.
The case of the postglacial drowning of the
continental shelf south of Australia, fulfilled all

of these conditions. Man is an animal who in terms
of his artifacts leaves within the archaeological
record, investigatable traces of his actions, and
behind them his motives and decisions. Complex
though he is, he is the only one whose behavioural
responses can be investigated in detail in the
past.

OFFSHORE ISLANDS: AREA, DISTANCE AND USE

Men on the distant land

The pattern of human occupation of the islands
south of the Australian continent was a source of
considerable surprise to the European maritime
explorers who charted those seas at the very end of
the 18th century (Fig.1). The fact that Aborigines
lived there was the main reason that southern
Tasmania, originally called Cape Van Dieman, was
assumed to have been a peninsula joined to the
mainland. The contemporaneous expeditions of Baudin,
Flinders and Bass showed that islands lying more
than about 5-10 km offshore were all devoid of man
or his works, a situation which held from Rottnest
and the Archipelago of the Recherche off the southwest of the continent to the large islands of
Kangaroo, King and the Furneaux Group off the south
and southeast (Baudin 1800-1803; Flinders 1814).
On these unoccupied islands, the vegetation was
thick and usually unburnt; kangaroos, wombats and
emus were tame; no smokes rose from the bush and
there were no signs of huts, tracks, artifacts or
middens which were such prominent features of the
continental coastline. Yet Tasmania itself, lying
to the south of all these, was the home of man, and
as Flinders in 1798-9 proved by sailing around it -
was also an island, separated from the mainland by
250 km of stormy seas. How could it be, mused
Flinders, 'that men should have reached the more
distant land, and not have attained the islands

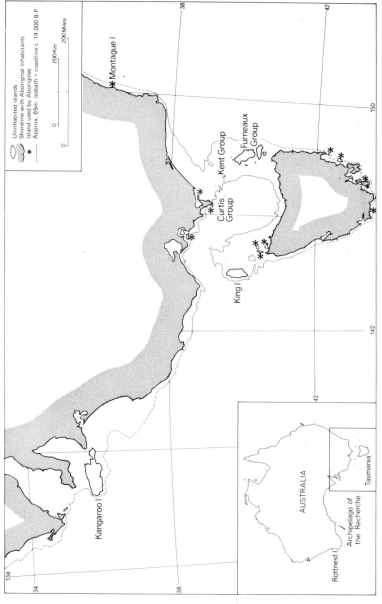

Fig.1.   Map of south eastern Australia and Tasmania showing the differential Aboriginal use of
the various mainland and island coastlines at the time of ethnographic contact.

intermediately situated' (1814:cxxxvi-cxxxvii).

Tasmania, with an area of 67,000 sq km and a coastline of 1700 km is by far the largest of more than 100 islands forming the Bassian archipelago its area being 17 times as large as all the other islands put together (Lakin 1972:40). Some 4000 Aborigines lived there at an average density of one person per 12 sq km, or since the economy of most bands was focused on the sea shore, at a rate of about two people per km of coast[2] (Jones 1974:326). This population was divided between some 75 land owning bands, each consisting of about ten families. The bands themselves were regionally agglomerated into nine linguistic and social units which can be called tribes (Jones 1974:327-30); tribal populations varying from 200 to 700 people (Table 1). The location of the tribal territories and the main seasonal movements of the constituent bands of two tribes is shown on Fig.2.

Tribe	Area (sq) km	Coastline (km)	Ethnographic population (central estimate)	Calculated population $p = \dfrac{A}{19.2} + \dfrac{C}{1.98}$	Extreme range of seasonal movements Km
North West	3,400	550	450	455	400
South West	2,100	370	300	296	400
South East	3,100	550	450	439	160
Oyster Bay	8,500	510	700	700	160
Big River	7,800	0	350	406	480
North	4,700	110	250	300	290
North Midlands	6,700	160	450	430	310
Ben Lomond	2,600	0	175	135	?
North East	5,700	260	450	428	?
TOTAL	44,600[1]	2510	3,575	3,589	

Area = 5,000 ± 2,200 sq km (N=9)

Ethnographic Population = 400 ± 140 (N=9)

Range of seasonal movements = 314 ± 113 kms (N=7)

1 Does not include unoccupied land in the western mountains.

Table 1.   Tasmanian tribes: showing for each the areas and coastlines of their territories, the extreme ranges of their annual seasonal movements and their populations.

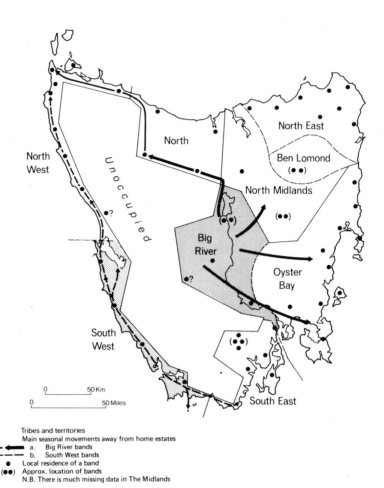

Fig.2. Location of band estates and tribal territories in
Tasmania. The seasonal movements of two of these tribes –
the Big River and the South West are shown.

Performance of Tasmanian watercraft

Tasmanian Aborigines living along the western
and southern coastlines (Fig.3) made watercraft
consisting usually of three bundles of paper bark
(*Melaleuca* sp.) or stringy bark (*Eucalyptus obliqua*),
up to 4.5 m long and 400 kg in weight; each bundle
being bound with a polygonal network of bark fibre

Fig.3. Distribution of ethnographically recorded sightings of Tasmanian watercraft, important river crossings and offshore islands which were exploited. Seasonal movements involving some visits to islands during an annual cycle are shown, together with the resultant 'seasonal catchment' of each island.

Fig.4. Detail from C.A. Lesueur's plate of Tasmanian
watercraft, originally drawn in south eastern Tasmania in
1802 during N. Baudin's expedition. From Lesueur and
Petit 1812 *Atlas* Plate XIV; accompanying *Voyage de
Découvertes aux Terres Australes*, 1807-1816 by F. Péron
and L. Freycinet, Paris.

and grass string, and tapered at both ends (Fig.4).
The central bundle of these canoe rafts provided
most of the buoyancy, the side ones acting as
stabilisers, leaving a well in the middle where
the passengers sat or stood, sometimes warmed by a
small fire held in a hearth of clay. They were
propelled by a long pole or by swimmers pushing
them along (Jones 1976:239-50 for details,
discussion and further references). Tribes in
northeastern Tasmania neither made nor used watercraft, nor could the men swim.

Calculations from specifications within the
ethnographic literature, laboratory tests on the
various materials (C. Turner in Jones 1976:247),
and field experiments with full sized replicas
(Fig.5), have confirmed eye witness accounts of the

Fig.5. Reconstruction of a Tasmanian watercraft made
from *Melaleuca* paperbark at Rocky Cape, 1974.

good performance of these craft in rough, rock-
snagged water and of their carrying capacity,
normally of two or three people but potentially up
to six or seven. Floating high out of the water,
and with inefficient propelling devices, they had
only limited ability to make headway against wind
or current. A further limitation on their
effective range was the fact that when saturated,
the bark had a density similar to water, so that
buoyancy depended on air cavities trapped within
the bark itself. The rate of saturation meant that
after a few hours, a craft tended to lose its
rigidity and thus to wallow like a bundle of kelp
in the sea.

Residential, seasonal and unoccupied islands

On the western, southern and southeastern
coasts of Tasmania, these watercraft were used to

cross rivers and to travel to offshore islands
(Fig.3). Islands with areas greater than 90 sq km
and with minimum water crossings of up to four km,
such as Robbins, Maria, and Bruny each served as
the home estate of a land owning band (Table 2).
Such bands of approximately 50 people had their
home bases on these *residential* islands, from which
they periodically ranged onto the mainland as well
as to other islands; and in return acted as hosts
for adjacent mainlanders paying reciprocal visits
(see Jones 1974 and 1976 for details and references).

Islands of less than 70 sq km in area down to
mere rocks, and with minimum crossings to reach
them extending from less than a kilometre up to
eight km, were visited *seasonally* (Table 2, Fig.3);
the more remote, or those involving the most
hazardous crossings, being handled by specialist
parties of experienced adults (e.g. Robinson,
24 June 1830 in Plomley 1966:183). An island with
a combination of area distance parameters
intermediate between these two classes of islands,
namely Schouten Island, had an intermediate social
use, being part of a band's estate, the rest of
which was on the adjacent southern tip of Freycinet
Peninsula (Plomley 1966:971-3).

Islands involving single water crossings
greater than about 13-15 km, no matter what their
areas - in the case of the combined Furneaux Group
ranging up to 2000 sq km - were never visited; or
at least, no record of any visit has yet been
substantiated (Table 2). The Furneaux Group, with
its 700 m high hills clearly visible from the cliffs
of Cape Portland, was the place to which dead men
went (Robinson, 14 August 1831 in Plomley 1966:400).

If intensity of use, measured both in terms of
residential versus seasonal occupation, and in
terms of visits by the whole spectrum of the
community as opposed to a few of its fittest members,
be considered as a cultural analogue to species

Island and its Type of Aboriginal Use			Area Sq Km	Minimum Cross—Sea Distance Km
A)	**Residential Islands**			
	(i)	Bruny	360	2
		Robbins (and Walker)	110	1.5
		Maria	93	4
	(ii)	Island forming part of a band's estate		
		Schouten	26	2
B)	**Seasonal Islands**			
	Hunter)		73	6
	Three Hummock) N.W.		65	) 4 from Hunter
	) Tas.			) 11 from Tasmania
	Trefoil)		1	2.5
	The Doughboys)		1	1
	Tasman		0.5	1; but nearest practical landing = 8
	Wedge)			
	Betsy) In Storm Bay		1 each	approx. 1 — 1.5 each
	Sloping			
	De Witt)		6.5	6.5
	Flatwitch) S.W.		1.5	) 5.5 from De Witt
	) Tas.			) 8 from Tasmania
	Maatsuyker)		2	) 1.5 from Flat Witch
				) 7 from De Witt
				) 10 from Tasmania
	Green		0.5	1
C)	**Uninhabited and not visited**			
	Albatross		1	10 from Hunter
	Black Pyramid		<0.5	18 from Hunter
	Furneaux	(Clarke	1,890	19 from Cape Portland, N.W. Tas.
		(Cape Barren		
		(Flinders		13 from Swan Island, situated between Clarke Island and Cape Portland
	King		1,100	60 from Tasmania
	Kangaroo		4,400	14.5 Backstairs Passage from South Australia

Table 2. Tasmanian offshore islands: their areas, distances from their nearest neighbours or adjacent mainland and the ethnographically recorded uses made of them by the Aborigines.

diversity, then a glance at Fig.6 shows that the
Tasmanian exploitation of offshore islands followed
neatly what Diamond (1973:760) called the
'fundamental law of island biogeography' that
'species diversity...increases with island area and
decreases with distance from the colonising source'.

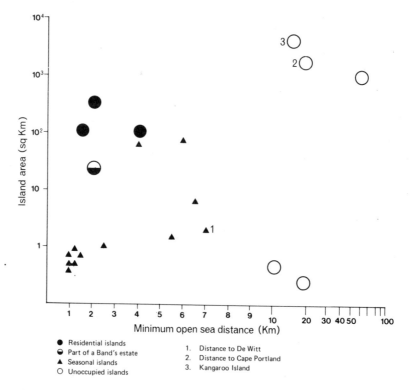

Fig.6. The areas of Tasmanian offshore islands and Bassian
islands plotted against the minimum open sea distances to
get to them, showing that intensity of ethnographic Aboriginal
use of these islands can be related to the interplay of these
two parameters.

On the north or continental shore of Bass
Strait, similar constraints of maritime distance
were exerted on the mainland Australian Aborigines,
some of whom used rigid walled canoes of tied or
pegged *Eucalyptus* stringy bark. Whereas Montague,

Broughton, Glennie and other small islands up to
about 8 km off shore from the coasts of southern
New South Wales and Victoria were visited
seasonally (Jones 1976:256; Sullivan 1975; Wright
1975), those further away such as Rodondo, the
Hogan and Kent Groups in Bass Strait, or even
Kangaroo Island off South Australia, with only a
minimum distance of 14.5 km across Backstairs
Passage to get to it, were beyond effective
Aboriginal maritime technology to reach (Fig.1).
To the Aborigines on the adjacent mainland of South
Australia, Kangaroo Island was 'Karta', the land of
creatures of the Dreaming (Tindale 1937).

Profit and cost of island use

With men and women making voluntary trips to
some of these islands and eschewing others, we are
faced with the sum of a series of decisions made
between the economic attraction of islands and the
cost of getting there. Islands were important
resource areas because they served as breeding and
resting grounds for seals and for birds such as
albatrosses, gulls and the extraordinary migratory
shearwater (*Puffinus tenuirostris*). Also, since
for geometrical reasons the length of coastline per
unit area of an island tends to increase the
smaller it is, even the seemingly insignificant
offshore islands used by the Tasmanians have a
combined coastline measuring some 600 km, excluding
rocks and reefs. The seashore, with its coastal
heaths and lagoons behind, and its rocks and reefs
in front, constituted by far the most important
ecotone within the economy of the Tasmanians. We
can see therefore that even with their limited
capacity, Tasmanian watercraft increased potential
access to this type of resource zone by more than
35%. The role of these islands within the total
economy of the western, southern and southeastern
bands is shown on Fig.3, where it can be seen that
seasonal visits to at least one island formed an
important element in the scheduling of the annual

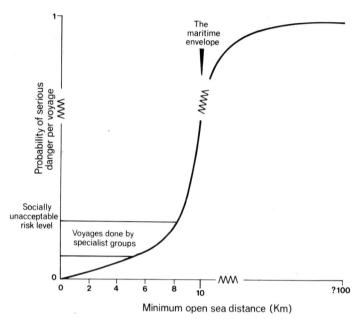

Fig.7a.   A qualitative estimate of the probability of serious
danger per sea trip plotted against the minimum open sea
distance to be crossed.

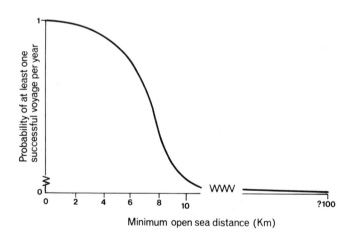

Fig.7b.   A qualitative estimate of the probability of at
least one successful sea crossing per year plotted against
the minimum open sea distance to be negotiated.

movements of most bands in those regions. Some
bands travelled a minimum distance of 150 km from
their own estates to do this (Jones 1974).

Balanced against such attractions, were the
negative factors of effort and danger. The
distributional pattern of Aboriginal use of the
islands, suggests that within the technological
constraints already described, the probability of
serious mishap must have risen sharply as the
minimum sea crossing increased beyond 6-8 km, as
shown qualitatively on Fig.7a. The Tasmanian
literature contains several accounts of
reminiscences of drownings and of accidents with
seals and sharks, whilst making such voyages (e.g.
Robinson, 15 December 1831 in Plomley 1966:554).
On the opposite end of the continent, Tindale (this
volume) has documented that two Kaiadilt sea
voyages of about 13 km each on rafts, resulted in
an average death rate of 50%.

Clearly sane men do not take such risks for
routine economic goals. I am not stating that it
is *impossible* to travel in a Tasmanian type canoe-
raft across the 13 km of open Banks Strait to
Clarke Island, or even in exceptionally favourable
circumstances the 80 km to King, simply that the
archaeological and ethnographic data imply that
this was not in fact done, even over a period of
several thousand years.

The Aboriginal use of the resources of the
shores of Bass Strait thus presents an interesting
contrast (Fig.1). The mainland coasts of both the
continental shore, and of Tasmania itself
constituted major resource zones for the Aborigines
and were thus densely populated, compared with
adjacent inland territories. Out from these
occupied coasts, islands up to about 8 km offshore
were utilised for their seasonally abundant foods.
However, islands in the middle of the Strait,
further away than this, were not occupied by man.

Some of these, such as King with 1100 sq km, the
Furneaux Group with 2000 sq km and Kangaroo Island
with 4400 sq km, were major blocks of land with
rich resources unused by man, because the social
costs of life and effort to get to them were
considered too high for the rewards.

TAKING THE LOW ROAD

Twenty thousand years ago, the road to
Tasmania lay open and dry. Unlike Moses, the
ancestral Tasmanians needed no special divine act
to facilitate their journey; rather the glacio-
eustatic lowering of the sea to about 100 m below
its present level exposed the floor of the Bassian
bridge, the critical sill linking island to
continent lying between the 55 m and the 65 m
isobaths (Jennings 1959, 1971; Jones 1968:197-8;
McIntyre *et al*. 1976; Chappell and Thom this volume).
That man had indeed taken this opportunity to claim
the most southerly, ice-locked knuckle of the
Australian Great Dividing Range, long predicted
(e.g. from Howitt 1904:21-4; to Jones 1968:197-201),
has finally been demonstrated archaeologically in
three recently investigated sites.

At the basal level of her excavation at Cave
Bay Cave (Figs 8, 9) on Hunter Island, 6 km off the
northwest tip of Tasmania, Bowdler (1975b and this
volume) has obtained a carbon date of 22,750 ± 420
BP (ANU-1498) associated with a hearth and artifacts
consisting of quartz flakes.

On Tasmania itself, a limestone solution hole,
Beginner's Luck Cave (Figs 8, 9), situated at an
altitude of 400 m in the Florentine Valley running
south from the Derwent Valley in the south central
mountainous region, has yielded three stone flakes,
two with secondary retouch, cemented in a breccia
of solifluction origin and dated on a charcoal

Fig.8. Map of Tasmania showing place names and archaeological sites mentioned in the text.

sample 12,600 ± 200 BP (R 5001/4 AG 16) (Goede and
Murray 1976; Murray 1976). During the 'ethnographic
present' this region was not occupied by the
Tasmanian Aborigines because of its dense *Nothofagus*
rainforest vegetation (Jones 1974).

Where the present Derwent meets its estuary,
on its eastern bank are wind blown sand deposits
believed on geomorphological grounds to have been
formed when the river flowed in a trench related
to the last glacial low sea level, its mouth being
some kilometres to the south in present-day Storm
Bay. At the Old Beach site (Figs 8, 9), stone
flakes were excavated *in situ* from such a deposit
and Sigleo and Colhoun (1975) have argued
persuasively for a late glacial date for these.

In the dry eastern parts of Tasmania,
especially the Midlands graben and the northeastern
coastal plain, are found sand sheet deposits, lake-
side lunettes and linear dunes, many now tentatively
dated to the latter parts of the last glacial stage
c. 20,000 to 10,000 years ago, and seen as
reflections of the strengthened westerly winds and
increased continentality of climate that affected
the whole of southeastern Australia during the
time of maximum sea lowering (Bowler 1975:81;
Colhoun 1975:19-27; Macphail 1975b). Stone tools
have been found eroding from many of these deposits
(e.g. pers. observation with J. Allen and B. Meehan
1967; Lourandos 1970; W. Sigleo pers. comm.), and
it remains for further fieldwork to demonstrate a

Fig.9. Tasmania and Kangaroo Island during the last Glacial
period, showing the presumed treeline at c. 18,000 BP and
the coastline at c. 14,000 BP. Dated archaeological sites
and surface stone tool finds thought to be of Pleistocene
age are also plotted.

Fig.10. The Tasmanian Archipelago and Kangaroo Island during
the early post Pleistocene period, the sea having just
reached its present level. Basal Tasmanian shell midden
sites are shown as are the islands which lost their human
populations.

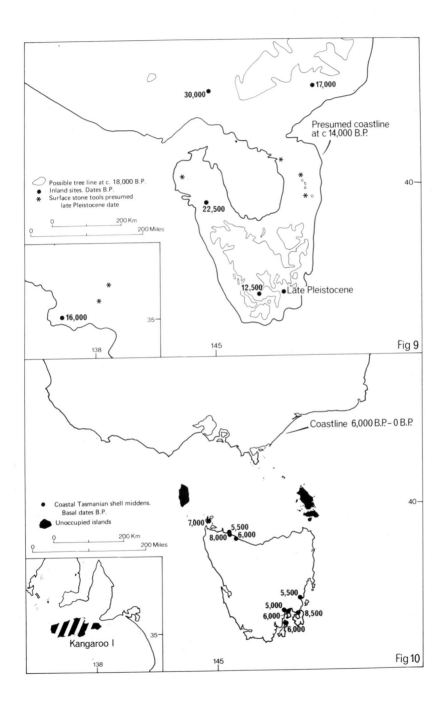

Fig 9

Fig 10

systematic human use during late glacial times of
these eastern lowlands, which on a tiny scale
resembled the geomorphologic environments of the
Murray-Darling river system, several hundred km to
the north-northwest - a theatre for human experience
over the past 40,000 years (Bowler *et al.* 1970;
Allen 1972; Mulvaney 1975:147-53; Shawcross 1975).

However during the height of the last glacial
period, the bulk of what is now the island of
Tasmania was inhospitable to human occupation
(Fig.9). The central highlands supported ice sheets
above c. 600 m in the wet southwest and c. 1200 m
in the drier east (Davies 1967). Active periglacial
activity occurred commonly down to 450 m, and even
down to present sea level on slopes steeper than
about 15 degrees on brittle, strongly jointed rocks
in the northwest (Chick and Colhoun 1972; Colhoun
1975:15-6). Macphail's pioneering pollen analyses
(1975a, 1975b) have shown that late glacial
Tasmania was even more treeless than previously
postulated (Galloway 1965:605; Jones 1968:192-3).
Along the west coast, the timber-line was close to
present sea level; whereas in the east, under the
combined influences of glacial temperatures and
reduced precipitation, exaggerated perhaps by
heightened rain shadow effects, the tree-line was
at about 200 m, but most of the lower country
supported only sparse steppe grassland and open
woodlands, with sedges and alpine herb-fields on
the upper slopes (Macphail 1975a:298-9; Colhoun
1976).

The vegetation of the Bassian floor itself is
difficult to ascertain and the few palaeo-botanical
data available do not give many clues as to the
late Pleistocene location of the rainforest and
wet scrub associations which in mid-post glacial
times were destined to dominate the wet, western
Tasmanian slopes (Jennings 1961; Colhoun 1975:298,
1976; Bowdler and Hope 1976; Bowdler this volume).
The possibility of extensive salt marshes in low

lying areas of the floor has been mooted by Macphail (1975a:298; cf. also Chappell and Thom this volume), and a large river system fed by the ancestors of the north Tasmanian and south Victorian rivers must have drained out of the central west of the basin, potentially affording a prime foraging environment at its mouth. In the east, strong winds in late summer might have whipped up sands to form dunes on the now drowned plain as well as on the adjacent edge of northeastern Tasmania and the Furneaux Islands (Sutherland and Kershaw 1971; Colhoun 1975: 21-2). Eighteen thousand years ago, along the eastern and southern coasts of the Bassian peninsula, the mean surface sea temperatures may have been about 4°C below present values (McIntyre *et al.* 1976:134).

Some stone tools (see below) found eroding from sand deposits on several of the large Bass Strait islands (Fig.9) were probably dropped there by Pleistocene hunters wandering over the lower slopes of hills rising from this Bassian plain. About 150 km to the north, Clogg's Cave, in the sheltered valley of the Buchan River in the foothills at the southern edge of the Victorian Great Dividing Range (Fig.9), had to wait until 17,000 years ago for human occupation (Flood 1974), which then continued intermittently throughout the period which saw the removal of the last permanent ice from the adjacent mountains (Bowler 1975:81). However, it seems likely that human penetration of the high southern tablelands and of the highlands proper, only took place in fully postglacial times (Flood 1973). I doubt if any area along the entire spine of the southern Great Dividing Range, including the hills of the Bassian plain and the Tasmanian mountains themselves, supported more than a slender or transient population during the full glacial period.

Clearly, such a statement, standing the risk of interpretation as a fundamentalist one of 'presence' or 'absence' ought to be re-cast in

probabilistic terms. It is worth reminding oneself
at this stage that the few scrapers and bone points
in the first 15,000 years in Cave Bay Cave, and a
similar order of density at Beginner's Luck Cave
do not add up to a high probability of a visit to
these sites in any one year, or even in any one
millennium. This is in stark contrast with, for
example the quantities of artifacts from the mid-
Recent Crown Lagoon sand dune site (Lourandos
1970), or Rocky Cape (see below), to say nothing of
the West Point midden (Jones 1966). The entire
corpus of Pleistocene artifacts so far discovered
in Tasmania can be matched in number by the
artifacts contained in one eight-litre bucket of
West Point deposit, itself the average product of
three hours occupation of the site. I will never
deny the existence of heroic acts nor even desperate
ones in prehistory, but alas, like those of Great
Men, they are seldom recorded in the levelling
processes of garbage accumulation. We archaeologists
of the Stone Age mostly deal with 'percentages' and
our language should more conscientiously follow
that of our bookmaking bretheren.

I re-assert that during last full glacial
times, in what is now Tasmania, only the stream and
lake systems of the Midlands, the lower Derwent
Valley and the small northeastern plain afforded a
feasible though relatively harsh permanent inland
habitat for hunter/gatherers. The Beginner's Luck
site does however show the dynamism of opportunity
which sometimes accompanies environmental change
(Goede and Murray 1976). Between the melting of
the periglacial uplands and their filling with
dense and unburnable rainforest, lay a moving phase
of exploitable open hunting ground, in a process
analogous with that proposed for late and post-
glacial highland New Guinea by Hope and Hope (1976;
see also Hope 1976:7).

The short low Pleistocene road to Kangaroo
Island had also been taken, as shown by Lampert's

16,000 year old basal date for occupation of the
Seton site (Lampert in press; see below) (Fig.9).
There would have been no especial ecological
problems associated with this event, since the
island itself forms but an extension of the
environment of the adjacent mainland. It now
enjoys a Mediterranean climate, but then perhaps
it was subject to a higher dose of desiccating
late summer westerly winds, which helped to form
the lunettes and longitudinal dunes on its landscape (Lampert pers. comm.; Bowler 1975:80).

RESPONSES TO THE SEA LEVEL RISE

Seithenyn's response according to legend, was
a flask of mead, when in customary alcoholic stupor
he forgot to close the sea dykes, and so Cantref
Gwaelod (The Bottom Hundred), its bells now tolled
by the flow of the tide, was lost beneath Celtic
waves.

'Dinas dawel môr o heli,   (Silent city of the
Hafan y dwfn ydyw hi'   salty sea,
(Williams-Parry 1924:33)   Haven of the deep
                                   is she)

Northwest Tasmania

Low lying Bassiania, so beguilingly exposed
to the wind, was also destined to be reclaimed by
a sea, fed once more by the melting waters of the
world's glaciers. The responses of its human
inhabitants, as the sea reached and formed the
present coastline in northwest Tasmania, can be
investigated in some detail through analysis of
long archaeological sequences in several
geomorphologically similar, old sea-formed cave
sites as shown graphically in Fig.11. Cave Bay
Cave, in pre-Cambrian shale (Meston 1936:155;
Bowdler 1974a, 1974b, 1975a, 1975b and this volume)

overlooks a small bay on the east coast of Hunter
Island (Fig.8). The North and South Caves at
Rocky Cape, and Blackman's Cave, Sisters' Creek
(on Breakneck Point), were cut into pre-Cambrian
quartzite which forms an old sea cliffline facing
Bass Strait some 75 km to the east (Figs 8, 10)
(Jones 1966, 1971). These sites provide a
composite faunal and artifactual sequence from
ethnographic times back to 22,500 years ago, and
are augmented in the recent two or three millennia
by numerous rich open shell middens such as at West
Point on the Tasmanian west coast and at Little
Duck Bay on Hunter Island (Fig.8).

The late glacial situation

Bowdler (1975b, this volume) has pointed out
that the Pleistocene occupation of Cave Bay Cave
was mostly confined to half a metre of deposit
corresponding to a period of only about 2000 years
between c. 22,800 and 20,800 BP, followed by
sporadic occupation associated with a phase of
heavy rock fall. After this there is half a metre
of deposit with no sign of man except for one
hearth in its middle dated to c. 15,000 BP (Fig.11).
The initial deposits, consisting of thick ash
layers with quartz flakes, a few tools and numerous
burnt and smashed bones of wallabies and other land
prey may have represented the camps of hunting
groups, foraging perhaps on the inland edge of
their coastal territories (Fig.9), with the sea
itself being of the order of 30-40 km away to the
west.[3] During the very peak of the glacial episode,
with heavy natural weathering inside the cave, it
was virtually abandoned. What remains there are,
represent only the odd visit, and certainly no more
than a handful over 10,000 years to what was then
a remote inland site. Twenty thousand years ago is
now seen as having been the time of the peak of the
west Tasmanian glacial episode (Colhoun 1975:13),
and the thick periglacial scree slope deposits
mantling the cliffs of Rocky Cape down almost to

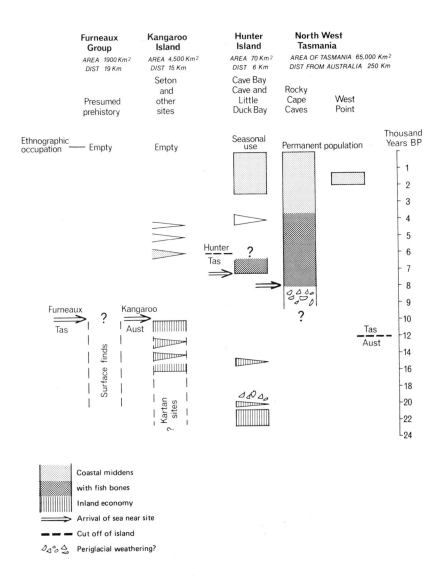

Fig.11. Schematic portrayal of the main archaeological sequences discussed in the text, showing the different responses of the human inhabitants in different parts of the Bassian landscape. The contrasts between the sequences in Tasmania, Hunter Island, Kangaroo Island and the Furneaux Group, can be explained by referring to the area/distance parameters shown above each section column.

the sea shore were being formed then (Chick and
Colhoun 1972; Colhoun 1975:17). Perhaps the great
angular blocks of rock and sterile leached grit and
sand older than 8000 years at the base of the Rocky
Cape South Cave deposits belong to the same causes
and epoch. Certainly, in my excavations, there
was no sign of human occupation or of charcoal in
them, a sterility confirmed in grits and sand at
the base of the North Cave and at Blackman's Cave,
Sisters' Creek also.

The arrival of the sea

    A fundamental change occurred 7-8000 years ago
when the rising sea first reached the present coast
(Figs 10, 11). At Rocky Cape dense shell midden
deposit was laid down, with a basal date of 8120 ±
165 BP (GXO 266) (Reber 1965), a time which
corresponded exactly with the arrival of the sea at
the foot of the cliffs which plunged below present
sea level to a depth of 30 m within a kilometre
from the cave (Jones 1968:198). Since that time,
until the arrival of the Europeans, a continuous
sequence of 6 m of shell midden accumulated in the
two caves. Numerous ashy hearths, burnt and
smashed animal bones, stone and bone tools etc.
indicated occupation as a base camp. Calculations
based on the total food energy represented in the
middens, show that a party of a few families could
have camped there on average for a week or so, each
year of the eight millennia (Meehan 1975:246; Jones
in press b). Even the first occupants of the cave
had an overwhelmingly coastal flesh diet eating fur
seals (*Arctocephalus* sp.) and elephant seals
(*Mirounga leonina*), *Pseudolabrus* sp. fish, and the
rocky coast gastropods, *Notohaliotis*, *Subninella*,
Dicathais and *Cellana*. Thus some 95% of the total
calorific intake from flesh foods was foraged from
the tidal zone or the immediate offshore environment,
the remaining 5% coming for the odd wallaby and
some small wet scrub marsupials (Jones 1971, in
press b).

This preponderance of coastal foods continued right through the sequence, only one feature of which I will comment upon here. Between c. 3800 and c. 3400 years ago, fish (teleosts) dropped suddenly and totally out of the diet - a pan-Tasmanian phenomenon, the implications of which I have discussed in detail elsewhere (Jones in press b). Briefly, I can find no satisfactory ecological reasons for this, and have suggested that we have to look for a cultural explanation within the realm of dietary prohibition. Although such an abnegation would have caused considerable dietary hardship during lean times of the year, for example winter, it was nevertheless maintained for over 3000 years until the arrival of the Europeans. I have linked the disappearance of fish within Tasmanian diet with other strange losses such as bone tools as shown in the Tasmanian archaeological record; possibly the items made with these tools; some wooden tools such as boomerangs and barbed composite spear heads, hafted edge ground axes, and the concept of hafting as such, as inferred from the archaeological and ethnographic records on both sides of Bass Strait (Jones in press a, in press b). This diminution I see as having been one of the consequences of the isolation of the Tasmanian segment of society from the wider continental social network. Perhaps there is here some cultural analogue of the loss of useful arts with the reduction of species on continental islands. At the very least, isolation may have allowed the persistence of economic maladaptations, through protection against more efficient systems replacing them from outside. Nowhere in the Tasmanian archaeological record, do we get any sign of the numerous technological innovations which occurred in mid-Recent and later mainland sequences. No dingoes reached Tasmania. It seems that Bass Strait, once re-formed, served as a completely isolating barrier, separating the Aborigines on both its shores for probably 12,000 years.

Responses to the arrival of the sea at Cave Bay Cave were more complex than at Rocky Cape. Lying immediately on top of culturally sterile late Pleistocene deposit, was a 15 cm layer of dense shell midden, its base being dated to c. 7200 years ago, the approximate time of the arrival of the sea at the foot of the cliffs in front of the cave (Bowdler 1975b). This midden consisted of rocky coast gastropods, together with bones of small macropods and mutton birds (*Puffinus*) and a few fish bones as in contemporary middens at Rocky Cape (Bowdler 1974a:6-7, 1975b). Above this midden there was a small hearth dated to c. 4000 BP followed by 25 cm of culturally sterile deposit, found in all soundings in the cave. Finally the top 25 cm consisted of lenses of shell midden and hearths, the base of which was dated to 2580 ± 70 BP (ANU-1362). The top midden contained no fish bones, this absence according with the absence of fish remains elsewhere in northwest Tasmania at this time (Fig.11).

Bowdler's convincing explanation for this sequence is that the initial midden was laid down as soon as the sea had reached the present coastal cliff, but that the block of land was still briefly joined as a 'Hunter Peninsula' to the adjacent mainland.[4] Coincident with the final severance from the main, the new formed island was abandoned for several thousand years (Bowdler 1975a:219, 1975b). Possibly the odd sign of occupation between the two midden deposits, such as the c. 4000 year old hearth, represents extremely rare visits to the island, perhaps to be measured in terms of only a few per millennium (Fig.11), and of no immediate consequence from the point of view of its recolonisation; but eventually of interest in giving a numerical calibration to the probability curve of frequency of highly stressful crossings close to the limiting practical value of cross-sea distance (Fig.7b).

At any rate, just over two and a half thousand years ago, Hunter Island was re-incorporated systematically into the Tasmanian economic world by cross-water travellers who exploited its sea shore resources (Bowdler 1974b:8).

A regionally co-ordinated economic system

Such an enlargement of the ecological space of the Aborigines of northwest Tasmania from about this time onwards is consistent with evidence from Rocky Cape, West Point and other mainland Tasmanian sites as previously postulated (Jones 1966:9, 1971) (Fig.11). In my top two 'analytical units' in the North Cave at Rocky Cape, with a basal date of c. 2500 BP there was a somewhat greater contribution to the diet from wallabies and coastal birds especially cormorants. Stone tools were imported ready made or as roughouts from quarries up to 100 km away on the west coast, instead of being made entirely on the spot from immediately local stones as was the case previously (Jones 1966, 1971, in press a, in press b). The two large, home base middens at West Point, have basal dates of c. 2000-2500 BP (Reber 1965; Jones 1966). The inhabitants at these sites received about half their flesh energy from elephant seals (Coleman 1966), and they manufactured and used tens of thousands of stone tools there, most being made from a high quality 'spongolite' chert mined locally, and being carried as far afield as Rocky Cape on the north coast and Macquarie Harbour down the west coast (Jones 1966, 1971; Sutherland 1972). Perhaps only a coincidence, but worth bearing in mind, is the fact that the rock carving site of Mount Cameron West (Fig.8), situated halfway between West Point and Cape Grim opposite Hunter Island, was also first carved about 2000 years ago (personal field-work with H. Lourandos, F.D. McCarthy and others). This is the greatest of all Tasmanian rock carving sites and its execution might possibly reflect some attainment of new levels of leisure or morale.

It fell into disrepair about 1000 years ago, the
same time as the abandonment of the West Point
midden, possibly due to the local extinction of the
elephant seal breeding population there (Jones
1966). Whether the re-claiming of Hunter Island
resulted in improvements in water crossing technology
and knowledge of the dangerous rips and tides of
the straits (e.g. Bowdler 1974a:8), or whether it
occurred in response to an appreciation of the
advantages of incorporating the island resources
within a wider economic system then being
established in the northwest, is not yet known.

Open shell middens on the west coast of Hunter
Island, such as the Little Duck Bay site and the
Mutton Bird Rookery site, belong to this latest
cross-water phase of Hunter Island use (Bowdler
1974b and pers. comm.), and although they look
similar to contemporary open middens on the mainland
Tasmanian west coast, they are about a quarter to a
tenth the size and only contain a limited range of
artifactual material - what stone tools there are,
being almost all made from local materials
(Sutherland 1972; Bowdler 1974b; and pers.
observation). The impression of less intense
occupation on the island vis à vis the neighbouring
Tasmanian mainland is strengthened by comparing the
top midden at Cave Bay Cave, with the contemporary
shell midden in Rocky Cape North (Jones 1971;
Bowdler 1974b). All this evidence is consistent
with Hunter Island being occupied seasonally by
people, perhaps specialised foraging groups who had
left their main base camps and perhaps certain
vulnerable elements of their society back on the
adjacent mainland. This system continued until the
ethnographic present, where it can be studied in
great detail in the ethnographic records (Figs 2, 3)
(Jones 1974:331-6, 343-6, 1976:251-4).

The archaeological evidence from northwest
Tasmania demonstrates both the Aboriginal
reclamation of Hunter Island, and the integration of

the resources of the west coast with those of the
north coast into a single economic domain of a
tribal sized group of people. In support of the
archaeological evidence, greater economic control of
adjacent inland areas is suggested by the fire-formed
foraging grounds of Surrey and Hampshire Plains
(Jones 1975:26-8). Do we see here the re-assertion
of an optimal regional equilibrium from a previous
period of fragmentation and of economic imbalance,
which was caused by a radically changed environment,
due both to the rising of the sea and the adaptation
of the flora to postglacial conditions? If so,
then this process might be interpreted as a cultural
equivalent of Diamond's 'faunal relaxation' (1972).
Within the particular environment and technological
régimes under discussion, it can be seen that the
'cultural relaxation' took a period of some 5000
years, from c. 7500 BP to c. 2500 BP to be
consummated.

The rest of Tasmania

Such a detailed picture has not yet been
obtained elsewhere in Tasmania, but it is relevant
to note that the arrival of the sea at its present
coastline in the southeast also heralded the
formation of middens on the new shoreline (Fig.10),
as indicated by the 8700 BP date from the base of
the Carlton Midden (Reber 1965:266), a date of
c. 4700 BP at Little Swanport (Lourandos 1970), and
dates of c. 5-6000 BP from several middens on the
east bank of the Derwent (Reber 1965; Colhoun 1975:
31-2; R. Vanderwal pers. comm.; A. Wallace pers.
comm.) - the slightly varying dates corresponding
well with the adjacent submarine topography. This
is ample evidence that coastal using peoples were
pushed back up the short, steep slope from the full
glacial, low sea levels in the southeast too. The
dry open woodland and grassland nature of the
hinterland throughout this period, would have
presented no special problems of re-adaptation to
the slightly higher land. Bruny Island (Figs 8,

10), has a midden with a basal date of c. 6000 BP,
and another with one of c. 5200 BP (Reber 1965),
presumably after its severance from the adjacent
mainland; there are also several others with dates
of about 2500 (Reber 1967). Whether or not there
was continuous across-water use of Bruny right from
the period of severance, or whether its use was
discontinuous as at Hunter, is a question that
awaits field investigation, but I strongly suspect
the former. This would imply that watercraft of
some sort, were even then part of the technology
of the newly isolated Tasmanians, and not something
which had to be invented later.

The prehistory of the Aboriginal use of the
islands of the Maatsuyker Group off the extreme
tip of southwestern Tasmania (Figs 2, 3, 8), is
under current investigation by R. Vanderwal.
Incorporation of these exposed islands, in the
teeth of the westerly gales, into the economy of
the southern tribes was one of the great maritime
exploits of hunting and gathering man, and it will
be fascinating to see to what extent this process
mirrored similar events on the other side of the
island in the northwest.

The Bass Strait islands

As regards the ethnographically unoccupied
Bass Strait islands, stone tools have been found on
at least four of them (Fig.9) - King Island (pers.
observation of struck flakes found eroded from a
dune by a Currie school master and shown to W.D.
Jackson in Hobart in 1965); Cape Barren Island
(R. Littlewood pers. comm.); Flinders Island
(Tindale 1941; D. Casey 1968; R. Littlewood pers.
comm.); and Erith Island (D. Anderson and S. Murray-
Smith pers. comm.). The tools from Erith and some
from Flinders are made from hard calcrete, to be
found outcropping nowadays only on the eastern Bass
Strait islands (L. Sutherland pers. comm.).

Typologically, several from Cape Barren and Flinders are large, steep-edged core scrapers, and concave and nosed scrapers. Stratigraphically coming from old, eroded dune blow outs, they support Tindale's suggestion (1941) that they were dropped onto the landscape when the islands were inland hills rising out of the Bassian plain.[5] No shell middens nor any other debris definitely referable to the postglacial prehistoric period, have ever been found on any of these islands, despite systematic search by several archaeologists and informed natural scientists (e.g. R. Littlewood pers. comm.; J. Hope pers. comm.; Reber 1965:267-8; see also Jones 1976:257-9). Ranga Cave on Flinders Island (Fig.8) while containing a rich land fauna dating as recently as c. 8000 years ago, contained traces of neither artifacts nor hearths (Hope 1973: 167-70). It would appear therefore, that while these islands were once the home of men and women, they lost their human populations as soon as they became islands (Fig.10). The absence of any shell middens argues against the survival of a stranded population for any appreciable length of time.

Kangaroo Island

The Seton site, excavated by Lampert (1972, 1975, 1976, in press) is a small cave in calcareous aeolianite overlooking a freshwater lagoon 8 km from the present south coast of Kangaroo Island. It was first occupied about 16,000 years ago by people who used it fleetingly as a hunting camp, eating game which included the now extinct large kangaroo-like *Sthenurus* sp., and manufacturing a few small scrapers. There was sparse intermittent use of Seton over the next few thousands of years, when the site would have been some 40 km from the seashore (Fig.9). Then at about 10,500-11,000 years ago, there was a short period of intensive occupation by people who had a varied inland subsistence with a substantial contribution from the modern grey kangaroo, and who used bone and

stone tools, the latter also certainly being
manufactured at the site (Lampert in press). It
remains to be seen whether or not this late intensive
use was related to the fact that it was now within
easy walking distance of the new coast, and could
thus be incorporated within the day by day hunting
strategy of people whose other focus was the seashore, but it is significant that some marine shellfish formed part of the diet (Lampert pers. comm.).
Immediately following this episode, the site from
then onwards was totally abandoned (Fig.11). The
timing of this event coincided with the final
severance of the land-bridge across the Investigator
Passage between the island and Yorke Peninsula to
the north, the critical sill being at about 28-33 m
below the present sea level. The much shorter
Backstairs Passage to the Fleurieu Peninsula would
have been sundered earlier as it is deeper, though
the effects of tidal scouring cannot be discounted.

Reversing a previous suggestion Lampert now
sees the Kartan industry which includes large
pebble choppers, horse-hoof core tools and waisted
core tools as having beeing a continental and not
an island phenomenon (Lampert 1976, in press).
That is, these tools were made by people occupying
an area of at least 100,000 sq km which included
present day Kangaroo Island and the adjacent
peninsulas, when all formed parts of one landmass.
Furthermore, Lampert also perceives a typological
sequence involving the steady replacement of heavy
core tools made on quartzite by small scrapers made
on quartz and flint, and that this already had been
substantially completed by the time of occupation
of the Seton site (Lampert 1976, pers. comm.).

For a long while, it appeared that definite
postglacial sites were absent on Kangaroo Island,
but intensive field research by Lampert over the
past two years has resulted in the discovery of six
sites attributable to the period after its
separation from the mainland (Fig.11).[6] Of these,

four are coastal sites and consist of scatters of
flakes with some marine shells, one being a rockshelter with midden deposit and one a tiny
stratified shell midden, half of which was
processed to yield a carbon date of c. 6000 BP.
The other two are inland stratified open sites with
scattered flakes and a few small scrapers. One is
dated to c. 5200 BP and the other to c. 4300 BP.

These latter two postglacial inland sites may
be contrasted in number with the 100 plus Kartan
inland sites, some extending over hectares of
ground, which had been occupied during perhaps a
roughly equivalent preceding time period. Likewise,
the middens, numbering one per 100 km of coast for
the 6-8000 years of the present sea level, can be
contrasted with the adjacent southern coast of
South Australia, where R. Luebbers' similarly
detailed survey has recorded approximately 1000
sites from an equivalent space/time unit (pers.
comm. and pers. observation). On the Arnhem Land
coast, Meehan (1975:239) showed that during a
single year, a band of 35 Gidgingali people ate
250,000 shellfish equivalent to a total midden of
500,000 valves measuring eight cubic metres, dropped
onto the landscape at three main home bases and
some 50 'dinner-time' camps. Perhaps the entire
postglacial Kangaroo Island shell material that has
survived is less than this. For postglacial
Kangaroo Island, while there was some occupation,
as a quantum of human activity this was several
orders of magnitude less than on similar blocks of
land on the adjacent mainland, which were occupied
continuously at full 'carrying capacity' (see
Birdsell this volume) over an equivalent length of
time. There is nothing in the Kangaroo Island
data suggesting large scale continuous occupation
for any appreciable time, rather it looks to me
like the result of sporadic, rare and relatively
short occupations.

To try and explain these data, let us consider

several scenarios for the loss of the island
population:

  1. The entire population supported by the block
     of land about to become an island remained
in situ and became extinct some time after. This
is unlikely to have been the case since the
approximate 400-500 people who were probably
involved (Jones 1976:258) (Table 3) would have left
far more substantial traces of their presence than
has been found in the field, especially if it
included archaeologically highly visible shell
midden material.

  2. In being abandoned by the bulk of its
     population, a segment, say the size of a
band or two, chose to stay behind. In the detailed
process of depopulation, this probably did occur,
but any such bands must have also left the island
soon afterwards without establishing a long-term
permanent population. McArthur has shown by her
simulation models that extremely small populations
run a high risk eventually of becoming extinct - a
sample run of 20 populations, each consisting of
three men and three young women, resulted in nine
extinctions, three doubtful cases and eight
successes (some reaching more than 250 persons)
over a period of 300 years (McArthur 1976:55).
Average Aboriginal bands are however significantly
larger than these samples - numbering say ten women
of reproductive age and ten immature girls at
least. The ultimate demographic fates of such
band-sized groups are more likely to have been
like those documented from historical sources by
Birdsell (1957:49-53), where two groups, one with
eight women and six men, and the other with 11
women and four men, both grew to c. 350-400 persons
in only five generations.[7] Thus, given this
scenario, the growth period from an initial isolated
band on Kangaroo Island up to the presumed full,
ecologically sustainable population level would
have occurred so rapidly, that at a distance of
8-10,000 years it would be barely archaeologically

Island	Area sq km	Coast km	Isobath Defining Island m.	Date of Separation Years B.P.	Population $p = \dfrac{A}{19.2} + \dfrac{C}{1.98}$	Notes
Greater Tasmania						
a) Total	125,000	2,000	64			Still attached as a peninsula
Inhabitable portion	75,000	2,000			4,900	
b) Total	115,000			13,500		The new formed island
Inhabitable portion	65,000	2,000	55	12,000	4,400	
Greater King Island	3,300	300	46	10–12,000	320	
Greater Furneaux Island	4,600	350	28	8,500–10,000	420	A single island about to break up into a group
Kangaroo Island						
a) Present day	4,400	410			440	
b) + 10% area	5,000	410	28–33	c. 10,000	470	

Table 3. The Bassian Islands at the critical points of their separation: suggested geographical parameters and the potential population of hunter/gatherers capable of being supported by them.

visible. In any case, we have no evidence during
the past 8000 years of any phase when there was an
island population of the same order of density as
on the adjacent mainland.

    3. A band-sized group remained, but maintained
        its existence more or less constant by
cultural means, eventually to become extinct through
the vagaries of chance. Whereas one can imagine
such a model, there is no evidence that it
corresponds to any real situation. In Australia
at least, Aboriginal population levels everywhere
were highly correlated with resources (Birdsell
this volume), implying that available 'ecological
space' was rapidly filled.

    4. A tiny group, for example a family or a few
        couples, stayed behind, their lineage
surviving for a period but eventually becoming
extinct. Here McArthur's data (1976) are
especially relevant. The odds are high that even
after a few hundred years the fate of such a group
would already have been resolved - either death or
success: translated archaeologically this would
mean either no sites after 1000 years or so, or as
dense a number as on the mainland. Neither is the
case. Using this particular model, which at first
glance is attractive, the archaeological data demand
the calculation of the odds for an extraordinary
unlikely biological event, namely the survival of
a group of people never exceeding in number more
than a few families, yet maintaining itself year
after year for no less than 250 generations until
4000 BP. If the archaeological data were one day
to show that this in fact is what did happen (e.g.
if an unbroken archaeological sequence lasting
until mid-Recent times were to be discovered, and/
or one containing some unique cultural traits not
found in contemporary adjacent mainland sequences),
then it would have profound implications concerning
the capacity of human society to transmit cultural
information.

    5. In my opinion, the most likely explanation
        for the Kangaroo Island sequence is the one

suggested by the biogeographical theories outlined
above. Firstly, the island was abandoned at or
soon after its separation from the mainland, with
any small remnant group(s) quickly becoming
extinct. Secondly, there was always a low
probability of recolonisation from the adjacent
mainland (Fig.7b). Such colonists, possibly
accidental voyagers or fugitives, might indeed have
spent many years or even lifetimes on the island,
but because of the demographic factors discussed by
McArthur (1976) they were never able to establish
a viable long-term island population, nor did their
experience cause the island's resources to be
re-incorporated systematically into mainland
economic networks.

Lampert's fascinating data suggest that such
colonisations occurred several times, but perhaps
only at the rate of say one or two per millennium;
and that the frequency of such visits was
diminishing, the island having been inviolate for
several thousand years before Matthew Flinders'
and Nicolas Baudin's almost simultaneous visits in
1802. Archaeological proof of prehistoric crossings
might be afforded by the discovery on the island of
an exotic mainland raw material, by a tool type
restricted in mainland assemblages to mid-Recent or
later times, or by the bones of a dingo fellow
traveller. The situation is complicated by the
fact that in Australia, both dogs and the
distinctive backed microliths are dated to more
recently than c. 5000 BP, a period of time when
trips to Kangaroo Island might already have ceased.
An indirect impression of the complex process of
human abandonment of the island should be forthcoming from faunal and pollen analyses now being
carried out (Lampert and G. and J. Hope pers. comm.),
a declining frequency of the use of fire sticks
having been a powerful agent in the vegetation
succession.

'FOR THE WORSE KIND OF SCARCITY A NATION
CAN SUFFER FROM IS LACK OF INHABITANTS'
(Rousseau 1755:151)

From these diverse data, four conclusions and
one further inference emerge, concerning the human
response to the drowning of the Bassian plain:

1. As the shoreline progressively rolled back
     onto higher ground, people living off it,
while maintaining their coast-focused economic
strategy, were forced to relocate themselves as
shown schematically in Fig.12. Since in this
region the inland areas had previously been mostly
uninhabitable, the contraction need not necessarily
have involved dislocation of other totally inland
groups.

2. As the continental shelf became cut up into
     islands of various sizes, some were abandoned
by man, not as a result of direct inundation but
because of their engirdlement by water. Furthermore,
it seems that *size* was the main determinant as to
whether or not a particular island lost or
maintained the presence of man. Thus the islets of
the Hogan Group, King Island, the Furneaux Group
and even Kangaroo Island became depopulated,
whereas Tasmania itself maintained its population.

3. There is no sign of relict populations
     surviving and establishing themselves for
archaeologically significant lengths of time. This
suggests deliberate abandonment of a smaller landmass
as a water barrier started to separate it from an
adjacent larger one.

4. There was also constantly a background of
     potential recolonisation or use of abandoned
islands, due to planned or random sea voyaging from
adjacent occupied lands. The chance of this being
successful was a function of the sea *distance* to be
crossed. Within distances 5-8 km, there seems to
have been a high probability of eventual success;
the islands being re-incorporated into a wider
economic system as happened, possibly after several

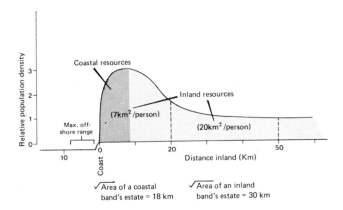

Fig.12a.   Relative Tasmanian Aboriginal population densities
along a transect at right angles to a coastline.

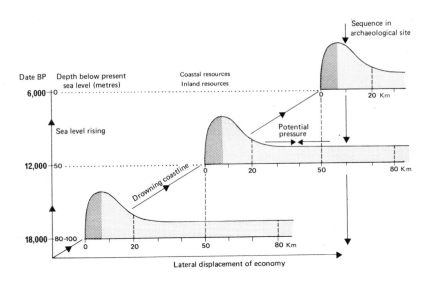

Fig.12b.   Model of coastal hunters' response to a drowning
coastline.

attempts, on Hunter Island. With distances up to
15 km, as in the case of Kangaroo Island, it seems
that although rare successful crossings were made,
they did not lead to any systematic re-use of the
islands concerned. For all practical purposes, a
sea distance of more than about 15 km constituted
an impassable envelope, at least within the context
of the number of different situations and the time
limit available in postglacial Bassiania. On the
other hand, it is likely that some islands, such as
Robbins and Bruny, being separated from their mainlands by distances of only one or two km were never
abandoned, especially if watercraft were available
from the beginning. The question is of course
archaeologically investigatable.

5. A further hypothesis can be made, that an
island was abandoned not when initially
severed, but only when the sea passage had reached
the point of critical distance to its seasonal
negotiators (say 8 km), or when other factors such
as unpredictable tidal rips made the journey too
dangerous for the resultant economic rewards.

THE CRITICAL LIMITING SIZE FOR A SELF SUFFICIENT
HUNTING AND GATHERING SYSTEM

Areas of newly formed islands

We can now attempt to use this 'experiment of
nature' (Diamond 1973:759) to measure the size of
the minimum viable habitat for a hunting and
gathering society in this environment, and hence to

Fig.13a. Approximate dates of formation of the various
islands of the Bassian Archipelago as the sea progressively
rose.

Fig.13b. 'Greater King Island' and 'Greater Furneaux
Island' shown as they appeared when the minimum cross
water distance to get to them from Tasmania approached
c. 5-8 km.

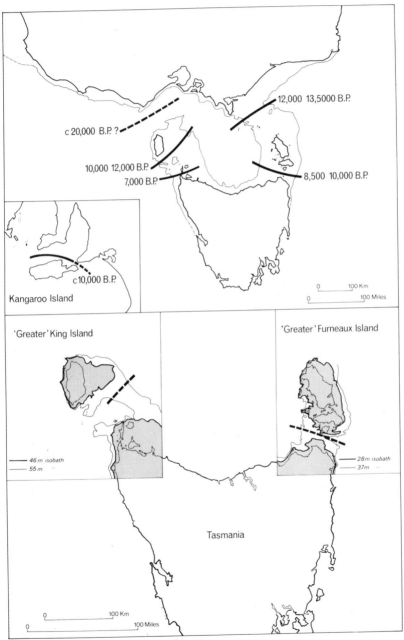

Fig 13

calculate the smallest viable unit of humanity
prepared to exist indefinitely on its own. Instead
of measuring the present areas of the islands, as I
did in my previous attempt (Jones 1976:257-61), one
ought to take them as they were when first formed,
or rather, when the closest cross-water distance to
reach them approached the order of 5-8 km (Fig.13,
Table 3).

Tasmania itself was severed from the mainland
between the Kent Group and Wilsons Promontory, some
12,000-13,500 years BP (Fig.13a). A sea level rise
of only 9 m from the present 64 m isobath to the
55 m one, flooded a corridor 65 km wide to form a
strait 60 km wide, with only the rocky stacks of
the Curtis and the Hogan Groups situated halfway
across (Jennings 1959, 1971; Jones 1968). The
'Greater Tasmania' thus cut off, consisted of some
115,000 sq km (taking the 55 m isobath). From the
human point of view, some 50,000 sq km of its late
glacial upland interior was not usable for reasons
previously discussed, leaving about 65,000 sq km
and 2000 km of coast to support the newly isolated
human population. 'Greater King Island' at its
critical point of abandonment 10-12,000 years BP
can be reconstructed by taking the 46 m isobath,
giving it an area of some 3300 sq km (Fig.13b).
The 'Greater Furneaux Island', as defined by the
28 m isobath, was a single island 4500 sq km in
area, being split, northwest of Cape Portland,
between 8500 and 10,000 years ago (Fig.13b).
During the previous 3000 years, the peninsula of
which it had been the core, was reduced in area by
a factor of about two-thirds, and the final stages
of sea level rise eventually cut it up into the
three large and 20 small islands which form the
group at present. Finally, I have estimated that
the newly formed 'Greater Kangaroo Island', which
required a minimum 8 km voyage to get to it, was
about 10% larger than its present size. Greater
precision is difficult, since voyaging of this
scale could have been made across the deep and

slowly widening Backstairs Passage for a short
while after the severing of the flatter and
shallower Investigator Passage.

*Populations capable of being supported by these
islands*

To calculate the Aboriginal populations which
could have been supported by these islands, we
have to consider both coastal and inland resources.
A previously published table (Jones 1974:326) shows
each of the nine ethnographically recorded Tasmanian
tribes, the number of its constituent bands and
thus its estimated population,[8] together with the
length of coastline and area of its territory
(Table 1). Plotting for each tribe the area in
sq km per person (A), against the length of coastline in km (C), I have found that they have an
inverse linear relationship according to the
regression equation

A = -9.7 C + 19.2 : with a coefficient of
correlation
r = 0.90 (n=9), significant at better than 0.1%
level.

Solving in turn for A=0, and C=0, we find that with
no coastal increment, the area required to support
one person = 19.2 sq km; and with no inland area,
the coastline to support one person = 1.98 km.
Furthermore, in calculating the population of any
tribe it appears that these two increments can be
added arithmetically according to the formula[9]

$$P \text{ (population)} = \frac{Area}{19.2} + \frac{Coast}{1.98} \text{ (in km)} \quad .. \text{ (1)}$$

Using the area and coastline parameters of the
Tasmanian tribes, I calculated their predicted
populations according to this formula and compared
the results with the ethnographic figures (Table 1).
The result is shown in Fig.14 where it can be seen
that there is an excellent correlation between
calculated and ethnographic values, the coefficient

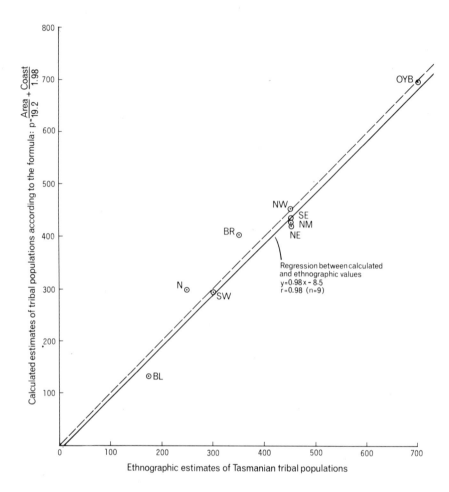

Fig.14. Populations of Tasmanian tribes : calculated
estimates according to a formula discussed in the text
plotted against the original ethnographic figures,
showing a high degree of fit throughout the entire
range of tribal sizes.

of correlation r = 0.98 (n=9) being significant at
better than the 0.1% level. This relationship is
maintained through the entire range of coast/inland
ratios, and with populations ranging from c. 175 to
c. 700 people.

Before applying this formula to the break-up
of the Bassian plain, I will make two assumptions.
Firstly, I will assume that both coastal and inland
resource densities were roughly comparable to
contemporary values. It has been argued in certain
geomorphic situations, that resources on an
actively inundated coastline might have been less
than those developed after a long period of
stability - e.g. as described by Lampert and Hughes
(1974) for the coast of New South Wales, where
postglacial, estuary-blocking sand barriers were an
important part of the food producing system.
However, at least at Rocky Cape and Cave Bay Cave,
the first inhabitants arrived on the ascending
shoreline, eating the full complement of coastal
foods, so it is likely in the relatively high
energy, rocky environments of Bass Strait that the
coastal ecosystem was able to keep pace with the
shore without an archaeologically appreciable lag.
With a mean summer temperature of the order of 5°C
- 10°C lower than present, it is possible that the
gross biological productivity per unit area, during
full glacial times was also less. In terms of the
insulation of King, Furneaux and Kangaroo Islands,
however, the time periods involved belong to early
postglacial times, so I do not think this
temperature factor would have been significant.
In the case of Tasmania itself, I have tried to
accommodate it by noting the largely uninhabitable
uplands not included in my calculations.

Secondly, I am assuming that the people themselves would have deployed a roughly comparable
technology onto the environment as recorded
ethnographically. Given the archaeological
demonstration of cultural continuity within
Tasmania going back throughout this entire sequence,
I feel that this is reasonable. Even in recent
times on the adjacent mainland of southeast
Australia, where the technology was considerably
more diverse than that of Tasmania, it seems that
population densities were comparable on both sides

of Bass Strait thus suggesting the existence of
fundamentally similar ecological relationships, not
transcended by what technological differences that
did exist (Jones in press a; cf. Birdsell 1957:61).

    Applying formula (1) to the measurements of
the 'greater' Bass Strait islands (Table 3), we
arrive at an estimate of the probable population
that each was supporting at the critical point of
its separation from a larger neighbour. It can be
seen that gross populations ranging from 300 to say
450 people were not viable units in these particular
historical and geographical circumstances. A
population of some 4000 people on 'Greater Tasmania'
however, did not abandon the pinched-off peninsula,
and furthermore was able to survive for 500
generations in total cultural and genetic isolation
from then on. By using comparable ethnographic
and census data from occupied islands off the north
coast of Australia, I have tried to narrow down
this range (Jones 1976:260), and have suggested
that the critical minimum long-term viable human
population is close to 500 people.

The minimum acceptable territory

    In searching for the causes of the non-
viability of isolated populations of less than this
size several explanations have been mooted,
depending on the historical circumstances of the
depopulation (e.g. Tindale 1937; Bauer 1970; Jones
1976:257-61; Lampert in press; Diamond this volume;
see also Bayliss-Smith 1974). If island populations
persisted for varying lengths of time after
insulation, one might consider the local extinctions
of small human groups, since it can be shown for all
animal populations that extinction probability
increases with decreasing population size and with
decreasing reproductive potential (Leigh 1975;
Diamond this volume). Causes for such a process
might include the frequency of natural disasters
such as storms, droughts or the depletion of an

important food resource; accidents especially to
crucial members of the population such as women of
child bearing age; excessive warfare or other
violence; genetic non-viability or the lack of
marriage partners, especially if cultural
restrictions on potential mates were enforced, e.g.
through strict kinship categories and rules for
local group exogamy. Trace element deficiency has
also been suggested in the case of Kangaroo Island
(Bauer 1970).

Catastrophe was a fact of Aboriginal life, and
its social and biological effects on their history
have not yet been fully appreciated. Tindale
showed that drownings accounted for some 13% of all
recorded Kaiadilt deaths on Bentinck Island (Tindale
1967:347) and that a combination of a tidal wave
salting their water holes, drought, warfare and sea
voyage accidents reduced their population by a
factor of some 50% in two years. The ultimate fate
of the surviving 70 Kaidilt was in considerable
doubt until the intervention of Europeans (Tindale
1962). Meehan (1975:231-8, in press, this volume)
has documented how a single freshwater flood
emanating out of the mouth of the Blyth River in
Arnhem Land, almost wiped out the molluscan fauna
over a 12 km front of open coast, a resource which
in the previous year had been one of the major
foods of the Gidjingali people living there. Hiatt
(1965) amongst several other social anthropologists,
has shown how local groups such as clans, and even
dialect units, can become rapidly extinct due to
the vagaries of the demographic structure.

The archaeological data have however, introduced
a new subtlety, that the actual process of loss of
human populations on the now uninhabited islands
was not due to the local extinctions of isolated
populations, but that the islands became abandoned
at the time of their severance from adjacent larger
land areas (see also Lampert in press). Thus the
problem is no longer one pertaining to the

demographic arithmetic of the probabilities of
births against deaths, but becomes a cultural one.
People made decisions to abandon blocks of land
because these were smaller than their perception
of what constituted a minimum acceptable living
space for a human society. Furthermore, we can
show that this concept of minimum space was
consistently maintained as having been greater than
3000-4500 sq km (Table 3).

Through being unwilling to split up their
societies, and consign groups of up to 400 people
to live for ever more on their own, these decisions
were made at a tremendous cost. Cumulatively, they
necessitated the immediate loss of some 13,000 sq
km of living space (Table 3). Even after the
stabilisation of the sea, there was an ultimate loss
of some 7500 sq km of unoccupied islands. This was
at a time when there must have been considerable
local population pressure due to the steady
inundation of lands (cf. Mulvaney 1975:136). We
can suggest for example that the original population
of Greater Tasmania (defined between the 64 and 55 m
isobaths), deployed as it was along some 2000 km of
coast would need to be reduced by some 20% by the
time of the final stabilisation of the island's shore,
the loss of coastal resources outweighing the gain of
inland ones which were released by the disappearing
periglacial conditions (Tables 1 and 3). It should
be noted that this suggestion is at variance with
Bowdler (this volume) who has based her calculations
on the 100 m isobath not the 64-55 m ones used here.
These latter would seem to be more realistic given
that the 100 m low sea appears to have been
achieved only twice and relatively briefly during
the past 55,000 years (Birdsell this volume).

We can see that this original Greater Tasmania
of 115,000 sq km was considered large enough not
to be abandoned, and carried a population intact
into 12 millennia of isolation from the continental
network.

Tribes and annual territories

Australian and Tasmanian Aboriginal tribes are probably best seen as agglomerations of land-owning local groups, who shared the same language and culture, tended to intermarry with each other, met together periodically for ceremonial and other social purposes and foraged on each other's lands to a greater extent than they did with bands of neighbouring tribes (Hiatt 1962; Meggitt 1964; Birdsell 1970; Berndt 1959; Tindale 1974; Jones 1974). Although there was some fluidity in their membership, tribes were important linguistic, genetic and social units. The tribal territory, being the land of its constituent bands, was almost contiguous with the 'annual territory' (Higgs 1975) of those bands, there being some movement outside for seasonally abundant or unusual foods, or to obtain specialised resources such as ochre or stone tools, or to carry out religious obligations. Such extra-territorial movements were sanctioned by custom and usually involved reciprocal arrangements with host bands.

Birdsell (1953, 1971) has brilliantly shown for mainland Aborigines, that population density was proportional to bio-production, as measured most conveniently by effective rainfall. Sociologically, this population density gradient was deployed in terms of an inverse relationship between the size of tribal territories and rainfall. Thus the Aborigines tended to maintain their tribal sizes around a statistically definable norm (c. 350-500 people) and in maintaining this as a constant, it was tribal area which varied with resources. In the rich areas of the coast, it was a case of more tribes per unit area, and not bigger ones, in the desert it was fewer tribes and not smaller ones. Units of this order of size and complexity can be seen as having satisfied such powerful sociological needs that their integrity was maintained, transcending variations in the environment.

Looking now at Tasmanian tribes (Jones 1974),
we see that their population distribution was
400 ± 140 (n=9), occupying tribal territories of
5000 ± 2200 sq km (Table 1). The areas of the
abandoned 'greater' Bassian islands, together with
the populations which they might have supported
(Table 3) fall into the middle of these distributions.
This fact clearly questions my argument. In the
opinion of the terminal Pleistocene occupants of
the region, territories of the same order of size
as those of ethnographic Tasmanian tribes were not
big enough to avoid being abandoned. Looking at
the actual seasonal movements of Tasmanian bands
however, we find that their annual territories
were in fact considerably larger than these formal
tribal ones. I will summarise the movements of
the bands of only two tribes, but ethnographic
details for the rest are documented (Jones 1974).

During a single year, bands of the South West
Tribe with their estates at Port Davey, visited the
Maatsuyker Islands off the southern coast and
possibly even Recherche Bay near South East Cape.
In the opposite direction they foraged north
certainly as far as West Point, and probably to
Cape Grim. The total range of these movements from
one apex to the other measured along the routes
which they took, add up to 400 km (Fig.2). These
extensive movements took place in the warmer months
of the year to exploit seasonally abundant foods
such as birds' eggs and seals. During winter, the
leanest time of the year, bands returned close to
their own estates, spaced out along the coast, and
ate shellfish and other littoral foods.

Bands of the Big River Tribe had their estates
in the upland country near the Great Lake in central
Tasmania. During the colder period of the year they
moved to lower land, some bands making regular trips
to the east coast. In the opposite direction, the
ochre mines and wet sclerophyll and plains country
of the Surrey Hills were visited, with some people

going to Cape Grim. The extreme range of these
movements along their roads was some 450 km (Fig.2).

The ranges of the bands of the seven tribes
for which we have adequate information are shown on
Table 1: their distribution being 314 ± 113 (n=7)
km. Looking again at the large Bassian islands at
the point of their formation (Fig.13), we see that
the greatest possible ranges, (measured in the same
way), within 'greater' King, Furneaux or Kangaroo
Islands, could only have been of the order of 100
to 150 km, significantly smaller than the
ethnographic Tasmanian figures.

We may here be at the solution to the problem.
Where an inundation cut across the annual territory
of the bands of a tribe, the smaller block of land
isolated was abandoned. Where the island being
formed encompassed the annual territory of the
bands of one or more tribes, these remained *in situ.*
Thus along the minus 55 m shoreline of Greater
Tasmania, there would have been enough room for at
least five or six overlapping annual territories,
so that the splitting up of the putative territories
of the residents of the Bassian saddle would have
had no immediate effect on those of others along
the western, southern and southeastern shores.
This was not the case with any of the other three
islands, though Kangaroo Island must have been
almost big enough.

Discussing Kangaroo Island, Lampert (in press)
has pointed out that the actual severance across
such putative seasonal movements need not have been
a catastrophic single event, but could even have
taken place over a period of decades or even several
generations. There is also the possibility of the
temporary emergence(s) of bridges due to slight
oscillations in the process of transgression (Hope
1973:165; Chappell and Thom this volume). Thus the
process of the abandonment could have been done
gradually, with fewer and fewer of the fitter

members of society making the steadily more
difficult journey, until one year a decision was
made that the costs outweighed the advantages. I
have made the untestable suggestion that it was to
a similar decision that we owe the strange absence
of watercraft, the knowledge to make them, the use
of close offshore islands and even the ability of
the men to swim in northeastern Tasmania (Fig.3),
in contrast to the rest of the island. Not only
might journeys to the receding Clarke - Furneaux
Islands have been discontinued, but also any
possible means to attempt the journey (Jones 1976:
257).

     In the minds of the people making these
decisions, might have been the sharp realisation
that it was only by fully marshalling the diverse,
seasonally deployed resources of their environment,
by a pattern of extensive movements, that they
could have maintained their population densities at
existing levels. Nevertheless, the astonishing
fact remains that in the splitting up of an annual
territory, the smaller segment was abandoned rather
than the social unit itself being divided. This
pattern of terminal Pleistocene decision making,
while serving to maintain social cohesion, consigned
a total of 13,000 sq km of land to the realm of the
dead and the Dreaming.

                 CONCLUSIONS AND IMPLICATIONS

     I have tried to show how some well-known
concepts of island biogeography can be used to
analyse the Aboriginal use of the archipelago south
of the Australian continent. From a study of the
human reactions to the eustatic inundation of the
continental shelf, a general rule for the region
can be proposed. When the sea broke up a single
block of land into two, the smaller one was
abandoned:

1. as the distance between them approached a
   critical point - in these particular contexts
c. 5-8 km, and
2. if the area of the smaller one was less than
   that of the annual territory of a social
group, the same order of size and structure as an
ethnographically recorded Tasmanian or southeast
Australian tribe.

In the Bassian environmental and cultural context,
islands became empty because 4000-5000 sq km were
deemed to be too small for a permanent population;
and they remained empty because a 10-15 km cross-
sea voyage was too great for recolonisation, or
re-incorporation into a wider economic system.

With different parameters, these general rules
might also have applied to other hunting societies
caught in the same situation. In Australia, it
can be shown in the case of coastal groups, that
annual territories tend to decrease in size as one
moves from temperate into tropical latitudes. This
is partly because of greater biological productivity
in the lower latitudes, but more importantly because
resources are more evenly distributed, both spatially
and temporally, through the annual cycle. Thus the
formally owned territory of the four communities of
the Gidjingali tribe of some 300 people on the
north coast of Arnhem Land (Meehan 1975:25, and
this volume), is only of the order of 650 sq km,
with an annual territory of some 1000 sq km, and
with an overall population density of six people
per km of coast, three times as great as in
Tasmania. One might predict therefore that the
minimum acceptable habitat will decrease with
decreasing latitude. This may well explain why
islands such as Groote Eylandt and Bentinck, to
say nothing of the Andaman Islands, were able to
maintain hunting and gathering populations, while
in absolute area being slightly smaller than some
of the abandoned Bass Strait ones (Jones 1976:258-
60; Radcliffe-Brown 1922:15-16; Erickson and
Beckerman 1975:107; Tindale this volume).

The Flandrian transgression had a profound
effect on Australian palaeo-ecology. Firstly,
something over 2,500,000 sq km of continental shelf
were drowned. Apart from Bassiania, its effects
on human populations have been documented on the
Nullarbor Plain by Wright (1971) and on the Torres
Plain by Golson (1972). Both Tindale (1967) and
Mulvaney (1975:136-7) have pointed out its probable
disruptive effects on the population of the Sahul
Shelf, where, unlike on the southern shore, human
groups could not fall back on a largely empty
hinterland - empty because of cold in Tasmania, and
dryness on the Nullarbor. Great as they were, these
effects were small compared to those on the Sunda
Shelf, where the entire configuration of the
province was transformed from being a continental
sized peninsula of Asia, into the world's largest
archipelago.

The Pleistocene Period, in terms of temperature
fluctuations, had little effect on the tropical
region of Sunda and Sahul, except on the very
highest peaks. However, the rise and fall of water,
rather than its lateral movement in a frozen state,
was the most important cyclical geographic factor
affecting human life in the region (see also
Tindale 1967).

Finally, the Tasmanian maritime data show what
an extraordinary event the initial human colonisation
of Australia must have been. Even during periods
of low sea level, the minimum ocean voyage was of
the order of 60 km (Birdsell this volume). The
survivors must have been of both sexes to reproduce
themselves, and as McArthur has pointed out (1976,
pers. comm.), the odds against the long-term
survival of a tiny founding population of a few
people are high indeed. Thus there was a combination
of many odds against this event happening - yet
happen it did, some time before 40,000 years ago
(Mulvaney 1975:153; Shawcross 1975; Jones 1975).
The archaeological record suggests man's presence

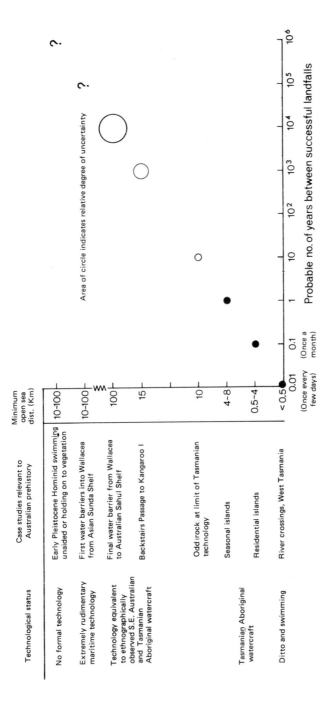

Fig.15. The probable number of years between successful landfalls plotted against the minimum open sea distance, as suggested by various prehistoric events in the Sunda-Sahul region, discussed in the text.

on the continental island of Java in early
Pleistocene times; his arrival across some water
barriers together with an elephantid and a large
rat on Timor and Flores in probable middle/upper
Pleistocene times (Glover and Glover 1970); and
finally his presence as the sole large placental
land mammal on the continent of marsupials, in the
late upper Pleistocene. Displayed on a logarithmic
chronological chart (Fig.15), this gradual migration
to the southeast of Asia gains a coherence when
viewed in terms of the formidable barrier that the
sea has been (Fig.7b), and particularly if the
maritime technology was of the level recorded in
ethnographic southern Australia. One of the
paradoxical things about the world's driest
continent is that its history has always depended
on man's ability to cross water.

ACKNOWLEDGEMENTS

I should like to thank Sandra Bowdler and
Ronald Lampert for the quality of their fieldwork
and for their intellectual generosity in rapidly
publishing their preliminary results concerning
the prehistories of Kangaroo and Hunter Islands.
Conversations with Jared Diamond made me aware of
some of the wider implications of the Tasmanian
data, and John Beaton and John Terrell led me
originally to his published works. I gratefully
acknowledge the stimulus which I received from
discussing the draft of this paper at Vancouver
with Joe Birdsell, David Harris, Norman Tindale
and Doug Yen. An airing at Cambridge provoked
useful discussions with Tim Bayliss-Smith, Nic
Shackelton and Geoff Bailey. Jim Allen provided
informed criticism of the text. Betty Meehan
suffered several early drafts, and has been exposed
to the slowly developing problem over the past six
years. A dug-out canoe voyage with her, Jackie
Butjaraga and Peter Djakandara to Buthya Islet,

8 km from Cape Stewart, Arnhem Land (see Meehan
this volume), finally convinced me, that viewed
from just above the level of the waves, we were a
long way from the shore. On the other side of the
continent, an experimental reconstruction of a full
scale Tasmanian bark watercraft with the aid and
exhortations of Professor N.W.G. Macintosh, Tom
Haydon, Ron Vanderwal and Charlie Turner served to
show the potentialities of the craft but not of the
navigator. Michael Turner demonstrated that a
sense of balance is the first requisite for a
putative Bassian traveller.

FOOTNOTES

[1] Slogan seen in the Oakland City Museum,
California, 1975.

[2] Calculated excluding the uninhabited west coast
mountains but including occupied offshore islands
as discussed below.

[3] The precise distance is hard to ascertain since
it is possible that this period between 22,750 ±
420 BP (ANU-1498) and c. 20,800 BP (Bowdler 1975b)
occurred slightly before the time of the lowest
retreat of the sea.

[4] Studies of the submarine topography of the present
straits between Hunter Island and northwest
Tasmania are not much help in investigating this
possibility because of deep tidal scouring channels
in the sea floor subsequent to inundation (Jennings
1959; Bowdler 1975b).

[5] Inspection of the artifacts and geomorphological
considerations cause me to change a previous view
(Jones 1968:200).

[6] Since this information has not yet been published
in an unrestricted form and is under active
analysis by Lampert, I will refer to it only in
general terms, acknowledging my debt to him for the
personal communication.

[7] By an interesting coincidence, one such group was
founded last century by Tasmanian and Australian
Aboriginal women and European sealers on the islands
of the Furneaux Group. Thus they re-occupied,
physically and ecologically, the empty niche
abandoned 8000 years previously, presumably by the
direct ancestors of some of the women. Birdsell
(1957:51) points out that this group lived largely
through hunting and gathering, concentrating
especially on coastal resources such as seals,
mutton birds, fish and shellfish. He suggests that
there was a tendency for budding off by emigration
to occur when population levels reached close to
350 people, this being some 85% of the theoretical
equilibrium of 400 people for this population in
this environment as estimated previously by Tindale.
Although living mostly on Cape Barren Island during
this century, the Islanders used the coastal and
inland resources of the whole Furneaux Group,
especially before intensive White settlement
occurred on Flinders Island in the years following
the First World War. This observed population
equilibrium level is remarkably consistent with my
independently derived estimate of the probable
population - c. 400 persons - capable of being
supported under a hunting and gathering regime on
these islands (Jones 1976:258) (Table 3).

[8] Presumably about half being adults and half
children.

[9] The details of this analysis will be published
elsewhere. Note that since area and coastline
are expressed in terms of different powers of the
linear measurement unit, it might be best to

consider the coast not as a line but as an area of
resources extending out 1 km at right angles to it
and thus expressed also in sq km. Alternatively,
when discussing the ratio between the areal and
coastal increments, these might best be expressed
as $\sqrt{A/C}$. In the Tasmanian case the ratio is 2.2.
For the South West Tribe, following a visit to
Macquarie Harbour, Tasmania, in 1975, and
discussions with J. Allen and R. Vanderwal concerning
the nature of the southwestern coastal region, I
have reduced the usable coastline by 80 km and
usable area by 775 sq km, the changes having been
made before commencing the present calculation. I
note the similarity of my formula (1) with that
proposed for the Andaman Islands by Erickson and
Beckerman (1975).

REFERENCES ·

Allen, H. 1972 *Where the crow flies backwards: man
and land in the Darling Basin.* Unpublished PhD
thesis, Australian National University, Canberra

Baudin, N. 1800-1803 [1974] *The journal of Post
Captain Nicolas Baudin... assigned by order of
the Government to a voyage of discovery*
(translated and edited by C. Cornell). Adelaide:
Libraries Board of South Australia

Bauer, F.M. 1970 The Kartans of Kangaroo Island,
South Australia: a puzzle in extinction. In
A.R. Pilling and R.A. Waterman (eds) *Diprotodon
to detribalization*:198-216. East Lansing:
Michigan State University Press

Bayliss-Smith, T. 1974 Constraints on population
growth: the case of the Polynesian outlier
atolls in the precontact period. *Human Ecology*
2:259-95

Berndt, R.M. 1959 The concept of 'the tribe' in
the Western Desert of Australia. *Oceania* 30(2):
81-106

Birdsell, J.B. 1953 Some environmental and cultural factors influencing the structuring of Australian Aboriginal populations. *American Naturalist* 87:171-207

1957 Some population problems involving Pleistocene man. *Cold Spring Harbor Symposia on Quantitative Biology* 22:47-69

1970 Local group composition among the Australian Aborigines: a critique of the evidence from fieldwork conducted since 1930. *Current Anthropology* 11:115-31

1971 Ecology, spacing mechanisms and adaptive behaviour in Aboriginal land tenure. In R. Crocombe (ed.) *Land tenure in the Pacific*: 334-61. Melbourne: Oxford University Press

Bowdler, S. 1974a Pleistocene date for man in Tasmania. *Nature* 252:697-8

1974b An account of an archaeological reconnaissance of Hunter's Isles, northwest Tasmania, 1973/4. *Records of the Queen Victoria Museum, Launceston* 54:1-22

1975a Caves and Aboriginal man. *Australian Natural History* 18:216-9

1975b Further radiocarbon dates from Cave Bay Cave, Hunter Island, north-west Tasmania. *Australian Archaeology* 3:24-6

and G.S. Hope 1976 *New evidence for late Pleistocene environments in northwest Tasmania.* Paper delivered at 47th Congress of the Australian and New Zealand Association for the Advancement of Science, Hobart, May 1976 (*Abstracts* vol.2:391. Hobart: University of Tasmania)

Bowler, J.M. 1975 Deglacial events in southern Australia: their age, nature, and palaeo-climatic significance. In R.P. Suggate and M.M. Cresswell (eds) *Quaternary studies:*

*selected papers from IX INQUA Congress,
Christchurch, New Zealand 2-10 December 1973*:
75-82. Wellington: Royal Society of New
Zealand, Bulletin 13

          , R. Jones, H. Allen and A.G. Thorne
1970 Pleistocene human remains from Australia:
a living site and human cremation from Lake
Mungo, western New South Wales. *World
Archaeology* 2:39-60

Casey, D.A. 1968 *Prehistory of Flinders Island.*
Unpublished

Chick, N.K. and E.A. Colhoun 1972 Tasmania. In
Research on Quaternary shorelines in Australia
and New Zealand. *Search* 3:413

Coleman, E. 1966 *An analysis of small samples from
West Point shell midden.* Unpublished BA (Hons)
thesis, University of Sydney

Colhoun, E.A. 1975 *A Quaternary climatic curve
for Tasmania.* Paper delivered at the
Australasian Conference on Climate and Climatic
Change (Royal Meteorological Society), Monash
University, Melbourne, December 1975

          1976 *The Quaternary environment of
Tasmania.* Paper delivered at 47th Congress of
the Australian and New Zealand Association for
the Advancement of Science, Hobart, May 1976
(*Abstracts* vol.2:392. Hobart: University of
Tasmania)

Darlington, P.J. 1957 *Zoogeography: the
geographical distribution of animals.* New York:
Wiley

Davies, J.L. 1967 Tasmanian landforms and
quaternary climates. In J.N. Jennings and
J.A. Mabbutt (eds) *Landform studies from
Australia and New Guinea*:1-25. Canberra:
Australian National University Press

Diamond, J.M. 1972 Biogeographic kinetics: estimation of relaxation times for avifaunas of southwest Pacific islands. *Proceedings of the National Academy of Sciences, U.S.A.* 69: 3199-3203

　　　　　 1973 Distributional ecology of New Guinea birds. *Science* 179:759-69

Erikson, P. and S. Beckerman 1975 Population determinants in the Andaman Islands. *Mankind* 10(2):105-7

Flinders, M. 1814 *A voyage to Terra Australis...,* (vol.1). London: Nicol

Flood, J.M. 1973 *The moth hunters.* Unpublished PhD thesis, Australian National University, Canberra

　　　　　 1974 Pleistocene man at Cloggs Cave: his tool kit and environment. *Mankind* 9(3): 175-88

Galloway, R.W. 1965 Late Quaternary climates in Australia. *Journal of Geology* 73:603-18

Glover, I.C. and E.A. Glover 1970 Pleistocene flaked tools from Timor and Flores. *Mankind* 7(3):188-90

Goede, A. and P. Murray 1976 *Pleistocene man in south-central Tasmania: evidence from a Florentine Valley site.* Paper presented at 47th Congress of the Australian and New Zealand Association for the Advancement of Science, Hobart, May 1976 (*Abstracts* vol.2:396. Hobart: University of Tasmania) (To be published 1977 in *Mankind* 11(1))

Golson, J. 1972 Land connections, sea barriers and the relationship of Australian and New Guinea prehistory. In D. Walker (ed.) *Bridge and barrier: the natural and cultural history of Torres Strait*:375-97. Canberra: Australian National University, Research School of Pacific

Studies, Department of Biogeography and
Geomorphology, Publication BG/3

Hiatt, L.R. 1962 Local organisation among the
Australian Aborigines. *Oceania* 32(4):267-86

          1965 *Kinship and conflict*. Canberra:
Australian National University Press

Higgs, E.S. 1975 *Palaeoeconomy*. Cambridge:
Cambridge University Press

Hope, G.S. 1976 Reflections on the 47th ANZAAS
Hobart, May 1976. *Australian Quaternary
Newsletter* 8:7-8

Hope, J.H. 1973 Mammals of the Bass Strait islands.
Proceedings of the Royal Society of Victoria
85:163-96

          and G.S. Hope 1976 Palaeoenvironments
for man in New Guinea. In R.L. Kirk and
A.G. Thorne (eds) *The origin of the Australians*:
29-53. Canberra: Australian Institute of
Aboriginal Studies

Howitt, A.W. 1904 *The native tribes of south-east
Australia*. London: Macmillan

Jennings, J.N. 1959 The submarine topography of
the Bass Strait. *Proceedings of the Royal
Society of Victoria* 71:49-72

          1961 Sea level changes in King
Island, Bass Strait. *Zeitschrift für
Geomorphologie* Supp.-Bd 3:80-4

          1971 Sea level changes and land
links. In D.J. Mulvaney and J. Golson (eds)
Aboriginal man and environment in Australia:
1-13. Canberra: Australian National University
Press

Jones, R. 1966 A speculative archaeological
sequence for northwest Tasmania. *Records of
the Queen Victoria Museum, Launceston* 25:1-12

1968   The geographical background to the arrival of man in Australia and Tasmania. *Archaeology and Physical Anthropology in Oceania* 3:186-215

1971   *Rocky Cape and the problem of the Tasmanians.* Unpublished PhD thesis, University of Sydney

1974   Tasmanian tribes.   In Tindale 1974: 319-54

1975   The neolithic palaeolithic and the hunting gardeners: man and land in the Antipodes. In R.P. Suggate and M.M. Cresswell (eds) *Quaternary studies: selected papers from IX INQUA Congress, Christchurch, New Zealand, 2-10 December 1973*:21-34. Wellington: Royal Society of New Zealand, Bulletin 13

1976   Tasmania: aquatic machines and off-shore islands. In G. de G. Sieveking, I.H. Longworth and K.E. Wilson (eds) *Problems in economic and social archaeology*:235-63. London: Duckworth

in press a   The Tasmanian parodox.   In Wright in press

in press b   Why did the Tasmanians stop eating fish?   In R.A. Gould (ed.) *Frontiers of ethnoarchaeology*. Santa Fe: School of American Research, and Alburquerque: University of New Mexico Press

Lakin, R. 1972   *Tasmanian year book no.6.*   Hobart: Government Printer, for Australian Bureau of Statistics, Tasmanian Office

Lampert, R.J. 1972   A carbon date for the Aboriginal occupation of Kangaroo Island, South Australia.   *Mankind* 8(3):223-9

1975   Kangaroo Island.   *Australian Archaeology* 3:39

1976 *Variation in Australia's Pleistocene stone industries*. Paper delivered at 9th Congress of the International Union of Pre- and Protohistoric Sciences, Nice, September 1976 (*Abstracts symposium XVIII*:44. Nice: Université de Nice)

in press Kangaroo Island and the antiquity of Australians. In Wright in press

and P.J. Hughes 1974 Sea level change and Aboriginal coastal adaptations in southern New South Wales. *Archaeology and Physical Anthropology in Oceania* 9:226-35

Leigh, E.G. 1975 Population fluctuations, community stability, and environmental variability. In M.L. Cody and J.M. Diamond (eds) *Ecology and evolution of communities*: 51-73. Cambridge (Mass.): Belknap Press of Harvard University Press

Lourandos, H. 1970 *Coast and hinterland: the archaeological sites of eastern Tasmania*. Unpublished MA thesis, Australian National University, Canberra

McArthur, N. 1976 Computer simulations of small populations. *Australian Archaeology* 4:53-7

MacArthur, R.H. and E.O. Wilson 1967 *The theory of island biogeography*. Princeton: Princeton University Press

McIntyre, A. and other CLIMAP Project Members 1976 The surface of the Ice-Age earth. *Science* 191: 1131-1137

Macphail, M. 1975a Late Pleistocene environments in Tasmania. *Search* 6:295-300

1975b *The history of the vegetation and climate in southern Tasmania since the late Pleistocene (ca. 13,000-0 BP)*. Unpublished PhD thesis, University of Tasmania, Hobart

Meehan, B. 1975 *Shell bed to shell midden.*
Unpublished PhD thesis, Australian National
University, Canberra

        in press (1977) Hunters by the seashore.
Journal of Human Evolution 6

Meggitt, M.J. 1964 Indigenous forms of government
among the Australian Aborigines. *Bijdragen tot
de Taal-, Land- en Volkenkunde* 120:163-80

Meston, A.L. 1936 Observations on visits of the
Tasmanian Aborigines to the Hunter Islands.
*Proceedings of the Royal Society of Tasmania
for 1935:*155-62

Mulvaney, D.J. 1975 *The prehistory of Australia,*
(rev.ed.) Ringwood (Victoria): Penguin Books

Murray, P. 1976 Investigations of late Pleistocene
cave deposits in Tasmania. *Australian
Quaternary Newsletter* 8:13-14

Plomley, N.J.B. 1966 *Friendly mission: the
Tasmanian journals and papers of George
Augustus Robinson, 1829-1834.* Hobart:
Tasmanian Historical Research Association

Radcliffe-Brown, A.R. 1922 *The Andaman Islanders.*
Cambridge: Cambridge University Press
(Reprinted 1964 New York: Free Press of Glencoe)

Reber, G. 1965 Aboriginal carbon dates from
Tasmania. *Mankind* 6(6):264-8

        1967 Additional carbon dates from
Tasmania. *Mankind* 6(9):429

Rousseau, J.-J. 1755 [1973] *A discourse on
political economy* (edited and translated by
G. Cole, J.H. Brumfitt and J.C. Hall). London:
Everyman Library

Shawcross, W. 1975 Thirty thousand years and more.
Hemisphere 19:26-31

Sigleo, W.R. and E.A. Colhoun 1975 Glacial age
man in southeastern Tasmania. *Search* 6:300-2

Sullivan, M.E. 1975 An archaeological survey of
    Montagu Island, N.S.W. *Australian Archaeology*
    2:37-44

Sutherland, F.L. 1972 The classification,
    distribution, analysis and sources of materials
    in flaked stone implements of Tasmanian
    Aborigines. *Records of the Queen Victoria
    Museum, Launceston* 42

              and R.C. Kershaw 1971 The
    Cainozoic geology of Flinders Island, Bass
    Strait. *Proceedings of the Royal Society of
    Tasmania* 105:151-75

Tindale, N.B. 1937 Relationship of extinct
    Kangaroo Island culture with cultures of
    Australia, Tasmania and Malaya. *Records of
    the South Australian Museum* 6(1):39-60

              1941 The antiquity of man in
    Australia. *Australian Journal of Science* 3:
    144-7

              1962 Some population changes among
    the Kaiadilt people of Bentinck Island,
    Queensland. *Records of the South Australian
    Museum* 14(2):297-336

              1967 Peopling the lands southeast of
    Asia. *Colorado Quarterly* Spring 1967:339-53

              1974 *Aboriginal tribes of Australia.*
    Berkeley: University of California Press, and
    Canberra: Australian National University Press

Williams-Parry, R. 1924 *Yr Haf a cherddi eraill.*
    Y Bala: Gwasg y Bala

Wright, R.V.S. (ed.) 1971 *Archaeology of the
    Gallus site, Koonalda Cave.* Canberra:
    Australian Institute of Aboriginal Studies

              1975 Broughton Island, N.S.W.:
    recent use of an offshore ocean island.
    Australian Archaeology 3:18-23

(ed.) in press *Stone tools as cultural markers: change, evolution and complexity*. Canberra: Australian Institute of Aboriginal Studies

SEA TRAFFIC, TRADE AND EXPANDING HORIZONS

JIM ALLEN

Department of Prehistory
Australian National University

INTRODUCTION

Current archaeological research in lowland and island Melanesia continues to emphasise the role of maritime trade in the reconstruction of the prehistory of the region. This paper sets out to review the available evidence for the antiquity of these systems, and discusses some of the implications of trading as an economic basis for one of these trader groups, the Western Motu from the Port Moresby area of central Papua.

SETTING

While trade in one or more of its various forms[1] is common to many human groups the social and economic complexities of the Melanesian maritime trading systems have long excited anthropologists. The work of Malinowski decreed that the *Kula* system become the outstanding example of the maritime systems in the region, but it is now possible to suggest that many characteristics of the *Kula* are shared by other Melanesian maritime systems which virtually ring the entire coast of Papua New Guinea and beyond. But while Malinowski's emphasis on the ceremonial aspects of the *Kula* has prevailed to the extent that for generations of students the word has conjured up the vision of armshells and necklaces in endless opposite orbit through the lives and deaths of the islanders in the system, latter day commentators (e.g. Uberoi 1962; Lauer 1970; Brookfield with Hart 1971) have demonstrated that

the exchange of *Kula* valuables enabled a vast array
of utilitarian trade in food and manufactured goods
between participants in the system and between
participants and others outside the *Kula*. 'Without
the valuables there would be little incentive for
regular transfer, and hence for the continuity of
long-distance trade on which the scale of
specialization in other parts of the ring depended.'
As well 'the economic role of the clockwise and
anti-clockwise circulation of valuables was to
integrate the system (Uberoi 1962), and at the same
time to create a "ring" in an entirely modern sense
by restricting the profits of the trade to the Kula
participants' (Brookfield with Hart 1971:327).

Such an assessment of the *Kula*, as a regional
integrated trading system involving long-distance
canoe travel and specialised merchants or middlemen
making a living by exchange surplus and/or trading
manufactured goods against food items, provides a
view in which the institutionalised ritual and social
aspects of the exchange of valuables are integrated
into a wider economic reality.[2] As such, the *Kula*
can more readily be equated with a number of other
maritime trading systems in the region. At the
same time such economic models have attracted the
attention of the archaeologists in the region, who,
ordained by the nature of their evidence to
emphasise technology, economics and ecology, see
some real hope of explaining their evidence more
readily in an economic rather than socio-ritual
framework. They may then be able to extend their
interpretations to the non-material aspects of
culture which have preoccupied many anthropologists
in Melanesia and elsewhere.

If areal integration through trade is as
complex and distinctive in coastal and island
Melanesia as Harding has argued (1967:241, but see
Sahlins 1972:294) it seems reasonable to ask how it
came about, and when. In New Guinea itself exchange
has a long antiquity, with coastal shell reaching

the highlands as early as 9000 BP or earlier (White
1972:147), but Hughes (1971:361) contrasts the network of highland trading links in New Guinea with
the maritime systems on the coast. Thus coastal
and island Melanesia can be considered separately.

LAPITA, OBSIDIAN AND CULTURAL STATUS

Arguing mainly from linguistic evidence Pawley
and Green (1976:54) date the expansion of
Austronesian speakers into island Melanesia at
about 6000 years ago, reaching New Caledonia by at
least 4000 years ago (Green 1976:57). These people
are considered by Pawley and Green to have
introduced agriculture, domesticated animals and
pottery. Within this generalised maritime expansion
the later manifestation now called Lapita, and
principally identified by the highly distinctive
Lapita style pottery,[3] is seen by Green as a new
and more specialised innovation correlated with the
advent of more efficient water transport (the
double canoe) which was 'dependent on the evolution
of an efficient internal-exchange network maintained
by effective two-way voyaging over distances up to
600 km' (Green 1976:57).

Firm evidence for this interpretation comes
from the recent results of obsidian sourcing carried
out by Ambrose (1976; Ambrose and Green 1972) which
has demonstrated that obsidian recovered from Santa
Cruz in the Eastern Solomons came from Talasea on
New Britain. A single flake from the same source
was excavated by Golson on the Ile des Pins at the
extreme end of the Melanesian island chain. More
recently obsidian from the northern New Hebrides
has been sourced to Lou Island in the Admiralties,
a straight line distance of some 2700 km. Temper
analysis of Lapita sherds from the New Hebrides
(Dickinson 1971) confirms that at least some of the
pottery was also imported, as seems to be the case

in other Lapita sites (see for example Dickinson and Shutler 1971). Green (1974:256-7) refers to the importation of other items into the Reef-Santa Cruz Lapita sites involving distances of 26 km to 400 km and beyond. The import of this new data is its implication for assessing the cultural status of the Lapita people.

Earlier excavators of Lapita sites pursued ceramic analysis with an almost admirable single-mindedness until Groube (1971:312), largely on the basis of his Tongan evidence, characterised Lapita potters as Oceanic 'strandloopers', people without a developed horticultural base who rapidly expanded ahead of the agricultural frontier. Almost immediately the Reef-Santa Cruz sites produced sufficient economic evidence (Green 1974:255) to throw serious doubt on this interpretation, and Green (1973, 1974, 1976) has since portrayed the Lapita people as seafarers and traders, a view already reiterated by Bellwood (1975:13) and to a lesser extent by Specht (1974:235-6) but questioned by Ambrose (1976:372-4) who cautions against a too simplistic equation of 3000 year old Lapita people and modern ethnographic trading systems on a number of grounds.

However the equation has already been drawn, and this new view of the cultural status of the Lapita people has generated comment that present day trading systems may have a long antiquity. Specht hazards the suggestion that trade was 'already formalised, if not institutionalised, in the early Austronesian cultures, perhaps closely linked with a status-achieving and/or status-maintaining system based on the redistribution of the products of both natural and human resources' and 'that trading of this kind was practiced [sic] by the original Austronesian settlers of Melanesia before they reached Buka Island' (1974:235, 236). Current archaeological evidence against which to test this viewpoint is both meagre and uneven, but the Papuan

south coast provides one area where some concerted
research has taken place and where such trading
systems were in existence at the time of European
contact.

ARCHAEOLOGICAL EVIDENCE

The earliest known pottery using and producing
communities appear on the south coast of Papua
around 2000 years ago. Details of the subsequent
sequence have been published elsewhere (Allen 1972,
in press a; Vanderwal 1973; Bulmer 1975) and a
brief résumé will suffice. From Mailu in the southeast to the Papuan Gulf (Fig.1) culturally related
sites have been located with basal dates all within
a century or so of each other. Culturally the
people concerned are viewed as a back migration of
Austronesian speakers presumably from somewhere in
island Melanesia although an exact derivation is
yet to be suggested (Vanderwal 1973:233).
Significantly the earliest levels of these sites
contain pottery similar and presumably generically
related to Lapita (Allen 1972:121; Vanderwal 1973:
204-8). The best expression of this early
manisfestation is Vanderwal's Oposisi site on Yule
Island, where the associated adze forms, *Trochus*
shell bracelets and other artifacts strengthen the
Lapita connection (Vanderwal 1973:230). Subsequent
developments at this and other early sites imply a
'Melanisation' of these migrants during the first
millennium AD.[4] In many respects these people
appear to be an example of 'human supertramps' (see
Diamond this volume) rapidly occupying what seems on
present evidence to have been an unoccupied economic
niche in an underpopulated region, if the absence of
any earlier sites (with the single exception of
Kukuba Cave which dates to 4000 BP) can be taken as
a guide (see Allen 1972:122). The economic data
from these sites suggests an undifferentiated mixed
gardening, hunting and fishing subsistence. While

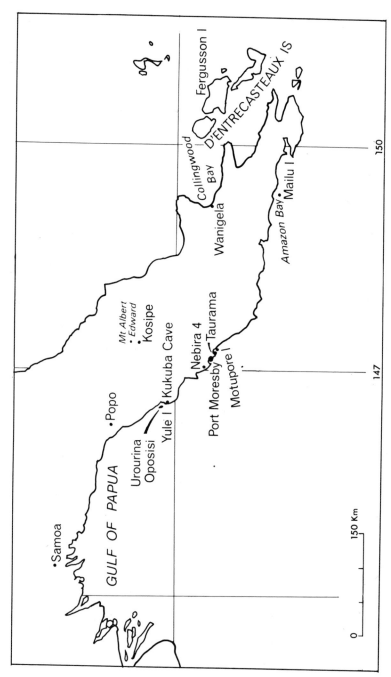

Fig.1. Map of southeast Papua, showing archaeological sites mentioned in text.

the main concentration is undoubtedly maritime,
sites like Nebira 4 near Port Moresby demonstrate
gradual adaptation to inland environments (Allen
1972:116-20). At the same time long distance
movement of raw materials is attested to by the
presence of Fergusson Island obsidian in these sites,
but apart from a suggestion of *Trochus* armshells as
imports (Vanderwal 1973:179) other possible long-
distance trade commodities remain uncertain and
indeed trade to any appreciably extent is not evident,
although the parallel evolution of ceramic types
over a thousand year period for sites as far apart
as Nebira 4 and Oposisi argues for close intra-
cultural ties, and emphasises an important addition
to the technology of the region: efficient sailing
vessels (Ambrose 1976:374).

This picture of gradual adaptation appears to
be disrupted about 1000 AD with the termination of
a number of long occupied sites. In the Port
Moresby and Yule Island areas groups appear who
cannot be derived from the coastal occupants of the
previous 1000 years on archaeological evidence;
ceramic styles alter radically and other artifactual
changes occur. Site locations and settlement patterns
become much more eco-specific, as does subsistence.
The obsidian trade from Fergusson Island now passes
no further west than the Aroma coast.[5] Such changes
are exemplified by Motupore, a site some 15 km east
of Port Moresby. First occupied some 750 years ago
and probably abandoned somewhere before 1700 AD,
this small offshore islet represents the typical
extreme coastal location and economic orientation
of people considered by me, on the basis of the
evidence in the site, to be antecedents of the
present day Motu. Motupore is rich in faunal remains
which attest to the occupants' heavy dependence on
shallow reef and estuarine fish and shellfish, some
domestic animals (dog and pig) and large quantities
of wallaby (*Macropus agilis*) from the nearby
inland. If the Motupore people were hunting on the
mainland themselves we might reasonably expect other

land fauna - cuscus, cassowary and reptiles to be
present also, but there is virtually no evidence of
these animals in the site. The Motupore faunal
remains appear rather to reflect the ethnographic
accounts of inland groups seasonally hunting large
numbers of wallabies and trading the smoked
carcasses to their coastal neighbours. Inland
polished axes, present in the earliest levels of the
site, strengthen the view that these new arrivals
quickly articulated inland trading links.

As described below, the single most important
occasion of the ethnographic Motu trade calendar
was the long distance canoe expedition called *hiri*.
Archaeological indications of the antiquity of the
hiri are few, although the occupants of Motupore
manufactured pottery and shell disc beads - both
items traded on that expedition. However all that
can be observed in the Motupore sequence is an
increasing simplification in ceramic decoration,
which might be in keeping with the sort of pottery
mass production recorded in ethnographic accounts
(e.g. Groves 1960:18). The archaeological solution
to dating the *hiri* lies in excavating recipient
village sites to the west, and a concerted effort on
this task has not begun. However a preliminary
examination of the site of Popo, an ancestral Erema
village, produced pottery which stylistically could
be equated with the upper levels only of Motupore
(J. Rhoads pers. comm.), evidence which accords
well with the oral traditions of the Motu, which
indicate an antiquity for the *hiri* (at least in its
modern form) of only several hundred years (Oram
in press).

A remarkably similar picture has emerged in
the Amazon Bay region some 300 km to the east of
Port Moresby, where Irwin's connectivity analysis
of prehistoric sites has demonstrated that during
the first millennium AD the most connected site was
on the mainland, despite the natural locational
advantages of the offshore island of Mailu. About

800 years ago a ceramic, if not cultural,
discontinuity occurred similar to that already
described for the Port Moresby region, and from that
time Mailu grew increasingly more important and
centrally located in respect of other existing
villages. By 1890, when it is known to have been
the centre of a flourishing trading system, it was
dominant in its location (Irwin 1973, 1974, pers.
comm.). Neatly complementing and confirming this
picture, X-ray fluorescence analysis of the pottery
from a number of the sites involved indicates that
2000 years ago pottery in the area was manufactured
from at least 5 discrete clay sources, suggesting
that a number of villages were producing pottery.
By several hundred years ago pottery appears to have
been made exclusively on Mailu Island and distributed
widely through trade (Irwin pers. comm.).

The Mailu and Port Moresby evidence, together
with that from the Yule Island area (Vanderwal 1973)
suggests that the last 1000 years of prehistory on
the south Papuan coast is marked by the growth of
localised and more specialised economies (Allen in
press b). Since such specialisation is basic to all
of the Melanesian ethnographic maritime trading
systems we can expect that in this region trading
was escalated to the complex levels observed in the
ethnography only within the last 500-800 years, that
is beginning some time after we can observe a
significanct disruption in the archaeological record
right along this coast. This more recent period I
see as reflecting a significantly higher ordering of
economic specialisation than can be observed during
the first millennium AD, although trading patterns
established then, particularly coast-inland contacts,
would have laid a basis for the rapid acceleration
suggested during the second millennium. This 'higher
order complexity' thesis I suggest offers a better
fit for the available evidence than the 'gradual
development' model recently proposed by Ambrose (1976:
374).

Turning to other areas the evidence grows ever
more meagre, but some incidental points can be
observed. The Port Moresby area was one of two
principal sources for the *Spondylus* discs used in
the manufacture of necklaces for the *Kula* (Malinowski
1922:506-7; Saville 1926:161; Tueting 1935:26). On
the Port Moresby evidence here reviewed it appears
unlikely that the discs were being produced on a
large scale before 800 years ago, which places this
upper limit on their inception into the *Kula*.
Tubetube, the most centrally placed location in the
Kula ring and the community which subsisted almost
entirely on middleman trade (Brookfield with Hart
1971:327) provided Seligman with detailed traditions
of their arrival on that island (1910:428-30), again
suggesting no great antiquity for their place in
the *Kula*. Another well-placed *Kula* group, the
Amphlett Islanders, who traded pottery against
foodstuffs, considered their position so important
that they were prepared to live a day's sailing
away from their source of pottery clay on Fergusson
Island (Malinowski 1922:283). Both Malinowski and
Lauer (1970:227) assert that the Amphlett potters
held a monopoly on the pottery trade from the
Trobriands to Dobu immediately prior to European
contact, but the archaeological evidence suggests
that it was a monopoly of no great antiquity.
Egloff's (1971) Collingwood Bay sequence is divided
into four phases - Early Ceramic, Expansion, Refuge
and Historic-Modern. The Early Ceramic Phase dates
to sometime prior to 1000 BP; the Expansion Phase
begins about 1000 years ago, with the Refuge Phase
beginning about 600 BP. Two of Egloff's Trobriand
sites contain Early Ceramic Phase pottery and are
associated with stone arrangements. Whereas
contemporary Trobrianders ascribe little importance
to these monuments and claim no association with
them, they do however place extreme importance on
a series of burial caves which contain, in addition
to the bones of their ancestors, pottery belonging
to the Expansion Phase, dating to about 1000 years
ago. During this period D'Entrecasteaux wares

increase in popularity, and somewhere before about 600 BP they have entirely replaced the mainland Collingwood Bay wares (Egloff 1971:131-2). On this evidence the Amphlett monopoly would seem to be not much older than about 600 years; and secondly some general cultural disruption seems to occur, as on the south Papuan coast, around 1000 AD.

Similarly in Specht's Buka sequence the Mararing Style appears about 1000-1200 AD (Specht 1969:310-11), accompanied in Specht's view by a number of social customs which continue until recent times. Among these is the earliest appearance of the *kepa*, a ceremonial vessel used now in association with *menak*, a prestation pudding made by men. In recent times no single Buka group owned the tools and ingredients needed to prepare *menak*, so that all groups had to import one or more items. Further north Mararing wares are the first of the Buka sequence to reach Ambitle Island (Ambrose pers. comm.). While the same does not hold true for Kaplan's analysis of a pottery collection from Nissan Island, where three sherds are attributed to the Buka Hangan Style of 500 AD (1973:25), she also notes (1973:34) that trade in pottery may have involved restricted areas of southern New Ireland by 1000-1200 AD. In general this evidence again suggests an increasing trade tempo at this time.

How far the similarities in the dates of these changes are coincidental would require a fuller study than has so far been made. However in discussing the disruption along the south Papuan coast Vanderwal (1973:209-10) has drawn attention to one particular decorative technique for pottery, that of combing, and examined its distribution throughout island Melanesia. He has noted its presence in Fiji about 900 years ago, in New Caledonia about 1000 years ago, in the northern Solomons in an undated context, in Specht's Buka sequence beginning between 1000-1200 years ago, and on the Tami Islands between New Guinea and New

Britain, where one sherd was recovered from an
undated archaeological context. In the Buka
sequence combing first appears in the Malasang Style
pottery, which Specht suggests may have been a
purely local development, but it is the only major
stylistic element which continues into the Mararing
Style (Specht 1969:310), comment on which has been
made above. It should however be noted that Kaplan
(1973:23-4) prefers to see the Mararing Style
developing from the Malasang. Vanderwal (1973:210)
also notes several ethnographic examples, all in
the vicinity of the southeast corner of New Guinea,
and extends his general comparison to include a
number of motifs which recur throughout the region.

This review strongly suggests that the last
millennium has seen fundamental changes in island
and lowland Melanesian prehistory which are as yet
only partially understood in social and economic
terms. On the south Papuan coast at least, the
evidence points to the rapid acceleration of
localised specialisation, one association of which
is the maritime trading systems recorded in the
ethnography, and in this region at least the
antiquity of these systems would seem to be
reckoned only in hundreds of years rather than
thousands. Elsewhere the evidence is more uneven,
but hints of the same increasing specialisation
occur. In the absence of contrary evidence there
seems no reason to expect any great antiquity for
the highly specialised systems of Melanesian
maritime trade, especially those incorporating
middleman traders such as the Motu, the Mailu, the
Siassi, the Manus Tru and several groups in the
Kula, to mention only the larger ones.

HYPOTHESES ON THE EVOLUTION OF THE HIRI

While recent research both in archaeology and
in oral history (Oram in press) agree on no great

time depth for the *hiri*, a demonstrable rational
explanation for its development is yet to be advanced.
Recent commentators (Groves 1973; Dutton and Brown
in press; Oram in press) all stress the infertile
nature of the immediate coast occupied by the
Western Motu at the time of European contact, and
the need to seek food sources outside this region.
There can be no doubt that this need existed at the
time of contact, given the environment, population
sizes and their distribution on the landscape. For
all this the environmental stress hypothesis remains
nothing more than an explanation for the developed
system as first recorded by Europeans, and not
necessarily an explanation of why it developed in
the first place.

Although archaeological research in the Port
Moresby area has not yet been specifically directed
to comparative site analysis, the presence in a
large site near Boera of ceramic types closely
related to the earliest levels of permanent
settlement in Motupore (P. Swadling pers. comm.) and
Urourina further west (Vanderwal 1973) suggests a
general cultural replacement right through present
Western Motu territory around 800 years ago.[6] Given
what is known of the subsistence patterns from
Motupore and the nearby Taurama site (Bulmer 1975:
53-4), together with the ethnographic evidence, it
is a safe assumption that prehistoric groups in
Western Motu territory articulated trading links
inland and further west but population densities and
levels of trade are unknown.

Turning to Bootless Bay itself, in which
Motupore is situated, the evidence is more
substantial. At contact the village of Tubusereia
at the eastern end of the bay was the westernmost
Eastern Motu village; Pari, situated west along the
coast from Bootless Bay, represented the most
easterly Western Motu village. Although it is
certain that the bay was used for subsistence
procurement, in terms of permanent settlement the

western part of Bootless Bay was no-man's-land.
This picture is in contrast to the very recent
prehistoric picture, where in addition to substantial
village sites at Motupore and Taurama a further
dozen sites are known from the immediate perimeter
of the bay - a figure which might be doubled with
more systematic survey. It is not assumed that all
these were permanent habitation sites, indeed the
majority would appear to be temporary gardening and
fishing camps, but most contain pottery closely
related to the upper levels of Motupore. In short
the field evidence points strongly to a significant
build-up of population in the immediate area of the
bay from about 500 years ago, and a rapid
depopulation to the situation recorded at contact.

Oral traditions recorded by Oram (in press)
complement the picture. Although oral references
to Motupore are few, they suggest that people moved
from there to Taurama, which was subsequently sacked
by the Tubusereians, with survivors moving further
west to Port Moresby, and it thus seems likely that
the abandonment of Motupore was also the result of
war. Reasons for this warfare are not clear, but
from the archaeological evidence competition for
local resources seems a likely cause. Further,
Oram has demonstrated that the western zone to which
these refugees moved is considerably less fertile
than the Bootless Bay region which they vacated. A
sudden influx of people into this new region may
have severely strained existing subsistence patterns,
a likely result of which may have been the
intensification of long distance trading into the
sago areas of the west.

Perhaps the most widespread and consistent
tradition of the Western Motu concerns the inception
of the *hiri* and relates how a Boera man, Edai Siabo
was taken by a spirit into a cave beneath the sea
and instructed how to make the large trading canoe,
lagatoi (Fig.2), and how to undertake the voyage.
According to Boera informants Edai Siabo lived 10

Fig.2. A Motu *lagatoi* or trading canoe in Port Moresby harbour,
photographed in 1885 by J.W. Lindt.

generations ago ascending from a man aged 60 (Oram
in press), and the consistency and widespread nature
of the tradition strongly suggests that Edai Siabo
was closely connected with the initiation or
intensification of long distance trade to the west.
The association of the *hiri* with a single historical
individual is a strong suggestion that its inception
was a rapid and radical change of subsistence
behaviour which is consistent with the historical
reconstruction offered here. At some variance with
this reconstruction is the suggestion of
intensification of pottery manufacture in the upper
levels of Motupore and the association of styles of
this period with pottery from the Erema site of
Popo, presumed to be associated with the *hiri*
(mentioned earlier in this paper) but it may be
simply that intensified trading had begun while
Motupore was under stress but before it was finally

abandoned.

Within the context of this reconstruction the
environmental stress hypothesis looks more
rational.   Nevertheless it may still be superficial
on a number of grounds.   Looking at the ethnographic
picture of the developed *hiri* expedition a number of
questions spring to mind.   If for example alternative
food supplies existed nearer to home what
justification existed to divert time and manpower to
travel 800 km for them?   Why not attempt to
infiltrate nearer more fertile and less populated
regions?   Why involve a significant number of able
bodied men in ritual and secular preparations for
the voyage at the time Motu gardens required
clearing and fencing and planting, then face the
distinct possibility, often a reality, of loss of
life and cargo during an open sea voyage?   What
socio-economic platform was required to launch such
an organised expedition?

Clearly a model encompassing answers to these
sorts of questions must go beyond the environmental
stress explanation of the *hiri*'s beginnings.   We
may begin with the economic question of subsistence.
The *hiri* cannot be seen as a simple annual
expedition to supplement local food production at
one point in the year.   Instead it has to be seen
within the full round of Motu trade.   While the *hiri*
was away in the west the central Western Motu
villages would be visited by traders from villages
further east, bringing shell valuables to exchange
for pots, and fishing on the Motu grounds and
supplying the remaining Motu with fish.   They would
await the return of the *hiri* and a share of the
sago.   More sago would arrive later in an expedition
from the west, and a second *hiri*-like voyage west
(*hirilou*) might be undertaken in times of famine
(Dutton and Brown in press; Oram in press).   In
addition however, internal trade between Western
Motu villages appears to have been a year-round
activity arising from minor differences in local

resources and perhaps village specialisation.
Finally inland trade with Koita and Koiari groups,
where pots and coastal products moved more or less
continuously against hunted meat, vegetables,
stimulants and forest raw materials, has suffered
in comparison with the more spectacular *hiri*, but
should be seen as a basic underpinning of the
structure of the Western Motu trading economy.
Figs 3 and 4 illustrate the nature of Motu trade;
the data here is gathered from a number of ethnographic sources, and not even rough estimates of
quantity (and therefore relative importance) can be
attempted although both exports and imports via the
hiri were by volume the most important, and thus
this expedition can be regarded as the most important
single trading occasion. They do, however,
illustrate the *nature* of Western Motu trade. Of
items terminating with the Western Motu 69% are
either food or stimulants, 12% raw materials and
19% manufactured items. By including goods which
flow through the Western Motu central exchange, of
which they extract a percentage, the figures alter

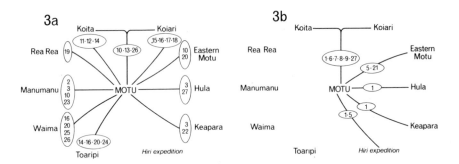

Fig.3.   Imports (Fig.3a) and exports (Fig.3b) in and out of the
central Western Motu exchange (excluding those shown in Fig.4).
Key: 1. Pottery; 2. Crabs; 3. Petticoats; 5. Boars tusks; 6. Dogs
teeth necklaces; 7. Net bags; 8. Salt; 9. Woven rope;
10. Vegetables; 11. Wallaby meat; 12. Netting fibre; 13. Bark
cloth; 14. Betel pepper; 15. Tobacco; 16. Betel; 17. Ginger;
18. Lime; 19. House timber; 20. Bananas; 21. Pigs; 22. Wooden
bowls; 23. Mangrove fruit; 24. Bows and arrows; 25. Sugarcane;
26. Feathers; 27. Fish.

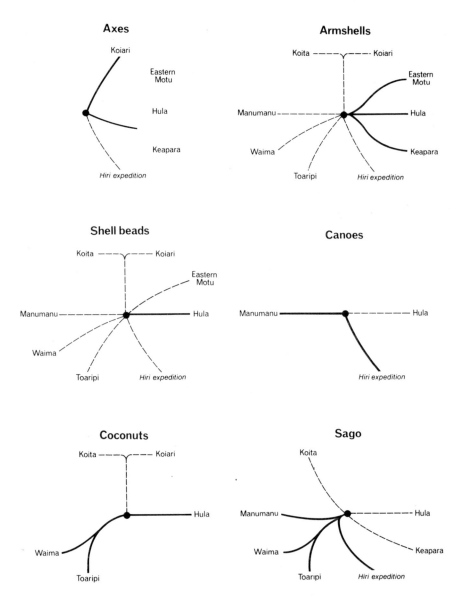

Fig.4. The movement of specific traded items into (solid line) and out of (dotted line) the central Western Motu exchange.

to: food/stimulants 60%; raw materials 16%;
manufactures 14%; and valuables 9%. While these
data are poor and these estimates only approximate,
they do support Belshaw's (1957:104) assertion 'that
the Motu depended very largely on it [trade] for
their food supply, leaving the agricultural skills
of the coast in the hands of their Koita neighbours.
This does not imply that gardening was not well
handled by the Motu - there is much evidence,
including that of ceremonial requirements, to the
opposite effect - but that they placed much
emphasis on trade'. In general terms the Western
Motu were a fishing and manufacturing group of
middlemen and traders and it is as a part of an
integrated trading economy that the *hiri*, while
still assuming large quantitative proportions,
begins to make more sense.

Elsewhere (Allen in press a) I have proposed
various defensive and socio-economic advantages for
various non-Motu groups entering into trade with
the Motu. Fig.4a illustrates one important reason -
shell valuables, and armshells in particular, which
were received from each of the eastern contact
groups and redistributed by the Western Motu both
inland and further west along the coast. In the
case of the *hiri*, armshells were used to reinforce
trading partner relationships, purchase canoe hulls
and also to purchase special conical packages of
sago which had ceremonial value in Motu villages
(Groves 1973:102). Thus while armshells were not
directly used in the purchase of the common packages
of sago, which were exchanged against pots, they
were nevertheless fundamental in facilitating the
sago/pottery exchange and are thus reminiscent of
the trade-creating valuable exchanges in the *Kula*
ring. By virtue of their location the Western Motu
villages controlled the westward movement of
armshells in a monopolistic fashion, but this still
fails to explain why they were not merely passed to
their nearest westward neighbours for sago which
those neighbours might acquire further along the

chain. According to Chalmers (in Lindt 1887:124-5)
the Motu obtained armshells from the east in exchange
for sago, and then exchanged the armshells in the
west for sago 'in bulk'. This suggestion of a
middleman surplus to be gained by bypassing the
villages immediately west of Western Motu territory
seems a plausible explanation but at this distance
in time it is impossible to know whether greater
returns offset the time, energy and considerable
danger attached to a *hiri* expedition. More telling
might be that at contact at least, pottery was being
manufactured by a small Motu group at Delena in Roro
territory west of the Western Motu, and shortly
after by the Roro themselves (MacGregor 1890:81;
Vanderwal 1976). MacGregor asserts that by 1890
Roro traders were exchanging their own pots for sago
in the Gulf. Since pottery was the principal item
that the Western Motu had to exchange in the same
area for the same commodity, sago, it would appear
that the two groups were competitors in the same
market. Was this belated development an attempt by
'squeezed' Roro entrepreneurs to break into the
Western Motu 'monopoly'?

Of relevance here is the fact that at some time
in the past Motu villages existed on Yule Island
which may have provided a trading link between the
more easterly Motu villages and the sago regions to
the west. It is tempting to speculate as Oram (in
press) has done that the disappearance of such links
may have resulted in the appearance of the *hiri* as
an alternative form of access to western sago
already established when the Motu and Erema were
nearer neighbours. At present however, it is
impossible to verify.

Despite the economic imperatives examined here
it is impossible to separate the *hiri* as a subsistence
expedition from the *hiri* as a social institution,
for in the *hiri*, as much if not more than in many
other activities of Motu life, socio-political and
economic objectives were closely intertwined. In a

series of articles Groves (1954, 1963, 1973) has
demonstrated that the major traditional objective of
a Motu man was to acquire prestige within his
village or village section (*iduhu*). The heads of
iduhu, the big men, competed at the highest levels
and lesser men at lower levels, acquiring prestige
and status not by the accumulation of wealth and
food but rather by the distribution of these things
on certain public occasions such as the payment of
brideprice and the cycle of mortuary rites. Groves
has argued that sponsoring a dance was the only way
a man 'might visibly display and commemorate his
ascendency over others' (1954:81), so that at the
highest levels of political competition the system
was essentially a closed one - in effect, to be a
big man one had to sponsor dances, but to sponsor
dances one had to be a big man since it involved
not only the sponsor's wealth and initiative but
also the power of his kinsmen and allies who owed
him allegiance. The *hiri* provided an important
entrée into this system. It was in one sense 'non-
visible' inasmuch as it was an experience outside
the village which irrevocably separated those who
went from those who stayed behind. It required
rigorous ritual preparation beforehand, and courage
and skill during the voyage; because exchange was
conducted on a face-to-face basis kin allegiance
disappeared and crew members competed with each
other and thus opportunities were made for individual
prowess to come to the fore. A successful *hiri*
elevated the status of all who went, and for more
junior men provided entry into higher levels of
reciprocal obligation. As Groves has summed-up,
'the *hiri* was one of the two major enterprises...in
which Motu entrepreneurs *at all social levels*
publicly displayed the cards they held in the power
game' (1973:105) (my emphasis).

It is in this wider view of the Western Motu
socio-economic system that the *hiri* is to be fully
rationalised, but in historical terms such a
description of how the *hiri* is integrated into

Western Motu lifestyle does not sit well with our earlier historical scenario. If we accept that Edai Siabo initiated the *hiri* only 10 generations ago we must postulate some fundamental alterations to both Western Motu economics and society in a very short space of time or else accept that the *hiri* was an economic enterprise which could be accommodated with ease in an existing system of trade and prestige acquisition developed since the ancestors of the Motu arrived on that coast some 800 years ago.[7] To me the latter seems more plausible, but must seriously weaken the environmental stress hypothesis. If the *hiri* was merely the intensification of an already existing adaptive mechanism (i.e. trade) under the impetus of population displacement, then the solution to the problems of subsistence in that environment were already at hand. In such a model the Western Motu were not *forced* by their immediate environment to trade in the west for food, but because trading was an already developed strategy, it was the obvious option among a possible number of alternatives, and thus environmental stress fails to explain how or why the *hiri* began, that is, why complex maritime trade was a viable socio-economic alternative. However if we can rely on the evidence from Motupore it may well prove to be the case that the ancestors of the Western Motu arrived with developed skills as manufacturers and traders and found not an infertile and hostile coast, but one which, with its protected coastline and abundant littoral resources, suited their specialised lifestyle and fostered its development.

CONCLUSIONS

If as suggested here the ethnographically recorded Motu trade system was both recent and socially complex then it implies some fundamental changes in the socio-economic history of the Papuan coast over the last millennium, and although the evidence is very meagre the same picture may well emerge elsewhere in Melanesia. In this sense the present paper is open-ended, or indeed ends where it should begin. It is offered here as a demonstration of current research in Melanesia and of the difficulties of integrating diverse sources of evidence. Hopefully it also indicates the fascination and possibilities of such data. Among the diverse strands of information it is already possible to predict that many of the maritime systems will be seen to share common characteristics such as the emergence of prosperous middleman groups; the location of trader villages not in terms of local subsistence resources, but rather in terms of trade strategy; and the growth of population in such trade centres and their dependence upon inland food sources. We may well be able to detect the effects of growing trade on social and political organisation and vice versa - were the normal Melanesians acephalous political structures adaptive factors in the development of maritime trade, or might the growth of trade eventually have altered these structures, given time? These and other themes must be taken up elsewhere.[8] Clearly however, maritime trade in Melanesia did integrate areas across ethno-cultural boundaries. Hughes (1971:367) was correct in observing that for most of the participants any concept of integration 'extended no further than the horizon' but in the last millennium at least, maritime trade extended that horizon significantly in Melanesia.

ACKNOWLEDGEMENTS

I am grateful to Sue Bulmer, Roger Green, Nigel Oram, Pam Swadling, Jim Specht and Ron Vanderwal for comments on a draft of this paper. They are not responsible for my interpretations of their data.

FOOTNOTES

[1] In this paper 'trade' and 'exchange' are
   synonymous and stand as glosses for a range of
terms such as 'exchange', 'barter', 'transfer',
'reciprocal transfer' etc found in current
anthropological literature.

[2] Which is not to enter into any argument of which
   is the more important aspect of the *Kula*, the
ritual or the economic aspect. Each appears to
complement the other.

[3] Principally but not entirely. In addition
   Bellwood (1975:13) lists a range of shell adzes,
arm rings and necklace units, and stone adzes of
various cross-section.

[4] At Oposisi Vanderwal (1973:232-6) argues for a
   physical and cultural break in the sequence
between the earliest deposit (the 'Initial Ceramic
Phase') and the following sequence: 'Besides lime
spatulae, pottery is the only other material item
introduced by the Oposisi people that characterises
the subsequent sequence, though the succeeding
pottery is different in type. The distinctive bone
industry and the diagnostic adzes disappear and the
narrow range of non-ceramic material culture that
succeeds, with its adzes of rounded cross-section
and its stone club heads presents a much more "New
Guinea" face' (1973:235). In no other South Papuan
early ceramic site is this separation so distinct
as at Oposisi, but even at this site there is no
clear indication of whether this change represents
the entry of a new group or a cultural fusion of
intrusive pottery users and local residents. Of
relevance to this problem is a unique artifact from
the early ceramic site of Samoa in the Papuan Gulf
(S. Bowdler pers. comm.) - a conventional New Guinea
disc clubhead manufactured from tridacna shell. The
fusion of Oceanic technology and local form adds
some limited weight to the idea of rapid

acculturation of these early pottery people.

[5] Sue Bulmer (1975:54) claims obsidian at Taurama
through 'all phases of occupation' in a site
which spans both the earlier (pre-1000 AD) and later
(post-1000 AD) occupation periods in the Port Moresby
area. This evidence is at variance with the remaining
data for this region. Extensive site surveying in
the area, where almost 100 sites are known dating to
the second millennium AD, has to my knowledge failed
to produce any with obsidian. Of excavated sites of
this period, apart from Taurama, Leask's (1943)
excavation of a midden produced no obsidian; Sue
Bulmer's Nebira 2 site (1975:55-6) has some 'tiny
flakes of Fergusson Island obsidian' but this site,
while predominantly of the later ceramic period,
has a layer of earlier ceramics at the base (Bulmer
1969:233 and Plate A), and it is not clear where
the obsidian flakes appear in the site. No obsidian
is reported from Bulmer's (1975:56) rockshelter site
of Eriama 1. On Motupore, where perhaps 200,000
flake stone artifacts have been excavated, only a
single flake of obsidian has been recovered.
Examination of the hydration layer on this piece
suggests that it is highly likely that it was flaked
well before Motupore was first settled, and that it
came onto the site as an 'antique' (W. Ambrose
pers. comm.).

Further east survey and excavations in the Hood
Peninsula area (Johnston n.d.) in 1971 located 19
sites, 17 of which appear to date to the second
millennium AD on stylistic ceramic evidence. Flaked
chert was recovered from 12 of these sites, but
obsidian occurred in none of them. However recent
sites along the Aroma coast further east, surveyed
in 1972 by G. Irwin and myself, produced an
abundance of large obsidian flakes.

West of Port Moresby obsidian recovered by
Vanderwal (1973:127) comes exclusively from first
millennium AD sites, none being present in the late

site of Urourina. In view of this accumulated data
it is difficult to accept the Taurama obsidian as
'indicating continued coastal trading as far as
Fergusson Island' (Bulmer 1975:54). This is not to
say that trade links did not extend this far, but
that obsidian seems not to have passed further west
than Maopa on the Aroma coast during the last 1000
years. The only possible explanation for the
Taurama obsidian which occurs to me is that the
later occupants may have been re-using obsidian
flakes from the first millennium AD occupation
period at that site.

[6] Since this was written I have received a draft of
   a paper by Pamela Swadling in which she argues
for cultural continuity in the Port Moresby region
during the crucial period c. 800-1200 AD. The
point is a complex one, involving Sue Bulmer's
'Massim style' ceramics, and I remain unconvinced
by Swadling's data and arguments to the extent that
I am presently aware of them. My point is that the
Motupore sequence cannot be derived from the previous
major cultural occurrence in the region, referred
to here as the early ceramic period and elsewhere
as the 'red slip' period. It is to be hoped that
Swadling's excavations throw light upon what is a
nagging temporal break in the Port Moresby sequence
at present. However in the absence of clear
information the question cannot be taken further
here.

[7] This date is based on the archaeological evidence.
   While genealogies do not comfortably stretch back
as far as this, the longer ones collected by Oram
(in press), of 16 or so generations, show a general
agreement with the archaeological evidence,
particularly if some latitude is allowed for the
telescoping of the genealogies. The linguistic
evidence is not so complementary. Using glotto-
chronological evidence, Pawley places the divergence
of Motu from its immediate neighbours at between
1500 and 2000 years ago and associates this with

the archaeological evidence for the arrival of the earliest pottery using groups at about that time (1975:93). As discussed earlier in this paper the break in the archaeological record 800 to 1000 years ago is so distinct that it is not possible to derive the later occupants from the earlier, and there appears to be no immediate solution to this conflict of evidence.

[8] In a paper entitled 'The Emergence of the Melanesian Middleman: Hypotheses on the Maritime Trading Systems of Melanesia' to be presented at a symposium on *Exchange Systems in Australia and the Pacific* being held to commemorate the 150th anniversary of The Australian Museum, Sydney, in August 1977.

REFERENCES

Allen, J. 1972 Nebira 4: an early Austronesian site in Central Papua. *Archaeology and Physical Anthropology in Oceania* 7:92-124

in press a Fishing for wallabies: trade as a mechanism of social interaction, integration and elaboration on the Papuan south coast. In J. Friedman and M.J. Rowlands (eds) *The evolution of social systems.* London: Duckworth

in press b Management of resources in prehistoric coastal Papua. In Winslow in press

Ambrose, W.R. 1976 Obsidian and its prehistoric distribution in Melanesia. In N. Barnard (ed.) *Ancient Chinese bronzes and Southeast Asian metal and other archaeological artifacts*: 351-78. Melbourne: National Museum of Victoria

and R.C. Green 1972 First

millenium BC transport of obsidian from
New Britain to the Solomon Islands. *Nature*
237:31

Bellwood, P. 1975 The prehistory of Oceania.
Current Anthropology 16:9-28

Belshaw, C.S. 1957 *The great village: the economic
and social welfare of Hanuabada, an urban
community in Papua.* London: Routledge

Brookfield, H.C. with D. Hart 1971 *Melanesia: a
geographical interpretation of an island
world.* London: Methuen

Bulmer, S. 1969 Recent archaeological discoveries
in Central Papua. *Australian Natural History*
16(7):229-33

            1975 Settlement and economy in
prehistoric Papua New Guinea: a review of
the archaeological evidence. *Journal de
la Société des Océanistes* 31:7-75

Dickinson, W.R. 1971 Temper sands in Lapita-style
potsherds in Malo. *Journal of the Polynesian
Society* 80:244-6

                and R. Shutler Jr. 1971 Temper
sands in prehistoric pottery of the Pacific
Islands. *Archaeology and Physical
Anthropology in Oceania* 6:191-203

Dutton, T.E. and H.A. Brown in press Hiri Motu:
the language itself. In S.A. Wurm (ed.)
*New Guinea area languages and language study,
III. Language, culture, society, and the
modern world.* Canberra: Linguistic Circle of
Canberra, Pacific Linguistics Series C, No.40

Egloff, B.J. 1971 *Collingwood Bay and the
Trobriand Islands in recent prehistory.*
Unpublished PhD thesis, Australian National
University, Canberra

Green, R.C. 1973 Lapita pottery and the origins
of Polynesian cultures. *Australian Natural*

History 17(10):332-7

    1974 Sites with Lapita pottery: importing and voyaging. *Mankind* 9(4):253-9

    1976 New sites with Lapita pottery and their implications for an understanding of the settlement of the western Pacific. In J. Garanger (ed.) *La préhistoire océanienne* (symposium XXII of IX Congress of the International Union of Pre- and Protohistoric Sciences, Nice, September 1976):55-87. Paris: Centre National de la Recherche Scientifique, preprint.

Groube, L.M. 1971 Tonga, Lapita pottery and Polynesian origins. *Journal of the Polynesian Society* 80:278-316

Groves, M.C. 1954 Dancing in Poreporena. *Journal of the Royal Anthropological Institute* 84: 75-90

    1960 Motu pottery. *Journal of the Polynesian Society* 69:3-22

    1963 Western Motu descent groups. *Ethnology* 2:15-30

    1973 Hiri. In I. Hogbin (ed.) *Anthropology in Papua New Guinea*:100-5. Melbourne: Melbourne University Press

Harding, T.G. 1967 *Voyagers of the Vitiaz Straits.* Seattle and London: University of Washington Press

Hughes, I.M. 1971 *Recent neolithic trade in New Guinea.* Unpublished PhD thesis, Australian National University, Canberra

Irwin, G.J. 1973 *Research prospects in coastal southeast Papua.* Typescript in Department of Prehistory, Research School of Pacific Studies, Australian National University, Canberra

1974   The emergence of a central place in coastal Papuan prehistory: a theoretical approach. *Mankind* 9(4):268-72

Johnston, G. n.d. *Archaeological site survey on the Hood Peninsula, Central District, Papua.* Typescript in Papua New Guinea Archaeological Survey Files, University of Papua New Guinea, Port Moresby

Kaplan, S. 1973 *A style analysis of pottery sherds from Nissan Island.* Chicago: Field Museum of Natural History, Solomon Island Studies in Human Biogeography 2

Lauer, P.K. 1970 Amphlett Islands pottery trade and the Kula. *Mankind* 7(3):165-76

Leask, M.F. 1943 A kitchen midden in Papua. *Oceania* 13(3):235-42

Lindt, J.W. 1887 *Picturesque New Guinea.* London: Longmans Green

MacGregor, W. 1890 Despatch reporting visit of inspection to the St Joseph River district. In *British New Guinea Annual Report for 1889-90*:76-86. Brisbane: Government Printer

Malinowski, B. 1922 *Argonauts of the western Pacific.* London: Routledge

Oram, N. in press Environmental factors determining migration and site selection in the Port Moresby coastal area. In Winslow in press

Pawley, A. 1975 The relationship of the Austronesian languages of Central Papua: a preliminary study. In T.E. Dutton (ed.) *Studies in languages of Central and South-East Papua*:3-105. Canberra: Linguistic Circle of Canberra, Pacific Linguistic Series C, No.29

and R.C. Green 1976 Dating the dispersal of the Oceanic languages. *Oceanic*

Linguistics 12:1-67

Sahlins, M. 1972 *Stone age economics*.   Chicago
and New York: Aldine-Atherton

Saville, W.J.V. 1926 *In unknown New Guinea*.
London: Seeley, Service

Seligman, C.G. 1910 *The Melanesians of British
New Guinea*. Cambridge: Cambridge University
Press

Specht, J.R. 1969 *Prehistoric and modern pottery
industries of Buka Island, TPNG*. Unpublished
PhD thesis, Australian National University,
Canberra

          1974 Of menak and men: trade and the
distribution of resources on Buka Island,
Papua New Guinea. *Ethnology* 13:225-37

Tueting, L.T. 1935 *Native trade in southeast New
Guinea*. Honolulu: Bishop Museum, Occasional
Papers 11(15)

Uberoi, J.P. Singh 1962 *Politics of the Kula ring*.
Manchester: Manchester University Press

Vanderwal, R.L. 1973 *Prehistoric studies in
Central Papua*. Unpublished PhD thesis,
Australian National University, Canberra

          1976 Tradition, history and
potting: a Papuan example of changing
settlement and economy. *Oral History*
(Port Moresby) 4:2-15

White, J.P. 1972 *Ol tumbuna: archaeological
excavations in the eastern central highlands,
Papua New Guinea*. Canberra: Australian
National University, Research School of
Pacific Studies, Department of Prehistory,
Terra Australis 2

Winslow, J.H. (ed.) in press *The Melanesian
environment: change and development*.
Canberra: Australian National University
Press

PART 4

THE ETHNOGRAPHIC WITNESS

In many parts of Australia, Melanesia and
Southeast Asia, economic systems of great
antiquity have survived until the present day.
Archaeologists become ethnographers and conversely,
ethnographers are increasingly looking to the
prehistoric record to analyse the historical
processes which led to the societies amongst
whom they are living. The belief that both
disciplines should be integrated as they once
were during the very birth of anthropology, is
what has given such a distinctive flavour to the
style of prehistoric research in the region.

Archaeologists have had to do their own
ethnographic observations because the questions
they want to ask have not been dealt with by the
social anthropologists who have monopolised the
field over the previous 70 years.

The four papers in this section deal with
economics, or more precisely with the methods of
subsistence and the ecological relationships of
man within his biological environment. They
provide the information in quantitative terms,
the food being described in numbers, in weights
and in terms of lists of species. There is an
insistence on describing the situations as they
really are, not in some romantic and mythical
'continuous present' which ignores the tin cans,
the clothes or the trade because these might be
deemed embarrassing or unaesthetic. Too often
these have been excised from the published
monograph and from the memory of anthropological
observers.

Separately, these papers are individual case studies, corporately they document the dynamic nature of hunting and horticultural economies when studied in minute detail. Such dynamic processes acted out on a long time scale are what we see reflected in the archaeological record.

SUBSISTENCE STRATEGIES ACROSS TORRES STRAIT

DAVID R. HARRIS

Department of Geography
University College London

INTRODUCTION

Ecological inference has long suggested that the time-honoured dichotomy between Australian 'hunter-gatherers' and Melanesian 'horticulturalists' does more to obscure than to clarify the real complexity of traditional subsistence economies. It is now acknowledged that Aborigines in Australia traditionally procured food in a great variety of ways, some of which approximated closely to 'agricultural' techniques of cultivation, harvesting and storage (Allen 1974; Campbell 1965; Irvine 1970; Tindale in press). Conversely horticulturalists in Papua New Guinea continue to exploit a wide range of wild food resources, particularly in lowland Papua north of Torres Strait (Ohtsuka this volume; Williams 1936).

As evidence of the diversity of traditional subsistence practices accumulates, the question raised by White (1971) and Golson (1972) of why Aboriginal populations in tropical Australia did not adopt horticulture from their northern neighbours across Torres Strait loses much of its problematic character, or more precisely, requires reformulation. Instead of posing the question in terms of a dichotomy between horticulture and foraging, we need to examine as comprehensively as we can the whole range of subsistence strategies practised by aboriginal populations in varied ecosystems at different times in the past. As I have previously argued (Harris in press a, b) it is only by adopting a spatially and temporally comparative approach that we can hope to reach a *general* understanding of the

processes that lead to change in the overall
orientation of subsistence economies.

It was with this objective in mind that I
undertook an investigation of traditional subsistence
across Torres Strait. The region offers a unique
opportunity to students of the origins and
development of tropical subsistence economies both
because indigenous peoples, from lowland Papua to
the southern Cape York Peninsula, practised a wide
variety of subsistence strategies within a broadly
uniform climatic environment, and because the
ethnographic and historical record is richer than
for most areas of equivalent size and significance
in the tropics. From the Oriomo Plateau of southwestern Papua New Guinea southward across the Torres
Strait as far as the southern Cape York Peninsula a
strongly seasonal rainfall regime prevails. This
regime is reflected in the areal dominance of open-
canopy 'savanna' woodlands adjusted to the seasonal
alternation of wet and dry conditions; although the
very extent of these woodlands tends to obscure the
existence of more restricted plant communities,
such as areas of rainforest, swamp, and coastal
thicket, that have been of disproportionate
importance in providing the plant foods traditionally
used by indigenous peoples.

Within this great tract of country of
relatively uniform climate, stretching some 950 km
from north to south, aboriginal populations were
practising a variety of subsistence systems when
sustained contact with Europeans began in the latter
half of the nineteenth century. These systems
varied along a gradient from north to south. In
lowland Papua and the northern Torres Strait islands
mixed systems existed which blended limited
horticulture with foraging; whereas in the southern
Torres Strait islands and the Cape York Peninsula
subsistence was almost completely non-horticultural
and a wide range of wild plant and animal resources
was exploited. It was the existence of this sub-

sistence gradient across Torres Strait that
encouraged me to undertake fieldwork and historical
research on traditional uses of plant foods in the
area. By doing so I hoped both to contribute to
specific knowledge of traditional patterns of plant
food procurement among Australian Aborigines, Torres
Strait Islanders, and coastal Papuans, and also to
illumine the general question of what processes
lead to, and maintain dependence on, tropical
horticulture and foraging respectively.

In order to gain a comparative perspective I
carried out fieldwork in five ecologically contrasted
zones: open-canopy woodland in the southern Cape
York Peninsula; closed-canopy rainforest in the
southeastern Cape York Peninsula, specifically on
the Atherton Tableland and coastal mountains between
Cairns and Mossman; mixed coastal ecosystems around
Lloyd Bay, mainly in the Lockhart Aboriginal Reserve;
insular ecosystems of the western Reserve islands of
Torres Strait; and littoral woodland and swamp along
the Papuan coast west of Daru, including the islands
of Saibai and Boigu. In this paper I summarise some
of the results for four of these zones (Fig.1) - the
rainforest is excluded - and present some preliminary
conclusions. A more complete account of traditional
subsistence in the region will be given in a
forthcoming monograph. The patterns of plant food
procurement characterised are those that are thought
to have prevailed at or shortly before the time of
European contact.

PLANT USE IN OPEN-CANOPY WOODLAND:
SOUTHEASTERN CAPE YORK PENINSULA

The open-canopy or 'savanna' woodlands are not
as uniform, structurally and floristically, as
casual impressions suggest (Fig.2), but they are
much less diverse than the eastern rainforests and
coastal ecosystems of the Peninsula and their yield

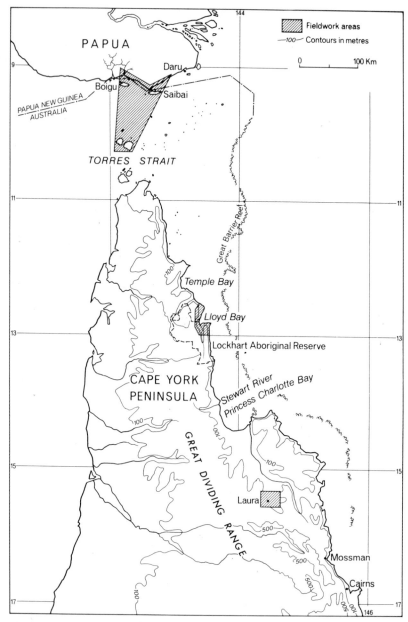

Fig.1.   Cape York Peninsula and Torres Strait: location map
showing fieldwork and Reserve areas; Reserve areas from
Department of Aboriginal and Island Affairs map of *Queensland
showing Reserves for Aboriginals*, Brisbane, 1973.

Fig.2. Open-canopy woodland dominated by *Eucalyptus* spp.; view east from near Mt Carbine 135 km northwest of Cairns (27 August 1974).

Fig.3. Freshwater swamp with water lilies (*Nymphaea gigantea*) and paperbark trees (*Melaleuca* sp.) 70 km north of Coen (26 September 1974).

of wild plant foods is relatively meagre. A few of
the smaller trees and shrubs of the woodland, such
as *Parinari nonda* and *Persoonia falcata*, provided
edible fruits which were valued principally as
snack foods eaten on hunting trips, but most of the
staple plant foods were obtained from localised
habitats or micro-environments within the woodland
ecosystem. The most distinctive and probably the
most important of these micro-environments in terms
of plant food procurement were the stream channels
and freshwater swamps that supported hygro- and
hydro-phytic plants through the long dry season
(Fig.3). Perennial plants with fleshy leaves, stems
and roots, such as palms, pandans, sedges and water-
lilies, were intensively exploited. Collectively
they represent the principal source of starch-rich
vegetable food available within the woodland
ecosystem which complemented the animal proteins and
fat obtained from terrestrial mammals, fish, birds
and other game.

Scarps and other relatively steep slopes
represent another type of micro-environment that
contributed staple plant foods to the traditional
diet. Rock outcrops frequently punctuate the steeper
slopes and allow pockets of deeper, damper soil to
accumulate. Yams and related tuberous plants
flourish better in these more mesic sites than on the
exposed slopes and plateau surfaces. Furthermore,
such sites are sometimes associated with freshwater
springs and with rockshelters, as in the Laura area
(Rosenfeld 1975), so that their attraction as living
areas is greatly enhanced. Drier, more exposed
slopes appear also to have functioned as foci of
plant food procurement in the woodland ecosystem,
particularly where they are dissected by the gullies
and minor stream channels that are commonly occupied
by stands of cycad (*Cycas* spp.).

These conspicuous, palm-like plants produce
starchy but poisonous seeds in large, easily
harvested quantities (Figs 4 and 5) and being highly

Fig.4. Burned and regenerating stand of cycads (*Cycas media s.l.*) in open-canopy woodland on scarp slope of the Atherton Tableland 15 km northwest of Cairns; the stand was severely burned in the dry season of 1973 (6 September 1974).

Fig.5. Mature seeds (ovules) on fertile leaves (sporophylls) of cycad (*Cycas media s.l.*); scarp slope of the Atherton Tableland 15 km northwest of Cairns (6 September 1974).

resistant to fire, they are differentially favoured by burning. The seeds appear to have been a staple food, despite the need to detoxify them, and it is likely that in pre-European times cycads were a managed rather than just a gathered resource. Their attraction as a food source lay in their abundant yield of large seeds, in the ease of harvest, in the possibility of storage, and in their occurrence in concentrated stands. Table 1 shows that the main Peninsula species, *Cycas media*, has an exceptionally low shell:kernel ratio and a relatively high nutrient status. My calculations of average yield, based on field sampling, demonstrate that average annual food production per seed-bearing plant is approximately 1625 kcal, and if this figure is related to data on the spatial occurrence of seed-bearing plants we find that a cycad stand of medium size, occupying some 200 m^2, yields in one year approximately 13 kg of edible kernel. This is equivalent to 65 gm or 131 kcal per m^2. Such a yield per unit area greatly exceeds the quantities of food that can be gathered from most wild plants, and even compares favourably with the yield of some cultivated crops.

Average weight in grams			%	%	%	%	%	%	
Shell	Kernel	Shell:Kernel Ratio	Moisture	Protein	Carbohydrate	Fat	Fibre	Ash	Kcal per 100g
4.8	6.5	1.0:1.3	49.91	5.09	43.52	0.22	0.55	0.71	201.28

Table 1. Average weight and proximate nutrient analysis of the seeds of *Cycas media* (*sensu lato*).

These data reinforce the view that cycads were a plant food resource of major importance to Aboriginal populations in the open-canopy woodlands of the Peninsula, as Rhys Jones' and Betty Meehan's recent observations (pers. comm. 1974) show them still to be in Arnhem Land. Because cycads combine extreme fire tolerance with unusual longevity - up to 200 years or more for individual plants - they are exceptionally well adapted to an ecosystem, such

as the open-canopy woodland of the Peninsula, in
which seasonal burning is dominant over long periods
of time. To a seasonally mobile human population
they offer a highly productive, quite nutritious,
easily harvested resource, the seasonal and spatial
availability of which can be predicted, and the
productivity of which can be enhanced by the
judicious deployment of fire to clear competing
vegetation. Burning also makes seed harvesting
easier, and stimulates asexual reproduction. The
fact that cycads are capable of fixing nitrogen
(Thieret 1958:30) may give them a further competitive
advantage over other plants when soil fertility is
low and/or has been reduced by burning. How far
Aborigines of the Peninsula went in managing cycads
to increase yields is unknown, but both fieldwork
observation and inference from the biology of the
plants suggest that the large stands of cycads
extant today may be, in large measure, the result of
Aboriginal manipulation of the woodland ecosystem.
Perhaps we should regard these stands as much the
ecological artifacts of a particular pattern of
plant food procurement as we do the gardens of
horticulturalists in the Torres Strait islands or
lowland Papua.

PLANT USE IN MIXED COASTAL ECOSYSTEMS: EASTERN CAPE YORK PENINSULA

In the east-central Cape York Peninsula, where
the Great Dividing Range and its associated uplands
approach the coast between Princess Charlotte Bay
and Temple Bay, the major plant communities of the
Peninsula reach their maximum diversity. Here too,
rainfall is higher than it is in the interior and
the dry season is somewhat less severe. The plant
communities vary from strips of rainforest on the
mountains parallel to the coast and along the larger
valleys to open-canopy forests and woodlands and
smaller areas of heath, grassland, mangrove

vegetation and saltpan.   There is also much variation
within the major communities, particularly close to
the coast where littoral thickets and swamps of
fresh or brackish water often occupy a narrow zone
between the beach or rocky foreshore and the forest,
woodland and heath communities inland. Within a
radius of 5-10 km from many points along the coast
great ecological diversity exists, both floristically
and in terms of plant life forms.   Indeed, when the
overall range of plant communities is considered, it
is clear that the east-central coast offered a
greater choice of plant resources to Aboriginal
inhabitants than any other region of the Peninsula.
This generalisation applies with particular force to
the coast and hinterland around Lloyd Bay in the
vicinity of Lockhart River and Settlement (Fig.6)
where I undertook fieldwork.

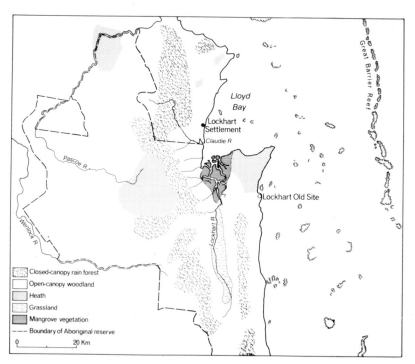

Fig.6. The Lockhart area: location map showing plant communities.
From Pedley and Isbell (1971:map) and fieldwork.

Whereas reconstruction of traditional patterns
of subsistence in the woodlands of the southeastern
Peninsula is necessarily based largely on inference
from ecological, historical, and archaeological
evidence, at Lockhart it was possible to work
directly with Aborigines who still retained much
traditional knowledge of wild food procurement.
While there I collected specimens of, and/or
information on some 86 species and varieties of food
plant and classified them in relation to the seven
main types of plant community in which they most
commonly grow.

The pattern of traditional plant food
procurement that emerges from an analysis of these
data is a broad-spectrum one in which the varied
resources of the mixed coastal ecosystems around
Lloyd Bay were exploited differentially in terms of
their accessibility and seasonal productivity. The
seven types of plant community that I distinguished
ecologically - riparian rainforest, open-canopy
forest and woodland, heath, grassland, mangrove
vegetation, freshwater swamp, and littoral thicket
- correspond quite closely to the Aborigines' own
perception of different plant food resource zones,
with the addition of an eighth community - montane
rainforest farther inland - which I was unable to
investigate. The seven plant communities can be
ranged along a gradient from least to most
productive of wild plant foods. Thus areas of
grassland and heath (Fig.6) contributed least to
traditional plant food procurement, although they
were valued as areas in which to hunt wallaby,
scrub fowl, and other game. The open-canopy forests
and woodlands provided a variety of fruits, most of
which were eaten raw, and some starchy stems and
roots, as well as non-edible products such as wood,
bark, resin, fibres and fish stupefacients which
were used in food procurement; but as far as staple
foods were concerned they were valued more for the
game they sheltered than as a source of plant food.

The riparian rainforests provided a number of
preferred wild plant foods, particularly figs and
other tree fruits and perennial herbs such as wild
banana (*Musa* sp.) and wild gingers (*Hornstedtia
scottiana* and *Amomum dallachyi*). These, together
with other perennial plant food such as pith from
the stems of palms (*Archontophoenix alexandrae* and
Gulubia costata) growing in the rainforests, were
especially valued because they were available
throughout the year.

The plant communities at or close to the coast
- mangrove vegetation, freshwater swamp and littoral
thicket - were the main source of staple plant foods.
Only two species of mangrove were reported as used
for food, but one of them, *Bruguiera gymnorhiza*,
proved to have a surprisingly high nutrient status
(Table 2). The processing of its fibrous fruits to
produce an edible pulp is laborious and the mangrove
has previously been described (e.g. by Hale and
Tindale 1933:115 and Flecker *et al.* 1948:12) as a

	% Moisture	% Protein	% Carbohydrate	% Fat	% Fibre	% Ash	Kcal per 100g
Bruguiera gymnorhiza	11.46	4.45	70.00	0.35	11.05	2.69	308.40
Dioscorea sativa var. *elongata (thampu)*	72.40	2.28	23.31	0.14	1.28	0.59	106.18
Dioscorea sp. *(kuthay)*	75.40	1.24	21.30	0.11	1.33	0.62	93.40
Dioscorea sp. *(ka-aatha)*	70.06	2.77	24.25	0.45	1.54	0.93	114.83
Tacca leontopetaloides	55.10	3.32	39.17	0.14	1.35	0.92	175.47

Table 2. Proximate nutrient analysis of the edible parts of
one species of mangrove, three varieties of yam, and Polynesian
arrowroot.

'lean-period' or 'famine' food. However it appears
to have been a staple food in the Lockhart area, as
it was also in the southern Torres Strait islands
and the Papuan coastal zone, and its processing by
repeated pounding, mashing through a basket, and
washing should be seen as part of an established
technique of refining other coarse and toxic foods

of the beach environment, such as matchbox bean
(*Entada scandens*) and 'Polynesian arrowroot'
(*Tacca leontopetaloides*).

The small freshwater and brackish swamps that
characteristically occur near the coast inland of
beach ridges made a major contribution to food
supplies. They are still favoured places in which
to hunt feral pigs and magpie geese (*Anseranas
semipalmata*) and in the past the plant foods they
provided were mainly roots, rhizomes, and tubers
rich in carbohydrates. These included water-lilies,
sedges of the genus *Eleocharis*, and at least two
forms of so-called 'taro'. One of these is a species
of *Colocasia* which is regarded as native to the
area and the roasted tubers of which were said to
have been a staple food. The other is said to have
been introduced from New Guinea or the Torres Strait
islands and to have somewhat bitter tubers. It
could not be identified because feral pigs root it
out before it reaches maturity, but it may be the
taro-like aroid *Alocasia macrorrhiza* which appears
also to have been a former plant food in the western
Torres Strait islands and lowland Papua.

The littoral thickets that commonly fringe the
back of sandy beaches are rich in wild plant foods,
particularly tubers and sweet fruits. The most
highly valued of the latter appears to have been
Manilkara kauki, the *wongai* of the Torres Strait
islands, which yields sweet fruits abundantly in
the middle of the dry season (July-August). But
the yams and other tubers which grow most abundantly
in littoral thicket eclipsed in importance all other
products of this plant community. Ten varieties of
'yam' were reported to me at Lockhart, but not all
are necessarily true yams of the genus *Dioscorea*.
However the five forms that I was able to collect
are all true yams and three of them - known locally
as *thampu* or long yam (*Dioscorea sativa* var. *elongata*),
kuthay (*Dioscorea* sp.), and *ka-aatha* (*Dioscorea* sp.)
- apparently represent former staple foods. *Thampu*

and *kuthay* yield 'sweet' tubers that can be eaten
after roasting or boiling (Figs 7 and 8), whereas
the tubers of *ka-aatha* (Fig.9), together with those
of 'Polynesian arrowroot' (Fig.10), need to be
peeled, mashed and leached in water before being
cooked and eaten. The place of these two bitter
tubers in traditional diet, despite the labour
involved in processing them, may be explained by
the fact that they contain more protein and have
higher calorific values than the 'sweet' yams
native to the area (Table 2).

Before wheat flour, sugar, rice and other
commercially produced carbohydrates became available
at government settlements, yams appear to have been
the principal starch-yielding staples of the
Lockhart area. There is no evidence that they were
formerly cultivated, but neither were they
indiscriminantly gathered. I was told that 'in
grandfather's time' the places where yams could be
found were well known, especially those in littoral
thickets along the backs of the beaches. When the
leaves on a yam vine turned yellow and withered at
the end of the wet season (March-April) it was a
sign that the tubers were ready for harvesting.
They were then dug up as needed through the dry
season, the digger marking the place by snapping a
convenient branch in the thicket and leaving it
hanging, or by breaking off a branch and placing it
in the bush where the vine grew. This served as a
sign of 'ownership' and insured that no one else
would harvest yams from that spot. Although there
was no formal ownership of yam grounds, permission
to dig for yams in a particular area had traditionally
to be sought from the male head of the family or
clan in whose customary territory the grounds lay.
Such permission would not necessarily be given only
to members of the family group but might extend to
members of another group in exchange for permission
to gather or hunt in their territory.

The need to insure continuity of the yam supply

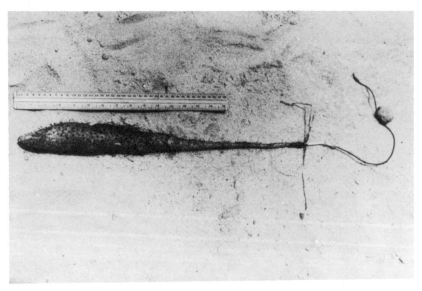

Fig.7. Tuber of *thampu* or long yam (*Dioscorea sativa* var. *elongata*) showing regeneration of vine from apex of tuber (pebble holds vine in place); ruler 38 cm long (4 October 1974).

Fig.8. Tubers and thorny vine of *kuthay* yam (*Dioscorea* sp.) growing in sandy soil beneath littoral thicket at back of beach, Lockhart Settlement (6 October 1974).

Fig.9.   Tubers of *ka-aatha* yam (*Dioscorea* sp.), littoral thicket
at back of beach, **Lockhart Settlement** (6 October 1974).

Fig.10.   Tuber **and dead stalks of 'Polynesian** arrowroot' (*Tacca
leontopetaloides*) in sandy soil beneath littoral thicket at
back of Restoration Beach 16 km north of Lockhart Settlement
(30 September 1974).

from year to year appears also to have been recognised.
I was told that it used to be common practice at the
time of harvest for the top of the tuber from which
regeneration takes place to be either left in the
hole or broken off and replanted in the same or a
nearby hole. This practice has been reported from
elsewhere in the Peninsula (e.g. McConnel 1957:2)
as well as from Arnhem Land, where it is reputed to
have applied to other roots and tubers as well
(Specht 1958:481). At Lockhart yams were said
never to have been deliberately planted near houses
or camp grounds because they would be less likely
to flourish in open areas away from their natural
habitat, and in particular, because children and
dogs would be liable to break the vines and dig up
the tubers before they were mature. I was told
however, that yams were sometimes planted on offshore islands to extend their distribution and to
ensure a 'reserve' supply. In general the
combination of regulated harvesting and frequent
replanting reported from Lockhart suggests that yams
were a managed rather than just a gathered resource
there. Indeed it may be said that their exploitation
approximated in several ways to horticulture, without the labour involved in tillage and the higher
yields per plant that cultivation affords.

Examination of traditional wild plant food
procurement in the mixed coastal ecosystems of the
Lockhart area indicates that a diverse and highly
productive subsistence system existed which focused
upon the micro-environments of the coast - reef,
shallows, inter-tidal zone, littoral thicket and
woodland including mangroves, and freshwater and
brackish swamps behind the beach - but which
extended both seaward and inland to exploit the
resources of deeper water on the one hand and of
rainforest, grassland, and heath communities on the
other. Exploitation was necessarily geared to the
alternation of wet and dry seasons, but although the
early wet season (December-January) was regarded as
a relatively lean time, food was never really scarce

and famine was said never to occur. The first half
of the dry season (April-July) was a time of
particular abundance when many plants reached
maturity following sustained growth during the wet
season. At this time a wide variety of ripe fruits
and seeds was available. Tubers too had by then
completed the process of bulking which takes place
rapidly in mid-wet season and slows down as the
above-ground parts become senescent with the approach
of the dry season. Towards the end of the dry and
into the wet season plant exploitation focused more
upon perennially available resources: those of
freshwater swamps, such as water-lilies, wild taros
and sedges; those of riparian and to a lesser extent
montane rainforests, such as wild gingers, palm
stems, wild bananas and figs; and those of the coastal
mangrove swamps.

Plant food procurement was complemented by
fishing, hunting and gathering animal foods. Green
turtle (*Chelonia mydas*), dugong (*Halicore dugong*),
salt and freshwater fish and shellfish contributed
more animal food than did terrestrial animals and
birds, although kangaroos, wallabies, cuscuses,
goannas (*Varanus* spp.), cassowaries (*Casuarius
casuarius*), the mound-building brush turkey (*Alectura
lathami*) and scrub fowl (*Megapodius freycinet*) which
provided eggs as well as flesh, geese, ducks and a
variety of other birds and animals were all hunted.
These animal foods contributed essential protein
and fat which was balanced by the carbohydrates
obtained from plant foods, especially from the yams
and other tubers. Considerable quantities of plant
protein were, however, derived from such sources as
the mangrove *Bruguiera gymnorhiza* and the tuber
Tacca leontopetaloides.

It is clear that the coast itself provided the
best habitat in the Peninsula for people practising
a subsistence system based on wild food procurement.
Not only does it represent an optimum location in
relation to the spatial distribution of resources,

but it is also a delightfully congenial environment
in which to live. The Aborigines of the east coast
between Lockhart and the Stewart River called
themselves 'people of the sand beach' and in so
doing they neatly epitomised their choice of the
optimum habitat in which to live. Not only is the
coast itself spacious, beautiful and rich in food
resources, but it transects an ecological mosaic of
great diversity and productiveness.

PLANT USE IN INSULAR ECOSYSTEMS: WESTERN TORRES STRAIT

The western islands of Torres Strait (Fig.11)
consist of the eroded remnants of volcanic rocks,
chiefly tuffs and granites, that are the above sea
level expression of the submerged Cape York-Oriomo
Ridge (Jennings 1972:34). Their soils are relatively
infertile, but the southern islands in particular
are surrounded and interspersed by extensive fringing
and platform reefs inhabited by numerous fish,
shellfish, turtles and dugong. The Strait experiences
the same strongly seasonal climate that affects the
Cape York Peninsula, so that although rainfall
increases northward across the Strait, the dominant
feature of the climatic regime is the alternation of
dry (April-November) and wet (December-March)
seasons.

The vegetation of the islands has been
substantially modified by human action, but open-
canopy woodland occupies uncleared parts of the
larger islands and probably represents the dominant
native vegetation of these islands in the past.
The smaller islands support mainly coastal
communities of littoral thicket and woodland as well
as mangrove vegetation, strips of which also fringe
the shores of the larger islands. Freshwater and
brackish swamps exist on some of the low islands
such as Sasi, and small areas of closed-canopy

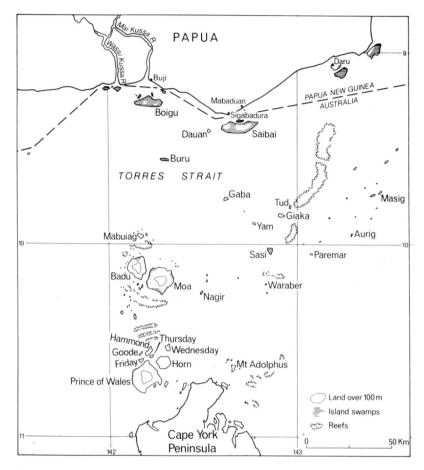

Fig.11. Western Torres Strait: location map. Indigenous and
European island names from Macgillivray (1852:chart) and
Haddon (1935:xvi).

sclerophyllous forest clothe steep, relatively
moist slopes on some of the higher islands,
particularly Dauan. There are however, no areas of
closed-canopy rainforest. Grasslands occur in the
interior of the larger islands, but on Moa and Badu
at least, there is evidence that these are the
result of the burning and clearance of woodlands
for subsistence purposes. Ecologically therefore,

the plant communities of the islands resemble, on a
smaller scale, the dry-seasonal and coastal
communities of the Peninsula. Floristically too,
the Strait represents less of a discontinuity between
Papua New Guinea and tropical Australia than was
formerly thought (Webb and Tracey 1972; Hoogland
1972; Wace 1972) and many of the species significant
for Aboriginal subsistence in the Peninsula were
available to, and appear to have been similarly used
by, the Islanders of the Strait.

In the course of fieldwork I was able to visit
six of the seven inhabited western Reserve islands:
Moa, Badu, Mabuiag, Dauan, Saibai and Boigu.
Traditional subsistence activities have declined
rapidly in recent decades as a result of increases
in social service payments to, and opportunities for
cash employment among, the islanders (Duncan 1974),
but by combining fieldwork with data from the
historical record it is possible to reconstruct, in
part at least, the subsistence patterns that existed
in the mid-nineteenth century when sustained European
contact began.

The particular interest of traditional
subsistence systems in the Torres Strait islands
lies in the fact that they incorporated in varying
degrees both wild food procurement and horticulture.
Detailed information on the use of wild plant foods
is difficult to obtain through fieldwork, and
historical references to such foods are usually
imprecise. Early European observers comment more
frequently - and more approvingly - on the
Islanders' 'gardens' than they do on the gathering
of wild plants, so that the role of horticulture in
the local economy tends to be over-emphasised in
historical accounts. There are however, some
historical sources that describe wild plant food
procurement, pre-eminent among which is O.W. Brierly's
record of Barbara Thompson's account of her four
years stay on Prince of Wales or Muralug Island in
the 1840s (Moore 1974). From this account there

emerges a clear picture of the heavy dependence of
the inhabitants of Muralug and nearby islands on a
variety of wild plant foods, particularly yams and
mangrove fruits (almost certainly the same
nutritious species, *Bruguiera gymnorhiza*, that was
exploited in the Lockhart area).

Barbara Thompson's testimony includes a
fascinating description of the small-scale cultivation
of yams in 1848 and 1849 (Moore 1974:A43). The
special interest of this description lies in a
statement that the planted yams were regarded as a
standby, if the wild yams should get scanty, rather
than as a staple crop. The implication is clear
that this activity was supplementary to the
procurement of wild plant and animal foods.
Furthermore, cultivation did not take place every
year (Moore 1974:A48). The only other crop that is
described as definitely planted on Muralug at this
time is sugar cane, although yams and sugar cane,
as well as sago and tobacco leaves, are reported as
having been brought to Muralug from nearby Nagir
(Mt Ernest) Island (Moore 1974:A37-8, A48, A66).
The evidence as a whole suggests that cultivation
was only small-scale and sporadic on Muralug and
that no sustained effort was made to develop
horticulture despite knowledge of a variety of crops
and techniques of cultivation.

North of the islands of the Prince of Wales
group horticulture was more firmly established. Yams
appear to have been the principal root crop, with
sweet potatoes, taro, bananas and sugar cane also
raised as staples. They were grown mainly in swidden
plots, although bananas and various tree crops,
particularly mango and coconut, were - and still
are - also raised in house gardens. Today
horticulture based on these traditional crops
persists least altered on the three northernmost
islands of Dauan, Saibai, and Boigu where a variety
of food crops is still raised in mixed plantings on
large, raised mounds (Figs 12-13). In the southern

Fig.12. Yams (*Dioscorea* sp.) planted in linear mound, Dauan Island (25 October 1974).

Fig.13. Rectangular mound planted with taro and mulched with grass; in background manioc, sugar cane, bananas, and coconut palms, Boigu Island (26 October 1974).

islands of Badu, Moa and Mabuiag horticulture has
declined much more. Yams for example are no longer
cultivated systematically because - as I was told -
it was too much hard work. Haddon describing the
situation at the beginning of the century notes
(1912:146) that yams were planted on the more wooded
land which had rich soil and good shade, and there
is no doubt that replacement of much open-canopy
woodland by shrubs and grasses, which has accompanied
the 'Europeanisation' of the islands during the last
hundred years, is one factor in the decline of
swidden horticulture in general and of yam cultivation
in particular; but a more potent cause has been the
general collapse of the subsistence economy in
recent decades which has gone further in the
southern than in the northern Reserve Islands.

In attempting to reconstruct the traditional
subsistence systems of the islands at the time of
European contact it is necessary to judge how far
the greater emphasis on horticulture in the northern
islands observable today is a result of the
differential decline in the subsistence economy this
century, and how far it reflects a long established
division between northern island economies that
emphasised horticulture and southern ones in which
plant foods were obtained mainly by gathering.
Documentary and field evidence (the latter in the
form of abandoned field systems) indicates that
horticulture was better developed and more diverse
on the southern reserve islands in pre- or early
European times than it is now. In addition it
appears that more intensive horticulture was
practised on the smaller islands of Mabuiag, Dauan
and Nagir than on the larger islands of Badu, Moa,
Saibai and Boigu.

The conclusion which both the fieldwork data
and the documentary evidence point to is that the
importance of horticulture in the traditional
subsistence systems of the western islands not only
increased along a gradient from south to north across

the Strait but also varied in relation to differences in the size and physical resources of individual islands. Thus, at least by the mid-nineteenth century, horticulture was relatively well established on the three northern islands, less important on Badu and especially Moa, and practised only sporadically with very few crops on Muralug and other islands of the Prince of Wales group; although within this broad pattern it was disproportionately developed on the smaller islands of Dauan, Mabuiag and Nagir. Given the evidence that knowledge of horticultural crops and techniques was general throughout the islands, even on those where planting was practised only casually or not at all, the differential importance of horticulture cannot be explained by assuming simply that some islanders had learned of it - from other islands or from nearby Papua - and others had not. Instead an explanation must be sought in the context of the overall subsistence systems of particular islands or island groups.

Although wild terrestrial plants and especially animal foods are meagre on all the islands relative to the mainlands to the north and south, they are more diverse and abundant on the large islands with more varied relief, such as Muralug, Horn, Moa and Badu, than on the smaller and more physically uniform islands. The abundance of maritime animal foods varies less with island size than with island position in relation to the more productive reefs and marine grazing grounds, particularly in terms of the availability of the islanders' two major sources of animal protein and fat: turtle and dugong. In general the clear seas around the southern islands, especially the reef-filled channels between Muralug and Mabuiag, are richer in fish, shellfish, turtles and dugong than the muddy waters off the Papuan coast which surround the northern islands.

For the islands of the Prince of Wales group, and for Moa (where horticulture was less well

established than on neighbouring Badu), a subsistence
system may be postulated that focused on the
seasonally adjusted harvesting of wild plant foods,
especially yams in the dry and mangrove in the wet
season, complemented by the year-round exploitation
of shores, inter-island reefs and submarine grazing
grounds, for fish, shellfish, turtle and dugong.
Terrestrial animal foods also have been relatively
more abundant on these larger islands. Scrub fowls
for example are present, and on Moa I observed many
of their nest mounds, now abandoned and grass-
covered. The abundance of these mounds may imply
that this forest bird was a former food source of
some importance, and they may also provide evidence,
as on Melville Island (Stocker 1971), of the former
extent of forest on the island. Some horticultural
products were no doubt occasionally obtained as
gifts or trade items from nearby islands where
cultivation was practised more systematically, as
the reported transfer of some foods from Nagir to
Muralug indicates; but it is reasonable to suppose
that the people of Muralug and Moa remained
basically foragers and fishers because this life
style provided sufficient food on their larger
islands and involved more varied and less arduous
work than horticulture. The proximity of Muralug
and nearby islands to the northern extremity of the
Cape York Peninsula, with whose inhabitants the
Kaurareg of Muralug were in close contact, would
also have tended to reinforce the non-horticultural
economy of the southernmost islands through exchange
of food and other goods, as well as simply by virtue
of a shared preference for hunting, fishing and
foraging.

On Mabuiag, and to a lesser extent on Badu,
subsistence depended more heavily on horticulture.
The amount of wild plant food available on Mabuiag
would have been much less than on Moa or Muralug,
the total areas of which are respectively some ten
and fourteen times greater than that of Mabuiag.
Badu, which is about seven times larger than

Mabuiag, would have yielded more adequate supplies
of wild plant food to a seasonally mobile population;
and the existence there of a tradition that
horticulture - and specifically the mound-cultivation
of yams - was introduced by the legendary figure
Yawar (Haddon 1890:36-8) may refer back to a time
when the island was wholly or mainly non-horticultural.
On Mabuiag however, it is difficult to envisage any
permanently established community supporting
themselves exclusively on wild foods, even allowing
for the richness in marine resources of the
surrounding sea.

Subsistence on the smaller islands of Nagir
and Dauan evidently incorporated quite intensive
horticulture. Macgillivray who visited Nagir in
1848 describes (1852:36) the careful cultivation
there of yams, of a root crop which may be the
aroid *Alocasia macrorrhiza*, and of tobacco; and
Moresby who visited Dauan in 1873 comments (1876:
132) on the 'richly cultivated valley, producing
taro' that he observed on the northeastern side of
the island. On both islands there was very little
terrestrial animal food available and subsistence
probably focused from an early time on horticulture,
associated with fishing, turtling, dugong hunting
and limited exchange of foodstuffs and other
products with neighbouring larger islands.

This examination of traditional subsistence in
the western islands reveals greater diversity in
insular economies than casual generalisations about
the Strait as a 'frontier' between horticulture and
hunting and gathering suggest. This diversity can
be understood by reference to variations in the
position, size, and physical resources of individual
islands and island groups, but the viability of
insular subsistence systems, particularly those of
the smaller islands not in close contact with
adjacent mainland areas, depended ultimately on
effective checks to increases in the human
populations they sustained. There are unfortunately

no demographic data available on the populations of
the western islands in the early decades of contact
with Europeans, but Haddon was able to collect some
information at the end of the nineteenth century.
It is clear from his observations that direct and
indirect methods of limiting population were widely
practised. He specifies (1890:359) three such
methods: abortion, for which (unidentified)
medicinal plants were sometimes used; infanticide;
and prolonged suckling, which meant that 'another
child is rarely born until the previous one is
three or four years old'. The relative importance
of these methods and of other checks on the build-
up of island populations such as fighting, emigration,
death at sea, etc cannot be assessed, but as Haddon
himself remarked (1890:359) after his first visit
to the islands: 'the small size of the islands and
the difficulty in procuring food, especially of a
vegetable character, were very strong reasons for
limiting the population'.

PLANT USE IN LITTORAL WOODLAND AND SWAMP:
PAPUAN COASTAL ZONE WEST OF DARU

West of Daru, the administrative headquarters
of the Western Province of Papua New Guinea, a
coastal zone of low muddy shores fringed with
littoral woodland stretches westward towards the
Mai Kussa and Wassi Kussa Rivers (Fig.11). The
zone includes the two low-lying, alluvial islands
of Saibai and Boigu, which, although politically
part of Queensland, are physically more an extension
of the Papuan coast than of the western granitic
islands of Torres Strait. Isolated granitic outcrops
do occur along the Papuan coast, as at Mabaduan,
but they do little to relieve the low, muddy
monotony of the coastal zone.

Subsistence in this zone today blends swidden
and house-garden horticulture with the procurement

of wild plant, terrestrial animal, and aquatic
foods. There is limited production of crops such
as coffee and peanuts for sale, but village
economies are still largely subsistence oriented.
As in the western Torres Strait, yams, sweet
potatoes, taro, sugar cane and bananas constitute
the traditional pre-European staple crops of the
Papuan coastal zone, but a significantly greater
number of wild plant foods are incorporated into
the subsistence economy here than in the Torres
Strait islands. Many of these plants have a dual
status as wild and tended or cultivated species.
The most conspicuous example of such a semi-
domesticated food plant is sago (Ohtsuka this volume),
which in this zone makes a major contribution to
carbohydrate supplies and bundles of which are
shipped by canoe to the Daru market. But there are
numerous less well known food plants that are
sometimes gathered wild and sometimes planted in or
near the village areas. They include, for example,
fruit trees such as *Manilkara kauki*, species of
Eugenia and 'wild' mango; kernel-yielding trees
such as Indian almond (*Terminalia catappa*), candlenut (*Aleurites moluccana*), a cashew-like species of
Semecarpus and species of *Canarium*; and herbs such
as wild gingers of the genus *Hornstedtia*. Most of
these plants were also traditionally used for food
in the Torres Strait islands and in the Lockhart
area, but there they were normally harvested in the
wild rather than planted. In addition to these
dual-status plants there is a wide range of wild
food plants that are still exploited in the Papuan
coastal zone. Some of these, such as cycads (*Cycas
circinnalis*) and the edible mangrove *Bruguiera
gymnorhiza*, were reported to me as having been used
until very recently as staple foods in the coastal
villages of Mabaduan, Sigabadura and Buji. Others
constitute minor or snack foods consumed more
casually on hunting and fishing trips.

The wide range of wild and cultivated food
plants that contribute to traditional diet is

paralleled by a diversity of animal foods,
particularly fish, shellfish and waterfowl from the
rivers, swamps and shallow seas of the coastal zone.
Aquatic resources are likely to have been particularly
important in the subsistence economies of Saibai and
Boigu islands, both of which consist largely of

Fig.14.   Linear, canal-like channel connecting flooded areas
of swamp, 2-3 km inland from village, northwest Saibai Island
(29 October 1974).

swamps which severely restrict the amount of
cultivable land.   On Saibai there are several
linear, canal-like channels a few metres wide and
of unknown length (Fig.14) which are said to connect
permanently flooded parts of the interior swamp.
They carry water in the wet season and whenever
tides are exceptionally high.   They may be natural
features, but their straightness suggests an
artificial origin.   They are referred to as 'old
roads' by the villagers and are reputed to have

been dug 'long time ago' to give access to the
interior by canoe. I was told that 'in those days'
villages were located inland to give protection
from raiding Papuan head hunters. Local tradition
concerning the artificial origin and purpose of the
'old roads' seems more likely to be correct than
that they were dug to drain land for cultivation,
although they may have served this purpose too. If
they were canals for canoe travel between areas of
permanent open water they would not only have served
as escape routes from raiders but would also have
given access to the best 'inland' areas for fishing
and for hunting waterfowl. I was unable to trace
fully the extent and direction of the channels, but
closer study would be worthwhile and might resolve
the question of their origin and use.

Terrestrial animal foods were less important
in the traditional diet of the Papuan coastal zone
than aquatic resources, particularly on the offshore
islands. On the mainland wild pigs, wallabies,
cassowaries, bandicoots and other small marsupials,
lizards and snakes were all hunted and eaten, but
their collective contribution to protein intake was
relatively small. It is doubtful whether wild pigs
were established on Saibai and Boigu in pre-
European times. Today they are regarded as a threat
to gardens - which are not fenced - and any found in
the bush are shot. Other terrestrial animals were
also less abundant than on the mainland, although
the mound-building scrub fowl was and still is
present on Saibai and Boigu.

In general, traditional subsistence in the
littoral woodlands and swamps of the Papuan coastal
zone appears to have been based on limited
horticulture including the tending of semi-wild
species, on the gathering of wild plant products and
shellfish, on fishing and to a lesser extent turtling
and dugong hunting, and on the hunting of wild pigs,
wallabies, other small marsupials, lizards, snakes,
land birds and waterfowl. There is little evidence

of resource specialisation having developed within
this broad-spectrum mixed economy, except insofar
as the adoption of limited horticulture can itself
be regarded as a form of specialisation. And the
major contribution of wild foods to traditional
diet in this zone further undermines generalisation
about the role of Torres Strait as a 'frontier'
between horticultural and hunter-gatherer subsistence
economies.

THE DIVERSITY AND DEVELOPMENT OF
TRADITIONAL SUBSISTENCE SYSTEMS

Two major conclusions emerge from this
investigation of traditional subsistence systems in
the Torres Strait region: first, that a clear
distinction cannot always be made between horticulture and the exploitation of wild plant foods;
and second, that dependence on horticultural crops
is only one of several forms of resource specialisation
practised in the region in pre-European or early
historic times.

Examples have been given of fruit trees and
tubers that are exploited both as wild and as
planted species. Such species cannot be regarded as
exclusively wild or cultivated plants and it is
often difficult or impossible to determine their
original natural distribution. One notable example
of such a plant, not so far mentioned, is the
coconut. Its presence is sometimes regarded as
indicative of a horticultural economy (e.g.
Vanderwal 1973:166), but it is capable of establishing
itself naturally following chance dispersal. It was
probably established at a few points along the east
coast of the Cape York Peninsula in pre-European
times - either as a result of natural dispersal or
having been carried in canoes south from Torres
Strait - but there is no evidence that coconut palms
were deliberately planted or tended there by

Aborigines before the arrival of Europeans.
Similarly, evidence of the intensive exploitation of
yams for food does not necessarily indicate a
horticultural economy. As we have seen, this can
vary from the regulated exploitation of wild species
in their natural habitats, as at Lockhart, to the
occasional planting of yams in prepared ground
despite continued dependence on gathered wild yams
as a staple food, as on Muralug, to a full horticultural commitment to the mound-cultivation of yams,
as on Dauan, Saibai, and Boigu. Other tubers, such
as *Tacca leontopetaloides*, *Alocasia macrorrhiza*,
and species of *Colocasia*, were also harvested 'wild'
in the Peninsula and on some of the islands, while
in other of the islands they were probably - and in
the case of *Colocasia esculenta* definitely -
cultivated.

The status of such fruit trees and tubers as
wild or cultivated food resources has thus varied
spatially and temporally according to the overall
orientation of the local subsistence economy towards
foraging or towards horticulture. But, as was
pointed out previously by Golson (1971), it is the
continuities in use of these plant foods from the
Peninsula to lowland Papua, despite contrasts in
their modes of exploitation, that is most striking.
These continuities no doubt relate to the initial
availability, palatability, and nutritional value
of particular plant products, as well as to the
establishment of customary food preferences, and
they point to the second general theme that emerges
from this investigation, that of resource
specialisation.

Although all the subsistence systems examined
were broad-spectrum in character - compared with
more specialised systems of food procurement
practised elsewhere - there is nevertheless
considerable evidence of intensive or specialised
use of particular resources within the broad-spectrum
patterns. In the coastal ecosystems of the Lockhart

area and the insular ecosystems of western Torres
Strait specialised exploitation of marine animal
resources developed, complemented by some parallel
specialisation in the use of terrestrial plant foods.
The procurement of fish, shellfish, turtles and
dugong was a major subsistence activity in both areas.
It played a central role in social life and was
supported by elaborate techniques of fishing and of
canoe building, especially in the Torres Strait
islands (Haddon 1912:154-71, 205-17). Complementing
the coastal and marine orientation of animal food
procurement was the specialised use of littoral plant
foods, chiefly tubers that grow in sandy soils near
the beaches and mangroves that occupy saltwater and
brackish swamps along the coast. It is not surprising
therefore, that intensive use should have been made
of yams - as wild or cultivated plants - particularly
as they yield carbohydrate abundantly which helps to
maintain a dietary balance with the fats and protein
obtained from fish, turtles and dugong. The use of
Bruguiera gymnorhiza as a staple food is also
explicable in terms of its high nutrient status and
the fact that it was available in the wet season
when few tubers could be harvested. It thus affords
an interesting example of resource specialisation
developing in the context of the seasonal scheduling
of wild food procurement (Harris in press a,
especially System C in Fig.1b).

In the Papuan coastal zone and the open-canopy
woodlands of the southeastern Peninsula there is
some evidence for the intensive use of particular
plant foods, but in neither area is the development
of resource specialisation as evident as in the
Lockhart area and the western Torres Strait islands.
Along the Papuan coast the adoption of limited
horticulture can be interpreted as a minor shift
towards resource specialisation, and in the open-
canopy woodlands of the southeastern Cape York
Peninsula specialised use appears to have been made
of the rhizomes and tubers of hydrophytic and
hygrophytic plants, such as water-lilies and sedges

growing in freshwater swamps, as well of the seeds
of cycads growing mainly on thin soils and dry
slopes in the woodlands. Both these resources were
exploited intensively in the long dry season of the
southern Peninsula and it is probable that stands
of cycads - despite the toxicity of the seeds - were
'managed', chiefly by seasonal burning, to enhance
their productivity. Certainly the harvesting and
processing of cycad seeds affords another example of
resource specialisation related to the seasonal
scheduling of wild food procurement, although in
the context of a broad-spectrum economy focused on
inland rather than on coastal and marine resources.

Seen in this comparative perspective horticulture in the western Torres Strait islands and in
lowland Papua takes its place as one of several
trends towards resource specialisation that developed
within the broad-spectrum subsistence economies of
the Peninsula and the Strait. To ask why Aboriginal
'hunter-gatherers' in the Peninsula did not adopt
horticulture is to assume a fundamental dichotomy
where in reality there was variation within a
subsistence continuum. What is required is an
explanation of the evolution of subsistence systems
in the region as a whole which would account for
this variation and in particular for the development
of the known and inferred patterns of resource
specialisation. There is as yet insufficient
evidence on which to base an explanation, but a
tentative hypothesis may be suggested by way of
conclusion.

The clearest evidence for specialised use of
plant foods comes from the smaller islands of the
western Strait, where horticulture was well
established. In these islands populations were less
mobile than they were in the more extensive woodland
and coastal ecosystems. Inter-island migrations did
take place in the Strait, as both Macgillivray (1852:
40) and Haddon (1890:353) indicate, but short-term
and seasonal movements of population were probably

neither as frequent nor as integral a part of
subsistence in the islands as they were on the mainlands to north and south. The populations of the
smaller islands are likely to have lived more
exclusively within the spatially more restricted
ecosystems to which their subsistence strategies
were primarily adapted, and this in itself partly
accounts for their specialised dependence on horticulture. But the adoption and development of
horticulture, as well as the intensified exploitation
of marine foods, may have been directly related to
increases in population.

In the absence of demographic data relating to
the pre-European populations of the islands it is
only possible to speculate about the relationship of
demographic change to changes in subsistence. It is
known however, that - other things being equal -
relatively sedentary human groups tend to experience
more rapid population growth than seasonally mobile
ones (Harris in press b). If populations increased
within the islands then more intensive use of
particularly abundant or palatable foods, both wild
and cultivated, is likely to have developed.

Thus the populations of the smaller islands -
particularly those of Mabuiag, Dauan and Nagir -
may have increased within their restricted territories
sufficiently to necessitate an intensification of
food procurement. Such an increase could have
occurred either internally on the islands or as a
result of emigration from Papua or elsewhere.
Alternatively, if one postulates an intensification
of food procurement sufficiently far back in time,
it can be envisaged as following from a reduction
in available territory as the Sahul Shelf flooded
during the post-glacial rise of sea level, resulting
ultimately in the concentration on the islands of
formerly more widespread populations. Whichever
process or combination of processes occurred, it is
apparent that at some time in their history the
populations of the islands intensified food

procurement by adopting horticulture.

As the areas of origin of the crops cultivated lie outside the islands, mainly in Southeast Asia and Melanesia, it is clear that the crops themselves, and no doubt also techniques of cultivation, were introduced to the islands from elsewhere, presumably from Papua New Guinea. But availability of crop plants and knowledge of cultivation does not alone result in the adoption of horticulture. Positive inducement is required to undertake the laborious business of clearance, tillage, planting, tending and harvesting the crops. Horticulture may initially have been established on the islands by immigrant 'gardeners' from Papua, or it may have been adopted piecemeal over a long period of time by populations already living on the islands, but in either case it is unlikely to have been sustained unless population pressure or some other stress factor made a continuing commitment to it advantageous.

The prevalence in the nineteenth century of infanticide and other methods of regulating population, which Haddon reports, suggests that population pressure on resources was experienced. Such pressure is likely to have been most compelling both on the smaller and on the less physically diverse islands which were nevertheless continuously occupied. Such islands are precisely those - for example Nagir, Mabuiag, Dauan, Saibai, and Boigu - on which horticulture appears to have been most firmly established. On the larger and more diverse islands such as Badu, Moa, and Muralug, with their greater terrestrial resources and access to the most productive marine ecosystems, pressure of population on resources would have been less intense. Greater seasonal mobility among the populations of these larger islands may also have tended to reduce demographic pressure by favouring lower rates of increase than prevailed among the more sedentary populations of the smaller and less diverse islands. If so, then this helps further to explain the fact

that groups living on the larger islands did not
commit themselves fully to horticultural resource
specialisation, as is most clearly attested by the
seasonally mobile population of the largest island,
Muralug.

    This line of reasoning does not however imply
that the differences in the subsistence systems of
the western islands observed in the nineteenth
century were environmentally determined or immutable.
They were rather the result of the complex interplay
of environmental, demographic and cultural variables
operating through time since the post-glacial
flooding of the Sahul Shelf. In the absence of
archaeological evidence (Vanderwal 1973), changes
in the subsistence systems of the islands cannot
yet be traced back beyond the limit of the historical
record. In particular, the length of time horticulture has been practised on the islands and its
impact on their vulnerable ecosystems cannot be
assessed. Pollen analysis might successfully be
applied to swamp deposits on some of the islands
and could yield valuable information on the history
of woodland clearance; and such clearance may, by
reducing the availability of wild food resources,
have encouraged the adoption of horticulture,
especially on the smaller islands. At present
therefore, we must be content to frame working
hypotheses that have some tentative explanatory
value, without being able to test them satisfactorily
against empirical evidence. There is insufficient
evidence from the mainland areas of coastal Papua
and of the Peninsula, as well as from the islands
of the Strait, with which to trace past changes in
subsistence, but comparative ecological study does
afford some understanding of the diversity and
development of traditional subsistence systems. It
demonstrates that, in all four of the ecological
zones examined, aboriginal populations were sustained
by broad-spectrum systems which incorporated some
degree of resource specialisation, whereas in the
island zone, where population pressure on resources

is likely to have been greatest, more specialised systems developed which focused to varying degrees on the exploitation both of horticultural crops and of marine resources.

ACKNOWLEDGEMENTS

I gratefully acknowledge the financial support I received for fieldwork from the Leverhulme Foundation, the Australian Institute of Aboriginal Studies, and the Central Research Fund of the University of London. The investigation was made possible by my appointment in 1974 as Visiting Fellow in the Department of Human Geography, Research School of Pacific Studies, Australian National University, Canberra.

I wish to thank all those who helped so generously with the fieldwork, and in particular, the following. At Lockhart Alick Sandy, Johnson Butcher, and David Thompson; I owe Athol Chase of Griffith University, Brisbane, a very special debt of gratitude for accompanying me to Lockhart and introducing me to the community.

In the Torres Strait I am grateful to the Councillors and people of each island that I visited for welcoming me so warmly, to John Buchanan of the Department of Aboriginal and Island Affairs at Thursday Island for helping to arrange my itinerary, and to George Hapgood of the Queensland State Health Department and Ron Shipway, owner of the MV 'Tambo Lady' for allowing me to join them on an anti-malaria spraying voyage through the western islands.

In Papua New Guinea I wish to thank Colin Middleton, Assistant District Commissioner, Western Province, who arranged for me to accompany a coastal patrol from Daru to the Mai Kussa River; Professor W.C. Clarke of the University of Papua New Guinea for much valuable assistance while I was in the country; and my fellow passengers, Nawe Akisa, Samote Wamu, and Sisa Keapi, who taught me much about the plants and people of the Western Province. I also make acknowledgement to the Papua New Guinea Government for permission to carry out research in the Western Province.

REFERENCES

Allen, H. 1974   The Bagundji of the Darling Basin: cereal gatherers in an uncertain environment. *World Archaeology* 5:309-22

Campbell, A.H. 1965   Elementary food production by the Australian Aborigines. *Mankind* 6(5):206-11; (6):288

Duncan, H. 1974 *Socio-economic conditions in the Torres Strait: a survey of four Reserve Islands.* Canberra: Australian National University, Research School of Pacific Studies, Department of Economics

Flecker, H., G.B. Stephens and S.E. Stephens 1948 *Edible plants in north Queensland.* Cairns: North Queensland Naturalists' Club

Golson, J. 1971   Australian Aboriginal food plants: some ecological and culture-historical implications. In Mulvaney and Golson 1971: 196-238

        1972   Land connections, sea barriers and the relationship of Australian and New Guinea prehistory. In Walker 1972:375-97

Haddon, A.C. 1890   The ethnography of the Western Tribe of Torres Straits. *Journal of the Royal Anthropological Institute* 19:297-440

        (ed.) 1912 *Reports of the Cambridge Anthropological Expedition to the Torres Straits,*

IV. Arts and crafts. Cambridge: Cambridge University Press

(ed.) 1935 *Reports of the Cambridge Anthropological Expedition to the Torres Straits, I. General ethnography.* Cambridge: Cambridge University Press

Hale, H.M. and N.B. Tindale 1933 Aborigines of Princess Charlotte Bay, north Queensland. *Records of the South Australian Museum* 5(1): 63-116

Harris, D.R. in press a Alternative pathways towards agriculture. In C.A. Reed (ed.) *The origins of agriculture.* The Hague: Mouton

in press b Settling down: an evolutionary model for the transformation of mobile bands into sedentary communities. In J. Friedman and M.J. Rowlands (eds) *The evolution of social systems.* London: Duckworth

Hoogland, R.D. 1972 Plant distribution patterns across the Torres Strait. In Walker 1972: 131-52

Irvine, F.R. 1970 Evidence of change in the vegetable diet of Australian Aborigines. In A.R. Pilling and R.A. Waterman (eds) *Diprotodon to detribalization*:278-84. East Lansing: Michigan State University Press

Jennings, J.N. 1972 Some attributes of Torres Strait. In Walker 1972:29-38

Macgillivray, J. 1852 *Narrative of the voyage of HMS 'Rattlesnake'... during the years 1846-1850...,* (vol.2). London: Boone

McConnel, U. 1957 *Myths of the Mungkan.* Melbourne: Melbourne University Press and London and New York: Cambridge University Press

Moore, D.R. 1974 *The Australian-Papuan frontier at Cape York, II. Documentary material.* Typescript in the library of the Australian

Institute of Aboriginal Studies, Canberra

Moresby, J. 1876 *Discoveries and surveys in New Guinea and the D'Entrecasteaux Islands. A cruise... of HMS 'Basilisk'.* London: Murray

Mulvaney, D.J. and J. Golson (eds) 1971 *Aboriginal man and environment in Australia.* Canberra: Australian National University Press

Pedley, L. and R.F. Isbell 1971 Plant communities of Cape York Peninsula. *Proceedings of the Royal Society of Queensland* 82:51-74

Rosenfeld, A. 1975 Air to ground. *Hemisphere* 19:21-5

Specht, R.L. 1958 An introduction to the ethnobotany of Arnhem Land. In C.P. Mountford (ed.) *Records of the American-Australian Expedition to Arnhem Land, III. Botany and plant ecology:* 479-503. Melbourne: Melbourne University Press

Stocker, G.C. 1971 The age of charcoal from old jungle fowl nests and vegetation change on Melville Island. *Search* 2:28-30

Thieret, J.W. 1958 Economic botany of the cycads. *Economic Botany* 12:3-41

Tindale, N.B. in press Adaptive significance of the Panara or grass seed culture of Australia. In R.V.S. Wright (ed.) *Stone tools as cultural markers: change, evolution and complexity.* Canberra: Australian Institute of Aboriginal Studies

Vanderwal, R. 1973 The Torres Strait: prehistory and beyond. *Occasional Papers* 2:157-94. St Lucia: University of Queensland, Anthropology Museum

Wace, N.M. 1972 Discussion on the plant geography around Torres Strait. In Walker 1972:197-211

Walker, D. (ed.) 1972 *Bridge and barrier: the natural and cultural history of Torres Strait.*

Canberra: Australian National University, Research School of Pacific Studies, Department of Biogeography and Geomorphology, Publication BG/3

Webb, L.J. and J.G. Tracey 1972 An ecological comparison of vegetation communities on each side of Torres Strait. In Walker 1972:109-29

White, J.P. 1971 New Guinea and Australian prehistory: the 'Neolithic Problem'. In Mulvaney and Golson 1971:182-95

Williams, F.E. 1936 *Papuans of the Trans-Fly*. Oxford: Clarendon Press

THE SAGO EATERS:
AN ECOLOGICAL DISCUSSION WITH SPECIAL REFERENCE TO THE ORIOMO PAPUANS

RYUTARO OHTSUKA

*Department of Human Ecology
University of Tokyo*

INTRODUCTION

Sago palms of the genus *Metroxylon* are important food plants in freshwater swamplands from Southeast Asia to Melanesia, and especially in New Guinea. Species of the *Metroxylon* group appear to have spread in some distant epoch from Indonesia to New Guinea, extending throughout the Melanesian chain to Fiji, with the exception of New Caledonia (Barrau 1959). Barrau also points out that in territories other than New Guinea and the neighbouring islands where varieties of *Metroxylon* exist, their use as food is now discontinued. When and why these plants dropped out of the food register in these areas is unknown. According to Yen (1974), in eastern Melanesia the *Metroxylon* species are said to be planted to provide thatching leaf for house building, with the extraction of starch from the inner pith of the trunk as an emergency food or dietary change being a secondary utilisation. It is of historical significance that the original Proto-Melanesian word for the sago palm means 'thatch' (Chowning 1963). Where the palm is known in Micronesia and Polynesia it seems to have been used mainly for building materials (Barrau 1961:60). However, the value of starch extracted from the sago pith as a food has been, and still is high for peoples inhabiting low swamplands of New Guinea. According to Lea (1972) the flood plains and swampy areas of the Sepik, Fly and Purari rivers of New Guinea still contained some 90,000 sago-eaters in the 1960s. The genus *Metroxylon* in Oceania consists of eight species, *M. rumphii*, *M. sagu*, *M. amicarum*, *M. bougainvillense*, *M. salmonens*, *M. warburgii*, *M. vitiense* and *M. upolense*, the first two being important as food (Barrau 1959). Elsewhere Barrau (1958:37) lists *M. oxybracteatum* as growing on the mainland of New Guinea. This report deals almost exclusively with the two food species, *M. rumphii* and *M. sagu*.

Sago palms grow 10 to 15 m in height and have trunks 50 to 75 cm in diameter. The palm flowers and fruits only once during its life span, and continues to store starch in the trunk before flowering. For this reason the palm is not worth felling until it is 10 to 15 years old. After the tree bears fruit it gives out a number of shoots from its root system, and therefore sago stands tend to be naturally dense. In many areas seedlings or shoots are transplanted[1], while in others propagation is understood if not practised. For example the Sanio-Hiowe living in the upper Sepik region, who rely entirely on wild stands of sago, are aware that sago can be planted by cutting and replanting young shoots (Townsend 1974). Sago can be harvested throughout the year, irrespective of the seasonal climatic cycle[2], and as Table 1 indicated, the yield of crude sago from a single tree varies considerably.

According to Townsend (1974) a Sanio-Hiowe woman produces 2.2 kg of sago on the average in one hour of work, and if walking between the hamlet and the sago grove is regarded as a component of the work, production drops to 1.9 kg of sago per hour. This productivity is similar to my data for the Oriomo Papuans and it can be assumed that sago production averages around 2 kg per hour.

Prehistorically, man's initial crossing of Wallace's Line from west to east took place in

Place	Number of trees studied	Weight of crude starch (kg) average (range)	Property	Reporter
Kiwai I. estuary of the Fly	—	90—140	wild & planted	Beaver (1920)
Abelam, east Sepik	2	219	planted	Lea (1964)
Sanio—Hiowe upper Sepik	5[1]	86 (28—205)	wild	Townsend (1974)
West Irian in general	—	110—160 (highest=410[2])	planted	Barrau (1959)
Oriomo	8	66 (29—104)	wild & planted	the present author

[1] Among the seven trees reported, two are omitted here by the present author, because sago-working of the two trees was not fully observed.

[2] Naturally sterile palm.

Table 1. Comparison of crude starch production from a single sago palm for five Papua New Guinea areas.

the Upper Pleistocene. Subsequently the post-glacial rise in sea level separated Australia from New Guinea (Golson 1971b), and one of the most striking differences between the two regions lies in the fact that in Australia human subsistence based on hunting and gathering persisted until European settlement, while in New Guinea horticulture has a long antiquity (see Golson this volume). The sago palm is absent in Australia also (cf. Golson 1971a, 1972), but whether any causal relationship between sago and horticulture exists has yet to be determined.

As well as illuminating one pattern of adaption in the freshwater zone of the tropics the study of sago palms and their utilisation may also contribute to a greater understanding of the prehistory of Sunda and Sahul. One effective approach is to investigate how contemporary people depending on sago utilise it for food and what part it plays in their subsistence economy as a whole,

whether that economy is basically a food producing
or foraging one. This paper is based mainly on
data gathered in the Oriomo Plateau and is directed
towards several specific questions about sago
utilisation. Firstly, what differences exist
between wild stands and planted stands in terms
of their value as a food resource? Secondly, while
the common method of pounding pith and washing
out starch has been regarded as a fairly developed
technology, what are the prehistoric implications
of this and other techniques reported in the
literature? Thirdly, if sago is compared with
other staple foods (yam and taro[3]) in the study
area, what can be said in respect of productivity,
the stability of sago as the main food resource and
the population carrying capacity of land?

RESULTS OF FIELDWORK IN THE ORIOMO PLATEAU

The people of Oriomo

The fieldwork on which this report is based
was carried out for a short period in 1967, and for
about seven months from July 1971 to March 1972 in
a village called Wonie (Wonio) on the Oriomo
Plateau (Fig.1); a preliminary report has been
published in Japanese (Ohtsuka 1974). The Oriomo
Plateau is one of the areas in which the people
depend heavily on sago for their diet. It is 450 km
in length, stretching from the River Digoel in West
Irian to the Fly River delta, and has an average
width of from 80 to 125 km. The plateau rises
some 60 m above the surrounding marshlands.
Average monthly temperature ranges within three
degrees, from 25°C to 28°C. The annual rainfall
reaches 2000 mm; about 80% of it falls in the wet
season between December and May, and the remainder
during the dry season, June to November. Dominant
vegetation types in the southern region of the
plateau (including the study region) are savanna

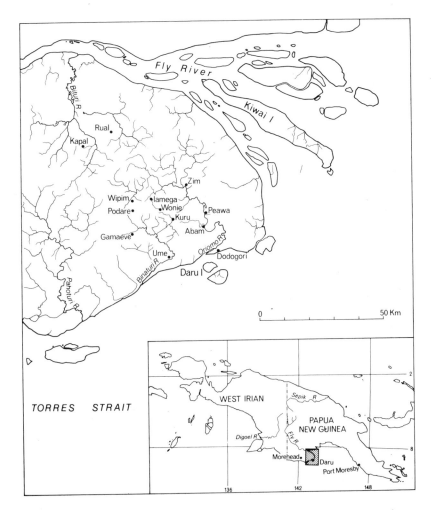

Fig.1.   The eastern end of the Oriomo Plateau, Papua New Guinea, showing position of Wonie village and Fly River.

and monsoon forest, while riverine forests and small patches of savanna woodland occur.   The natural vegetation in the area has been disturbed to a considerable degree by shifting cultivation practices (cf. Paijmans 1971).

The language spoken by the inhabitants of Wonie is called Gidra, one of the four languages

belonging to the Eastern Trans-Fly Family of the
Trans-Fly Stock (Wurm 1971:145) and spoken by
about 1600 people inhabiting 13 villages (Fig.1).
These villages vary in population from 50 to 200
and are located 10 to 20 km apart. The people
change village sites every five to ten years,
moving distances of 1-10 km. Population density
of the region is approximately one person per
square kilometre. In 1972 the population of Wonie
was around 100. There were 19 households, each
forming a basic economic unit, which consisted of
15 nuclear families, three polygamous families and
one widow's family. The traditional age-grade
system (Table 2) is still maintained. Young

Male	Estimated age	Female
miid		
	50	nanyu-konga
nanyu-ruga		
	40	
ruga-jog		
	20	konga-jog
kewal-buga		
	15—16	
yam-buga		ngamugai-buga
	7—8	
sobijog-buga		sobijog-ngamugai

Table 2. Traditional age-grade system of the Wonie villagers.

children belonging to *sobijog-buga* and *yam-buga*
for boys and *sobijog-ngamugai* and *ngamugai-buga*
for girls are cared for by their parents and other
adult villagers. *Kewal-buga* males part from their
parents to live alone or in a separate group.
While they learn how to hunt animals, come to know
who owns which sago stands, and familiarise
themselves with the topography, the vegetation and
the network of paths in their land, they depend to
a great extent on adult villagers for their daily
food. Men of *ruga-jog, nanya-ruga* and *miid* are

heads of household and women of *konga-jog* and
nanya-konga are housewives, both providing
sustenance for the community. The social
organisation is patrilineal. Infants of either
sex belong to their father's clan and do not
change, and the most valuable properties, i.e.
sago stands and coconut stands, are inherited
through the male line, usually from a father to
his sons.

Cash has started circulating in this area,
but the purchasing power of the people is still
very small. Popular foreign goods are steel axes
and knives, clothing such as shirts, shorts,
skirts and blouses, kitchen utensils such as pots
and bowls, matches and tobacco, all of which are
commonly used by all villagers. However foreign
foods are seldom brought to the village so that
the daily menu of the people consists, as a rule,
of local products.

Importance of sago

Food-getting activities consist of slash-and-
burn horticulture, hunting, fishing in small creeks,
collecting wild plants and small animals, and the
utilisation of sago starch and coconuts which appear
to belong partly to agriculture and partly to
collecting. One of the most striking features is
the lack of animal husbandry, but hunting is
frequent to provide animal foods. Judging from my
data on the time spent in food-getting activities
(Table 3) and the quantity of food intake (Table 4),
production of sago, slash-and-burn horticulture
and hunting are the major subsistence activities
and provide the bulk of the diet. Table 5 shows
the proportion of calorie intake according to
foodstuff. This table and Table 4 indicate the
high significance of plant foods, especially sago,
in the diet. Sago provides about 70% of the total
calorie intake, and adding calories provided by
banana and taro, the proportion reached 85%; among

plant foods taken separately, these values rise to 75% and nearly 95% respectively.[4]

DRY SEASON

Age-grade	Hunting	Fishing	Horti-culture	Exploitation of sago	Exploitation of coconut	Gathering
miid & nanyu-ruga	20	0	171	27	0	0
ruga-jog	71	0	133	169	19	0
kewal-buga	96	15	10	16	0	9
nanyu-konga	0	0	104	117	15	6
konga-jog	0	0	125	187	23	0

WET SEASON

Age-grade	Hunting	Fishing	Horti-culture	Exploitation of sago	Exploitation of coconut	Gathering
miid & nanyu-ruga	0	4	130	92	0	0
ruga-jog	43	0	75	74	24	0
kewal-buga	19	3	9	40	0	0
nanyu-konga	0	9	60	89	24	0
konga-jog	0	12	78	88	32	0

Table 3. Average daily time in minutes spent in food-getting activities. Data based on two surveys each of 14 consecutive days, for each season and for all adult villagers. All time away from the village settlement is regarded as working time.

	Sago	Coconut	Taro	Banana	Pineapple	Papaya	Other garden crops	Wild plants	Meat	Fish
dry season	9.6	0.7	4.0	3.2	1.1	2.8	0.2	2.4	1.4	0
wet season	10.9	0.4	0	8.2	0.3	2.6	0.1	0.3	1.7	0.1
average	10.1	0.5	2.0	5.7	0.7	2.7	0.1	1.3	1.5	0.1
total	10.1	0.5			10.0			1.3	1.5	0.1
by method or place	sago grove	coconut grove		slash—and—burn garden				gathering	hunting	fishing

Table 4. Average daily food consumption (kg) of 17 people from four households. Data are based on two surveys each of 13 consecutive days for each season. Composition of the sample group is three adult men, five adult women and nine children.

	% Calorie among plant foods			% Calorie among all foods		
	Dry season	Wet season	Average	Dry season	Wet season	Average
sago	72.2	79.5	75.9	66.4	71.6	69.1
coconut	1.7	1.0	1.4	1.6	0.9	1.2
taro	12.6	0	6.3	11.6	0	5.7
banana	6.4	16.5	11.4	5.9	14.8	10.4
papaya	2.8	2.5	2.6	2.5	2.2	2.4
pineapple	1.1	0.3	0.7	1.0	0.2	0.6
other crops	0.6	0.1	0.3	0.5	0.1	0.3
wild fruits	2.7	0.2	1.5	2.5	0.2	1.3
(meat)				8.0	9.5	8.8
(fish)				0	0.4	0.2

Table 5. Proportion of calorie intake by foodstuff. Data are based on average values for wet and dry seasons as represented in the sample given in Table 4.

Exploitation of sago compared with other plant foods

Methods of obtaining plant foods may be divided into three groups. These differ according to the nature of the plants and the technology employed. However, while we can delineate a system of collecting of wild plants, one of garden horticulture and one of exploitation of sago starch and coconuts, it should be remembered that the three co-exist as complementary parts of the subsistence pattern.

Wild plants collected are not curated nor are they owned by specific people or groups. The most productive are fruits of *Canarium vitiense* (collected from September to November) and *Gnetum gnemon* (from December to February). Naturally occurring trees of *C. vitiense* are fairly abundant so that villagers utilise those located within half an hour's walk from the village. The tree is cut down with an axe, and the fruits are plucked off the fallen tree. A collecting party will consist of one or two men belonging to *ruga-jog* or *kewal-buga* age-grades and several adult women and

children. The men fell the tree and the women and
children collect the fruit. Since collecting
parties usually contain women and children from
different households the fruit will be distributed
to more than one household. *G. gnemon* may be an
introduced species, and the trees are few in
number in the area. Since fallen fruit only is
collected, gathering is not organised. Instead one
or more villagers, mostly women and children,
collect them usually on the way back from the
garden to the village. The collected fruit is
not normally distributed since members of each
household can collect the fruit as they like.

Differences between the system of slash-and-
burn horticulture and that of exploiting sago
starch and coconuts appear to be a product of the
fact that it takes less than one year for most
garden crops to mature, while it takes 10 to 15
years for sago and coconut. Thus while all
garden plots are moved frequently, as with most
slash-and-burn horticulture, sago and coconut
grow naturally or are planted in semi-permanent
groves. Forest in the savanna and along rivers,
and also woodland savanna are selected for gardens,
usually within half an hour's walk from the village.
Sago groves grow exclusively on swampy land, of
which there are several large areas in Wonie
territory. In all of these, sago palms have
proliferated and most of the Wonie sago comes
from these large groves although there are many
small natural sago groves as well. Moreover, the
people have made small sago groves along creeks
by transplanting sago shoots. Unlike the garden
plots the sago groves lie scattered over Wonie
land, regardless of distance from the village.
Whoever clears a garden plot and plants suckers,
cuttings or seeds holds ownership of the garden
and the crops; usually garden crops are owned by a
husband and his wife or wives. Gardens are not
inherited. In contrast, sago and coconut stands
are each owned by married men, and sometimes they

are inherited. When a man marries he inherits some
sago stands from his father, alive or dead. These
vary in number according to the number of sago
stands owned by his father and the number of his
brothers. After this he will increase his sago
palms by planting suckers. Therefore the young
married man in many cases possesses a small number
of matured sago stands for 10 to 15 years after
marriage. A further distinction is that while sago
and coconuts can be harvested almost evenly
throughout the year, some garden crops cannot. Of
the eight major garden crops, taro, yam and sweet
potato can be harvested only in the dry season, and
sugarcane mainly in the wet season, while banana,
papaya, pineapple and perhaps cassava may be
harvested at any time.

Due to the seasonal availability of some crops,
especially taro, horticulture requires a yearly
cycle of labour. In the early dry season, from
August to October, members of each household clear
one or two new, big gardens, the men felling trees
with axes while the women clear shrubs and grasses
with bush-knives. When dry, the grass, shrubs and
trees are burnt in the mid or late dry season.
After this planting takes place. Before the
planting however, the gardens are occasionally
fenced in by men to prevent damage by wild pigs.
Besides these new gardens, every household usually
possesses one or more small gardens adjacent to the
village or at the margins of old gardens, where
perennial plants such as banana and papaya are left
growing. The kinds of crops planted in both types
of gardens are almost identical, with the proportion
of taro being much lower in the small gardens.

The planting is usually done by women using a
digging stick. Between planting and harvesting, a
new garden is weeded once or twice unsystematically,
generally by women. Old gardens where only
perennials grow are never weeded. Harvesting does
not require much labour input and is done little

by little as the food is required. Normally a
member of each household, usually the wife,
fetches the various kinds of crops almost every
day. Any crop is eaten within one or two weeks,
although unripe fruits, especially banana, are
sometimes harvested to be kept in the house in the
village. Harvests from the gardens are rarely
presented between households, because the kinds
of crops raised by every household are virtually
identical.

Sago exploitation involves only the initial
planting of a sucker and the eventual harvesting,
i.e. starch-making, both able to be done
throughout the year. In addition some of the
utilised sago stands are self-propagated ones.
According to the villagers, wild stands and
transplanted stands co-exist as sago groves,
although I was unable to determine the proportions.
As stated, the transplanting of the suckers is
done by married men. Individual holes are dug for
each sucker, after which no special care is
required until harvesting, but a married man will
inspect his own sago palms while on hunting
expeditions or while women of his group are
actually working sago at a grove. These frequent
visits play a useful role in determining the
right time to cut palms.

Sago production is carried out by groups which
include not only the owner of the sago palm to be
cut and his wife or wives, but also in many cases,
other villagers who wish to gain starch at the
moment. While sago-making parties are informally
constituted, a young couple possessing only a small
number of matured stands will tend to cooperate
with close relatives such as parents and elder
brothers; a widow or a wife in a polygamous
household will tend to join any group. As well,
the brothers and sisters of the owner, together
with their respective spouses, may join the
sago-making party. The produced starch is not

presented between households very frequently simply
because the composition of these parties ensures
distribution through a number of households.
However where a woman has been sick for a long
time or has just given birth, the redistribution
of starch to her household will normally occur.

Comparing the exploitation of coconuts with
sago it is found that planting methods, ownership,
inheritance, and the organisation of a collecting
party are almost identical. The major difference
is in the complexity and time involved in producing
sago starch. Harvesting coconuts merely involves
the men in climbing the trees to obtain the nuts
and the women in husking them.

The exploitation of sago is distinguished from
gardening and wild fruit collecting in the four
following ways:

1. Sago palms are individually owned by
   married men, while garden crops are usually
   owned by a married couple and wild trees by
   nobody;
2. Sago palms only are inherited;
3. Differences of time and effort are involved
   in each of the three cases, as discussed
   above;
4. The distribution of the various products in
   the village is different.

Sago starch extracted from a single palm is
usually shared by two or more households depending
on the composition of the sago-making part, and
the fruits of *C. vitiense* from a single tree are
shared in a similar manner. On the other hand
garden crops, and the fruit of *G. gnemon* which are
harvested as easily as garden crops, are, as a
rule, not presented between households.

Two further observations on sago seem relevant
at this point. The first is that although there is

strict ownership of sago palms by married men,
women from different households do the processing
at the same time and take the produce back to their
own households, somewhat in the way that the wild
fruits of *C. vitiense* are harvested and distributed.
This means that the sago palm takes on something
of the character of common property at the village
level. It is possible that this arises from the
fact that, like *C. vitiense*, little or no labour
is involved in managing sago before the actual
harvest, particularly since a man inherits stands
from his father and controls natural stands. The
system of ownership, inheritance and distribution
appears to contribute to the stable utilisation of
sago starch, and this, together with the long
maturation period of the palm itself, leads to the
second observation, that because of these factors
it is very difficult for people to migrate far
from their village, to the extent that they continue
to rely on their own sago stands.

With regard to productivity, the people obtain
around 2 kg of crude starch or around 7000 kcal per
man-hour's work without undue exertion. It is very
difficult to compare this with horticultural
productivity in which the labour input varies from
season to season. Only an approximate estimate can
be made using the record of time consumption (Table
3) and the quantity of food intake (Table 4).
While the former includes all of the time spent
out of the village, a considerable part is used
for travelling between the settlement and the
various working places and for resting and talking
as well. Men in particular use little of their
time for actual work when present in the gardens
or sago groves. Similarly, if not to the same
extent, the length of time a woman spends in a
garden is only a crude indication of the time spent
gardening. With these reservations the data from
Tables 3 and 4 indicate that one man-hour's labour
provides 1020 kcal by gardening and 3160 kcal by
the exploitation of sago. In general terms it can

be concluded that the exploitation of sago is more productive than horticulture in the sense of calorie return for time spent.

Sago starch-making

It is the men's task to cut down the sago palm at about 40 to 70 cm above the ground with a steel axe and, when it is lying on the ground, to remove with the axe the upper half of the surface wood, the width of which is around 2 to 4 cm, along the length of the tree, thereby exposing the pith which fills up the whole interior of the trunk.[5] The women then begin[6] by scraping out the sago pith and pounding it into a fibrous mass. This work usually involves two or more women each performing the same task at separate points along a single trunk. The pounding is done with a special wooden tool called *abol*, which is operated in the same way as an adze (Fig.2) and at an average interval of 1.2 seconds between strokes. When loosened pith is accumulated, the second stage of operations, washing out the sago powder from the pith, commences. This task takes place in a sort of trough made of a sago frond, the wider end raised to a slanting position by a strut made of a sago frond or wooden sticks. Fixed just above the lower end of the trough is a filter made of a spathe of coconut palm. The trough leads into a large vessel lying on the ground, which is made of a frond of wild palm. The woman engaged in washing out sago fills the trough with the pounded pith and pours in large amounts of water, which she brings from some small spring near the working place. Then she begins to knead the pith and the water in the trough, pouring more water in at intervals (Fig.3). The suspended sago starch runs with the water through the filter into the vessel, while the pith remains in the trough. In this fashion the vessel is filled with water, dark orange in colour, in which the starch is left to sink gradually to the bottom. After a while the

Fig.2. Women pounding out sago pith, using the special wooden tool, *abol*.

Fig.3. Woman washing sago pith. The starch is suspended in the water and passes the filter which catches the pith. It is eventually caught in a receiving vessel, the water removed, and the powdery sediment retrieved.

woman removes the water by tilting the vessel,
leaving a white powdery sediment which dries to
lumpy sago flour. The woman usually wraps up a
small part of it in young leaflets of sago palm or
leaves of cane to take and eat on the spot. The
rest is wrapped with a sago frond into bundles to
be carried back to the village.

Assuming that all the tasks of sago producing
were performed by a single man and a single woman
without interruption, the man's work would require
about an hour and the woman's some 20 hours,
judging by my records. In actual fact it is about
half as much again, because of the time spent
resting and talking.

DISCUSSION

Wild sago versus planted sago

Planted stands and wild stands of sago have
rarely been distinguished here because the
villagers themselves do not care whether the sago
to be utilised has been planted or self-propagated,
and also because my data suggests that there is no
significant difference in starch production between
the wild palm and the planted one. Such a
conclusion is supported, at least tacitly, by other
workers (Beaver 1920:161; Conroy and Bridgland
1947:73; Barrau 1958:38), who report co-existence
of wild stands and planted stands without drawing
any clear distinction between them. However,
P.K. Townsend (1974) reports starch yields from
Abelam planted palms at 0.2 kg/m^3 compared with
only 0.08 kg/m^3 from Sanio-Hiowe wild palms and
concludes that the Abelam may have better yielding
sago because they plant it and practise selection
of varieties. A more important measure may be
labour productivity. Townsend states that 154
man-hours are required to obtain 1 million kcal

among the Abelam and 157 man-hours among the
Sanio-Hiowe. My data for the Oriomo Papuans
indicated 137 man-hours. On these figures it
would appear that the people produce similar amounts
of starch per unit of labour, irrespective of the
wild or planted status of the sago palm.

One potential advantage derived from
transplanting sago is to expand the area in which
sago palms grow. However this potential is limited
because sago grows only in swampy areas. Among the
Oriomo Papuans it would appear that such specific
locations are already occupied by sago and that
attempts to transplant sago shoots in places along
a number of creeks have met with only partial
success. These new sago groves contain only a
small number of sago palms and yield little starch.

Technology of processing

Techniques of sago-making consisting of felling
a palm, pounding pith and extracting starch are
similar throughout New Guinea[7], although variations
exist. For example the Keraki of the Morehead
River and the Wiram of the middle Fly do not wash
out pounded pith in a trough, but pack it into a
close-woven bark bag and then stamp it (Williams
1936:422-3). As to the implements for sago-making,
steel axes have replaced stone tools for cutting
palms almost everywhere, and in some places the
top of the sago-pounder traditionally made of hard
wood or a bamboo node has been fitted with a round
iron plate at the striking edge. Other implements
used in the process are made of local materials
and therefore are unlikely to have changed. The
use of iron for the sago-pounder may have not
changed labour efficiency very much, but although
the Oriomo Papuans know this new type of implement,
most of them continue to use the traditional type.
On the other hand one may consider that the steel
axe is much more effective than the stone
implement, although according to W.H. Townsend

(1969) who studied the Heve living in the middle
Sepik area, the sago-cutting stone implement is
about as efficient as the steel axe for this
purpose and both tools were observed being used
alternately to fell the same trunk in 1967.

Such crops as taro and yam are introduced
species (Barrau 1968; Yen 1971). In contrast to
these, sago might be indigenous. If so, the
invention of sago-making techniques must have
made possible the utilisation of this productive
food resource at any time in the past. To date,
studies have not made clear when the invention and
diffusion of these techniques took place, nor where
nor how; however Nakao (1967:356) discussing the
techniques of leaching developed in temperate
climates for exploiting some kinds of nuts and
roots, suggests that pounding and washing out of
sago pith are so advanced a technology that sago
processing did not occur during Barrau's 'shifting
agriculture' stage.[8]

Apart from the sago-making techniques
mentioned above, an unusual method of extracting
starch from sago pith was reported by Wollaston
(1912:91): 'very often the natives of the Mimika
(Irian Jaya) eat the crude sago, that is to say,
the pith simply as it is cut out of the tree,
without having been washed or pounded. The stuff
is roasted in the usual way and the separation of
the sago is done in the mouth of the eater, who
spits out the uneatable fibre.' Watanabe has
observed that 'this example suggests that wild
sago-palms could have been utilised as food by
pre-horticultural peoples even if they did not
know the complicated techniques of sago-processing'
pers. comm.; also in Golson (1972:377). On this
point it is both necessary and important to
investigate the extent to which this method of
separation of sago starch is effective for the
purpose of utilising sago as a food.

Comparison of sago with other plant foods

Comparing the number of man-hours needed to produce 1 million kcal among several different subsistence economies, P.K. Townsend (1974) places sago production on a comparable level to swidden cultivation. Among the Oriomo Papuans, the labour efficiency of sago production is superior to that of garden crops. This is in part due to the collecting nature of most of the labour required in the utilisation of sago. Sago is characterised by year-round availability whereas most wild roots and fruits and some garden crops are not. Moreover sago tends to be little damaged by wild animals like pigs and rats or by abnormal climate. Also the potential storage period of sago starch is fairly long, varying from several weeks to several months according to the methods of preservation; however in many societies where sago starch is utilised as a daily food it is not stored for long periods. For instance among the Oriomo Papuans it is usually consumed within two weeks of making it.

Along with the advantages of a system of subsistence based on sago, there are some disadvantages. The system depends upon a very specific habitat, namely low swampy land, and is restricted to this environment. Thus it is impossible for people depending on sago, wild or planted, to migrate out of the low swampy land unless they change their staple food. This geographical restriction may affect the density of human population; for peoples depending on wild sago palms, the density of palms in their land is one of the main factors determining the human population density, and even for peoples depending on planted sago palms it is impossible to raise the density of palms beyond the capacity of the swampy areas. Thus human population density would seem automatically delimited. A further disadvantage stemming from this geographical restriction is that the swampland where sago eaters live is generally unfavourable to health.

Nutritionally speaking, emphasis is placed on the fact that sago starch contains little value other than carbohydrates. According to Hodges *et al.* (1947) and Peters (1957) sago starch per 100 gm is composed of 0.1-0.2 gm protein, 71-83 gm carbohydrate, 17-27 gm water. This amount of sago yields 285-349 kcal. While any staple foods, tubers or cereals, are regarded as caloric sources, sago is extremely so. However this staple required dietary supplements, especially animal foods being rich in protein. Unless domestic animals are available as daily or semi-daily foods, natural resources must be exploited by hunting and/or fishing; alternatively some researchers (e.g. Fountain 1966) have stressed the importance of sago grubs (fam. Cerambyidae) as a protein source.[9] Generally speaking, sago eating people inhabiting coastal or riverine localities depend on fishing while those inhabiting inland areas tend to hunt. The population density of the latter may depend not only on the density of sago palms but also on the amount of wild animal meat available. On the other hand the population density of the former may depend to a lesser degree on the amount of fish, because fish resources are less likely to be affected by human exploitation than land animals; the more fishing technology improves, the greater the catch. P.K. Townsend (1971, 1974) points up another nutritional problem. Sago is not suitable as a food for infants and therefore breastfeeding is necessary for a long period after birth. She supposes this to be one of the factors enforcing the practice of infanticide among the Sanio-Hiowe. I obtained no information about infanticide among the contemporary Oriomo Papuans.

Whatever the reason, the low density of sago palms, the low density of wild animals, the unfavourable conditions for health, or the poor nutritional levels, the population density of

human groups heavily dependent on sago is low,
and they live in small groups, although some of
them have made permanent or semi-permanent
settlement; these factors appear to inhibit them
from elaborating their socio-political organisation.
As well, though the system of subsistence
depending on sago appears to be stable not only
throughout the year but also over periods
of years, it is severely restricted to low,
swampy land.

ACKNOWLEDGEMENTS

Financial assistance for the fieldwork was
provided by a Wenner-Gren Foundation for
Anthropological Research grant (#2125) awarded
to Professor H. Watanabe. The Wonie villagers'
friendliness to me was indispensable in my
fieldwork. I wish to thank Professor Watanabe
for six weeks' cooperation in the field and for
support and suggestions. Thanks are also due to
the New Guinea Research Unit of The Australian
National University in Port Moresby, especially
Professor R. Crocombe in 1967 and Dr. M. Ward in
1971 and 1972 for assistance in arranging
fieldwork; to the Research School of Pacific
Studies of The Australian National University in
Canberra, especially Professor J. Golson, for
providing the opportunity for gathering information
concerned with this study there in 1974; and
finally to my colleagues in the Department of
Human Ecology, University of Tokyo, for their
continuous support.

FOOTNOTES

[1] According to Landtman (1927:101) the Kiwai Papuans
do both.

[2] Heinen and Ruddle (1974) report that the starch

content of 'moriche' palm (*Mauritia flexuosa*), exploited as a food among the Warao of the Orinoco Delta, is greatest between February and April, just prior to the onset of the rainy season and lowest during June and July, when rainfall is at its heaviest. In pointing to this observed coincidence between pattern of rainfall and cycle of starch formation, they cite Corner (1966:225) who, summarising worldwide research of the history of palms, laments that neither the physiological nor environmental (climatological) factors which trigger flowering are known.

[3] It is generally accepted that the first garden crops of Oceania were probably taro and yam and some other aroids (e.g. Barrau 1968; Yen 1971). Moreover, according to Spencer (1963) mainland and island Southeast Asia were once characterised by the yam-taro-sago crop complex.

[4] The consumption of taro was greatest in the early dry season, i.e. July to August, after which it dwindled gradually to zero in November or December at the latest. I assume that in July and August the quantity of taro eaten was about the same as that of sago, but provided only one third of the caloric value of the sago. Since the records of food intake in the dry season shown in Tables 4 and 5 were made from 25 October to 6 November, the actual amount of taro consumed on the average in the dry season is likely to have been a little greater than this value.

[5] According to the villagers, a few harvested sago trunks are not full of pith when felled, although I failed to witness such an example. This might be caused by the misjudgement of maturation by the owner of the palm.

[6] Pounding and washing are done mainly by men among some other peoples e.g. the Dobuans (Malinowski 1922:377-8), the Wogeo (Hogbin 1938-9:306-7), and

the Tikopians (Firth 1939:135). However these
groups depend on sago much less than the Oriomo
Papuans.

[7] According to K. Ruddle (pers. comm.) and Suarez
(1968) cited by P.K. Townsend (1974), techniques
of obtaining starch from 'moriche' palm *(Mauritia
flexuosa)* by the Warao of the Orinoco Delta are
also very similar to techniques found in Papua New
Guinea.

[8] On the basis of the subsistence patterns found
amongst contemporary Melanesian communities,
Barrau (1958: 33-6) presents an hypothesis for the
evolution of subsistence systems in the region,
as follows:
1. Foraging
2. Shifting agriculture
3. Agriculture with bush-fallowing rotation
4. Semi-sedentary agriculture with artificial
   fertilisation of soil
5. Sedentary agriculture with rotation and
   manuring.

[9] The sago beetles lay eggs in the pith of the
fallen sago trunk. Grubs (or larvae) are eaten
and also occasionally the adult beetles. To
deliberately harvest sago grubs men fell the sago
palms and leave them lying on the ground and
collect the grubs later. In the Oriomo area
however, the people collect small quantities of
grubs from the unworked portion of the sago trunk.

REFERENCES

Barrau, J. 1958 *Subsistence agriculture in
Melanesia*. Honolulu: Bishop Museum,
Bulletin 219

          1959 The sago palms and other food
plants of marsh dwellers in the Pacific
Islands. *Economic Botany* 13:151-62

          1961 *Subsistence agriculture in
Polynesia and Micronesia*. Honolulu: Bishop
Museum, Bulletin 223

          (ed.) 1963 *Plants and the migrations
of Pacific peoples*. Honolulu: Bishop Museum
Press

          1968 L'humide et le sec: an essay on
ethnobotanical adaptation to contrastive
environments in the Indo-Pacific area. In
A.P. Vayda (ed.) *Peoples and cultures of the
Pacific*:113-32. Garden City (N.Y.): Natural
History Press

Beaver, W.N. 1920 *Unexplored New Guinea*. London:
Seeley, Service

Chowning, A. 1963 Proto-Melanesian plant names.
In Barrau 1963:39-44

Conroy, W.L. and L.A. Bridgland 1947 Native
agriculture in Papua-New Guinea. In
Nutrition Survey 1947:72-91

Corner, E.J.H. 1966 *The natural history of palms*.
London: Weidenfeld and Nicolson

Firth, R. 1939 *Primitive Polynesian economy*.
London: Routledge

Fountain, O.C. 1966 *Wulkum: land, livelihood and
change in a New Guinea village*. Unpublished
MA thesis, Victoria University of Wellington,
New Zealand

Golson, J. 1971a Australian aboriginal food plants:
some ecological and culture-historical
implications. In D.J. Mulvaney and J. Golson
(eds) *Aboriginal man and environment in Australia*:
196-238. Canberra: Australian National University
Press

          1971b Both sides of the Wallace Line:
Australia, New Guinea, and Asian prehistory.
Archaeology and Physical Anthropology in Oceania
6:124-44

          1972 Land connections, sea barriers and
the relationship of Australia and New Guinea
prehistory. In D. Walker (ed.) *Bridge and
barrier: the natural and cultural history of
Torres Strait*:375-97. Canberra: Australian
National University, Research School of Pacific
Studies, Department of Biogeography and
Geomorphology, Publication BG/3

Heinen, H.D. and K. Ruddle 1974 Ecology, ritual
and economic organization in the distribution
of palm starch among the Warao of the Orinoco
Delta. *Journal of Anthropological Research*
30:116-38

Hodges, K., C.F. Fysh and K.G. Rienits 1947 New
Guinea and Papuan food consumption tables.
In *Nutrition Survey 1947*:270-80

Hogbin, I. 1938-9 Tillage and collection: a New
Guinea economy. *Oceania* 9(2):127-51;
(3):286-325

Landtman, G. 1927 *The Kiwai Papuans of British
New Guinea*. London: Macmillan

Lea, D.A.M. 1972 Indigenous horticulture in
Melanesia. In R.G. Ward (ed.) *Man and
landscape in the Pacific Islands*:252-79.
Oxford: Clarendon Press

Malinowski, B. 1922 *Argonauts of the western
Pacific*. London: Routledge

Nakao, S. 1967 Nōgyō kigen ron (On the origin of agriculture). In S. Morishita and T. Kira (eds) *Shizen - seitakugaku-teki kenkyū*:329-494. (*Nature: ecological studies*:329-494). Tokyo: Chūōkōron-sha. (In Japanese)

Nutrition Survey 1947 *Report of the New Guinea Nutrition Survey Expedition, 1947*. Sydney: Government Printer, for Department of Territories

Ohtsuka, R. 1974 Oriomo-chihō papua-jin no seitai (Ecology of Oriomo Papuans). In R. Ohtsuka, J. Tanaka and T. Nishida *Jinrui no seitai*:92-130. (*Human ecology*:92-130). Tokyo: Kyōritsu-shuppan. (In Japanese)

Paijmans, K. 1971 Vegetation, Forest resources, and ecology of the Morehead-Kiunga area. In K. Paijmans, D.H. Blake, P. Bleeker and J.R. McAlpine *Land resources of the Morehead-Kiunga area, Territory of Papua and New Guinea*: 88-133. Canberra: Commonwealth Scientific and Industrial Research Organisation, Land Research Series No.29

Peters, F.E. 1957 *Chemical composition of South Pacific foods: an annotated bibliography*. Noumea: South Pacific Commission, Technical Paper 100

Spencer, J.E. 1963 The migration of rice from mainland Southeast Asia into Indonesia. In Barrau 1963:83-9

Suarez, M.M. 1968 *Los Warao: indigenas del delta del Orinoco*. Caracas: Instituto Venezolano de Investigaciones Cientificas

Townsend, P.K. 1971 New Guinea sago gatherers: a study of demography in relation to subsistence. *Ecology of Food and Nutrition* 1:19-24

        1974 Sago production in a New Guinea economy. *Human Ecology* 2:217-36

Townsend, W.H. 1968 Stone and steel tool use in a
    New Guinea society. *Ethnology* 8:199-205

Williams, F.E. 1936 *Papuans of the Trans-Fly.*
    Oxford: Clarendon Press

Wollaston, A.F.R. 1912 *Pygmies and Papuans.*
    London: Smith, Elder

Wurm, S.A. 1971 Notes on the linguistic situation
    in the Trans-Fly area. *Papers in New Guinea
    Linguistics* 14:115-72. Canberra: Linguistic
    Circle of Canberra, Pacific Linguistic Series
    A, No.28

Yen, D.E. 1971 The development of agriculture in
    Oceania. In R.C. Green and M. Kelly (eds)
    Studies in Oceanic culture history, (vol.2):
    1-12. Honolulu: Bishop Museum, Department of
    Anthropology, Pacific Anthropological Records
    No.12

        1974 Arboriculture in the subsistence of
    Santa Cruz, Solomon Islands. *Economic Botany*
    28:247-84

MAN DOES NOT LIVE BY CALORIES ALONE:
THE ROLE OF SHELLFISH IN A COASTAL CUISINE

BETTY MEEHAN

RMB 148 via Bungendore, NSW 2621

INTRODUCTION

The role played by shellfish in the total diet of a group of contemporary hunters and gatherers has received little attention so far from researchers in either anthropology or archaeology. Considering the frequent occurrence of shellfish remains in the archaeological record throughout the world, and the desire of many archaeologists to assess the importance of various components in the diets of prehistoric peoples, this paucity of comparative ethnographic data is puzzling. Here an attempt is made partially to remedy that situation by presenting a case study from the north coast of Australia, where an opportunity arose to make a year long quantitative record of the total diet of a group of coastal hunters and gatherers.[1]

The Anbara are a group of Gidjingali-speaking Aborigines (Hiatt 1965) who live around the mouth of the Blyth River in Arnhem Land (Figs 1-2). There, over the past decade or so, they have modified their traditional hunting and gathering lifestyle so as to incorporate various aspects of European culture, mainly material, medical and educational, which were considered to be useful or desirable. At the same time they maintained a largely traditional social structure; foraged all their flesh foods from their own territory; and supported a continuing and vigorous program of secret and secular ceremonies (Meehan 1975:13-72). On 334 days between July 1972 and July 1973, I made systematic quantitative observations of the diet of the Anbara people who were camped at the Blyth

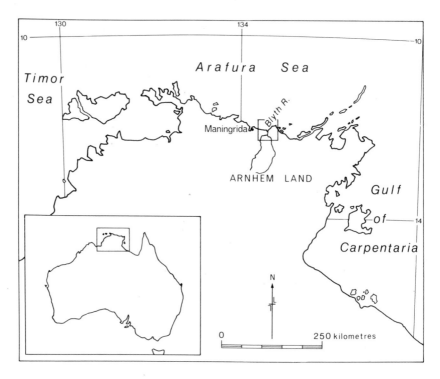

Fig.1.   Map of Arnhem Land showing location of fieldwork area.

River, the average size of this group being 34
people.   This fieldwork was carried out in
collaboration with Rhys Jones of the Department of
Prehistory, Australian National University.

THE YEAR'S SHELLFISH HAUL

During this period the Aborigines collected a
total of 7000 kg gross weight of shellfish over
194 days, i.e. 58% of all observed days (Table 1).
Altogether, 30 different species of shellfish were
eaten, but of these, six species constituted 95% of
the gross yield.   The favoured species were: the
gastropod *Melo amphora* and the bivalves *Tapes*

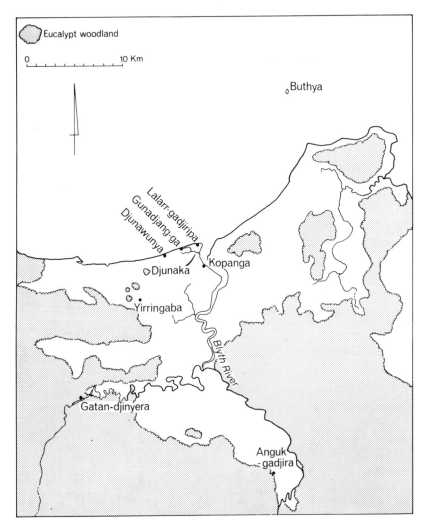

Fig.2. Map of Blyth River region showing Gidjingali country and sites mentioned in text.

hiantina, Batissa violacea, Modiolus micropterus, Anadara granosa and *Mactra meretriciformis*. One of these, *Tapes hiantina*, was especially important, contributing no less than 65% of the total gross weight collected.

Gross weight	=	7000 kg
Weight flesh	=	1500 kg
Weight protein	=	300 kg
Energy	=	1,200,000 kcal

	Quantities: observed day	Quantities: shell gathering day
	(N = 334)	(N = 194)
Gross weight per head	0.6 kg	1.1 kg
Weight flesh per head	0.1 kg	0.2 kg
Weight protein per head	0.03 kg	0.05 kg
Energy per head	106 kcal	182 kcal

Average population	=	34
Days of observation	=	334
Days shells collected	=	194

Table 1. Dietary contribution of shellfish during the year.

To convert these gross figures into useful dietary units, I carried out experiments in the field to ascertain flesh weight to shell weight ratios for each of the important species (Meehan 1975:Figs 9.1, 9.2). From these I estimated an average of 21% of the gross weight of all shellfish was edible flesh, the number of kilo calories (kcal) per kilogram of steamed flesh being assumed at 800, a figure based on calculations by Thomas and Cordon (1970:14) and Shawcross (1967:121-2). The protein content has been placed at 20 gm of protein per 100 gm of flesh, again based on Thomas and Cordon's (1970:14) analyses for steamed scallops and oysters (Table 2).

Thus, over the year, a total of 1500 kg of flesh, representing 300 kg protein, or 1,200,000 kcal was obtained from shellfish. Each individual

Category	% Gross weight eaten	Gm of protein per 100 gm flesh	Kcal per kg flesh
Shellfish	21	20	800
Crustacea	55	18	930
Fish	80	20	1370
Reptiles	70	20	1500
Birds	70	18	3000
Mammals	75	19	3000
Nuts	4	20	6000
Fruits	95	1	600
Vegetables	100	2	1300
Honey	100	0.8	1680
Bought food	80	10	3700

Table 2. Food values.

Anbara received an average of 0.6 kg gross weight of shellfish every day of the year or 1.1 kg each day that shells were collected. The amount of flesh per person per day of observation was 0.1 kg and per shell gathering day 0.2 kg. This was equivalent to 0.03 kg of protein each observed day, or 0.05 kg each shell collecting day. In terms of energy, each person derived about 106 kcal from shellfish each day of observation, and 182 kcal each shell gathering day (see Table 1).

THE TOTAL DIET

My analysis of the total diet of the Anbara is not final as many assessments of food content have still to be refined. However, what follows gives some indication of the order of the dietary intake and in that context the significance of the shellfish contribution can be assessed. Jones has kindly made his journals available to me for this section, so that I could include food collected by the men.

I selected the four months of September 1972
and January, April and May 1973: periods which were
representative of the late dry season; the onslaught
of the monsoon; the late wet season and the early
dry season respectively. This choice was made
particularly difficult because of the unusual
nature of the 1972-3 wet season (Meehan 1975:42).
Other factors complicating the selection were the
number of days of observation. September, for
which I have 17 days of observation at the Kopanga
camp (Fig.2), was a reasonably good example of the
late dry season. January was chosen because by
then the northwest monsoon winds and rains had
begun to occur in earnest, though rain had already
fallen well before. It was also the first month
that the Lalarr-gadjiripa camp (Fig.2) was occupied.
Normally April would have been part of the early
dry season, but in 1973 it was still mature wet,
when cyclonic winds had eased but rain continued to
fall. May was representative of the early dry
season, though hardly a classic example of it. The
rains had eased and the temperature dropped, and
normal dry season pursuits were carried out
especially those related to the collection of the
vegetable foods *Dioscorea transversa* and *Eleocharis
dulcis*.

Conversion of dietary components to edible flesh, protein and energy

Table 2 lists the major categories of foods
together with the percentage weight of each that
was eaten, the protein contents of its flesh and
the number of kcal per kg of flesh. These figures
are based on standard food analyses (e.g. Fysh *et
al.* 1960:138; Shawcross 1967:122; Thomas and Cordon
1970), and in some cases are approximations based
on figures for equivalent foods, since the food
values of most of the plants and animals of Arnhem
Land have never been ascertained.

Animal flesh

The Anbara ate a greater percentage of most
items of food than Europeans do. McArthur (1960a:
25, 1960b:98-123) discussed Aboriginal eating habits
in some detail, stating 'There is no refinement of
food, no storage, little waste and no leaching of
vitamins and minerals in cooking water.'
Preparation and cooking of shellfish has been
described in detail elsewhere (Meehan 1975:132-64
and in press). Suffice it here to say that, apart
from gastropod radulae, everything contained inside
the slightly steamed shells was eaten.

Crustacea included several species of crabs
and prawns. The Anbara were especially interested
in the colour and quality of the 'fat' from inside
crab bodies and occasionally threw away specimens
that they considered to be 'too thin'. They
normally ate all the soft parts within the crabs
and left only the carapace, pinchers and filter
processes.

A fish was usually cooked whole in the ashes
and most of its carcass was consumed with the
exception of the skeleton (though bones were always
sucked), scales, charred outer skin, gills and a
small part of the guts. Flesh from the head,
including the eyes and brains, was relished.
Stingrays and sometimes sharks, included here with
fish, were a highly prized item of the diet,
especially those with 'young' and 'fat' livers. A
complicated cooking procedure was used to prepare
stingray in which the flesh was ultimately dipped
in a 'gravy' made from the liver. People took
portions of flesh up with their finger tips, dipped
them in the 'gravy', then ate them.

Reptiles eaten during the year were mostly
goannas (*Varanus* spp.) and freshwater turtles
(*Chelodina* sp.). Others included the blue-tongued
lizard (*Tiliqua* sp.), several species of snake and

saltwater turtle. Eggs belonging to most of these
species were also eaten and greatly prized. On
several occasions Jones, being with the men, saw
saltwater turtle eggs being hidden so that the
owner would not have to share them with people who
arrived later. The white flesh of the goanna,
often compared with *balanda* or 'white man' chicken
by the Anbara, was a popular food and the bright
yellow 'fat' contained in some specimens was
particularly savoured. The head was usually
discarded because it was 'too small' but the rest
of the body was eaten excepting the skeleton, skin
and a small part of the guts. Once the carapace
and skeleton of the turtles had been discarded,
most of the flesh was also eaten, their cleaned
intestines being regarded as 'good'. On the few
occasions that I saw large saltwater turtles
butchered in the camp, the many metres of
intestines were washed out in salt water and
carefully divided between the various waiting
eligible relatives. All other reptilian species
were prepared in a similar fashion, eggs were eaten
after being lightly cooked, even when they contained
small embryos.

Most of the birds consumed during the year
were ducks, geese and some plain turkeys. I made
an estimate of food values using figures for these
species. Feathers and skeletons were discarded
though all bones were sucked and suitable ones
broken to obtain marrow. Bird flesh was *mindjak*
or 'flesh with blood inside', and was normally
eaten after light cooking. I only saw one emu
eaten during the year, which was brought from the
other side of the river as a gift from some Matai
people. This particular animal was clothed with a
thick layer of yellow fat of which the Anbara ate
so much that several of them were afterwards sick.

Only a few species of mammals formed part of
the 1972-3 diet - wallabies and kangaroos being the
main ones, plus feral cats and some small marsupial

mice and rats. Wallabies (*Macropus agilis*) were
the most common species eaten on the western bank
of the Blyth; the larger kangaroos (*Macropus
antilopinus*) being located in the forests on the
eastern bank. Wallabies were cooked whole in their
skins, parts of the intestines being discarded after
the carcass had been singed. After further cooking
in the ashes, the only parts not eaten were the
skin, gall bladder, parts of the guts and skeleton,
though long bones were cracked for marrow. The
liver, heart, kidneys and brains were especially
valued. A similar cooking procedure occurred for
cats. I saw only a few rats and mice eaten, but
they appeared to be cooked whole and eaten thus
with the exception of skin and bones.

Plant foods

In the monthly diet lists (Tables 3-6), fruits
and nuts are combined under a single heading. The
main nuts eaten were *Sterculia quadrifida*, which was
very like a peanut, and pandanus nuts which resembled
pine nuts. On one major expedition (Meehan 1975:
162) I had the opportunity to calculate the nut
content of pandanus fruits - about 4% of the total
fruit weight. Despite the low yield from this
species, the nuts were highly prized by the Anbara
and at certain times of the year, notably in the
middle to late dry season, a characteristic sound
in the camp was that of someone somewhere chopping
the hard husks of a few pandanus. They removed the
small, deeply embedded oily nuts with a special
implement - in the past, a long skewer of hard wood,
nowadays a spatula-shaped piece of metal with a
wooden handle. On some occasions I was able to
weigh various hauls of nuts and fruits, but in
general it was an impossible task. Fruits and nuts
were eaten by anyone at anytime that they were
available - swiftly taken from the tree and popped
into the mouth. People resented any slowing down
of this process and readily showed their discontent,
so I desisted. A large variety of fruits was

Food category	Gross Weight		Nett Weight		Protein Weight		Kcal	
	kg	%	kg	%	kg	%	Number	%
Shellfish	239	24.3	50	9.5	10	11.1	40,000	3.6
Mangrove 'worms'	6	0.6	6	1.1	1	1.1	5,000	0.5
Crustacea	14	1.4	8	1.5	1	1.1	7,000	0.6
Grubs	0.5	0.05	p	p	p	p	p	p
Fish	221	22.4	177	33.7	35	38.9	242,000	22.0
Reptiles	100	10.2	70	13.3	14	15.6	105,000	9.5
Birds	30.5	3.1	21	4.0	4	4.4	64,000	5.8
Mammals	87	8.8	65	12.4	12	13.3	196,000	17.8
Fruits & nuts	141	14.3	10	1.9	2	2.2	33,000	3.0
Vegetables	6	0.6	6	1.1	p	p	8,000	0.7
Ant bed	0.5	0.05	p	p	p	p	p	p
Honey	8	0.8	8	1.5	p	p	13,000	1.2
Bought food	131	13.3	105	20.0	10.5	11.7	388,000	35.2
Totals	984.5		526		90		1,101,000	

Table 3. Total diet for September 1972.

Days observed = 17

Population = 31

p = present

Food category	Gross Weight		Nett Weight		Protein Weight		Kcal	
	kg	%	kg	%	kg	%	Number	%
Shellfish	800	48.5	168	19.7	34	26.2	134,000	8.9
Mangrove 'worms'	–	–	–	–	–	–	–	–
Crustacea	20	1.2	11	1.3	2	1.5	10,000	0.7
Grubs	–	–	–	–	–	–	–	–
Fish	354	21.5	283	33.2	57	43.8	388,000	25.8
Reptiles	32	2.0	22	2.6	4	3.1	33,000	2.2
Birds	15	0.9	10.5	1.2	2	1.5	31,500	2.1
Mammals	91	5.5	68	8.0	13	10.0	204,000	13.6
Fruits & nuts	120	7.3	114	13.4	1	0.8	68,000	4.5
Vegetables	6	0.4	6	0.7	p	p	8,000	0.5
Ant bed	–	–	–	–	–	–	–	–
Honey	–	–	–	–	–	–	–	–
Bought food	212	12.8	170	19.9	17	13.1	629,000	41.8
Totals	1650		853		130		1,506,000	

Days observed = 31
Population = 30
P present

Table 4. Total diet for January 1973.

Food category	Gross Weight		Nett Weight		Protein Weight		Kcal	
	kg	%	kg	%	kg	%	Number	%
Shellfish	683	30.0	143	10.6	29	16.9	114,000	4.5
Mangrove 'worms'	1	0.1	1	0.1	p	p	1,000	p
Crustacea	50	2.2	27.5	2.0	5	2.9	26,000	1.0
Grubs	—	—	—	—	—	—	—	—
Fish	500	21.9	400	29.5	80	46.5	548,000	21.4
Reptiles	86	3.8	60	4.4	12	7.0	90,000	3.5
Birds	7	0.3	5	0.4	1	0.6	15,000	0.6
Mammals	10	0.4	7.5	0.6	1	0.6	22,500	0.9
Fruits & nuts	275	12.1	144	10.6	1	0.6	44,000	1.7
Vegetables	160	7.0	160	11.8	3	1.7	208,000	8.1
Ant bed	2	0.1	p	p	p	p	p	p
Honey	6	0.3	6	0.4	—	—	10,000	0.4
Bought food	500	21.9	400	29.5	40	23.3	1,480,000	57.8
Totals	2280		1354		172		2,558,500	

Days observed = 30

Population = 35

p = present

Table 5. Total diet for April 1973.

Food category	Gross Weight		Nett Weight		Protein Weight		Kcal	
	kg	%	kg	%	kg	%	Number	%
Shellfish	437	20.8	92	6.5	18	8.2	73,000	2.5
Mangrove 'worms'	–	–	–	–	–	–	–	–
Crustacea	48	2.3	26	1.8	5	2.3	25,000	0.9
Grubs	1	0.1	1	0.1	p	p	p	p
Fish	882	42.0	706	49.5	141	64.1	967,000	33.6
Reptiles	73	3.5	51	3.6	10	4.5	77,000	2.7
Birds	9	0.4	6	0.4	1	0.5	19,000	0.7
Mammals	–	–	–	–	–	–	–	–
Fruits & nuts	25	0.8	24	1.7	p	p	14,000	0.5
Vegetables	90	4.3	90	6.3	2	0.9	117,000	4.1
Ant bed	–	–	–	–	–	–	–	–
Honey	2	0.1	1.8	0.1	p	p	3,000	0.1
Bought food	534	25.4	427	30.0	43	19.5	1,580,000	55.1
Totals	2101		1425		220		2,875,000	

Days observed = 31
Population = 37
p = present

Table 6. Total diet for May 1973.

available in the Anbara range - some large, some
small, some sweet, some sour, but all relished. I
have made a general estimate of the quantities
consumed, incorporating any actual weights that I
managed to obtain. However the fruit and nut
weights must be seen very much as minimum quantities.
The food values for these fruits and nuts have been
extrapolated from some analyses contained in Thomas
and Cordon (1970:15-17) such as those for black-
berries, currants, figs, gooseberries and pine nuts,
because these species resembled those available to
the Gidjingali. One item in the list of fruits,
water melons, was sometimes collected in large
quantities from Kopanga camp. These had
spontaneously germinated in old midden heaps where
seeds from melons purchased at Maningrida (Fig.1)
had been discarded (Jones 1975:24-5).

Most of the gathered tuberous vegetables were
either the yam *Dioscorea transversa* or the corm of
the spike rush *Eleocharis dulcis*. These were
roasted and eaten, nothing being discarded. For an
assessment of the content of these foods, I have
been guided by analyses done by Fysh *et al.* (1960:
138).

The 'sugar bag', as the wild honey was called,
was eaten entirely - wax, bees and all. Together
with stingray liver and goanna fat, honey was one
of the most valued foods in the Anbara menu.

A few foods collected in small quantities
during these months have not been included in Table
2. *Dungonbara*, or witchetty grubs, were occasionally
collected and highly prized. *Gonogotjula* or mangrove
'worms' are really molluscs but were never recognised
as such by the Anbara, so I have kept them separate
for most of the calculations. They were regarded
as very good food. Several times, old women
collected quantities of ant bed which they ate.

European carbohydrate food

Most of the European food brought from the
store at Maningrida consisted of white flour, white
sugar and white rice. I have estimated a 20% loss
of these items, which I think is conservative. I
possess copies of all the orders and dockets
relating to goods that came to the Anbara community
from the store at Maningrida - that is, I have a
maximum coverage of these foods as opposed to the
minimum coverage of the hunted foods. However, much
of the bought food, especially flour and sugar, was
never consumed. Some got spoiled on the journey
out, either by being soaked or spilled and some was
even returned to Maningrida by 'holiday makers'!
Much was ruined during periods of rain because
people failed to protect it properly, or because
their houses leaked. Flour in the form of a thick
paste, *bupuru*, was fed to good hunting dogs, and
the half-starved 'rubbish' dogs often helped
themselves to flour and sugar if it was left on the
ground. Some dogs even managed to climb onto
storage platforms when really hungry. People wasted
flour and sugar by the way they prepared damper and
tea, flour being tipped onto bags so that damper
could be kneaded and afterwards shaken off, while
large quantities of sugar were added to billy cans
and cups of tea, much of which was left behind after
the tea was finished. If a child or dog did not
finish this off, it was wasted. Occasionally, I
saw European food that had been stored at
unoccupied home bases, ruined because of faulty
containers.

Distribution of food within the community

Males, and active mature men in particular,
probably had more flesh to eat than females, as
they often cooked fish, stingrays, wallabies etc
at dinnertime camps in the company of other males.
On these occasions, according to Jones, they ate
large quantities, often considerably more than a

kilogram each, bringing only what was left back to
camp. They also had greater access to livers and
fat which were such valued items of the diet. On
the other hand, mature women with families tended
to eat less, in favour of their children, almost
never refusing a request for food from their own
children and those of close relatives. Thus there
was a great incentive in the Anbara lifestyle to
accompany foraging expeditions, even if one did not
participate in them. Almost invariably any food
procured was prepared away from the base camp at a
dinnertime site, and everyone present received an
ample share of the repast. The rest was taken back
to the base camp to be distributed to relatives
that had stayed behind. Many of these were old
people, especially women, whose diet was probably
deficient in many ways. Old men usually received
plenty of animal food from other men, especially
during ceremonies. I rarely heard old men
complaining that they were being neglected, but
frequently old women asserted that no-one was
looking after them.

STUDY MONTHS

September 1972

About 31 Anbara were camped at Kopanga during
September 1972. The hinterland, by this time, had
dried up and bushfires were a common part of the
daily landscape. People were moving freely all
over the country. Thirteen species of shellfish
were collected during the month, *Tapes hiantina*
being the major contributor by gross weight.
Stingray (one species) and fish (at least 13 species)
were also eaten. The main reptiles obtained during
this time were goannas (69.0 kg) and freshwater
turtles (20 kg). At this time of the year goannas
were plentiful and 'fat'.

Most of the birds caught comprised two species of duck and some geese. The latter were highly prized and said to be 'fat'. All the mammals were wallabies.

Two nuts were included in the diet for September, the most important being that of the pandanus (136 kg gross weight minimum) which yielded 5 kg of nut. A small amount of *Sterculia quadrifida*, some coconut which was washed up onto the beach, some *Tamarindus indicus* from Gulala territory and a few other small fruits were also eaten.

A small quantity of tuberous vegetables including *Dioscorea transversa*, *Eleocharis dulcis* and *Ipomoea* sp. were procured during the month too, but never in large quantities, and never from a major foraging activity but always as an adjunct to some other expedition such as goanna hunting.

Several hauls of mangrove 'worms' were made from the mangroves lying to the south of Kopanga, as well as a few witchetty grubs and two species of ant bed. Bought food contributed a gross weight of 131 kg.

The gross weight contributed by all these food categories appear on Table 3 together with corresponding amounts of nett weight, protein and calories. It can be seen from this table, and graphically from Fig.3 that shellfish contributed 24% of the gross weight of food available during the 17 days of September. This was equivalent to 10% of the nett weight, 11% of the protein, and 4% of the calories. If the animal foods only are taken into account, then shellfish contributed 35% of the gross weight, 14% of the flesh and 7% of the calories.

Taking the total diet for the month of September, then, the gross weight of food available

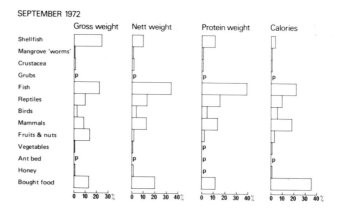

Fig.3. Percentage graph of contribution of various food items to total diet for September 1972.

for each person each day was approximately 1.9 kg, or 1.0 kg nett, and thus 0.17 kg of protein. This gave a total of 2090 kcal for each person per day, of which shellfish (including mangrove 'worms') had contributed 85.

January 1973

In January the Anbara wet season camp was established at Lalarr-gadjiripa. Here people eventually built themselves long, low houses which provided good protection from the fierce winds, rain and mosquitoes that characterised the period. For the first half of this month, before the real onslaught of the wet season, people were very lethargic and spent a lot of their time resting or sleeping under fragile shades on the beach; it was too hot and humid for much activity. During the second half of the month, after the rains and winds had commenced, and after the wet season houses had been constructed, many people remained equally inactive, spending long periods, that is, days, in the houses, venturing outside only when really necessary to defecate, or to collect fuel for the constantly burning fires. It was during this month

that live shellfish were washed up onto the beach
and so the 800 kg of shellfish eaten during this
month contained some deep water species
(approximately 17 kg) not normally available to the
Anbara. *Tapes hiantina* still provided the highest
gross weight, 580 kg.

Crabs and large prawns were collected as well,
usually in the net fishing activities, though some
crabs were procured from the junction of the
mangroves and the Lalarr-gadjiripa dune where they
had been washed up by the high tides.

Approximately 82 kg of the fish caught during
January consisted of four species of stingray,
while 20 species of fish constituted the remainder
of the 354 kg. Much of the fishing was done at the
mouth of the Djunaka Creek (Fig.2) with a long net.

Reptiles were not in abundance at this time of
the year. Everyone said that there was 'too much
grass' to get goannas. Those procured were usually
trapped by one of the hunting dogs. The prize
reptile food for January was bundles of small 'tree
snakes' called *manmarrk-manmarrk* which were collected
from the branches of pandanus and other trees. A
small salt water crocodile (8 kg) was also eaten.

Birds caught were mostly ducks. Mammals
included wallabies and two smaller marsupials, one
of which, *djingombula* (*Rattus colletti*) was
considered very good food.

January was a good time for two fruits - the
'red apple' (*Eugenia suborbicularis*), which was
nearing the end of its season, and *Morinda
citrifolia* which was just beginning. Both these
fruits were large and contained ample flesh.
Several coconuts, some fermenting, were washed onto
the beach and were promptly devoured.

The supply of tuberous vegetables was at an all

time low for the year, the jungle patches being at
this time dense with vegetation and mosquitoes.   A
few water-lily products were tried and a quantity of
Cycas media which had been soaking in a pool on the
other side of the river for six months, was eaten.

Bought carbohydrate food was in short supply
due to the fact that the Maningrida people had not
been able to get to the Blyth River because of bad
weather.   A lot of flour etc that arrived eventually
was ruined because its owners were unprepared for
the sudden onslaught of the monsoon rains.

Approximate weights available of all food
categories appear on Table 4 and are shown
graphically on Fig.4.   Eight hundred kg gross weight
of shellfish was collected in January.   This yielded
168 kg of flesh, 34 kg of protein and a total of
134,000 kcal.   Shellfish made up 48% of the gross
weight of food, 20% of the nett weight and 26% of
the protein.   Of the total number of calories,
shellfish contributed 9%.

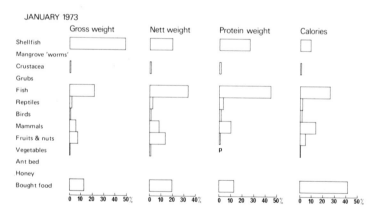

Fig.4.   Percentage graph of contribution of various food items
to total diet for January 1973.

In terms of animal flesh only, however, shellfish contributed 61% of the gross weight, 30% of

the flesh and 17% of the calorific content.

How well off were the 30 people living at Lalarr-gadjiripa during January 1973? They had at least 1.8 kg gross weight of food per head per day. This meant about 0.9 kg nett or 0.14 kg of protein. The number of kcal available for each person per day was about 1620, of which shellfish contributed 144.

April 1973

Normally April should have been a month of that delightful season in the Northern Territory called the 'early dry'. In 1973 however, it was still the wet season - hot and humid, with lots of mosquitoes and long grass. The Anbara at Lalarr-gadjiripa were becoming impatient by being trapped on the coast. So the women, almost invariably *without* children began to penetrate the hinterland to get, amongst other things, yams.

The 683 kg gross weight of shellfish collected in April was made up of 16 species, of which *Tapes hiantina* contributed 607 kg.

Two species of crab and prawns contributed to the crustacea weight, many of these being caught in the fish trap at Gunadjang-ga (Fig.2). Five species of shark and stingray, plus 16 species of fish contributed 500 kg gross weight to the diet during April. Again, many of these came from the fish trap at Gunadjang-ga.

The reptile season, with goanna and blue-tongued lizard hunting, was really opening up at this time. Most were caught by the hunting dogs which were directed by women; all the goannas were young, small and 'fat'. One large saltwater turtle was consumed at Lalarr-gadjiripa, having been caught at Buthya Islet (Fig.2). It weighed about 38 kg. Saltwater turtle nests of eggs were also important.

Mammals consisted entirely of feral cats, one being
the size of a small dog.

Six species of fruit, including water melon,
and three species of sweet grasses were procured
during the month. Two hundred and sixty kg of water
melon were collected from Kopanga. The wet season
fruit, *Morinda citrifolia*, was still available, but
early dry season fruits, such as *Pouteria sericea*,
were beginning to mature.

Women collected 160 kg of vegetable foods in
April. Six species were gathered, including some of
the water-lily products (*Nymphaea* sp.) and yams.
Mangrove 'worms' (1 kg), honey (of at least two
types) and ant bed (two kinds) were also collected.

The gross weights of various foods procured
during April are shown on Table 5 and Fig.5. Shellfish contributed 30% of the total gross weight, 11%
nett, 17% of protein and 4.5% of the calories during
this month.

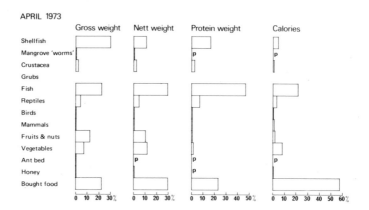

Fig.5. Percentage graph of contribution of various food items
to total diet for April 1973.

The gross weight of food available to each

person for each day of April was 2.2 kg, the nett
weight was 1.3 kg and the amount of protein was
0.16 kg. Thus, the number of kcal available for
each person each day was about 2400.

Again in terms of animal food only, shellfish
contributed 51% of the gross weight, 22% of the
flesh, and 14% of the total number of calories. In
other words, people ate shellfish at the rate of
0.7 kg gross weight, 0.1 kg flesh and 110 kcal per
head per day.

May 1973

Climatic conditions were beginning to improve
in May, but sudden, heavy showers were still
interrupting normal gathering patterns. However,
the population (37) resident at Lalarr-gadjiripa
during this time lived well, as will become clear
from the figures presented below.

They collected 437 kg gross weight of shellfish
comprising 13 species. Again, however, the 302 kg
of *Tapes hiantina* was the major contribution.

Five species of stingray and shark yielded
62 kg gross weight, and no less than 37 species of
bony fish contributed 820 kg. It is no surprise
that the Anbara said that this period of the year
was 'fish time'.

Reptiles eaten included at least two species of
goanna, some large carpet snakes and saltwater
turtle eggs. Only a little bird flesh was obtained.

No mammals were eaten during May. I know that
one large buffalo was shot (Meehan 1975:228) by
Bandarpi. This animal arrived at Lalarr-gadjiripa
one day and everyone went after it. Most people soon
tired, and by the time it had reached Djunawunya,
Bandarpi was the only hunter left. Apparently, he
followed it several more kilometres inland to

Yirringaba (Fig.2) where he shot it. When asked
why he had not brought any flesh with him, he
replied: 'Knife, I bin leave 'im.' Sometime after,
we saw the carcass where it had been despatched.
It was Bandarpi's first buffalo kill and he had
pursued it as if he was determined to score.
Despite the fact that 500 kg of 'beef' was lying at
Yirringaba, nobody was prepared to walk that distance
to get it. This was not because buffalo meat was
despised. On the contrary, during a visit to
Gatan-djinyera, Gurmanamana and Jones helped two
Gunadba hunters to kill a buffalo. A large amount
of this was brought back to a delighted group of
Kopanga people.

Nine fruits, three sweet grasses and some sweet
sap from bark were consumed during May. The wet
season fruit, *Morinda citrifolia*, was still being
harvested. Also available now were dry season
fruits such as *Mimusops elengi* and *Tacca
leontopetaloides*. Ninety kg of vegetable foods were
harvested in this time consisting of four species,
but mainly *Dioscorea transversa* and *Eleocharis
dulcis*. A small amount of witchetty grub (1 kg) and
honey (2 kg) was also collected.

As can be seen from entries on Table 6 and
Fig.6, 21% of the gross weight of food collected
during May was shellfish. This represented 6% of
nett weight, 8% of protein and 3% of kcal. When
animal foods only are considered, shellfish
contributed 30% of the gross weight, equivalent to
10% of animal flesh and 6% of the calories derived
from that source.

Thus the population at Lalarr-gadjiripa in May
1973 had 1.8 kg gross weight of food per head per
day, or 1.2 kg nett, or 0.19 kg protein -
equivalent to about 2500 kcal. Of this energy
shellfish provided an average of 64 kcal per head
per day.

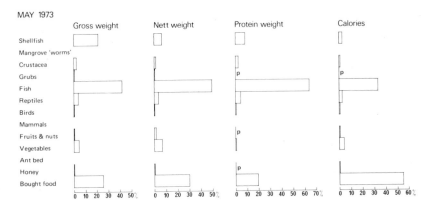

Fig.6. Percentage graph of contribution of various food items to total diet for May 1973.

QUALITY OF ANBARA DIET

Nutritionists have formulated the concepts of recommended dietary allowances, i.e. the optimum intake of various nutrients and energy to maintain life (e.g. Thomas and Cordon 1970:53-5). Whereas these recommended intakes have not so far been based on direct ergonometric studies of Aboriginal populations living in traditional situations, and are known to vary somewhat between races, nevertheless a meaningful extrapolation can be made for the purposes of this study.

McArthur (1960a, 1960b), working in 1948 with Arnhem Land Aborigines living under similar conditions to the Gidjingali at the Blyth River, calculated recommended dietary allowances for each of the communities studied. These were based on quantities listed by the National Research Council of America but incorporated adjustments made for the special features of the Aboriginal populations, such as lower body weights. In terms of energy requirements, the means of the recommended allowances ranged from about 1600 to 2050 kcal per head per day,

the latter figure being applicable to populations
living on settlements that she also visited. Her
corrected recommended allowance of kcal per head per
day for adult males was 2350, for females 1750, and
for children 5-14 years of age, 2200. Adolescents
13-20 years of age required more than the recommended
allowances for adults. Similar studies have been
made by Taylor (1972:19-22, 1973:8-9, 22-7, in
press) on the diets of some Cape York settlement
Aborigines. He used the sex-age profile of these
communities and the standard dietary allowances for
white Australians derived from Thomas and Cordon
(1970:53-5). My preliminary extrapolation from
Thomas and Cordon's data onto the Anbara population
profile, produced a similar order of mean daily
calorific requirements as McArthur's assessments -
2050 kcal, which I will use in the following
calculations:

	Mean daily consumption of kcal	% of recommended intake (100% = 2050 kcal)
September 1972	2090	102
January 1973	1620	79
April 1973	2400	117
May 1973	2500	122

My estimates of the calorific content of Anbara
diet, based on the four months discussed above, are
probably underestimates as I was unable to be everywhere for detailed recording. However, despite the
crudity of my methods, the results are of the
correct order of magnitude, giving me confidence
that the major parameters of the diet have been
recorded.

During January, their month of lowest calorific
intake, no-one seemed to be particularly hungry.
Most people sat motionless for long periods, beneath
their shades on the beach, or in their long houses,
after the heavy rains of the monsoon weather had
begun, rain and heat combining to inhibit strenuous

activity. Altogether, January was a month of
minimum activity, a fact which may help to explain
the low energy intake for that period. The highest
daily intake of calories per head of population
occurred in May, the early dry season. This was a
time of reasonably pleasant weather when everyone
was preoccupied with plans for the future - new
camp sites, the commencement of ceremonies, the
'readiness' of new foods. The level of activity in
the camp increased markedly. Foraging expeditions
became more numerous and energetic, and production
of items of material culture, almost non-existent
for the past few months, suddenly began to flourish.
The entire population was in high spirits, full of
expectation and confidence. The seasonal differences
evident in these data confirmed qualitative
impressions that I had formed during the year. Data
for the other eight months, which have not yet been
fully analysed, appear to support this pattern.

There is no doubt that the diet enjoyed by the
Anbara during 1972-3 was a good one. In general, it
provided an excess of the recommended intake of
energy including an abundant supply of protein in
various forms. Because of the diversity and
freshness of the foods consumed, it probably also
was rich in trace elements and vitamins, though at
this stage, I have not investigated these aspects.
A feeling of well-being existed amongst the
population; many people especially children,
exhibiting great energy, alertness and enthusiasm
for most tasks undertaken. Apart from respiratory
diseases, normally contracted through contacts with
the wider Australian community, and of leprosy and
tuberculosis, both of which having now been brought
under control by the medical authorities, the health
of the Gidjingali people living in the bush appeared
to be good (Sister Maija pers. comm.).

OTHER ABORIGINAL GROUPS

It is interesting to see how this Anbara diet resembled those of other Aboriginal groups within Australia. Such an assessment is difficult to make because no comparable data exists either in terms of the length of time of the study, nor in the quantitative base. There are several generalised accounts of Aboriginal diets which are couched in terms of the species eaten and of their seasonal availability. Some of these are based on analyses of literature (e.g. Hiatt (see Meehan) 1967-8; Allen 1972), others on direct observation (e.g. Roth 1900; Thomson 1948-9; Peterson 1973), but none of these have a detailed quantitative content.

McArthur's work, carried out in Arnhem Land in 1948 (1960b:90-135) is useful. In this case however, the groups studied were asked by researchers not to eat flour and sugar during the study periods: 4 days at Hemple Bay, 3 days at Bickerton Island, 4 days at Port Bradshaw and 11 days at the inland Fish Creek. The normal diet of these people was probably similar to that of the Anbara's during 1972-3, being an amalgam of European and hunted foods. At Hemple Bay, McArthur found that the daily intake of kcal per head of the population was 2160 or 116% of the recommended intake; at Bickerton Island it was 1170 or 74%; at Port Bradshaw 1380 or 79%, and at Fish Creek it was 2130 or 104%. The Anbara diet, for the months so far assessed, suggests that they were perhaps better off than the groups studied by McArthur.

Taylor (in press) found that at the Edward River settlement in Cape York, the total calorific intake during February 1970 was 103% of the recommended figure. Two years later, in July 1972 (Taylor 1973:27) this same community's intake had dropped to 70% of the recommended quantity. At Mitchell River, Cape York, in January 1972, the calorific intake of the population living there was

89% of the recommended intake (Taylor 1972:22). The low calorific intake of the people living at both these settlements, occurred despite the fact that there was more cash available in the communities. This decline in standards can be seen as being part of a widespread phenomenon associated with Aboriginal populations living in settlement conditions. A similar contrast could be seen in Arnhem Land where people appeared to be healthier when living on their own lands rather than in the centralised settlements. Whether this was due solely to the superior quality of the bush dwellers' diet or to other factors associated with being in charge of their own lives away from the pressures of the European style towns, it is not yet possible to say.

HUNTERS OUTSIDE AUSTRALIA

As is the case within Australia, quantitative descriptions of the diets of hunters and gatherers elsewhere in the world are scarce. Some information is however available from Africa. Marshall, Silberbauer and Lee, have described Bushman diet as consisting of between 40% and 60% of vegetable food, the rest being meat (Lee 1965:170). For a period of 28 days, Lee (1965:167-70) recorded all the food collected by a camp of 42 people. The daily intake per head during that time was 0.2 kg of meat and 0.7 kg of vegetable food consisting of Mongongo nuts and various roots. If we assume that the meat contained about 3000 kcal per kg, and that the vegetables about 2500 kcal per kg, then each person received an average of approximately 2300 kcal per day.

A dietary study was carried out by Bose (1964: 298-310) between 17 December 1963 and 15 January 1964, amongst the Onge, a group of hunters and gatherers living on Little Andaman Island in the Bay of Bengal. The gross weights of each food

collected each day was noted together with the size
of the population. From this data, I calculated an
approximate calorific intake per head of population
by processing Bose's quantities from the values
contained in Table 2. Food values for pig are from
Wu Leung *et al.* (1972:107). The results can be
seen on Table 7. Given an average daily population
of 41, the data indicates that each person received
about 1720 kcal per day, of which shellfish
provided only 0.09%.

Food Category	Gross weight kg	Edible flesh kg	Number kcal
Pig	575	472	1,460,000
Turtle	34	24	36,000
Fish	224	179	245,000
Bivalves	14	3	2,000
Crab	22	12	11,000
Vegetables	259	259	337,000
Honey	15	15	25,000
Fruits	0.5	p	p
Totals	1144	964	2,116,000

Days observed (Bose 1964) = 30

Population = 41

p = present

Table 7.   The Onge Diet.

SHELLFISH IN THE TOTAL DIET

A problem

It is difficult to make a final assessment of
the role of shellfish in the total diet of the
Anbara people, because in some ways, the evidence

is contradictory. It can be seen from the above
discussion (particularly Tables 3-6), that in terms
of the weight of animal flesh alone, the contribution
made by shellfish ranged from as low as 10% in May
to 30% in January. When these contributions were
converted into calories, the percentages were lower,
6% in May to 17% in January. Thus at no time during
the year was shellfish more than a supplementary
food even in the flesh diet. Only in January,
perhaps, was its calorific contribution crucial -
9% at a time when the total intake of kcal per head
per day was only 1620. The Anbara may well have
suffered hardship during this month if shellfish
had not been readily available. The relative
importance of shellfish in January may explain why
the Anbara characterised the wet season as 'shellfish time'. Being in the same style as other
Anbara comments about their diet, this did not mean,
as I originally anticipated it would, that shellfish
was the most important food in terms of flesh weight
eaten during that period, rather that it was more
important then than at any other time of the year.

If the assessment of shellfish's importance was
left at this point, it would remain vastly under-
rated. Shell gathering, as an activity, occurring
on 58% of observed days was as recurrent as fishing,
and both took place far more frequently than any
other foraging pursuit. In addition a large number
of people collected shellfish, the total number of
'people days' involved being higher than for any
other single food category. This was so, in spite
of the fact that, next to pandanus nuts, shellfish
has the lowest yield of flesh per unit of gross
weight of all foods eaten by the Anbara.

The Anbara regarded shellfish, especially
Tapes hiantina, as one of the prime resources in
their territory, and proximity to shell beds was a
major consideration in the location of base and
dinnertime camps. Furthermore the Anbara
characterised themselves as 'beach people' living

off the resources of the river mouth, such as fish
and shellfish, and contrasting this with the 'forest
people' - such as the Matai and Gunadba - who resided
immediately inland and who dined on red meat and
honey.

MAN DOES NOT LIVE BY CALORIES ALONE

An explanation for the above apparent
contradictions in the importance of shellfish in the
Anbara world can be presented in the following terms.

The gathering of shellfish involved the
participation of a broad spectrum of the population
both in terms of age, physical fitness and skill.
People who played little part in the foraging arena,
such as old women, heavily pregnant women and
children, as well as the normal range of huntresses,
all took part. In general, shell gathering required
no special physical strength nor skill, nor the
expenditure of much energy. In this respect it was
unlike other foraging pursuits carried out by the
serious women such as goanna catching or yam digging,
both of which were considerably more demanding.
Such expeditions normally involved walking long
distances, up to 20 km return, as well as the
digging of holes and hauling of substantial weights
back to home base. Whilst working on the open sea
shell beds, women could have their small children
with them if necessary without the children being
in any danger, nor interfering overly with the
gathering yields (Figs 7,8). However the presence of
too many dependent small children on goanna or yam
expeditions, seriously lowered a woman's productivity.

The actual time devoted to the gathering of
shellfish on any one day was small - about two hours,
depending on the state of the tide. During that
short time a skilled woman could collect shellfish
equivalent to about 2000 kcal. For the rest of the

Fig.7. A group of Matai women and children (far background) and an Anbara woman and her children (foreground) collecting *Tapes hiantina* from beds adjacent to Lalarr-gadjiripa during the wet season. The dogs are a normal part of shell gathering expeditions and are said to keep the sharks away. The upright stake in the foreground marks the general shell bearing areas.

Fig.8. Nguraba Nguraba, a young Anbara girl, collecting *Tapes hiantina* from the beds near Lalarr-gadjiripa after the tide had left the beds completely exposed.

day women were free to participate in other
activities if they so desired. Even on the long
trips to Lalarr-gadjiripa from Kopanga, much of the
time was actually spent engaged in other foraging
pursuits or relaxing in the dinnertime camp.

Shellfish was one of the dependable food
sources in the Anbara diet. Together with fish, it
was potentially available at all seasons of the year.
However it was even more dependable than fish because
it was a guaranteed source. Its collection was not
regulated by the skill of the gatherers, nor by the
intricacies of the behaviour of the prey. If
absolutely necessary, some kinds of shellfish could
have been collected every day of the year. They
were there for the taking, like food on a supermarket
shelf with which they were sometimes compared. Once
gatherers were actually on the beds, it was simply
a matter of mining in the shell-producing areas.
Women could, within certain limits, designate the
amount of shellfish they wanted to collect; the more
effort they put into the process, the more they
reaped from it.

Because shellfish were collected consistently,
they provided a small, constant source of fresh
protein, the importance of which should not be
underestimated. Certainly one wallaby provided a
larger quantity of flesh, protein and energy than a
single haul of shellfish, but even in good seasons
such large mammals may only have been available
every four or five days at the most. For example,
during the 17 days of observation in September 1972,
wallabies were caught on 3 days, whereas shellfish
were collected on 11. During April no wallabies
were caught, domestic cats being procured on 3 days,
but shellfish gathered on 28 days! Bandarpi's
buffalo could have provided about 900 kcal per head
per day for the entire population for May - about
one third of their daily intake for that period.
Still, nobody stirred from the camp to collect even
part of the flesh. Even if the animal had been

slaughtered close to the camp, its flesh would not
have lasted more than two or three days at the most,
because of the tropical nature of the Arnhem Land
climate. 'Freshness' of food was important to the
Anbara; in many ways they were fastidious about it.
Before cooking or eating food that was a few hours
old, they always smelled it. The state of a fish's
eyes was always discussed and sometimes seemingly
fine fish were discarded only a few hours out of
the water because they were 'too old'. On the
return trip from a site up the Blyth River, Anguk-
gadjira (Fig.2), two cooked wallabies were thrown
away only a few kilometres from Kopanga, because
they were 'no good'; they had been cooked the night
before. During his trip to Canberra in 1974,
Gurmanamana, my chief Anbara informant, was at first
most suspicious about food that came out of the
refrigerator - 'old one aye?' It is in this context
of the Anbara preference for fresh food, that shellfish once again has some importance. It could be
collected daily if necessary and eaten 'fresh'. As
such, it was a valuable source of flesh that
remained available between major hauls of fish and
other animal foods.

The foraging strategy employed by the Anbara
had two major components. On the one hand, there
were opportunistic activities which involved various
degrees of luck, skill and strength. These included
most of the mammal hunting, and many types of
fishing. The other component in the strategy
depended on low-key pursuits such as shellfish and
vegetable gathering, and some forms of line fishing.
The food provided from these activities was
dependable and could be used as a last resort when
the more flamboyant and less reliable part of the
subsistence strategy had failed.

The Anbara in no way resembled a hunting
society clinging onto life by eating any foods that
were available. Rather in terms of the food they
ate, they were affluent hunters with high

gastronomic standards. They had a clear idea of
what constituted a good diet and were confident that
their environment provided all the necessary
ingredients. Shellfish was one of these ingredients,
and for the special features it contributed to the
total diet, it was highly valued. The attributes of
open sea bivalve flesh were often discussed and
frequently, after fish had been the staple for
several days at a time, people expressed a specific
desire for shellfish flesh because it was 'wet',
not 'dry' like fish. The Matai made regular visits
to the coast to collect shellfish, and on several
occasions, gifts of *Tapes hiantina* were taken to the
inland people, the Gunadba at Gatan-djinyera, in
exchange for buffalo meat. There can be no doubt
that shellfish, especially those from the open sea
beds, and *Tapes hiantina* in particular, held a
special place in the Anbara culture which was not
altogether due to their nutritional content.

It is only within this wider cultural context
that the real significance of shellfish in the
Anbara economy can be fully appreciated. Perhaps
the persistence of the activity of shellfish
gathering over periods of thousands of years by
coastal hunters in many parts of the world, as
exemplified by the prominence of shell middens in
the prehistoric record, indicates that the importance
of molluscs in those economies also was not measured
solely in terms of their gross energetic contribution
to the diet. True, debris from shell gathering tends
to withstand the ravages of time better than that
from most other foraging activities and is thus
perhaps over-represented in the archaeological
record, but we should not let this factor blind us to
the subtle role that shellfish may have played in
ancient hunting economies.

ACKNOWLEDGEMENTS

This article is based on research carried out whilst enrolled as a PhD student in the Department of Prehistory and Anthropology, School of General Studies, Australian National University, Canberra. The work was supported by grants from the Australian Institute of Aboriginal Studies.

The large number of people and institutions who assisted me between 1972 and 1975 while I was carrying out the research have been thanked in my thesis (Meehan 1975:iii-vii). Here I will simply reaffirm my indebtness to Frank Gurmanamana, Nancy Bandeiyama, their family and to the Gidjingali community with whom I lived during my fieldwork.

FOOTNOTE

[1] For a description of fieldwork conditions and techniques, including a record of the pattern of observation, see Meehan 1975:73-84. Copies of this thesis are available in the following institutions: the Menzies Library in the Australian National University, the Australian Institute of Aboriginal Studies Library in Canberra, the Haddon Library in Cambridge, and the University Library in Berkeley.

REFERENCES

Allen, H. 1972 *Where the crow flies backwards: man and land in the Darling Basin*. Unpublished PhD thesis, Australian National University, Canberra

Bose, S. 1964 Economy of the Onge of Little Andaman. *Man in India* 44:298-310

Fysh, C.F., K.J. Hodges and L.Y. Siggins 1960 Analysis of naturally occurring foodstuffs of Arnhem Land. In Mountford 1960:136-9

Hiatt (Meehan), B. 1967-8 The food quest and economy of the Tasmanian Aborigines. *Oceania* 38(2):99-133; (3):191-219

Hiatt, L.R. 1965 *Kinship and conflict: a study of an Aboriginal community in northern Arnhem Land.* Canberra: Australian National University Press

Jones, R. 1975 The neolithic, palaeolithic and the hunting gardeners: man and land in the Antipodes. In R.P. Suggate and M.M. Cresswell (eds) *Quaternary studies: selected papers from IX INQUA Congress, Christchurch, New Zealand, 2-10 December 1973*:21-34. Wellington: Royal Society of New Zealand, Bulletin 13

Lee, R.B. 1965 *Subsistence ecology of !Kung Bushmen.* Unpublished PhD thesis, University of California, Berkeley (University microfilms, Ann Arbor, 1967)

McArthur, M. 1960a Food consumption and dietary levels of the Aborigines at the settlements. In Mountford 1960:14-26

1960b Food consumption and dietary levels of groups of Aborigines living on naturally occurring foods. In Mountford 1960: 90-135

Meehan, B. 1975 *Shell bed to shell midden.* Unpublished PhD thesis, Australian National University, Canberra

in press (1977) Hunters by the seashore. *Journal of Human Evolution* 6

Mountford, C.P. (ed.) 1960 *Records of the American-Australian Scientific Expedition to Arnhem Land, 2. Anthropology and nutrition.* Melbourne: Melbourne University Press

Peterson, N. 1973 Camp site location among Australian hunter gatherers: archaeological and ethnographic evidence for a key determinant.

Archaeology and Physical Anthropology in Oceania
8:173-93

Roth, W.E. 1900 *A report to the Under-secretary,*
Home Department, on the Aboriginals of
Pennefather (Coen) River Districts, and other
coastal tribes occupying the country between
the Batavia and Embley Rivers (8th January
1900). MS in Mitchell Library, Sydney

Shawcross, W. 1967 An investigation of prehistoric
diet and economy on a coastal site at Galatea
Bay, New Zealand. *Proceedings of the*
Prehistoric Society 33:107-31

Taylor, J. 1972 Anthropologist's report. In
Twenty-seventh annual report of the Council:
19-22. Brisbane: Queensland Institute of
Medical Research

        1973 Aboriginal child health. In
Twenty-eighth annual report of the Council:
8-9, 22-7. Brisbane: Queensland Institute of
Medical Research

        in press Diet, health and economy: some
consequences of planned social change on an
Aboriginal community. In R.M. Berndt (ed.)
Aborigines and change: Australia in the '70s.
Canberra: Australian Institute of Aboriginal
Studies

Thomas, S. and M. Cordon 1970 *Tables of composition*
of Australian foods, (5th ed.) Canberra:
Australian Government Publishing Service

Thomson, D.F. 1948-9 Arnhem Land: explorations
among an unknown people. *Geographical Journal*
112:146-64; 113:1-8, 53-67

Wu Leung, W.T., R.R. Butrum and F.H. Chang 1972
Food composition table for use in East Asia, I.
Proximate composition, mineral and vitamin
contents of East Asian foods. Washington:
Department of Health, Education and Welfare,
Publication No. (NIH) 73-465

IMPLICATIONS OF CONTEMPORARY AND PREHISTORIC EXCHANGE SYSTEMS

JEAN TRELOGGEN PETERSON and WARREN PETERSON

Department of Anthropology
University of Illinois

Throughout its history, anthropology, like other disciplines, has focused on categorisation. Kuhn (1970:15-22) has described a pre-paradigmatic state common to all young or developing disciplines: a state through which all scientific disciplines pass. This pre-paradigmatic state is characterised by a concern with definition, class and measurement, in other words with descriptive tasks. Archaeology is at that point of development. There is no commonly shared paradigm and a concern with explanation is relatively new and controversial. Recent attempts (e.g. Binford 1968) to formulate the discipline's primary goals, 1) the reconstruction of culture history; 2) the reconstruction of life way; 3) the elaboration of process, reflect the pre-paradigmatic state of archaeology. Two of these goals are descriptive in nature, and the third, while explanatory in nature, is poorly understood and seldom attempted. Most archaeologists are descriptively oriented and when a concern with disciplinary goals is evident at all, the reconstruction of culture history is the focal point. It is quite clear that the developmental stage frameworks used by culture historians to generalise at the descriptive level about prehistoric events are nothing more than elaborate classifications. Such frameworks are used as pigeon-holing devices to organise descriptive data along lines of space and time.

The research efforts of archaeologists are still confined to excavation, descriptive analysis and the preparation of descriptive site reports, perhaps because of the time consuming nature of our techniques. Our professional obligations are considered fulfilled when these tasks have been accomplished. Those few archaeologists motivated to generalise in terms of culture history will then proceed to fit the archaeological sites into existing stage frameworks. If necessary the framework will be revised or expanded to encompass the new material and occasionally an entirely new framework is devised. It appears however, that stage frameworks are characteristically in a state of revision due to the fact that every archaeological site is unique to some degree (W. Peterson 1974a). Thus our comparative techniques gloss over differences in the search for similarities between sites. The result is inadequate stage frameworks and inadequate culture histories.

The traditional approaches of archaeology have not been satisfactory for the Sunda-Sahul area, possibly because so many of the comparative classificatory techniques rest on the typological analysis of tool morphology. There are tool assemblages which have few or no recurrent forms (types). This aspect of some assemblages from island Southeast Asia has been noted by several researchers. Hutterer (1974:292), for example, says of the Sohoton, Philippines industry, 'The industry is strictly a flake industry without any evidence of blade making. The most striking characteristic of the lithic assemblage is its apparent formal amorphism.' A similar statement is made by van Heekeren (1972:139-40) in reference to the difficulty of classifying the lithic artifacts from some Indonesian sites. The Dimolit Site (W. Peterson 1974b) is an excellent example of such an 'unclassifiable' assemblage. The entire collection consists of very small, irregular flakes of a reddish-brown jasper plus fragments of sandstone mortars and their matching quartzite grinders. There are *no* instances of recurrent form. Such assemblages make it extremely difficult to construct

developmental frameworks since a traditional means
of comparison is absent.

There are also several examples of unusual
persistences of prehistoric adaptive strategies
with their associated technologies for island
Southeast Asia. One such example is Pintu Rock
Shelter (W. Peterson 1974b). This site is located
in the Sierra Madre Mountains of northern Luzon and
was used until the last 20 years as a frequentation
site by broad-spectrum hunter-collectors. Excavation
produced a lithic assemblage distinctively
Hoabinhian in nature, associated in the upper layers
with sparse, plain earthenware sherds. The
Hoabinhian is thought by many to fall between
10,000 BC and 5000 BC. The C-14 dates for the site
indicated, unexpectedly, that it was a late expression
running from c. 2200 BC to after the birth of Christ.
There are other examples of technological persistence
from Southeast Asia, including the assemblages from
Samar (Hutterer 1971), Tabon Caves (Fox 1971), and
Timor (Glover 1973). No one has suggested a
reasonable explanation for the persistence phenomenon.

The remainder of this paper will explore some
of the ecological implications of territorial and
social boundaries for prehistoric as well as modern
times. There is a basic assumption necessary to the
analysis; that ecological principles and structures
operative in the present were also operating in the
past. Such an assumption (a principle) is identical
in form to the assumption of uniformitarianism in
geology and is clearly warranted. If it is possible
to isolate ecological structures and processes in
the present, it can be assumed that the same
structures and processes were characteristic of the
past. Recent research by J.T. Peterson (1974)
suggests that one such process or structure in
ecology involves ordered exchange across boundaries.
Processes occurring on one kind of social or physical
boundary today, may well occur on other social or
physical boundaries contemporaneously, and in the

past. Such boundary processes may in fact typify
boundaries within other kinds of systems.
Exploration of these processes is therefore
potentially a very fruitful endeavour.
J.T. Peterson's ecological analysis of the modern
exchange system operating between Agta hunters and
Palanan agriculturalists demonstrates that such
exchange systems level resource variation and
broaden the food web across territorial and social
boundaries.

CONTEMPORARY EXCHANGE

Generally, inter-ethnic exchange has been
viewed as being of two types, both involving the
concept of diffusion. Prehistorians have acknowledged
a steady flow of pots, adornments, and so forth
through space. They and students of contemporary
behaviour have also recognised the potential for an
exchange of ideas. However, surprisingly little
attention has been given to the potential of
critical food exchanges occurring. Where energy
(food and labour) exchanges have been examined (Lee
1969; Harris 1971:203-18) attention has focused
largely within cultural systems, not between
cultural systems. Regular and critical food
exchanges between hunting peoples and adjacent
sedentary peoples appear to be common.[1] However
they have been fully reported only by Turnbull (1965)
and J.T. Peterson (1974).

Within Southeast Asia these relations are well
known for the Negritos of the Malay Peninsula and
throughout the Philippines. In each case relations
are strikingly similar, and persist even where gross
environmental change occurs. For example, in one
area where we lived on the western watershed of the
Sierra Madre in northern Luzon, logging and lowland
farming emigrants have largely eliminated the forest.
Nonetheless, former hunters continue to gather herbs,

rattan and bamboo, and to fish and hunt small animals
in the remaining forest. They trade these items to
sedentary peoples for carbohydrate foods. Near
Clark Air Force Base they scrounge on trash piles,
and nearer Manila, maintain a broad-spectrum
subsistence involving prostitution and herb selling.
Persistently these peoples opt for a low labour
intensive system in association with exchange with
sedentary populations. Such exchanges have been
largely ignored because for too long social
boundaries have been regarded as vertical tunnels
through time, as the containers of cultural
traditions and barriers to exchange and interaction.
Detailed examination of one case from northeastern
Luzon involving lateral exchange may illuminate the
value of exploring processes on boundaries.

The environment in northeastern Luzon

The Palanan Bay watershed on the northeast
coast of Luzon is one of the more isolated and
environmentally less hospitable areas of the
Philippines. Access to Palanan is effectively
limited to hiking for most people, although a
trading launch visits annually and light planes may
be chartered to cross the mountains. The trip by
foot across the Sierra Madre Range requires up to
six days. North and south along the coast there
are only two communities, each as isolated as
Palanan. Radios and outdated newspapers and
magazines rarely reach Palanan; the only other
communication is provided by two sporadically
functioning shortwave radios and an equally
unreliable telegraph service. Much of the coastline
is rugged and hillsides are forested. The mean
monthly dry season temperature is 28°C and rainfall
exceeds 250 cm annually (Spencer and Wernstedt 1967:
54, 423). The rainy season which begins in September
and tapers off in January, is often characterised by
constant, unbroken cloud cover and incessant rain,
further limiting internal mobility and eliminating
external contact. Thirty two percent of all typhoons

reaching the Philippines strike the northeast coast
of Luzon. Disease as well takes its toll on life
in Palanan. Nineteen percent of children of the
sedentary people and one-third of the hunters'
children die before the age of two. Many people,
especially children and the elderly, die of
bronchitis during the rainy season. A government
doctor visiting the area in 1970 estimated that
more than half the adult population was affected by
tuberculosis and stated that malaria is endemic in
the area.

The people: past and present

Archaeological excavation (W. Peterson 1974a
and b) indicates the existence of seasonal occupation,
with people using relatively substantial structures,
along the coast between 550 and 3500 BP. Archaeo -
logical survey suggests the existence of a classic
Neolithic culture of unknown date on the coast and
up the Palanan River. According to Keesing (1962:
258) early Spanish records report two pagan
populations in the area, the Agta and the Irraya.
The present-day inhabitants refer to the inland
mountainous area to the west as Irraya and use the
same term to describe the swiddening peoples
inhabiting that area. Whether these Spanish accounts
refer to a population separate from the present-day
Palanan farmers is a matter of speculation.

Presently two ethnically and physically
distinct populations inhabit the area. About 10,000
Palanans, a farming people, are distributed
predominantly in the flatland areas along the
Palanan and Disukad Rivers and adjacent coastal
strips (Fig.1). Palanan settlement in modern times
until World War II was confined to the lower Palanan
River valley around Centro. During the Japanese
occupation in that area, many Palanans, fearing
abuse from the Japanese, moved up and down the
coast and up the river valleys, leading to the
present-day distribution. This pioneering endeavour

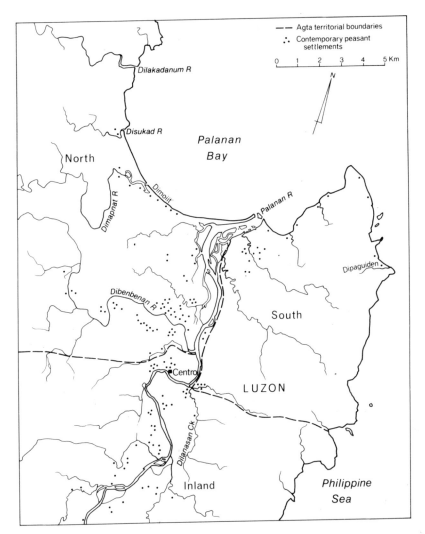

Fig.1.   Map of the Palanan Bay area of northeast Luzon,
showing contemporary Palanan farming settlements and
boundaries separating North, South and Inland Agta
territories.

continues as the farming population seeks new lands.
The 800 Negritos, who are known to themselves as
Agta and to others as Dumagat or Aeta, live largely

by hunting and fishing in areas fringing peasant
settlements. Agta and Palanan speak a mutually
intelligible language with only two phonemic shifts
and some vocabulary referring to forest products
and activities, and to kin relations, being known
only by the Agta. Headland and Wolfenden (1967:596)
designate Agta as an Austronesian language.

Peasant subsistence

The Palanan farmers produce mostly corn and
roots (especially yams and manioc) and only small
amounts of rice. Average land holdings are five to
ten hectares of flatland per household, less if the
family is young. While a pioneer may originally
clear a forested area, it is always with the intent
to cultivate that ground permanently. An average
farmer produces just under 40 *cavan*[2] of corn, just
over eight *cavan* of rice and a variety of roots.
This breakdown of productive activity is efficacious
from several perspectives. First, by focusing
predominantly on corn and roots the farmer is
reducing his labour output as these two crops require
less care than rice. Second, corn and roots may be
planted in the same fields at the same time, and
productivity may actually be thus enhanced. Third,
corn and roots are nutritionally superior to rice,
particularly considering that the leaves of root
crops are regularly consumed. Finally, corn is a
crop which thrives in dry years. The variety of
wet rice grown in Palanan, which is generally
planted by broadcasting in dyked fields and is
dependent on rainfall for irrigation, fails when
rain is not abundant. Thus diversification between
these two crops provides some assurance of adequate
food in spite of climatological variation.

Other domestic flora are minimally cultivated.
While many families would like to maintain kitchen
gardens, few are able to do so because of a lack of
seed. Fruits and vegetables raised include pineapple, eggplant, tomatoes, two types of squash and

beans.   Perennials and tree crops are somewhat more common and include jackfruit, papaya, coconut and banana.

Domestic animals are notably sparse in Palanan. Typically a family might own four *carabao* (water buffalo), 30 chickens, four of which are laying hens, and one pig. While all of these animals may be eaten, they rarely are. *Carabao* are primarily draft animals and may not legally be butchered unless the animal is too old or ill to work and permission is obtained from the mayor to kill it. Owners of pigs and chickens regard them less as a food source than as an investment. They are rarely killed to provide daily food. Chickens, and much more rarely pigs, may be butchered to provide meat for life crisis events such as weddings, funerals and death anniversary ceremonies. Hens are kept for their eggs and roosters for weekly cock fights. All domestic animals are primarily raised to be butchered and sold for cash in emergencies. If for example a family member requires expensive medical care, a child is to be sent to school away from Palanan, or a house needs repairs, an animal might be killed and sold to neighbours or at market. Typically, chickens are sold whole and large live-stock is sold in one kg lots.

Hunter-gatherer subsistence

Agta production, focused as it is on hunting and fishing, provides a striking contrast to what we have described for the Palanans. The Agta produce little in the way of domestic vegetable foods. Cultivation is confined to small swidden plots, usually on hillsides. Occasionally an Agta may 'borrow' or sharecrop a portion of a peasant field. The aged, those too old to hunt or fish, are most prominently involved in planting. Draught animals are rarely used; most planting is done with dibble sticks, and the plots abandoned after two or three years. Some Agta have never planted, 12%

(n=52) were not planting in 1968, 1969, or both,[3] and 25% planted exclusively roots. These latter cultivate not more than 0.5 hectares, often less than 0.25 hectares, and sometimes fewer than half a dozen plants. Only 50% of Agta plant regularly, and 38% usually, but not always.

Only 56% of Agta plant a few vegetables and 46% claim tree crops, usually only one or a few coconut palms or banana plants. Collecting of wild vegetables accounts for some vegetable intake in roughly 15% of Agta meals.

Only 37% of Agta own domestic food animals other than dogs, and these are kept only for sale to peasants. Agta have a strong aversion to domestic meat of any kind and refuse to eat it. Wild game and fish account for the vast majority of Agta food production. For Palanan as a whole, Agta per-family production of boar totals 12 kg/month, for deer just under 3 kg/month, and just over 43 kg/month of fish. Other foods - wild fruit, grasses, roots and tubers, monkeys, snakes and birds - are hunted and collected incidentally. Shellfish are collected regularly and are stockpiled in tide pools. Tops of wild roots are replanted to propogate for collection later.

There is significant areal variation in these production figures. Agta recognise three distinct bounded territories within Palanan. The resources of each territory may be tapped only by its residents and their visiting kinsmen from other territories. Marital alliances are managed to provide optimal access to resources to extended families. The regional variation is illustrated in Table 1. These boundaries also represent a means of channelling exchange and interaction. Seasonally Agta exploit kin ties in other areas in order to equalise resource variation.

	North	South	Inland
Production (kg/week)			
boar	6+	0	2.5
deer	−1	0	−1.5
fish	5+	−12	11.0+
Consumption/production ratio (%)[1]			
corn	26.6	2.4	34.1
camote (yam)	44.0+	−80.0	−100.0
Trade and exchange			
trade ratio[2]	.207	1.28	.36
average no. trades/week	1.360	.83	1.20
% Agta not claiming *ibay*	5	30	0
Average land holding (hectares)[3]	−1.5	+.75	+1.5
Agta/Palanan ratios			
land holdings (individual)	1:2.5	1:0.36	1:1.6
demographic (families)[4]	1:1.7	1:0.25	1:1.4

1 The percentage of corn or *camote* consumed by Agta that is produced by Agta. The remainder is obtained in trade. Wild vegetable foods are utilised in 15% of Agta meals.

2 These figures represent mean fish traded over mean corn traded and provide an indication of the favourability of trade. A higher value represents trade more lucrative for Agta. The Southern figure here is somewhat deceptive as it includes exchanges in town; local exchanges in this area are much less lucrative for the Agta.

3 While these figures for the northern and inland areas are the same, Inland Agta till this much land without prompting, while in the north cultivation has been strongly encouraged by Panamin.

4 These figures are based on census of all persons in selected sample communities in each territory.

Table 1.   Resource variation in Agta territories.

Interdependence

Clearly, Agta and Palanans present optimum opportunity for economic interdependence. The Agta are a people with limited carbohydrate and the

Palanans have limited protein foods. Through trade
each supplies the other with needed foods. The
extent and nature of their interdependence as
expressed through food production is illustrated in
the bar graph in Fig.2.

Food exchange represents only a part of Agta-
Palanan economic interdependence. Access to cleared
land and Agta labour are other dimensions of
exchanges between the two populations. As noted,
Agta swidden small plots of land which they then
leave. They may move on to other forests, or
abandon cultivation altogether for a year or more.
They retain the right to return to that land at
their discretion. Their primary interest is in
territory, that is, access to resources on the land.
Many Palanans on the other hand, are eager to acquire
more land to cultivate permanently. Palanan ownership concerns, unlike the Agta, are with land as a
resource, as property. Whenever possible they
prefer to take over land already cleared by Agta,
since this saves them a significant amount of labour.
They estimate 175-200 man hours of labour expended
for each hectare of forest land cleared in Palanan.
Since this clearing takes place only on the
peripheries of Palanan settlements, it is difficult
to amass a large enough labour force to clear a
significant amount of land at once. Agta who clear
often do so piecemeal, requiring one to two years to
complete clearing of a single hectare. Because Agta
dibble they are not concerned with removal of tree
stumps; thus, in order to plough, Palanans who clear
their own land must take into consideration this
additional labour expediture. A prosperous Palanan
may hire Agta or peasant neighbours, but pioneers
are seldom prosperous. It is therefore highly
advantageous for pioneering peasants to take over
land from Agta. It is cleared and any remaining
tree stumps left rotting. Agta, who prefer to remain
on the forested fringes, the ecotone of peasant
settlement where game is most abundant, have
relatively little interest in returning to abandoned

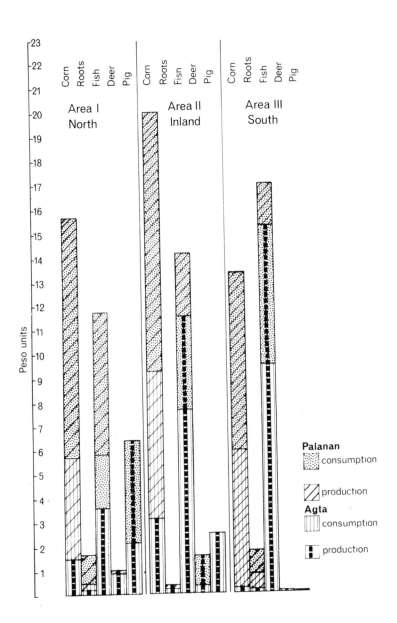

Fig.2.   Agta-Palanan exchange.

plots (J.T. Peterson 1975).   Palanans acquire access
to Agta plots by two means: purchase and land-grabbing.
Where relations between the two peoples are most
felicitous the peasants compensate the Agta for their
land, with compensation agreed upon by both parties.
It might range from a simple pledge of future support
by the Palanan to gifts of cloth, beads and cooking
pots, or of *carabao* or ploughs.   In most of these
cases Agta retain rights to any permanent crops
they may have planted on the land.   In areas where
relationships between Agta and Palanans are tense,
the latter simply take over abandoned Agta land.
Fewer than half a dozen Agta have made tax
declarations on their land, the first step to a
legal claim; their land therefore can easily be
usurped.   Even those Agta who have a nebulous idea
of the appropriate procedure for making land claims
have little recourse because of their ignorance and
illiteracy.   In short, the politically and legally
more sophisticated peasants encounter few obstacles
in acquiring Agta land without.compensation.   Unable
to exercise their legal rights, the Agta prefer to
move on and avoid unpleasant confrontations when
their land is taken.

Palanans also frequently call on the Agta as
a labour source. The reluctance of most peasants
to work for wages and the scattered settlement
pattern of much of Palanan makes it difficult to
assemble a sufficient number of persons for clearing,
planting, and harvesting.   While Agta are reluctant
to assume long term agricultural work which seriously
inhibits their hunting and fishing activities, they
will work a few days at a time when the labour need
is critical.   In exchange for their work they
receive food and/or wages.

The medium for most of these transactions
between Agta and Palanans is the *ibay* (special
friend) relationship, a term used by both Palanans
and Agta.   An *ibay* relationship involves one Agta,
usually married and usually male, and one peasant,

also usually married and male. The two friends, or
partners, recognise a mutual commitment to provide
goods and services to each other. Typically, the
Agta provides protein foods to his partner in
exchange for carbohydrate foods. The extent of
this commitment is reflected in the fact that
peasant *ibay* plant 10-30% in excess of their own
consumption needs in anticipation of Agta requests
for trade. Agta, on the other hand, place the
protein needs of their *ibay* as a high priority in
distributing the protein they procure. While non-
ibay exchanges of protein for carbohydrates do occur,
the *ibay* relationship is unique in that it demands
a commitment for regular exchanges, it allows for
extension of credit, and it commits the partners to
other economic transactions as needed. For example,
an Agta who has been unable to obtain protein may,
nonetheless, ask his *ibay* for sufficient carbohydrate
foods to see him through days or even weeks, with
the implicit understanding that he will provide
protein when he is able. Conversely, a Palanan may
request that his *ibay* supply him with a specified
amount of game for a life crisis event or to feed
field workers during planting or harvesting. *Ibay*
may depend on each other in crises, such as when an
Agta needs medical attention, or a peasant needs a
guide and bearer to cross the mountains. Finally,
peasants may rely on their *ibay* to work as field
labourers when the occasion demands it, and they
frequently approach *ibay* to purchase abandoned
fields. There are social, political, and religious
ramifications of this relationship as well
(J.T. Peterson 1974, 1976).

The complementarity of this relationship is
revealed in the fact that the two partners in an
ibay relationship seldom agree on how or when the
relationship began or why it exists. Most peasants
acknowledge the primary purpose of the relationship
as being access to Agta labour, and cite the first
employment of their partner as the inception of the
relationship. Agta, on the other hand, invariably

indicate that access to carbohydrate foods is the
reason for seeking an *ibay* and date the relationship
to the first exchange of food.

About a third of all peasants and nearly all
Agta have an *ibay*. Another third of the peasant
population regularly trade with Agta. Interpreting
this in the light of the preceding graph (Fig.2),
we can safely say that two-thirds of the present
population are receiving 30-50% or more of their
protein food from Agta, and nearly all the Agta
are dependent on peasants for anywhere from 70% to
nearly 100% of their carbohydrate foods.

Effectively, Palanan-Agta exchange represents
a labour specialisation which coordinates the two
populations in a higher order economic system. The
efficacy of this specialisation can be illustrated
by exploring the integration of their relative
economic roles.

To an extent, resource limitation places a
ceiling on Palanan animal domestication. *Carabao*
require pasturage which might better be utilised
for cultivation. Pigs and chickens in Palanan
exclusively feed themselves by foraging. Since most
of Palanan habitation is concentrated in long-
settled, heavily cultivated areas far removed from
the forest, these animals must forage on human
refuse or in cultivated fields. Any rise in
domestic animal population might well create a more
serious threat to field crops.

Alternatively, Palanans might deliberately
cultivate a root or grain surfeit explicitly to feed
pigs and chickens, but a number of factors tend to
deny that this is a desirable adaptation. As it
stands two-thirds of the Palanans with *ibay* (n=39)
do cultivate 10-30% in excess of their needs in
order to provide grain or roots for their trading
partners. Five percent cultivate over 30% in excess
of their own needs in order to trade. Of those

interviewed 10% could not calculate excess production
accurately, but acknowledged 'some' deliberately
cultivated surfeit, and only 18% of Palanans denied
any deliberate effort to cultivate a surfeit for
trade. In exchange for this trading surplus and
thus the additional expenditure of land and labour
required to produce it, they receive half, or
slightly less, of all protein foods from Agta. The
same quantity of grain and roots fed to pigs and
chickens might well produce less protein for
consumption. While it is impossible to predict with
any degree of accuracy how much domestic protein
could be produced by expending a given quantity of
carbohydrate in Palanan, we can at least consider
that it may be cheaper to feed Agta to provide fish
or wild animals, who feed themselves in the forest,
river, or sea, than to feed domestic animals.

Several other facts support this argument.
First, most meat or fish is provided by Agta in
quantities that can easily be consumed by a single
domestic unit, that is, in two to four kg lots.
Domestic production and slaughter would require
either cash sale or some kind of reciprocal or
redistributive exchange network. Palanans, as
noted, have only sporadic need for cash, and thus
there would seem to be little purpose in
substituting a less satisfactory intra-cultural
exchange network or the complexities of a market
for an inter-cultural network. Furthermore, Agta
protein is supplied with considerable regularity.
Again, to achieve this regularity with domestic
animal production would demand greater cultural
complexity.

Therefore the existing system of exchange in
Palanan may well be providing the peasants with
adequate protein with less direct labour output.
Certainly indirect labour expenditure is reduced
through exchange. Increased production of domestic
animals would require either controlled feeding
and/or construction and maintenance of fences, both

with concomitant labour intensity.

A further obvious advantage of maintaining exchange with Agta is that the hunter-gatherers provide not only protein but an important source of labour and a variety of other services. In short, by opting for inter-cultural exchange over domestic animal production, Palanan peasants are widening and diversifying their food web. Such widening and diversification of the food web has been acknowledged elsewhere (W. Peterson 1974a; J.T. Peterson 1974; Lewis 1972) as an effective means of assuring survival without increasing labour intensity.

Inter-cultural exchange is important to the Agta as well. Relative to protein production, surfeit represents at least as great a problem as deficit (cf. Woodburn 1968:106). Most commonly, Agta hunters spend one to three days at a time in search of game and take all the animals they can kill. Even a single boar or deer represents a food surfeit. One domestic unit, or even a camp group cannot easily consume this quantity of meat before it spoils. The problem then is one of maximising means of exchanging a protein surfeit.

Deficit is a problem in terms of carbohydrate foods. Garvan (1963:27) referring to Philippine Negritos, and Lee and DeVore (1968:7) commenting on hunters and gatherers in general, conclude that collection of carbohydrate staples is at least as critical a problem, often a greater problem, than protein production. For the Agta, receipt of carbohydrate foods from peasants represents a relatively stable food supply, and one which requires little labour output as compared to collecting, preparation, and preservation of non-domestic carbohydrate foods. Certainly it involves less labour than does production of domestic carbohydrate foods. Furthermore non-domestic carbohydrate foods do not store well; the opportunity of inter-cultural exchange represents an actual storehouse full of

food to which Agta can lay some claim without
increasing their own work efforts.

Hunting and gathering as a way of life requires
relatively low labour output on the whole. The Agta
labour three to five hours a day as compared to four
to eight hours among some long fallow cultivators,
and as many as ten or more hours a day for short
fallow systems (Boserup 1965:43-51). A number of
scholars have explored the implications of
maintaining a low labour output system (W. Peterson
1974a; Sahlins 1972; Lee and DeVore 1968). The Agta
are able to maintain such a system largely because
of exchange with peasants.

Maximisation of cultivation is not only labour
intensive, it is not compatible with maintenance of
hunting and gathering as a lifestyle. While
transition of one to the other can of course be
effected, long term maintenance of both technologies
poses problems on any other than a seasonal basis.
Fields ideally must be weeded, cultivated, harvested
and guarded against theft. In short, the abandonment
of the cultivated site for hunting will at least
lower its productivity. Attention to field labour,
on the other hand, reduces the potential for hunting
and fishing activity.

In addition to increasing labour output,
increased cultivation by Agta would throw them into
direct competition with Palanans over land. As it
stands, the limited cultivation practised by Agta
can be effectively carried out predominantly on
peripheral hillside land which holds little
attraction for the peasants, and peasants exploit
land that has relatively little appeal to Agta.
Open conflict would quite probably result if Agta
were attracted to the same resources as Palanans.

The combination of hunting and gathering with
exchange and limited cultivation offers an
extraordinarily wide food web. It is characteristic

of the diversity Agta manifest in many realms.
While hunting and fishing are the most prominent
activities, they also collect, swidden and plant
permanent fields. In all these they are attracted
to a great diversity of foods. In terms of allocation
they practise simple sharing, generalised and
measured reciprocity, and actual selling.
Diversification of direct and indirect food-getting
strategies is an effective adaptation for a
population with a limited technology.

In short, the union of culture-specific
specialisation and inter-cultural exchange allows
particularly effective utilisation of land and
labour resources. We should note that the same
principle applies to the territorial exchanges that
occur between Agta. As well, it may effectively
increase carrying capacity without increasing labour
output. This tandem specialisation does represent
intensification of land use. In a sense, a single
area is being exploited for two diverse resource
bases, i.e. a kind of dual technology 'double-
cropping' (cf. Barth 1959:8-9). Where it is
established, such a relationship may be critical
for the maintenance of existing population size for
both populations.

IMPLICATIONS FOR PREHISTORY

The modern variation in subsistence strategies
among the Palanan Agta (i.e. the Agta groups who
trade with the Palanan) may also be seen as a
synchronic manifestation of a diachronic
intensification process leading from hunting and
collecting to agriculture. The intensification
process was first hypothesised for modern agricultural
systems by Boserup (1965) as a throw-off insight
resulting from her attempts to explain the variations
in agricultural subsistence techniques. The same
process was identified and made more explicit in a

model presented by W. Peterson (1974a) where land-use intensification triggered by local population pressure is seen as an explanation for change in prehistoric technology and subsistence. While the land-use intensification process in human ecology is not the topic of this paper, it is germane to that topic. Exchange adaptation appears to operate as an alternative to intensification or at least as a stop-gap measure which delays the shift to a more labour intensive subsistence mode. It is a related process.

The Palanan Agta consist of small subsistence populations which display great variation in terms of their reliance on plant manipulation and their dependence on exchange with neighbouring agriculturalists. Some Agta subsistence groups appear to be moving toward a significant reliance on the cultivation of domesticated plants, while others primarily obtain carbohydrate foods from agriculturalists in exchange for protein foods such as pig, fish and deer. Ebukid Negrito hunters from nearby territories maintain a traditional hunter-collector pattern where neither trade nor plant cultivation is practised.

If present ecological processes can be assumed for the past, then the synchronic variation exhibited by the Agta has a number of diachronic implications. First, similar subsistence mode shifts occurred in the past. Second, prehistoric subsistence mode shifts were paralleled by changes in the nature of boundaries. Third, the shift from hunting and collecting to primary dependence on plant manipulation caused a drastic set of changes in boundary systems. These changes and their ramifications are the subject of the current analysis.

We have diagrammed the system (Figs 3 and 4) as consisting of linked simple and complex feed-back loops. Unlike similar representations presented by Maruyama (1968:304-13) these are not reversible

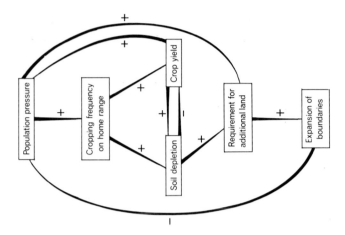

Fig.4.   Boundary expansion system.

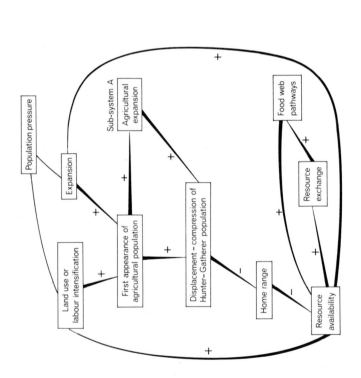

Fig.3.   Exchange adaptation system.

systems because they include a time factor. At the
same time they should not be mistaken for flow
diagrams. Fig.4 is a representation of an embedded
system or subsystem of the system presented in Fig.3.

Given a geographically bounded space such as
Palanan, one can assume a point in time when
agriculture as a subsistence technique was first
introduced, *provided* such a subsistence mode is
currently represented in the area. The exact time
is a matter of historical interest only. Such an
introduction is due either to internal processes of
labour or land-use intensification or to the
intrusion of agriculturalists from outside the area
under consideration. Both are assumed to be the
result of local population pressure.

The utility of using population pressure or
growth as a causal factor has recently been
challenged by a number of individuals (Cowgill 1975;
Flannery 1972). We can only answer that explicit
basic assumptions such as this are perfectly
legitimate; the burden of disproving the assumption
falls on other shoulders. In fact, we see no
difficulty. As Bateson (1972:430) points out,
'Every species has a primary Malthusian capacity.
Any species that does not, potentially, produce
more young than the number of the population of the
parental generation is out. They're doomed.' The
weight and simplicity of the argument is undeniable.
Our species, like all successful species, is
characterised by growth. That does not mean
population growth is characteristic of all places
at all times, but it does imply that the assumption
of population pressure in the system is valid
without specific evidence to the contrary.

Once agriculture as a subsistence mode is
established in a bounded space, a number of drastic
changes occur. Many of these changes are related to
the fact that the boundaries of areas being exploited
by agricultural techniques are characteristically in

a state of expansion. There are two primary reasons
for this. First, the increased growth rates indicated
for agriculturalists as opposed to hunters (Kolata
1974) create demands for additional yields and land.
Second, cropping of any sort depletes soil nutrients
and lowers crop yield progressively. Soil depletion
can be counteracted by fertilisation techniques, but
it is also possible to solve the problem of soil
depletion by moving to new land. If Boserup (1965)
is correct, it is less labour intensive to move, as
do swiddenists, than to replenish soil nutrients by
fertilisation. It is likely that expansion will
occur rather than labour intensification, provided
the land is held by hunters. The two populations
will view the resources differently; hunters, as
noted, are primarily interested in the availability
of wild resources on the land, while agriculturalists
must have land itself in order to raise crops. The
'expansion problem' of agriculturalists is chronic
in the sense that solution of the soil nutrients
problem in whatever way simply leads to increased
population pressures. Crop yield increase equals
more available food supply which in turn raises the
limits on maintainable population numbers. There
is of course, a limit to expansion without conflict,
but we suspect that limit has only recently been
reached for most areas of the globe. Today in
Palanan, one can document the expansion of
agriculturalists into hunter-collector territories.

   We have portrayed a feasible structure of this
expansion problem in Fig.4; it is integral to the
understanding of exchange. Population pressure is
seen as leading to an increase in home range
cropping frequency, which in turn causes soil
depletion to increase and yield to increase. The
increasing yields, as stated above, raise the limits
to population growth, which results in additional
population pressure. Increases in cropping speed
the soil depletion process which eventually affects
the yield adversely. In time, the soil is exhausted
and action must be taken. One solution, not

illustrated, is to fertilise. The more prevalent
solution for much of prehistory was to acquire new
land by expansion into adjacent space. This has
the effect of reducing population pressure until
the growth rate once more drives the cropping
frequency for the larger home range over the limits.

We have assumed in the exchange adaptation
system (Fig.3) that the soil nutrient problems
faced by agriculturalists result in a continual
demand for additional land, a demand augmented by
population pressures from food surpluses. There are
limits to expansion, of course; it can be prevented
by warfare and is limited by the availability of
arable, undefended land. In a very general sense
expansion is a delaying tactic opted for prior to
intensification. The model presented in Fig.3 is
designed to illustrate the diachronic effects of
agricultural expansion and to explain the functions
of exchange across ethnic and territorial boundaries.
It is a time dependent system triggered by the first
appearance of agriculturalists. The need for new
land resulted in expansion into hunter-collector
territory. This occurs today in Palanan; land is
gained at the expense of Agta hunters who have
little or no interest in land as property. Hunter-
collector groups occupying territory adjacent to
agriculturalists find themselves caught between
expanding agricultural boundaries and resource areas
controlled by other territorially organised hunters.
This dilemma results in a progressive decrease of
the home range which in turn reduces the available
resources in the home range. A number of alternatives
become possible to the pressured hunters. First,
they can shift to a new subsistence pattern with
its greater labour demands. Second, they can
expand into new territory (if available) or take
new territory by force from adjacent hunters.

The solution adopted by the modern Agta in
Palanan has been to maintain (and increase) resource
availability by exchange with agriculturalists and

among themselves. Exchange across hunter-
agriculturalist boundaries constitutes an improvement
in the efficiency of energy flow for both populations
by lowering labour expenditure and broadening the
food web. The extended food web results in an
increase in resource availability for all groups
involved. Exchange creates a food web which
transcends ethnic and territorial boundaries and
which provides greater resource variety and an
improved safety margin. Exchange adaptation can
also be seen as a means of surviving on an
insufficient home range.

CONCLUSION

The foregoing analysis has been based on
ethnographic and archaeological information. The
ethnographic information was of much greater value
in the construction of the model; indeed the
insights could not have been achieved from
archaeological data alone. However the model (*a
priori* in that it requires testing against new data)
provides some intriguing insights for archaeology
and indicates realms which require attention in the
future.

Ethnographic observations and ecological
analysis of the Agta hunters of Palanan have
suggested the relationships operating in the
exchange processes, in the incursions into hunter
territories by agriculturalists, and in the
displacement-compression phenomenon. Whether the
relationships and feedbacks as portrayed in the
systems are an accurate representation of reality
beyond the observations used in their construction
will depend on the results of future applications
of the models.

As with many models (Braithwaite 1970:268-75),
this one performs an important heuristic function

in that it identifies areas for future research as
well as illuminates problems other than those for
which the explanation was constructed. Some areas
illuminated by the present example include:

1. Exchange can operate as an alternative to
   other forms of intensification, or migration.
2. Hunter-collector/agriculturalist exchange is
   probably as ancient as agriculture.
3. Evidence of trade in prehistoric contexts may
   have ecological implications.
4. Exchange adaptation can operate to delay
   intensification and therefore technological
   change.

All of these warrant additional attention. The last
point is particularly suggestive, when one considers
the pattern of late persistence of hunter-collector
lithic technologies for Southeast Asia. Pintu Rock
Shelter (W. Peterson 1974a), the Samar area (Hutterer
1971), and the Tabon Caves of Palawan (Fox 1971) are
relevant examples. Such persistences could be the
result of exchange adaptation. It is not a
conclusive answer - they could also be due to lack
of population growth - but it is a highly possible
one which needs further research.

Some of the problem areas delimited by the
model are:

1. The inability of archaeology to distinguish
   types of trade from archaeological evidence.
2. The lack of appropriate ethnological and
   ecological information on modern hunter-
collectors and agriculturalists.
3. The need to work out archaeological 'markers'
   of ecological processes.

The problem areas clearly show theoretical and
technical domains which need investigation or which
must at least be recognised as areas for which data
is problematic.

We find that the ethnographic data on the

exchange between hunters and agriculturalists is
best interpreted as an ecological process which is
not unique. A systems model presents a version of
the process. In addition, a soil exhaustion
process, also not unique, is presented as a related
ecological process, i.e. a separate but embedded
system. Research directed toward the isolation of
other such processes is needed and the authors
encourage refinements and criticisms of the systems
presented. The implications are extremely
significant for archaeology and other ecologically
oriented disciplines. If we are isolating
ecological structures and/or processes which apply
regardless of location in time and space, then we
are obviously dealing with a realm of inquiry which
has tremendous powers of prediction, explanation
and generalisation.

FOOTNOTES

[1] Relationships of hunters with sedentary peoples
   are reported, for example, for the Birhor of
India (Sinha 1972:386-7; Williams 1968:128), the
Paliyans of India (Gardner 1972:405, 416-7, 441-2),
the !Kung Bushmen (Lee 1972:331-4), the Hadza
(Woodburn 1968:50), the Malay Negritos (Skeat and
Blagden 1906:255), and the Negritos of the
Philippines (E. Fox 1956; Garvan 1963:32, 41, 76,
79, 80, 85, 146, 158, 163, 241, 261; Maceda 1964:
46-8; Reed 1904:44; Vanoverbergh 1925:157, 431ff;
Schebesta 1954:156-60).

[2] A *cavan* equals approximately 2.12 bushels.

[3] Many of the individuals who were not cultivating
   during this period were not included in our
sample because they were hunting away from settled
areas, and therefore were never available for
interview. Thus the number of non-cultivating Agta
is higher than these figures suggest.

REFERENCES

Barth, F. 1959   The land use pattern of migratory tribes of south Persia. *Norsk Geografisk Tidsskrift* 17(1-2):1-11

Bateson, G. 1972 *Steps to an ecology of mind.* New York: Chandler

Bicchieri, M.G. (ed.) 1972 *Hunters and gatherers today.* New York: Holt, Rinehart and Winston

Binford, L.R. 1968   Archaeological perspectives. In S.R. and L.R. Binford (eds) *New perspectives in archaeology*:5-32.   Chicago: Aldine

Boserup, E. 1965 *The conditions of agricultural growth.* Chicago: Aldine

Braithwaite, R.B. 1970   Models in the empirical sciences.   In B.A. Brody (ed.) *Readings in the philosophy of science*:268-75.   Englewood Cliffs (N.J.): Prentice-Hall

Cowgill, G. 1975   On causes and consequences of ancient and modern population changes. *American Anthropologist* 77:505-25

Flannery, K. 1972   The cultural evolution of civilisation. *Annual review of ecology and systematics* 8:399-426

Fox, E. (tr.) 1956   Bisayan accounts of early Bornean settlements in the Philippines recorded by Father Santaren. *Sarawak Museum Journal* 7(7):22-42

Fox, R. 1971 *The Tabon Caves*.   Manila: National Museum, Monograph No.1

Gardner, P.M. 1972   The Paliyans.   In Bicchieri 1972:404-47

Garvan, J.M. 1963 *The Negritos of the Philippines*, (edited by Hermann Hochegger).   Vienna: Institut für Völkerkunde der Universität Wien,

Wiener Beiträge zur Kulturgeschichte und Linguistik 14

Glover, I.C. 1973 Late Stone Age traditions in South-East Asia. In N. Hammond (ed.) *South Asian archaeology*:51-65. London: Duckworth

Harris, M. 1971 *Culture, man, and nature*. New York: Crowell

Headland, T. and E. Wolfenden 1967 The vowels of Casiguran Dumagat. In M.D. Zamora (ed.) *Studies in Philippine anthropology*:592-6. Quezon City: Alemar-Phoenix

Heekeren, R. van 1972 *The Stone Age of Indonesia*, (2nd ed.) The Hague: Nijhoff

Hutterer, K. 1971 *Cultural evolution in Samar, Philippines*. Paper presented at the 70th Annual Meeting of the American Anthropological Association, New York

        1974 The evolution of Philippine lowland societies. *Mankind* 9(4):287-99

Keesing, F. 1962 *The ethnohistory of northern Luzon*. Stanford: Stanford University Press

Kolata, G. 1974 !Kung hunter-gatherers: feminism, diet and birth control. *Science* 185:932-4

Kuhn, T. 1970 *The structure of scientific revolutions*, (2nd ed.). Chicago: Chicago University Press, International Encyclopedia of Unified Science, Vol.2(2)

Lee, R.B. 1969 !Kung Bushman subsistence: an input-output analysis. In A.P. Vayda (ed.) *Environment and cultural behavior*:43-79. Garden City (N.Y.): Natural History Press

        and I. DeVore (eds) 1968 *Man the hunter*. Chicago: Aldine

Lewis, H. 1972 The role of fire in the domestication of plants and animals in southwest Asia: a hypothesis. *Man* n.s.

7:195-222

Maceda, M. 1964 *The culture of the Mamanua.*
Manila: Catholic Trade School

Maruyama, M. 1968 The second cybernetics:
deviation-amplifying mutual causal processes.
In W. Buckley (ed.) *Modern systems research
for the behavioral scientist*:304-13. Chicago:
Aldine

Peterson, J. Treloggen 1974 *Ecological
implications of economic and social behavior
among Agta hunter-gatherers, northeastern
Luzon, Philippines.* Unpublished PhD thesis,
University of Hawaii, Honolulu

              1975 *The merits of margins.*
Paper presented at the Midwest Conference on
Asian Affairs, Athens, Ohio

              1976 Folk traditions and
interethnic relations in northeastern Luzon,
Philippines. In A.L. Kaeppler and H.A. Nimmo
(eds) *Directions in Pacific traditional
literature*:319-30. Honolulu: Bishop Museum,
Special Publication 62

Peterson, W. 1974a *Anomalous archaeological sites
of northern Luzon and models of Southeast
Asian prehistory.* Unpublished PhD thesis,
University of Hawaii, Honolulu

              1974b Summary report of two
archaeological sites from north-eastern Luzon.
*Archaeology and Physical Anthropology in
Oceania* 9:26-35

Reed, W.A. 1904 *Negritos of Zambales.* Manila:
Bureau of Public Printing, Philippine
Islands Ethnological Survey Publications,
Vol.2(1)

Sahlins, M. 1972 *Stone age economics.* Chicago:
Aldine

564   J.T. AND W. PETERSON

Schebesta, P. 1954 *Die Negrito Asiens, II.*
     Ethnographie der Negrito, 1. Wirtschaft und
     Soziologie. Vienna-Mödling: St Gabriel Verlag,
     Studia Instituti Anthropos 12

Sinha, D.P. 1972 The Birhors. In Bicchieri 1972:
     371–403

Skeat, W.W. and O. Blagden 1906 *Pagan races of*
     the Malay Peninsula, (2 vols). London:
     Macmillan

Spencer, J.E. and F.L. Wernstedt 1967 *The*
     Philippine island world. Berkeley and
     Los Angeles: University of California Press

Turnbull, C. 1965 *Wayward servants: the two*
     worlds of the African pygmies. Garden City
     (N.Y.): Natural History Press

Vanoverbergh, M. 1925 Negritos of northern Luzon.
     Anthropos 20:148–99, 399–442

Williams, B.J. 1968 The Birhor of India and some
     comments on band organization. In Lee and
     DeVore 1968:126–31

Woodburn, J. 1968 An introduction to Hazda ecology.
     In Lee and DeVore 1968:49–55

PART 5

SAUER'S HYPOTHESIS: DEVISING THE TESTS

A theory almost completely lacking in factual basis may still be stimulating and provocative and may be especially useful if it can be subjected to critical tests which would prove it wrong. I can think of no such tests to apply to Sauer's theory. His two principal hearths occur in regions where few archaeological remains have so far been found and where the climate almost precludes the long-term preservation of herbaceous cultigens. Practically all of his conclusions, although unsupported by evidence, are still virtually impossible to disprove. Indeed if one sought, as an exercise in imagination, to design a completely untestable theory of agricultural origins and dispersals, it would be difficult to improve upon this one. In creating such a theory, the author has at least demonstrated that there are still huge gaps in our knowledge of man's history.

Paul Mangelsdorf 1954

(In a review of Carl Sauer's *Agricultural Origins and Dispersals* (1952) published in *American Antiquity* 19:87-90)

HOABINHIAN HORTICULTURE?
THE EVIDENCE AND THE QUESTIONS
FROM NORTHWEST THAILAND

D.E. YEN

Bishop Museum
Honolulu, Hawaii

INTRODUCTION

The first plant remains associated with the
artifactual complex of a Hoabinhian site were
excavated by Chester Gorman at Spirit Cave in
northwest Thailand. When Gorman (1969, 1970,
1971) published his reports on the site,
prehistorians were prepared to accept the
redefinition of the Hoabinhian 'technocomplex'
and the early associated dates. A variable
reception however, attended the ethnobotanical
aspects, particularly after Solheim (1972)
appeared to stress the tentative plant
identifications from the excavations as evidence
for the precedence of a Southeast Asian origin of
agriculture over the Near East. The 'authenticity'
of the evidence was rashly questioned by Harlan
and de Wet (1973), while Flannery (1973),
regretting the extravagance of interpretation,
called the presentation of plant identifications
careful and circumspect.

Among the participants in the study of the
plant materials of Spirit Cave, acceptance of the
identifications was also varied. The existence of
doubt was reflected in the effort to establish
firmer methodology for ethnobotany in the extension
of the northwest Thailand project by Gorman and the
present writer. The plans, formulated as Gorman's
original reports were in preparation, include these
considerations:

1. *Recovery of additional plant remains*: to
increase if possible the numbers of specimens,
particularly of genera critical as possible
domesticates. Among other considerations concerned
with increasing confidence in identifications, this
would permit dissection of material, which could
not be risked because of the number of single
specimens recovered from the first excavation at
Spirit Cave.

2. *Collection of present flora*: with concentration
on plant parts corresponding to those
represented by the archaeological specimens, the
feasibility of identifications might be satisfied,
at least as far as adaptation to present climate is
concerned. Since few detailed studies of the flora
in this region have been made (see review in Gorman
1970) this step was deemed to be necessary for some
improved degree of certitude in suggesting what
plants had been exploited by the early inhabitants
of the region.

3. *Examination of the agricultural systems*: the
cultural groups of the region, as defined by
Lebar *et al.* (1964) include the Northern Thai and
those who are regarded as immigrants of hundreds
rather than thousands of years standing - the Shan
or Thai Yai, Lahu, Lisu, Meo and Karen. The
agricultural systems of these groups form an
interesting study in contrasts, with possible
historical significance, but the relevance of this
phase of fieldwork is the plant collection of
cultivated species. Seeds or other plant parts
could be compared with equivalent parts of the
archaeological plant specimens and of wild species
collected from present flora. Ethnographic
information on useful plants both cultivated and
wild is a further aspect of this part of the study.

This paper summarises the ethnobotanical
results of the expedition to northwest Thailand,
October 1973 - March 1974, after Gorman had
further developed the Spirit Cave excavation and
investigated two further cave sites in this

mountainous region, Banyan Valley Cave and Tham Pa
Chan. The material from the original excavation is
also considered. While this account concentrates
on the archaeological material, supporting data
from the ethnographic aspects of the study will be
introduced where they are relevant. The
archaeology of the sites and its interpretation
are in preparation for publication by Gorman.

THE PLANT MATERIALS

The identifications of the plant remains from
the three northwest Thailand sites are set out in
Table 1.

Class A

The one identification questioned in class A
is *Aleurites* on the score of its present-day
distribution. It was not found during forest
collection, despite the distribution of the genus
in various specific forms throughout Malaysia
(Burkill 1966). The archaeological sample of
numerous seed-shell fragments is similar to
remains excavated in Hawaii in internal and
external structural features, and on this evidence
might be assigned to the pan-Pacific *A. moluccana*
Willd., the candlenut. Whether this represents a
former inland Thai adaptation cannot be confirmed,
but certainly the coconut, *Cocos nucifera* L.,
often associated in the Pacific with candlenut,
has been adapted to cultivation in the valleys of
northern Thailand. If the fragments represent the
coastal adapation of *A. moluccana*, then the
nearest source for its seeds would be at the
Gulf of Martaban, now a straight-line distance
of some 240 km southwest of the Spirit Cave area
and probably more in late Pleistocene and early
Recent times. Since the sizes and shapes of the
original seeds cannot be determined from

	Spirit Cave (Sample i)	Spirit Cave (Sample ii)	Banyan Valley	Tham Pa Chan
A				
Aleurites	(2)			
Areca	(1)	X (2)		
Canarium	(2,1)	X (4,3,2,1)	X (3,2,1)	X (5,4,3,2,1,S)
Madhuca	(2)	X (4)		
Piper	(2)			X (4)
Prunus	(3)		X (?)	X (S)
Terminalia	(3)			X (?)
Castanopsis	(3)			
		Gramineae (bamboo) (4)	X (5,1)	X (3)
		Celtis (1,2)		X (S)
		Euphorbiaceae (2)		
		Richinus (4)		
			Calamus (1,4)	
				Mangifera (1)
B				
Cucumis	(3)		X (?)	
Lagenaria	(3)	X (2)	X (2)	
Trapa	(3)			
		Cucurbitaceae (1)	X (?)	
		Momordica (?)		
		Nelumbium (1)	X (4)	
		Trichosanthes/Luffa (5,4,3,2,1)		
			Oryza (2,1)	
C				
Pisum/Palmae (4)		X (4,2,1)	X (4,1)	X (2)
Phaseolus/Glycine (4)			X (2,1)	X (5,4)
Vicia / Phaseolus (2)				

X indicates a repeated identification

Numbers in brackets refer to excavation levels

S = surface

For Spirit Cave sample i, the levels are dated (Gorman 1969)

(1) c. 7600 BP

(2) c. 8-9000 BP

(3) c. 9-11,000 BP

(4) c. 11,000 – BP

reconstruction of the excavated seed-coat fragments, perhaps the most reasonable explanation is that the local forest species of *Aleurites* was missed in collection for seasonal or other reasons. In the inland situation of our plant collections, we had expected to find forms of the tung-oil tree or its relatives, *A. fordii* Hemsl., *A. montana* Wilson, or perhaps *A. cordata* R. Br.

A common indigenous use of *Aleurites* nuts is for lighting, due to the kernel's high oil content, but other uses in the Pacific include body decoration and use as a condiment and medicine. None of these of course could be confirmed ethnographically for northwest Thailand, but Table 2 summarises the uses of the other forest plants in Table 1 by present occupants of the region that *might* represent their utilisation in the past. A reasonably wide range of food plants seems to be indicated in class A plants, representing edible fruits and nuts.

.By far the dominant one, judging by numbers recovered, is *Canarium*. It is perhaps significant that not a single sample of seed of the genus was

Table 1. Identifications of plant remains from Spirit Cave, Banyan Valley Cave and Tham Pa Chan, all in northwest Thailand. The vertical division separates the Spirit Cave identifications from those found at the other two sites, while the Spirit Cave materials are further divided into (i) those reported by Gorman (1969) from the first excavation and (ii) from re-excavation. Horizontally, the table divides into three sections: A) trees and perennials of present-day primary and secondary forests; B) annual and perennial plants represented in the region now by cultigens, found in mixed swiddens, kitchen gardens or small pond areas of the rice farmers. Some have wild or seemingly wild analogues or closely related species; C) possible annual crop plants, now cultivated in small fields in rotation with rice, or often in mixed plantings. The divisions A, B and C may also be regarded as a scale of decreasing confidence in identifications, with class A the most positive in both qualitative and comparative (with modern floral elements) standards, and quantity of material.

Genus	Plant Part	Quantity		Condition[1]	Possible Use
Aleurites	seed shells	5	C	fragments	lighting/medicine/ food (kernel)
Areca	fruit section	1	U	fibrous fragment	betel chew (kernel)
	fruit petiole	2	C	2/3 cm length	
Canarium	seed sections	> 50	C/U	many fragments	food (kernel)
Madhuca	seed shells	3	C	fragments	food (fruit) poison (kernel)
Piper	seed	5	U	whole	betel chew (leaf) condiment (seed)
Prunus	seed shells	2	U	large fragments	food (kernel?)
Prunus	seed shell	1	U	half	food (fruit)
Terminalia	seed shell	2	U	fragments	food (kernel)
Castanopsis	kernel	1	C	whole	food (kernel)
Gramineae	bamboo stem	7	U/C	short sections	extractive tools/ building/cooking utensil (stem)
Celtis	seed	11	U	whole	food (fruit)
Euphorbiaceae	fruits	3	U	whole	poison (fruit)
Calamus	seed	2	U	whole	food (fruit)
Mangifera	seed	1	U	whole	food (fruit)

[1] C = carbonized; U = uncarbonized

Table 2.   The possible uses of forest products from the northwest Thailand sites (see Table 1, class A).

recovered whole: carbonised or not, they were all
fragmented, as if purposely broken by smashing
across the mid-section of the hard seed to obtain
the kernel. Thus there were over 50 rough cross-
sections of the seed which confer confidence in the
identification. Fig. 1 illustrates this point, and
also contrasts the present local variation and
other Pacific species. It can be seen in the

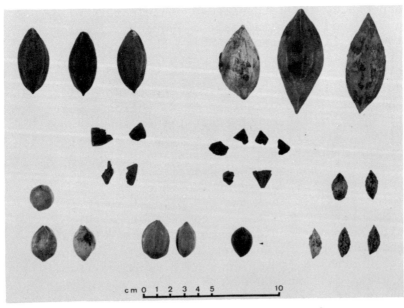

Fig.1. *Canarium* seed fragments from Spirit Cave, with
representatives of the genus from the region in northwest
Thailand and from the western Pacific. Centre row. Seed-
end pieces from excavation: left, carbonised; right,
uncarbonised. Lower row. Left, 3 from feral tree; middle,
3 from 2 village trees, both groups possibly *C.alba*.
Right, 5 from trees close to village, used for their
fleshy fruit. Upper row. Left, from Indonesia; right,
from Santa Cruz, Solomon Is.

photograph that the ends of the archaeological
specimens appear to be much more pointed, more
acutely angular than the larger of the local
forms, which are recognised by informants to be

feral, as well as being purposely cultivated on
the rising slopes of hills surrounding irrigated
rice fields of the Shan. Within the territories
of the swidden cultivators, like the Lahu and Lisu,
the large *Canarium* trees within secondary or
recovery forest seem to indicate survival through
burning in field preparation. It would be tempting
to suggest that reconstruction of the excavated
specimens, the wild forms of *Canarium*, and
especially the large-seeded contemporary wild/
cultivated forms indicate a sequence of selection
towards large kernels. While this may be so, the
present major use of the genus is for its fruit,
pickled or preserved. Thus present-day *Canarium*
cultivated in the region may represent a divergent
and more recent direction of selection toward
fleshier character of fruit rather than kernel
size. Certainly in our attempts at reconstruction
of the remains, one anatomical character is
consistent through the excavated levels: the
tri-locular structure of the inner seed is
maintained, so that the nut product is three
small rather than one larger kernel per seed;
cf. the mono-locular (with 2 degenerate) Eastern
character of the Solomon Island *Canarium* for
which prehistoric selection is proposed (Yen 1974).
A great deal more needs to be known about the
botany of *Canarium* in Thailand before any firm
pronouncement can be made on the history of the
genus there. The taxonomic treatment of the
genus by Leenhouts (1955a, 1955b, 1958) is limited
to the Malay Peninsula, the Indonesian islands
and western Oceania, but from our limited work it
is likely that analogous variation in the
structural characters will be found in northwest
Thailand, at least at the species level.

Of the other plants in Class A, the
ethnographic information suggests varied uses, the
slender basis for whose application to the
prehistoric situation should be emphasised again.
Betel chewing may be associated with the latter

part of the Spirit Cave sequence, while sources
of poison - one *(Madhuca)* with possible food use
as well, the other (Euphorbiaceae) with little
alternative use except as low quality firewood -
were perhaps of use in hunting. The latter
however, may be an incautious speculation since
no hunting points were excavated. Bamboo
fragments may be the signal for raw material in
the manufacture of extractive tools, and perhaps
for minor construction in the caves; none of the
fragments however, had sufficient features to be
even suspected as hunting points or parts thereof.
Should the identification of bamboo require
support, the carefully excavated ash remains of
seemingly fibrous material in the fifth level at
Banyan Valley Cave was identified and demonstrated
by local informants as the bamboo leaves
remaining in elephant dung, a commonly used fuel
for slow cooking.

Resin and gums can be obtained from *Canarium*,
Madhuca and the Euphorbiaceae, and are used by the
Shan today. The archaeological remains demonstrate
indirectly that these products were available to
the more ancient cultures of the region, and
perhaps of use for tool hafting and pottery
coating.

Class B

The low quantities and poor condition of
some of these specimens as described in Table 3
preclude overall confidence in the identifications.
The Cucurbitaceae photographed as Fig.2 further
illustrate the material. As identified, all are
food plants at the present time, and have been
recently described by Herklots (1972) and
Purseglove (1968); however, the plant parts
excavated would indicate other uses. The
Lagenaria fruit shells, for example, would be
used as containers in their whole condition; if
the *Luffa* identification is correct, the fruit

Genus	Plant Part	Quantity	Condition[1]		Characteristics	Cu/W[2]
Cucumis	seed case	1	U	nearly whole	unrimmed, flat, point broken: length c.6 mm breadth 2—3 mm; resembles *C. melo* L. var. *conomon* Makino	Cu
Lagenaria	fruit shell	Many	C/U	mostly small fragments	Thin sectioned, resembling variety *L. siceraria* (Mol.) Standl., cultivated as vegetable cf. varieties for water containers, seed storage, betel lime	Cu/W
Trapa	seed case	2	C	fragments	like 'horned' shell of nuts of *T. bicornis* Osbeck	Cu
Cucurbitaceae	seed case	1	C	complete	large, rough surfaced unrimmed; no identification	?
Momordica	seed case	2	U	small fragments	thin, irregular surface cavity, like *M. charantia* L.	Cu/W
Nelumbo	seed	2	U	whole	Ovoid, 5—6 mm long; resembles *N. nucifera* Gaertn.	Cu
Trichosanthes	seeds	6	C	halves, fragments	shape like *T. cucumerina* L., thick irregular encasement, cavity clear	Cu
Luffa	fruit skin	1	U	section mature fruit skin	lineal markings like *L. cylindrica* (L.) M.J. Roem.	Cu/W
Oryza	spikelet husks	57 53	U U	whole or near halves or quarters	size and shape of rice, *O. sativa* L.	Cu/W

[1] C = carbonized; U = uncarbonized
[2] Cu = recorded cultivated in N.W. Thailand
W = recorded wild in N.W. Thailand

Table 3.   Identifications of possible annual plants (see Table 1, class B).

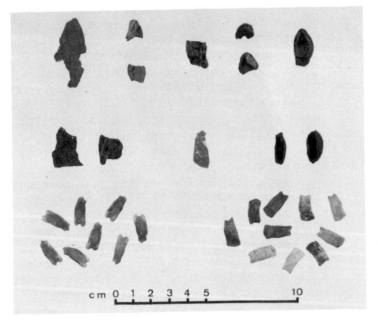

Fig.2. Cucurbitaceae: top and middle rows excavated. Top
row. Left, a portion of fruit skin of possibly *Luffa*;
remainder, seed fragments, showing corky fringing formation
suggesting *Trichosanthes*. Middle row. Left 3, two
carbonised and one uncarbonised fragments of fruit shell
determined as *Lagenaria*; right 2, fragments of unknown cucurbit
seed. Lower row. Left group, seeds of *Lagenaria siceraria* of
a variety grown in northwest Thailand; right group, seeds of
an unknown wild cucurbit of the region.

that the skin fragment represents would be too
mature to eat, and perhaps the fibrous skeleton
of the mature fruit would have a small-cloth
function, as in many of the village households
now. The finds of *Oryza* in such relative
quantity, so carefully and jubilantly excavated
by Gorman from the Banyan Valley Cave, endows
the identification with as much confidence as that
of *Canarium*, and furthermore gives opportunities
for further analysis of which we were deprived
in most of the other samples. This will be
reported in the following section of this paper.

It will be noted that Table 3 records whether

the genera are found wild. These were collected
with local informants, but because of the field
contexts of secondary growth, I was unsatisfied
that they were wild forms rather than garden
escapes or the remains of earlier gardening. One
exception was *Luffa cylindrica*, collected from an
uncultivated stream bank in Meo forest territory
in which Shan had recently trespassed to cut
large trees for their own use. Because I like
the vegetable form of *Momordica* I conducted,
contrary to local advice, a cooking and tasting
test of the alledgedly wild fruits and indeed
these small-fruited forms of bottle gourd, *Luffa*
and bitter melon were too bitter to eat. The
latter two species also suffered in contrast to
their equivalent cultivated forms in the thinness
of their flesh. While these characteristics may
all be the product of growth under the more
natural competitive conditions of the environment,
this was denied by informants, Shan and Lahu, who
subscribed to 'like produces like'; also adverse
features of taste tend to be accepted as the
superficial differentiations between wild and
cultivated forms (e.g. Schwantitz 1966).

Rice however presented a different story.
All of the cultural groups visited, except the
Thai Yai, described wild rice as possessing
edible, shattering heads whose main harvesting
problem was in the competition with birds. Not
prized, the Lahu call it *ja tuh*, 'wild rice', in
the most literal way, but the Shan, one group of
whom live near the site of the first of Gorman's
excavations, Spirit Cave, call it *kao pi* or spirit
rice (*kao* - grain, including rice, millet, etc.),
surely appropriate. Too late to collect it in the
field, except for dried stubble, we were given two
samples allegedly gathered in September by a
Lahu group who said that the natural stands were
situated in open sloping forest close to their
village at an estimated altitude of 600 m. A
Shan informant provided a sample of a small-seeded

variety which his people had grown for generations, and which they had found feral when they arrived from Burma. These samples were included in comparisons with the archaeological rice.

Class C

This group of identifications has borne the brunt of criticism, and perhaps justifiably. There were only single specimens of each alternative subclass identification, e.g. *Pisum*/Palmae; this form of presentation was itself meant to suggest high uncertainty. With re-excavation, the numerical position was only somewhat improved, to a total of nine classed as *Pisum*/Palmae and six as *Phaseolus/Glycine*, while unfortunately *Vicia/Phaseolus* remained at one. In the field we sought analogues among the seeds of over 60 feral legumes - trees, vines, shrubs and herbs - without significant success; the cultigens produced somewhat better, but still tenuous correspondence. *Phaseolus* and *Glycine* were unexpectedly found in cultivation, the latter, in fact, sometimes as a dry season element in the rotation cropping of irrigated rice fields, and having a large number of varieties. *Phaseolus*, grown most in swiddens and kitchen gardens of mixed plantings, was found as *P. aureus* Roxb., *P. angularis* (Willd.) Wight, *P. aconitifolius* Jacq., *P. calcaratus* Roxb. and the American *P. vulgaris* L.

Fig.3 however, demonstrates the uncertain nature of the identifications. The *Vicia* identification has been made on my experience as a plant breeder with that genus, when small varietal forms from the Mediterranean were grown in New Zealand. Unadapted, the seeds harvested were the same shape and size as the Spirit Cave specimen, but generally showed what was diagnosed as a physiological condition that affected cotyledon development. This was evidenced in the scar-like depression that developed on one or both outside

surfaces of the seed, a symptom noted at times even
in adapted larger seed varieties in New Zealand.

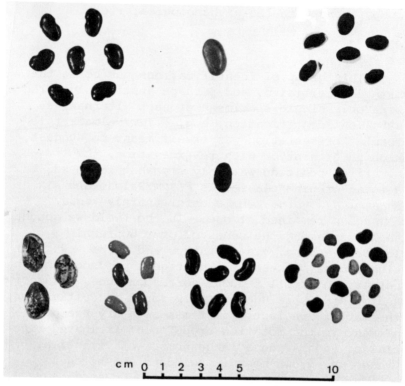

Fig.3. Bean-like carbonised plant remains. Middle row.
Excavated samples. Left, identified as *Vicia/Phaseolus*; centre,
Phaseolus/Glycine; right, *Phaseolus/Glycine*, from Tham Pa Chan
(others, Spirit Cave). The top and bottom rows are for
comparison. Top row. Left, group of 7, *Phaseolus calcaratus*;
centre, unknown legume, cultivated and gathered by Shan; right,
P. angularis. Bottom row. Left, group of 3, unknown garden
legume; group of 5, possibly *P. aconitifolius*; group of 7,
American *P. vulgaris*; right, group of 17, mixed *Glycine max*
(soybean) varieties.

The archaeological specimen exhibited just such
a scar, evident despite carbonisation. This of
course does not positively identify the specimen,
which could be of another leguminous species
susceptible to this growth defect. *Vicia* is grown

sporadically among the people of northwest
Thailand and prized for its roasted seed as a
snack food, but cultivators say its yield is
rather erratic and may prefer other beans because
of this.

Pisum is rather more widely grown in kitchen
gardens in the sugar pea form (*P. sativum* L. var
saccharatum), in a number of variable varieties.
The first carbonised archaeological specimen had
been identified simply on its roundness, size and
a slight indentation that may have been the
original hilum of the seed. The increase in the
number of 'peas' from the excavations confirmed
this character in five other individuals (three
carbonised, two uncarbonised), and an effort was
made to determine whether the round bodies were
dicotyledonous (to support the *Pisum* identification)
or monocotyledonous (Palmae). The two other
partial 'peas' excavated were not clearly enough
the product of splitting of pairs of cotyledons,
since the flat surfaces that should result were
eroded. Sectioning however has been inconclusive
in the four attempts so far, because of the crumbly
internal texture, whether carbonised or not.

Two genera of Palmae were found in the vicinity
of the Spirit Cave, whose fruits might be confused
with *Pisum* in an archaeological context. One was
Livistona, whose olive-like fruits produce, inside
the easily cracked seed-coat, a round seed with
a conspicuous, hilum-like structure, while the
other, *Caryota*, produces a smaller rounded fruit
that might be carbonised directly in the green
state to form spherical pea-like remains.

The unconvincing status of the evidence for
peas is represented in Fig.4. The doubt still
rests with the identification of the specimens
themselves. The other argument, of a 'most
extraordinary assemblage of tropical Southeast
Asian and cool-season Mediterranean plants'

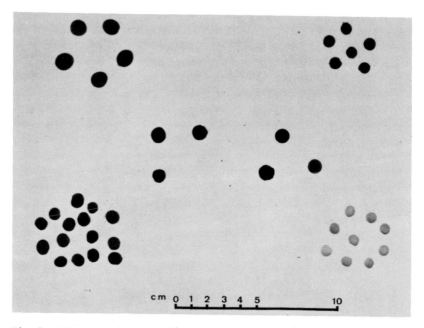

Fig.4. The questionable *Pisum*/Palmae identification. Centre. 6
"peas" excavated from Spirit Cave. Top row. Left, kernels of
Livistona palm; right, seeds of *Caryota* palm. Bottom row. Left
and right groups, varieties of sugar peas (*Pisum*) from northwest
Thailand.

(Harlan and de Wet 1973), cannot be maintained,
not only in the light of the fieldwork of this
project, but also in the assignment of plants of
Mediterranean origin to Southeast Asian
distribution by many writers (e.g. Burkill 1966;
Purseglove 1968; Herklots 1972). In fact, the
low night temperature conditions of the dry
season in northwest Thailand (recorded in Spirit
Valley, January and February 1974, at 4.4 - 7.2°C
minima) seem less than tropical, at least seasonally.

RICE STUDIES

The discovery of rice (Figs 5a,5b) by Gorman at

Banyan Valley Cave promoted several lines of
enquiry, to be summarised here.

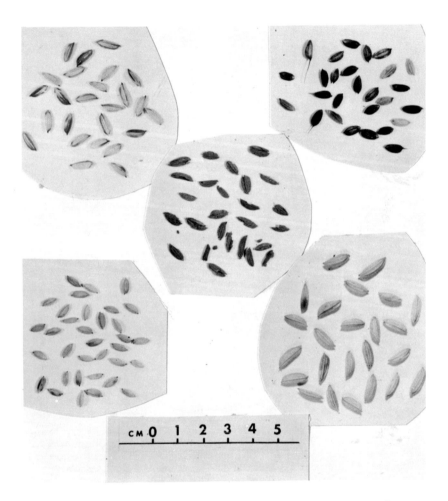

Fig.5a.   Archaeological *Oryza* from Banyan Valley Cave, and
contemporary subsistence rice varieties of the region.   Centre
group.   Sample 57 from level 2 of excavation by C. Gorman.
Other groups.   Some contemporary rices including claimed wild
variety (upper right) and variety of claimed wild ancestry
(lower left).

Fig.5b. Close-up photograph of excavated *Oryza* husks showing
breakage pattern, the posited result of hand milling by a method
different from those applied by the contemporary subsistence
farmers of northwest Thailand.

Metric data

The *Oryza* spikelet remains resembled
cultivated rice in dimensional and structural
features with palea and lemma parts clearly
distinguished. So a collection of 128 local rice
varieties was made in the field, representing

varieties from a number of cultural groups, including irrigation and swidden farmers, the former usually differentiating between wet and dry varieties in their integrated subsistence systems. These varieties, including the three varieties claimed to be gathered from wild stands or descended from a wild progenitor, were compared dimensionally. Twenty grains of each variety were measured to obtain the mean measures that are represented diagrammatically in Fig.6. Table 4 gives the data on the archaeological rice; it should be noted that the total number measured is at variance with the total number given in Table 3, because only near perfect spikelets were measured.

Sample No.	No. whole husks measured	Length mm		Breadth mm	
		Range	Mean	Range	Mean
56a	18	7.2 – 8.3	7.7	2.6 – 3.6	3.3
56b	7	8.6 – 9.4	9.0 .	3.2 – 3.9	3.6
57	23	8.0 – 8.5	8.2	3.0 – 3.9	3.3
73	1	(7.8)	(7.8)	(2.4)	(2.4)

Table 4. Dimensions of archaeological rice from Banyan Valley Cave.

The mean values for grain length and width were then plotted on to the scattergram representing the northwest Thailand rices of today. Grain depth or thickness, also a useful statistic, could not be used for the archaeological material, so is omitted from the presentation. It will be noted that sample 56 (Gorman field no.) was divided into two grain types, on the advice of Dr. T.T. Chang, geneticist at the International Rice Research Institute, Los Baños, Philippines.

Standards of length and breadth similar to those applied by Vishnu-Mittre (1962) to Indian prehistoric material were used to attempt to differentiate Indica (I) from possible Japonica (J) forms. In terms of grain width, it appeared that the two types might be within the varietal array,

but the length index seemed to the contrary. The
length:width ratio was calculated for each variety
and the indices 3.1 to 3.5 for I and 1.4 to 2.9 for
J (Grist 1965) were applied. The diagonal line
separates the few varieties that might fall into
the Japonica grouping from the majority that
conform with the Indica, including the
archaeological samples. Even if the one-spikelet
sample from excavation (73) is omitted from
consideration, the excavated samples fall into
the smaller-grained quadrant of the diagram,
along with those with putative 'wild' histories.
In fact, the smallest is the Shan-claimed
domesticate.

Anatomical data

     Microscopic examination of the lemma of all
the archaeological spikelets possible, confirmed
the field identification notes that none exhibited
awn formation. This was the first note of caution
in attempting to identify the samples as *O. sativa*.
Shastry and Sharma (1974), in defining the·
phylogenetic ranking of sections of the genus
Oryza, have specified the absence of awn as a
feature of the Section Padia, along with perennial
habit; the more advanced Section Oryza, to which
the annual cultivated rice belongs, is
characterised by well-developed awns, although
this character is often bred out by modern

Fig.6. Dimensional comparison of husks of archaeological *Oryza*
from Banyan Valley Cave and contemporary varieties of *O.sativa*
cultivated in northwest Thailand. Length, width and length/
width ratio standards for Japonica and Indica types of rice are
indicated by J and I. Black squares indicate the archaeological
rice samples; circles, contemporary rice; dotted circles, those
claimed as wild or with immediate wild ancestry. In addition,
cross-barred circles indicate the irrigated variety, unbarred
circles indicate swidden rice. Shaded circles equal glutinous
rice; unshaded equal non-glutinous. Circles marked \ indicate
husks showing awn development; those with / indicate husks
showing hair development on surfaces; and those with | indicate
sterile glume development, above normal size.

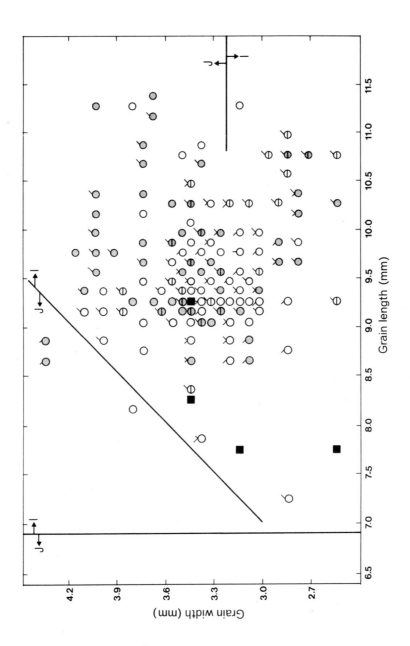

breeders. Of the 124 subsistence varieties
collected 40 exhibited awning of the lemma
(see Fig.6).

The scientists at the International Rice
Research Institute, using an imprint method, SUMP
(Kihara and Katayama 1960), to study the surface
cell structure of the husks, gave us further and
firmer cause for caution of interpretation of the
archaeological 'rice'. Chang (pers. comm.) wrote:

> We are quite sure that the markedly ragged
> glume surface is more indicative of a wild
> type, because both *sativa* and *glaberrima*
> cultivars have more symmetrical, round-edged
> and shallower cross-ridges. We have compared
> it with several specimens of *rufipogon*
> (perennial, wild), *nivara* (wild, annual)
> *spontanea* (introgressed hybrid, annual) and
> *sativa* and we are quite certain that your
> sample, because of its elevated and
> irregular ridges, came from a wild form. On
> the other hand, the glume dimensions fall
> between *sativa* and *spontanea*.

Further comparisons were made with wild rice
species from the Bishop Museum Herbarium,
O. ridleyi, *O. minutae* and *O. longiglumis*, and
the collection of modern rices of claimed 'wild'
source or ancestry, without being able to
establish close resemblances with the excavated
specimens. It should be added however, that there
is some variation in surface cell structure among
the samples 56a, 56b and 57.

The co-operative work is still in progress.

Breakage patterns

The field identification of the husk remains —
there were no grain or endosperm remains recovered
in excavation — also revealed a pattern of

breakage suggesting that the grains had been
expressed prior to the discarding of husks
(Fig.5b). Therefore samples of husks after milling
by contemporary subsistence farmers were collected.
Briefly, the study of this material showed that the
two methods of vertical pounding and one of
circular grinding of the whole grain did not
produce the breakage patterns of the excavated
husks. By experiment, firstly with laboratory
mortars and pestles, then with stone pounding
implements from Hawaii with similar conformation
to the Spirit Cave Hoabinhian grinding stones
illustrated by Gorman (1970), we were able to
imitate the breakage of the archaeological
material on fresh whole grain. This, achieved by
using the rounded 'handle' end as the grinding
surface in a rocking kind of action on a gently
elliptical surface, suggests an adaptation that is
the transformation of use instead of the
introduction of a new type of tool. A full
account of these experiments is to appear later
(Yen and Davis in preparation). It would seem
that further investigation of this posited
conversion of tool usage could be more directly
made on the tools themselves; there may be
evidence of silica-derived particles on the 'handle'
ends of the implements, embedded in the vesicular
matrix.

The results of these studies leave us with a
confirmation of the presence of a rice-like grain
at Banyan Valley and indications of its use as
a food. The dates for the site range from 3500 BC
to 700 AD (Gorman pers. comm.), but the
correlations of the grains with the excavated
sections and the position of artifacts have yet
to be made.

The inability to identify the husk remains
securely leaves open the possibility that we could
be dealing with some intermediate form/forms in

what appears on present genetic knowledge (Shastry
and Sharma 1974) to have been a complex course of
evolution of a cultigen. Were this a secure
interpretation, the interesting speculation is
that the cave remains may represent a horticultural/
selection phase in northwest Thailand prehistory,
later, however, than the generally accepted
Hoabinhian time levels.

THE ROOT CROPS

In regions where a root crop domestication
antecedent to that of grains has been so strongly
promulgated in issues of the origin of agriculture
the rarity of evidence for such early domesticates
in archaeological remains is a characteristic
frustration. The case of the putative Southeast
Asian 'cradle of agriculture' of Sauer (1952) is
such an example, for so far no macrofossil remains
or evidence from pollen have been turned up to
show the presence of roots in prehistoric diets.
In northwest Thailand then, their presence has to
be based on deduction from comparison of the
present flora and that indicated in the archaeological
record, and the present utilisation of roots.
From our preceding account of the useful plants of
the Hoabinhian technocomplex, based on the analysis
of present-day use, it is fairly safe to assume
that the past natural flora of the region was
essentially similar in composition to today's.
Eight feral species of *Dioscorea* were recorded,
and it is significant that the five which were
named were identified on their fruiting and
flowering (and female and male) characteristics.
Thus the opportunity for hybridisation is ever-
present, and may account for the variations that
guide the subsistence farmers in the region in
their selection of wild types in the gathering
(and hunting) component of their economic systems.

Other root-producing plants so gathered are the leguminous *Pueraria* and *Dolichos* and the aroids *Amorphophallus* and *Alocasia*, the latter two being mainly cooked for pigfeed. Although claims were made for wild taro, *Colocasia esculenta* (L.) Schott, no collection in the region yielded convincing examples. Most appeared to be derived from previous cultivation. The cultivated yams were largely of the species *D. alata* and *D. esculenta* but wild varieties of the former, inseparable from the cultivated, were common and sought by the Lahu and Lisu to supplement the roots from swidden fields.

At best then, the presence of yams in the food roster of the early dwellers of Spirit Cave and its environs may be a logical enough deduction.

THE QUESTIONS

Gorman (1971) has divided the Spirit Cave sequence into two general cultural levels, the first of which spans the period c. 10,000-7000 BC and is designated Hoabinhian Orientations; the more recent cultural level, incorporating only excavation layer 1 and the top of layer 2, and dating from c. 7000-5600 BC is referred to by Gorman as Hoabinhian with new technological introductions such as adzes, pottery and slate knives. The introduced artifactual complex indicates a change that Gorman has cautiously suggested might be associated with the introduction of domesticated rice into the Hoabinhian areas and a general phasing out of upland settlement in favour of the lowland adaptation. The later occupation spans represented by Banyan Valley Cave at 3500 BC to 700 AD and Tham Pa Chan at 5500 BC to 3600 BC (Gorman pers. comm.) might reflect this process, but the evidence may be more secure when the final archaeological evaluations from those two sites appear. The spasmodic occurrence

of rice could provide strong support for such an
hypothesis, but as we have seen, the identity of
the *Oryza* remains is in question. The same
cloudy picture now applies to the *Oryza* imprint
finds of Bayard (1970). Dated at prior to 3500 BC
from excavation at the lowland Non Nok Tha,
northeast Thailand, these are now questioned
because of the cellular structures revealed.
Chang (1976:146 *fn*) interprets this sample as
representing an intermediate between the wild
annual and the annual weed forms of *Oryza*. The
carbonised grain (endosperm) remains that Bayard
recovered (Solheim 1970) in the same site and
associated with a date c. 3000 BC, however at
least fit metrically with Vishnu-Mittre's (1962)
identifications of rice in Indian sites of
generally later date.

Other botanical remains from northeast
Thailand, this time in Gorman's most recent
excavations on the Khorat Plateau at Ban Chiang,
have produced further examples of *Oryza*, largely
as temper in pottery making (Higham 1975).
Recovered in deep burial sites, the datings
associated with these remains are expected to
overlap with the dates from northwest Thailand.
We cannot predict the coming results of *these*
identifications, but the continuing finds of
rice-like remains (even if not domestic forms as
we know them today) in early archaeological
contexts will surely produce a phylogenetic
model for rice domestication that involves human
intervention in the earlier courses of evolution.
These dispersed finds, at overlapping or similar
time levels, with differing cultural contexts as
indicated by associated artifacts, and in varying
environments, may be the signals of plant
domestication as a process in which the 'modified'
Hoabinhian plays but a part. Furthermore, the
confused identities of these remains suggest that
the human role in domestication proceeded at
interspecific rather than solely intraspecific

levels of selection. In other words selection was
applied to the 'more wild' species at the same
time as the 'primitive' forms of *O. sativa*. Thus
eventually we may expect to find evidence for
the disappearance of the products of divergent
directions of selection in favour of the
cultivated *sativa* forms as we know them today.
What is being suggested, then, is a selection
stage that may merge into a horticultural
identification intermediate between the modern
interpretations of rice origins, namely that:

1. Southeast Asia was the probable centre of
   origin of the genus (Shastry and Sharma
   1974); and
2. *Oryza sativa* in its present form evolved
       from an annual progenitor whose distribution
extended from eastern India across Upper Burma,
northern Thailand and Indochina to southern China
(Chang 1976).

It may well be that Banyan Valley cave
remains of *Oryza* could represent the termination
of one avenue of selection in favour of the more
successful adaptation of rice agriculture in the
more extensive lowlands of other areas. This
hypothesis does not preclude the position that
the inspiration for such divergent selection
originally came from lowland areas; but it
follows that the features of rice agriculture
in the northwest area - irrigation systems on
the valley floors and swiddening at intermediate
altitudes - were diffused elements arriving later.
The absence of early open sites in the river
systems of the region despite extensive
archaeological surveys carried out in 1973-4 (Davis
pers. comm.) may lend some support to this
contention. The presence of many wild species
in the region however, and especially that
of forms that are firmly claimed, ethnographically,
as gathered by the rice farmers of today, requires
more investigation.

With regard to the earlier Hoabinhian and the
possibility of horticulture extending back over
10,000 years, the evidence presented is even less
certain - with no more certitude than when the
preliminary plant identifications were first
published, and speculated on. A wide-ranging
exploitation of the local environments by the cave
dwellers is suggested, with *Terminalia* and
Canarium representing the valley forests generally
dominated by dipterocarps, and *Castanopsis* the
higher areas in which evergreens dominate and *Pinus*
appears in often open, grassy vegetation. While
some of the tree and perennial genera (*Areca*, *Piper*,
Canarium, *Prunus*) and all of the annuals identified
from excavations are represented in the range of
present cultivars, there is little evidence among
the remains for purposeful planting that could have
been the prelude to local effort towards the
domestication of *Oryza*. They are all largely
indicative of direct use rather than conservation
for planting. In eliminating *Pisum* and *Vicia* as
possible misidentifications or cases of confusion
with other gathered resources whether Palmae or
other wild Leguminosae, and with the difficulty of
accounting for the presence of Near Eastern and
Mediterranean plants *at that time*, the horticultural
case must be regarded as almost closed on the
evidence from northwest Thailand. What does
remain are the annuals (*Nelumbo*, *Trapa*, *Trichosanthes*)
which could not be found in feral settings. Their
assignment to Chinese and Indian centres of
domestication poses further questions that remain
unanswerable, though the assignment itself may need
to be qualified due to the general rethinking of
the definition of Vavilovian centres of origin of
cultivated plants (Harlan 1961).

The one shred of evidence left for
horticulture in the Hoabinhian context comprises
the annuals found wild in the region. Are their
remains from the caves representative of the
same bitter wild forms found today? Were they

rendered edible by preparation methods unknown today? Are they the evidence of selected forms less bitter than the average wild types? Were they cultivated in less competitive environments to produce less bitter fruits?

Finally we have to consider the distribution of wild yams in the region, accepted as close to the centre of domestication of the genus, but without benefit of proof or presence in archaeological evidence to date. Our observations show that the genus is gathered on a selective basis even today, and that the major cultivated form has a utilised wild analogue. If the precedence of root culture over rice is acceptable in the area, then this would be an indication of early horticulture. However, in the light of the seeming absence of feral taro (*Colocasia*), one is compelled to question the earliness of yam domestication, for early consumption of these roots could simply be maintained on a gathering basis, without cultivation.

So the argument has to be extended - away from this evidence and remote from this region, but appropriate to this volume, since Sahul becomes involved. It is generally accepted that the Austronesian speakers who eventually populated the far reaches of the eastern Pacific originated in Southeast Asia; as horticulturists, they were responsible for the diffusion of rootcrop agriculture with yam-taro dominance, before rice became the general staple in much of Asia. Presentations of this view are numerous in the ethnobotanical literature of the Pacific, but in this instance, perhaps it will suffice to quote the latest, based on archaeological and linguistic criteria. Shutler and Marck (1975) place the advent of the 'Austronesian horticulturists' into island Melanesia at c. 4000 BC, following a migration route that began from a general region incorporating the northern hinterlands of the

mainland Southeast Asian peninsula and southern
China, 'the Thai/Kadai/Austronesian homeland',
to Formosa c. 9000 BC. It can be inferred without
doubt that yam and taro were together the
terrestrial economic base that was to survive the
cultural and linguistic transformations that are a
part of Pacific prehistory. In Sahul itself the
possible implications of the New Guinea highlands
evidence for the early spread of a yam-taro
dominant rootcrop agriculture are discussed by
Golson (this volume).

Obviously this study has not produced the
clear-cut answers that were sought. At least some
requirements for future research appear to have
been indicated, and as Flannery (1973) has
remarked, one of the keys lies in the cereal rice.
For regardless of the time depth that may be
accorded its domestication, the material from
archaeological excavation often lends itself to
a number of qualitative and quantitative analyses
that may produce meaningful hypotheses on the
processes of biological change under varying
degrees of human guidance. In these may be
reflected the changes in the economic aspects of
human history itself, since rice became dominant
in the tropical Asian subcontinent. But it is
the early rices found that will provide a
benchmark for the backward projection to
horticulture, and what prepared people for the
major change.

ACKNOWLEDGEMENTS

Drs Wilhelm Solheim II and Chester Gorman
were principal investigators of the northwest
Thailand archaeological project, funded by
National Science Foundation, Washington, D.C.
(Grant no. GS - 29133) through the Social Science
Research Institute, University of Hawaii. In

Thailand the expeditions were sponsored by the
Department of Fine Arts, while botanical
determinations were made by Dr T. Smitinand,
Director of the Forest Herbarium, Royal Forestry
Department. Dr T.T. Chang, geneticist and
leader of the Genetics Resources Program, and his
assistant Mrs Genoveva Loresto, at the International
Rice Research Institute, Los Baños, Philippines,
initiated the metric study on rice and have
maintained a continuing cooperation in the husk
surface analyses. At Bishop Museum Dr Peiter van
Royen, head of the Department of Botany, assisted
with the determination of archaeological plant
remains, while Peter Gilpin has been responsible
for the photography in this paper.

To these individuals and institutions I owe
my sincere thanks; they are not however to be
held responsible for any of the interpretations
of the data.

REFERENCES

Bayard, D.T. 1970 Excavations at Non Nok Tha,
    northeast Thailand, 1968: an interim report.
    Asian Perspectives 13:109-44

Burkill, I.H. 1966 *A dictionary of the economic
    products of the Malay Peninsula*, (2 vols)
    (rev.ed.) Kuala Lumpur: Ministry of
    Agriculture and Co-operatives

Chang, T.T. 1976 The rice cultures. In *The early
    history of agriculture*:143-55. London: Royal
    Society, Philosophical Transactions B.
    Biological Sciences, Vol.275

Flannery, K.V. 1973 The origins of agriculture.
    Annual Review of Anthropology 2:271-310

Gorman, C.F. 1969 Hoabinhian: a pebble-tool
    complex with early plant associations in

Southeast Asia. *Science* 163:671-3

   1970a Excavations at Spirit Cave,
north Thailand: some interim interpretations.
Asian Perspectives 13:79-108

   1970b The Hoabinhian and after.
World Archaeology 2:300-20

Grist, D.H. 1970 *Rice*, (4th ed.) London: Longman

Harlan, J.R. 1961 Geographic origin of plants
 useful to agriculture. In R.E. Hodgson (ed.)
 Germplasm resources:3-19. Washington:
 American Association for the Advancement of
 Science, Publication No. 66

   and J.M.J. de Wet 1973 On the quality
of evidence for origin and dispersal of
cultivated plants. *Current Anthropology* 14:
51-5

Herklots, G.A.C. 1972 *Vegetables in South-east
 Asia*. London: Allen and Unwin

Higham, C.F.W. 1975 A Late Hoabinhian hunting
 pattern in north Sundaland. In *13th Pacific
 Science Congress, Vancouver, August 1975.
 Record of proceedings, I. Abstracts of papers*:
 376. Honolulu: Pacific Science Association

Kihara, H. and T. Katayama 1960 Application of
 SUMP method in taxonomic studies in *Oryza*. In
 Annual report no.10, 1959:39-40. Misima
 (Sizuoka-ken): National Institute of Genetics,
 Japan

Lebar, F.M., G.C. Hickey and J.K. Musgrave 1964
 Ethnic groups of mainland Southeast Asia. New
 Haven: Human Relations Area Files Press

Leenhouts, P.W. 1955a Florae Malesianae
precursores XI. New taxa in *Canarium*.
Blumea 8(1):181-94

   1955b *The genus Canarium in the
Pacific*. Honolulu: Bishop Museum, Bulletin
216

in collaboration with C. Kalkman
and H.J. Lam 1958 Burseraceae. In
C.G.G.J. van Steenis (ed.) *Flora Malesiana,
series 1. Spermotophyta, 5. General chapters
and revisions*:209-96. Groningen: Noordhoff,
for the Botanical Gardens of Indonesia, Bogor,
and the Rijksherbarium, Leyden

Purseglove, J.W. 1968 *Tropical crops: dicotyledons,*
(2 vols). New York: Wiley

Sauer, C.O. 1952 *Agricultural origins and
dispersals.* New York: American Geographical
Society

Schwanitz, F. 1966 *The origin of cultivated plants.*
Cambridge (Mass.): Harvard University Press

Shastry, S.V.S. and S.D. Sharma 1974 Rice. In
Sir Joseph Hutchinson (ed.) *Evolutionary
studies in world crops*:55-61. Cambridge:
Cambridge University Press

Shutler, R., Jr. and J.C. Marck 1975 On the
dispersal of the Austronesian horticulturalists.
Archaeology and Physical Anthropology in Oceania
10:81-113

Solheim, W.G., II 1970 Northern Thailand, Southeast
Asia and world prehistory. *Asian Perspectives*
13:145-62

1972 An earlier agricultural
revolution. *Scientific American* 226:34-41

Vishnu-Mittre 1962 Plant economy in ancient
Navdatoli-Maheshwar. In *Technical reports on
archaeological remains*:11-52. Poona: Deccan
College Postgraduate and Research Institute

Yen, D.E. 1974 Arboriculture in the subsistence of
Santa Cruz, Solomon Islands. *Economic Botany*
28:247-84

and B.D. Davis in preparation
*Contemporary milling methods and archaeological
remains of rice in NW Thailand*

NO ROOM AT THE TOP: AGRICULTURAL INTENSIFICATION IN THE NEW GUINEA HIGHLANDS

JACK GOLSON

Department of Prehistory
Australian National University

An important feature of the archaeology of New Guinea, as of other areas of Sunda and Sahul, is the extent to which it is yesterday's ethnography. This essay in agricultural history is heavily dependent on the work of students of the contemporary scene.

New Guinea exhibits a great variety of ecological situations and a wide spectrum of locally adjusted subsistence patterns, to which plant foods are basic. Staples range from a naturally occurring, minimally managed resource like sago to plants requiring some form of cultivation. The same cultivated plants appear, in different combinations and with differing degrees of dominance, in systems covering a great range of technical elaboration and of ecological impact. The systems support varying densities of population organised in units and patterns of settlement of different nature, size and extent (e.g. Brookfield with Hart 1971:94-124).

Apart from sago, the basic food plants, tubers like yam, taro and sweet potato and fruits like banana and coconut, are not in the main indigenous to New Guinea. With different degrees of certainty and with the definite exception of the sweet potato, a plant of tropical American ancestry, they have their origins in Southeast Asia (on this and what follows Yen 1971, 1973; Powell 1976). Yet New Guinea is floristically rich enough, being the eastern province of that Indo-Malaysian plant geographic region to which Southeast Asia itself belongs, and its settlement, dating beyond 25,000 years ago,[1]

sufficiently long, to raise the possibility of
independent origins for plant domestication there.
The indigenous contribution to the register of
secondary plants in New Guinea agriculture is
important, while in the swampy lowlands sago is the
staple of thousands and in the interior various kinds
of pandanus constitute a significant seasonal
resource. The island is suspected of a formative
role in the evolution of sugar cane and the
Australimusa section of bananas, and in their
further dissemination, particularly into Oceania.
Furthermore some of the less important yams, *Dioscorea
bulbifera, D. nummularia, D. pentaphylla, D. hispida*,
may be indigenous to New Guinea and could have been
taken into independent domestication there.

A number of situations exist for which the
sedentism favourable to the development of plant
domestication and/or to the reception of incoming
domesticates can be argued (Allen in press). They
include the various interfaces between coast, river,
swamp, rainforest and savannah; all providing a
range of resources within limited compass. These
are of course, lowland occurrences, and as yet none
of them has been investigated archaeologically.
Only in the New Guinea highlands has enough
appropriate research been done for the beginnings
and course of agricultural development in one part
of them to be described and tentatively interpreted.

THE CHARACTER OF HIGHLANDS AGRICULTURE

Until less than 50 years ago outsiders thought
of the New Guinea highlands as a single, uninhabited
mountain chain. Subsequent exploration revealed the
existence above 1400 m of substantial populations,
perhaps a third of the island's population overall,
inhabiting large intermontane basins and the valleys,
plateaux and hill slopes above them, in places up
to 2770 m. These populous communities, and equally

large numbers of pigs, living in the midst of
extensive grasslands relieved by planted groves of
Casuarina and bamboo, were maintained by the produce
of large orderly fields of cultivated crops, amongst
which the sweet potato, an unimportant plant in
lowland New Guinea agriculture, was absolutely
dominant.

Scholarly research over the past 20 years has
defined the nature of highlands agriculture and
settlement and indicated their parameters (e.g.
Brookfield with Hart 1971:97-105, 111-6 and
references; Waddell 1972:202-20). Though there is
considerable variation in agricultural practice
dependent on local conditions of topography, soil
and rainfall, sweet potato fields are commonly
segregated from mixed plantings of other crops, like
bananas, sugar cane, taro, yam, beans and a number
of greens, and accorded more elaborate and labour-
intensive techniques of cultivation. Though the
procedures of simple swidden agriculture find a
role in parts of most systems, soil preparation
through tillage is widespread, particularly in the
service of the sweet potato, as is the control of
fallow by deliberate planting of *Casuarina* and
conservation of regrowth species like *Trema* and
Dodonaea. In addition, the practice of raised-bed
cultivation of the staple is general, with and
without mulching, in small mounds, large mounds or
flat-bed plots formed within a grid of garden
ditches. Finally cultivation is extended into areas
of more difficult terrain through devices of soil
retention on steep hillsides and drainage in swampy
valleys. The populations supported by this
agricultural technology are commonly of the order
of 40 persons per km^2 and locally may rise to 120
and even 200.

The technology is seen as allowing frequent
agricultural re-use of grassland, where simpler
techniques of cultivation are ineffective, at
altitudes where slower weed growth facilitates

their employment. It is thought to have been
developed in response to a situation where, in
conditions of slow natural regeneration due to
elevation, the sustained practice of bush clearance
under shifting cultivation would tend to degrade
forest and eventually replace it by grassland, which,
once established, would be maintained by periodic
firing in the hunting of grassland animals (e.g.
Bulmer 1968:312, 314). Soil preparation through
tillage would then become necessary to break up the
root mat, remove grass roots and aerate the soil
(Clarke 1971:192-3). Planting and conservation of
trees, perhaps originating in an effort to safeguard
an economic resource diminishing as a result of
deforestation, would be the agency for refertilisation
no longer provided by natural forest regeneration.
Raised-bed cultivation would be a further means of
securing agricultural production in an altered
environment, in the way that similar forms of raised-
bed cultivation have been widely developed in
similar circumstances by cultivators throughout the
Old World tropics (Denevan and Turner 1974).

If agricultural intensification in the highlands
is related in these ways to forest degradation and
the development of grasslands, both have been seen
ultimately as the result of population growth. In
this context explicit reference has been made (e.g.
Clarke 1966) to Boserup's (1965) propositions about
the evolutionary development of agricultural systems:
that population growth leads to progressive
shortening of the fallow period in the cycle of
shifting cultivation; that ecological changes
consequent upon this require developments in
agricultural technology designed to ensure the
productivity of more intensively cultivated land;
and that each stage along the continuum from the
most extensive of bush fallowing to multi-cropping
requires higher labour inputs and yields lower
outputs per man-hour.

Discussion of these issues in the highlands

situation has been overlain by debate about the sweet
potato, the plant in whose service the intensive
techniques of highlands agriculture are employed,
and specifically about the extent to which these
techniques, the grassland environment in which they
operate and the large populations which they sustain,
developed only as a result of it (Watson 1965a,
1965b, 1967; Brookfield and White 1968).   The
question was thought to be important since the
sweet potato is a relatively recent addition to the
New Guinea crop register and an introduction within
the past 400 or so years, following European
penetration of island Southeast Asia, has been
generally accepted (see Yen 1974:249-60).   The
debate took the form it did however, because of
questions relating to the performance at altitude of
the older crops of New Guinea agriculture and to the
type of subsistence and settlement regime that could
have been supported in the highlands before the
sweet potato came along.

THE LIMITING CONDITIONS OF HIGHLANDS AGRICULTURE

The fact that the older plants of New Guinea
agriculture were approaching their limits of
cultivation in the great highlands basins that
afforded such favourable conditions for agricultural
settlement has figured prominently in speculations
about highlands agricultural history and the part
played therein by the sweet potato with its greater
altitudinal tolerance (e.g. Brookfield 1964:21-2;
Bulmer and Bulmer 1964:45-6; Bowers 1971:22; see
also Yen 1974:317-25).   Yam falls out of cultivation
by about 1800 m, *marita* pandanus shortly afterwards
and by 2100 m bananas, sugar cane and a number of
vegetables are also not cultivated.   Beyond 2100 m
there remain the various semi-cultivated and wild
types of nut or *karuka* pandanus, some wild forms
growing up to 2900 m, and the hardy taro.   Clarke
(1973) records taro as being planted as high as

sweet potato, at 2600-2750 m, amongst the most
extreme altitudes at which tropical crops are grown
(Yen 1974:324; cf. Brookfield 1961:437). However
it is commoner below 2100 m than above and in
elevated plantings it may take as much as 18 months
to mature, compared with up to 12 months for sweet
potato, and its yields are smaller (Clarke 1973).

It is obvious therefore that under climatic
conditions like those of the present there would
have been a ceiling on productive agriculture
without the sweet potato which would have been
appreciably lower than with it. For sweet potato
agriculture the ceiling ranges from as low as 1825 m
to as high as 2770 m and is governed by the level
of persistent cloud formation and, where this is
not a factor, by frost (Brookfield 1964:29-31).
The incidence of frost is seen by Waddell (1975:
especially 252-6) as the crucial element in the
subsistence and social strategies of the Enga of
the Wabag area. Those Enga who live between 1500 m
and 2200 m cope with the mild inversion frosts
which they occasionally experience by planting in
the tops of large mounds where temperatures are of
the order of 2°C higher than at ground level as a
result of cold air drainage, and further elevated
by about 1.2°C within the mound by the decomposition
of incorporated mulch. Above 2300 m, where minor
frosts occur almost annually and killing frosts
every 10 to 30 years, there are responses at the
local, regional and extra-regional levels attuned
to the severity and duration of the blight. In
1972 ground frosts struck on upwards of 30 nights
between June and October above 2300 m, with
individual incidences as low as 1650 m (Waddell
1975:250-1). The implications of such occurrences
for agriculture based on less hardy plants than the
sweet potato need no emphasis. Climatic stress may
have been more pronounced at times in the past when
minor ice advances and active periglaciation took
place on the high mountains (Hope and Peterson 1975:
160-1; Hope 1976:657).

If the zone of close settlement in the highlands is sharply delimited above, it is equally
sharply delimited below, over a range from about
1225-1525 m. Under the present agricultural regime
this is due to a complex of local and regional
factors in which steep and rugged terrain, persistent
cloud, proneness to drought and the incidence of
malaria are to be numbered (Brookfield 1964:31-4),
and it is reasonable to suppose that the same
constraints operated in the pre-sweet potato past.

Thus today highlands agriculture operates in a
highly favourable but laterally and vertically
constricted zone (Brookfield 1964:22-3), with four-
fifths of the populations it supports inhabiting a
series of intermontane valleys between 1400 and
2000 m (Brookfield 1964:35). Within this same zone
must have been concentrated the activities and
agents of the older New Guinea agriculture, beneath
a lower effective ceiling on sustained upwards
expansion.

The proximity of this ceiling has its effects
on the maturation and productivity of the older
crops of highlands agriculture, including the hardier
taro, and all compare unfavourably with the sweet
potato. Yen (1974:40-75) has documented the
agronomic superiority of the sweet potato over the
older cultigens of New Guinea - and Oceanic -
agriculture: not only its speedier production and
higher and temporally more extended yield, but its
capacity to produce over a wider range of ecological
and edaphic conditions. Clarke's recent (1973)
studies of taro in New Guinea emphasise these
points. This plant is grown in naturally rich
soils or as a first crop in ground newly cleared
from bush, with sweet potato following in rotation.
It is rarely planted twice in immediate succession,
whereas sweet potato is often planted several times
without a fallow period. In two experimental plots
at 1650 m near Mount Hagen township (Clarke 1973:
table 1) sweet potato produced ten times as much as

taro by weight at a site which local gardeners
classed as having poor soils and which had been in
cultivation for the preceding 10-15 years.
Maturation time for the sweet potato was eight
months as against 13 months for taro. At a site
described as having good soils with at least eight
years under *Miscanthus* grass, sweet potato produced
three and a half times more than taro, maturing at
eight months as against twelve. Sweet potato yield
at the poor site was close to twice that of taro at
the good site. Yen (1974:72-3) describes how the
productivity of the sweet potato plant lasts longer
than that of taro and much longer than that of yam:
its shallow rooting allows partial harvesting of
individual plants; the roots left behind continue
to grow; prolific secondary rooting takes place,
with the development of new tubers and the
possibility of harvesting for up to two years.
This, combined with its ability to grow in poorer
soils and thus as a follow-up crop in a rotational
system, allows the sweet potato to effect a 'spatial
and temporal expansion of garden production' (Clarke
1973).

Before the arrival of the sweet potato the need
of the major crops for substantial periods of fallow
to allow fertilisation of the soil through forest
regeneration would have combined with the slower
rate of such regeneration at these altitudes to
require larger areas of land for the cycle of
shifting cultivation to operate. The effects of
any growth of population in this context could only
have been temporarily cushioned by expansion into
new territories, given the boundaries set to such
expansion by the factors discussed above.
Eventually the effective filling up of the available
space would have turned the pressures inwards,
leading to progressive shortening of the fallow
period bringing severe ecological changes in its
wake. If productivity were to be maintained in
these changing conditions, particularly at existing
levels of population, advances in agricultural

technology would be needed. These propositions
will be considered in the light of the empirical
evidence bearing on the history of highlands
agriculture.

THE HISTORY OF HIGHLANDS AGRICULTURE

The diachronic data essential for the
reconstruction of agricultural history in the
highlands is being provided by archaeological,
palynological and, latterly, geomorphological
studies (see Fig.1b for major localities mentioned
below).

Serious archaeological work did not begin
until 1959 and has been almost exclusively confined
to the eastern half of the island, now known as
Papua New Guinea. Susan Bulmer, who pioneered this
work, has recently provided a convenient summary of
it up to mid-1973 (Bulmer 1975). Early effort was
directed to the problem of defining archaeological
sequences through excavations at rockshelters and
it is impossible to interpret the results of these
satisfactorily in terms of agricultural history
(e.g. White 1972:144-5). The difficulties arise
not only from the nature of the data recovered, but
also from the small number of investigated sites,
the smaller number published, the less than
desirable tightness of the dating and problems in
comparing the typological categories used by
different workers in stone tool analysis.

Palynological research is even younger than
the archaeological and its results have been
reviewed in a variety of publications for a number
of different purposes (Flenley 1972; Hope 1976;
Hope and Hope 1976; Hope and Peterson 1975; Powell
1970b; Powell *et al.* 1975; Powell and Hope in
Paijmans 1976:101-4; Walker 1970). Currently about
14 pollen diagrams are available, from a relatively

small area of the Papua New Guinea highlands but
spanning a large altitudinal range. For the upper
Wahgi Valley near Mount Hagen township there are
six diagrams in the zone of major settlement, of
which five have been published (Powell *et al.* 1975):
two from the Manton site at 1580 m and three out of
the four from Draepi-Minjigina at 1885 m. Some
archaeological work has been done in association
with the palynological research at both these sites.
Unfortunately the Manton pollen sequence does not
begin until about 5000 years ago and there is a
gap in the Draepi-Minjigina sequence between about
15,000 and 5000 years ago, so that the period vital
for agricultural beginnings is not covered. There
have been no archaeological investigations of
significance in the Wabag region for which three
diagrams have been constructed. One of these, at
Birip at 1900 m in the Lai valley east of Wabag, is
published only in thesis form (Flenley 1967): it
begins about 2500 years ago. The others are from
neighbouring sites west of Wabag, towards the
upper margins of the agricultural zone (Flenley
1972): Flenley's Lake Inim diagram at 2550 m and,
in preliminary form, Walker's diagram from the
Kayamanda swamp at Sirunki at 2500 m. The remaining
five diagrams are at high altitude on Mt Wilhelm,
between 2740 and 3910 m and above the limits of
agriculture and settlement (Hope 1976).

    The archaeological work now to be described
has been specifically directed to the study of
agricultural history. It forms part of a continuing
project on the undeveloped eastern half of Kuk Tea
Research Station, at 1550 m altitude 13 km east of
Mount Hagen township in the upper Wahgi Valley
(Fig.1a). The Station is established on a block of
280 hectares of drained swamp excised from a larger
area of swampland, one of a number that are widespread in the upper Wahgi.

    Before its recent drainage, water ran over the
surface of the Kuk basin from a number of small

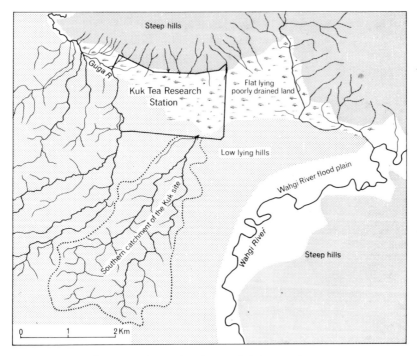

Fig.1a.   The Kuk site and its setting.

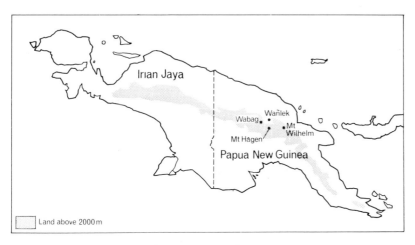

Fig.1b.   locality map.

catchments on the steep ridge that borders it to the
north and particularly from a large catchment in
low, tephra-mantled hills to the south. Besides a
slight fall from north to south, there is an
imperceptible watershed across the basin that
deflected water west to the Guga Gorge and
east to the Wahgi River, 4 km and 5 km away
respectively from the southern boundary of the
Station. The natural fall over these distances is
less than 1 in 200. The stratigraphic units in the
Kuk basin, which go back beyond the range of radiocarbon dating, contain sediments washed in from the
catchments on its margins. A record of the
beginning and development of plant husbandry in the
area is provided by the upper inorganic formations
in the basin and by the evidence of its periodic
reclamation and abandonment as land for planting.

The assumptions are that events in the basin
reflect developments in the subsistence system as
a whole and that the scale of effort involved in
its management indicates that regional rather than
purely local factors are at work. The attempt is
made to test these assumptions against appropriate
evidence from other archaeological sites, few though
these are, and against the pollen record, which may
be expected to monitor in broad terms the impact of
agricultural man on his environment.

Depending, as we shall see, on the way the
evidence is interpreted, there are five or six
distinct phases of management in the Kuk basin.
All will be discussed, though it is Phase 3 and
subsequent phases which are most germane to the
subject of this paper.

Phase 1: c. 9000 BP, and Phase 2: c. 6000-5500 BP

The most notable element in the upper inorganic
formations at Kuk is a large wedge of grey clay,
thickest where the water from the large southern
catchment funnels into the basin across the

southern boundary of the Station and thinning out
from there. Its deposition beginning about 9000 BP,
it represents a marked increase in the rate of
sediment accumulation and is interpreted as the
inwashed products of accelerated erosion due to
bush clearance for gardening in the catchment from
a date close on the attainment of climatic
conditions like those of the present in the highlands. This interpretation, and its implications,
are discussed in detail elsewhere (Golson and Hughes
1976; also Golson in press b). Recent claims for
the presence of pigs in the region by this date
(Bulmer 1975:18-9, 36, in press) are seen as
lending support to the case, since as a non-indigenous
animal not likely to have made its independent way
into New Guinea from islands to the west, the pig
probably came in with man as an already domesticated
animal. If this indeed were so, it is possible that
domesticated plants were introduced at the same time,
and perhaps that presently important cultigens of
Southeast Asian origin like taro and particular
varieties of yam were part of the crop register
from the very beginning of at least New Guinea highlands agriculture (Golson and Hughes 1976:95-6;
Golson in press b). However, new evidence allows
other views to be canvassed as to the plants of
this early horticulture.

Recent fieldwork strongly suggests that early
gardening was not restricted to dry land at Kuk and
that the wet basin itself was also utilised. A
complex of archaeological features - gutters,
hollows, pits and stakeholes - has now been found
beneath grey clay to add to the shallow basins
already reported and to raise questions about the
previous interpretation of the latter as due, in
whole or in part, to pigs (Golson and Hughes 1976:
89-90; Golson in press b). Of crucial importance
to our understanding of this phase at Kuk has been
Hughes' demonstration, against the scepticism of
project colleagues, including myself, that a 2 m
wide by 1 m deep channel close to and contemporary

with the archaeological features discussed above is
an artificial and not a natural feature. Its
purpose, like that of the similar channels of all
subsequent management systems, was to intercept
the water from the southern catchment flooding
across the Kuk basin at its narrow point of entry
and carry it off to a suitable outlet on an
established natural drainage system (Fig.2). The
fact that this operation was itself sufficient to
fit the Kuk basin for utilisation, without the
need for supplementary drainage works, shows that
the area was much more easily managed than it
subsequently became: the term wet land will be used,
in contrast to swamp, to describe the situation at
this stage. Douglas Yen, who has seen some of the
evidence in the field, warns against overlooking
the possibility that it is part of a regime based
entirely on indigenous New Guinea plants, amongst
which Australimusa bananas could have served as a
staple and characteristic greens, for example
Oenanthe javanica, are naturally wet land plants.
Phase 2 in the Kuk basin, discussed below, provides
some suggestive data on this point.

Whatever the activity associated with Phase 1
at Kuk, it seems to have been shortlived. There is
no evidence of the disposal channel being recut, as
is common in later systems, and the lower part of
its fill is thought by Hughes to have been quickly
deposited; it is from this level that the radiocarbon
sample dated at c. 9000 BP was obtained. The upper
part of the channel fill is the grey clay already
mentioned as the inwashed erosional products of
bush clearance for gardening in the catchment, which
thickly covers the channel, associated archaeological
features and a large area of the contemporary land
surface. Grey clay does not appear before this
point in the depositional sequence only because
when the channel was active, sediments from the
catchment were carried out of the basin, not laid
down there. When grey clay deposition did begin,
it continued for about 3000 years and ceased when

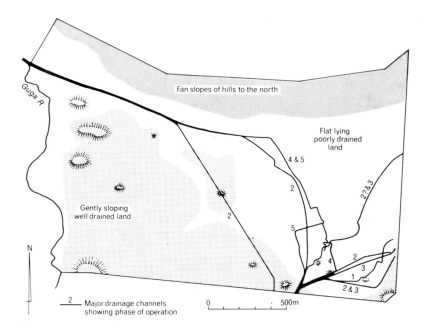

Fig.2. The major disposal channels of the five phases of basin management at Kuk.

the digging of the disposal channels inaugurating
Phase 2 in the Kuk basin allowed renewed removal of
sediment from the catchment through and out of it.

There are at least four large channels belonging
to Phase 2 (Fig.2). Up to 2 m wide and deep, they
have been traced, two northwest and two southeast,
as far as the boundaries of the Station, a distance
in some cases of 2 km, and they presumably
continued to outfalls at the Guga and the Wahgi.
There is clear evidence for some of them being
cleaned out and recut. The relationship of certain
volcanic ash bands to their fill shows that
different channels, and the field systems dependent
on them, were in use at different times. As in
Phase 1, there are no supplementary drainage works
and the disposal channels themselves seem to have
been sufficient to allow wet land operations.

Indeed one type of field system associated with
them seems designed to retain water as well as to
dispose of its excess. This has been described
previously (Golson and Hughes 1976; Golson in
press b) but is now more fully known. It consists
of a web of short channels, so disposed as to define
roughly circular clay islands of about a metre
diameter (Fig.3). The intersections of these
channels form small basins, whose bases are not only
slightly lower than those at the central point of
the channels which connect them but also than the
base level of the channels in the system that
directly articulate with the major disposal drains.
The arrangement seems well suited to the cultivation
of water-tolerant crops like taro in the basins,
with plants requiring drier conditions on the intervening islands, whose surfaces were no doubt
elevated with the spoil from channel digging.

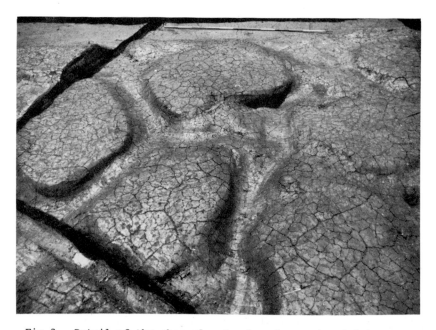

Fig.3. Detail of the channel network and associated island
beds forming one part of the Phase 2 field system on top of the
grey clay level at Kuk. The two straight drains belong to
Phase 3.

Recent investigations have given evidence of another kind of system, side by side and fully contemporary with the one described. Its individual features and the apparent lack of an overall pattern in their disposition have a similar character to Phase 1 beneath grey clay and may represent a continuity of horticultural practices over three millennia. If this is so, it could well be that the practices in question were to do with horticulture based on indigenous New Guinea plants, as Yen has suggested as a possibility, while the new, highly organised system that makes its appearance with Phase 2 marks the introduction of taro and other plants of Southeast Asian origin into the region.

Like Phase 1, Phase 2 at Kuk is short-lived and there is little evidence outside Kuk against which to test explanations for both the inception and the abandonment of the two episodes of wet land management. The regional pollen diagrams, at Mantons and Draepi-Minjigina, respectively 9 km SW and 17 km NW of Kuk, begin shortly after Phase 2 has closed. All display proportions of woody non-forest to forest taxa, and of particular trees within each category, that are interpreted as reflecting an already substantial degree of clearance for agriculture by 5000 BP (Powell 1970b; Powell *et al*. 1975:zone A of Fig.9, base of zone J of Figs 7, 8, 11). The lower altitude Manton site shows a forest to woody non-forest ratio rather less than at Draepi- Minjigina, which might mean that clearance was more advanced in the Wahgi Valley than on the Mt Hagen volcanic plateau. If this were so, Kuk, in the middle of the valley, would be even more affected than Mantons, towards its margins.

The ecological effects of deforestation can hardly account even for Phase 2 in the Kuk basin however, since the pollen diagrams show a continuing decline in the forest to woody non-forest ratio well after Phase 2 had ended. Other evidence supports this conclusion. Christensen (1975:31)

reports the absence of charcoal of any other tree
type than pandanus in deposits at Manim rockshelter
before 6000 BP, which may mean that bush clearance
did not begin in its vicinity until that date,
which is also when the first ground stone tools
appear at the site. Manim rockshelter, now in
grassland, is at 1770 m on the western edge of a
side valley of the Wahgi, 15 km SW of Kuk and 6 km
SW of the Manton site, where admittedly very
limited excavations (Golson *et al.* 1967; Lampert
1967) did not reveal the equivalents of Kuk Phases
1 or 2. At Kuk itself what local inhabitants
claimed was bark of a tree of the 'true bush',
possibly *Nothofagus*, was found at the base of a
Phase 2 basin. As yet incompletely analysed
botanical remains from the basal fill of major
channels belonging to Phase 1 and early Phase 2 -
branches, leaves and seeds - also testify to the
local presence of primary forest at the time the
two earliest basin management systems were
operating.

Yen has advised (pers. comm.) that experimental
ventures in horticulture are to be expected in the
highlands situation at these early periods, not all
of which would prove successful or worthwhile and
that this might account for the short-lived
character of Phases 1 and 2. Phase 1, as we have
seen, must stand very close to the beginnings of
horticultural activity of any kind in the highlands.
Phase 2, as we have seen, could represent a chapter
in the adaptation of new crops, of Southeast Asian
origin, to the local conditions. An important
point is that in both phases fairly simple measures
- the digging of a large disposal channel - were
enough to make the Kuk basin usable. On the other
hand constant attention would have been needed to
keep it so. All profiles across them show a
tendency for the disposal channels to silt up, due
to their length and their minimal gradient. The
labour involved in their maintenance may not have
been felt in the circumstances always worthwhile.

Alternatively the groups involved may have lost control of the outlets on which the whole system depended.

Phase 3: c. 4000 - c. 2500 BP

The first true drainage systems at Kuk belong here. Large disposal channels were dug as in previous phases (Fig.4). There are at least three of them and they run northeast from the southern catchment, presumably to an outfall at the Wahgi; the western half of Kuk is not utilised during this phase, perhaps because the Gumants outfall was unavailable. Articulating with the major channels are long individual drains (Fig.4) with a few tributary branches, themselves branching in turn. The long individual drains seem to represent the spine of loose systems of integrated drainage serving areas of contemporary cultivation, though

Fig.4. The long trench follows one of the main field drains of Phase 3; smaller field drains of Phase 5 can be seen crossing it. They are all exposed in the surface of the grey clay prior to removal of infill.

excavation has not yet defined the total extent of
any of these. The evidence suggests that only part
of the swamp was being drained and cultivated at
any one time. The disposal channels had a longer
life than the individual systems they served and
were cleaned out and recut over time. They
themselves however were not necessarily in
contemporary use. Only a few field features, apart
from drains, have been found in so far limited
investigations. It is difficult therefore to
characterise the farming regime involved, but it
seems to lack the specialised character of later
systems.

The existence of tributary drains, though by
no means as numerous as in subsequent phases,
suggests that conditions in the basin had
deteriorated, possibly as a direct result of man's
previous interference with it. As the earlier
disposal channels ceased to be properly maintained,
there would have been a tendency for the sediments
they were transporting not to be carried away
through the outfalls but to be deposited over the
land surface short of them. Natural drainage
throughout the basin, inefficient at all times,
would therefore have been even less efficient when
it resumed with the decay of the artificial channels.
The fact that what was now becoming more truly swamp
was nevertheless reclaimed indicates some need to
do so.

The beginning of Phase 3 seems to be
contemporary with a low point in forest values in
the pollen diagrams, extreme at Mantons (zone B),
less so at Draepi-Minjigina (zone J) (Powell *et al*.
1975:Figs 9, 10 and 7, 8, 11 respectively). This
low point is not as securely dated as might be
wished, but it is consistently registered and a
central date of about 4000 BP is not unreasonable
for it. It reflects the effects on the environment
of millennia of shifting cultivation. Powell
(1970a:149) interprets the Manton diagram as showing

degraded and locally cleared areas within the forest
rather than wide expanses of grassland; at Draepi-
Minjigina regrowth shrub and grassland vegetation
were extensive (Powell 1970a:177).

Sustained use of reclaimed land as in Kuk
Phase 3 could well have been undertaken in response
to problems created by the clearance of primary
forest and the various inhibitions on its recovery,
including presumably growth of population, however
slow. Reinterpretation of the excavated evidence
at Mantons suggests that the prehistoric field
systems described there (Golson *et al.* 1967; Lampert
1967) belong to this period, the digging stick
dated at 2300 BP marking its close. There appears
then to have been a general response to a general
problem. If this interpretation is correct, the
response was successful, for the Manton pollen
diagrams show a marked recovery in forest values,
followed by the stabilisation of the forest to
woody non-forest ratio (Powell *et al.* 1975:zone C
of Figs 9, 10). Powell's interpretation (1970a:
162, 1970b) is that farming of the swamps allowed
sustained forest regeneration on the hillslopes,
combined with their continued agricultural use.
Forest recovery is registered, though less markedly,
in the Draepi-Minjigina diagrams, followed by
stabilisation as at Mantons (Powell *et al.* 1975:
zone J of Figs 7, 8, 11). Powell (1970a:183) says
a dynamic mosaic of grassland, regrowth and forest
vegetation is reflected here.

Phase 3 ends at Kuk with a marked change in
the nature of sediment deposition in the swamp:
sediments in the form of dark clay give way to
others in the form of soil aggregates. The last
drains of Phase 3 are in use when this change
occurs. The interpretation is that soil preparation
through tillage has made its appearance in the dry
land sector of agriculture and that its products
are washed into the swamp; the success of the
innovation allows swamp reclamation for agriculture

to be given up without disturbing the environmental
balance which it had effected.

Some innovation in the technology of dry land
agriculture such as this is necessary to explain
why the environmental deterioration which we have
suggested as accounting for Phase 3 in the Kuk
swamp, was also checked where no great areas of land
were available for reclamation, as in the Wabag
region. The lack of such land may account for
evidence implying high-altitude (2500 m) forest
destruction in the Sirunki area west of Wabag,
though not apparently at nearby Inim, beginning at
an inferred age of 4300 BP, around the time that
Phase 3 starts at Kuk. In the opinion of Walker
and Flenley (pers. comm.), if the vegetation
changes in the Sirunki pollen sequence are to be
attributed to man, their scale and persistence,
over an inferred period of 1300 years, suggest
continuous residence rather than occasional visits.
In the lower-altitude Birip diagram, east of Wabag,
at 1900 m in the agricultural zone, there is a low
point in forest values, a sharp recovery and a
subsequent stabilisation, very much on the upper
Wahgi pattern but later in time (Flenley 1967:
Fig.7.5). The forest decline is halted between
2000 and 2500 BP, close to the date suggested by
the Kuk evidence for the innovation of soil tillage
and possibly resulting from it.

It is possible that the evidence provided by
the open settlement site of Wañlek at 1710 m
altitude on the northern fringes of the highlands
(Bulmer 1975:40-1) relates to this phase of
agricultural history. In a level producing two
dates of about 2850 BP - but another of around
5450 BP from its base - was found a rich assemblage
of stone tools, including a number of tanged blades
of slate, interpreted as digging tools. There
appears to be more than one variety of working edge
represented, a wide curving type functionally
suited for cutting turf and possibly a more pointed

type, similar to an early, unstratified find from
Kuk (Allen 1970:180, 181; 1972:187), which could
also have served agricultural purposes, including
the tilling of soil. These possible functions are
discussed at greater length elsewhere (Golson in
press a); here it is sufficient to note that they
conform to agricultural needs in an environment of
degraded regrowth vegetation.

Phase 4: c. 2000 - c. 1200 BP

Phase 4 is characterised by a more intensive
drainage regime, both of disposal channels and
field ditches. There is at least one large main
channel (Fig.2) with which a number of major
tributary channels articulate. Together they
assemble the water from the western three-quarters
of the site and carry it towards the Guga Gorge;
an outfall at the Wahgi River may at this stage
have been unavailable. The character and extent of
this disposal network, so different from the single
channels of earlier phases, suggest on the one hand
that swampiness of the area had further increased
and on the other that larger areas than previously
were in simultaneous or at least co-ordinated use.

The field ditches, typically gutter-like
features deeper than wide (30-50 cm as against 20-
40 cm) and much more closely spaced than the field
drains of Phase 3, are disposed in grids whose
dimensions are yet to be fully investigated. They
seem to represent a far more systematic and perhaps
specialised use of the swamp than in Phase 3,
possibly marking the existence of crop segration in
the agricultural system, with differing environments
and techniques being reserved for different plants.
Thus taro could have been appropriately grown in
the swamp plots, while yams were planted in the dry
land gardens, served by the new technique of soil
tillage in the manner noted for yam cultivation in
the Kainantu area today by Watson (1967:91, 95).
The situation may have been something like that

described by Yen (1971:9) for the island of Uvea in
western Polynesia, where shifting cultivation of
yams, bananas, taro and *Alocasia* on hillside and
plateau areas is combined with permanent swamp
cultivation of taro in the valleys in raised
rectangular plots in chequer-board patterns.

Since the system was so soon abandoned, it can
hardly have been instituted for this purpose, though
it may have taken this form while serving some other
need. The fact that no equivalent phase is evident
in the small area investigated at Mantons may mean
that the need was local. However, some drainage
took place at least at the margins of the small
Minjigina swamp, apparently towards the end of Phase
4 at Kuk, so that the Kuk experiment may have been
evoked by developments of a more general character.
As we shall see, this is strongly suggested by the
circumstances under which Kuk Phase 4, and the
equivalent phase at Minjigina, came to an end.

Abandonment at Kuk took place shortly before a
volcanic ash fall about 1200 years ago, whose
products lie so low in the fill of major channels
and so near the base of the latest field drains
that the systems were without doubt fully operable
when they were given up. The same volcanic ash has
been recorded in similar circumstances at Draepi-
Minjigina, and in two of the pollen diagrams there
(Powell *et al*. 1975:Figs 7, 11) it marks a level
after which relative forest values begin to fall
after the long period of stability in the forest
to woody non-forest ratio established early in Kuk
Phase 3. The same fall in forest values is recorded
in the unpublished Birip diagram further west
(Flenley 1967:Fig.7.5), at a level marked by a grey,
silty volcanic ash (Flenley 1967:Fig.7.3, Table 7.1)
which, loosely bracketed by dates of 1500 BP and
300 BP, could well be the 1200 BP ash of the upper
Wahgi sites. In other publications (especially in
Powell *et al*. 1975:44-7; also Golson in press b) I
have interpreted this pollen evidence as registering

renewed and sustained forest clearance at 2000 m
and above and used its coincidence with the
abandonment of swamp drainage at lower altitudes as
part of a case to argue the arrival of the sweet
potato in New Guinea some hundreds of years earlier
than the c. 400 BP date generally accepted. The
interpretation fits well with the model proposed by
students of highlands agriculture about the likely
effects of sweet potato introduction (Brookfield
with Hart 1971:124 *fn*; Waddell 1972:219; Yen 1971:
7, 1973:80).

The decline in the forest component in the
pollen diagrams at Draepi-Minjigina and Birip from
1200 BP is accompanied by a marked rise in the
values for two trees, *Trema*, a genus of disturbed
woodland, and *Casuarina*, a tree of stream banks,
previously present in the diagrams only in small
amounts. A similar rise in *Casuarina* values is
even recorded at the same date in high-altitude
bogs at Mt Wilhelm, the pollen funnelled up above
the tree line from settled areas in the upper
Chimbu valley (Hope 1976:656). Today the
conservation of *Trema* and the deliberate planting
of *Casuarina* constitute the practice of tree
fallowing which we have noted as part of the
intensive agricultural technology of the highlands,
and the pollen diagrams suggest its appearance 1200
years ago. Are we to suppose that the practice was
handed over together with the sweet potato when
that plant made its entry into those areas of the
highlands with which we are now concerned?

There is an alternative possibility. Since the
pollen diagrams we are using are not based on
absolute counts, it is possible that the forest
decline is not real, but simply a deflection of the
forest curve due to the increased contribution of
Casuarina and *Trema* to the woody non-forest component.
If this is so, what we may be seeing in the
abandonment of drainage at Kuk and Minjigina, is
the result of the introduction of tree fallowing

into the dry land sector of agriculture. The
practice could account for developments at the
northern margin of the Kuk basin, where increased
deposition of sediment from 1200 BP could reflect
the first extensive clearances of the steep, thin-
soiled slopes for sustained cultivation.
Alternatively (Golson in press b) this could result
from the introduction of the sweet potato into the
horticultural system.

The context for the widespread adoption of the
innovation is possibly supplied by evidence for
renewed high altitude clearance in the pollen at
Sirunki and Inim. According to Walker and Flenley
(pers. comm.) this began at an inferred date of
2000 years ago at Sirunki, persisting for about
500 years to the top of the sequence there. The
clearance at Inim, starting about the same time,
was intensified within the last few hundred years,
with *Casuarina*, *Trema* and open ground indicators
becoming abundant (Walker and Flenley pers. comm.).
The inauguration of this late intensive phase can
be attributed with reasonable confidence to the
arrival of the sweet potato, initiating the
formation of the present cultural landscape.
Flenley (1967:305) estimates it as beginning about
260 BP, which would fit with the accepted view of
the recency of the sweet potato in New Guinea.
Whatever the nature of the preceding subsistence
regime involving forest clearance from about 2000
BP, its appearance at these high altitudes might
mean the existence of stresses within the
agricultural system at lower altitudes, which the
practice of tree fallowing was designed to alleviate.

Phase 5: c. 400 - c. 100 BP

Initially Phase 5 is characterised by an
extensive and elaborate framework of large disposal
drains collecting water from the entirety of the
site, and apparently beyond it to the east, and
transporting it via the major channel shown in Fig.2

to an outfall at the Guga Gorge to the west. Within
this framework is a grid of small, flat-bottomed
field ditches, sometimes wider than they are deep.
The details of the system are yet to be investigated,
but some gross differences are clear between it and
the situation after the fall of a distinctive
volcanic ash which forms a marker horizon at around
250 BP (Blong 1975). More than half the eastern
part of the site was abandoned after this date,
while in the area that continued to be used, the
field grid assumed a tighter mesh, though
articulating with some of the original disposal
drains and served by the same main channel. Also,
for the first time in the history of its utilisation,
there are houses scattered through the swamp, with
women's houses adjacent to the gardens.

In earlier publications (Golson 1976:212-9,[2]
in press b, in Powell *et al.* 1975:48) Phase 5 as a
whole has been interpreted as the cultivation of
sweet potato in the swamp, for a number of reasons:
the more intensive nature of the drainage network,
reflecting the sensitivity of the plant to moisture;
continuity in the use of major disposal channels
and the typological identity of the gridded field
ditches throughout the phase; the similarity of
these latter to the field ditches of modern dry
land sweet potato agriculture in the Wahgi; and
finally the discovery of fragments of charred sweet
potato in two excavated houses. The abandonment of
land after the volcanic ash fall, and the tightening
of the field grid, were seen as responses to
deteriorating conditions in the swamp, making its
drainage more difficult.

An alternative explanation is possible and
will be tested in future fieldwork. The extensive
drainage of the pre-ash period, with its more open
grid, may be a renewal of the Phase 4 regime, in
the specialised service of taro; the restricted,
more intensive drainage which follows may mark the
replacement of taro by sweet potato in the swamp

system, with the houses of the women moving in close to the concentrated area of intensive food production. On this interpretation Phase 5 at Kuk would have to be divided into two, Phase 5, taro-based, before 250 BP, and Phase 6, sweet potato-based, after. To avoid confusion this terminology is not used here.

At Kuk it is the Phase 5 drainage works which are those visible from the air and it is reasonable to suppose that the drainage systems shown by aerial photography to be widespread through the upper Wahgi swamplands belong to the same phase. It is certainly represented, though originally misinterpreted, at the Manton site. If however, Phase 5 at Kuk should really be divided into an earlier extensive taro stage and a later less extensive sweet potato stage, it could be that some at least of the aerially visible systems at other swamps are the equivalent of the earlier stage at Kuk: this seems to be the case at Mantons where a fence post found lying in the very top of the gardening zone is dated at about 470 BP (Powell 1970b). In other words, it is impossible on present evidence to assess the extent of swamp drainage specifically for sweet potato cultivation in the upper Wahgi. Perhaps the lack of tradition regarding such large-scale drainage amongst the Mount Hagen tribes today (I.M. Hughes pers. comm.) is not only a function of its almost total disappearance beyond the memory of anyone alive today, but due also to its having been by no means as widespread as I had originally supposed (Golson 1976:216-7, in press b, in Powell *et al.* 1975:48-9). This would go some way also to explaining why the abandonment of swamp cultivation has not led to any general pressures on available dry land today and why moreover most upper Wahgi swamp was readily alienated to the Australian Administration in the post-war years.

Whatever the plant involved at the beginning of Phase 5 at Kuk, taro or sweet potato, the extent

of drainage there and throughout the upper Wahgi is
likely to reflect the renewed onset of basic
problems in the conduct of productive agriculture
in an environment of degraded regrowth after the
relief offered by the innovations of 1200 BP,
whether these were restricted to tree fallowing or
included the sweet potato as well. Were the sweet
potato a later arrival, its adoption might have had
effects generally throughout the upper Wahgi that
we see in microcosm at Kuk around 250 BP - the
abandonment of large areas of large-scale drainage.
Perhaps there was only limited and local need to
adapt the swamp systems for the cultivation of the
new plant; such adaptations as were made, including
that at Kuk, had been given up by the time of
European exploration in the 1930s.

It is probable that an important factor in land
use at this stage was the appearance of a final
innovation in the agrarian technology, that of
cultivation in raised beds. The particular form
this takes in the Wahgi is the grid of normally
shallow flat-bottomed garden ditches generally
around 25 cm wide enclosing plots of varying sizes
but clustering around 2-3 metres square, over which
the spoil from ditch digging is spread. Gridded
plots are a feature of swamp agriculture at Kuk in
Phases 4 and 5 and the field drains of Phase 5 are
very close in size and shape to those of modern dry
land agriculture. In the post-ash stage of Phase 5
the tightening of the grid and the stratigraphically
visible disposal of the more abundant spoil on the
surface of the plots brings the swamp system close
to the modern dry land form. In the swamp these
were devices necessary to successful cultivation of
the sweet potato, the garden ditches controlling
the water table, the plot surfaces raised from their
spoil not only providing friable soil for planting
but also lifting the tubers even further above the
moisture level. A less obvious aspect of the
operation is the apparently fertilising effect of
bringing subsoil onto the garden surface, renewed

as ditches were cleaned out and redug (cf. discussion
on 'sub-soiling' in UNESCO 1962:60, 95-6, 105,
106-7). This is presumably the factor which permits
long-term usage of the same garden plots. The
suggestion made here is that the practice was
learned in the swamps. Once learned, it was
capable of being diffused to areas with no direct
or large-scale experience in swamp cultivation, as
in lower Chimbu.

CONCLUDING REMARKS

This paper has sought, in a preliminary and
tentative fashion, to explain the periodicity and
pattern of use of the Kuk basin for agriculture in
the light of evidence regarding land use in the
upper Wahgi and beyond derived from palynological
and, where available and appropriate, archaeological
evidence. Specifically it has attempted to show
how the particular features that characterise the
intensive agricultural technology of the highlands
today were developed at particular points in the
past in response to problems arising from a series
of limiting conditions on agricultural operations.
A complex of variously unfavourable environments
below and a ceiling, or series of ceilings, on crop
productivity above concentrated agriculture and
settlement into a favoured but laterally and
vertically constricted zone between about 1400 and
2000 m. Within this zone of concentration the
preference of presumed important crops like taro
and yam for richer and less degraded soils, added
to the slower regeneration of the forest on which
refertilisation under a system of shifting
cultivation depended, inaugurated, with growth of
population, an irreversible process of environmental
change, whereby the natural vegetation succession
was deflected to secondary forest and finally to
grassland.

Given the evidence for agricultural clearance shortly after 9000 BP, the process was a slow one, due presumably to low initial and only slowly expanding populations and to the ready availability, at least at first, of bush resources, including the seasonally important pandanus growing up to high altitudes. The upper Wahgi populations had reclaimable land through which to cushion the effects when these began to show themselves. Phase 3, involving the first real drainage of the site, begins at the period when the upper Wahgi pollen diagrams show their lowest values for forest pollen (c. 4000 BP) and ends when one of the important characteristics of contemporary highlands agricultural practice, soil tillage, makes its appearance about 2500 BP. I have argued that this innovation was adopted over a wide area and accounts for the alleviation of pressures on the forests of the Wabag area, where no reclaimable land is available and where the pollen diagrams seem to indicate high altitude clearance for a period of about 1300 years from around 4300 BP.

From this point forwards the agricultural technology increasingly takes on the character that we know today: tree fallowing by 1200 BP and raised bed cultivation, at least in the upper Wahgi, perhaps around 250 BP. It does so, we may presume, as the environmental transformation to a landscape of regrowth and grassland moves towards completion throughout the continuously occupied zone, with the populations within it more and more dependent on agriculture for subsistence as forest resources disappear or become remote (e.g. Waddell 1972:213). The renewal of swamp cultivation in Kuk Phases 4 and 5 may thus reflect the pressures with which agricultural technology had to cope.

Whenever it arrives, the sweet potato is incorporated into an agricultural system already well along the road of dynamic adaptation to a radically changed environment. In such conditions

the contribution it makes to the intensification of
production, through its higher yields, quicker
maturation, longer productive life and greater
tolerance of naturally poor and agriculturally
degraded soils, is more likely to be picked up
archaeologically than palynologically, and the post-
250 BP abandonment of the larger part of the Kuk
swamp can be suggested as a possible instance of
this. Where the pollen record should be sensitive
to the arrival of the sweet potato is at the
higher altitudes, where for the first time the new
plant allowed sustained and widespread agriculture
and settlement; hence perhaps the intensified
forest clearance revealed within the last few
hundred years by the Inim diagram from 2550 m is a
reflection of it. In both these ways the sweet
potato created room at the top where this had been
in short supply before, in the sense of an
agricultural zone limited within and above by the
characteristics of the crops on which subsistence
depended. The highlands are still adjusting to the
potential - and limitations - of the recently
adopted staple.

ACKNOWLEDGEMENTS

Acknowledgement is due to the Papua New Guinea
Government for permission to carry out the research;
to the PNG Department of Primary Industry for
allowing it to be carried out at one of its research
stations; and to the successive managers of Kuk, the
late John Morgan, Douglas Grace and Batley Rowson,
and their staff, for their every help and co-operation.

Because this paper attempts to summarise five
years work, the debt I owe to project colleagues,
field assistants and voluntary helpers for their
labours and their discussions is too large to be
individually detailed here. I must however, make
specific acknowledgement to specialist co-workers:

Russell Blong (geomorphology and volcanic ash chronology) to whose participation Macquarie University, Sydney, has made an appreciated contribution; Ian Hughes (traditional land use and settlement); Henry Polach (radiocarbon dating); Jocelyn Powell (pollen analysis and swamp strati- graphy); and especially Philip Hughes, who has worked on a great variety of problems relating to the Kuk sediments and contributed importantly to the interpretations of them offered here.

   The project as a whole has been almost entirely funded by the Australian National University through the Research School of Pacific Studies. I am indebted to the Wenner-Gren Foundation for Anthropological Research (Inc.) for contributing to the cost of labour during the 1974 and 1975 seasons (grant 3016).
   In preparing this paper I have benefitted from discussions with Douglas Yen, who is however, not responsible for my use of his comments. I am grateful to Donald Walker and John Flenley for allowing me access to unpublished palynological results.

FOOTNOTES

[1] All dates in this paper are based on uncalibrated
   radiocarbon ages using the 5568 year half life,
except for that relating to the introduction of the
sweet potato which is based on historical evidence.

[2] Although only recently published, this article
   was completed in 1973. Our better understanding
of the complex Kuk systems, together with the range
of important new data recovered in subsequent field
seasons means that this article is now substantially
outdated.

REFERENCES

Allen, J. 1970 Prehistoric agricultural systems in
    the Wahgi valley: a further note. *Mankind* 7(3):
    177-83

        1972 The first decade in New Guinea
    archaeology. *Antiquity* 46:180-90

        in press The hunting neolithic:
    adaptations to the food quest in prehistoric
    Papua New Guinea. In J.V.S. Megaw (ed.)
    *Hunters, gatherers and first farmers beyond
    Europe*. Leicester: Leicester University Press

Blong, R.J. 1975 The Krakatoa myth and the New
    Guinea highlands. *Journal of the Polynesian
    Society* 84:213-7

Boserup, E. 1965 *The conditions of agricultural
    growth*. London: Allen and Unwin

Bowers, N. 1971 Demographic problems in montane
    New Guinea. In S. Polgar (ed.) *Culture and
    population*:11-31. Cambridge (Mass.) and London:
    Schenkman, for Carolina Population Center

Brookfield, H.C. 1961 The highland peoples of New
    Guinea: a study of distribution and localization.
    Geographical Journal 127:436-48

        1964 The ecology of highland
    settlement: some suggestions. In Watson 1964:
    20-38

        with D. Hart 1971 *Melanesia: a
    geographical interpretation of an island world*.
    London: Methuen

        and J.P. White 1968 Revolution or
    evolution in the prehistory of the New Guinea
    highlands: a seminar report. *Ethnology* 7:43-52

Bulmer, R. 1968 The strategies of hunting in New
    Guinea. *Oceania* 38(4):302-18

Bulmer, S. 1975 Settlement and economy in prehistoric Papua New Guinea: a review of the archaeological evidence. *Journal de la Société des Océanistes* 31:7-75

    in press Between the mountains and the plains: prehistoric settlement and environment at Wañlek, a site in the Bismarck-Schrader Range. In Winslow in press

    and R. Bulmer 1964 The prehistory of the Australian New Guinea highlands. In Watson 1964:39-76

Christensen, O.A. 1975 Hunters and horticulturalists: a preliminary report of the 1972-4 excavations in the Manim valley, Papua New Guinea. *Mankind* 10(1):24-36

Clarke, W.C. 1966 From extensive to intensive shifting cultivation: a succession from New Guinea. *Ethnology* 5:347-59

    1971 *Place and people: an ecology of a New Guinea community*. Berkeley and Los Angeles: University of California Press and Canberra: Australian National University Press

    1973 *A change of subsistence staple in prehistoric New Guinea*. Paper read at the Third International Symposium on Tropical Root Crops, Ibadan

Denevan, W.M. and B.L. Turner II 1974 Forms, functions and associations of raised fields in the Old World tropics. *Journal of Tropical Agriculture* 39:24-33

Flenley, J.R. 1967 *The present and former vegetation of the Wabag region of New Guinea*. Unpublished PhD thesis, Australian National University, Canberra

    1972 Evidence of Quaternary vegetational change in New Guinea. In P. and M. Ashton (eds) *The Quaternary era in Malesia*:99-108. Hull: University of

Hull, Department of Geography, Miscellaneous
Series No.13

Golson, J. 1976 Archaeology and agricultural
history in the New Guinea highlands. In
G. de G. Sieveking, I.H. Longworth and
K.E. Wilson (eds) *Problems in economic and
social archaeology*:201-20. London: Duckworth

    in press a Simple tools and complex
technology: agriculture and agricultural
implements in the New Guinea highlands. In
R.V.S. Wright (ed.) *Stone tools as cultural
markers: change, evolution and complexity*.
Canberra: Australian Institute of Aboriginal
Studies

    in press b The making of the New Guinea
highlands. In Winslow in press

    and P.J. Hughes 1976 The appearance of
plant and animal domestication in New Guinea.
In J. Garanger (ed.) *La préhistoire océanienne*
(symposium XXII of IX Congress of Pre- and
Protohistoric Sciences, Nice, September 1976):
88-100. Paris: Centre National de la Recherche
Scientifique, preprint

    R.J. Lampert, J.M. Wheeler and
W.R. Ambrose 1967 A note on carbon dates for
horticulture in the New Guinea highlands.
Journal of the Polynesian Society 76:369-71

Hope, G.S. 1976 The vegetation history of Mt
Wilhelm, Papua New Guinea. *Journal of Ecology*
64:627-64

    and J.A. Peterson 1975 Glaciation and
vegetation in the high New Guinea mountains.
In R.P. Suggate and M.M. Cresswell (eds)
*Quaternary studies: selected papers from IX
INQUA Congress, Christchurch, New Zealand,
2-10 December 1973*:155-62. Wellington: Royal
Society of New Zealand, Bulletin 13

Hope, J.H. and G.S. Hope 1976   Palaeoenvironments
     for man in New Guinea.   In R.L. Kirk and
     A.G. Thorne (eds) *The origin of the Australians:*
     29-53.   Canberra: Australian Institute of
     Aboriginal Studies

Lampert, R.J. 1967   Horticulture in the New Guinea
     highlands: C14 dating.   *Antiquity* 41:307-9

Paijmans, K. (ed.) 1976   *New Guinea vegetation.*
     Canberra: Australian National University Press

Powell, J.M. 1970a   *The impact of man on the
     vegetation of the Mt Hagen region, New Guinea.*
     Unpublished PhD thesis, Australian National
     University, Canberra

          1970b   The history of agriculture in
     the New Guinea highlands.   *Search* 1:199-200

          1976   Ethnobotany.   In Paijmans 1976:
     106-83

          , A. Kulunga, R. Moge, C. Pono,
     F. Zimike and J. Golson 1975   *Agricultural
     traditions of the Mount Hagen area.*   Port
     Moresby: University of Papua New Guinea,
     Department of Geography, Occasional Papers
     No.12

UNESCO 1962   *Symposium on the impact of man on
     humid tropics vegetation, Goroka, Territory
     of Papua and New Guinea, September 1960.*
     Canberra: Commonwealth Government Printer, for
     Administration of the Territory of Papua and
     New Guinea and UNESCO Science Co-operation
     Office for South East Asia

Waddell, E. 1972   *The mound builders: agricultural
     practices, environment, and society in the
     central highlands of New Guinea.*   Seattle and
     London: University of Washington Press

          1975   How the Enga cope with frost:
     responses to climatic perturbations in the
     central highlands of New Guinea.   *Human Ecology*
     3:249-73

Walker, D. 1970 The changing vegetation of the montane tropics. *Search* 1:217-21

Watson, J.B. (ed.) 1964 *New Guinea: the central highlands*. *American Anthropologist* 66(4, part 2), Special Publication

    1965a From hunting to horticulture in the New Guinea highlands. *Ethnology* 4: 295-309

    1965b The significance of a recent ecological change in the central highlands of New Guinea. *Journal of the Polynesian Society* 74:438-50

    1967 Horticultural traditions in the eastern New Guinea highlands. *Oceania* 38(2): 81-98

White, J.P. 1972 *Ol tumbuna: archaeological excavations in the eastern central highlands, Papua New Guinea*. Canberra: Australian National University, Research School of Pacific Studies, Department of Prehistory, *Terra Australis* 2

Winslow, J.H. (ed.) in press *The Melanesian environment: change and development*. Canberra: Australian National University Press

Yen, D.E. 1971 The development of agriculture in Oceania. In R.C. Green and M. Kelly (eds) *Studies in Oceanic culture history*, (vol.2): 1-12. Honolulu: Bishop Museum, Department of Anthropology, Pacific Anthropological Records No. 12

    1973 The origins of Oceanic agriculture. *Archaeology and Physical Anthropology in Oceania* 8:68-85

    1974 *The sweet potato and Oceania*. Honolulu: Bishop Museum, Bulletin 236

INDEX